The Psychobiology of Aggression

Harper's Physiological Psychology Series
under the editorship of H. Philip Zeigler

The Psychobiology of Aggression

K. E. Moyer

Carnegie-Mellon University

Harper & Row, Publishers
New York, Hagerstown, San Francisco, London

Sponsoring Editor: George A. Middendorf
Project Editor: Cynthia Hausdorff
Designer: Emily Harste
Production Supervisor: Kewal K. Sharma
Compositor: American Book–Stratford Press, Inc.
Printer and binder: Halliday Lithograph Corporation
Art Studio: Danmark & Michaels Inc.

**The Psychobiology
of Aggression**

Library of Congress Cataloging in Publication Data

Moyer, Kenneth Evan, Date -
    The psychobiology of aggression.

    (Harper's physiological psychology series)
    Bibliography: p.
    Includes index.
    1. Aggressiveness (Psychology) 2. Violence. 3. Psy-
chobiology. I. Title. [DNLM: 1. Psychophysiology.
2. Aggression. WL102 M938pa]
BF575.A3M65   152.4   76–1884

ISBN 0–06–044641–2

To Shawn and Brett and Joy

Contents

Preface, ix
Introduction, xiii

1. **A Physiological Model of Aggression** 1
   Definitions, 1
   Kinds of Aggression, 3
   The Model, 4
   Summary, 20

2. **Neural Factors in Aggression in Man** 22
   Kinds of Aggression in Man, 23
   Brain Dysfunctions Relating to Aggression, 24
   Brain Lesions and Aggression Control in Man, 44
   Direct Brain Stimulation, 50
   Summary, 57

3. **Blood Chemistry Changes and Aggressive Behavior in Man** 59
   Endocrinology of Aggression in Male Humans, 60
   Aggression and the Premenstrual Syndrome, 66
   Aggressive Behavior as an Allergic Reaction, 69
   Hypoglycemia and Aggression, 74
   Drug-Induced Aggression, 78
   Aggression Inhibition by Drugs, 88
   Summary, 94

4. **The Control of Aggression   96**
The Need for Control, 97
Nonphysiological Methods of Control, 99
Physiological Methods of Control, 103
The Limitations of Physiological Methods of Aggression Control, 120
Ethical Problems, 122

5. **Kinds of Aggression   I: Introduction, Predatory Aggression, Inter-male Aggression   130**
Early Attempts to Classify Kinds of Aggression, 131
Dimensions on Which the Kinds of Aggression Vary, 132
Definitions and Characteristics of Different Kinds of Aggression, 135
General Summary, 174

6. **Kinds of Aggression   II: Fear-Induced, Maternal, Irritable, Sex-Related   176**
Fear-Induced Aggression, 176
Maternal Aggression, 180
Irritable Aggression, 186
Sex-Related Aggression, 204

7. **Territoriality?   209**
Summary, 226

8. **Physiological Substrates of Different Kinds of Aggression   227**
Neurological Basis of Predatory Aggression, 227
Endocrinology of Predation, 238
Endocrinology of Inter-male Aggression, 239
Neurology of Inter-male Aggression, 254
Neurology of Fear-Induced Aggression, 256
Endocrinology of Fear-Induced Aggression, 262
Physiology of Maternal Aggression, 263
Neurology of Irritable Aggression, 263
Endocrinology of Irritable Aggression, 270
Summary of the Physiological Substrates of the Different Kinds of Aggression, 272

9. **Some Theoretical Considerations   275**

Appendix, 285
Glossary, 289
Bibliography, 301
Author Index, 373
Subject Index, 387

Preface

My concern with the problem of aggressive behavior began in 1966 in an attempt to understand what appeared to me to be a significant increase in senseless violence. That was the year that Richard Speck killed eight young women in a nurses' residence in Chicago, Charles Whitman climbed to the top of the clock tower of the University of Texas with a high-powered rifle and shot innocent passersby, killing 14 and injuring 31 more, and Robert Smith, a high school senior, coolly and without motive shot five women and two children through the head after forcing them to lie on the floor in the form of a cartwheel.

Initially, my motive was to find out what was known about the physiology of this bizarre hostile behavior in order to determine whether the field of physiological psychology (broadly defined) could make any contribution to the control of irrational aggressive tendencies. It can, as Chapter 4 will show. However, in the pursuit of knowledge in this complex field it became apparent that an adequate understanding of control had to be based on a great deal of fundamental material. My progress has involved wider and wider fields of study ranging from anthropology to zoology with aggression as the unifying theme.

Most of the critical experiments on the physiology of aggression have been done on animals, and it was therefore necessary to have a knowledge of that field. In order to gain an adequate understanding of the results of animal experiments in the laboratory, it was necessary to become familiar with the behavior of subjects in their natural habitat, making essential the study of ethology. The study of subhuman species gave direction to the kinds of questions that might reasonably be asked about aggressive behavior of man.

This book is an attempt to organize the large amount of material on some aspects of aggression in a systematic way, in order to achieve a better understanding of that kind of behavior. Although there are still wide gaps in our knowledge, what is known does imply actions that can be taken to help man reduce some kinds of aggression. However, some of the available methods give us pause and demand intelligent concern about the potential for abuse.

Finally, it is hoped that a better understanding of aggressive behavior will contribute in some measure to a better understanding of behavior in general, and provide some insight into man's most complex problem—man.

ACKNOWLEDGMENTS

The major concepts in this book have been developed over a period of several years and have been presented at various symposia. Earlier versions of different portions of the book have been published elsewhere and, although all of the material has been updated and all of it revised, I have quoted freely from my earlier writings. At the request of Markham Press, eight of these earlier papers were collected in a single volume entitled *The Physiology of Hostility,* published in 1971.

The basic ideas for the physiological model in Chapter 1 were presented at the Symposium on Brain Research and Human Behavior in the Plenary Session on How Brain Research Can Contribute to World Peace under the joint sponsorship of UNESCO and the International Brain Research Organization, March 11–15, 1968, in Paris, France. The model was further elaborated and presented at the AAAS symposium on The Physiology of Fighting and Defeat, December 28, which was subsquently published in 1971 under that title by the Plenum Press, as edited by B. E. Eleftheriou and J. P. Scott.

The initial elaboration of the concept that there are different kinds of aggression and that each has a different physiological basis (Chapters 5 and 6) was published under the title "Kinds of Aggression and Their Physiological Basis" and appeared in *Communications in Behavioral Biology,* 1968, 2, 65–87.

Much of the material in Chapters 3, 5, and 6 relating to differences between the sexes was contained in a paper titled "Sex Differences in Aggression," which was presented at the symposium Sex Differences in Behavior conducted by the International Institute for the Study of Human Reproduction, September 30–October 3, 1973, edited by R. C.

Friedman, R. M. Richard, and R. L. Vande Wiele and published by John Wiley and Sons, Inc., 1974; it is used by permission of the publisher.

The information on the physiological control of aggression (Chapter 4) was originally presented at a symposium entitled Cognitive and Physiological Factors in Violence and Aggression, held at the City University of New York, June 6, 1969. It was published in a book edited by J. L. Singer, *The Control of Aggression and Violence: Cognitive and Physiological Factors,* New York, Academic Press, 1971. The material was later revised and updated and presented at the Seventh Annual Conference on Current Concerns in Clinical Psychology, sponsored by the Department of Psychology of the University of Iowa. That paper, "The Physiological Inhibition of Hostile Behavior," was published in the book *The Control of Aggression,* edited by John F. Knutson and published by Aldine Publishing Company of Chicago. It has been further revised and expanded for this book.

Portions of the last chapter on theoretical considerations were an outgrowth of discussions during the University of Virginia Sesquicentennial Symposium on Allegiance and Hostility, Man's Mammalian Heritage, held October 8–11, 1969, and organized by Frederick Richardson. Some of this material was revised and presented as an invited address at the First Latinamerican Congress of Psychobiology held in Sao Paulo, Brazil, December 9–14, 1973, and organized by E. A. Carlini. Some of the theoretical aspects of this work were presented at the Houston Neurological Symposium, March 9–11, 1972, and is published in W. S. Fields (Ed.), *Neural Bases of Violence and Aggression,* St. Louis, Green, 1975.

I am grateful to the organizers of all the symposia for the opportunity to present my views and to the many participants who challenged some of the concepts and forced me to clarify and revise some of my thinking. The exchange of ideas with my colleagues and my students has also been of considerable value to me. Although many have influenced my thinking, I particularly appreciate the discussions I have had with Jim Korn, Len Jarrard, Dick Bandler, Mike Crabtree, Judy Gibbons, and Gordon Barr.

This book has been improved because of the many comments by the Psychology Editor of Harper & Row, Dr. Philip Zeigler. He went over early drafts of the material in great detail and suggested many omissions, inclusions, changes, and reinterpretations. As a result of his comments, I found it necessary to rethink many of my ideas. Sometimes I agreed with him and made the suggested changes. Many times, however, further thought only reinforced my original ideas. Phil is therefore completely absolved from responsibility for what I have said here. His considerable help, however, is gratefully acknowledged. Thanks are also due to Dr. Douglas Candland, who read the entire manuscript and made many helpful suggestions.

Mrs. Geri Wilkinson also deserves thanks for her tireless typing and retyping of the manuscript, and for the meticulous care of an extensive filing system.

And once again, my thanks are due to Dusty, whose love makes all things possible.

K. E. M.

Introduction

Aggression is one of man's most important and most controversial topics of study. Much of the disagreement about the meaning and the causes of aggressive behavior derives from the fact that different authors are talking about different things but calling them by the same name. Further, there has been a tendency by many writers to oversimplify the causal factors and to exclude from consideration important areas of relevant data. It must be stated and emphasized at the beginning of any discussion of aggression that a number of different behaviors are subsumed under that general rubric. It is therefore essential that terms be clearly defined and areas of consideration clearly indicated. It must be further emphasized that each of the different kinds of aggression is determined by an interwoven complex of *internal*, *external*, and *experiential* factors. Because these three factors are constantly interacting in any organism during an aggressive act, it is possible to separate them only for purposes of discussion.

There is no single cause of aggressive behavior. However, for theoretical purposes it is essential to recognize that each of these factors does play a role and to attempt to understand how each contributes to the total behavior pattern. This book is an attempt to delineate the role of the internal or physiological components of aggressive action.

Physiological structures are innate and, in general, the functions of those structures are genetically determined. It is obvious, however, that from the moment of conception the environment begins to influence

both structure and function. Experience is a constant influence that
interacts with the genetic material to produce behavior. As a result
of learning and interactions with the environment, the physiology of
the organism is constantly being altered. Some changes, such as those
that occur in the neurons of the central nervous system during learning,
are impossible to detect with techniques currently available. Other
changes, such as the modification of the hormonal output of the pituitary
adrenal axis, which indirectly influence the central nervous system are
gross enough to be measured. Because of the constant alteration of
physiology by environment, it is unreasonable to think of aggressive
behavior, or any other behavior, for that matter, as a fixed, predeter-
mined, and unmodifiable characteristic that must be expressed because
it has innate physiological substrates. A somewhat more detailed discussion of the role of heredity in the expression of aggression is given
in Chapter 1.

Some of the controversy about aggressive behavior results from the
generalization of data from one species to another. Much of what is
known about aggression has, of course, been derived from the study
of animals. However, some of that knowledge is highly specific. A
given finding may relate only to one strain of a particular species for
one kind of aggression, and, at times, only to the specific experimental
test situation in which the animal has been studied. Certainly, data
obtained from one species are useful in the generation of hypotheses
about other animals. However, it is never safe to assume that an experimental finding in one type of laboratory subject is characteristic of
other kinds of animals, even closely related. There are, for example,
wide differences between strains of laboratory mice in the probability
that they will fight when two males are paired after a period of
isolation (Southwick & Clark, 1968). Some strains fight fiercely whereas
others manifest essentially no aggressive behavior. Amygdalectomized
rhesus monkeys in a laboratory situation lose their normal fears and
consequently much of their fear-induced aggression. However, in a
more naturalistic environment they appear to be more rather than less
fearful (Kling, Lancaster, & Benitone, 1970).

It is even more hazardous to attempt to attribute experimental findings obtained in animal studies to man, and vice versa. The study of
animals is certainly useful in gaining an understanding of man. Obviously, certain types of experiments can only be done on animals.
However, particularly in the physiological area, when one finds that
an experimental manipulation has a similar effect in a broad range of
species, there is presumptive evidence that similar relationships *may*
be found in man. The evidence is, however, presumptive until it can be
confirmed at the human level. The data from animals may be very useful
in indicating the directions that human research should take, the kinds

of variables that should be considered, and hypotheses that should be tested. However, it is never safe to make the assumption that what is true for a given animal is also true for man.

It is equally unwise to generalize from man back to the lower animals. Much of the writing on aggression attributes to subhuman species the feeling states and cognitive processes that the writer can observe only by introspection. Thus in an inter-male contest when the weaker animal assumes a posture that functions to inhibit further aggressive behavior from the victor, it is said to manifest an effort toward friendly harmonic social integration and to be requesting "love" from the superior animal (Schenkel, 1967). Such anthropomorphizing is of little value as an explanation and may, in fact, lead one to a theoretical dead end. The feeling states and mental processes of animals are forever unknowable and it is gratuitous and misleading to assume that one knows what an animal thinks or feels about an event.

REASONS FOR THIS BOOK

There are as many different approaches to the study of aggressive behavior as there are approaches to the study of man. Concern with this problem has resulted in a significant number of volumes devoted to the topic. The recent upward surge in violent behavior in the United States has motivated many more investigators to give serious consideration to a variety of aspects of aggression with the result that there is a rapidly expanding literature in this field. However, of the 85 or so books currently available, only the following three have been devoted primarily to the biological basis of aggressive behavior and none of them was written to be a complete exposition of the material.

Mark, V. H. & F. Ervin. *Violence and the Brain.* New York: Harper & Row, 1970.
Moyer, K. E. *The Physiology of Hostility.* Chicago: Markham, 1971.
Eleftheriou, B. E. & J. P. Scott (Eds.). *The Physiology of Aggression and Defeat.* New York: Plenum, 1971.

The Eleftheriou and Scott book is the result of an AAAS symposium. The Moyer book is an edited collection of his individual papers. The one by Mark and Ervin is a relatively small book devoted primarily to an exposition of the highly sophisticated clinical work of the authors. However, an extensive amount of experimental and clinical evidence is now available on the physiological substrates of aggression, and there is considerable need for an integrated presentation of that information.

As indicated, there are many possible approaches to the understanding of aggressive behavior. Some of them are inadequate and misleading because they do not take into account what is known about the physiological substrates. Although it is clear that a variety of approaches to the problem is necessary to provide a complete understanding of aggression phenomena, it is also clear that each of these approaches must take into account the findings of the others. It is possible to create a useful and predictive model of aggression at a level of discourse that does not deal with its biological basis. However, no explanation is a good one if it is contradicted by or incompatible with the available evidence. Thus one of the aims of this book is to provide a systematic presentation of the work that has been done on the biological aspects of the problem.

VARIETY OF INFORMATION SOURCES

The evidence on the physiology of hostile behavior is scattered over a variety of fields and will be found in a diversity of journals. A perusal of the bibliography at the end of this book will show that the primary fields include anatomy, anthropology, biochemistry, biology, ecology, electroencephalography, endocrinology, ethology, general medicine, genetics, neurology, pharmacology, physiology, primatology, psychiatry, psychology, sociology, and zoology, as well as the following disciplines, which border on two or more fields: clinical endocrinology, experimental therapeutics, neuroendocrinology, neuropharmacology, neurophysiology, neuropsychiatry, neurosurgery, physiological psychology, physiological zoology, psychopharmacology, psychosomatic medicine, and social psychology. Each of these fields makes a contribution to our understanding of aggressive behavior.

Because the information is so scattered and because science tends to be compartmentalized, it frequently takes a considerable amount of time for a significant contribution in one area to influence the research of an investigator in another area. All experimenters tend to suffer from information overload in their own fields and frequently do not have ready access to recent developments in related areas. With the development of computers with large memory storage, techniques are just now being developed for the dissemination of knowledge according to specific topics. The task of integrating the many research findings, however, is still left to the individual author.

An attempt is made here to bring together information from all of the various areas of knowledge and to organize it in the hopes that the work of the neurologist will influence the work of the psychologist, who may provide ideas for the endocrinologist, whose inspiration will have an effect on the thinking of the ethologist, etc. If this book stimulates further research and the development of theoretical structures that ultimately contribute to the development of rational control measures for hostile behavior, it will have served its purpose.

WHAT THIS BOOK IS NOT

It is also important to indicate what is not covered in this book and to emphasize that many important aspects of the total problems of aggressive behavior are not included. A complete exposition of what is known about the field would require an encyclopedia. A general and very broad coverage is now available in Roger Johnson's book, *Aggression in Man and Animals,* Saunders, 1972.

No attempt has been made to review the now vast literature on the social and learning aspects of the problem. Albert Bandura's book, *Aggression: A Social Learning Analysis,* Prentice-Hall, 1973, provides a recent analysis of that material. Two earlier books, *Aggression: A Social Psychological Analysis,* by Leonard Berkowitz, McGraw-Hill, 1962, and *The Psychology of Aggression,* by Arnold Buss, Wiley, 1961, also present much of that information from two other viewpoints. The social and learning aspects of aggressive behavior are critical to an understanding of the phenomenon but they are not the central thrust of this book.

The evolution of aggression is an interesting area of study in its own right and not infrequently contributes to our understanding of the behavior of higher organisms. However, an extensive coverage of that area of knowledge would take us too far from the central concern of this book.

There are, of course, hundreds of references on the aggressive behavior of fish and birds, not to mention the social insects. However, this book is concerned primarily with mammals. Other organisms are considered only when comparable relevant information is not available on mammalian species.

ORGANIZATION OF THIS BOOK

Chapter 1 is devoted to a preview of the physiological model of aggressive behavior. Terms are defined, the model is outlined, and enough evidence is presented to provide general support for the basic premises and corollaries. This model essentially determines the structure of the rest of the book, which deals in detail with the psychobiological evidence relating to each of the concepts considered in the model.

The neurological bases of aggressive behavior in man are presented in detail in Chapter 2. Chapter 3 considers the changes in blood chemistry that influence man's aggressive tendencies.

Chapter 4 considers the implications of a physiological model of aggressive behavior for the control of hostile, asocial activities in both normal individuals and those with various pathologies. Both physiological and nonphysiological methods are discussed. The potential for the control of aggression is so great that it raises new ethical questions, which are considered in the last section of Chapter 4.

Chapters 5 and 6 present evidence supporting the position that aggression is not a unitary concept but is a general term that covers a variety of behaviors having different response topographies, different eliciting stimuli, and different physiological bases. Chapter 5 introduces the concept and covers predatory and inter-male aggression. Chapter 6 considers the evidence for fear-induced, maternal, irritable, sex-related, and instrumental aggression.

Chapter 7 considers the concept of territoriality and presents evidence to show that it is not useful to consider territoriality as a separate kind of aggressive behavior and that although it may be a useful descriptive term for some kinds of behavior, it has relatively little explanatory value.

The neural and endocrinological substrates of each of the different kinds of aggression are presented in Chapter 8.

In the final chapter consideration is given to the differences between this model of aggression and others.

Because this monograph includes material from a large number of scientific and clinical fields, many readers will encounter vocabulary with which they are unfamiliar. In order to minimize this problem an extensive glossary has been included, starting on page 289.

The Psychobiology
of Aggression

1

A Physiological
Model of Aggression

The model presented in this chapter attempts to integrate the large amount of material on the physiology of aggressive behavior and to show the relationships among the many aspects of the different physiological mechanisms. It will thus provide a framework that will enable the reader to organize the information into a unified structure so that he can see the forest and not just the trees. The various facets of the model are extensively documented in the rest of the book. Some readers may prefer to skip this chapter and come back to it before reading the final chapter. In that case it is suggested that the summary of this chapter (p. 20) be read.

DEFINITIONS

Any attempt at precision in thinking or writing requires definition of terms. When the terms to be defined are in the common domain they mean different things to different people, although there is frequently a core of agreement. One is then faced with two possible solutions to the definition problem. New words can be created and rigorously defined or the ones in common usage can be redefined. In the first approach there can be no confusion about meaning as a result of the idiosyncratic experience of the reader with the defined term. However, neologisms are not readily learned or accepted and the reader must constantly engage in a translation procedure that interferes with smoothly flowing processes. Therefore the lesser of two evils has been chosen and the more common words have been used, with an attempt to make an explicit statement regarding the connotations to be assigned to them.

There have been a number of attempts to define *aggression* and the terms relating to aggressive behavior (Buss, 1961; Kaufman, 1970; Dollard et al., 1939; Montagu, 1966; Frank, 1967; Welch, 1969; Rothballer, 1967; Davis, 1964; Holloway, 1968; Berkowitz, 1962; Carthy & Ebling, 1964; Daniels et al., 1970; Boelkins & Heiser, 1970). The following definitions do not quite agree with any of them. However, a definition is never wrong, it is only more or less useful. The following terms provide a basis of understanding from which further concepts may be developed.

Aggression. Overt behavior involving intent to inflict noxious stimulation or to behave destructively toward another organism. Aggressive behavior may be direct or indirect. Under conditions of aversive stimulation or frustration, aggressive, destructive behavior may be directed toward inanimate objects. The important variable is the intent or the perceived intent of the behaving individual. A small boy who vigorously attacks but is unable to injure a larger boy is behaving aggressively. The poor marksman who shoots at his wife but misses her is aggressive, whether she is injured or not.

Intent. Intent is also included in this definition in order to exclude from the concept of aggression those accidental acts that may result in noxious stimulation to some organism. Intent implies goal direction, is always a private event, and can only be inferred from behavior. In humans intent can frequently be inferred from verbal behavior. One can ask the human if he intended to produce noxious stimulation and frequently (although obviously not always) infer intent from his answer.

Aggressive behavior in animals is somewhat more difficult to deal with. However, the concept of intent is important here also. An elephant walking through the veldt may, without awareness, step on a field mouse. That behavior may result in noxious stimulation to the mouse. However, in this text the elephant would not, in that instance, be considered aggressive. One can infer aggressive intent in an animal if it persists in destructive behavior toward the same or similar stimulus objects at different times. With this approach it is possible to discriminate between accidental and intentional behavior. Destructive behavior can be defined without much difficulty. Whether the animal intends to produce noxious stimulation is, of course, unknowable. Thus that portion of the definition cannot apply to subhuman species.

There are many conditions under which men and animals behave destructively toward inanimate objects. However, in the sense that the term is used here, few of them involve aggression. The man who rakes up leaves in the fall and burns them is engaged in destructive but not aggressive behavior. However, the frustrated driver who kicks a flat tire is aggressive, as is the rat that bites the bars through which it is being shocked. Destructive behavior toward inanimate objects is only considered aggressive if frustration or aversive stimulation are involved. Frustration is here considered to be any condition that blocks or prevents the fulfillment of intent as we have operationally defined it.

Symbolic aggression. Much of man's behavior is symbolic and his expression of aggression may also be symbolic. He may produce noxious stimulation through sarcasm, gossip, or character assassination. He may also hurt others by destroying their property. All of these behaviors are considered aggressive.

Achievement and aggression not the same. Popular usage of the term aggression includes some behaviors that are specifically excluded from the definition as it is used here because it is felt that quite different physiological mechanisms are involved. People who work hard toward the achievement of a particular goal are not considered to be aggressive unless their behavior includes the intent to do injury to others along the way. Assertiveness (that is, the positive statement or affirmation of a point of view) is not considered aggressive unless an intent to demean or otherwise hurt another person is involved.

Hostility and hostile behavior. These terms are the equivalent to aggression and aggressive behavior and will be used interchangeably in this book.

Aggressiveness and aggressivity. These terms refer to a relatively enduring state of the organism that reflects the ease with which aggression can be elicited.

Fantasy aggression. Covert behavior in which the individual imagines situations in which he is engaged in hostile behavior. This may involve the planning or rehearsal of a specific aggressive act, or it may involve ruminations unrelated to any intentions to overt behavior.

Threat. Behavior that attempts to communicate the intent to behave aggressively. In humans threats may be verbal or involve postures and gestures. In animals threats usually involve species-specific postures and gestures.

Anger. An aroused state involving particular autonomic and muscle tone patterns. During anger the individual's threshold for aggression is lowered.

Violence. A form of human aggression that involves inflicting physical damage on persons or property. Violent behavior is frequently intense, uncontrolled, excessive, furious, sudden, and at times seemingly purposeless (Daniels et al., 1970).

KINDS OF AGGRESSION

There are a variety of behaviors that may be subsumed under the preceding definition of aggression, including fighting between males, a mother defending her young, an animal driving intruders from its territory, and the verbal hostility of a young lady during her period of premenstrual tension.

Chapters 5 and 6 make clear that there are different kinds of aggressive behavior, just as there are different kinds of consummatory behavior. Eating, drinking, and the consumption of salt by an adrenalectomized animal can all be classified as consummatory behavior, there are, to be sure, certain similarities in the kinds of responses and in the physiological mechanisms involved. In each case something is ingested. It is obvious, however, that the details of the neurological and blood chemistry substrates for these three kinds of consummatory behavior are very different. Any attempt to find a single physiological basis for consummatory behavior would therefore lead to a rash of contradictory and unreproducible experiments.

In Chapters 5 and 6 an attempt is made to classify the various kinds of aggression. Chapter 8 presents the evidence indicating that each kind of aggression has a different physiological basis. At this point it is sufficient to state that there are a number of different types of aggression and that any consideration of aggressive behavior must take that fact into consideration.

THE MODEL

It is obvious that if there are many kinds of aggression and each has a different physiological basis, it will not be possible to construct a model that will fit each of them in detail. It may, however, be possible to identify mechanisms of types of mechanisms that, although differing in detail, are similar for all or most aggression types. Further, since aggression is a complex behavior that in this text is not considered to be fundamentally different from other complex basic behavior patterns, this model may be useful in clarifying some of the mechanisms involved in those behaviors also. An attempt will now be made to elucidate some of those mechanisms.

Neural Systems for Aggression

The first premise of this model indicates that there are in the brains of animal and man innately organized neural systems that when active in the presence of particular complexes of stimuli result in a tendency for the organism to behave destructively toward those stimulus complexes. In addition, the different kinds of aggression result from the activity of different, although undoubtedly sometimes overlapping, systems.

It should be emphasized that although these neural systems exist and are innately organized, aggression is not necessarily inevitable, nor is it uncontrollable. The activity of these neural systems is constantly being modulated by input from other neural systems, including changes in the nervous system produced by learning and by a variety of changes in the blood chemistry. The factors that determine whether the neural systems for aggression are activated and whether or not that activity results in overt aggressive behavior are discussed later.

As the term is used here, *neural system* refers to a complex of neurons involving several brain levels. Although each neuron in the system has many possible connections, the system tends to function as a unit. Other things being equal, when neurons within the system are activated, there is a greater probability that other neurons in the system will be fired in preference to those not so included. Thus because of some innate mechanism there is less synaptic resistance (broadly defined) among neurons within a particular system than among neurons in general.

Sensory Input

A given neural system has a variety of inputs from the different sensory systems. However, only particular patterns of activity in the sensory neurons are adequate to activate the various neural aggression systems. In most laboratory rats, for example, the neural system for predatory aggression is activated by the total sensory pattern input of a frog or a turtle, but in relatively few by the sensory pattern of a mouse, and in almost none by the sensory input of a rat pup (p. 137).

The pattern of the stimulus input for each of the different kinds of aggression is different. Thus the total stimulus pattern of an animal's natural prey activates the system for predatory aggression and has no effect on the one for inter-male aggression. That system, however, is activated by the stimulus pattern of a strange male.

Output to Motor Neurons

Any given aggression system governs the activity of particular patterns of motor neurons, with the result that in some kinds of aggression the response topography is characteristic of that particular aggression type. Male deer fight other males by lowering the head and locking antlers. However, predators are attacked by rearing and striking out with hooves (Tinbergen, 1953). Thus one part of the output of the neural system for inter-male aggression in the deer involves the activation of those motor units that result in the lowering of the head. However, the activation of the neural system for defensive aggression in that species results in an inhibition of those motor units with an activation of those that bring the head back as a part of the rearing response that brings the front hooves into striking position.

The motor units governing the head action in these two kinds of aggression in the deer, are, of course, only a small part of the total pattern of motor neural activity involved in the execution of a particular aggressive act.

Sensorimotor Feedback

The neural system for a particular kind of aggressive behavior dictates the general motor predisposition of the organism. The detailed movements are under the control of the sensory input in a feedback type of mechanism in which changes in the pattern of stimulation result in changes in the specifics of the behavior. Thus the particular pattern of attack is constantly shifting as a function of changes in the pattern of stimulation.

Stimulus Change Turns Off Aggression

The attack behavior, if it is effective, results in changes in the stimulus input. Therefore there is a constant interaction between the stimulus pattern and the motor movements of the attacking organism. When the stimulus situation changes sufficiently, the attack behavior ceases because the stimulus is no longer adequate to elicit an attack. For example, the live rat is an adequate stimulus to elicit an attack by a predatory cat. However, if the attack is successful, the live rat becomes a dead one, and a dead rat is not an adequate stimulus to elicit attack, so the predatory behavior ceases. Or if the rat is successful and escapes through a hole in the wall, the attack behavior also ceases. There may still be activity in the cat's neural system for predatory aggression, but since aggression is stimulus-bound and since the adequate stimulus is gone, there is no manifest aggressive behavior.

Sensory Sensitivity Increased by Aggression System Function

Activity in a neural system for aggression tends to increase the sensitivity of certain portions of the sensory systems. In a pioneering study by Mac-Donnell and Flynn (1966a, 1966b) it was shown that electrical stimulation of a particular area of the hypothalamus of the cat resulted in predatory aggression. Stimulation of that same area produced a sensory field in the muzzle area of the cat the size of which varied with the intensity of the stimulation. When this sensitized muzzle area was stimulated by touching, there was a resultant opening of the mouth. It has also been shown that the activation of the hypothalamic system for predation results in an increased probability that the cat will react with a lunging and jaw-opening response to the stimulus of a mouse presented to the side contralateral to the stimulated hypothalmic site (Bandler & Flynn, 1971).

The facilitating effect of the neural system for aggression on the sensory systems may be an indirect one, through the reticular activating system (to be discussed later). However, there is also evidence that the aggression system has a direct facilitating effect. In a study by Vanegas et al. (1969–1970) it was shown that hypothalamic stimulation enhances the responses of some individual cells of the visual cortex to specific stimuli even after the destruction of the midbrain reticular formation.

The result of this facilitating interaction between the aggression systems and the sensory systems is twofold. If a particular system for aggression is active in the absence of a relevant stimulus complex and the individual encounters an appropriate object of attack, it is more likely to respond to it appropriately. And, as indicated previously, an appropriate stimulus is capable of activating a given aggression system even though that system is not at the moment active.

Reciprocal Action; Aggression and Reticular Systems

A reciprocal facilitating interaction exists between each of the neural systems for aggressive behavior and the reticular activating system. As a result, activity in any of the aggression systems tends to alert the animal and produce a generalized state of arousal. The animal is then more responsive to its environment and its general muscle tone is increased. Amygdaloid stimulation in man, which results in an intense anger reaction, also produces a state of high arousal (King, 1961). Activity in the reticular activating system puts the animal in a general state of readiness and the activity in the aggression system provides the direction for that aroused state.

The reticular activating system also sends facilitating neurons back to the neural system for aggression with a resulting enhancement of activity within that system. It is important to note that activity in the system for arousal *enhances* but does not initiate activity in that aggression system. Sheard and Flynn (1967) have shown that stimulation of certain sites in the midbrain reticular formation at a particular intensity produces only mildly alerting responses in the cat. The activation of those sites, however, facilitates the attack of a cat on a rat when that attack is initiated by stimulation of the lateral hypothalamus. Sheard has also shown that hypothalamically induced predatory attack is also enhanced by intraperitoneal injections of amphetamine and suggests that the amphetamine action is similar to direct electrical stimulation of the reticular system (Sheard, 1967).

Neural Systems Other Than Aggression

There is considerable evidence that a variety of neural systems in the brain act as the substrates for complex behaviors other than aggression. It is postulated in this model that there is a constant interaction among these different systems. The ultimate behavior of the organism is a function of those interactions, which are partly under external control.

Activity in some of these systems tends to facilitate the functioning of particular neural systems for aggression, whereas activity in others tends to be inhibitory. The interactions among these systems must be quite complex and the details are not going to be worked out for some time. It will be necessary not only to determine which portions of the brain inhibit or facilitate a particular neural substrate, but also to determine whether that area is a part of some other neural substrate, and if so, which one.

Systems Facilitating Aggression

In addition to the facilitating effects of the activation of the midbrain reticular activating system on hypothalamically induced predatory aggression, Flynn and his colleagues have identified other brain areas that have a similar facilitating effect (Egger & Flynn, 1963; MacDonnell & Flynn, 1964; Wasman & Flynn, 1962). (See Chapter 8 for more detail.)

It is proposed here that similar facilitating mechanisms exist for all the different kinds of aggression. The system for irritable aggression may be used as an example. Even though the studies have not yet been done to demonstrate increases in neural sensitivity in this neural system by the activation of neural substrates of other complex behaviors, one can draw such an inference from certain behavior studies.

A number of different states increase the tendency for the subject to manifest irritable aggression in the presence of an appropriate stimulus. These include aversive stimulation, particularly pain (Ulrich, 1966); a variety of deprivation states, such as food deprivation (Davis, 1933; Scott, 1948), sleep deprivation (Laties, 1961), morphine deprivation in addicted rats (Boshka, et al., 1966); and frustration produced by withdrawal of reinforcement (extinction-induced aggression) (Azrin et al., 1966; Thompson & Bloom, 1966; Kelly & Hake, 1970). (See Chapter 6.)

All the preceding conditions function as stressors and, if long continued, may produce endocrine changes that may influence the sensitivity of the aggression system (see the following discussion); however, the relatively rapid onset of aggression after some of these stressors implies a neural facilitation.

Systems Inhibiting Aggression

As we have indicated, the sensitivity of the aggression systems also appears to be influenced by inhibitory input from other neural systems. The absence of an aggressive response does not mean, of course, that the underlying system is actively being inhibited. The system may simply not be active, or it may be active and specific motor systems may be blocked, or some of the essential units of the motor system may be preempted by a competitive activity. However, there is considerable experimental evidence lending support to the idea that there is some direct inhibition of the neural system for aggression. Flynn (1967) has elaborated the brain areas in the cat that tend to decrease the sensitivity of the hypothalamic portions of the predatory system (and to some extent the system for what is probably irritable aggression). Flynn refers to those inhibitory systems and to the facilitating systems already mentioned as modulating structures. Delgado (1960) has shown that aggressiveness in the monkey can be specifically inhibited by stimulation of particular points in the head of the caudate nucleus. The normally hostile monkey loses its aggressiveness and does not attempt to bite the experimenter if given an opportunity. However, this does not appear to be an arrest reaction. The animal's motility or motor responsiveness to sensory stimulation is not lost during the caudate stimulation.

Stimulation and lesion studies indicate that systems for irritable aggression and escape behavior are probably controlled by separate but overlapping anatomical areas within the amygdala (as well as other places in the brain) (Kaada, 1967). It also seems likely that a portion of the amygdaloid area that when stimulated induces escape behavior also has inhibitory functions in relation to those areas of the amygdala associated with irritable and predatory aggression (Fonberg, 1965; Egger & Flynn, 1963; Wood, 1958). Stimulation of the central nucleus of the amygdala of the dog results in fear and escape responses (Fonberg, 1965). The same is true for the cat (Anand & Dua, 1956; Wood, 1958). Lesions in the same area, however, result in a reduced threshold for irritable aggression in both animals. The cat with lesions in the central nucleus will, according to Wood (1958), readily attack other cats. The dog with the same lesion shows great irritability to normal restraints, and once started in a rage response becomes more wild, exhibiting what Fonberg calls an avalanche syndrome. Thus it seems likely, as suggested by both authors, that the central nucleus, which appears to be a part of an escape system, also functions to inhibit the activity of the system for aggression. Lesioning this nucleus results in release of that inhibition, with the resulting excessive irritability.

Reciprocal Inhibition
All these studies that relate to the decrease in sensitivity of the aggression systems by neural inhibition lead to the conclusion that the inhibitory neural influences may also be related to the activation of other motivational or motor-predispositional systems. These mechanisms may function in a manner similar to the reciprocal innervation mechanism in muscle control. Thus the intense activation of the neurological substrate for the euphoric or fear response may be neurologically incompatible with the

simultaneous activity of the irritable aggression system because the activation of one system involves the inhibition of the other.

Levels of Sensitivity of Aggression Systems

The interacting neural systems may account for some of the changes in tendencies to hostility over time. Input from other neural systems may either enhance or inhibit the functioning of a given neural aggression system. It is proposed here that there are three possible sensitivity states (which blend into a continuum) of any aggression system. First, the system may be completely insensitive. In this condition the threshold is so high that it cannot be activated by the usual sensory stimulation that provokes attack. One example of this state can be found in the immature or castrated male rat, which will not respond with aggression or threat postures to the stimulus complex of a strange male conspecific, although that stimulus complex is adequate to elicit inter-male aggressive behavior in the normal adult animal.

If the immature or castrated rat is administrated testosterone, the adequate stimulus for inter-male aggression does, in fact, elicit fighting behavior (Levy & King, 1953; Beeman, 1947). Thus it appears that testosterone in some way sensitizes or lowers the threshold of the brain system involved in inter-male aggression so that it is fired by the adequate stimulus complex. This, then, is the second state: the system is sensitized but is inactive until it is activated by the appropriate stimulus. If the sensitivity is slight, fewer cells may be activated by the stimulus situation and the resultant attack may be halfhearted, elicited only by a narrow range of the most appropriate stimuli. On the other hand, if the sensitivity is high, the subject will respond to a wider range of stimuli and the attack behavior will be more intense.

In the third state the threshold for a particular aggression system may be so low that it is spontaneously active even in the absence of the appropriate stimulus, that is, it is activated by the normal metabolic processes in the brain. In this case the cells of the system are firing and the organism is restless, is aroused, and may engage in exploratory behavior. It does not, however, make aggressive motor movements. It will respond more readily to the appropriate stimuli because activity in that system sensitizes the relevant sensory modalities so that the receptors are more easily fired.

In humans it seems likely that activity in certain of the neural systems for aggression is accompanied by subjective feelings of anger and hostility (Schwade & Geiger, 1956; Treffert, 1964; Woods, 1961). The individual may engage in extensive aggressive fantasies and a large number of stimuli will suffice to elicit aggressive thoughts. It is unknowable, of course, whether animals have any comparable subjective state.

Blood Chemistry Influences on Neural Sensitivity

A variety of changes in the blood chemistry of an organism can contribute to the sensitization or desensitization of the neural systems for aggression. (See Chapters 3 and 6 for more details.) The influence of testosterone on inter-male aggression has already been mentioned. There is recent evidence that these androgenic effects may be masked or inhibited by the administration of estrogens (Suchowsky et al., 1969). Irritable aggression in the female in certain species is cyclical (Pearson, 1944) and can be manipulated by hormone injections (Kislak & Beach, 1955).

There is clinical evidence to indicate that similar mechanisms exist in man. Progesterone reduces the irritability manifested as a part of the premenstrual tension syndrome (Dalton, 1964; Greene & Dalton, 1953), and the administration of androgens has been reported to increase aggressiveness in males (Sands, 1954; Sands & Chamberlain, 1952; Strauss et al., 1952). Castration (Hawke, 1950; LeMaire, 1956) and the administration of stilbestrol (Dunn, 1941; Sands, 1954) in some cases reduce aggressive tendencies.

It is generally recognized that frustration and stress, particularly if prolonged, are likely to result in increased irritability and aggressive behavior. It may well be that frustration-induced irritability results from the sensitization of irritable aggression systems in the brain by the particular hormone balance that characterizes the stress syndrome. At this point there is no experimental verification of this hypothesis, but the experimental designs for the testing of the hypothesis are obvious.

The blood chemistry influence on aggressive behavior does not appear to be limited to hormonal factors. Hypoglycemia, for example, is a dysfunction in the blood chemistry that evidently results in an increased sensitivity of the neural substrates for aggression. In a much-neglected paper by Wilder (1947), a remarkable amount of evidence is compiled that implicates low blood sugar as a causal factor in hostility and crime. He indicates that the aggressive tendency associated with hypoglycemic states is manifest in certain matrimonial relationships, homicidal threats and acts, destructiveness, and cruelty toward children. Although well-controlled research on this problem is minimal, low blood sugar as an underlying cause of hostility and irritability is suggested by several other authors. (See Chapter 3 for a more complete discussion of this relationship.)

Mechanisms for Blood Chemistry Influences

It is not clear at the moment whether the endocrine changes in the bloodstream increase the sensitivity of the aggression systems directly or do so indirectly by differentially influencing the amounts of neurotransmitters in particular portions of the brain, with a resulting change in the sensitivity of particular systems. There is good evidence, for example, that the brain chemistry of aggressive animals (isolated mice) is different from that of normals, including difference in turnover rates of serotonin (Giacalone et al., 1968) and norepinephrine and dopamine (Welch & Welch, 1969). Sigg et al. (1966) have shown that isolation-induced aggression does not develop in castrated mice. The endocrine-brain chemistry interactions and the causal relationships to the aggressive behaviors remain to be worked out.

In light of the experimental evidence there can be no doubt that different kinds of aggression are in part a function of particular hormonal balances and that the levels of aggressiveness can be directly manipulated by endocrine changes. It is inferred here that the endocrine-induced changes in aggression result from direct or indirect sensitization or activation of particular brain systems.

Permanent Influence of Early Blood Chemistry

The sensitivity of the aggression systems and the consequent tendency to behave aggressively may also be *permanently* influenced by the endocrine, particularly gonadal, status of the organism shortly after birth. A study by Conner and Levine (1969) indicates that rats castrated as neonates fight less under conditions of shock (irritable aggression) than do either weaning-age castrates or intact rats. Further, the fighting level of the weaning castrates can be brought up to normal by exogenously administered testosterone, but the fighting behavior of the rats castrated as neonates remains unaffected by testosterone. Conner and Levine concluded from this that the neural substrates that are modulated by the androgens in later life are permanently changed by the early castration. Other evidence also indicates that these same neural substrates can be altered by the administration of testosterone propionate to female mice on the day of birth. When female mice are so treated and subsequently isolated, they respond to the administration of testosterone in the same manner as males castrated at weaning, that is, with increased fighting (inter-male aggression). However, females treated with oil within the first 24 hours after birth do not fight when isolated and given testosterone (Edwards, 1968). Edwards thus concludes, "One may presume that the stimulation by endogenous testosterone in the male (and exogenous testosterone in the female) can organize or cause the differentiation of a neural substrate for fighting." (See Chapter 8 for more detail.)

Hereditary Influences on Neural Sensitivity

There is reasonable evidence that some of the factors that contribute to the sensitivity of the neural substrates for aggressive behavior have an inherited component. (The general topic of behavior genetics as it relates to aggressive behavior is not covered in this book; however, an excellent review of this material can be found in McClearn, 1969.) There can be no doubt that animals can be bred specifically for particular kinds of aggression; for example, fighting cocks, fighting bulls, and pit dogs have been selectively bred for fighting behavior. There are clear-cut strain differences in the probability of predatory attack. Seventy percent of Norway rats kill mice, whereas only 12 percent of the domesticated Norways kill mice (Karli, 1956). A significantly higher percentage of Long-Evans hooded rats kill chickens than do Sprague-Dawley albinos (Bandler & Moyer, 1970).

There are also strain differences in inter-male fighting (Scott, 1942; Southwick & Clark, 1968). A number of experimenters have shown that it is possible, through selective breeding, to develop aggressive and non-aggressive strains of animals. In these cases the behavior studied was also inter-male aggression (Hall & Klein, 1942; Lagerspetz, 1964; Stone, 1932; Yerkes, 1913). The most extensive study of the genetics of aggression has been done on mice selectively bred for high and low aggressiveness according to a seven-point scale of behavior during a period in which formerly isolated mice were paired. It is interesting to note that the selection process was carried out only on males, since the females did not show enough aggression to score. Table 1 shows the mean aggression score for each successive generation. As McLearn (1969) points out, "In combination with the differences among inbred strains in aggressiveness, this success in selective breeding for aggressive behavior constitutes unassailable evidence of the importance of hereditary factors in determining individual differences in mouse aggressiveness."

There is, of course, no comparable data on man. However, the model

Table 1
The Selective Breeding Experiments

Genera-tion	Number of selected males		Age at selec-tion (months)	Range of test scores of selected animals		Number of successful matings		Number of offspring	
	A	N		A	N	A	N	A	N
P	3	3	3–6	5.3–7.0	1.8–2.1	4	3	10 8	12 8
S_1	4	4	4½	4.1–5.9	1.5–1.9	5	4	25 8	7 10
S_2	6	4	4½	4.1–6.6	1.3–2.4	7	7	29 22	22 19
S_3	6	6	4½	5.0–6.2	1.1–1.9	7	7	20 15	22 14
S_4	7	7	4½	6.1–7.0	1.0–1.7	6	6	30 24	27 23
S_5	7	8	4½	5.9–6.9	1.4–1.7	9	9	31 37	26 31
S_6	9	9	4½	6.4–6.9	1.0–1.6	10	13	34 30	28 34

K. Lagerspetz, Studies on the aggressive behavior of mice, *Annalis Academiae Scientiarum Fennicae,* 1964, Series B, 131, p. 51, Table 4.

presented here would predict that there would be hereditary factors contributing to the determination of individual differences of some kinds of aggression in man. Certainly there are vast inherited differences in the human nervous and endocrine systems. If, as suggested in this model, there are specific neural systems that are responsible for particular types of aggression, one would expect genetic variability in the sensitivity of those systems. If, as appears to be the case, the sensitivity of these systems varies as a function of level of certain circulating hormones (see Chapters 3 and 8), one would also expect genetic variability in the factors that contribute to the determination of the hormone levels in the bloodstream. This is not to imply that these genetically determined factors cannot be modified or that they are uninfluenced by interactions with the environment. It does indicate, however, that other things being equal, some individuals are more likely to behave aggressively in a given situation than are others.

Although much more evidence is needed before a firm statement can be made, some chromosomal abnormalities in man may result in a lack of impulse control, with a resultant increased tendency to aggressive behavior. One of these is the Klinefelter syndrome (Burnand et al., 1967) and the other is the XYY syndrome (Kessler & Moos, 1970).

Learning and the Manifestation of Aggressive Behavior

The important role of learning and experience in aggressive behavior of all kinds is not covered in detail in this book. As indicated on p. xvii, there are already several reviews of this material available.

Aggressive behavior, like all other basic behaviors, is strongly influenced by experience. An animal can be readily taught to overeat (Williams & Teitelbaum, 1956) or undereat (Lichtenstein, 1950; Masserman, 1943) through the use of reinforcement, regardless of the state of deprivation. Similarly, animals can be taught to exhibit or inhibit aggressive behavior.

Instrumental Aggression and the Law of Effect

It is possible to increase the probability of occurrence of any aggressive or destructive response, no matter what its initial motivational source, if that response is followed by a positive reinforcement. The law of effect operates just as effectively to facilitate motor responses that are labeled aggressive as to facilitate those that are not. In the classification system outlined in Chapters 5 and 6, aggressive behavior, so determined, is referred to as instrumental aggression. A particularly pure case of instrumental aggression is demonstrated in the study of Stachnik et al. (1966a, 1966b). By reinforcing successive approximations to aggressive behavior in rats through positively reinforcing brain stimulation, these investigators were able to induce rats to attack other rats, monkeys, and even cats. They note, however, that the occasional pain-elicited aggressive attacks resulting from counterattack by a control rat presented a noticeable contrast to the topography of the conditioned attack. We have used the same procedure to reinforce the attack on a mouse by a nonpredatory rat. It is relatively easy to induce the rat to chase, harass, and nip at the mouse. However, although we have tried repeatedly, we have been unable to induce mouse killing by this procedure. The rat's typical predatory response of biting through the spinal cord of the mouse just never occurs in the nonpredatory rat and thus cannot be reinforced.

Another experiment from our laboratory illustrates the distinctiveness of instrumental aggression. Karli (1956) has shown that nonpredatory rats will starve to death with a live mouse in the cage. It is possible, however, to induce mouse killing in nonpredatory rats by gradually teaching the rat that the mouse is a source of food (Moyer, 1968, unpublished). Most rats, when deprived of food, will eat a dead mouse with the skin of the back slit. After a series of trials with that food object and, subsequently, with an intact dead mouse, and a live but totally anesthetized mouse, these rats will attack and kill a lightly anesthetized mouse that is still mobile but sluggish in its behavior. Again, however, it is easy to discriminate this instrumental behavior that results in the death of the mouse from the typical predatory response either naturally or chemically induced. These rats never kill by bites on the back of the neck. Their attack is directed at the tail, feet, and belly of the mouse. The approach is tentative and the latencies of attack and the time between attack and kill are much longer than in the natural predatory response. It would seem unlikely that any manipulation of the physiological basis for predatory aggression would have a considerable effect on this instrumental response.

Reward Value of the Aggressive Response
Any positive reinforcement can be used to increase the tendency to behave aggressively. However, there is also evidence that the opportunity to express aggression can be used to reinforce new learning.

It would appear that the aggressive act is only reinforcing when the relevant neural system for that particular kind of aggression is either active or highly sensitized. Thus non-mouse-killing cats will learn a Y-maze in order to obtain a rat to kill if the hypothalamic system for predation is stimulated during the learning process. However, performance quickly deteriorates when trials are given in the absence of the brain stimulation (Roberts & Kiess, 1964). Predatory rats will learn a maze to obtain a mouse, whereas nonkiller rats will not (Myer & White, 1965).

The opportunity to behave aggressively can be used to reinforce learning if that opportunity is provided in situations that normally elicit aggression. Tail shock produces "reflexive" aggression in monkeys. These animals will also learn a chain-pulling response in order to obtain a canvas-covered ball that they may bite (Azrin et al., 1965). Pigeons frequently behave aggressively during the extinction of a response that has previously been reinforced. During extinction they will also learn to peck a key that produces another bird that can then be attacked (Azrin, 1964).

Although aggressive behavior may be positively reinforcing when the relevant neural system is functioning, activity in the neural system itself may be either positively or negatively reinforcing, depending on the kind of aggression involved. There is as yet relatively little hard data available on this concept. There is little doubt that activity in the neural system for aggression that is, produced by aversive stimulation has negative reinforcement value. The monkey, which will learn a response for the opportunity to bite a ball under the stress of tail shock, will certainly learn a response to terminate the tail shock and the resultant neural activity.

Although the evidence is complex and difficult to interpret, some inferences may be drawn from studies that use brain stimulation to induce aggressive behavior. If an animal will work to terminate the stimulation activating a neural system that produces aggressive behavior, one might infer that activity in that system is associated with negative affect. If the animal will work to turn the aggression-inducing stimulation on, positive affect might be inferred. Both kinds of evidence exist. Monkeys will lever-press to terminate brain stimulation that appears to produce irritable aggression (Polotnik et al., 1971). In another study monkeys pressed a bar to receive stimulation that produced inter-male aggression (Robinson et al., 1969). However, there are other interpretations possible. The current may activate more than one neural system at the same time. These systems may be functionally discrete even though they are anatomically proximal. Thus the affective state generated by the stimulation may be irrelevant to the manifest behavior. More definitive information on this problem must come from work with humans who can provide verbal reports on the affective states that accompany the different kinds of aggression.

Punishment of the Aggressive Responses

Just as aggressive behavior can be facilitated by reward, it can be inhibited by punishment. Predatory aggression can be readily suppressed by punishment of the attack response (Myer, 1968). In spite of the fact that noxious stimulation produced irritable-aggressive behavior (Ulrich, 1966), it can also, if sufficiently intense, inhibit aggressive tendencies. Aggressive behavior is suppressed in monkeys if the punishing shock is more intense than the shock that elicited the fighting (Ulrich et al., 1969).

The negative reinforcement in defeat during inter-male aggression results in a decrease in aggressive tendencies (Kahn, 1951; Lagerspetz, 1961). Miller et al. (1955) have clearly shown that it is possible to manipulate social hierarchies in monkeys by punishing a dominant animal in the presence of a subordinate, and Ulrich indicates that when a monkey is severely bitten by an opponent, there is an obvious decrease in the aggressiveness of the bitten subject.

Dominance, Submission, and Learning
In an established colony where animals have a frequent opportunity to interact, it is easy to see that the preceding learning mechanisms could account for the development of dominance hierarchies. A given animal could easily learn to respond to the cue complex of one animal in the colony with aggressive responses but to another with avoidance, submission, or aggression-inhibitory responses. One would certainly expect these learned responses to interact with the other internal states of the organism such as the activity of particular aggression systems. If an animal is punished in the presence of food, the eating responses of that animal, in the presence of the cues associated with punishment, will be inhibited, regardless of the amount of deprivation (and presumed activity in the neural systems for hunger or consummatory behavior). One would expect no less of an influence of learning on the manifestations of aggression. As Plotnik et al. (1971) and Delgado (1963, 1966) have shown, the brain stimulation-induced aggressive behavior of monkeys is related to the animal's prior experience. The effects of lesions involving the aggression systems are also influenced by the animals' earlier learning (Rosvold et al., 1954; Sodetz & Bunnell, 1967a, 1967b). It is more rare for the activity of the aggression systems to be so intense that they appear to override well-established habit patterns, although this has been reported in monkeys (Robinson et al., 1969) and humans (Schwade & Geiger, 1956).

Modeling Aggressive Behavior
An extensive series of experiments has shown that an individual may learn aggressive behavior through a simple observation of another person behaving aggressively. (See Bandura, 1973, for a complete review of this material.) In a classic experiment of this type, nursery school children were permitted to observe the behavior of an adult solving a problem. The behavior of the adult included the punching of an inflated Bobo doll as well as other responses that were irrelevant to the solution of the problem. When the observing children were put into the situation and given the problem to solve, they imitated many of the behaviors of the adult model, including the irrelevant aggressive responses of hitting the inflated doll (Bandura & Huston, 1961). A number of theories have been

suggested to explain why modeling occurs (Bandura, 1970). However, further considration of them is beyond the scope of this book.

Mechanism for Learning Influence

There is little experimental evidence on the neural mechanisms involved in learned inhibition of aggressive responding. It could, according to this model, occur at any one of several levels. As indicated previously, the inhibition may occur at the level of the integrating aggression system itself. For example, the subjective feeling of anger in the human (which would be indicative of activity in the system for irritable aggression) could be replaced by a sufficiently intense fear such that the irritable aggression system would be inhibited and the individual would no longer have the subjective experience of anger. The inhibition could also occur at the muscular level producing the extreme tension state of inhibited rage. In this instance the muscles in opposition to those used in attack are sufficiently activated to prevent attack behavior. Under this circumstance, however, the central integrative aggression system would continue to fire and the human would continue to experience the subjective state of anger.

Aggression, Learning, and Man

Man, of course, learns better and faster than any other animal. It is therefore reasonable to expect that the internal impulses to aggressive behavior would be more subject to modification by experience in man than in any other animal. In addition, because of man's additional ability to manipulate symbols, and to substitute one symbol for another, one would expect to find a considerable diversity in the stimuli that elicit or inhibit activity in the aggression system. One would also expect that the modes of expression of aggression would be more varied, diverse, and less stereotyped in man than in other animals.

Chronic Behavior Tendencies

The interactions of all the preceding factors contribute to the determination of the aggressive tendencies of a given individual at a given time. One might be thought of as having a chronic behavior tendency to hostility if these factors function to produce activity in or a sensitivity of the neural systems for aggressive behavior over a prolonged period of time. The underlying factors that contribute to a chronic behavior tendency may vary considerably from one individual to another. The following are some examples.

A particular person may frequently react with anger to a wide variety of stimuli because his heredity has determined that the threshold for the activation of his neural substrates for hostility is relatively low.

The heredity of another individual may dictate that his neural substrates for aggression have a threshold well within the normal range. However, his environment may be such that he is subjected to constant frustration and stress, which may result in a hormone balance that sensitizes the neurons in the hostility system so that they are readily activated by a wide range of stimuli.

In another case an individual may be born with a neural system for some positive affect with a particularly low threshold. Other things being equal, he may have a chronic behavior tendency to react to many stimuli with positive approach tendencies. If inhibitory neurons to the neural substrates for aggression are a part of that system, that individual will have less of a tendency to behave aggressively.

It is also possible for an individual to have a chronic behavior tendency to hostility without having the neural systems for aggression particularly involved. He may simply have learned that aggressive behavior is what is expected of him if he is to receive the kinds of approbation that are rewarding to him. This is well illustrated by Claude Brown in *Manchild in the Promised Land.*

> I was growing up now, and people were going to expect things from me. I would soon be expected to kill a nigger if he mistreated me, like Rock, Bubba Williams, and Dewdrop had. Everybody knew these cats were killers. Nobody messed with them. If anybody messed with them or their family or friends, they had to kill them. I knew now that I had to keep up with these cats; if I didn't I would lose my respect in the neighborhood. I had to keep my respect because I had to take care of Pimp and Carole and Margie. I was the big brother in the family. I couldn't be running and getting somebody after some cat who messed with me.[1]

Interactions of all the determining factors are, of course, the rule. The individual with an inherited low threshold for the activation of the neural system for hostility will be even more readily and intensely aroused to anger if he lives in a deprived, frustrating, and stressful environment. If, on the other hand, he is surrounded by love and protected from much of the harshness of the world and is exposed to relatively little provocation, his aggressive behavior will be limited.

Neurological Set

Chronic behavior tendencies refer to the long-run probabilities of a particular kind of behavior. Set, however, involves the proclivities toward a given kind of behavior at the moment. It should be emphasized here that the reaction to the environment is an interaction between what is going on in the environment and what is going on at the same time in the

---

[1] Claude Brown, *Manchild in the Promised Land.* New York: Macmillan, 1965, p. 121. Copyright © Claude Brown, 1965.

nervous system. It is obvious that what constitutes a provocation at time A, is not necessarily a provocation at time B. If there is ongoing activity in the neural system for aggression or if it is highly sensitized, the amount of provocation required by a relevant external stimulus to elicit an aggressive action will be less. The reason for the neural activity or hypersensitivity is irrelevant.

A teenage girl may have a highly sensitized neural system for irritable aggression because of the hormone balance characteristic of the third day before her menstrual period. At a different time that neural system may be sensitive or active because she has been frustrated by the cutting and sarcastic remarks of a high school teacher. In either case she has an increased probability of responding aggressively to any appropriate external stimulus. Whether this increased probability of aggressive responding actually results in aggressive behavior in a given instance is determined in part by her previous experience with the eliciting stimuli. If she has been negatively reinforced for expressing hostility toward her parents, she will be less likely to make that response. However, if she stumbles over her dog, she may very well swear at it or kick it.

In the second instance, in which the girl's neural system is activated by the sarcasm of her teacher, her act of kicking the dog is referred to as displaced aggression. In the traditional psychoanalytic formulation the aggressive "energy" is transferred from one subject to another. In the analysis presented here it will be seen that the two instances are not essentially different, except in the manner in which the neural system was initially activated or sensitized. In both instances the tendency to respond aggressively may be the same, and in both cases the particular stimulus responded to depends on the individual's reinforcement history.

It is also possible to have a neurological set in which the tendency to aggression is decreased. If the individual is in a "happy" frame of mind, it will take more provocation to elicit an aggressive response. As suggested, this is due in part to inhibitory neurons from the neural substrate of the "happy state of mind" that tend to block activity or reduce the sensitivity in the neural substrates for hostility.

SUMMARY

Aggression is defined and it is suggested that the concept of intent is essential to a useful definition of the term. An operational definition of intent is given and aggression-related terms are defined.

Aggression is not a unitary concept. There are different kinds of aggression that may be classified on the basis of the topography of the response and the types of stimuli that elicit the particular type of aggression.

Some of the experimental evidence is examined to support the proposition that there are organized neural systems in the brain for the various kinds of aggression. When these systems are active in the presence of particular stimuli, the organism behaves aggressively. Thus aggressive behavior is stimulus-bound and dependent on the functional integrity of the relevant neural systems.

There is a constant interaction among the sensory, motor, and aggression neural systems. A specific pattern of activity in the sensory system activates a neural system for aggression that induces patterned activity in the motor system. Activity in the motor system interacts with the input from the sensory system in a feedback mechanism that permits directed and coordinated movement. Activity in an aggression system also acts to sensitize specific portions of the sensory mechanisms.

A reciprocal action exists between the neural system for aggression and the reticular activating system. Activity in an aggression system initiates functioning of the RAS. Activity in the arousal system enhances but does not initiate functioning in an aggression system.

There are neural systems in the brain for complex behaviors other than aggression. The interactions among these systems are complex and activity in one system may inhibit or facilitate activity in another and the interactions between some systems may be reciprocal. For example, the neural substrates for irritable aggression and for euphoria may be mutually inhibiting.

Although the exact mechanism cannot yet be specified, the sensitivity of the neural systems for aggression may be raised or lowered by specific blood components, particularly from the endocrine system. If some hormonal influences occur early in the life of the organism, the effects on the neural systems may be permanent.

Evidence exists that the sensitivity of the neural systems for the different kinds of aggressive behavior is in part determined by heredity.

Learning has an important influence on aggressive behavior just as it does on any other behavior. Aggressive behavior that is rewarded tends to be repeated, and that which is punished tends to be inhibited. In certain circumstances the completion of an aggressive act is in itself rewarding.

The variables that influence the sensitivity of the neural system for aggression may function to increase the sensitivity over a prolonged period of time. In that circumstance the individual may be said to have a chronic behavior tendency to hostility.

If the sensitivity of an aggressive system is relatively transient, the individual may be considered as having a neurological set for hostile behavior.

2

Neural Factors
in Aggression in Man

According to Pope, "The proper study of mankind is man." Although we can learn much from animals, man must be the ultimate subject of our study if we are to discover the substrates of his behavior. In the next two chapters the physiological bases of aggression in man will be examined and in Chapter 4 the implications of that understanding for control of aggression in humans will be considered. Later in the book the physiology of the various kinds of aggression found in animals will be presented.

Ethical considerations usually preclude well-controlled physiological experimentation on man; however, it is possible to derive considerable understanding of physiological bases of aggression from the study of a variety of natural dysfunctions that alter behavior. Further, knowledge can be gained from the careful analysis of well-controlled therapeutic procedures.

There are a number of physiological changes that occur in man that can alter the ease with which he can be aroused to anger and hostile behavior. Some of these changes are clearly pathological and may result in uncontrollable rages and violence, whereas others involve only moderate fluctuations in metabolic processes and physiological functions and result in minor changes in the threshold for irritable behavior. By one process or another these physiological changes alter the functioning of the neural systems for aggression that man has derived from his animal heritage.

This chapter is concerned with various forms of brain damage that influence man's hostile tendencies, some of the therapeutic interventions designed to reduce aggression, and some of the results of direct brain stimulation in man that provide some further insight into the neural systems involved in aggression. The next chapter considers some of the changes in blood chemistry that enhance our understanding of aggression in man.

KINDS OF AGGRESSION IN MAN

There seems to be little doubt that there are different kinds of aggression in humans in that hostile and destructive behaviors may have more than one physiological substrate. However, it is much more difficult to define these different kinds of aggression in man than it is in animals. As Chapters 5 and 6 will show, the kinds of aggression in animals vary on a number of dimensions. Two of the most useful for the classification of aggression in animals are the types of stimuli eliciting the behavior and the topography of the response. In man, however, these dimensions are not useful in the development of a system of classification. Man's outstanding capacity for learning and for symbol manipulation permits him to interchange the object of his aggressive intent and to substitute one object or type of object for another much more readily than is possible for animals. The symbol against which the aggressive behavior is directed may be more than once or twice removed from the original eliciting stimulus and mechanisms such as repression may make it difficult even for the individual himself to recognize the original target of his hostility.

It is also not possible to differentiate among the various kinds of aggression in man on the basis of the response topographies as it is in animals.[1] Except for the possibility of a few expressive movements that may have an innate basis (Eibl-Eibesfeldt, 1972), man has no automatically elicited behavior patterns. Even the expressive movements are readily subject to modification and control through the learning process. There are many ritualistic aspects to certain aggressive behaviors in man, but these are culturally determined and vary from one culture group to another. Man's use of tools further complicates any attempt to differentiate the different kinds of aggression on the basis of response topography. A knife may be used in a confrontation between rival males (inter-male aggression); in an attack on a frustrator (irritable aggression); in a sadistic assault on a victim during a sexual frenzy (sex-related aggression); or during a paroxysm of fear when cornered by a bully (fear-induced aggression).

It is conceivable that the different kinds of aggression in man might

[1] The classification of aggressive behaviors in animals includes predatory, inter-male, fear-induced, maternal, irritable, sex-related, and instrumental. (See Chapters 5 and 6.)

someday be differentiated on the basis of the verbal reports of the subjective feelings that accompany the hostile impulses. A young National Guard member may be able to explain that he felt angry (irritable aggression) or terrorized (fear-induced aggression) or was simply following orders (instrumental aggression) when he fired into a crowd of rioting students. However, there is no relevant experimental work on this problem to date.

In spite of our inability to define the various kinds of aggression in man, it is important to recognize that different kinds do exist. Thus a particular physiological manipulation may alter the tendency to hostility in one individual but have no effect on another. This may well be due to the fact that the substrates of the aggressive behavior may be different in the two individuals.

BRAIN DYSFUNCTIONS RELATING TO AGGRESSION
Brain Tumors

As neoplasms of the brain grow, they may produce the intermittent activation of brain cells in the immediate area. Ultimately, of course, the normal cells in the area of the tumor are destroyed. The symptomatology of brain tumors varies widely. Headache, nausea, and vomiting generally result from an increase in intracranial pressure. However, there are also a wide variety of psychological symptoms, ranging from hallucinations to an impairment of mental faculties and psychotic episodes. When various portions of the limbic lobe are involved, changes in personality and in affect frequently occur, and may result in disorders of emotional expression and fundamental drive states. The patient may have inappropriate bouts of laughter, euphoria, or depression. He may become hyperphagic or anorexic and manifest either hypo- or hypersexual behaviors. Of interest here is the well-documented evidence that a frequent behavioral result of limbic system tumors is an increase in irritability, temper outbursts, and even homicidal attacks of rage (Kletschka, 1966). The resulting personality changes are frequently completely out of keeping with the individual's behavior patterns prior to the onset of the pathological state.

Temporal Lobe Tumors

Malamud (1967) describes nine cases of confirmed tumors in the temporal lobe that showed psychiatric symptoms. Three of these patients showed increased tension and aggressive behavior, ranging from intense sibling rivalry to unpredictable assaultive tendencies. Two violent patients with tumors of the temporal lobe are described by Sweet et al. (1969). One man, a powerful individual, attempted to kill his wife and daughter with a butcher knife. When brought to the hospital, he was in a full-blown rage reaction, during which he snarled, showed his teeth, and attempted to hit or kick anyone who came close enough. History taking revealed that over a period of six months, his personality had gradually changed and that he had complained of blurred vision and intense headaches. When the tumor that was pressing on the anterior temporal lobe was removed, his symptoms rapidly abated. Another patient who had shown hyperirritability for years began to show serious destructive rages. He drove his car recklessly and began to direct his outbursts of rage against his wife and son. Although intellectually capable as a chemist, he was unable to hold a position for longer than a few months because of his volatile and irritable behavior patterns. After the removal of a slow-growing tumor that had evidently invaded the temporal lobe over a period of several years, his symptoms disappeared. He became more stable, more placid, and functioned adequately as a chemist during the 19-month follow-up. Vonderahe (1944) describes the onset of sudden outbursts of aggression in a female patient who on autopsy was found to have a tumor the size of a cherry on the anterior and inner aspect of the left temporal lobe encroaching on the amygdala.

Temporal lobe lesions, including tumors, may also result in paroxysmal symptoms that include various affective disturbances and automatisms in which the patient carries out "automatic" activities in a state of impaired consciousness. During this period he is apparently unable to make decisions and is not amenable to reason. The individual may continue to drive his car and engage in other activities at an automatic level and yet show amnesia for his behavior during the period of the fuguelike state. During the period of the automatism the patient may engage in highly destructive behavior, breaking furniture and assaulting others (Mulder and Daly, 1952).

Charles Whitman

One of the most celebrated cases of extreme hostility that may have resulted from temporal lobe pathology was that of Charles Whitman. It is particularly instructive because he recognized his impulses to violence, was concerned about them, and sought help from a psychiatrist. He was also an introspective young man who kept extensive notes in an attempt to understand his own obviously pathological motivations. He was also concerned that others understand his behavior so that individuals with problems similar to his own could get help before it was too late. One letter, which was started before he killed his wife and his mother and finished after the double murder, provides some insight into the thought processes of an individual whose mental world is governed in part by what appears to be excessive activation of the neural systems for hostility.

> I don't quite understand what it is that compels me to type this letter. Perhaps it is to leave some vague reason for the actions I have recently performed.
>
> I don't really understand myself these days. I am supposed to be an average, reasonable and intelligent young man. However, lately (I can't recall when it started) I have been a victim of many unusual and irrational thoughts. These thoughts constantly recur, and it requires a tremendous mental effort to concentrate on useful and progressive tasks. In March when my parents made a physical break I noticed a great deal of stress. I consulted a Dr. Cochrum at the University Health Center and asked him to recommend someone that I could consult with about some psychiatric disorders I felt I had. I talked with a doctor once for about two hours and tried to convey to him my fears that I felt overcome [sic] by overwhelming violent impulses. After one session I never saw the doctor again and since then I have been fighting my mental turmoil alone, and seemingly to no avail. After my death I wish that an autopsy would be performed on me to see if there is any visible physical disorder. I have had some tremendous headaches in the past and have consumed two large bottles of Excedrin in the past three months.
>
> It was after much thought that I decided to kill my wife Kathy, tonight after I pick her up from work. . . . I love her dearly, and she has been a fine wife to me as any man could ever hope to have. I cannot rationally pinpoint any specific reason for doing this. I don't know whether it is selfishness or if I don't want her to have to face the embarrassment my actions would surely cause her. At this time though, the prominent reason in my mind is that I truly do not consider this world worth living in, and am prepared to die, and I do not want to leave her to suffer alone in it. I intend to kill her as painlessly as possible. . . .

Later in the night he killed both his mother and wife, and then wrote:

> I imagine it appears that I brutally killed both of my loved ones. I was only trying to do a good and thorough job.
>
> If my life insurance policy is valid please see that all the worthless checks I wrote this weekend are made good. Please pay off all my debts. I am 25 years old and have never been financially independent. Donate the rest anonymously to a mental health foundation. Maybe research can prevent further tragedies of this type.[2]

During his consultation with the psychiatrist several months earlier, Whitman had revealed that he sometimes became so angry that he would like to go to the top of the university tower and start shooting people. The morning after having written the preceding letter, he did just that. He took a high-powered rifle with a telescopic sight and several hundred rounds of ammunition to the tower. He killed the receptionist, barricaded

[2] R. Johnson, *Aggression in Man and Animals.* Philadelphia: Saunders, 1972, p. 79.

the door, and spent 90 minutes shooting anyone he could bring into his powerful sight. He was a good marksman. When he was finally killed by the police he had wounded 24 and killed 14 innocent people. Autopsy revealed that Whitman had a malignant infiltrating tumor (glioblastoma multiforme). Because there was extensive damage to the brain from gunshot wounds, the neuropathologist was not certain of the precise location of the tumor, but it was probably in the medial part of one temporal lobe.

It is not possible to determine after the fact whether the temporal lobe malignancy actually caused the extreme aggression displayed by Whitman. Valenstein (1973) concludes that it is unlikely because Whitman's actions were planned and not typical of a burst of impulsive rage characteristic of the dyscontrol syndrome. That is, of course, true, but it is beside the point. The Whitman case is, in fact, more typical of the progressive effects of expanding tumors. As indicated in other parts of this section, the change in the individual's personality may occur over a period of years. In some instances the only symptom is an increase in irritability. As the tumor growth progresses, the patient may become more and more irritable and ultimately homicidal. There are now a significant number of cases in which progressive irrational aggression of several years duration has been alleviated by the removal of a limbic tumor.

Tumors in Other Parts of the Limbic System,
Frontal Lobe, and Hypothalamus
Tumors in other areas of the limbic system also result in excessive irritable behavior and rage responses that are not characteristic of the patient's normal personality and that he does not understand. Tension, ambivalence, negativism, and hostility characterized one patient with a tumor that involved primarily the white matter of the cingulate gyrus. Another with tumor damage in the cingulum and left frontal lobe was described as having had attacks of assaultiveness and convulsions. Between attacks, as the tumor progressed, he became increasingly irritable and abusive (Malamud, 1967).

Zeman and King (1958) report a number of cases in which tumors of the septal region result in restlessness and irritability with some maniacal outbursts. These patients showed an excessive startle reaction, temper "flare-ups," and irrational assaultiveness. One became homicidal, attempted to stab her husband with a paring knife, and threatened to poison him. Frontal lobe tumors also result in pathological affect. Over half of one series of 85 patients with frontal lobe tumors had affective disturbances and the most frequent change was in the direction of increased irritability. In many cases it was the first and in some it was the only mental symptom during the course of the disease. Some of the patients were reported to be "raging" (Strauss & Keschner, 1935, 1936).

Finally, as might be expected from our knowledge of the neural systems involved in aggressive behavior in animals (see Chapter 8), tumors in the hypothalamus result in a facilitation of hostile impulses. Alpers (1937) reports a case of teratoma in the third ventricle that resulted in damage to the anterior hypothalamus; in this case the patient's character changed radically and became very aggressive. About a year prior to other tumor symptoms he became irritable, aggressive, argumentative, and unreasonable. He frequently flew into rages over trivial matters. Reeves and Blum (1969) have recently reported a case in which the ventromedial hypothalamus was destroyed by a neoplasm, which resulted in manifestations of many of the symptoms found when similar lesions are made in animals. The patient developed hyperphagia, became obese, and had a very low threshold for aggression. At times she would become uncooperative and hostile without apparent reason and would hit, scratch, and attempt to bite the examiner. Subsequently, she would sometimes express regret for her unprovoked hostility. A similar case is reported by Killeffer and Stern (1970). Sano (1962) has reported on 1800 cases of brain tumor of which 297 were in the limbic region. He concluded that increased irritability and rage attacks characterized patients with tumor involvement in the anterior hypothalamus.

The evidence from brain tumors demonstrates again that man's neural systems for aggression can be activated by internal physiological processes that result in the individual feeling and behaving in an inappropriate, hostile manner. As with other neurological dysfunctions, the behavior could result from an irritative focus of the tumor that activates some of the neurological mechanisms for aggression, or it could result from the destruction of inhibitory mechanisms.

Miscellaneous Brain Trauma

Personality changes that include loss of impulse control with increases in irritability accompany a wide variety of different types of brain lesions. In some instances it is possible to specify the area damaged; in others the trauma may be diffuse. Head injuries caused by falls or automobile accidents frequently result in loss of consciousness. As the individual regains consciousness he goes through a period of uncontrolled violence and aggression toward those around him (Mark & Ervin, 1970). The behavior of children is particularly affected by injury to the brain. The child's personality may show a complete reversal; the child may change from a lovable youngster to an antisocial and unmanageable one. Such children show emotional instability with a characteristic unrestrained aggressiveness and a lack of impulse control. They may be cruel and show such asocial behaviors as lying and stealing (Blau, 1937; Kasanin, 1929; Strecker & Ebagh, 1924).

There are a variety of disorders that involve generalized damage to the central nervous system, including cerebral arteriosclerosis, senile dementia, Korsakoff's syndrome, and Huntington's chorea. These dysfunctions frequently present a common symptomatology referred to as chronic brain syndrome, which is characterized by memory deficit, orientation loss, and affective disturbances. There are wide fluctuations of mood and a general emotional instability, but the affective pattern is dominated by anger, rage, and increased irritability (Lyght, 1966).

Rabies

The cry "mad dog" has always meant that a dog is loose that will attack anyone or anything that crosses its path. The dog has no restraint on its aggressive behavior and its selection of victims is indiscriminate. If the animal bites and infects a human and the disease process is not blocked by rabies vaccine, the sequela may involve bizarre behavior changes, which may include excesses in sexuality, alcoholism, and violent rages involving irrational assaults. During the terminal stages of the disease the patient manifests extreme irritability and is subject to pronounced spasms of the throat muscles, which cause excruciating pain. The spasms are precipitated by any attempt to drink water, with the result that the patient refuses all fluids in spite of severe thirst, thus the name *hydrophobia*. Death occurs within three to five days from exhaustion, general paralysis, or asphyxia.

Rabies (derived from the Latin word meaning "rage") is caused by a filterable virus transmitted to the victim in the saliva of the infected animal. Being neurotrophic, it travels up the peripheral nerves to the spinal cord and then to the brain. The entire brain is affected to some extent in that nerve cells are damaged and there is a generalized menengial and cerebral edema with multiple minute hemorrhages. As might be suspected from the behavioral symptomatology there is a particular involvement of the limbic system with damage most extensive in the temporal lobe. Negri bodies containing the rabies virus are most concentrated in the cell bodies of the hippocampus, providing the definitive postmortem diagnosis (Lyght, 1966).

The evidence from the victims of rabies implies that there are neural systems for rage behavior and that the virus provides an irritative focus that produces the activation of those neuron complexes with the resultant hyperaggressivity. It seems remarkable that the rabies virus not only has an affinity for the nervous system, but has a particular proclivity to infect that specific part of the nervous system that is related to aggressiveness. Although the specificity is far from perfect, it is sufficient to suggest that there is a considerable potential for the development of pharmacological agents that may be used in the precise manipulation of certain types of hostile behavior in man.

Encephalitis

In Romania in 1915 a few cases of encephalitis lethargica began to appear. The disease rapidly spread to other countries and became a worldwide epidemic by 1924. A part of the symptomatology of this disorder frequently included a radical change in personality characterized by a loss of impulse control, including violent displays of temper. After the acute phase of the disease process, about 54 percent of the patients who showed mental symptoms continued to manifest them, frequently for prolonged periods (Wilson, 1940). The behavior disorder was most common in children between the ages of 3 and 10. Not uncommonly, the personality change occurred prior to the onset of identifiable neurological symptoms. The conduct disorder sometimes occurred immediately after the acute infection but was at times delayed for a period of months or even years. Brill (1959) gives a good description of the characteristics of these children.

> a marked destructiveness and impulsiveness, with a tendency to carry primitive impulses into headlong action. Children who had previously been normally behaved would lie, steal, destroy property, set fire, and commit various sexual offenses, without thought of punishment. The motivation was less comprehensible and less subject to immediate control than in the so-called psychopathies, but the capacity for real remorse was strikingly well retained. There was marked instability of emotion which, coupled with disinhibition of action, led to serious aggression, usually against others, but occasionally against the patient himself, resulting in gruesome self-mutilation [p. 1167].

A Case Study

The following case study is illustrative of this syndrome.

> Roy was admitted to the Child Guidance Home in February 1927, at the age of 13 years. It was stated that the boy had been a behavior problem for two and one-half years. . . . There were 4 siblings, 3 boys and 1 girl, all in good health and all doing well at school. They presented no behavior problems. The developmental history showed that Roy's birth and early development had been normal. He had had chickenpox, measles and whooping cough. The ages at which he contracted these were not stated. The boy had an attack of acute epidemic encephalitis at 9 years of age.
>
> At the Child Guidance Home the physical examination disclosed no significant abnormality, but there were positive neurologic findings in the form of pyramidal tract changes. The boy had an intelligence quotient of 122. From the moment he entered the Child Guidance Home it was noted that he was extremely difficult to control. He was impulsive, egocentric, depressed and suspicious. He exhibited violent temper tantrums during which he was unmanageable. His emotional instability was pronounced. The children obviously annoyed him and he did not hesitate to bite pieces out of their arms and legs when he became angry. There was no one with whom he could get

along. He was extremely irritable and a serious sex problem. He ran away five and six times a day. There was no way of appealing to him or obtaining his cooperation. He did as he pleased and did not hesitate to destroy or injure anything or anyone in his path. He had unusual physical strength and on one occasion tore a tie off of one of the children. In forcibly removing the tie he almost choked the boy. On the other hand, there were times when Roy appeared to be tractable and affectionate. At such times he would put his arms around anyone at the Home and act in a tender and loving manner, but a moment later his mood would change and he would try to injure the object of his former affection. Such bizarre behavior as plucking hair from a child's head or sticking another with pins was of frequent occurrence. He could not be left alone with the other children, and because of his unusual physical strength no adult person at the Home was able to handle him alone. The children were in mortal terror of him. In psychiatric interviews, contacts were on an extremely superficial level because of the boy's apprehensiveness, antagonism and unwillingness or inability to respond. Attempts to reassure him and to get him into a more responsive frame of mind were unsuccessful. In most of the interviews he refused to answer at all and would sit with his head in his lap. Occasionally he spoke about his family. He was bothered about the poor economic conditions in his home. He felt that his mother did not have enough money to take care of the family properly. He showed many fears, particularly of the laboratory tests. There was no evidence of delusions or hallucinations.

It was felt that the boy had had an attack of lethargic encephalitis with resultant psychiatric disturbances, principally in the sphere of volition. It was recommended that he be institutionalized. The parents were both ununderstanding and uncooperative, and made no attempt to carry out the recommendation. A year later the mother reported that the boy had been committed to the boys' industrial school (a state correctional institution) as a result of conviction on a charge of assault and battery. The boy's record at the industrial school was bad. He did not adjust in any way. He was paroled in March 1929 and returned to his home. A short time later he was arrested and sent to a state hospital for the mentally ill, where the same diagnosis as that given at the Child Guidance Home was made. Later in that year, another report from the hospital stated that he had become much more difficult, was quarreling with the other patients, attacking them and threatening every one with assault. In October 1931, the state hospital reported that Roy was home on trial visit. He was attending classes in high school. However, after being home for eight months, he had to be returned to the hospital because the family could not control him. Each year Roy's behavior has become more difficult. In January 1946, at the age of 32, he was still in the state hospital, where it was reported that his behavior was both bizarre and unpredictable. His intelligence quotient was still 122.[3]

[3] J. V. Greenbaum and L. A. Lurie, Encephalitis as a causative factor in behavior disorders of children. *Journal of the American Medical Association*, 1948, *136*, 929.

Encephalitis in Adults and Types of Neural Damage

Similar behavior problems appeared in adults who contracted the disease but the symptoms were not as intense. The impulsive-aggressive behavior has a peculiar compulsive quality to it, as though the individual is *driven* to his hostile action. The patient's conduct is particularly distressing to him because, as with the children, the adult retains his capacity for remorse and is capable of adequate and insightful self-criticism.

When the neurological signs do appear, they are most characteristically of the parkinsonian type, including tremor, rigidity, and masklike face. The onset of symptoms is slow and insidious and once started tends to progress in an irregular fashion. Brill (1959) suggests that the syndrome characteristic of chronic encephalitis lethargica differs from that brought about by the residual damage caused by other encephalitic disorders in that the later symptoms are more diffuse and are relatively fixed. With chronic encephalitis lethargica, there are clinical and pathological indications of a chronic and progressive inflammation.

The neural damage from encephalitis lethargica, although more localized and specific than that found in other encephalitic disorders, is still rather diffuse and it has not been possible to relate particular behavioral symptoms to the brain area damaged. The hypothalamus, mesencephalon, and brain stem (particularly in the area of the periaqueductal gray matter) generally sustain neuron loss (Brill, 1959). The temporal lobes are also frequently involved (Himmelhoch et al., 1970). The basal ganglia and the substantia nigra are also damaged, which accounts for the parkinsonian symptoms (Brill, 1959).

Such a diffuse pattern of neuron necrosis tells us little about the specific neural mechanisms that underlie aggression in man. It should be noted, however, that the temporal lobe, the hypothalamus, and the mesencephalon are involved and have been shown to be important in the neural circuitry of aggression in lower animals (p. 263). The characteristic behavior patterns could result from either the activation of the hostility systems by the inflammatory process or the loss of neurons in the neural systems that function to suppress activity in the aggression systems once it is started. The impulsive, compulsive aspects of the behavior appear to make the latter interpretation plausible.

An interesting side note is that individuals with the encephalitic syndrome are frequently misdiagnosed as having functional psychiatric disorders. Such was the case in seven of eight cases reported by Himmelhoch et al. (1970).

The Lesch-Nyhan Syndrome

Another disorder of childhood that results in aggressive behavior is the Lesch-Nyhan syndrome. Although relatively little is known about this disease it is included here because it is a neurological dysfunction resulting in directed aggression that appears to be completely beyond the child's control. This syndrome was initially described in 1964 (Lesch & Nyhan, 1964) and there are now a total of somewhat more than 100 identified cases in the world.

Children with Lesch-Nyhan syndrome are retarded, have spastic cerebral palsy, and display random involuntary spasmodic movements characteristic of chorea and athetosis. The most disturbing and bizarre symptom is a persistent uncontrollable self-mutilation. They bite their cheeks, lips, and fingers so persistently that the lower lip may be completely chewed away. Some have actually chewed off parts of their fingers, including the bone. There is no evidence of anesthesia. Lesch-Nyhan patients show every evidence of feeling pain and are extremely distressed by their own self-destructive behavior. As they hurt themselves they cry, and can verbalize—"it hurts." They are, of course, kept under restraint. If the restraints are removed, the child appears frightened and pleads that they be replaced.

The behavior is not due simply to reflexive biting. One child accidentally cut his lip falling against the crib. He then persistently banged his lower lip against the floor, the crib, or the wall and kept the lip split open most of the time. Others have learned to lacerate themselves with their braces and to use the spokes of their wheelchairs for self-injury.

Other people are also the objects of their aggression. They pinch nurses, knock eyeglasses off, hit and bite people who happen to be in range. Externally directed aggression may occur when the child is angry or when he is not. He may behave aggressively and laugh about it. There is also evidence of verbal aggression. Some patients develop a vocabulary of four-letter words, which they use appropriately (Dismang & Cheatham, 1970; Nyhan et al. 1969; Nyhan, 1970).

The Lesch-Nyhan syndrome is a genetic disease of the male, transmitted as an X-linked recessive character. It is due to a disorder of purine metabolism that has been traced to the inactivity of an enzyme hypoxanthineguanine phosphoribosyltransferase (HGPRT) (Kelley, 1968; Beardmore et al., 1970). The result is an enormous overproduction of purine. It is not yet clear how the deficiency of HGPRT produces the behavioral problem. Work is currently under way to develop an animal model of the disorder so that experimental work can be done to relate the neurobiochemistry to the behavior. Large doses of purines (trimethyl purine and theophylline) given to rats produces a self-mutilation of the paws and abdomen. These animals are also aggressive toward other rats (Hoefnagel, 1968). Some rats with hippocampal lesions also become self-destructive (Jarrard, 1970). Relatively little has been done as yet but there is considerable potential for an increased understanding of some of the chemical factors involved in a particular kind of aggression that has a counterpart in humans. Whether the results will have a bearing on non-pathological aggression in man remains to be seen.

Epilepsy and Aggression

Epilepsy is a disorder involving abnormal spontaneous activations of various neural systems on the brain. It is not a disease entity but a symptom of nervous system dysfunction. The etiology of epilepsy is highly varied and may be the result of brain trauma, cerebral circulation defects, various toxins, birth injury, metabolic disorders, or brain tumors. In about two-thirds of the cases, no specific cause can be determined and it is therefore referred to as idiopathic. The classification usually used for epileptic disorders includes *grand mal, petit mal,* and psychomotor or temporal lobe epilepsy (Lennox & Lennox, 1960). *Grand mal* involves the characteristic convulsion in which the patient falls to the floor in a fit of generalized muscular contractions and loss of consciousness. The seizure is usually followed by a period of confusion and drowsiness and amnesia for the seizure period. *Petit mal* is characterized by a temporary loss of consciousness in which the individual may stare straight ahead and automatically repeat the acts in which he was engaged at the time of the attack. There is no major muscle involvement. Psychomotor epilepsy, which is the most common form in adults (Ward et al., 1969), usually includes more subjective experiences, such as compulsive thinking, anxiety, impaired awareness, dream states, depressive seizures, and paraoxysmal behavior disorders. One reason for the higher incidence of psychomotor epilepsy is the likelihood of bilateral temporal brain lesions from contusions of the head. According to Jonas (1965), "following contusions of the head, the two edges of the perifalciform regions are damaged since they are crushed by the countercoup against the sharp edges of the lesser wing of the sphenoid" (p. 90).

The Ictal-Interictal Continuum

The behavior of the epileptic is frequently dichotomized as ictal or interictal. The former refers to that behavior reflecting a massive and excessive discharge of central nervous system neurons. Interictal behavior is presumably not related to this excessive neuronal activity. This is a useful but somewhat naive classification that may reflect the state of the art of electroencephalography. Subcortical recordings have demonstrated that some of the presumed interictal behavior may, in fact, be related to excessive localized neuron discharges not reflected in the surface EEG (Monroe, 1970). Ictal phenomena must be considered as being on a continuum, as Jonas so succinctly indicates:

> Biological laws would demand the existence of a continuum extending from
> the intense focal and generalized electrical discharges in *grand mal* down to

the normally firing brain. It is also probable that the brain, in its complexity, could not function unceasingly without the occurrence of abnormal discharges resulting from occasionally overburdened circuits. Such manifestations, however, may escape detection because of the innocuous and inconsequential aspects of the systems [Jonas, 1965, p. 15].

Jonas goes on to make the important point that spontaneous firing in the motor system may result in the twitching eyelid or the activation of whole muscle groups such as in nocturnal jactations during light sleep. Thus it is most reasonable to expect that the spontaneous activation of some of the neural systems for aggression might result in feelings of irritation, anger, or rage. If that activity is of sufficient intensity, the hostile impulses may be acted on.

Epilepsy and the EEG

The electroencephalogram is useful in the diagnosis of epilepsy (see Penfield & Jasper, 1954), but it is by no means infallible (Goldensohn, 1963). The EEG can be negative even in the presence of overt epileptic fits, and such factors as acid-base balance, blood sugar concentration, and toxic metabolites occasionally produce patterns similar to those seen in epilepsy. About 10 percent of the population has EEG evidence of cortical dysfunction similar to that found in *grand mal,* but less than half of 1 percent actually have seizures, and about 20 percent of those individuals showing *grand mal* have normal EEG records (Jonas, 1965).

As the use of implanted electrodes has increased, evidence has been accumulating that considerable spiking and abnormal firing can occur in the depths of the brain, particularly in the limbic system, and not appear on a surface EEG recording (Wilder, 1968; Mark & Ervin, 1970; Monroe, 1970). Electrical activity associated with activation of the amygdaloid nucleus (which might be well expected to result in hostile reactions) cannot generally be detected with scalp electrodes or even in leads placed directly on the cortex (Narabayashi et al., 1963). There is also evidence that rhinecephalic neural disturbances are associated with the disordered behavior occurring during episodes of behavioral disturbances (Monroe, 1959).

Epilepsy and Behavioral Disorders

Since epilepsy is an indication of some brain damage it is not surprising that one finds a higher percentage of behavior disorders among epileptics. There is now a considerable literature on this topic, which has been reviewed by others (Bingley, 1958; DeHaas, 1958; Cazzullo, 1959; Jonas, 1965; and Monroe, 1970). Although there are some studies that take exception (Small et al., 1962; Stevens, 1966), it has generally been concluded that individuals manifesting temporal lobe epilepsy show a higher percentage of personality disorders than do persons with other types.

One might expect a variety of dysfunctions, depending on where the damage is in the temporal lobe and which neural systems in the brain are activated by the epileptic process. Although our concern is with the deviations in aggressive behavior, it should also be noted that problems also occur, although much less frequently, in the sexual sphere. Epstein (1969) summarizes some of the literature on disordered sexual behavior associated with temporal lobe dysfunction, including epileptic manifestations, and case reports are available on patients who experience sexual activity and sexual sensations in association with seizures (Currier et al., 1971). Hyposexuality is most commonly reported as being associated with temporal lobe epilepsy and it is not infrequently alleviated, if not converted into hypersexuality, by temporal lobe surgery (Walker, & Blumer, 1972; Blumer, 1970).

It is certainly true that temporal lobe epilepsy is not necessarily accompanied by an increased tendency to impulsiveness and hostility. There are a number of reports that disclaim any relationship between epilepsy and aggression or crime (Livingston, 1964; DeHaas, 1963). However, most of the evidence on the subject supports the contention that there is a significantly greater probability that disorders of impulse control and aggressiveness will be found in the population of epileptics than in a normal population.

Ictal Emotions

Ictal rage[4] does occur but it is less common than either fear or depression (Weil, 1959; Williams, 1965). Rage is most likely to occur as an ictal emotion when the recorded EEG discharges are from the anterior temporal regions (Williams, 1969a). It is, however, relatively rare for ictal rage to be converted into effective aggressive behavior. During the seizure state and the period of confusion that usually follows it, the individual is sufficiently disorganized that attack behavior usually occurs only if the patient is restrained and in his confusional state misinterprets these attempts at restraint (DeHaas, 1963; Monroe, 1970). Monroe (1970) describes a case in which a father attempted to loosen the belt of a patient during a seizure. The boy jumped up and began to beat the father and indiscriminately break up the furniture.

It occasionally happens that the ictus is relatively prolonged and the patient engages in what has been described as "automatic behavior." During this period the individual may engage in a variety of actions in a mechanical, unmotivated, or driven manner and generally shows amnesia

---

[4] Recognizing the difficulties with the ictal-interictal dichotomy previously indicated, it is useful, and common in the literature, to refer to ictal behavior as that which accompanies an actual seizure or massive discharges recordable with scalp electrodes.

for the period. The patient may then awaken in a portion of the city strange to him and have no memory for how he got there or what actions he may have been involved in during the forgotten period. In some cases that ictal behavior may involve considerable aggression or even homicide. Although a number of cases have now been reported and reasonably well verified (MacDonald, 1961; Gunn & Fenton, 1971; Fenton & Udwin, 1965; Dinnen, 1971; Brewer, 1971; Walker, 1961), ictal homicide actually appears to be quite rare. Gunn and Fenton (1971) concluded that "automatic behavior is a rare explanation for the crimes of epileptic patients."

Interictal Aggression

Although well-directed ictal aggression is a relatively rare phenomenon, there is abundant evidence that uncontrolled, impulsive, assaultive behavior is not uncommon as an interictal behavior pattern, particularly among temporal lobe epileptics. Gastaut (1954) concludes that the "psychomotor epileptic behaves, in the interval between his fits, like an animal presenting a state of continuous rhinencephalic excitation, and during his fits, like an animal presenting a paroxysmal rhinencephalic discharge." In describing the behavior difficulties that psychomotor epileptics display during the interval between fits, Gastaut says, "Subjects become impulsive, aggressive and inclined to angry, violent reactions, sometimes dangerous. Sometimes perverse character traits associated with sensitiveness and hypocrisy render them insupportable in their social milieu and even in their family" (Gastaut, et al., 1953, quoted in Gastaut, 1954).

Falconer et al. (1958), reporting on 50 patients, indicated that 38 percent of them showed spontaneous outbursts of aggression. Psychomotor epilepsy is the most difficult to control with medication and seizure control is ineffective in about 30 percent of the cases. About half of those patients develop destructive behavior and paroxysmal bursts of anger as a part of a behavior disorder (Schwab et al., 1965). Glaser et al. (1963) also indicate that impulsive, aggressive, and unstable states characterize some of their psychomotor patients. The aggressiveness noted in patients afflicted with temporal lobe epilepsy has a peculiar aspect to it. Outbursts of anger, abusiveness, and assaultiveness occur with little or no provocation and contrast with the patient's usual good-natured behavior. The change is abrupt and striking (Walker & Blumer, 1972). Serafetinides (1970) indicates that aggressive behavior was the most common interictal behavior pattern in temporal lobe epilepsy and among 100 consecutive temporal lobe epileptics selected for temporal lobe resection, 36 displayed overt physical aggression (Serafetinides, 1965). He also concludes that aggression is more common among younger patients whereas depression is more common among older patients.

Among children showing temporal lobe epilepsy, there is a high incidence of aggressive behavior (Nuffield, 1961; Keating, 1961). Ounsted (1969) reported that 36 of 100 children with psychomotor epilepsy that had been followed for a decade showed outbursts of catastrophic rage.

It is important to emphasize that the subjects in the preceding studies were from a highly selected population of individuals with epilepsy. They were, in general, persons who had been committed to an institution or were candidates for surgery. There are, of course, thousands of epileptics who are making an adequate adjustment in the real world and do not suffer from personality disturbances, impulsiveness, or uncontrolled aggressive tendencies. The individuals with very serious antisocial tendencies are removed from society and institutionalized. It is thus possible for studies that involve those patients remaining in society to show no more criminal or antisocial behaviors than are found in the rest of the population (Livingston, 1964; DeHaas, 1963). Whether a patient manifests a lack of hostility control may depend on whether or not the spontaneous neural activity resulting from the lesion involves the neural systems for aggression. Another possibility, as suggested previously in another connection, is that there is damage to those neural systems that are important in the inhibition or suppression of the neural systems for aggression. In addition, there is necessarily an interaction between the dysfunction in the central nervous system, the learning experiences, and the rest of the environmental input. Except in extreme cases, which involve massive output from the hostility systems, the individual is subject to the same kinds of socialization and inhibitory training as is the rest of the population. However, because of the lower thresholds or increased spontaneous activity of those brain mechanisms that bring on irritability or rage, socialization training is less effective. This may be another way of stating the thesis of Taylor (1969), who suggests that the important variable involved in the hyperaggressiveness of epileptic patients is the damage to the structures necessary to learn adequate controls, and Keating's (1961) position that behavior disorders of epileptic children result largely from their reaction to environment and handling.

There is at least some evidence to suggest that the underlying neural mechanisms for the seizure are different from those that are important in the impulsive-aggressive syndrome. A common complication in the treatment of psychomotor epilepsy is the tendency for the psychiatric symptoms to become more manifest when the seizures are satisfactorily reduced by medication (Bailey & Gibbs, 1951). Effective anticonvulsant medication frequently results in an increase in irritability and dyscontrol. Phenothiazines can be used to reduce the behavior problems, but they frequently exacerbate the seizures. Further, surgical intervention in the form of discrete lesions may bring about an improvement in either the fits or the behavior problems without having an effect on the other (Ervin et al., 1969).

Aggression and the Abnormal EEG

Another indicator of brain dysfunction is an abnormality in the electro-encephalogram. Although there is considerable disagreement on the details and the interpretation of the findings, it can be concluded that individuals manifesting a variety of behavior disorders, particularly aggression, are significantly more likely to have an abnormal EEG than does the general population (Ellingson, 1955). (Also see the review by Bonkalo, 1967.)

Abnormal EEG and Behavior Disorders in Children

A number of studies show that children with behavior disorders are more likely to have an abnormal EEG that may reflect a diffuse brain pathology. From 5 to 15 percent of normal children show a variety of EEG abnormalities, but 50 to 60 percent of those with behavior disorders have abnormal records (Monroe, 1970). In a study of 200 problem children, Bayrakal (1965) found 100 with abnormal EEG tracings. Among the disturbed behaviors that correlated with the abnormal EEGs were poor impulse control, inadequate social adaptation, and hostility. The overwhelming majority of the abnormal records were found in the temporal lobe and the subcortical regions. One hundred disturbed children whose principal symptoms were hyperactivity, temper tantrums, destructive behavior, aggressiveness, and antisocial behavior were studied by Aird and Yamamoto (1966). Forty-nine percent had abnormal EEG records and 67 percent of those abnormalities had a temporal lobe focus.

Gross and Wilson (1964) suggest that an EEG should be taken routinely on all children who manifest behavior disorders and learning problems. They found over half of the children referred to a suburban psychiatric clinic had abnormal EEGs. Forty-five of the children, although they showed no tendency to seizures, were given anticonvulsants as their only treatment; half of them showed significant improvement, and ten of the cases showed dramatic improvement.

Abnormal EEG and Abnormal Aggressive Behavior

Although temporal and subcortical foci are most frequently reported to be associated with the aggressive-behavior disorders, Cohn and Nardini (1958) describe an abnormality with an occipital focus. The abnormal waves were bilateral, slow, and synchronous and were found in young adults who were hostile, hypercritical, irritable, nonconforming, and lacking in adequate impulse control. Treffert (1964) found that psychiatric patients with EEG abnormalities in the temporal lobe but without overt epilepsy tended to be combative with rage episodes and paroxysmal symptoms in the form of blackouts and hallucinations. Control subjects with a matched diagnosis, however, tended to have disorders of thought.

The diagnosis "psychopath" tends to be a catchall category and is sufficiently ambiguous that some investigators tend to avoid it (Williams, 1969b). However, several studies have shown that individuals given that diagnosis are far more inclined to show EEG abnormalities (Silverman, 1949; Murdoch, 1972; Gibbens et al., 1959; Hill & Watterson, 1942; Hill, 1944; Hill, 1952). Whereas only 15 percent of normals have abnormal EEGs, 48 percent of the psychopathic group had abnormalities. When the aggressive psychopaths were differentiated from those classed as inadequate, 65 percent of the aggressives showed abnormalities but only 32 percent of the inadequate subjects did (Hill & Watterson, 1942).

Abnormal EEG and Aggressive Crime

Most of the psychopaths studied either were prisoners or had criminal records, and there is general agreement that prisoners, in general, show more EEG abnormalities than the rest of the population (see Knott, 1965). Studies of juvenile delinquents in Japan have shown that EEG abnormalities are markedly higher in them than in the general population (Arai et al., 1966; Yoshii et al., 1961). The abnormal pattern showing theta waves in the delinquents were directly correlated with tendencies to habitual violence (Yoshii et al., 1964). Jenkins and Pacella (1943) concluded that delinquency per se was not related to EEG abnormalities but that habitual aggressiveness was. Abnormal tracings were more frequently found in delinquents with assaultive tendencies showing emotional instability, irritability, and poor impulse control.

In one study of 64 English murderers, it was found that only one of 11 who killed in self-defense or incidentally in the commission of another crime had an abnormal EEG. However, 73 percent of those individuals who committed murder without apparent motive showed electroencephalographic abnormalities (Stafford-Clark & Taylor, 1949). In another study of 32 insane murderers, the EEG records were read "blind" and compared with control subjects who were not patients. The incidence of abnormal records in the murderers was four times that of the control group (Sayed et al., 1969).

An extensive study of the EEGs of criminals in the London area was carried out by Denis Williams (1969b). He selected a sample of 333 subjects at random from his total population of 1250 criminally aggressive subjects who had been referred to him by prison officials during the past 20 years. He then compared the records of those individuals who were habitually aggressive with those who had committed a single major violent crime. Sixty-five percent of the records of the habitual aggressives were abnormal, but abnormalities were found in 24 percent of the second group. Williams places the percentage of abnormalities in the general population at 12 percent. When the records of individuals who were mentally retarded, had had a major head injury, or were epileptic were removed, the percentage of abnormalities among those subjects who had committed a solitary violent crime of major proportions was the same as that of the general population, 12 percent. However, the *habitual* aggressives still showed 57 percent abnormalities. In 64 percent of the habitually aggressive subjects the abnormalities were bilateral. The temporal lobes were affected in all the hypraggressives, and over 80 percent manifested rhythms known to be associated with temporal lobe dysfunction.

Interpretation of Data on Abnormal EEG and Aggression
Although the preceding evidence is, in general, mutually supportive, it should be mentioned that some investigators have not found the relationship between abnormalities in the electroencephalographic record and aggressive tendencies (Arthurs & Cahoon, 1964; Knott & Gottlieb, 1943). This probably reflects, at least in some measure, difficulties in definition of both aggression and EEG abnormalities. However, at best the EEG has very little prognostic value in regard to aggressive behavior. As the preceding statistics indicate, there are far too many false negatives and false positives for the EEG to have much predictive value. The various types of behaviors manifested by juvenile delinquents cannot be discriminated on the basis of the EEG record (Small, 1966). Gibbens et al. (1959) found that the abnormal EEG in criminal psychopaths did not, in general, give any indication of the prognosis for recidivism. However, as indicated previously, the EEG may be useful in predicting which individuals might benefit from some type of anticonvulsant medication (Gross & Wilson, 1964).

The relationship between abnormalities in the EEG and aggressiveness and crime in general is open to various interpretations. It might be hypothesized that the abnormalities reflect brain damage that directly affects the neural systems for aggression so that spontaneous firing occurs in the system with the resultant acting out of hostile impulses. Or there may be damage to the brain mechanisms that function to inhibit the neural mechanisms for aggression, so that the aggressive behavior threshold is functionally lowered. The abnormalities may also indicate a generally lowered level of neurological competence, with the result that the individual is unable to cope with the usual demands of society and resorts to criminal behavior as an adjustive mode.

The mechanisms may be even more indirect. The brain damage implied by the irregularities in the EEG may result in a very low tolerance for frustration that makes the individual more prone to hostile action and subsequent incarceration. Furthermore, there is no reason to believe that the several interpretations offered previously are mutually exclusive either across individuals or for any given individual. Finally, it should be recognized that any of the preceding dysfunctions interact with the individual's environment and the type of inhibitory training he has received. The possible neurological limitations previously indicated are neither a necessary nor a sufficient cause for criminal behavior. In most studies approximately half of the deviant populations investigated show no indication of abnormal EEG tracings. Obviously, anyone with a normal, adequately functioning brain can acquire any of these behavior deviations through learning. Moreover, a nonstressful, supportive, sheltered environment can protect the brain-damaged individual from environmental situations that are likely to provoke criminal activity. Thus any interpretation must take into account the many possible interactions among the various etiological agents.

6- and 14-per-second Spikes and Aggression

One EEG abnormality that appears to be specifically associated with impulsive, aggressive behavior is the 6- and 14-per-second positive spike. Schwade and Geiger (1960) conclude that the aggressive behavior that is correlated with the positive spike phenomenon can no more be controlled by the individual than a *grand mal* seizure can be controlled by an epileptic. After a study of over 1000 cases these authors (1956) characterize that form of aggressive behavior as follows, "The control by rage is so absolute that parents fear for their lives and those of others. Typical complaints are: extreme rage outbursts, larceny, arson, violent acts without motivation, sexual acts (aggressive), threats to stab, shoot, mutilation of animals, and total inability to accept correction or responsibility for the act" (p. 616).

The initial report of the 6- and 14-positive-spike phenomenon was made by Gibbs and Gibbs (1951). Since that time a considerable literature has accumulated on the topic. A short survey of the material will be covered here, but for detailed reviews of the nearly 200 studies on this topic the reader is referred to Henry (1963), Hughes (1965), and Monroe (1970).

Symptoms Associated with 6 and 14 Positive Spikes

A variety of symptoms have been indicated as being associated with the 6- and 14-per-second spike. These include a number of physical signs, such as vomiting, heart palpitation, sweating, nausea, dizziness, blurred vision, and headaches (Gibbs & Gibbs, 1955, 1963b). These patients are also described as showing less affection, less sensitivity, and less understanding of the consequences of their behavior (Greenberg & Pollack, 1966). The aggressive behavior shown by these subjects is not the more random and confused type sometimes found in the ictal and immediate postictal state. The rage and destructive attacks occur with little or no provocation and are frequently carried out with skill and precision. Under the impulse of an explosive episode of aggression, the individual appears overwhelmed by his own momentum and is unable to inhibit the act. The aggressive acting out is often followed by a relief of generalized tension and is generally unaccompanied by feelings of guilt or remorse (Monroe, 1970; Schwade & Geiger, 1960; Bender, 1953; Stehle, 1960). There have now been a number of murders, including several cases of matricide, committed by individuals showing the 6 and 14 positive spikes, and it has been generally held that the murders occured with relatively little motivation (Stehle 1960; Schwade & Otto, 1953; Schwade & Geiger, 1960; Woods, 1961; Winfield & Ozturk, 1959). Delinquents with 6- and 14-spike abnormality are more likely to be repeated offenders and are more likely to be involved in such crimes as murder, arson, and burglary (Yoshii et al., 1963). In a controlled study in which schizophrenic patients with and without the 6 and 14 positive spike were rated by psychiatrists who were not aware of the EEG findings, those subjects showing spiking were rated as significantly more aggressive than the controls (Greenberg & Pollack, 1966).

Population Showing 6 and 14 Positive Spikes
The 6- and 14-positive-spike abnormality is most frequently found in children and early adolescents. Small and Small (1964), however, report that the phenomenon occurs in approximately 4 percent of the adult patients admitted for acute psychiatric conditions and found no behavioral differences between patients showing the positive spiking and those not. It is found in as many as 72 percent of children diagnosed as impulsive and in up to 58 percent of problem children in schools. In unselected populations the positive spiking occurs in between 1 and 3 percent. The pattern is most common during the drowsy state, when the percentage in an unselected population may go as high as 12 to 13 percent (Hughes, 1965).

The preceding findings are most frequently supported but there have been some studies that throw doubt on the concept that the 6 and 14 spike is an indication of an abnormality. For example, one study reports that the incidence of this pattern was 58 percent in a group of 13-, 14-, and 15-year-old boys who were, at least presumably, normal (Lombroso et al., 1966). In another study the pattern was found in 25 percent of a nonclinical population of 17- to 25-year-old men during stage 1 and stage 2 sleep (Lond & Johnson, 1968). Both groups of investigators suggest that a larger percentage of individuals showing the pattern might be found if the EEG records were taken over a longer period and if repeated EEGs were taken on the same individuals. The significance of these findings is not immediately clear. It may be that many relatively normal individuals show this pattern if one tests for it long enough and often enough, but it can be found more easily and more frequently in individuals with an impulsive-aggressive disorder.

Physiological Basis of the 6 and 14 Positive Spike
There is considerable controversy over the physiological meaning of the
6- and 14-per-second pattern. It has not been possible to pin down the
anatomical origin of the wave form. Gibbs and Gibbs (1951) originally
suggested, from the wave form, that the focus was in the thalamus or
hypothalamus and the pattern has been reported in at least one case associated with a verified hypothalamic tumor (Bevilacqua & Little, 1961).
It has also been suggested that the focus is in the hippocampal region
(Neidermeyer & Knott, 1962; Refsum et al., 1960). One investigator has
suggested that the wave form reflects a blocking of inhibitory mechanisms
in the superficial layers of the cortex (Grossman, 1954). However, there
are no really good data to pinpoint the locus of the pattern. Dietze and
Boegele (1963) believe that patients with the 6- and 14-positive-spike
pattern do not comprise a well-circumscribed special group, but the finding is nonetheless useful as an indicator of more general brain damage
that is the basis of a behavior disorder.

Since relatively little is understood about the basis of the neurophysiological substrate of the 6- and 14-per-second pattern, there are no good
explanations of the relationship between the pattern and the behavior disorders. Although a causal relationship is implied in many studies, no real
neurological mechanism is apparent. Woods suggested in 1961 that the
dysrhythmia did not in itself induce violent action but functioned as a biologically determined stress. Henry (1963), in a similar vein, believes that
pattern may reflect a neurophysiological handicap that renders the patient
less capable of dealing with a stressful environment. He implies that the
impulsive-aggressive pathology may be a function of the interaction between the neurological handicap and the stress of the environment. In
terms of the general model presented in this monograph, the 6- and 14-
per-second pattern may reflect some damage in the inhibitory mechanisms
that reduces the threshold for aggression in these individuals, with the
result that they react more primitively in conditions of frustration than
would be found in a normal population.

BRAIN LESIONS AND AGGRESSION
CONTROL IN MAN

There are a variety of therapeutic reasons for making brain lesions, and
much can be learned about the neural mechanisms underlying aggressive
behavior through the brain lesion technique. Lesions in a variety of loci
in the brain result in the reduction of aggressive behavior. Wild cats, wild
monkeys, and a variety of other animals have been surgically tamed by
the ablation of precise brain areas that apparently interfere with the function of the underlying neural systems for hostility.

There have now been at least several hundred cases reported in which aggressive behavior in man has been reduced, in many instances dramatically, by specific brain lesions. Although these operations provide us with some general insight into the types of neural mechanisms involved in what is probably irritable aggression in man, there are many problems in interpreting the various studies. It is possible to determine the general areas of the limbic system that are involved, but an understanding of the precise brain areas included in the neurological substrates of aggression must await many more and far-better-controlled studies than have as yet been done on humans. Interpretation problems are created by both the neurological and behavioral evidence.

The lesions produced in almost all the following descriptions of surgery are relatively large and undoubtedly involve a number of mechanisms in addition to those concerned with aggressive behavior. Even the relatively precise amygdalotomy is a large lesion in terms of the complexity of the nucleus. As will be indicated in Chapter 8, some portions of the amygdala involve the facilitation of different kinds of aggression and others involve their inhibition. Other portions are a part of the neural substrate of fear-motivated behavior. Lesions in the amygdala also have a significant effect on the endocrine system, which is also important in the regulation of some kinds of aggression.

For many reasons, including the fact that most of the patients are still alive when the studies are reported, good histology is not available, so it is not possible to determine with precision the location of even the relatively large lesions.

On the behavioral side, as Valenstein (1973) points out, it is frequently difficult to make an independent judgment about the results of a given study because the clinical reports are generally written in a subjective style and objective test data are seldom included. In any given study there are relatively few subjects, and pre- and postoperative objective evaluations often are not made. Further, the individuals making the evaluations of the behavior frequently know the nature of the lesions and the expected results, and the behaviors reported on are not precisely defined behaviorally.

Of course the clinic is not a laboratory and surgeons are not generally trained in experimental procedures. They seldom have either the time for or the interest in rigorous scientific procedures. It is therefore important to interpret clinical material with caution. However, the clinical material is a valuable source for the generation of specific hypotheses and anyone working in this area must have a knowledge of what has been done. Consequently, it is critical to survey this now extensive literature. It is also important that future studies utilize good experimental designs and scientific procedures within the constraints of comfort for the patient and medical ethics.

Temporal Lobe Lesions

The experimental work of Kluver and Bucy, which involved bilateral temporal lobe ablation and resulted in surgically induced docility, inspired some surgeons to attempt the same operation on man in an attempt to modify aggressive behavior and agitation in schizophrenic patients (Terzian & Ore, 1955). As might be suspected from the results of Kluver and Bucy, this radical operation resulted in a variety of dysfunctions. (See Chapter 8 for details.) In one case report presented in detail by Terzian and Ore (1955), bilateral removal of the temporal lobes, including most of the uncus and hippocampus, exactly reproduced the Kluver and Bucy syndrome. Rage and fear were reduced, ability to recognize people decreased, and there were increased sex activity, bulimia, and serious memory deficiencies. Prior to the operation the patient had frequent attacks of aggressive and violent behavior during which he had attempted to strangle his mother and to crush his younger brother under his feet. After unilateral temporal lobectomy, he attacked the nurses and doctors and threatened some with death. After the second temporal lobe was removed, he became extremely meek with everyone and was "absolutely resistant to any attempt to arouse aggressiveness and violent reactions in him."

Temporal lobe lesions, both unilateral and bilateral, have been extensively used in man to control epilepsy that is not susceptible to drug therapy. A frequent side effect of the operation, in addition to seizure control, has been a general reduction in hostility compared to the individual's reactions prior to the operation (Green et al., 1951; Terzian, 1958; Scoville & Milner, 1957; Pool, 1954; Falconer, 1972, 1973; Falconer et al., 1955; Freeman, 1965; Hill et al., 1957; Turner, 1959; Blumer, 1967). Although cases have been reported in which aggressive behavior has been increased by the operation (Sawa et al., 1954; Woringer et al., 1953), the increase is generally temporary. Some authors report no change in psychiatric symptoms (Gibbs et al., 1958). Bailey (1958) indicates that temporal lesions do not generally reduce the psychiatric problems of the patient, except that in certain subjects the attacks of aggressive behavior were reduced or completely eliminated. He believes that the aggressive attacks were in fact phychomotor seizures. Falconer et al. (1958) report definite personality changes for the better after temporal lobe lesions and conclude that the most striking way in which they improved was in the reduction of aggressiveness. "Whereas, previously, the relatives of the patient might be very careful as to what they said to the patient for fear of provoking an aggressive outbreak, they can now talk freely and joke with him" (Falconer, 1958).

Vallardares and Corbalan (1959) removed the tip of the temporal lobe, including the uncus, specifically in order to modify their patients' aggressive impulses. Their sample included 16 oligophrenics, 7 psychopaths, and 13 individuals with psychopathic personalities. They indicate that the patients were examined from the medical, neurological, psychiatric, psychological, EEG, and pneumoencephalographical point of view, but they do not report the results of those examinations. In terms of the degree of reduction of aggressiveness and impulsiveness they report great improvement in 13 of the 36 patients, no change in 9 and no information on 1. Although they do not report the criteria for change, they indicate that only one patient showed an intellectual impairment. They imply that memory improved as aggressiveness was reduced.

Amygdaloid Lesions

Complete temporal lobectomy is, of course, a very radical operation. The experimental work on animals indicates that it should be possible to achieve a reduction in tendencies to hostility by much smaller lesions in the temporal lobe. The most precise control of aggressive behavior through brain lesions, and the one that involves the greatest promise, has been more recently developed and involves stereotaxic lesions in the amygdala. Lesions 8 to 10 mm in diameter have been produced by an injection of 0.6 to 0.8 ml of oil to which Lipiodol had been added (Narabayashi et al., 1963; Narabayashi & Uno, 1966) or by thermocoagulation (Narabayashi, 1961, 1972). These authors report that 85 percent of 51 patients showed a marked reduction in emotional excitability and a normalization of social behavior. It should be emphasized that except for the reduction in hostility, none of the signs of the Kluver-Bucy syndrome resulted from the bilateral destruction of the amygdaloid nuclei.

Similar results have been reported by Heimburger et al. (1966). They have lesioned approximately half of the amygdala using cryosurgery. The lesions were 8 to 10 mm in diameter. This operation has resulted in dramatic improvement in some patients and an overall improvement in 23 of 25 patients. Destructiveness, hostility, and aggression toward others were the behavior symptoms most frequently improved by the operation. The improvement in two of the patients was so great that they were released from mental institutions. Others were moved from solitary confinement to open wards. Some of them were observed to smile and laugh for the first time in their lives after the operation. Heimburger et al. conclude, "Stereotaxic amygdalotomy is a safe and relatively easy procedure for treatment of a select group of patients who have previously been considered untreatable." Schwab et al. (1965) use a very promising technique of implanting 48 pairs of recording electrodes bilaterally through the limbic system. Then they carry out a program of recording and stimulation over a period of several weeks in order to localize and limit as much as possible the precise area that, when destroyed, will relieve the symptoms. A radiofrequency lesion is then made through the indwelling electrodes. Ervin indicates that there is good reason to believe from their observations that the neural and neurochemical substrate for the motor seizure and for the interseizure assaultive and aggressive behavior are different. It is possible to eliminate the one without affecting the other (Ervin, personal communication).

The effects of amygdalectomy or amygdalotomy on uncontrolled aggression in man have now been demonstrated repeatedly in hospitals throughout the world and essentially confirm the expectations that one might derive from a survey of the animal experimentation. The amygdala in man, as in animals, is a critical portion of the neurological basis of certain kinds of aggression. (For other reports on amygdala ablation and aggression in man, see Anderson, 1972; Balasurbramaniam et al., 1972; Hitchcock et al., 1972; Mark et al., 1972; Umbach et al., 1972; Vaernet & Madsen, 1970, 1972; and Mempel, 1971.)

Cingulate Lesions

As with animals, the production of surgical docility in man is not limited to temporal lobe lesions. Following Ward's demonstration of the calming effects of cingulectomy on monkeys, Le Beau (1952) did cingulum ablations on humans in an attempt to control agitated behavior, obsessive-compulsive states, and epilepsy. He concluded that, "Cingulectomy is specially indicated in intractable cases of anger, violence, aggressiveness, and permanent agitation." Other investigators have found that lesions in the anterior cingular gyrus, although not eliminating outbursts of anger, have reduced the intensity and duration of such outbursts (Tow & Whitty, 1953; Whitty et al., 1952; Sano, 1962; Ledesma & Paniagua, 1969). Turner (1972) reports 80 percent of 30 cases given posterior cingulectomy lost their aggressive behavior.

One of the earliest reports on cingulotomy included the use of a control group in which four patients were given skin lesions and bone button removal and were provided with the same follow-up as the 24 patients given anterior cingulate lesions. None of the control subjects showed any improvement, whereas half of the lesioned patients were discharged and seven were rated as having shown moderate to good improvement. The majority of the lesioned patients showed striking mood changes characterized by an absence of hostility and fear (Livingston, 1951). Although postoperative reduction in aggressive behavior after cingulotomy is frequently reported, some authors have noted a tendency for these patients to relapse. It is not clear, however, why this occurs (Sano, 1962; Minigrino & Schergna, 1972).

Hypothalamic Lesions

Operating on the theory that pathological aggression is due to an imbalance in the ergotropic circuits and the tropotropic circuits with a dominance of the ergotropic, Sano (Sano, 1962, 1966; Sano et al., 1972) has performed what he calls sedative surgery. This involves lesioning the ergotropic zone (posterior hypothalamus) in order to normalize the balance. He reports remarkable success with patients showing intractable violent behavior. They became markedly calm, passive, and tractable and showed decreased spontaneity. Although they showed a recovery of the spontaneity within a month, the other changes persisted for up to three years and seven months, as long as the patients were followed up. Of course one need not accept Sano's theory in order to accept his results; he may very well be getting the right results for the wrong reasons. Sano's theory implies that aggressive behavior is the result of excessive arousal and can thus be eliminated by sedation. Sedation, however, is not essential to the limiting of aggression. It is quite possible to be hyperactive without being aggressive. For example, the Kluver-Bucy monkeys were extremely friendly but at the same time they were overactive and always ready to engage in play.

Thalamic Lesions

Lesions in several areas of the thalamus have been shown to exert a significant inhibitory effect on pathological aggressive behavior. Bilateral lesions of the dorsomedial nuclei result in a reduction in tension, anxiety states, and agitation. Aggressiveness and assaultive behavior subside and irritability tends to be replaced with euphoria (Spiegel et al., 1951; Spiegel & Wycis, 1949). Andy and his colleagues have reported that lesions of the centermedianum and intralaminar nuclei are particularly effective when aggression and destructive behavior form a major part of the behavioral dysfunction. Disturbances in affect are alleviated in some cases but not as reliably as is the symptom of excessive hostility (Andy, 1966, 1970; Andy & Jurko, 1972a). Poblette et al. have reported on three cases in which extreme hostility has been alleviated by lesions of the thalamus (Poblette et al., 1970).

Frontal Lobe Lesions

Lesions of the frontal lobes of man have been reported to have the effect of increasing aggressive behavior, decreasing it, and having no effect. It is not uncommon for all three effects to occur within the same study. Hetherington et al. (1972) report on the effect of a standard leukotomy in 11 patients showing hostility. Six were made worse, one showed no change, and four were improved. In another study of the effects of leukotomy, five aggressive patients showed no improvement, two showed an increase in aggressive behavior, and five showed a partial decrease (Siegfried & Ben-Shumel, 1972). Similar results are reported by Strom-Olsen et al. (1943).

Other investigators, using somewhat different lesioning procedures, have reported more favorable results. Eight of ten epileptics with explosive behavior were able to engage in gainful employment after obitoventromedial undercutting (Hirose, 1972). The same investigator in a follow-up of prefrontal patients reported considerable improvement in such traits as antisocial personality disorder and explosive tendencies, but no effect on shiftlessness, irresponsibility, and inability to feel guilt (Hirose, 1968). Strom-Olsen and Carlisle (1972), using bifrontal stereotaxic tractotomy, indicated that 17 patients with marked aggression preoperatively were improved by the tractotomy.

Lobotomies are so lacking in precision that it is not surprising that the results are contradictory and confusing and tell us little about man's neural systems for aggression.

Other Lesions
Although relatively little has been published on the effects, Sano (1957, 1966) has reported that lesions in the fornix have blocked aggressive behavior in epileptics manifesting explosive behavior. He has also reported similar results with lesions in the upper mesencephalic reticular formation (Sano, 1960, 1966).

DIRECT BRAIN STIMULATION
Direct stimulation of the brain is a therapeutic procedure that provides us with some insight into the neurological basis of aggressive behavior in the human. There are a number of different kinds of patients for whom there is good reason to believe that some kind of direct brain stimulation would be beneficial. When temporal lesions are being considered for the control of epilepsy, it is necessary to identify precisely the focal areas of abnormal electrical activity. This can be accomplished by recording from implanted depth electrodes and by stimulating in an attempt to replicate the details of the epileptic process (Mark & Ervin, 1970). Some patients with intractable pain resulting from terminal carcinoma can get relief (sometimes dramatic) from direct brain stimulation (Ervin et al., 1969). Small brain lesions are useful in the control of tremor caused by Parkinson's disease and the exact lesion location is determined by stimulation (Sem-Jacobsen, 1966). The procedure has also been used in patients with anxiety neurosis, involuntary movement (Delgado, 1965a), and chronic schizophrenia (Heath & Mickle, 1960).

With the development of the stereotaxic chronic implantation of electrodes in 1952 (Delgaro et al., 1952) it was possible to take brain stimulation out of the operating room and test the patient in relatively natural conditions, without anesthesia or sedation. The electrodes are well tolerated by the brain and there are relatively few side effects. Heath (1964a) reports on one patient with 125 implanted electrodes that remained accurately fixed in position for a period of two years. It is not possible to say how many patients have now experienced direct brain stimulation, but the procedure is no longer rare. Just one investigator reported in 1966 on

82 patients in whom 3,632 electrodes had been implanted (Sem-Jacobsen, 1966).[5]

Problems of Interpretation

There are a number of problems in arriving at a reasonable interpretation of the results of direct brain stimulation. These difficulties are well summarized by Ervin et al.

1. A synchronous electrical discharge is quite different from the exquisitely patterned afferent volley of physiologic signals.
2. In a complex neural aggregate the electrical input may activate excitatory and inhibitory, afferent, efferent, and integrative, or cholinergic and adrenergic systems indiscriminately.
3. The instantaneous state of cerebral organization—i.e., all the other influences acting on the object,structure at the time of stimulation—is unknown.
4. At best, the site stimulated is part of an integrated system, so that the stimulus is like a rock thrown in a pond—perhaps influencing by waves a distant lily pad. The stimulation of a structure says what it can do under certain circumstances, not what it does do normally.
5. It should be further emphasized that ablation is not the reciprocal of stimulation in other than very simple input and output systems.

    It might best be said that both stimulation and ablation experiments should be described with the emphasis on how the organism functions in the new state of cerebral organization necessitated by the experimental intervention.[6]

In summary, it is not possible to know with any degree of precision what is happening in the brain during an electrically activated motivation state. It will be necessary to combine this technique with many others in order to get a better understanding. However, there is now a considerable body of evidence to demonstrate that the brain of man contains neural systems specific to a variety of motivational states and that these states can be directly elicited by either electrical or chemical brain stimulation.

Emotional and Motivational Changes Produced by Brain Stimulation Although our interest in this section is on eliciting anger, it should be noted that brain stimulation has produced a wide variety of emotional and motivational states in man, ranging from sheer terror through rage to what has been described as drunken euphoria. It should be recognized that these moods and feeling states are not simply the aftermath of memo-

---

[5] For the interested reader the technique of electrode implantation and stimulation has been described in several sources. (See Delgado et al., 1952; Sem-Jacobsen, 1968; Randy et al., 1964; Sheer, 1961; Ramey & O'Doherty, 1960.)

[6] F. R. Ervin, V. H. Mark, & J. Stevens, Behavioral and affective responses to brain stimulation in man. In J. Zubin and C. Shagass (Eds.), *Neurobiological Aspects of Psychopathology*. New York: Grune & Stratton, 1969, pp. 54–55. Used by permission.

ries evoked by stimulation of the cortex. Penfield has reported that memories can be evoked by stimulation of the temporal cortex, but came to the conclusion that electrical stimulation could not evoke such emotions as anger, joy, pleasure, or sexual excitement, and that there were no specific cortical mechanisms directly associated with those emotional states (Penfield & Jasper, 1954). Sem-Jacobsen (1968) has listed the following mood changes that have occurred during stimulation of subcortical locations: relaxed, feeling of well-being, sleepy, restless, anxious, tense, sad, irritable, depressed, unhappy, angry, afraid, and orgastic responses. Feelings of loneliness and positive expressions of love have also been noted (Delgado, 1965a). Heath (1962), discussing 12 years of experience with brain stimulation in man, has indicated that the emotional and feeling changes that have occurred on stimulation have been fairly consistent from one patient to another.

There have been some failures to evoke emotional states by stimulation that need comment. Chapman et al. (1954) and Chapman (1958) stimulated spontaneously assaultive patients in the amygdaloid region and obtained reports of anxiety and fear. However, neither anger nor irritability were produced. Jasper and Rasmussen (1958) studied 46 epileptic patients using direct electrical stimulation of the amygdaloid region in an attempt to reproduce the onset of the patient's regular attack. They found only two patients who responded with a fear reaction during the stimulation. Other patients either did not respond or bcame confused. These authors were led to the conclusion that the amygdala was of relatively little importance in emotional responses. Ursin (1960) suggests that these failures to obtain emotional reactions may have been due to the fact that the electrodes were located in or near the epileptogenic focus (pathological tissue); thus the results were not meaningful for normal brain function. However, it is also quite possible that the electrodes were simply not in the correct location. It is clear from the animal experiments that the entire amygdala is not involved in emotional responding, and that sites that evoke a fear response on stimulation in the cat may lie within 1 mm of those that produce anger or no response at all.

Different Responses from Stimulation in the Same Brain Area
Both fear and anger have been produced by brain stimulation. Fear is perhaps more frequently found, and at times both fear and anger have been evoked from the same anatomical location with approximately the same stimulus parameters (Heath & Mickle, 1960; Heath, 1955, 1962, 1964b). This is not as surprising as might first appear. It has been shown repeatedly with animals that the brain stimulated subject generally reacts only to appropriate stimuli in the environment. When brain stimulation-induced aggression is evoked, the animal seldom attacks inappropriate targets. Brain stimulation studies in man are carried out in as friendly an

environment as is possible, so it is uncommon that there are appropriate targets for aggression except as the patient may misinterpret the situation. At the same time, however, the entire operative situation may cause anxiety or fear. The patient is justifiably fearful and concerned when his brain is to be stimulated. If there is already natural ongoing activity in the neural system for fear, it should require less intense electrical stimulation to elicit an overt response. Thus a fear raction may be evoked even though the electrode is not placed directly in the neural system for fear. Further, with the proximity of the neural systems for fear and anger, it would not be unlikely that an electrode could be placed near enough to both systems that either one could be activated with a given stimulation. Which reaction would be evoked would depend on the state of activity in the two systems, or the "neurological set," as explained in Chapter 1.

An anger reaction, in association with anxiety, has been produced by stimulation in the hippocampus with levarterenol bitartrate (Heath, 1964b) and by electrical stimulation in the posterior hypothalamus (Obrador, 1972). Intense rage accompanied by pain has resulted from stimulation in the rostral mesencephalon (Heath et al., 1955) and in the caudal hypothalamus (Heath, 1962). In these situations, the rage may be a consequence of the pain, since there is abundant evidence for a pain-aggression interaction. However, it is also true that not all pain produces hostile behavior.

Aggressive Reactions from Brain Stimulation
Aggressive reactions unmixed with other motivational states have also been reported. Stimulation of the hippocampus at a rate of four stimuli per second resulted in spike and slow-wave activity recorded from the septal region and an intense rage reaction (Heath, 1964a). One of the best-reported cases is that of Julia (Mark & Ervin, 1970; Mark et al., 1969; Mark et al., 1972; Delgado et al., 1968). Julia was a 22-year-old girl with a history of brain disease that evidently began with an attack of encephalitis before she was 2 years old. She had seizures with brief losses of consciousness, staring, lip smacking and chewing, frequently ending in a state of fugue in which she would find herself in a strange neighborhood alone and confused. Between seizures she showed severe temper tantrums, which were usually followed by intense remorse. On 12 different occasions Julia seriously assaulted people without apparent provocation. These included a near-fatal stabbing of a girl in the heart and an attack on a nurse in which she plunged scissors into the woman's lung. Julia had received extensive treatment, including psychotherapy, antiseizure medication, and a variety of other drugs. Finally, she was subjected to a course of 60 electroshock treatments. None of these treatments resulted in any improvement in either her seizure pattern or her assaultive behavior. An array of 20 electrodes was chronically implanted in each temporal lobe,

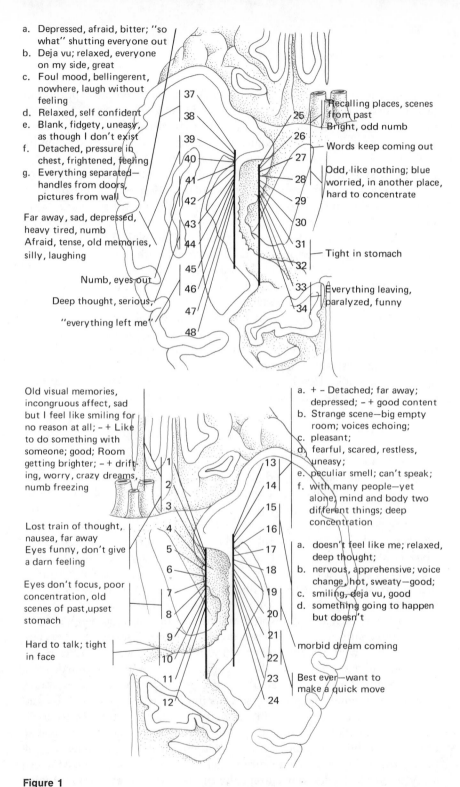

Figure 1

Summary of subjective states evoked by electrical stimulation superimposed on diagrammatic reconstruction of depth recording-stimulating points. (From J. R. Stevens et al., Deep temporal stimulation in man. *Archives of Neurology*, 1969, *21*, 162. Copyright 1969, American Medical Association.)

and over a period of time each electrode was stimulated in an attempt to duplicate her seizure pattern so that the appropriate area could be lesioned. These stimulations were carried out in the laboratory setting while her electrodes were connected to recording and stimulating equipment. In this situation she showed neither seizure activity nor hostile behavior. Only a "racing, restless" feeling was produced, which was typical of her preseizure response.

Later, however, Julia's electrodes were connected to a stimuloreceiver that could be activated remotely without attached wires. It was then possible to stimulate in the depths of the temporal lobe as well as record from it without connecting wires and in a natural setting. In one instance stimulation of the hippocampus, while she was talking to her psychiatrist, resulted in gradually increasing EEG and clinical abnormalities. Over a period of several seconds after the termination of the stimulation, she lost responsiveness to the examiner and suddenly began furiously to attack the wall with her fist. The attack coincided with bursts of high-voltage, spikelike EEG tracings from the right hippocampus and amygdala. In another instance stimulation was applied to the amygdala while she was playing a guitar and singing for her psychiatrist. Again, after a buildup lasting a few seconds, she lost contact, stared ahead blankly, and was unable to answer questions. Then, during a storm of subcortical electrical activity, she swung her guitar just past the head of the psychiatrist and smashed it against the wall.

Another case is reported in some detail by King (1961). A patient was stimulated in the amygdala with a 5-ma current and became verbally hostile, expressing a desire to tear things up and a plea for restraint. When the current was lowered to 4 ma she lost her aggressive tendencies. She was able to report on her earlier feelings and indicated that she felt as though she had no control over herself. When the 5-ma current was again applied she once again became hostile and threatened to strike the experimenter. She reported later that she felt no pain during any of the stimulations.

Prolonged Effects of Brain Stimulation
As in animals, the stimulation in the brain of man results in emotional and motivational states that generally do not outlast the duration of the stimulus. However, there is an increasing number of reports that indicate that stimulation in some areas results in delayed as well as prolonged effects. This implies that neurohumoral rather than neuroelectric processes are involved. One patient with electrodes implanted for the purpose of relieving intractable pain was stimulated at various points over a 1½-hour period. No changes in mood or in amount of pain were observed. Amygdala stimulation did result in a sharp rise in blood pressure that lasted for almost an hour after the termination of the stimulation. At the

end of the session the patient was returned to the ward. After a 20-minute delay, this mild-mannered, courtly and dignified man who had no history of brain damage or behavioral disturbance became extremely angry and would attack without provocation anyone close enough. He was incontinent and climbed on his bed and threw feces at anyone within range. He was finally sufficiently restrained to be given an injection of chlorpromazine, after which he calmed down and went into a deep sleep. When he awoke, he had total amnesia for the incident. Later, stimulation of the opposite amygdala resulted in a very similar reaction, although of shorter duration. The patient's death 12 days after treatment permitted the investigators to check the electrode locations. They were placed as intended, in the right and left amygdala (Ervin, Mark, & Stevens, 1969). Unfortunately the report does not indicate the specific location of the electrodes within the amygdala, which would have been more informative. Other cases of a similar nature are reported in the same paper and in Mark et al. (1972) and Stevens et al. (1969). Prolonged and delayed effects have also been reported for euphoric responses, relaxation, and pain relief. (See preceding references, Heath and Mickle, 1960, and Sem-Jacobsen and Torkildsen, 1960).

Inhibition of Aggression by Brain Stimulation
There are suppressor areas for aggressive behavior in the brain of man, as there are in the brains of animals, and there is good reason to believe that those suppressor areas are associated with other motivational systems. Heath (1963) described the reaction of a psychomotor epileptic patient to septal stimulation. The patient was exhibiting agitated, violent psychotic behavior when the septal stimulation was introduced without his knowledge. His behavioral state changed almost instantaneously from disorganization, rage, and feelings of persecution to happiness and euphoria. He described the beginnings of a sexual motive state and was unable to explain the sudden shift in his behavior when he was directly questioned about it. Heath goes on to point out that the case described is not unique, but has been repeated in a large number of patients in his laboratory. The same kind of dramatic change can also be produced by direct application of acetylcholine to the septal area through permanently implanted cannulae. In one patient described by Heath, the electrical recording characterized by spike and slow-wave activity in the septal area was normalized by the application of acetylcholine at the same time that the rage responses associated with it were reduced (Heath & Guerrero-Figueroa, 1965).

The aggression-suppression effects of brain stimulation may also have a relatively prolonged effect. Sem-Jacobsen and Torkildsen (1960) report that stimulation in the ventromedial frontal lobes had a calming effect on a violent manic patient. A similar effect resulted from stimulating the central area of the temporal lobe. When both points were stimulated in rapid succession the calming, antihostility effect was greater and of some duration. Peterson, in a discussion of the Sem-Jacobsen and Torkildsen paper, also reports that actively disturbed and antagonistic patients become quite placid and talk well after about 15 minutes of stimulation in the frontal medial area of the brain. This period of calmness may last for a day or even longer. There is no indication in any of the reports that the investigators were dealing with a general "arrest" phenomenon. The patients reacted normally but their mood level and affective tone was shifted in a more positive direction. Although the physiological basis for the effect is not clear, there is some evidence that the brain stimulation effects can extend over a period of months. One patient with psychomotor seizures who also exhibited assaultive behavior was given several periods of electrical stimulation to an undesignated area in the right amygdala. The results were said to produce long-lasting and gratifying improvement in his mood and thought content. The results were so favorable that the electrodes were removed and the patient was able to hold a good job and was relatively symptom-free in regard to both seizures and violence for a period of a year. He did, however, relapse completely (Sweet et al., 1969).

SUMMARY

Relatively little is known about the detailed neuroanatomy of the neural systems for aggressive behavior in man. However, the general outline is clear. The weight of the evidence seems to indicate that man, for all of his encephalization, has not escaped from the biological determinants of his hostility. Man has neural systems for aggressive feelings and behavior. When these systems are activated, by whatever means, he has aggressive feelings and may act aggressively. When the activity in the neural systems is blocked, either by surgical interruption or by suppression from inhibitory systems, man's tendency to hostility is reduced.

There are a variety of pathologies of the brain resulting in changes that increase the probability of activity in neural substrates for aggression, with a consequent lowering of the threshold for hostile thoughts and behavior. Subcortical tumors in various portions of the limbic system result in a gradual change in the individual's personality, with irritability as one of the predominant symptoms. A formerly reasonable, pleasant person may change to one who manifests persistent irrational, hostile thoughts and actions and who is unable to understand his own behavior. When the tumor is excised and the pressure is relieved, his adjustment may return to normal.

Several disorders, including miscellaneous brain trauma, rabies, and encephalitis, result in damage to particular portions of the limbic system with a consequent personality alteration in which inadequate control of aggressive impulses predominates. An individual's behavior may range from a moderate loss of impulse control to pathological aggressive and even homicidal tendencies.

The Lesch-Nyhan syndrome is a relatively rare disorder of purine metabolism in which the patient is unable to control both self-mutilating tendencies and aggressive behavior toward others.

In certain individuals with temporal lobe epilepsy the spontaneous activation of the neural systems for aggression results in periodic aggressive episodes. There is some reason to believe that the neural substrates underlying the convulsive process are not the same as those responsible for the aggressive outbursts. Surgery that excises a portion of the subcortex may result in an alleviation of the hostility without affecting the convulsions or vice versa. Some of the pharmaceutical agents that are useful in the control of the seizures may exacerbate the aggressive behavior, and medication to reduce the hostility may increase the seizure tendency.

Abnormal electroencephalographic records also indicate dysfunctions in the brain. Although there is considerable controversy in the literature, the consensus seems to be that there is a greater probability that individuals with abnormal EEG records will manifest more aggressive tendencies than will the normal population. It is clear, however, that the EEG cannot be used to predict aggressive tendencies.

Although there are limitations to its use as a practical therapy (see Chapter 4) it is of considerable theoretical importance that pathological, uncontrollable aggressive behavior can be eliminated by specific brain lesions. The neural systems for aggression course through much of the limbic system. Interruption of these systems at any one of several locations may result in a reduction or complete elimination of excessive hostile behavior. This has been accomplished with gross lesions in the temporal lobe, amygdaloid lesions as well as ablations in the cingulum, thalamus, hypothalamus, and fornix.

Finally, it has now been repeatedly demonstrated that aggressive behavior and feelings can be brought under control by direct stimulation of man's brain. Stimulation in particular portions of the amygdala and the hippocampus has resulted in angry feelings and reactions with no report of pain, even though the patient was unaware of the stimulation. These hostile reactions terminated as soon as the current was turned off. It has also been shown that direct stimulation in the septal and other brain areas can block an ongoing aggressive reaction and cause a shift to a more positive feeling tone.

In the next chapter we will consider the changes in blood chemistry that influence the sensitivity of the various neural systems for aggressive behavior.

3

Blood Chemistry Changes and Aggressive Behavior in Man

There are a number of changes in the blood chemistry that result in the alteration of the brain mechanism, with a consequent change in tendencies to aggression. In man, as in animals (see Chapter 8), many of these changes are in the endocrine system. However, this chapter also considers the role of hypoglycemia, certain allergens, and some hostility-inducing and inhibiting drugs.

Experiments and clinical observations on humans frequently present problems in interpretation. Because experiments frequently lack some desirable controls, it is difficult to determine the role of variables not specifically considered in a particular study. Manipulations of blood chemistry, either experimental or natural, do not occur in a vacuum. A large number of factors are, of course, constantly interacting to affect the changes in aggression potential that result from blood changes. There are wide individual differences in susceptibility to various drugs and hormones.

Changes in drug or hormone levels cause changes in subjective experience that may be interpreted differently by different individuals because of their prior learning. The individual's expectations may strongly influence his behavior, and the experience he has after a given manipulation will be influenced by his interpretations of the expectations of others about how he should be affected.

In spite of all the difficulties, however, it is possible to draw some tentative conclusions about the role of blood chemistry changes and aggressive behavior in man. Much of the evidence in this chapter is clinical and some of the studies have a small number of subjects and have fewer controls than one would find with comparable animal experiments. These findings must be interpreted with considerable caution. However, the results are frequently suggestive of hypotheses that should be followed up and tested more carefully in the future.

ENDOCRINOLOGY OF AGGRESSION IN MALE HUMANS

As indicated in Chapter 8, good evidence exists that various agonistic behaviors appear in a number of animals with the onset of sexual maturity. Despite wide individual differences, there appear to be dramatic increases in testosterone and androstenedione (a biologically active form of testosterone) levels in adolescent human males. There are differences between the sexes prior to puberty but after the age of 9, boys show a gradual increase in testosterone levels. At ages 10 to 15 the increase is on the order of tenfold. Adolescent boys do, of course, show an increase in aggressive behavior, but the increases in testosterone levels have not yet been related to any measures of aggression in adolescents (Hamburg, 1971c).

Until recently essentially no information has been available relating the endocrine function and affective response tendencies in man. However, with improvement in assay techniques (see Hamburg & Lunde, 1966) such studies are beginning to appear. A suggestive relationship was found between the activity of the pituitary (luteinizing hormone) testicular axis and feelings of hostility, anger, and aggression (Persky et al., 1968). A further study was undertaken on the basis of those findings using more refined techniques involving the measurement of plasma testosterone level and testosterone production rate (Persky et al., 1971). Two groups of men were studied. The 18 individuals in the younger group ranged from 17 to 28 years of age, and the 15 older men were between the ages of 30 and 66 years. The average testosterone production rate of the older men was about half that of the younger men and when all the subjects were considered as a group, a significant negative correlation ($r = -0.62$) was shown between age and testosterone production rate. This is an interesting finding in itself inasmuch as it has been shown that violent crime in the United States is most prevalent among males between the ages of 15 and 24.

This study also showed that in the younger men the production rate of testosterone was highly correlated with a measure of aggression derived from the Buss-Durkee Hostility Inventory,[1] and a multivariate regression

---

[1] The Buss-Durkee inventory provides a measure of aggression and hostility. It was developed through the use of standard test construction techniques. It was sub-

equation was obtained between the testosterone production rate and four different measures of aggression and hostility. This equation accounted for 82 percent of the variance in the production rate of testosterone for the younger men. In the older age group the only variable that correlated highly with testosterone production was age, and the regression equation that was highly predictive for the young men was not valid for the older age group.

In another study aggressive behavior and plasma testosterone were assessed in a young criminal population (Kreuz & Rose, 1972). The subjects were selected to provide a high-aggression and a low-aggression group using the number of times that an individual had been placed in solitary confinement as the index for assignment to the two groups. That index was associated with fighting behavior and resulted in highly differentiated groups. Fighters 'were defined as those individuals who had been in more than one fight during their imprisonment. Plasma testosterone was measured in six plasma samples taken within one hour of awakening. Although there was a significant difference between the two groups in terms of actual fighting behavior and verbal aggression, the differences on plasma testosterone were not significant. Paper and pencil tests were also given to the subjects. Hostility was measured by the Buss-Durkee Hostility Inventory but no significant correlation was found between the hostility test scores and fighting in prison, and the hostility scores did not correlate with plasma testosterone. However, an investigation of the type of crime for which the subjects were incarcerated revealed that those individuals who had committed violent and aggressive offenses during adolescence had a significantly higher testosterone level than men who had not committed that type of offense. There was also a significant correlation between the age of the first conviction for a violent crime and the plasma testosterone level. However, the past history of assaultive behavior was not correlated with either fighting in prison or hostility as measured by the paper and pencil test.

The results of the Kreuz and Rose study are somewhat surprising in light of the Persky et al. study, which used the same hostility inventory. It may well be that a variety of potent pressures in the prison setting influence the instrumental aggression of the subjects. Reinforcement in the prison tends to be swift and severe and may be a more important determinant of actual behavior than whatever internal tendencies to hostility are set up by the testosterone level. The behavior that did correlate with plasma testosterone took place outside the prison. The reasons for the lack of relationship between the scores on the Buss-Durkee inventory and testosterone level are not clear at the moment.

---

jected to an item analysis and factor analyris and a collection of norms are available. Responses to the items on the inventory seem to be relatively free from the influence of the social desirability variable. (See Buss, 1961.)

The preceding studies on blood levels of testosterone and aggressive tendencies use males as subjects, but it is not possible from the data to determine whether the hostility measured is a form of inter-male or irritable aggression, or some combination of both.

Although uncontrolled clinical studies must be interpreted with caution, several reports on humans offer support for the idea that exogenous androgens enhance aggressive tendencies. One series of schizophrenic patients showed a decrease in fearfulness and apprehension and increased self-confidence when treated with Diandrone (dehydroisoandosterone) (Strauss et al., 1952)..A decrease in feelings of inferiority, timidity, and apathy with an increase in self-confidence occurred in young males with "inadequate personality" after four days to four weeks of therapy with the same preparation (Sands & Chamberlain, 1952). Diandrone is also reported to exert an androgenic effect in the social and psychological rather than in the physical or sexual field. Masculine activity, aggression, and self-confidence are enhanced. The timid "shrinking violet" becomes more adequate and aggressive tendencies in individuals with manifest hostility are made flagrantly worse (Sands, 1954).

Although the evidence is far from conclusive, it certainly suggests a relationship between testosterone levels in the male and some indications of aggressive behavior. This is what one might expect from the numerous studies on animals. One could also expect the relationship to be less powerful because learning is such a potent factor in aggressive behavior in man. Learned inhibitions can, of course, prevent an individual from acting on relatively strong aggressive feelings that might occur because of the sensitivity produced in the neural systems for aggression by a relatively high androgen level.

Effects of Castration on Aggression in Humans

A further understanding of the role of androgens in the aggressive behavior of humans can be gained from a study of the effects of castration. This operation has been carried out on man from ancient times for a variety of purposes. Eunuchs were needed to guard the harems of sultans, and until the nineteenth century boy sopranos were castrated so that they would be able to retain their pure, high tones. In 1894 the first castration for the control of pervert sexual acts was performed by Dr. Pilcher of the State Training School of Winfield, Kansas. Denmark legalized the operation as a therapeutic measure for certain types of crimes in 1929 and other countries followed soon after—Nazi Germany in 1933, Norway in 1934, Finland in 1935, Iceland in 1938, and Sweden in 1944 (Bremer, 1959). Several authors have reviewed the results of these programs and concluded that castration, if it is combined with other therapeutic measures, is an effective method of dealing with sex crimes, particularly those of a violent nature (Kopp, 1938; Campbell, 1967; LeMaire, 1956; Hawke, 1950; Sturup, 1961).

Bremer (1959) did a follow-up study on 224 Norwegian cases and concluded that the sex drive was drastically reduced by castration: "It can be stated at the beginning that in all cases without exception the amount of sexual activity has been altered. It has been reduced or abolished, irrespective of the direction or the form of sexual urge—heterosexuality, homosexuality, fetichism, zoophilic actions, masturbation, exhibitionism, or fetichistic actions—which are those represented in the material" (p. 67). In two-thirds of the cases sexual interest and activity essentially disappeared within the first year after the operation and in most cases the asexualization occurred immediately or shortly after the operation.

About half of the cases considered by Bremer were dangerous. The others were considered to be merely asocial or troublesome, manifesting such offenses as exhibitionism, fetishism, and zoophilia. Castration was most effective in all respects when the sexual factor was the dominating cause of the criminal or disturbed behavior. Seventy-seven of the subjects were castrated in the hope of achieving a general pacifying effect to make the patients easier to control. Many of these individuals were low-grade oligophrenics and schizophrenics. Bremer reports that the operation was ineffective in controlling the disturbed mental cases and had no definite pacifying effect. This is an interesting and somewhat paradoxical finding in light of the animal literature, which seems to indicate that there is a reduction of inter-male and irritable aggression with a reduction of the androgen level in the blood.

Other investigators have found that castration (and androgen blocking by other means) does reduce hostility that is not directly associated with the individual's sexual behavior. Hawke (1950) describes several cases in which a generally aggressive individual has had his sexual aggression curbed and has been made less aggressive in other ways by castration. He also reports on a series of observations in which relatively large doses of testosterone were given to large groups of castrates over a period of several weeks. In a number of cases it was necessary to terminate the injections because the patients became generally destructive. They "had reverted to all of their antisocial tendencies, were attacking small children, starting fights, breaking windows and destroying furniture" (p. 222). When the administration of the hormone was stopped, the individuals became tractable once again within a few days and no longer created disturbances on the ward. Many of the 330 individuals in the Kansas sample treated by castration were brutal homosexuals who were generally unstable and constantly created disturbances. After the operation they became stabilized and could be paroled or became useful citizens within the institution.

Sex criminals treated by castration seldom repeat their crimes. Danish statistics indicate that the recidivist rate for individuals treated without castration and released is about ten times that of persons who have been castrated (Sturup, 1961). The figures are almost the same for Norway (Bremer, 1959). Hawke (1950) reports that a sex crime has never been committed by a parolee or a castrate who escaped from the Kansas institution.

Estrogens as Antihostility Agents in the Male

There are now a number of clinical studies indicating that female hormones may be used in the control of aggressive tendencies in men. Golla and Hodge (1949) indicate that estrogenic substances could be used as a form of chemical castration and would be more efficient than the operation itself because the estrogens would block the effects of adrenal androgens, which are not controlled by castration. A number of authors have reported series of cases in which the aggressive tendencies of adolescents and young adults were controlled by the use of stilbestrol (Sand, 1954; Foote, 1944; Whitaker, 1959). Stilbestrol is a synthetic drug that has been demonstrated to have the estrogenic qualities of natural estrogens. It depresses anterior pituitary gonadotropic function.

A case is reported in some detail by Dunn (1941) in which stilbestrol was used to control hyperirritable aggression and excessive libido. This patient was a 27-year-old male under maximum sentence for sexual offenses against female minors. He was a persistent troublemaker in prison and was frequently placed in solitary confinement for insubordination. The prisoner had abnormal amounts of male hormone and gonadotropic hormone in the urine before therapy and was preoccupied with his sex life. After four weeks of daily treatment with stilbestrol, he reported that his sexual responses, both physical and mental, were reduced. He had also adapted much better to prison discipline and was no longer considered a troublemaker. He continued relatively symptom-free for more than three months after discontinuance of the therapy. Subsequently, however, he had a return of his symptoms and requested a resumption of therapy.

Two investigators have used subcutaneous or intramuscular injections of long-acting estrogens (estradiol B.P.C. and oestrodiol valerianate) to avoid the necessity of daily oral therapy (Field & Williams, 1970; Chatz, 1972). This approach permits the release of otherwise highly dangerous individuals and does not depend on their cooperation in taking the medication. Both reports indicate that the aggressive behavior and the sexual offending were essentially eliminated while the patients were under the estrogenic therapy.

Antiandrogens as Antihostility Agents

There are now several substances available that have demonstrated anti-androgenic activity (Lerner, 1964). A-Norprogesterone (Lerner et al., 1960), chlormadinone acetate (Rocky & Neri, 1968), cyproterone acetate (Neuman et al., 1968), and medroxyprogesterone (Servais, 1968) have been shown to be potent antagonists of androgens. These synthetic hormones are steroids, as are the natural sex hormones. When administered to intact animals they produce, in some measure, chemical castration. Cyproterone acetate appears to block the use of naturally produced testosterone by competing with it at the receptor sites (Neuman et al., 1970), and medroxyprogesterone lowers the plasma level of testosterone from the testes (Money, 1970).

It is interesting that cyproterone acetate does not block inter-male aggression in either the gerbil (Sayler, 1970) or the mouse (Edwards, 1970a; Brain et al., 1973), but does appear to have some effect in the control of excessive libido and, apparently, sex-related aggression in man (Laschet, 1967; Laschet et al., 1967). Seven individuals convicted of indecent assault and sexual murder have been successfully treated and at least one has been placed on probation with an order for continued therapy (Laschet, 1973). There is not as yet sufficient evidence to evaluate the effectiveness of cyproterone on aggression, particularly in man. However, further work is certainly indicated.

Medroxyprogesterone (Provera, Upjohn), which is chemically very close to natural progesterone, is highly effective in lowering testosterone level. There is some evidence that it may be effective in the control of excessive and impulsive sexual behavior and aggression in man. Lloyd (1964b) indicates that sexually hyperactive and aggressive adolescent boys are made more tractable by Provera therapy. Although aggressiveness is not dealt with, as such, Money (1970) reports that Provera significantly and rapidly reduces a variety of illegal sexual behaviors in male offenders. In a preliminary study Blumer and Migeon (1973) found that a high level of Depo-Provera (300 mg every 10 days) successfully reduced sexual arousal and consequently sexual deviations, including one case of homosexual aggressiveness toward younger children. Perhaps even more interesting was the finding that one-third of the dose for sexual deviates was used successfully to control the episodic irritability and rage reactions of 11 temporal lobe epileptics. It should be emphasized that this is a preliminary study. The long-term side effects of Provera are not known and the risks involved are not yet clear.

Summary of the Role of Androgens in Aggression in the Human Male

Unfortunately data bearing on the relationship between the endocrines and aggressive behavior in man seldom come wrapped in a neat package with a good experimental design complete with an analysis of variance. However, the preceding section seems clearly to implicate the androgens in some forms of aggressive behavior in man. When the level or potency of androgens is reduced in certain populations of aggressive individuals, the tendency to aggressive behavior is also reduced. It is interesting that castration reduces the sex drive in essentially all individuals studied. More important for this discussion, however, it also essentially eliminated violent crimes and excessive aggressive or dangerous behavior in those subjects who were incarcerated for that reason. In the Bremer study castration effectively reduced aggression related specifically to sexual behavior. Sex-related aggression also appears to be reduced by either estrogenic compounds or antiandrogenic substances. There also appears to be some evidence that a reduction in androgen level or potency reduces the probability of irritable aggression.

This material is, at best, suggestive. However, it certainly merits further controlled investigation. Now that improved hormone assay techniques and several androgen-blocking agents are available, we can expect an increase in the number of studies relating to this problem, which should provide us with more precise data.

AGGRESSION AND THE
PREMENSTRUAL SYNDROME

Feminine hostility has, of course, many causes, but there is now reasonably good evidence that there is a periodicity to the irascibility of women and that it is related to the hormonal changes occurring over the course of the menstrual cycle. There is some evidence that during the period of ovulation, anxiety and feelings of hostility are at a relatively low level (Gottschalk, 1969). During the period just prior to menstruation, however, a significant number of women manifest a variety of symptoms that have been collectively called the premenstrual syndrome. This syndrome includes such physical changes as headache, edema, particularly of the face, hands, and feet; and significant weight gain. Changes in appetite, a craving for sweets, and unusual bursts of energy may also be a part of the syndrome (Sletten & Gershon, 1966; Altman et al., 1941). Emotional instability is a characteristic of a number of women during the premenstrual period. There is an increased tendency for women to seek psychiatric help during the premenstrual period (Jacobs & Charles, 1970) and a general increase in psychiatric symptomatology at that time (Glass et al., 1971; Torghele, 1957). Suicide attempts also increase (Dalton, 1959; Glass et al., 1971; Ribero, 1962; Mandell & Mandell, 1967).

Of particular interest here is the increase in various manifestations of irritability and hostility. Shainess (1961) describes it as defensive hostility. Ivey and Bardwick (1968), using Gottschalk's technique of analysis of verbal reports,[2] found consistent themes of hostility during the pre-menstruum. In a recent study of 1100 women who were the wives of graduate students in a large American university, 52 percent reported that they were markedly irritable in the premenstrual phase of some cycles and 30 percent reported marked irritability during their most recent cycle. The feeling of irritability was more marked than that of depression or tension (Hamburg, 1971c). Similar findings have been reported by other investigators (Coppen & Kessel, 1963; Sutherland & Stewart, 1965; Moos, 1968). Women in prison populations are more irritable during pre-menstrual and menstrual phases of the cycle (Ellis & Austin, 1971).

Aggressive Acting Out During the Premenstruum
Irritable feelings are frequently acted out. In the Ellis and Austin study significantly more aggressive acts occurred during the menstrual and premenstrual period. According to Dalton (1964), women prisoners themselves frequently recognize that their behavior during this critical period is likely to get them into trouble and, as a result, request to be isolated. School girls show more infractions of the rules and receive more punishment during the critical period in the cycle, and older girls with legitimate disciplinary power tend to mete out more punishments during their own menstruation (Dalton, 1960). The majority of women prisoners who are sufficiently violent so as to require removal to maximum security quarters menstruate during the few days of confinement (Smith, quoted in Shah & Roth, 1975). Women prisoners are more frequently reported for "bad behavior" during the critical period (Dalton, 1961).

There is also evidence that more crimes are actually committed during the irritable period in the menstrual cycle. A study of prison records revealed that 62 percent of the crimes of violence were committed during the premenstrual week and only 2 percent at the end of the period (Morton et al., 1953). However, the length of the "end of the period" was not indicated. A similar finding is reported by Dalton (1961). She found that 49 percent of all crimes were committed by women during menstruation or in the premenstruum. Thus the association between menstruation and crime is highly significant. One would expect only 29 percent of all crimes to be committed during the eight-day period if they were normally distributed. The probability of the obtained distribution occurring by chance is less than one in a thousand. The possibility of impulsive aggression and lawbreaking during the menstrual and pre-

[2] The Gottschalk-Gleser Content Analysis Scale is a method of determining from a verbal sample the individual's mood state. S. B. Sells summarizes the work on this scale as follows: "In summary, the Gottschalk-Gleser Content Analysis Scales appear to be reasonably valid and reliable measures of the manifest psychological states evidenced in verbal protocols. They thus provide a powerful psychometric tool in the diagnosis of psychological states of interest to clinical, researchers and practitioners" (Buros, 1972).

menstrual period is of sufficient magnitude that the criminal law in some countries recognizes menstruation as an extenuating circumstance (Deutsch, 1944). Severe premenstrual tension is placed in the category of temporary insanity in France (Podolsky, 1964).

Feelings of irritability, hostility, and other manifestations of the premenstrual syndrome are not confined to a few asocial individuals who get into difficulties with the law. Moderate or severe degrees of the syndrome occur in about a quarter of all women (Coppen & Kessel, 1963; Hamburg et al., 1968). Some authors estimate that as many as 90 percent of women undergo some irritability, hopelessness, depression, or other symptoms prior to or during menstruation (Janowsky et al., 1967; Pennington, 1957).

Physiology of Premenstrual Hostility
The underlying physiology of the tendencies to hostility associated with the menstrual-premenstrual syndrome is obscure. There seems to be rather general agreement that the symptoms are associated with a fall in the progesterone level and a relatively greater amount of estrogen in the estrogen-progesterone ratio (Hamburg et al., 1968; Morton, 1950; Lloyd & Weisz, 1972). (Bardwick, 1971, maintains that the symptomatology is due to the absolute fall in estrogen.) Several studies have shown that the symptoms can be alleviated by the administration of progesterone (Dalton, 1964; Green & Dalton, 1953; Lloyd, 1964a). Women who take oral contraceptives that contain progestagenic agents show significantly less irritability than do women who are not taking the pill (Hamburg et al., 1968; Wiseman, 1965; Paige, 1969, quoted in Bardwick, 1971). It may be that the irritability-reducing effects of the progestagens are a function of their direct effect on the neural systems in the brain that relate to hostility. However, the explanation may be much less direct. Janowsky et al. (1967) hypothesize that the irritability results from the cyclic increase in aldosterone inasmuch as weight changes, behavioral changes, and aldosterone changes seem to parallel each other. The resulting increase in sodium and water retention caused by aldosterone results in a secondary neuronal irritability and consequent psychic symptoms. It is not clear, however, why general neuronal irritability should affect the parts of the nervous system associated with irritable feelings and negative affect. The therapeutic effects of lithium (Ellis & Austin, 1971) and diuretics (Whinshel, 1959; Greenhill & Freed, 1940; Morton, 1950) in treating premenstrual tension may then be due to their tendency to reverse the aldosterone effect on sodium metabolism.

Another physiological characteristic of the premenstrual syndrome is hypoglycemia. Billig and Spaulding (1947) found evidence of hypoglycemia during the period immediately prior to the onset of the menses, and Harris (1944) noted an increase in the symptoms of hyperinsulinism in women at the same time in the cycle. Morton (1950) suggests that the increased sugar tolerance is due to the action of the unopposed estrogen on carbohydrate metabolism and indicates that many of the psychic symptoms as well as weakness and fatigue can be largely ascribed to the hypoglycemia. He recommends diet changes including supplementary protein as an adjunct therapy. The hypoglycemic states may also contribute to feelings of irritability and hostility, as is discussed later.

Although the evidence certainly indicates an increase in feelings of irritability and hostility in some women during the premenstrual period, there is no good physiological explanation of the cause as yet. It must be recognized that the menstrual process is a phenomenon loaded with psychological meaning in most cultures. It therefore seems unlikely that the psychological changes associated with the period just prior to the onset of the menses are exclusively or even primarily of physiological origin. As with most other manifestations of hostility, learning, culture, and the environment play an important role. However, the data do suggest the definite possibility that the particular endocrine balance characteristic of the premenstrual phase contributes to the feelings of irritability and hostility frequently found during that portion of the cycle. Further work on the physiology of this problem is clearly indicated.

AGGRESSIVE BEHAVIOR AS AN ALLERGIC REACTION

You wouldn't believe bananas. Within twenty minutes of eating a banana this child would be in the worst temper tantrum—no seizures—you have ever seen. I tried this five times because I couldn't believe my own eyes. He reacted with behavior to all sugars except maple sugar. We went to California the Christmas of 1962 to be with my parents. Robbie's Christmas treats were all made from maple sugar. He was asking for some other candy. My mother wanted him to have it and I told her allright if she wanted to take care of the tantrum. Of course, she didn't believe me but predictably within thirty minutes she had her hands full with Robbie in a tantrum. It made a believer of her. These discussions did not take place in front of the child if you're wondering about the power of suggestion.

If you go into this food reaction thing it will make you feel so sorry for people you can't stand it. After bad behavior from food, Robbie would cry and say he couldn't help it and feel so badly about it. You won't be able to read of a Crime of Violence without wondering if a chemical reaction controlled the aggressor—in fact, you'll be unable to condemn anyone for anything. . . .

The preceding case, quoted in a letter to me by Robbie's mother, was my introduction to the rather remarkable possibility that aggressive behavior could be the result of physiological changes brought about by a reaction to specific allergens. A search of the allergy literature reveals that aggression as an allergic response is a well-recognized phenomenon. As early as 1916, just ten years after the term *allergy* was coined by von Pirquet (1906, quoted in Speer, 1970a), Hoobler (1916) described certain allergic children as "restless, fretful, and sleepless." Shannon (1922) was one of the first to indicate that the behavior disorders were a primary allergic reaction and not simply a normal response to the discomfort caused by the other manifestations of the allergic reaction. The behavioral symptoms occurred without a history of preceding dermal discomfort, they were out of proportion to the primary allergy, and they were not always caused by the same allergen.

The Allergic Tension-Fatigue Syndrome
The term *allergic tension-fatigue syndrome* was introduced in 1954 to describe the allergic behavior pattern (Speer, 1954). It is important to note that behavior disturbances are only one of many possible allergic reactions and that all individuals with allergies do not show a behavioral alteration.

The most common descriptive term used in connection with this syndrome is *irritability* (Coca, 1959; Randolph, 1962), which is seldom defined behaviorally. However, the irritability syndrome (*irritable aggression* as used in this book) can be understood by the various synonyms used by different authors to describe the individuals so afflicted. Davison (1952) has referred to irascibility and impulsiveness as behavioral allergic symptoms. Other descriptive terms have been uncooperative "antisocial" (Pounders, 1948); cross and irritable, resisting all handling . . . spells of intense temper and fury (Kahn, 1927); peevishness, unhappiness, unruliness, rebellious behavior (Crooke et al., 1961); incorrigible (Rowe, 1930); disobedient, perverse, cantankerous, antagonistic (Schaffer, 1953); hot tempered, hard to please, sulky, temperamental, hotheaded, wild, unrestrained (Speer, 1970b); *aggressively* irritable, ill-natured, resentful, domineering, slow to forgive (Speer, 1954); combative, quarrelsome, delinquent (Fredericks & Goodman, 1969); snappish disposition, angry irritability, violent temper tantrums (Coca, 1959); negative, asocial, hostile, paranoid (Randolph, 1959). The descriptions are a veritable thesaurus of irritability. A classification of allergic reactions in the nervous systems includes the following:

> *Emotional Immaturity Reactions.* Included under this heading are temper tantrums, screaming episodes, whining, impatience and excitability. Patients of this type are inclined to be erratic, impulsive, quarrelsome and irresponsible. Many admit having "childish" compulsions.
>
> *Antisocial Behavior.* These patients are inclined to be uncooperative, pugnacious, sulky, and perhaps cruel. Most have learned enough self-control to avoid serious aberrations of behavior [Campbell, 1970a, p. 31].

The intensity of the symptoms may run from a mild irritable reaction in which the individual is a little more easily annoyed than usual to a psychotic aggressive reaction. Mandell (1969) describes a 10-year-old girl with intractable asthma in whom an attack was brought on by an ethanol test. She was completely amnesic for the three hours during which the test lasted. She became infantile and did not know her name and address. Her mood ran from silliness and restlessness to withdrawal. Several times during the prolonged reaction, she became extremely belligerent and tried to bite her mother, whom she was unable to identify. In a case described by Speer (1958), a 9-year-old boy reacted to wheat by awakening in a nightmare completely disoriented, not knowing who he was, who his mother was, or where he was. He struck his head against the wall repeatedly and engaged in high-pitched, uncontrolled screaming. Numerous other case studies are available to demonstrate all variations in intensity from mild to severe. (See the papers of the investigators previously mentioned.)

Many of the symptoms found in allergies of the nervous system are also characteristic of the syndrome of minimal brain dysfunction (MBD). In addition to those characteristics already mentioned, the allergic individual, particularly a child, is hyperactive, and his parents frequently describe his behavior as wild. He also tends to be overtalkative, restless, and inattentive, and has difficulty learning basic skills (Speer, 1970b). Schneider (1945) has indicated that allergy is one of the most important factors, frequently unrecognized, in the production of the hyperkinetic child syndrome. Kittler (1970) provides a number of case studies of children with the typical MBD syndrome who respond to allergy management and essentially lose the symptoms. The following case is typical:

G. L. was seen because of temper tantrums. He was believed aphasic because of poor speech development at age five years and one month. He was too uncontrollable to do initial IQ testing. Allergy tests were done and strong positive reactions found to yeast, chocolate, and milk. He had an electroencephalogram with 14-per-second spikes, large amount of sharp activity in the motor leads, temporal single polyphasic sharp waves, and a long run of sharp waves in the right temporal area. He was placed on a diet free of milk, chocolate, and cola drinks. His electroencephalogram in March, 1967, seven and one-half months later, was normal. In September 1967, he was learning better and his behavior was much improved. He was challenged again with the suspected foods for one week. Repeating the electroencephalogram showed 2½- to 6-per-second activity on the right, greater in the mid-temporal and parietal leads, accentuated by drowsiness. Light cerebral dysfunction was diagnosed. His behavior became quite uncontrollable again during the week he was challenged with foods.[3]

[3] F. J. Kittler, The effect of allergy on children with minimal brain damage. In E. Speer (Ed.), *Allergy of the Nervous System*. Springfield, Ill.: Charles C Thomas, 1970, p. 126.

It is of interest that both Benadryl and Dexedrine, which are effective in the control of MBD, are also useful as medication for allergy (Campbell, 1970b). The role of allergy in MBD provides an illustration of the compartmentalization in science. Although there is a reasonable literature on the topic, and Wender (1971) takes an eclectic approach to the etiology of the disorder, the term *allergy* is not even in the index of Wender's extensively referenced book.

It is difficult to determine how extensive a problem allergic aggression is. There are relatively few studies comparing aggressive tendencies in allergic individuals with controls. And since it is clear that all allergic individuals do not have nervous system involvement, such studies would not be particularly meaningful. Although there are a large number of case studies in the literature showing that individuals with allergic tension-fatigue syndrome lose that symptomatology under allergy management, the only reasonable way to determine whether the syndrome is an allergic one is to eliminate the allergen from the environment until the symptoms abate and then reproduce the symptoms by reintroducing the allergen into the environment, the so-called challenge technique. Crook et al. (1961) report on 50 patients who had five signs and symptoms of allergy: fatigue, irritability and other mental and emotional symptoms, pallor, circles under the eyes, and nasal congestions. The majority of the patients in this study had their symptoms relieved and reproduced by the challenge technique. The 50 patients reviewed in this research were seen in the group pediatric practice during a four-year period. The authors conclude that allergy as a systemic or generalized illness is much more common than is usually recognized by most allergy textbooks.

Allergens that can produce the allergic tension-fatigue syndrome are highly varied. It can be produced by pollens (Kahn, 1927); a variety of inhalants (Eisenberg, 1970; Randolph, 1962); drugs (Gottlieb, 1970a; Schaffer, 1953); and many foods, of which milk, chocolate, cola, corn, and eggs are the most common (Speer, 1970c; Crook et al., 1961). The sensitivity of the individual varies idiosyncratically and according to the type of allergen. One patient showed such exquisite sensitivity to onions that she could tell when they were being cooked, not by the odor but because she had sudden and intense nervousness and irritability (Fredericks & Goodman, 1969). Other individuals can tolerate moderate amounts of some allergens. It is not uncommon for a child to be allergic to milk but to manifest no reaction as long as the milk intake is limited to several times a week.

The Physiology of Allergy-Induced Aggression

The basic physiological cause of the irritable allergic reaction is not yet clear. It has been suggested that allergens have a direct effect on the nervous system (Speer, 1958; Piness & Miller, 1925). This is evident from the fact that some epileptic disorders have an allergic basis. In fact, early allergists hoped to demonstrate that all idiopathic epilepsy was due to an allergy (Speer, 1970a). Although that did not turn out to be the case, there is abundant evidence that in some individuals, convulsions and other epileptic phenomena can be produced at will by challenging the individual with the particular allergen to which he is sensitive. (An excellent review of the literature with several cases is given by Campbell, 1970c.)

Cerebral edema has been suggested as causing allergy-induced mental symptoms (Moore, 1958; Fredericks & Goodman, 1969), but generalized edema leaves much to be desired as an explanation of the specific symptomatology. Campbell (1970a) implies on the basis of the symptomatology that the limbic system is involved (as it must be), but gives no indication of what that involvement is. Perhaps the most reasonable hypothesis is suggested by Gottlieb (1970b), who considers the possibility that the symptoms are due to allergically caused circumscribed angioedema (noninflammatory swelling) of the brain. There is some evidence that such localized edema occurs in the brain as a result of allergies just as localized edema occurs in the skin. Both types of edema are reversible. As with the skin, there is evidence that the edema may be localized in different parts of the brain. Thus the number and kind of symptoms will be a function of the particular location of the resultant pressure in the brain.

The problem of detecting a transient localized edema in the central nervous system is obviously great. However, such edema has been detected in the optic nerve and in the retina in patients who were manifesting peripheral angioedema. The possibility that localized edema was also occurring in the brain seems to be indicated by the presence in these patients of cerebral manifestations that included unilateral paralysis, convulsions, sensory aphasia, motor aphasia, and partial loss of vision (Kennedy, 1926; Bassoe, 1932). Other transitory CNS signs have been noted in some allergy patients. These have included transient palsies, radiculitis, and scotoma and were associated with allergic hives and transient edema of the optic nerve and retina (Kennedy, 1936, 1938). Recurrent cerebral edema as a result of food allergies has also been described by Rowe (1944). These patients became somnolent and showed staggering gait, dizziness, and inability to focus the eyes.

It can be inferred from the preceding data that individuals with allergy-induced aggressive behavior may have angioedema in any one of several portions of the brain through which the neural system for irritable aggression courses. The pressure of the swelling may sensitize or activate those neural systems, or may deactivate some of the systems that have an inhibitory function, as appears to be the case with specific localized brain tumors. (See Chapter 2).

HYPOGLYCEMIA AND AGGRESSION

Hypoglycemia (low blood sugar) may be caused by hyperinsulinism resulting from tumors on the islands of Langerhans in the pancreas or from a therapeutic overdose. It can also be caused by endocrine secretions that are inadequate to counter a normal insulin level, as found in Addison's disease (hypoadrenalcorticalism) (Tintera, 1955, 1966), in hypothyroidism, and in several pituitary dysfunctions. It can occur during lactation, after starvation, and as a result of muscular exhaustion in certain predisposed subjects. Idiopathic blood sugar deficit, in which no cause can be determined, is also common (Wilder, 1940; Kepler & Moersch 1937; Jones, 1935). Hypoglycemia is particularly prevalent in children whose glucose-regulating mechanisms are less stable (Wilder, 1943, 1944). In adulthood it occurs more frequently in middle age (Kepler & Moersch, 1937). The physiological consequences of the hypoglycemic state are well summarized in Bleicher (1970) and need not be covered here. The important consideration for this section is the psychological symptoms that may accompany the disorder.

Hypoglycemia Symptoms

The symptoms of hypoglycemia are highly varied and are primarily psychological or neurological (Kepler & Moersch, 1937; Wilder, 1943). The individual may feel faint, dizzy, weak, disturbed, fatigued, and nervous. Patients frequently develop an exaggerated negativism during which they are inclined to reject any suggestions, even those obviously beneficial. The individual may refuse to take orange juice, for example, and hold his lips tightly closed even though his symptoms would be relieved by drinking it (Sonne, 1930). An intense abulia also occasionally develops and the individual is unable to initiate any action, even that of taking candy that he carries specifically to alleviate hypoglycemic attacks. Other mental changes may include exhilaration, euphoria, and hilarity, but these are relatively uncommon. The negative emotions are more frequent and include anxiety, depression, and impulsivity. Aggressiveness and irritability in one form or another are quite common. The patient may be morose, asocial, sullen, and generally misanthropic. He is often rude and profane and the aggressive reaction may develop into a full-blown rage in which the individual becomes violent and destructive, attacking both objects and people, at times with fatal results (Aldersberg & Dolger, 1938-1939; Greenwood, 1935; Podolsky, 1964; Rud, 1937; Billig & Spaulding, 1947; Ziskind & Bailey, 1937). Wilder (1947) has summarized a wide variety of crimes committed during a hypoglycemic state.

When the hypoglycemia is severe, the individual may become confused and disoriented and develop a fugue state in which he wanders aimlessly around the streets engaging in irrational and sometimes violent behavior. He may also show complete amnesia for the period of fugue. Several irrational murders have been committed and attempted by hypoglycemic patients and in some cases the subject has been judged not guilty by reason of temporary insanity (Clapham, 1965; Anderson, 1940; Hill & Sargant, 1943; Kepler & Moersch, 1937; Schwadron, 1965). The following case illustrates many of the symptoms of the hypoglycemic syndrome:[4]

K., 51 years of age, a very sedate businessman, had been taking insulin for six years. After the usual injection of 30 units at 7:30 A.M. and breakfast, he went to his office one day and performed routine work. About 10 A.M. he took some fruit, and then made a few calls. At noon he went home for lunch by trolley. He had already had a "light dizzy feeling," and his companion told him the next day that he was amazed at the silliness and incoordinated movements of the patient at that time. The patient felt the need for sugar which, incidentally, he always carried with him but he lacked the "power and will" to take it. What happened thereafter he could not recall. The conductor and the police officer agreed as to the following: K. entered the trolley behaving like a drunkard, opened his vest, set his hat on the side of his head, yelled and laughed. The perplexed conductor called the police officer who ordered K. to leave the trolley with him. K was obviously confused, resisted stubbornly, and had to be overpowered by the policeman who dragged him by force to the police station, followed by a curious crowd. He was rabidly violent. Some time later, with decreasing disorientation and confusion, he begged the police to obtain some bread for him. This done, he was soon in complete possession of his senses, greatly surprised at his arrest and his preceding actions. The police surgeon examined him and found on him the marks of numerous injections, arousing vigorous protests on the part of the patient because of the accusation of morphinism. In court his personal physician testified that he had been treating K. for some time and that similar confusions had occurred previously, but to a milder degree, and that probably this episode was due to hypoglycemia with transitory psychotic manifestations. The case was dismissed when evidence of previous similar episodes was produced.

Several times, while on the trolley, the patient overlooked his point of destination, being slightly confused, was picked up at the end of the line, and brought to a police station where the officers already familiar with his behavior called his wife to take him home. A month before his arrest, while visiting relatives, he began to make stupid and silly remarks, a symptom very familiar to his family as indicative of a reaction. He fought off the attempts of his family to give him some food, and finally had to be overpowered by several people so that a few pieces of sugar could be forced between his teeth. A year prior to his arrest he had had a severe hypoglycemic reaction after erroneously taking a double dose of insulin (confusing U-20 with U-40 insulin, a mistake not noted then by his wife). At dinner he behaved normally at first, but then towards the end he became completely psychotic. He danced about the table and juggled oranges. Soon after, he

---

[4] D. Aldersberg and H. Dolger, Medico-legal problems of hypoglycemia reactions in diabetes. *Annals of Internal Medicine, 12,* 1938–1939, 1809–1810.

lapsed into a coma from which he could not be aroused by the oral administration of sugar, but required hospitalization and intravenous glucose
therapy. The reaction of the patient to these attacks was one of embarrass-
ment and chagrin. He constantly proclaimed his innocence and insisted that
the statements and stupidities uttered during hypoglycemia were beyond
his control; that he could not even remember them. In fact, he was aware of
them only through information gathered from his family. These accidents
upset him greatly, for he was ordinarily very polite and correct, and could
not understand how he could have been so rude and discourteous.

An Experimental Test of the Hypoglycemia-Aggression Hypothesis
Most of the work on hypoglycemia was done in the two decades following the description of the syndrome of hyperinsulinism by Harris in 1924.
The many clinical studies appear to establish beyond a reasonable doubt
that a relationship exists between a drop in blood sugar and some forms
of aggressive behavior. There are a large number of studies showing that
a drop in glucose level results in an aggressive episode that can be
promptly terminated by sugar intake, and in some patients that sequence
of events may recur repeatedly. For obvious reasons there has been relatively little experimental work on the problem. However, an anthropologist has recently confirmed the relationship in a field experiment with
the Qolla Indians of the Peruvian Andes (Bolton, 1973). Bolton hypothesized that the exceptionally high level of social conflict and hostility
in the society could be explained, in part, by the tendency to hypoglycemia
among the community residents. Approximately 55 percent of these
villagers show instability in glucose homeostasis. Peer ratings of aggressiveness (which had an acceptable reliability) were studied in relationship to blood sugar levels as determined by a glucose tolerance test.
The aggression ratings were not known to the individual who read the
glucose levels. A χ^2 analysis of the data showed a statistically significant
($p < 0.02$) relationship between aggression ranking and the change in
blood glucose levels during the four-hour glucose tolerance test. In view
of all the other possible causes of aggressive behavior, this is a remarkable
finding and indicates that the relationship must be powerful.

Bolton proposes the interesting hypothesis that fighting is both initiated
and perpetuated in this society by hypoglycemic tendencies. He suggests
that the individual gets into a social altercation because of the irritability
associated with the low glucose level. However, as indicated earlier, a
number of other uncomfortable symptoms, such as faintness, dizziness,
and fatigue, accompany the hypoglycemic episode. When the person gets
into a fight his metabolism is changed and the output of adrenalin and
adrenal corticoids counter the insulin effects and cause liver glycogen to
be converted to glucose with the result that the uncomfortable symptoms
are reduced. He is thus rewarded for engaging in fighting behavior and is
thus more inclined to be aggressive when he again experiences the

Table 2
Distribution of Blood Glucose Conditions in the Sample
Population According to Aggressiveness Ranks

Aggression rankings (grouped by fourths)	Normal glycemia		Moderate hypoglycemia		Severe hypoglycemia	
	N	%	N	%	N	%
1 (high aggressors)	1	7.7	11	84.6	1	7.7
2	8	57.2	5	35.7	1	7.1
3	7	50.0	4	28.6	3	21.4
4 (low aggressors)	8	61.5	3	23.1	2	15.4

From R. Bolton, Aggression and hypoglycemia among the Qolla: A study in psycho-biological anthropology, *Ethnology*, 1973, *12*, 246.

physiological cues associated with the hypoglycemic reaction. Related to this hypothesis is a case report by Duncan (1935) describing the antidotal effects of anger on a diabetic during hypoglycemia produced by an insulin injection.

Hypoglycemia-CNS Relationship
The reasons for increased aggressive tendencies during hypoglycemia are not yet clear, although some of the effects of low blood glucose on the central nervous system give some indications. According to Ervin (1969), hypoglycemia is a well-known provocation for epileptic foci, and the limbic system appears to be particularly sensitive to it. Thus patients with minimal deep temporal lobe damage may only have episodes of aggressive dyscontrol under conditions of hypoglycemia. There is considerable evidence that low blood glucose levels are associated with disruptions in the EEG pattern. (See a summary of this evidence in Fabrykant & Pacella, 1948.) The hypoglycemic murderer studied by Hill and Sargant (1943) showed an abnormal EEG pattern only during periods of low blood sugar.

The brain, although it has stores of glycogen, is unable to convert glycogen to glucose when the need arises as other organs can. It is therefore dependent on the glucose in the bloodstream. If there is a deficiency of glucose, the brain loses its fuel supply and is less able to extract oxygen from the blood. One result is a loss of function of some of the neural systems. If, as in the case of alcohol, the systems first affected are the ones related to neural inhibition, the hyperaggressiveness associated with hypoglycemia might be expected to occur.

Hypoglycemic Aggression as a Practical Problem
It is difficult to determine whether the tendency to hostility produced by low blood sugar is a problem of practical significance. Greenwood in 1935 reported that routine estimates of blood glucose level showed that

2.8 percent of patients in general hospital wards and 4.35 percent of patients in psychopathic wards had levels of 70 mg per 100 cm^3 of blood (normal being 90 to 110 per 100 cm^3). It has been estimated that 0.5 percent of patients in general practice show hypoglycemic tendencies (Wilder, 1940). If one assumes the validity of these estimates, the absolute numbers of individuals is large indeed. Abramson and Pezet (1951) estimate the number of hypoglycemic patients at a minimum of 10 million in the United States and perhaps as many as 30 million. Although it is true that all hypoglycemic patients do not manifest overt aggression, and few become violent, it would seem that the irritability resulting from this disorder would at least contribute to the unhappiness of many patients and their close associates and, at worse, would account for some irrational crimes of brutality. There are, of course, adequate therapies for this disorder.

DRUG-INDUCED AGGRESSION

The ingestation of drugs is another method of changing the blood chemistry that in certain instances, and in certain individuals, results in an increase in the potential for aggressive behavior. This section will deal with drugs that have a facilitating effect on hostile behavior. Those that function to block aggression will be covered in the next section.

Amphetamines and Aggression Facilitation

The amphetamines, including amphetamine sulfate, amphetamine phosphate, dextroamphetamine sulfate, and methamphetamine, are widely used central nervous system stimulants that have recently come under strict federal controls because of their considerable potential for abuse. Therapeutically, the amphetamines (generally dextroamphetamine) are used in the treatment of obesity, narcolepsy, parkinsonism, depressive syndromes, and behavior disorders (Goodman & Gillman, 1965). They have the rather remarkable property of reducing the hostile tendencies of children with minimal brain dysfunction when given in moderate doses and precipitating violent aggressive behaviors in adults when used in large doses.

When taken in therapeutic doses the individual may feel slightly more restless and have a moderate lift in mood. Larger amounts result in increased restlessness, dizziness, tremor, insomnia, hyperactive reflexes, tenseness, anxiety, and irritability. There is general agreement that moderate use and occasional abuse of amphetamines does not result in violence (Tinklenberg & Stillman, 1970; Blum, 1969). In fact, Blum goes so far as to say that there is no research support linking amphetamines and violence. That appears to be true for moderate abuse, particularly if the drug is taken orally. However, long-term users of high doses are potentially dangerous. During acute intoxication the individual suffers from hyperirritability, aggressiveness, and loss of judgment (Kalant, 1966). His actions tend to be impulsive and may be violent (Cohen, 1969). Tinklenberg and Stillman (1970) report having observed a progressive deterioration of the amphetamine abuser's ability to control his behavior. The individual may recognize his impulsive destructive acts as being inappropriate but is unable to inhibit them. These investigators conclude that there is a "cumulative amphetamine effect that predisposes the user toward assaultive behavior" (p. 334).

The abuse potential and the severity of the assaultive tendencies are increased when the drug is taken intravenously. On intravenous injection the subject experiences a "rush," which is a generalized, intense, pleasurable feeling. After the rush the euphoric state gradually dissipates and in a matter of several hours the pleasant feelings are replaced by a general state of irritability, vague uneasiness, anxiety, and body aches. The user is then likely to administer another intravenous dose of the drug to avoid the discomfort and to reestablish the feeling of the rush. The pattern of self-administration of methamphetamine may continue every two hours for days or for more than a week. This prolonged administration is referred to as a "run." During the run the subject is constantly awake, eats very little or nothing, and frequently engages in repetitive purposeless activities. When the run is finally terminated, the discomforts associated with the down period after a single dose of amphetamine are magnified many times and it is at this point that the individual is most likely to be destructive and assaultive (Kosman & Unna, 1968; Kramer et al., 1967; Tinklenberg & Stillman, 1970). Paranoid symptoms begin to appear the second or third days of a run and become increasingly severe. Paranoia is characteristic of prolonged amphetamine intoxication and is the major feature of amphetamine psychosis when it develops. Some investigators (Breamish & Kiloh, 1960; Hampton, 1961) maintain that the paranoid tendencies associated with amphetamine abuse are little more than an exaggeration of a premorbid paranoid personality. Connell (1958) rejects that as a necessary factor.

There is little doubt that the subculture of the methamphetamine abuser (speed freaks) is dominated by suspiciousness and feelings of persecution, and it seems likely that the physiological effects of the drug are reinforced by the attributes of the culture. The subculture of the speed freak is also violence-ridden. Individuals who have or believe that they have been cheated in a drug transaction are expected by their peers to gain revenge and retribution. The probability of violence is further enhanced by the general tendency of the members of this particular subculture to carry concealed weapons.

Some amphetamine abusers develop an acute psychosis that may last for days or years after withdrawal from the drug. The major feature is paranoid delusions. The delusions may be disorganized as in paranoid schizophrenia or they may be well organized and internally consistent as in true paranoia. In the latter type of psychosis the individual's thinking is intact except for a set of circumscribed delusions. He may, for example, believe that the Mafia or the communists are plotting to kill him (Cohen, 1969; Connell, 1958; Ellinwood, 1967). Connell (1958) reports on 42 cases of amphetamine psychosis and indicates that 81 percent of the individuals had paranoid delusions and 22 percent were hostile and aggressive.

The paranoid panic accompanying acute amphetamine intoxication, which occurs during the down period after a run, may result in aggressive action. Ellinwood (1971) reports on 13 cases of homicide related to amphetamine abuse. In one case a 27-year-old truck driver shot and killed his boss because he believed that the boss was attempting to kill him by releasing poison gas into the back seat of the car in which he was riding. This subject had taken 80 mg of amphetamine in a 20-hour period in an attempt to complete a 1600-mile trip nonstop. He had not slept for 48 hours and had begun to have persecutory ideas six to eight hours before the murder. Masaki (quoted in Kalant, 1966) reported that 31 of 60 convicted murderers in Japan in May and June of 1954 had some connection with amphetamine abuse. Rylander (1969), reporting on 146 central stimulant addicts,[5] indicated that the aggressive crimes perpetrated by these individuals included murder, manslaughter, robbery, assault and battery, and destruction of property.

As Ellenwood (1971) is careful to point out, the precise role of the amphetamines in cases of murder and assault is difficult to assess because other factors such as specific environmental conditions, predisposing personality characteristics, and the use of other drugs are frequently involved.

Alcohol and Aggression Facilitation

There can be no doubt that alcohol and violence are related. In a study of homicides in Philadelphia between 1948 and 1952, it was shown that either the victim or the offender had been drinking just prior to the crime in 64 percent of the cases (Wolfgang, 1958). In a study of rape the results indicate that alcohol was present in one-third of the rapes, and in most instances both the victim and the offender had been drinking (Blum, 1969). Aggravated assaults are also significantly associated with alcohol. A study by the Commission on Crime of the District of Columbia found that 35 percent of the offenders in 124 cases of assault had been drinking prior to the attack, as had 46 percent of 131 victims (Report of the President's Commission on Crime in the District of Columbia, 1966). Drinking

[5] A number of these persons were abusing the drug phenmetrazine (Preludin), a CNS stimulant related to amphetamine.

delinquents commit more crimes of assault than do those who do not drink (Molof, 1967).

That alcohol and aggression are associated is a fact. What that fact means is not immediately clear. Obviously, all individuals who consume alcoholic beverages do not become homicidal, assaultive, or even have an increase in feelings of hostility. In fact, self-reports of mood changes during alcohol consumption have included increases in cheerfulness, lovingness, and friendliness (Fregly et al., 1967); increase in happiness (Kastl, 1969); less irritability, more relaxation, and more self-satisfaction (Nash, 1962). (See Wallgren & Barry, 1970, for further studies.) No doubt many readers can substantiate these data with their own subjective impressions. In this section we briefly examine the evidence relating alcohol and aggression and attempt to resolve the apparent paradox above.

Alcohol Consumption and Hostile Feelings
A number of studies have shown that alcohol, even in moderate doses, results in a statistically significant increase in evidence of hostile feelings. Aggressive fantasy as measured by the Thematic Apperception Test (TAT) increased significantly among college men after three to four drinks containing 1.5 oz. of an 86-proof alcoholic beverage. The TAT protocols did not change during a comparable period in similar situations (living room discussion groups or stag cocktail party) when nonalcoholic beverages were served. Aggression themes decreased between four and six drinks and were replaced by thoughts of physical sex. After six drinks the story themes showed a decrease in inhibitory thoughts regarding aggression restraint, fear anxiety, and time concern. Thoughts of physical aggression recurred with high frequency in subjects who drank very heavily (more than ten drinks) (Kalin & McClelland, 1965). Similar increases in themes relating to aggression and self-assertion, among other things, were found by Takala et al. (1957) when they compared the TAT protocols of young men in a social drinking (0.09 to 0.17 percent blood alcohol) situation with the protocols of control subjects. The same subjects also showed increases in overtly aggressive themes on the Rosenzweig Picture Frustration Test. The later finding, however, was not substantiated in a well-controlled study by Nash (1962), who found a decrease in extrapunitive or overt aggression themes among subjects with 0.065 percent of blood alcohol.

Young men under the influences of moderate amounts of alcohol rate cartoons as funnier than do those consuming a placebo, and the difference is greater for cartoons portraying hostile humor as opposed to those dealing with nonsense humor (Hetherington & Wray, 1964). Nathan et al. (1970) studied skid row alcoholics over a prolonged period during drinking and nondrinking sessions and found that most subjects became more sociable at the start of drinking but as drinking continued, anxiety, depression, and hostility as measured by a Mood Adjective Checklist increased significantly. Loomis and West (1958) reported that all of their subjects became more talkative and less inhibited with an alcohol blood level of 0.03 to 0.09 percent. However, about half of them also became argumentative. Tiredness and tendencies to withdraw from the group predominated when the blood levels reached 0.10 to 0.17 percent alcohol.

It is important to note in all the preceding studies that although statistically significant increases occurred in various measures of hostile tendencies, there was also considerable variability and all subjects did not react to alcohol consumption with increases in aggressiveness. Further, as indicated earlier, a number of studies report an increase in positive affect with no indication of hostility increases, and some such as Fregly et al. (1967) reported increases in positive affect in some subjects but increases in irritability, aggressiveness, and nervousness in others.

There are relatively few studies that provide an opportunity for actual overt aggression in the laboratory situation. However, Shuntich and Taylor (1972) and Taylor and Gammon (1975) have shown that college students involved in a competitive reaction time situation tend to set significantly higher shock levels after having ingested alcohol. The expression of physical aggression is related to the quantity of alcohol ingested. Low doses of alcohol (0.5 oz of 100-proof bourbon or vodka) appear to inhibit aggressive responding whereas high doses (1.5 oz) facilitate aggression responding when compared with placebo controls. The subject's judgment of his opponent was also influenced by the level of alcohol consumption. Those individuals receiving high doses of vodka rated their opponents as being bloodthirsty, aggressive, cruel, and revengeful. The authors point out that this negative affect appears to be exaggerated and inappropriate since, from the subjects' point of view, the opponent did not initiate the aggressive interaction.

In another experiment by Bennett et al. (1969) there was no evidence of a change in aggressive tendencies (level of shock set for an experimenter confederate) related to alcohol consumption. The mean blood alcohol concentrations of 0.030, 0.058, and 0.086 percent were observed at the three doses used. The discrepancy between the Taylor studies and the Bennett et al. study seems to be due to the nature of the experiment. In the latter case the subjects were directed to shock a helpless victim who could not retaliate for making errors in a pseudolearning experiment. In the other case, however, the subjects were engaged in a competitive situation in which the individuals' opponent could retaliate.

Alcohol and Crime

The relationship between alcohol and homicide has been extensively reviewed by Wolfgang (1958), Wolfgang and Ferracuti (1967), and Blum (1967, 1969) and will therefore be dealt with only briefly here.

As indicated earlier, alcohol is involved in 65 percent of homicides. The method of killing is more likely to be violent and brutal when alcohol is involved. When the method of killing used is stabbing, 72 percent of the cases involve the use of alcohol. When the method is beating, alcohol involvement occurs in 69 percent of the cases. For shooting it is 55 percent and for miscellaneous methods, only 45 percent. Among whites, alcohol is present in the majority of killings only when the method used is that of beating (Wolfgang, 1958). Several more recent studies have confirmed the essential findings of Wolfgang's earlier studies (Gillies, 1965; Guttmacher, 1967; Vos & Hepburn, 1968).

Alcohol is also associated with the more violent types of crime among women. A study of feminine felons in California showed that drinking was associated with 55 percent of the homicides, 62 percent of the assaults, and 43 percent of the robberies. On the other hand, alcohol usage was related to only 29 percent of the offenses against property (Ward, quoted in Mulvihill & Tunin, 1969).

Although the studies cited here have all been conducted in the American culture, similar results have been obtained in other countries. This material is succinctly summarized by Blum (1969).

A Mexican appraisal (De la Vega Llamosa, 1966) indicates that alcohol compared to marihuana and other narcotics is most often implicated in male criminality. A study in France (Muller, 1965–1966) shows alcohol involvement in fifty percent of the acts of homicide, seventy-eight percent of assaults, and eighty-seven percent of robberies as derived by a random sample of arrested offenders. A German review (Ulrich, 1967) reports a rising rate of juvenile offenses in which the offender had been drinking and in Argentina (Herreca, 1965–1966) alcohol, and in particular alcoholism, have been identified as major contributing factors in several crimes of violence, those of vengeance and passion, as in response to adultery, and those involving insult to self-esteem, that is a challenge to manliness arising out of social drinking among male companions [p. 1475].

Nonphysiological Factors in the Alcohol-Violence Relationship
There are many social, cultural, and learning factors involved in the tendency for an individual under the influence of alcohol to become aggressive. In some subcultures an individual is not considered responsible for his behavior when he is inebriated, with the result that the drinker's behavior is less restrained by his perception of social pressure. Because of past experience particular social groups expect certain individuals to become hostile after alcohol consumption, and some of the resulting aggressive behavior may be attributed to the fulfillment of the expectations of the group. The particular social situation in which the drinker finds himself may also precipitate aggressive behavior. A drinking companion is often a provocateur of violence. Although it may help, it is certainly

not necessary to be drunk to respond aggressively toward an obnoxious intoxicated companion. Homicide and assault victims are frequently involved in drinking at the time of the assault (Wolfgang, 1958). Alcohol may be only one element in a subculture where physical aggression is common, and in that sense alcohol may not be a causal factor.

The alcohol-aggression-crime relationship is obviously a complex one having many contributing factors. Any or all of the preceding variables may contribute to a given alcohol-aggression incident.

Physiological Factors in the Alcohol-Aggression Relationship
In addition to the psychocultural factors mentioned, there is good evidence that, for some individuals, physiological factors resulting from alcohol consumption interact with nonphysiological variables to increase the probability of aggression in the drinker. There appears to be a selective suppression of the neural mechanism for inhibition in the central nervous system by alcohol. In the patellar tendon reflex, for example, ethanol enhances the response and reduces reflex latency, which implies a reduction in inhibitory influences from higher centers (Tuttle, 1924; Travis & Dorsey, 1926). (See Wallgren and Barry, 1970, for a review of inhibition suppression by alcohol.) They conclude that both excitatory and inhibitory functions are suppressed by the ingestion of alcohol, but the inhibitory functions are suppressed somewhat more. It is common knowledge that social inhibitions are also reduced by alcohol consumption (Mulvihill & Tumin, 1969). If the stimulus situation contains factors increasing the probability that the neural systems for hostility will be activated, the likelihood is increased that the individual will both feel and act aggressively.

Pathological Intoxication
With alcohol, as with any other drug, there are wide individual differences in its effect. Some of these differences in physiological reaction relate to whether or not a threshold for aggressive action is lowered by the drug. In one study personality inventories were given to a population of subjects who were then divided into two groups on the basis of plethysmographic recordings under conditions of alcohol or placebo dosage. The results showed that individuals who reacted to alcohol (0.23 ml per pound body weight in tomato juice heavily spiced with Tobasco sauce) with vasoconstriction were significantly ($p < 0.01$) more hostile than those who reacted with peripheral dilation (Rosenberg et al., 1966). It is not clear how these findings relate to the effect of alcohol on the central nervous system, and there is no evidence that the hostility of these subjects was increased by the alcohol. However, there is evidence that a small percentage of individuals do respond to ethanol consumption with pathological aggressive reactions.

Pathological intoxication has been a recognized clinical entity and it was initially described by Krafft-Ebing in 1869 (quoted in Banay, 1944). The state is characterized by its dramatic and sudden onset. Although the duration is relatively short, a few moments to an hour or so, the reaction may continue for a day or more. Consciousness is frequently impaired and the perception of the environment is distorted by delusions that are always of a persecutory nature and hallucinations that have a hostile content. Maniacal outbursts occur and include terminal fits of rage and an irresistible desire for destruction. Movements are not well coordinated, but they are vigorous. The attack occurs early in intoxication and is not related to the quantity of alcohol consumed. The reaction is usually terminated by deep sleep and amnesia for the entire incident (Banay, 1944; Skelton, 1970).

There is evidence that some cases of pathological intoxication result from the action of the alcohol on the temporal lobe, which can be verified by electroencephalic records that show temporal lobe spiking. (See the section on epilepsy and aggression in Chapter 2.) In one study EEG records were taken on 402 patients because they had been involved in incidents of confusion, abnormal behavior, destructive rage, and other mental dysfunctions as a consequence of alcohol consumption. They were given alcohol in the form of beer, whiskey, or gin, depending on the type of beverage that had precipitated the incident for that individual. The results showed no diagnostic abnormality in 347 cases (86 percent). In 55 cases, however, specific anterior temporal lobe spikes were recorded. Forty-two of the cases showed unilateral spikes and 13 had bilateral temporal lobe spikes. Spiking appeared in from 25 seconds to 35 minutes after the first dose of alcohol. Eighteen patients had definite psychomotor episodes (Marinacci, 1963).

In another study of ten patients who showed the clinical symptoms of pathological intoxication, EEG spiking was, after alcohol administration, found only in two patients, and in them only when the recordings were made from electrodes implanted in the temporal lobe in the region of the amygdala. Thus it would appear that alcoholic activation of temporal lobe spikes cannot be ruled out even though they do not appear on a surface recording (Bach-y-Rita et al., 1970). A particularly interesting aspect of this study was the fact that alcohol was given intravenously and the subjects were not told when or if they would be given the drug. All of the patients showed signs of drunkenness, nystagmus, slurred speech, and grossly impaired gait, but only one of them recognized that he was drunk. None of the patients became violent during the study. The authors suggest that these apparently paradoxical results may be explained by the complexity of alcohol, aggression, brain dysfunction, and environmental interactions. In the experimental situation, conducted in a sterile hospital environment in which the welfare of the patient was of prime concern, there were no stimuli capable of eliciting an aggressive response. They suggest further that the experimental situation was supportive and nonstressful and that stress of some kind may be necessary to bring about the temporal lobe dysfunction during the application of alcohol. A number of case reports of pathological intoxication are on record (Banay, 1944; Skelton, 1970; Marinacci, 1963; Lion et al., 1969). The following case is typical.

A 27-year-old male had been perfectly normal until the age of twenty-three years, when a craniocerebral injury resulted in a right temporal skull fracture and an associated period of unconsciousness. Subsequently, following the ingestion of even a minor amount of alcohol he became belligerent, confused, and destructive. On one occasion, the patient had two cocktails five minutes before he walked into a liquor store to purchase additional liquor. On being refused the sale of the liquor he went into a rage, and the salesman attempted to subdue him. The patient picked up a knife from the counter and stabbed the salesman several times. He was overcome by several bystanders before the police arrived. The salesman was dead on arrival of the ambulance. An alcohol-activation electroencephalogram was requested by the public defender. The routine study showed generalized instability and isolated short spikes in the right anterior temporal area (region of the skull fracture). Following alcohol-activation, profuse spikes were recorded in the right anterior temporal area with spreading to the right parietal and temporal areas.[6]

Other Drugs and Aggression Facilitation

Increase in irritability, feelings of hostility, and overt aggressive behavior are side effects in some patients for several drugs. However, except in the case of the benzodiazepines this phenomenon has generally not been systematically studied. In the subculture of drug users, abuse of the barbiturates is considered likely to result in the sudden onset of aggressive incidents (Brill, 1969). Ban (1969) indicates that the euphoria found with barbiturate drug abuse is occasionally replaced by irritability, quarrelsomeness, and a generally hostile attitude with paranoid ideation. These same drugs may also increase the activity of, irritability of, and difficulty in managing hyperactive children (Resnick, 1971).

One of the first symptoms of overdosage with L-dopa is an increase in irritability along with agitation, helplessness, and insomnia. If the dose is further increased, anger, hostility, and overt violence with paranoid delusions may occur. Barbeau (1972) described one patient who concealed a knife under his pillow and had plans to use it on his roommate because of a paranoid delusion that the roommate was going out

[6] A. A. Marinacci, A special type of temporal lobe psychomotor seizure following ingestion of alcohol. *Bulletin of Los Angeles Neurological Society*, 1963, 28, 246.

with the patient's sister. Barbeau tentatively concludes that dopamine and cyclic AMP play a role in mania and aggressivity in man.

One study on four patients suggests that the antidepressant imipramine increases the expression of hostility as measured by the Gottschalk content analysis of verbal behavior. This preliminary finding has not yet been replicated (Gottschalk et al., 1965).

Benzodiazepine-Induced Aggression

One of the most interesting features of early animal studies on the benzodiazepines (chlordiazepoxide, diazepam, oxazepam, and nitrazepam) was their profound taming effect (Randall et al., 1960; Randall et al., 1961; Heise & Boff, 1961; Schekel & Boff, 1966). They also had a significant antiaggression effect in humans (discussed later). However, early in the clinical use of this class of drugs it was noted that in some individuals an acute "rage" reaction resulted from the administration of high doses (Tobin et al., 1960). Because the reaction appeared in a limited number of individuals and was contrary to the usual effect it was labeled *paradoxical rage*. Since the early reports there have been a number of clinical and experimental reports on benzoxiazepine-induced hostility in humans. Feldman (1962) reported that many patients receiving diazepam showed a progressive development of dislikes and hates. These patients were aware that their hateful feelings were irrational, but were, nevertheless, unable to control them. In some instances the hostile feelings were acted on, resulting in overt violence, such as throwing trays of food or attacking other patients.

In experimental studies designed to determine the effectiveness of chlordiazepoxide and oxazepam in the control of anxiety, DiMascio and Barrett (Barrett & DiMascio, 1966; DiMascio & Barrett, 1965) found an indication that the two drugs had different effects on hostility. Chlordiazepoxide tended to increase aggressive tendencies, whereas oxazepam had no effect on them. The data on hostility were not reported in those publications but were followed up in a carefully controlled double-blind study. High, medium, and low-anxious subjects (on the Taylor Manifest Anxiety Test) were given daily doses of 45 mg of oxazepam, 30 mg of chlordiazepoxide, or a placebo. The subjects were tested prior to any drug ingestion and again two hours after taking the final dose one week later on the Buss-Durkee Hostility Inventory (Buss & Durkee, 1957) and on the Gottschalk-Gleser Hostility Scales (Gottschalk et al., 1963). The placebo had essentially no effect on the level of hostility in any of the three groups. Oxazepam also produced no consistent changes in the hostility scores on the Buss-Durkee inventory. Chlordiazepoxide, however, produced a significant increase in the hostility measures for the high-anxiety group and a trend in the same direction for the medium-anxious group. The scores on the subscales indicated that the increase was greatest for indirect hostility, irritability, and verbal hostility. Chlordiazepoxide also significantly increased the ambivalent hostility scores on the Gottschalk-Gleser scale for the high anxious subjects. The authors suggest that oxazepam should be used for anxious patients who have inadequate impulse control and a history of aggressive or destructive behavior, and that chlordiazepoxide be used with anxious subjects who are inhibited and would benefit therapeutically from an ability to express aggression (Gardos et al., 1968).

There are currently no physiological data that help to explain these results.

AGGRESSION INHIBITION
BY DRUGS

Although some drugs appear to facilitate aggressive behavior, many more tend to inhibit both overt aggression and feelings of hostility. There is currently no drug that is a completely specific antihostility agent; however, a significant number of preparations are available that do reduce aggressive tendencies as one component of their action. The current state of the art is summarized nicely by Resnick (1971) when he says, "There is ample evidence to indicate that psychotropic drugs now available may help individuals who are aggressive, irritable, unstable, egocentric, easily offended, obsessive, compulsive and dependent, who demonstrate such symptoms as anxiety, depression, hysteria, agony, unexplainable and motiveless behavior, recurrent violent emotional upsets including temper tantrums and violent rages." It is not possible here to provide a complete and exhaustive coverage of the now vast literature on drug inhibition of aggression, but a number of studies are covered.

Some kind of a measure for aggressiveness is a part of the battery of screening tests used in the initial evaluation of psychotropic drugs on animals and many standard drugs are being evaluated for antiaggression effects. A review article by Valzelli (1967) provides some notion of the extent of these investigations. He reported 204 animal studies dealing with drug-aggression interaction. Eight of these studies reported drugs that produced an increase in aggressiveness; 24 reported no effect on the particular behavior studied. Of the 80 drugs covered in the studies reported by Valzelli, 74 of them inhibited some form of aggression in some animal studied. Thus the potential for the development of aggression-inhibiting drugs for humans is very great. It is important, however, to recognize that drug effects may be both species-specific and situation-specific. Valzelli is one of the few authors who makes an attempt to discriminate among the different kinds of aggressive behavior. His table of drug effects shows that some drugs tend to block one kind of aggression and facilitate another within the same species and that a given drug may block aggression in one species but facilitate it in another. In addition, there are wide individual differences in susceptibility to the taming effects of various drugs.

All the preceding factors are significant to understanding drug effects on hostile tendencies in humans. Aggressive behavior has many causes, and can result from overactivity or dysfunction in a number of different neural systems. It is therefore not surprising that a specific drug may be effective in reducing the hostility of some individuals and have no effect on others with similar symptoms.

Although there can be little doubt that a variety of drugs can have profound effects on the neural substrates for aggression, much of the evidence at this time is sketchy and limited to clinical studies using nonblind procedures in which suggestion can and sometimes does have a larger impact on the dependent variable than the drug. Many of these clinical reports should be considered as hypothesis-generating rather than hypothesis-testing studies, which permit the design of careful, well-designed experiments. There are, however, some pitfalls in research designs on drugs that must be understood in evaluating the results. A good double-blind crossover study showing that a given drug or drug combination decreases aggressive tendencies as indicated by some reliable measure is potent evidence for believing that the preparation has some antihostility actions. However, a good double-blind crossover study showing no antiaggression effect is not good evidence, and this goes beyond the obvious principle that one cannot prove the null hypothesis. Because there are different kinds of aggression, which, according to our model at least, have different neurological bases, and because there are wide individual differences in susceptibility to all types of pharmaceutical agents, it is quite possible for a given drug to have potent antihostility effects that do not reach statistical significance in a particular study even though that study was well designed. Many studies use a large, heterogeneous sample of patients composed of neurotics, schizophrenics, manic-depressives, sex deviants, and whatever other type of patient happens to be available to the experimenter. With this kind of sample it is conceivable that a given drug may have a real and profound antihostility effect on a small percentage of individuals and no effect at all on a large percentage of patients. The high variability in the data then washes out any possibility of statistical significance. If there are good clinical or theoretical reasons for believing that a particular drug should have aggression control properties, the negative finding in the initial study should be followed up by a study of the responders in which each subject serves as his own control with, of course, all the appropriate research controls and cautions. This is obviously an arduous and time-consuming task, but there is no way around it.

The Phenothiazines
The advent of the widespread use of phenothiazines led to a significant
reduction in psychotic hostility. Kline (1962) suggests that "wards
formerly filled with screaming denudative, assaultive patients now have
window curtains and flowers on the table." Quantitative estimates of the
reduction of destructive, assaultive behavior are difficult to find, but
Kline (1962) offers one that is dramatic in its simplicity. In 1955 prior to
the use of the major tranquilizers in the Rockland State Hospital, there
were 8000 windowpanes broken and three full-time glaziers were needed
to keep the windows in repair. By 1960, when full use was being made
of the psychotropic drugs, windowpane breakage was down to 1900 panes
a year. (Also see Brill's 1969 evaluation of the actions of the phenothiazines on aggression reduction.) It has been suggested that the sedative
action of the phenothiazines alone could account for the improved picture
in the mental hospitals. However, it must be recognized that potent
sedative hypnotics such as chloral hydrate and paraldehyde have been
known and used for three-quarters of a century.

The phenothiazines, or major tranquilizers, all appear to have a taming
effect over and above their sedative action (Goodman & Gilman, 1965;
Ban, 1969). They are the drug of choice for self-referred violent patients
who report to Massachusetts General Hospital because they have what
they perceive as uncontrollable destructive or homicidal tendencies (Lion
et al., 1968). Cole et al. (1966), reporting on a number of controlled
studies on the phenothiazines used for schizophrenic patients, conclude
that hostility and uncooperativeness are more frequently controlled than
are anxiety, tension, and agitation.

Perphenazine alone or in combination with the antidepressant amitriptyline has been useful in reducing the aggressive tendencies of depressed patients (Pennington, 1964), aggressive mental defectives (Mises
& Beauchesne, 1963), sex-deviated criminals (Buki, 1964), and aggressive
alcoholics (Bartholomew, 1963). In one study using a double-blind crossover design to compare the psychological effect of perphenazine and a
placebo, the investigators reported a significant reduction of the median
scores on hostility for 16 of 20 patients when they were on perphenazine
(Gottschalk et al., 1960).

The hostile tendencies of a wide variety of patients, from epileptic
psychotics (Wolpowitz, 1966; Kamm & Mandell, 1967; Pauig et al., 1961),
to disturbed adolescents (Rosenberg, 1966), mentally retarded patients
(Abbott et al., 1965; Allen et al., 1963), and hyperactive children (Alderton & Hoddinott, 1964), have been successfully controlled with thioridazine. A survey of the studies on thioridazine is given by Cohen (1966).

Other phenothiazines on which there is clinical evidence for the particular control of aggressive and combative behavior are propericiazine
(Jirgl et al., 1970; Turns et al., 1965), trifluoperazine (Smith, 1965; Vas-

concellos, 1960; Terrell, 1962), and fluphenazine (Traldi, 1966; Ziporyn & Stoner, 1964).

Diphenylhydantoin

Dilantin (sodium diphenylhydantoin) is a drug that has been used with considerable success in the control of seizures. Some years ago it came into popular prominence because of its apparent tendency to control hyperexcitability and hostility in nonepileptic patients (Rosenfeld, 1967). Zimmerman (1965), as early as 1956, studied 200 children with severe behavior disorders and reported that 70 percent of them improved under sodium diphenylhydantoin therapy showing less excitability, as well as less frequent and less severe temper tantrums.

Turner (1967) in a study of 72 subjects seen in psychiatric practice found that 86 percent showed drug-related improvement particularly in relation to anger, irritability, and tension (also see Maletzky, 1973). The drug is effective with individuals having both abnormal and normal EEG records (Ross & Jackson, 1940). There seems to be little qustion that Dilantin is useful in treating persons with a wide variety of disorders, including neurotics, psychotics, psychopaths, and emotionally disturbed children. The behavioral syndrome that seems to be common in such a diverse group of patients includes explosiveness, low frustration tolerance, irritability, impulsive behavior, compulsive behavior, aggressive behavior, erratic behavior, inability to delay gratification, mood swings, short attention span, undirected activity, and similar symptoms (Resnick, 1967).

Some double-blind studies, one on male delinquents (Lefkowitz, 1969; Conners et al., 1971) and one on children with severe temper tantrums (Looker & Conners, 1970), have not found Dilantin to be superior to a placebo in the control of aggressive behavior. As indicated earlier, a double-blind study showing lack of effect of a drug is not good evidence by itself that the preparation does not have antihostility properties. Other studies, equally well controlled, have reported that the drug's effect on those behaviors was significant. Stephens and Shaffer (1970), in a double-blind crossover study of neurotic outpatients, found it to be effective in reducing symptoms relating to anger, irritability, impatience, and anxiety. Resnick (1967) also reported that Dilantin significantly improved the hostile behavior of selected prisoners and juvenile delinquents. He gives revealing excerpts from tape recordings of interviews with the prisoners during the study that reveal the potency of the drug in manipulating negative affect.

Haloperidol

A number of studies have now shown that haloperidol can be used effectively to moderate the aggressive tendencies of several different types of individuals. LeVan (1971) compared the effectiveness of haloperidol and chlorpromazine in a double-blind study on mentally retarded children and concluded that haloperidol reduced the severity of hostility and aggressiveness in significantly more patients than did chlorpromazine. Adverse reactions were minimal. The same author (1969) reported that the drug significantly reduces hyperactivity, assaultiveness, and self-injury in hospitalized children and adolescents with behavioral disorders. These results are accomplished with no loss of mental alertness.

Psychotic patients also have reduced tendencies to hostility under haloperidol medication. Haward (1969) reports a significant reduction in verbal hostility and Darling (1971), who treated 30 chronically assaultive patients, indicates that 20 of them improved substantially. Phenothiazines had been tried on these patients without success. The drug is also therapeutically effective for agitated, overactive, and hostile elderly patients suffering from chronic brain syndromes (Sugerman et al., 1964).

Finally, haloperidol appears to be particularly effective in controlling the rather strange disorder Gilles de la Tourette's disease in which the individual has bouts of involuntary swearing and using of profanities and obscenities (Seignot, 1961; Challas & Brauer, 1963; Chapel, 1964).

The Benzodiazepines

Although there is good evidence that the benzodiazepines increase aggressive tendencies in some individuals, they have also been shown to have an antihostility effect on a wide variety of persons, from neurotic outpatients to raging psychotic criminals. Chlordiazepoxide (Librium) has been shown significantly to reduce "hostility outward" (statements of destructive or aggressive intent) and "ambivalent hostility" (statements blaming or criticizing others) in a group of juvenile delinquent boys. The study was done double-blind and the hostility measures were taken on the Gottschalk scale (Gleser et al., 1965). Podobnickar (1971) has also reported on the effectiveness of chlordiazepoxide in the control of hyperaggressiveness in a double-blind study of private patients suffering from various forms of anxiety and neurotic hyperaggression. Several clinical studies have also shown Librium (Mans & Senes, 1964; Denham, 1963) and Valium (diazepam) (Barsa & Saunders, 1964) to be useful in the control of irritability in neurotic patients. Monroe (1972) used chlordiazepoxide alone and in combination with primidone added to a basic phenothiazine regimen to reduce the aggressiveness in psychotic patients, 80 percent of whom had been relegated to the disturbed ward of a state hospital because of uncontrolled aggressive outbursts. Both Librium and Valium in combination with the primidone were effective. Diazepam has been used with "remarkable success" in eliminating the destructive rampages of psychotic criminals (Kalina, 1962, 1964). Kalina indicates that schizophrenia is unaffected by the drug, but the aggressive and destructive elements that make the patient difficult and dangerous to manage are eliminated.

Lithium

Chronic mania, which frequently involves considerable hostility and episodic hyperaggressiveness, can be successfully treated with lithium carbonate (Schou, 1967; Gattozzi, 1970). A number of clinical reports (summarized by Tupin, 1972; also see Shader et al., 1974) seem to indicate that this drug may be useful in the treatment of a variety of disorders having aggressiveness as a symptomatic component. These studies combined with the evidence that lithium reduces aggressiveness in animals (Sheard, 1970a, 1970b, 1971a; Weischer, 1969) have led some investigators to utilize lithium in the reduction of excessive aggressiveness in selected prisoners. Tupin and Clanon (1971), in a nonblind study of ten prisoners whose behavior was characterized by significant outbursts of violence and who had spent long periods in solitary confinement because of their uncontrollable aggressiveness, found a reduction in aggression while they were on the drug. The subjects took lithium for a three-month period during which time all except two were free of disciplinary infraction related to violence. It was also reported that the men showed a noticeable increase in frustration tolerance and were able to work in the prison program. Tupin et al. (1973) reported similar results in a population of prisoners with a long history of violent behavior.

In a single-blind study in a maximum security prison 12 chronically assaultive prisoners with a record of violence in the prison setting were given a three-month trial of one month on lithium, one on placebo, and a return to lithium during the final month (Sheard, 1971b). Aggressiveness was significantly reduced during the lithium trials. The aggression measures included a self-rating scale, clinical ratings of verbal aggression during clinical interviews, and the number of tickets received for aggressive behavior. Although a single-blind design was used for the study, two of the assessment conditions, the self-rating scale and the number of tickets given by the prison staff, were, in fact, done blind and both of them showed a significant difference between drug and placebo condition ($p < 0.01$).

Both Sheard and Tupin are continuing their studies of the usefulness of lithium in aggression reduction in humans under more controlled conditions. Although the initial studies indicate that lithium is another drug that may have a reasonably specific antihostility action, further work is clearly needed.

The Propendiols

Finally, the propendiols (meprobamate and tybamate) should be mentioned, not because they have a predominantly antihostility effect but because they are so widely used. Meprobamate was one of the first of the minor tranquilizers introduced in the early 1950s and it is still used by thousands for the control of anxiety. Ban (1969) surveys the literature on this drug class and concludes that the propendiols in general and meprobamate in particular are indicated for various psychoneuroses in which psychic tension and anxiety are associated with irritability.

SUMMARY

In spite of the many problems in interpreting studies on humans, it appears clearly justified to conclude that there are a variety of blood chemistry manipulations that affect the threshold of aggressive reactivity in man. The blood chemistry variables always interact with social and environmental and learning factors, but the evidence indicates that in many instances the physiological variables make an important and significant contribution to the overall aggressive potential.

Androgens are related to aggressive behavior in the male but there is still much to be learned about the exact nature of that relationship. Other things being equal, a higher level of androgen is associated with increased hostile behavior of some kind, and a reduction or blockage of androgenic compounds tends to reduce some kinds of hostile behavior in aggressive individuals. It is clear that the androgens are important in sex-related aggression and there is some indication that they may play a role in generalized irritable aggression. However, much more work needs to be done to establish that relationship unequivocally.

Endocrine factors also seem to be involved in the production of the irritability and feelings of hostility that accompany the premenstrual tension syndrome. Although there is no doubt that social, cultural, and experiential factors are important variables in this syndrome, it is possible to reduce the feelings of irritability by physiological manipulations including changes in the progesterone-estrogen ratio.

Although relatively little hard evidence exists on the underlying physiological mechanisms, there is good reason to believe that aggressive behavior may be a reaction to allergens just as urticaria can be an allergic reaction. The allergic aggressive reaction can be eliminated by removing the allergens from the individual's environment and reinstated by once again challenging the patient with the offending substance.

A precipitous drop in blood sugar may produce a pathological proclivity for aggressive behavior in some individuals which can be dramatically and immediately alleviated by restoring the blood sugar level to normal. Because the tendency to hypoglycemia affects a small but significant number of individuals in the total population, this dysfunction may be of some practical importance.

There is unequivocal evidence that a large number of drugs can profoundly influence the tendency to hostility. The threshold for aggressive behavior tendencies can be reduced in some individuals by alcohol, the amphetamines, and paradoxically by chlordiazepoxide and diazepam. Although no drug is a completely specific antiaggression agent, there are now quite a few that have an antiaggression component in their therapeutic spectrum. These drugs include the phenothiazines, diphenylhydantonin, haloperidol, lithium, and in many individuals chlordiazepoxide and diazepam as well as the other benzodiazepines.

Now that we have some understanding of the physiological substrates of aggressive behavior in man, we can go on to consider whether or not this knowledge leads to the possibility of the control of aggressive behaviors. Chapter 4 shows that a number of physiological methods are useful in the control of hostility in man.

4

The Control
of Aggression

Civilization rests, in part, on man's ability to control his aggressive tendencies and to exercise some modicum of control over other men who will not, do not, or cannot control their own hostile impulses. However, problems arise in deciding how much aggression should be controlled, by whom, and by what methods. The types of controls one considers as possible (although not necessarily desirable) depend on the kind of model one has of man. Much aggressive behavior is, of course, learned. Some authors, when they deal with the problem of aggression control, offer solutions to the problem based entirely on the premise that the behavior is *only* subject to control by techniques involving learning (Scott, 1962; Hinde, 1967; Bandura, 1973). Others, although accepting the basic idea that there are internal impulses to aggression, conceive of aggression in terms of an energy construct and consider control measures related to the draining off of the "aggressive energies" (Lorenz, 1966; Storr, 1968). None of them considers the possibility of the manipulation of the individual's internal environment. Scott (1971), in fact, is so committed to the construct that aggressive behavior is essentially learned that he concludes that drugs cannot be effective in aggression control because "we still have no drug that will selectively erase the effect of training" (p. 38).

It is obvious from earlier chapters that a variety of physiological manipulations result in the reduction of one or another kind of aggression. The model developed in this book has a number of implications for the control of aggression. This chapter considers some of those implications.

The potential effectiveness, the possible side effects, the probable problems, the potential for abuse, and the potential for further development are discussed. Further, whenever one man exercises control over another man's behavior, ethical problems are involved. The problems arise whether the controlling manipulations are the result of educational measures, the manipulation of the contingencies of positive reinforcement, the application of psychological or physical punishment, or direct changes in the physiological substrates of the individual's behavior. However, since control by physiological manipulation is relatively new, and also relatively powerful, there is currently considerable, justifiable concern about these methods. It is therefore necessary to devote some space to ethical considerations.

THE NEED FOR CONTROL

There is an increasing incidence of violence and violent crime in the world today and the potential for the further escalation of violence with the acceleration of population increase seems a distinct possibility. If civilization is to be preserved, means must be found to mute the expressions of hostility in large segments of the population in general, and in world leaders in particular. This general problem merits the consideration of specialists in many fields and the solutions will require the expertise of individuals in many disciplines. However, the emphasis in this chapter is on the control of aggression in indivduals.

The ability to deal with feelings of hostility and the tendency to overt aggressive action varies greatly from one individual to another. Some persons are pathologically violent and are unable to exercise any constraints on their tendency to injure either themselves or other people. If they and those around them are to survive, their aggression must be controlled. Many of these individuals, although not all, are mentally retarded, and their behavior requires institutionalization. Many of them have readily diagnosed brain pathology. The extremely hyperactive brain-injured child, for example, "is indiscriminately aggressive and impulsively violent. He may keep in constant and socially disruptive motion—running, shouting and destroying any object that he gets his hands on" (Mark & Ervin, 1970, p. 57). Andy and Jurko (1972b) describe a "hyperresponsive syndrome" the main characteristics of which are hyperkinesia, aggresssion, and pathological affect. The following excerpt from one of their cases is illustrative.

> D.D., 7-year-old. This mentally retarded child said single words at 2–3 years of age, and stopped talking at 5 years of age. At about 1 year of age, the patient began to have tantrums and fits with loud screaming which lasted 20 minutes or 2 hours. At 3 years of age, she developed spells of aggression consisting of biting, scratching, and kicking her mother and others in the family.

Her mother's arms and hands were scratched so badly that they bled. The child also bit and scratched herself. The attacks began by whining. Following one of these attacks, she sometimes slept for 3–4 hours. She frequently plugged her ears with her fingers, particularly for some sounds that were unpleasant. Her "temper tantrums" became more frequent and severe. She had one such episode the night prior to admission characterized by biting, scratching, turning over furniture, kicking the wall, etc.[1] [p. 125].

Heimburger et al. (1966) report a case of a retarded 15-year-old boy who had been institutionalized for years in a locked room without furniture because of his uncontrollable destructiveness and hostility toward attendants. Another sample of hyperaggressive patients was described as follows:

In this overly aggressive and hyperactive group the aides were almost continuously confronted with such behavioral problems as hostile aggressiveness (fighting, biting, scratching, kicking, pulling hair, slapping), passive aggressiveness (hollering, screaming, singing loudly, cursing, talking vulgarly, tantrums, denudation), destructiveness (pulling down curtains, breaking windows, throwing furniture, rending clothing), filthy habits (excretory soiling, smearing of feces, coprophagy, eating rags, plaster, etc.) and restlessness (excessive walking or running, insomnia, rapid ingestion of food).[2]

There are no reliable estimates of the number of these unfortunate individuals in institutions, but the number must run into the thousands.

There are also significant numbers of individuals who for a variety of reasons have episodic loss of control over their impulses to aggression and destructiveness. The etiology of many of the cases of episodic hostile behavior has been discussed in Chapters 2 and 3, and include such factors as epilepsy, various other brain dysfunctions, endocrine disturbances, allergies, hypoglycemia, and some pathological reactions to drugs. In many cases, however, there are no obvious physiological pathologies (Monroe, 1970; Lion, 1972). Charles Whitman, whose case has been discussed in some detail earlier, probably behaved aggressively because of a brain tumor. However, Whitman has counterparts in many universities and, of course, in the rest of society. These are globally hostile individuals who have homicidal impulses and the means to carry out their threats with firearms. This behavioral pattern is now being referred to as the Whitman syndrome. Kuehn and Burton (1969) provide three cases with this syndrome and recommendations on how they should be handled. These three individuals were globally hostile ("pissed off at the world"; hated all people, particularly those in authority; fantasized shooting

---

[1] O. J. Andy and M. F. Jurko, Hyperresponsive syndrome. In E. Hitchcock, L. Laitinen, & K. Vaernet (Eds.), *Psychosurgery*, 1972, p. 125.

[2] M. S. Terrell, Response to Trifluoperazine and Chlorpromazine, singly and in combination in chronic, "backward" patients. *Diseases of the Nervous System*, 1962, *23*, 42.

people from the university carillon tower, "just for the hell of it"). They were also paranoid, in the process of losing their controls, and had the means (access to firearms) to act on their homicidal impulses. Fortunately, they had come to the counseling service (as had Charles Whitman) for help because of their fears of loss of impulse control. These three students were seen in a relatively short time at a university of 16,000 full-time students and led the authors to conclude that there are "numerous severely disturbed and potentially dangerous people in a large university setting."

A significant number of people in the nonuniversity setting also have violent, sometimes homicidal impulses with sufficient concern about them to seek help, frequently unsuccessfully, from their physicians or from the hospital emergency room. This type of patient is discussed in detail in John' Lion's book *Evaluation and Management of the Violent Patient* (1972), and in a series of papers by Lion and his colleagues (Lion & Bach-Y-Rita, 1970; Lion et al., 1968).

Finally, there are many people, manifestly normal and in good contact with reality, who experience a chronic, relatively low level of hostility and who have a low threshold for the expression of angry feelings. These are the thousands of men and women, husbands and wives, who shout at each other, who, in moments of loss of impulse control, scream at their children and slap them, or worse, only to regret it a moment later, feel guilty, and fervently wish that they did not feel so "mean." Many of these individuals have a strong desire for better control over their hostile feelings and aggressive behavior.

NONPHYSIOLOGICAL METHODS OF CONTROL

Much aggressive behavior is learned and is subject to the same types of influence as any other learned response. In its purest form aggression based on learning may be completely unrelated to the physiological substrates for aggression discussed in earlier chapters. In has no underlying biological basis except in the sense that all behavior and all learned behavior has such a basis. Pure instrumental aggression will not be altered by physiological measures. It can only be controlled through therapeutic techniques based on an understanding of the basic principles underlying learned behavior.

Internal impulses to hostility are also, in some measure, subject to learned control, as are all internal impulses. Therefore therapeutic measures based on learning theory will be useful in helping all types of individuals to inhibit maladaptive hostile tendencies. Thus a number of investigators recommend the use of multiple approaches to aggression control (Bach-Y-Rita & Lion, 1971; Freed, 1962; Lion, 1972). Many, although not all, individuals whose neural systems for aggression are easily fired may still learn to inhibit overt behavior even though they feel extreme anger.

The nonphysiological methods of aggression control will be discussed only briefly in this section. This is certainly not to imply that they are unimportant; they are obviously very important, and, over the long run, civilization must depend primarily on learning as the major technique for the inhibition of interpersonal and international aggression. However, because the major concern of this book is the biology of aggression, biological control methods will be our major concern. Further, control measures based on social learning interactions have been discussed in detail by other authors. (See in particular Bandura, 1969; 1973; Berkowitz, 1962).

Punishment

Punishment is one of the oldest methods of reducing aggression known to man. It does, of course, work in certain circumscribed circumstances but obviously many problems result from its use (Skinner, 1971). It is frequently ineffective and may under some circumstances facilitate the learning of the responses against which it is directed. The punishing parent may serve as a role model for the child. Aggressive parents do produce aggressive children (McCord et al., 1961) and the factor most strongly related to the development of aggressiveness in children is the use of physical punishment (Feshback, 1970). For general reviews of the use, effectiveness, and limitations of punishment, see Skinner (1971), Bandura (1973), and Buss (1961).

Aversion therapy is a fairly recent technique that is closely related to the age-old method of punishment. It differs only in that the aversive consequences of aggressive behavior are systematically manipulated and the parameters of that manipulation are derived from a significant body of experimental work. This technique is the subject of the violent novel and motion picture *A Clockwork Orange* (Burgess, 1962). Aversion therapy has been used most frequently in cases of pathological hostility in which other methods have been unsuccessful. The procedure consists of assuring that physically painful consequences, usually electric shock, follow a clearly defined aggressive act. Chronic assaultive and violent behavior in a 31-year-old female schizophrenic was brought under control by the administration of shock after any of the following three types of behavior: (1) aggressive acts, (2) verbal threats, and (3) accusations of being persecuted and abused. Her general level of adjustment improved and she began to substitute more positive relationships for her previously combative responses (Ludwig et al., 1969). Aversion therapy has also been used successfully to reduce dangerous self-mutilating behavior in children. Children kept in restraints at all times to prevent them from doing serious permanent injury to themselves by head-banging, self-hitting, or self-biting can be released if each self-destructive act is systematically followed by painful shocks (Bucher & Lovaas, 1968).

Aversion therapy is a drastic form of treatment in which the cure can be worse than the disease. Because it is aversive, its use raises a number of ethical problems similar to those discussed under the physiological methods of control.

A less drastic form of aversion therapy consists of a brief time out from social reinforcement for clearly defined deviant behaviors. These behaviors have included aggression, tantrums, self-destruction, sibling aggression, continuous screaming, biting, and destruction of property. When the patient engages in any of the designated behaviors, he is placed in isolation in a "time-out room" for a relatively short period, which, in different studies, varies from 5 to 30 minutes. The procedure has been used successfully with both children and adults and in some cases is remarkably effective in the control of severe, long-standing behavior problems (Bostow & Bailey, 1969; Allison & Allison, 1971; White et al., 1972; Foxx & Azrin, 1972). (See Smolev, 1972, for a review of several studies of this type.)

Reward for Incompatible Responses

The systematic use of reward can also be useful in controlling destructive hostile behavior. Responses that are desirable and incompatible with the deviant behavior to be eliminated are specified, and when they occur the individual is given a positive reinforcement. The reward may consist of attention in the form of hugs and smiles, candy, or tokens that may be exchanged for money or other desirables at a later time. Vukelich and Hake (1971) describe a case of an 18-year-old severely retarded female whose dangerously aggressive behavior was rapidly reduced to a manageable level through the use of this procedure. Under a time-out contingency alone, the patient attempted to choke others within minutes of being released. When positive reinforcement in the form of attention and candy was provided continuously as long as there were no aggressive responses and the rewards were contingent on incompatible responses, her dangerous behavior was essentially eliminated. (Also see Neuringer and Michael, 1970; Smolev, 1972; Stedman et al., 1971).

Psychotherapy

Since aggressive behaviors are frequently maladaptive, it is not surprising that a variety of psychotherapeutic techniques have been used in attempts to bring it under control. Milieu therapy, in which the entire social environment is controlled, has been successfully used to deal with the aggressiveness of hyperaggressive boys (McCord & McCord, 1956). In several cases psychodrama has been useful in reducing the aggression of students (Ferinden, 1971; Logan, 1971). Maladaptive anger responses have been brought under control by systematic desensitization and reciprocal inhibition (Rimm et al., 1971; Evans & Hern, 1973; Herrell, 1971; Evans, 1970; Grazino & Kean, 1967). Finally, group therapy has been useful in helping violent outpatients to deal with their excessive aggressive tendencies (Lion & Bach-Y-Rita, 1970).

Some General Considerations for Aggression Control

One need not accept all the propositions of the frustration-aggression theorists to recognize that frustration plays a role in the generation and perpetuation of aggressive behavior. It has been proposed earlier that frustration and stress, particularly if prolonged, may activate the endocrine system to produce particular hormonal patterns that, in turn, sensitize the neural system for hostility. There is no doubt that a large portion of our population lives in conditions under which frustration, deprivation, and stress are dominant aspects of the life-style. One would expect that a reduction of those factors would mitigate some of the hostile tendencies of the people involved. These conditions for the ghetto residents in the United States have been well described and recommendations for their alleviation have been detailed in the Kerner report (Report of the National Advisory Commission on Civil Disorders, 1968).

Any method that contributes to an increase in empathy among individuals should decrease aggressive behavior because greater identification with the aggressee is then possible and the aggression is thus inhibited (Feshbach, 1964; 1971; Feshbach & Feshbach, 1969).

Cognitive restructuring may also reduce aggressive tendencies if the individual learns a more realistic, less threatening perception of certain aspects of his environment. This may be accomplished in individuals through role playing, for example (Toch, 1969), or through more conventional therapeutic or educational approaches (Feshbach, 1971).

Any shifts in the culture that reduce the number of violent role models after whom children may pattern their behavior may serve to reduce the general level of expressed aggression in the society (Wertham, 1954; 1966). The importance of television in this respect is currently under considerable debate (Feshbach & Singer, 1971; Baker & Ball, 1969; Comstock & Rubenstein, 1972).

Finally, the expression of aggression can be reduced by removing some of the cues that instigate aggressive behaviors. Berkowitz (1967) summarizes an outstanding series of studies demonstrating that individuals react with greater hostility in the presence of objects, such as guns, that have previously been associated with aggressive incidents.

Catharsis, the tendency for the expression of aggression to reduce further tendencies to aggressive behavior, is discussed in the last chapter.

PHYSIOLOGICAL METHODS OF CONTROL

Because there are physiological substrates for aggressive behavior, it is possible to alter hostile tendencies by altering the physiology of the individual. Four basic methods can be used to accomplish this: (1) A portion of the neural substrate for aggression may be lesioned in order to limit or reduce activity in that system. (2) The neural systems inhibiting the neural substrates for aggression can be activated by direct electrical stimulation. (3) Since particular hormone patterns sensitize the neural systems for aggression, and others tend to reduce that sensitivity, it is possible to reduce particular kinds of aggressive behavior by the direct manipulation of the hormonal status. (4) Finally, a number of drugs that are reasonably specific in their antihostility action can be used to help an individual gain control over unwanted hostile feelings and actions.

Brain Lesions

There can be no doubt that a large number of different brain lesions can reduce the tendency of an individual to both feel and express hostility. This is a finding of considerable theoretical importance, but the implications for the practical control of hyperaggressive patients must be considered. From a surgical standpoint the risk is relatively low and the results can be highly dramatic. However, the side effects of a number of the techniques are so great that no surgeon would suggest that they be used. The patient with a bilateral temporal lobectomy who shows all of the Kluver and Bucy syndrome, including loss of immediate memory, hypersexuality, and overeating, has been little helped by the operation even though his impulsive pathological aggression has been brought under control (Terzian & Ore, 1955). The results of the prefrontal lobotomy in reducing aggression are so variable and the side effects so unpredictable that it is now used relatively infrequently, and should probably not be used at all for aggression control.

Amygdalectomy

Of all the brain lesion techniques that have been used in aggression control, the amygdalectomy seems to have the greatest promise. (See

Chapter 2.) Precise lesions of 8 to 10 mm in diameter are made with the
aid of a stereotaxic instrument. The procedure generally produces less
trauma than other techniques, and the side effects reported have been
minimal. The side effects reported have included two cases of visual
field defects (Schwab et al., 1965), one case of hemiparesis (Freeman &
Williams, 1952), and one case of diabetes insipidus (Heimburger et al.,
1966). Sawa et al. (1954) have also reported two cases with severe
vomiting and abdominal pain, and one case of transient palsy was reported by Narabayashi et al. (1963). Only Sawa et al. (1954) have reported defects in memory as a result of this procedure and then only in
three cases who exhibited agnosia for persons and objects.

In general, intellectual functions have not been impaired by the
stereotaxic amygdalectomy. Heimburger et al. (1966) have concluded
that the surgical procedure has no effect on mental retardation, but
Narabayashi et al. (1963) have reported a gain in intellectual capacity
in five of nine retarded children in one series. He found no evidence
for memory difficulties and no deterioration of psychic function.

In a study of 16 patients with temporal lobe epilepsy who had received coagulation of the amygdala, no intellectual deficit was found.
Eight of the patients were lesioned in the right amygdala, six in the left,
and two bilaterally. Four subtests on the Wechsler Intelligence Scale
were used as well as various continuous performance tasks and the Stroop
Colour Word Test, a test for word fluency, and tests for learning and
memory. The subjects were tested pre- and postoperatively. Although
there was no indication of general intellectual loss, selective differences
were found in relation to the response to the novel situation at the
beginning of the learning process. No other information is given on those
differences (Anderson, 1970).

It should be pointed out that although gross deficits in intellectual
functions or radical changes in personality (except for the common finding of a drastic reduction in antisocial behavior) have not been reported
in the literature, it is not possible to determine what effects amygdalectomy or any other aggression-inhibiting lesion has on the patient. None
of the reports contain complete psychological work-ups on the patients
before and after the operation. It is quite possible that the individual
has been drastically changed (for better or for worse) in many aspects
of his total being. There may be many subtle changes in intellectual
functions, and there may be long-run limitations on the individual's
adaptability, flexibility, and social awareness. Only well-designed pre-
and postoperative evaluations will permit judgments on the total effects
of these various psychosurgical procedures. Further, such evaluations
should contribute considerably to our knowledge of human brain function.

In the real world many of the preceding questions, although important,
are academic. If the patient is, like Heimberger's patient described earlier,

retarded and locked in a room without furniture for years because of his uncontrollable hostility and destructiveness, it makes very little difference whether a brain lesion will produce subtle intellectual or motivational changes. If a patient's reaction to the testing situation is to destroy the test materials and attack the psychometrist, the evaluation will obviously not have much meaning. An amygdalectomy, however, may enable the patient to be released from a solitary and completely sterile environment and begin to interact socially within the hospital environment or even be released into the outside world. To argue that this patient is made "less of a person" by the operation is essentially meaningless (Breggin, 1972).

There are obvious problems in using lesions for the control of aggression. The most serious one is that they are not reversible. Once the lesion is made, nothing can be done to restore the individual to the preoperative state. When the operation is not successful the patient is brain-damaged to no avail. It therefore appears clear that surgery should be a last-resort therapy and should be used only after all other types of control, both psychological and physiological, have been tried.

If the various psychotherapeutic methods discussed earlier have been given an adequate trial, a variety of physiological methods should be attempted before psychosurgery of any kind is performed. As indicated in Chapter 3 there are now a number of drugs and hormone preparations that, in some patients, produce a clear reduction of hostility. However, since the state of the art is not yet refined, it is seldom clear at the outset which drug will be the most effective. Therefore a casual trial with a couple of the major tranquilizers in no way exhausts the possibilities for the less drastic physiological control techniques and does not justify attempts to control the behavior by brain surgery. There is evidence that in some of the hospitals around the world in which aggression control operations are performed, relatively little care is taken to ensure that brain surgery is, indeed, the "last-resort therapy" that is should be. (See Valenstein, 1973, for a further exposition of this point.)

Need for Further Work

None of the preceding operations is 100 percent successful, but as of now there are no good criteria for deciding which patients will be helped by which operation. Detailed behavioral analyses and psychological evaluations of all psychosurgical candidates may ultimately permit a more precise identification of the individuals most likely to have their symptoms alleviated. It has recently been suggested, for example, that the tendency to violence toward persons may have a different neurological substrate than the tendency to self-mutilation or the destruction of objects. In a series of 18 patients, seven of nine who showed interpersonal hostility were benefited by amygdalectomy, whereas none of nine patients who were either destructive of self-mutilating showed persistent improvement after the operation (Kilon et al., 1974). Heimburger (1966) has also suggested that more detailed analyses need to be made of the electroencephalographic records. Some patients whose EEGs have improved, that is, displayed fewer epileptogenic discharges, have not shown a behavioral improvement, whereas others who have improved behaviorally have shown no changes in their EEG record. Well-controlled sleep records, with temporal and sphenoidal leads and depth recordings during surgery, may also be useful in finding the type of patient for whom the operation is potentially successful.

It is a far cry from the first crude prefrontal lobotomies, with their massive damage, to the relatively precise amygdalotomy done with the stereotaxic instrument. By comparison, current techniques are highly refined, but they are in need of further refinement. The amygdala is a complex entity that has an influence on a number of behaviors. In animals there is evidence that it is involved in at least three different kinds of aggressive behavior and that the different nuclei may be involved in either the facilitation or the inhibition of one or more kinds of aggression (Chapter 8). Some of the failures to control antisocial behavior through operative techniques may very well be due to the imprecision in electrode location. Thus a great deal more research is needed to gain this relevant information.

Potential for Abuse

As with any other therapeutic technique, there is a potential for abuse. The operation may be used prematurely, when it is unwarranted, or by individuals who have the legal right but not the competence to undertake this type of surgery. It is also conceivable that surgery to prevent aggression might be used as a political tool for the control of dissidents or as a threat to control aggressive individuals in prisons. Psychosurgery for aggression control would not be a particularly effective political tool. There is no reason to believe, and no evidence to suggest, that the precise lesions currently available for the mitigation of uncontrollable violence would have any effect in reducing the aggressive behavior of an individual who has decided to resist oppression on the basis of intellectual processes rather than anger. Thus that kind of abuse would be the result of ignorance on the part of the user. It is, of course, true that brain operations are possible that could restrict an individual's political activity by reducing his general reactions to all stimuli and putting him into a coma or semicoma—by destroying portions of the arousal system, for example. That type of surgery, however, has no more relationship to therapeutic psychosurgery than does simple murder. This important point is developed later in the section on the limitations of physiological methods of aggression control.

Brain Stimulation and Aggression Control

There is now considerable evidence indicating the presence, in the brains of animals and man, of suppressor areas that, when activated, function to block ongoing aggressive behavior (Chapters 1 and 8). This has been accomplished repeatedly in both animals and man and thus provides another possible method for the direct control of intractably aggressive individuals. The evidence indicates clearly that the reaction to stimulation is not a general arrest phenomenon. In humans, depending on the site of stimulation, the patient's mood may change from a generalized feeling of hostility to one of euphoria, superrelaxation, or a sexual motive state.

Although there can be little doubt that suppressor systems exist and can function to block aggression, little is known about the details or the effects of the repeated stimulation of those systems. A great deal more work needs to be done before this technique can be demonstrated as safe and practical. Most of the technical hardware problems have been solved and will be discussed later; however, there is a real lack of knowledge of the potential physiological and psychological problems.

Risks Involved in Brain Stimulation

The surgical risk of mortality through electrode implants is even lower than that for stereotaxic brain lesions and can be considered negligible. There are, however, other serious side effects that merit a great deal more research before electrical stimulation of the brain of man can be considered risk-free. Although there are no data on man, it has been shown in mice, rats, cats, and monkeys that repeated brief, subthreshold stimulation of the amygdala results in a progressive lowering of seizure threshold and ultimately in behavioral convulsions. This increase in seizure potential resulting from brain stimulation has been referred to as the kindling effect. (See Goddard, 1972, for a detailed review of this phenomenon.) The kindling effect appears to be restricted to limbic system stimulation and the tendency to kindling appears to be directly related to the number of connections with the amygdala. Goddard concludes that the kindling effect is a relatively permanent transynaptic change resulting from neuronal stimulation and is unrelated to such factors as tissue damage, edema, or gliosis. There do not appear to be detectable histological differences between the brains of animals with low seizure thresholds from repeated stimulation and control animals that had the implants but not the stimulation. At least one case has been reported in which a human patient was stimulated in the lateral amygdala daily for a three-month period with no report of a lowered seizure threshold (Mark & Ervin, 1970).

Kindling only results when the stimulation is brief and intermittent, usually separated by a 24-hour period. It has been shown in the rat that if the stimulation is massed, that is, given at intervals of less than 20 minutes, the animals seldom develop convulsions. Further, if animals, previously kindled, are given continuous stimulation for many hours, they appear to adapt to the stimulation and cease having convulsions.

Thus it is possible that the kindling effect may be circumvented by massing the stimulation but until much more is known about that effect, procedures involving repeated electrical stimulation of the brain of man can hardly be considered risk-free.

Kindling results from repeated electrical brain stimulation. However, one study has shown that a single application of 1 μg of acetylcholine chloride bilaterally to the basolateral portion of the amygdala of cats resulted in relatively permanent abnormalities in the electrical activity of the brain. Within 4 minutes of the stimulation electrophysiological seizure activity was recorded from the point of stimulation. Overt motor seizures appeared within 10 to 15 minutes that were quite similar to epileptic attacks in humans. The behavioral seizures disappeared during the next 24- to 48-hour period but highly abnormal discharge patterns persisted during the five months of observation. Immediately after the seizure the animals were hypersensitive to all stimuli and made unprovoked but well-coordinated attacks on other cats and the experimenter. The "wild cat" behavior also persisted for the entire observation period. The formerly tame cats continued unprovoked attacks on conspecifics and on people and resisted all attempts at taming. Behavioral effects of chemical stimulation in other areas studied, including the hypothalamus, midbrain reticular formation, thalamus, and amygdaloid regions other than the basolateral area, did not persist for more than 30 to 60 seconds (Grossman, 1963).

Aside from this single study essentially nothing is known about this phenomenon. It is not known whether other brain areas can be affected in the same way by a single stimulation, nor is it known whether the abnormalities will persist indefinitely. However, the possibility that a single stimulation of the brain of man could result in convulsions, permanently wild behavior, and abnormal electrical spiking in the brain is indeed frightening. At least one human patient has shown delayed and prolonged increases in violent aggressive behavior from a single session of electrical stimulation in the amygdala (see p. 55). That patient showed an apparent recovery of his prestimulation, well-controlled behavior after a 24-hour period. However, it is not possible to determine whether there were long-term changes because the patient died (from other causes) soon after the stimulation session.

There is another side effect about which even less is known. It has been reported that one patient (and only one as of this date) has become addicted to electrical stimulation of the amygdala (Mark et al., 1972; Ervin et al., 1969). The patient was a 33-year-old engineer who had periodic attacks of extreme violence. He also presented symptoms of multiple pains, worry, dejection, and intense feelings of anxiety and tension. Bipolar stimulation of the lateral portions of the amygdaloid complex on either side resulted in symptom relief after a 10- to 30-second latency and a feeling of superrelaxation. Stimulation was given several times weekly for an unspecified period and the patient developed an addiction to the stimulation. He insisted on being stimulated and when the procedure was stopped for ten days he became irritable, depressed, and manifested his earlier symptoms. Placebo stimulation had no effect and stimulation of other sites did not relieve the symptoms.

The addictive process implies that some kind of positive affect may have been produced. In addition to the so-called addiction, the continuous electrical activation of positive areas may involve a number of as yet unrecognized psychological problems. Valenstein (1973) puts it succinctly when he says, "The belief that anyone could adjust in this world if a spontaneous orgasm followed by mental calmness was programmed at 10, 2, and 6 o'clock seems ludicrous" (p. 173). It is not clear what to make of this single case, and nothing is known about the possible mechanisms underlying the addiction, if that is, indeed, what it is. However, the case raises a red flag of caution for electrical brain stimulation in humans.

Potential Development of Aggression Inhibition by Brain Stimulation
It is clear from the preceding discussion of side effects that brain stimulation for the control of aggression is not currently a useful technique. It is, in every sense of the word, in the earliest experimental stage. The potential hazards are serious and quite possibly irreversible. At this point it is not possible to determine whether the potential problems can ever be solved so that the procedure could be used therapeutically. Much more research needs to be done and good animal models must be developed and explored in depth. These factors must be kept in mind in the following discussion of the possible adaptation of technology to these techniques. Brain stimulation may ultimately prove to be useful for a *limited number* of patients for whom less drastic measures have been unsuccessful. It is therefore useful to explore potential applications of the technique.

As indicated in Chapter 2 there is some reason to believe that brain stimulation may have prolonged effects. A significant body of animal literature establishes this possibility (Delgado, 1970; MacLean, 1965) and in at least one case in humans the aggression control effects lasted for months (Sweet et al., 1969). If the effect was indeed due to the stimulation and if further work results in sufficient understanding of the mechanisms so that a reasonable prediction of success can be made, it may be possible to facilitate an individual's control over his hostile impulses by a single series of amygdaloid stimulations, after which the electrode can be removed. It should be emphasized that such a procedure, although relatively safe surgically, is highly experimental and the possible long-term, and even short-term consequences, are not at all understood.

Self-stimulation for Aggression Control

Many patients have an intense desire to gain control over their irrational impulsive aggressive behavior. It is now technologically feasible, although it may not be desirable, for them to do so through the stimulation of their own brains. Health (1954) has developed a transistorized self-contained unit the individual can wear on his belt. The unit generates a preset train of stimulus pulses each time it is activated. This stimulator could be connected to an electrode implanted in an aggression suppressor area, and the patient would then have his own "antihostility button' which he could press to calm himself down whenever his irrational feelings of hostility occurred. [This device has already been used with a narcoleptic patient who, whenever he felt himself drifting off to sleep, could reach down and press his "on button" and once again become alert. His friends soon learned that they could press the button to get him back into the conversation if he fell asleep too rapidly to press it himself (Heath, 1963).]

Brain Stimulation Without Surgery

It may ultimately be possible to provide brain stimulation in limited subcortical areas without open surgery. Although this development may not be in the immediate future, the implications are of such importance that it should at least be mentioned. A stereotaxic instrument is now available[3] that can produce lesions as small as 0.5 to 0.1 mm by using low-frequency ultrasonic energy. It may ultimately be possible to use the ultrasonic source of energy at a lower level as a stimulator. C. W. Dickey, who developed the device, has already given some thought to that possibility (personal communication).

Radio-Controlled Brain Stimulation

Much of the work on the activation and inhibition of aggressive behaviors through brain stimulation has utilized a radio-controlled device that permits stimulation from a distance without having encumbering wires attached to the subject (Delgado, 1959, 1965b, 1965c, 1966, 1967; Robinson et at., 1969). The monkey wears a stimulating device on its back which is connected by subcutaneous leads to electrodes implanted in various brain locations. The leads are connected through a very small

[3] CDV Stereotaxic Ultrasonic System, from Baltimore Instrument Company, Inc., 716 West Redwood Street, Baltimore, Maryland 21201.

switching relay which can be closed by an impulse from a miniature radio receiver bolted to the animal's skull. The radio is activated by a transmitter that can be located some distance from the subject. In a classic experiment (Delgado, 1963) it was shown that remote stimulation of the caudate nucleus of the boss monkey in a colony blocked his spontaneous aggressive tendencies. His territoriality diminished and the other monkeys in the colony reacted to him differently. They made fewer submissive gestures and showed less fear. When the caudate was being stimulated it was possible for the experimenter to enter the cage and catch the monkey with bare hands. During one phase of the experiment, the button for the transmitter was placed inside the cage near the feeding tray and thus made available to all the monkeys in the colony. One of the submissive animals learned to press the button during periods when the boss monkey showed aggressive tendencies. When the boss made threatening gestures, the smaller monkey would frequently look him straight in the eye and press the button, thus directly calming him down and reducing his hostile tendencies (Delgado, 1963, 1965a).

Remote radio control of interacerebral stimulation is also possible in the completely free patient just as it is in the free-ranging monkey. Delgado et al. (1968) have already implanted electrodes in the brains of four patients and brought the leads out to a radio receiver attached

Figure 2

Elsa, pressing the lever, stimulates by radio the caudate nucleus of Ali (on right side of cage), producing behavioral inhibition. Elsa's attitude is significant because her attention is directed not to the lever but to Ali. It is unusual for lower-ranking monkeys to look straight at the boss of the colony because this evokes retaliation. (From J. M. R. Delgado, Cerebral heterostimulation in a monkey colony. *Science,* 1963, *141.* Copyright 1963 by the American Association for the Advancement of Science.)

to the patient's head and covered by the head bandages. (Also see Mark et al., 1969; Mark & Ervin, 1970; Delgado, 1969a.) It is thus possible to stimulate these patients from a considerable distance by activating the radio transmitter. Various effects have been reported to result from radio stimulation with this device, including "pleasant sensations, elation, deep thoughtful concentration, odd feelings, super-relaxation, and colored vision." In one patient outbursts of rage and assaultive behavior, similar to her spontaneous episodic anger responses, resulted from stimulation in the right amydala. It is also possible to record from the electrodes because the unit on the head includes a very small RF transmitter. If the electrodes were implanted in an aggression-inhibitory area, it would be quite possible to permit the patient to engage in his normal activities as long as he was within range of the transmitter. Periodically, the stimulator could be activated, thus keeping the patient in a nonaggressive state of mind.

Even though the unit just described weighs only about 70 g, there are still some obvious difficulties. It must be worn under bandages on the head (although one patient was able to hide the device completely with a wig) and it is necessary for the leads to the electrodes to penetrate the skin, thus producing a constant source of irritation as well as the ever-present possibility of infection. However, even these difficulties have been resolved by the recent developments in microminiaturization. At a symposium in 1969 Delgado reported that an entire stimulation unit had been reduced in size and shaped so that it could be implanted under the skin. It would therefore be possible for an individual to have an electrode implant in an aggression-inhibiting area attached to one of these devices (Delgado, 1969b). As soon as his hair grew back, he would not look different from any other individual. He could then return to all normal activities as long as he stayed within the range of the transmitter. Obviously, the range would depend on the transmitter's power. It would also be possible to give the subject a small, relatively inexpensive, transistorized radio transmitter similar to the units used for the remote opening of garage doors. He could then carry his transmitter with him in his pocket and as long as he possessed the initiative for his own impulse control, that control would be available to him. It would also be possible to make transmitter units available to responsible individuals for use during periods when the subject's violence was dangerous but not subject to his own wish to control it. The ethical implications of this type of device will be discussed.

Terminal Man

In Michael Crichton's superb book *The Terminal Man* (1972) the main character, because of his inability to control his violent impulses, has had an electrode implanted in his brain. He also has a micro-miniaturized computer implanted subdermally and connected to the electrode. The computer senses, on the basis of characteristic brain waves, when Mr. Benson is about to become aggressive and provides stimulation in an aggression suppressor area. Mr. Benson can then lead a normal life. However, things go awry, and thereby a very fine tale it told. How close is the "terminal man"? Closer than many would like to believe. Like all good science fiction writers, Dr. Crichton had done his homework well.

Delgado reported in 1969 that he had implanted electrodes in the brain of a chimpanzee and connected them to a miniaturized transmitter-receiver bolted to the animal's head. With this device it was possible to make EEG recordings from depth electrodes as well as to provide remote stimulation of deep brain sites. It was then determined that spontaneous spindles from the amygdala were correlated with excitement and attack behavior and that stimulation in the area of the central gray resulted in a negative response in the chimp. A computer was then programmed to differentiate the spindle waves from other EEG responses and to activate the electrode implanted in the central gray on the occurrence of the amygdaloid spindles. A reduction in the amount and frequency of spindle waves from the amydala resulted. Within two hours the amount of spindling was reduced by one-half and after a few days the spindles were essentially eliminated. The chimpanzee's behavior also changed. He became considerably more docile, had less appetite, and became somewhat lethargic. The behavior change persisted for a two-week period without further stimulation.

The interpretation of this experiment is not yet clear. Until the procedure is applied to humans it will not be possible to know what kinds of subjective experience are associated with either the spindles or the stimulation of the central gray. Central gray stimulation was negatively reinforcing for the chimp and has been associated with pain in man and thus would be undesirable as a locus for stimulation in the control of aggression. However, it has been shown that under certain circumstances violent behavior in man is preceded and accompanied by particular EEG tracings from the depths of the temporal lobe, particularly the amygdaloid and hippocampal regions (Mark & Ervin, 1970). As indicated earlier, stimulation in several brain areas results in an inhibition of hostility with the substitution of some positive affect. Thus it appears that the basic mechanisms for the computer control of hostility in humans have already been demonstrated. Once again, the hardware technology is available, and much more is known about that aspect of the problem than is known about the brain mechanisms involved. The possible complications and side effects of such a procedure are at the moment completely unknown.

Potential for Abuse

Brain stimulation for the control of aggression is a highly experimental technique, and relatively little is known about potentially dangerous and irreversible side effects. The evidence clearly indicates that the procedure can prevent aggressive behavior or block that which is ongoing. Those findings are, of course, of considerable theoretical importance. As of yet, however, there are relatively few patients for whom the therapy would be appropriate. However, when all else fails and the only alternatives are years of physical restraint, solitary confinement in a barren room, or brain lesions, this measure may in time be preferred.

The greatest potential for abuse appears to be similar to that for lesioning procedures. The technique may be used prematurely when it is not warranted, or by individuals who are inadequately trained. The sophisticated achievements in electronic hardware may lure some individuals to use the techniques before some of the serious possible problems are understood and resolved. The suppression of aggressive behavior by brain stimulation is of considerable theoretical importance. However, it should be emphasized once again that it is a highly experimental technique with many unknown risks and is not yet a practical therapeutic procedure.

Like brain lesions, brain stimulation for aggression control would not be a particularly good device for political suppression. There is no evidence that brain stimulation has any effect on instrumental aggression, and even if it were effective, the technical problems of controlling large numbers of individuals would be overwhelming.

Hormonal Manipulation for Aggression Control

It is clear from the material in Chapter 3 that the tendency to certain kinds of aggressive behavior in humans is a function of particular hormone balances and that alterations in the individual's hormonal status result in a change in the aggression potential. Except for the endocrinopathies, where the obvious therapy is the normalizing of the endocrine balance, there are essentially two types of aggressive behavior that appear to respond to endocrine manipulations. The first is the very serious problem of sexual violence. The second is the much less serious but frequently troublesome irritability associated with fluctuations in the menstrual cycle.

Sex-Related Aggression

Aggressive behavior that is directly associated with sexual behavior, either heterosexual or homosexual, can most generally be controlled by reducing or blocking the androgens in the bloodstream. The simplest and most obvious method of accomplishing this is through the operation of castration. There is now considerable evidence that this operative procedure is effective in reducing the level of sexual arousal regardless of its direction. This is, of course, a drastic therapy and a number of problems are connected with it. In cultures where manliness is commonly associated with sexual potency, the psychological effects of castration may be devastating. Almost one-third of a sample of castrates in Norway were extremely embittered after having undergone the operation (Bremer, 1959). Although some authors (Hawke, 1950) consider the physiological effects to be minimal and to some extent even beneficial, Bremer (1959) reported a variety of somatic complaints in 37 of 215 castrated subjects. These problems included troublesome weight gain, exceptionally aged appearance, polydypsia and polyuria, complaints of weakness, and deterioration in general health.

Although some of the effects of castration, including the reduction of sexual arousability, can be alleviated by hormone therapy, the operation is, of course, irreversible. In all countries in which castration is a legal therapeutic measure the operation is voluntary. That is, the individual is permitted to choose between preventive detention for an indefinite period and castration, although that is hardly a free choice. The advantage of indefinite tenure in prison is, of course, that the sentence can be terminated. It is not necessarily true, however, that the psychological and physiological damage done to the individual during a stay in prison (side effects) is reversible.

In summary, castration is a very effective method of controlling sex-related aggression when it is the result of excessive sexual arousal. The evidence is that it will control socially inappropriate behavior such as exhibitionism as well as the extremely brutal sexual assaultive, mutilative murders of small children. The latter must, of course, be controlled in one way or another. Because castration is a permanent and disturbing operation, other therapeutic methods should be tried first.

Although the evidence is certainly not extensive, there appears to be good reason to believe that sex-related aggression can frequently be controlled by estrogenic and antiandrogenic compounds. The problem of side effects must, of course, be considered. Most of the side effects of the estrogenic compounds, such as tenderness in the breast, loss of facial hair, redistribution of fat deposits, and so on, can be controlled by reduction or withdrawal of the medication. However, Laschet (1973) suggests that prolonged treatment with estrogens or progestagens may lead to irreversible damage of the Leydig cell functions.

If the potentially sexually violent individual is to be released into society, two other problems must be taken into consideration. First, there must be assurance that the individual receives the medication and, second, its effectiveness must be checked. When there is the possibility of a brutal child murder, self-medication obviously cannot be trusted. An individual may, under most circumstances, be very concerned about his violent tendencies and feel strongly about controlling them. However, as a therapeutic dose of a hormone or hormone inhibitor wears off and the state of extreme sexual arousal ensues, he may be unable to respond to his rational processes. Several attempts have been made to solve this problem with long-acting subcutaneous or intramuscular injections. Chatz (1972) indicates that intramuscular depot injections of estrodiol valerianate (Primogyn Depot Sherin Berlin) remain effective for a two-week period. The individuals are released into society and report to their personal physician or to the outpatient clinic every 14 days for another injection. If a dangerous offender fails to report he is rearrested and either given the injection or returned to an institution. Estradiol B.P.C. has also been used as a long-acting sex suppressant (Field & Williams, 1970). It is implanted subcutaneously by means of a trochar and cannula after the skin has been anesthetized. Implants of 100 mg at a time are made until the goal of impotence or near impotence is reached. The dosage has varied from 100 to 1200 mg. In this study a two-year follow-up revealed that sexual reoffending was essentially eliminated. Two of the antiandrogens, cyproterone acetate and medroxyprogesterone acetate, are also available in depot form (Laschet, 1973; Blumer & Migeon, 1973).

A prisoner who has committed a violent sex crime and has a life or indeterminate sentence is obviously highly motivated to provide evidence that his sex drive has been reduced under any kind of therapy. Thus the usual self-reports of frequency of masturbation, spontaneous erections, and sexual fantasies that are used as measures of potency are likely to be quite unreliable. There is therefore good reason to develop more objective measures of sexual arousability if hormonal suppressants are to be used in the control of sexual violence. Little work has been done on this problem to date. However, it should not be difficult to develop the necessary measures using various indicators of physiological arousal to the presentation of sexually prepotent stimuli. Field and Williams (1970) have suggested, among other things, the direct measurement of penile volume.

Premenstrual Irritability
The woman who continues to endure premenstrual irritability and tension month after month has a physician who either is not aware of the problem or has not kept up on the literature. A number of possible therapies are now available and, whereas a given therapy may not be satisfactory for a particular individual, there is a good probability of finding one that will control the symptoms without excessive side effects. These measures

have been indicated in the discussion of the physiological basis of the
syndrome and will not be covered in more detail here.

Pharmacotherapy and Hostility Inhibition

The complexity of the problem of the physiological control of hostility
is well illustrated by the attempts to use drugs for that purpose. A single
pharmacological agent may dramatically reduce the hostile tendencies
of one individual. It may just as dramatically *increase* the expressions of
aggression by a second individual and it may have no effect on these
tendencies in a third. Kalina (1962), for example, has successfully used
diazepam to eliminate the intense rage reactions of psychotic criminals.
However, DiMascio et al. (1969) report that the same drug may result
in assaultive and destructive behavior. Previously quiet patients were
seen to break up office furniture shortly after being placed on the drug.
Cases of violence and even murder, presumably resulting from the
"paradoxical rage reaction" induced by one of the benzodiazepines, have
also been reported.

These results are not too surprising when one recognizes that there
are a number of different kinds of aggressive behavior and that each of
them has a different physiological basis. Similar results have also been
reported in many animal studies (Valzelli, 1967). Because aggression
has many causes and can result from a variety of neural and endocrine
dysfunctions, the problem of predicting which drug will be effective in
the inhibition of hostility of a given individual is difficult. There are, as
yet, no good diagnostic tests that permit a rational pharmacotherapeutic
approach to hostility control. However, in spite of this lack of perfect
predictability in the matching of a particular drug to a particular patient,
the large number of substances capable of blocking both overt aggression
and feelings of hostility are a valuable adjunct to the therapeutic measures
available to relieve human misery. In many areas of medicine a lack
of knowledge of the details of the therapeutic process dictates that a
search must be made for the most efficacious drug. The simple dictum is,
if the first drug does not work, try the next one on the list. A wide selection
of pharmaceutical agents are now available that have hostility reduction
as a significant component of their effects and that have limited serious
side effects. Thus there is a high probability that irrational, incapacitating,
discomforting, aggressive behavior can be kept under control through
the use of drugs.

Side Effects, Positive and Negative

There is a general misconception in the popular literature and among
a surprising number of physicians that the drugs manifesting an antihostility effect, as well as psychotropic drugs in general, produce their

effects by reducing the individual's general level of awareness, making him stuporous, stupid, and unable to respond adjustively to the relevant stimuli in his environment. Individuals are frequently described as "drugged," implying the glazed look and general apathy of the heroin addict "on the nod." Research (and there is now a large body of literature on the problem) does not support that interpretation.

The most general finding has been that patients improve on various tests of intellectual functioning during the drug trials, or those processes are unaffected by the drugs. Baker (1968) has reviewed 89 studies on the effects of psychotropic drugs on test performance and finds relatively few deleterious effects. The interested reader is referred to Baker for details, but the general finding in regard to chlorpromazine is that it is an effective agent. That property of the drug enables anxious and highly agitated patients to direct their attention in the testing situation, with the result that they do significantly better on tests of intellectual functioning. Anxious subjects treated for six weeks with 800 and 1600 mg of meprobamate do significantly better on the digit symbol test of the WAIS than do placebo controls. The performance of normal subjects has generally been reported to be unaffected, except for one study in which the individuals received a dose of 1600 mg per day and did more poorly on the digit symbol test than controls.

The results of other studies not covered by Baker (1968) yield similar results. Dilantin sodium not only reduced the irritability of institutionalized epileptics, it also resulted in a general improvement in intelligence rating, which was particularly reflected in memory, reasoning and planning, and recognition of verbal absurdities (Ross & Jackson, 1940). Fish (1960) has reported an improvement in school performance by hyperactive children during therapy with Benadryl. Ninety-three percent of the children with behavioral disorders, among whom assault and self-injury were important characteristics, showed either no change or improvement on the Tulane Behavioral Test, indicating no loss of mental alertness during treatment with haloperidol (LeVann, 1969).

It is, of course, possible to give a large enough dose of any of the antiaggression drugs to reduce alertness. If the dose is high enough to interfere with the individual's general adjustment, there is a good possibility that a better agent may be found. It is also true that drowsiness is sometimes a side effect to which the patient habituates with continued treatment or with dosage reduction.

All the drugs used in the control of aggression may also have, in some individuals, unwanted physiological side effects, and the therapist must obviously be aware of them and be attentive to the possibility of an idiosyncratic reaction by particular individuals to certain of the drugs. Exactly the same precautions must be taken in the prescription of anti-hostility agents as with any other drug. The possible side effects of the

various drugs are listed in most of the manuals of drug use, such as the
Physician's Desk Reference, and will not be covered here.

Pharmacotherapy and Psychotherapy

The antihostility drugs discussed above function to raise the threshold
for hostile feelings and thus for hostile behavior. They are therefore
useful in providing the individual with a measure of control that is unavailable without them. In a sense they help to control his environment
in that he is an active participant in interpersonal interactions. Hostility
evokes hostility that evokes further hostility. Drugs with an antiaggression action contribute to the breaking of that type of vicious circle, since
the patient is less easily angered. In some cases that action in and of
itself may be all that is needed. However, anger frequently results from
an inappropriate interpretation of the environmental stimuli. That is,
the individual has learned to respond with anger in situations that would
not arouse that affective state in most people in his culture. Psychotherapy
in one form or another is necessary to help the patient learn to interpret
the cues in his environment differently and more appropriately. The drug
therapy may make the patient more accessible to psychotherapy and
facilitate the learning process. Therefore for many patients the optimal
therapeutic approach is a combination of both drug and psychotherapy.

Potential for Abuse

There is probably more potential for abuse (i.e., the inappropriate use)
of drugs for aggression control than for any of the other physiological
methods. Currently, all the drugs with an antihostility component to
their action require a prescription signed by a physician. None of them
give a very satisfactory "high" so they are unlikely to be abused by the
same group of individuals who abuse the various mood elevators. However, the ease with which drugs can be administered means that they
can be prescribed inappropriately without adequate evaluation of the
optimal therapy.

With drugs there is a *potential* for political abuse. The present author
has suggested (Moyer, 1968) that it might ultimately be possible to put
antihostility drugs in the water supply and that we should be concerned
about it. In April of 1974 a panel at the Seventh International Water
Quality Symposium considered the question, "Shall we add lithium to
drinking water?" As of this writing the conclusions of the panel are not
available, but it is clear that the unequivocal answer is NO!!, and that
no applies to lithium and any other psychotropic drug. There are obvious
ethical considerations, which will be discussed later, and there are
practical considerations almost too obvious to mention. These relate to
dosage, distribution, side effects, and a general ignorance of the effects
of mass distribution that would almost undoubtedly bring to light a

large number of unpredicted idiosyncratic and possibly paradoxical reactions.

As a political tool for the control of the masses of people to keep them happy with a given administration or political system, it would not be very useful. At best, the wide distribution of antihostility drugs, whether via water, milk, bread, or any other system, would reduce the probability of some kind or kinds of aggression. Intellectual, unemotional dissent (i.e., instrumental aggression) would not be controlled.

THE LIMITATIONS OF
PHYSIOLOGICAL METHODS OF
AGGRESSION CONTROL

The physiological methods of aggression control cannot be effectively used against either the "trigger man" for Murder Incorporated or the bomber pilot over North Vietnam. Both are engaged in instrumental aggression, and neither may have any feeling of hostility toward their victims. The bomber pilot may be essentially at peace with the world. He has had a good breakfast of steak and eggs and a very pleasant morning ride high above the clouds, which are bathed in sunshine far below. When his radar indicates that it is time to press a bomb release button, he may do so without the slightest feeling of antagonism. His bombs may destroy the homes and lives of hundreds of people. He has behaved as he has been trained to behave and emotional responses may not be involved at all. The "trigger man" for Murder Incorporated kills because he is financially rewarded for killing. He may not know his victim and may feel no animosity toward him whatsoever. Scott (1971, p. 38) was quite correct when he said "we still have no drug that will selectively erase the effect of training." It should be added that there is no other physiological manipulation that can selectively modify the effects of training. Further, with the current state of the art, no such method is likely to be found in the near future. It is not even clear where to start looking for that type of method. That type of control must await major, and as yet, quite unpredictable breakthroughs.

It is important to differentiate learned aggressive behavior from learned feelings of anger. Learned aggressive behavior, instrumental aggression, is similar to any other complex learned response such as driving an automobile. Once the response pattern is learned, there is little if any affective component connected with it. And, just as there is no physiological method of selectively manipulating the learned response of driving behavior, there is none for the learned response of aggressive behavior. It is true that a number of procedures may reduce general awareness, interfere with neuromuscular coordination, and through sedation interfere with performance. They do not, however, affect learning.

In addition to learning to respond aggressively to particular situations in order to gain some satisfaction or reinforcement, it is also possible to learn to become angry. Frustration, deprivation, or some other anger-evoking phenomenon becomes associated with the cues of a particular situation or individual. Those cues are then capable of eliciting a feeling of anger or hostility. The feeling of anger is subject to physiological manipulation because that feeling is dependent on a particular set of neural pathways in the limbic system that are subject to the various methods of physiological control considered in this chapter. It is possible to raise the threshold for feelings of anger, with the result that greater provocation is necessary before the individual feels the appropriate emotion.

The distinction between instrumental aggression and aggressive behavior containing an affective component has important implications for the abuse potential of the physiological control of aggression. As indicated briefly in connection with each method, none of them are particularly valuable as political tools, since they are capable only of reducing the intensity of or the threshold for the affective component. They may, in fact, be counterproductive for an individual who wishes to control the rebellious tendencies of a particular population. One reaction to oppression, political or otherwise, is to become angry and, as a result of that anger, to evolve a plan, which may involve aggressive behavior, to alleviate the oppression. Another reaction to oppression is to recognize it as such intellectually and to come to the conclusion that the oppression must be eliminated. A plan, which may involve aggressive behavior, is then worked out. Antihostility drugs in the water supply will affect only the anger, they will have no influence on the intellectual processes involved in the aggressive plans. In fact, if the anger is controlled, the plans may be more effective because they will not involve the impulsive quality that often results from the urgency of anger. Further, because the emotional component will not function as a distractor, the intellectual processes may function more efficiently.

In 1971 Kenneth B. Clark started a monumental controversy when he suggested that the necessary resources in terms of scientific personnel and research facilities be mobilized "to reduce human anxieties, tensions, hostilities, violence, cruelty, and destructive power irrationalities of man which are the basis of wars" (p. 1055). He further suggested that world leaders accept and use the first form of psychotechnological biochemical intervention that would reduce or block the possibility they would use their power destructively. He implies that the adequate use of the new physiological technology of hostility control could eliminate destructive wars. Since, as this book has shown, a great deal is now known about hostility control and the potential for further developments in those types of controls is great, it is important to attemp to relate these developments to Clark's proposals.

If one makes the assumption that modern wars result from the impulsive behavior of world leaders who are acting in anger, Clark's proposal would be a reasonable one, and adequate antiaggression therapy for world leaders would, in fact, significantly reduce the possibilities of armed conflict. Further, given the current status of our understanding, it is highly likely that a concentrated research program could develop pharmaceutical agents that, either singly or in combination, could eliminate feelings of anger and hostility and the irrational decision based on those feelings. A number of drugs are available now but considerable research is needed to establish the types of aggressive behavior affected and more needs to be known about possible side effects. When these drugs are perfected, as they certainly will be, and we know with some assurance that there are minimal risks of such effects as paradoxical reactions, I agree with Kenneth Clark that they should be taken by those who hold positions of political power. The world can ill afford the luxury of world leaders who are subject to fits of anger that may result in impulsive and irrational aggressive behavior.

However, the unfortunate fact is that although the psychotechnical revolution may ultimately reduce feelings of anger and its resultant behavior, it is not likely to eliminate destructive war. Much, if not most, of the aggression involved in war is instrumental. That is, it is directed at achieving certain gains—the acquisition of territory, the settlement of disputed boundaries, the expansion of a sphere of influence, or the economic exploitation of another country. Those motives may have essentially no emotional component and anger may play no role. Once again, it should be emphasized that no known physiological manipulation can selectively influence particular learned behaviors. The psychotechnological revolution is not even close to being able to influence those kinds of behavior; thus war based primarily on nonemotional motivations will not be curtailed by physiological manipulations.

Kenneth Clark's proposal implies the use of some kind of pressure to convince world leaders to take advantage of the predicted psychotechnical advances. William G. Scott (1973), however, proposes that, "Mind techniques will be used by the elite doing significant jobs to change themselves into significant people." His argument runs, in part, that the elite are overworked and constantly striving to improve their efficiency. Such factors as anxiety and unreasonable feelings of hostility interfere with clear thinking and the most efficient performance. Various types of mind control ultimately offer the possibility of reducing these distracting states of mind. Scott indicates that the moral grounds for the use of mind control techniques by "significant people" stem from the significance of their jobs, the superior execution of which will benefit large numbers of people. This is an interesting proposal, which time will test.

ETHICAL PROBLEMS

As indicated, there are now large numbers of methods that are useful for the control of aggressive behavior. These methods may be highly beneficial to individuals in terms of their own adjustment, happiness, and efficiency. They may also be beneficial to society in protecting it from the depredations of the irrationally hostile individual. However, controls always imply the limitation of freedom, and the limitation of freedom is the justifiable concern of most of mankind. The issues are complex but they cannot be ignored for that reason. The possibility of highly effective control of the aggression of individuals is here now, and the methods can only become more effective and efficient in the future. It is therefore critical that some of the problems be examined and some tentative suggestions for guidelines offered.

The Self-referred Patient and Informed Consent

Many individuals who exhibit aggressive behavior do not want to behave in that way but insist that they cannot help it. The annals of crime contain many cases of pathological murderers who plead with the police to catch them before they commit another murder. Many of the patients discussed here actively seek help in controlling their impulsive aggressiveness. Mark and Ervin (1970) indicate that half of a sample of 150 of their violent patients were driven to attempted suicide because of their despair over their uncontrollable violence.

The ethical problems involved in dealing with the self-referred patient appear to be relatively uncomplicated. As long as the patient gives *informed* consent, it would appear that any of the available therapies could be used as long as the welfare of the patient is paramount and the individual administering the therapy does not have a conflict of interest in the case. The patient, it is true, must have a certain amount of trust in the therapist because some of the therapies are highly complex and require a considerable background of knowledge before they can be reasonably well understood. Further, as has been emphasized repeatedly, aggressive behavior is most generally episodic and the individual's tendency to give consent, either informed or otherwise, may vary considerably as a function of where he is in the cycle. Charles Whitman actively desired help in the control of his globally hostile impulses and did seek such help from a psychiatrist. However, once he was engaged in the violent episode, it is clear that he was unwilling to consent to any control over his behavior.

The problem is dramatically illustrated by a case study presented informally at a symposium on the identity and dignity of man. This quotation is presented in full because it dramatizes so well the dilemmas involved in informed consent and the problems in the outer reaches of behavior control. The exchange is between Robert V. Bruce and Frank Ervin.

> *Bruce:* May I ask Dr. Ervin if he has ever been tempted to press a button to make the patient reasonable enough to understand the explanation of why the button should be pressed?
>
> *Ervin:* This leads to a very interesting kind of paradox. I will give you a specific example. We had a patient whom we had in fact operated on. We had done the diagnostic procedure and had wires in his brain. A guy who had a very dramatic "flip-flop" in his personality state, he was either aggressive, paranoid, litigious, difficult to deal with or he was a very sweet, reasonable, passive, dependent kind of neurotic. These were his two modes of existence. Long before he had also happened to have epilepsy which is why he had come to us. In fact, there were two patients. I had a choice as to which one to deal with. These two patients were a great stress on the wife of the single body in whom they were contained. On this occasion she broke down and wept and said, "Who are you, honey? I don't know who you are." He had gotten extremely upset on the ward. We could not hold him against his will in the hospital since our hospital is a voluntary hospital and he could only be there by his own choice. He threatened to leave and was, in fact, in the process of leaving, ostensibly to kill his wife. At least that is what he said he was going to do, and I rather believed him. In the course of the day, we managed to get him into the laboratory and stimulate this part of the brain that Hudson Hoagland mentioned this morning.[4] In about a minute he visibly relaxed. He took a deep breath and said, "You know you nearly let me get out of here?"
>
> *Bruce:* If I may quote history instead of the Bible for a change, you appealed from Alexander drunk to Alexander sober.
>
> *Ervin:* Precisely, and I said, "Yes, I couldn't have held you." He said, "You've got to do something to keep me from getting out of here. I think if you had the nurse hide my pants, I wouldn't have left." I thought that was a good suggestion and followed it. We had a very reasonable discussion and he was very grateful for my having stopped him. I said, "Well, I guess we won't have to go through this very much longer because tomorrow morning we have planned to make the definitive lesion and I wanted to talk to you about that. What we are going to do is burn out this little part of the brain that causes all the trouble." He said, "Yeah, that's great." Well, the next morning about 9:00 he was brought down and he said, "You're going

[4] This reference is to the amygdala.

to burn what out of my brain? Not on your bloody life you're not!" He would easily at the earlier point have signed anything I asked for. He was guilty; he was sweet; perhaps he was reasonable. But which of those two states I should deal with posed a real problem for me. So informed consent isn't all it's cracked up to be. Voluntary understanding has its problems (Ervin, 1973).[5]

Ervin's dilemma over whether the patient was being reasonable before or after the electrical stimulation is an exaggeration of the same problem in the normal man who sometimes makes decisions during a state of anger or during a state of calm. When the neural substrates for anger are activated by external stimuli the individual may make a decision to shout at his wife, beat her, or kill her. If he is restrained from any of these activities by circumstances and has an opportunity to calm down so that those neural substrates are no longer active, or are, in fact, inhibited by the activity in one of the neural substrates for positive affective behavior, his decision on how to behave toward his wife may be very different. He may be extremely grateful for the circumstances that prevented him from carrying out his decision during his anger state. I am not suggesting in any sense that individuals should be aided in their decision-making processes by direct amygdaloid stimulation, I merely wish to point up the fundamental similarity. In the case of Ervin's patient, the aggressive mental state was blocked directly by a handy electrode. It is conceivable that the patient's mood could have been changed by the manipulation of the external environment, calm therapeutic counseling, and so on.

The problems involved in the use of brain stimulation as a method of aggression control were discussed earlier. The case is used merely to point up the problem with the concept of informed consent. In spite of the difficulties, however, the principle of informed consent appears to be a valuable guide in deciding on the types of therapy to be used for those individuals who actively seek help in controlling their hostile feelings and actions.

The Patient Who Is Not Self-referred
The more difficult problem from an ethical standpoint lies in the control of aggression when the aggressor actively rejects the idea that his behavior should be controlled. When, under what circumstances, and by whom should controls be imposed from without? Obviously, this problem did not arise with the development of the recent behavioral and physiological control methodologies. Men have always been controlling other men, and since the code of Hammurabi in 1780 B.C., laws have been

[5] In P. Williams (Ed.), Ethical issues in biology and medicine, *Proceedings of a Symposium on the Identity and Dignity of Man.* Cambridge, Mass.: Schenkman, 1973, pp. 177–178.

used to limit that control. Law must ultimately limit the use of more sophisticated controls developed by technology.

Society must and will protect itself from the depredations of violent individuals regardless of the origin of their violence. It already has an elaborate, although frequently ineffective, system for protecting itself while protecting the civil rights of the individuals being restrained. Technology has now provided society with much more powerful tools for the control of aggressive individuals. Because these techniques have been developed only recently, there is no body of common law regarding them. Because they are powerful, they are subject to misuse and thus potentially threaten individual civil rights.

It should be recognized, however, that the techniques now available, or potentially available, provide the individual with considerably better alternatives than the traditional ones in general use. Some of the techniques discussed here are irreversible and because of that their use should certainly be limited and subject to the most stringent types of controls. However, it is not clear that they should be completely rejected on the basis of their irreversibility. Drugs, hormones, electrical stimulation, and lesions do make changes in the brain, some more permanent than others. However, it should be obvious that current prison management techniques also make changes in the brain and those changes may also be permanent. It would be naive to believe that prison conditions as described by many individuals (see Menninger's *Crime of Punishment*, 1968) do not have a permanent and deleterious effect on the behavior and the emotional stability of those incarcerated. Experience, and particularly traumatic experience, has its own powerful effects on the neural mechanisms that control our behavior.

The ideal technique for dealing with the violent individual is one that both protects society and enables the individual to gain some control over his actions. As detailed in Chapters 2 and 3, a number of disorders that are readily diagnosed result in behavior ranging from minor social disruption to murder. Persons subject to these disorders frequently break laws and are subject to the judicial process. Their tendency to violent behavior can frequently be readily eliminated by a physiological manipulation, and they are benefited little, if any, by incarceration. The uncontrollably hostile individual with a septal or temporal lobe tumor can regain normal behavior when the tumor is removed. Some psychomotor epileptics with episodic dyscontrol can have their periodic outbursts of violence eliminated when they are given adequate doses of Dilantin. Certainly most men would agree that physiological techniques should be used in those instances. These are "medical" problems, which should be dealt with medically. They require careful and complete diagnosis and therapy and although it may be necessary to take careful security precautions, the treatment should be handled by physicians and in a medical reather than a penal facility.

Many other violent individuals, however, who do not have readily diagnosable physical disorders may nevertheless be helped by physiological techniques. Special precautions must be taken to assure their rights are not abused by the misuse of modern technology. A number of actions are possible to assure such protection.

One of the potential problems is that the decisions to use drastic therapies may be made by individuals who have a particular vested interest in having the individual brought under control. Family members, prison officials, and some governmental units may find their purpose well served if the aggressive person can no longer express his hostility, and their concerns may very well not be in the best interest of the one whose behavior is to be altered. In order to minimize that risk, it would be useful to have an independent review board approve all procedures that are not a part of the traditional correctional methodologies. The board should be composed of physicians, lawyers, ethicists, laymen, and prisoner advocates.

In addition to the review board that must ultimately pass on whether or not a given procedure can be used in a particular case, the principle of informed consent should be utilized within the constraints set down by the judicial process. Obviously, consent, informed or otherwise, is not required before a man can be confined, even in solitary, for prolonged periods. However, even though some of the physiological techniques of behavior control are far less drastic than prolonged solitary confinement, informed consent should be required at least until those procedures have the sanction of prolonged usage. Informed consent in a prison situation leaves much to be desired. There are many pressures, some subtle and some blatant, that can be brought to bear on a prisoner to induce him to agree to a given procedure. It is for this reason that the prisoner's consent is not sufficient of itself for permission to be granted. The review board indicated earlier must help to protect the individual from those pressures. However, at this stage of knowledge, it seems that the greatest protection of civil rights would be served by not permitting the use of nontraditional techniques without the consent of the recipient.

The new therapies for the control of hostility are not equally risky and several criteria can be used to assess their relative desirability and priority of use. Clearly experimental techniques should not be used on a captive population that, because of the nature of its life situation, cannot give a reliable informed consent. Mark and Neville (1973) delineate two aspects of the concept of *experimental.* In the first sense a technique is experimental if it is done for the purpose of increasing fundamental knowledge and without the expectation that the recipient will derive benefit from it. In the second sense a procedure is experimental if "its effects are unpredictable, its mechanisms poorly understood, its risks highly variable, and its usefulness subject to widespread debate in the medical community" (p. 766). Mark and Neville go on to indicate that psychiatric neurosurgery is experimental in the latter sense even though there is now relatively little risk to life.

A procedure that provides the least amount of discomfort while providing the greatest amount of self-determination and that provides the least amount of risk of objectionable side effects is the most desirable. Finally, at this stage of technological development a procedure's desirability is partly a function of its reversibility. When these physiological procedures get beyond the experimental stage, nonreversibility may be a virtue. At the current stage of development, however, reversible effects are clearly preferred.

According to the preceding criteria, psychosurgery would be one of the least desirable techniques because it is clearly experimental and the effects are permanent. If there are any behavioral side effects, they are also frequently permanent. Aggression control by brain stimulation would also be undesirable because so little is known about it that it must be considered as highly experimental. Further, it is not yet clear what the possible side effects are, and whether they are transitory or relatively permanent. Castration as a treatment for sex crime would also be relatively less desirable than other types of treatment. The results are obviously permanent and, in some individuals at least, there are both psychological and physiological side effects that, although not critical, may be quite disturbing.

Hormone therapy and the use of pharmaceutical agents would seem to be a valuable addition to correctional procedures for specific kinds of critical violence as long as the safeguards previously outlined are provided. The effects of both of these procedures are readily reversed simply by withdrawing the medication. There is always the possibility of undesirable side effects but careful monitoring, particularly during the early phases of treatment, can usually prevent any serious damage and the side effects are generally eliminated by a reduction of the dosage or by discontinuing the treatment.

Finally, there is a general concern by some critics about all methods of physiological control over behavior. They suggest that aggressive behavior is an expression of the free will and that any direct physiological intervention that limits or prevents that expression is demeaning and degrading of human dignity. Mark and Neville (1973) put it very well when they reply to this argument, "This view is particularly inappropriate not because free will is to be denied but because the quality of human life is to be prized" (p. 772). They point out, as has been repeatedly indicated in this book, that many hyperaggressive individuals are most distressed by their own unacceptable behavior and their inability to control it and many are driven to the brink of suicide because of their deficiencies in impulse control. A physiological therapeutic measure that helps to alleviate an impulsive-aggressive syndrome provides the individual with more, not less, control over his own behavior and, "It enhances, and does not diminish, his dignity. It adds and does not detract, from his human qualities" (Mark & Neville, 1973, p. 772).

5

Kinds of Aggression
I. Introduction,
Predatory Aggression,
Inter-Male Aggression

Much of the understanding of the substrates of human aggression discussed in the preceding chapters is based on the study of animals. Because they are less complex and their symbolic activity is limited, it is easier to discern the different kinds of aggression and the variables of which they are a function. The next several chapters are devoted to what is known about the different kinds of aggression and their physiological bases in nonhuman animals.

A few examples from the laboratory serve to illustrate the point that there are different kinds of aggression. If a rat is placed in isolation in a single cage for a period of a month, it will become exceptionally aggressive. This reaction has been described as follows:

> In the more extreme cases, the reaction of the isolated rat to handling is quite dramatic. When the experimenter attempts to pick the animal up, it scurries frantically around the cage in an attempt to escape. If care is not taken to prevent it, the subject will leap out of the cage, two feet into the air, fall to the floor, and make a frenzied dash for any cover. When cornered the rat will resist being picked up and the more agitated subject will repeatedly bite the experimenter. A violent reaction such as this was never found in the control animals used in any of our isolation studies [Korn & Moyer, 1968].

In spite of the animals' behavior when an attempt is made to pick them up, these animals react with monumental indifference to another rat placed in the cage with them. Further, they show no increased tendency to attack and kill mice but will, in fact, permit an active mouse to crawl all over them.

Approximately 10 to 20 percent of laboratory rats react in a highly aggressive manner toward mice (Karli, 1956). A killer rat responds to a mouse placed in its cage with an immediate attack and kills the mouse in a matter of seconds, usually by a skillfully placed bite in the back of the neck that breaks the spinal cord. These same animals, however, may be quite docile toward the experimenter, who can, immediately after a kill, place his finger in the mouth of the rat without fear of being bitten.

It is possible to increase the aggressive behavior of a nonkiller rat by manipulating the contingencies of reinforcement. This procedure has already been described on p. 15. Reinforcing brain stimulation was used to teach non-mouse-killing rats to chase and bite a mouse. However, these rats never killed and did not show the predatory cervical bite so characteristic of the natural mouse killer.

Considerable hostility can be observed in a colony of mice. This manifest aggression, however, is highly selective. Most of it is carried out by a dominant male who periodically and without apparent cause attacks another male and chases it around the cage, with much squealing on the part of the victim. Fighting among females, however, is quite rare and the attacking male seldom attacks a female or juvenile.

All the preceding behaviors have been repeatedly referred to in the literature as aggression. They are all complex responses and do appear to have one common characteristic; that is, someone, a mouse, a rat, or an experimenter is likely to get hurt. However, are we talking about the same behaviors when we refer to the mouse killing by one rat, experimenter damage by another, and attack of one male mouse on a cage mate? It is proposed here that we are not. These behaviors differ on a variety of dimensions and there is good evidence that each has a different physiological basis.

EARLY ATTEMPTS TO CLASSIFY KINDS OF AGGRESSION

Several authors have suggested that aggression is not a unitary concept (Scott, 1958; Bevan et al., 1960; Jacobsen, 1961; and Valzelli, 1967). Bevan et al. divide aggressive behavior into two classes: spontaneous aggression and competitive aggression. In the first the only identifiable stimulus seems to be the "physical proximity of another animal." Competitive aggression occurs when two or more animals attempt to obtain some desirable goal object at the same time.

Jacobsen (1961) and Valzelli (1967) both found it necessary to postulate different types of aggressive behavior in order to understand the conflicting results obtained in the many research reports on the effects of drugs on behavior. Jacobsen's classifications were highly tentative but included a fear-flight-attack reaction, fighting for territory, fighting for females, and fighting to obtain social position. Under the last category he placed the fighting that is induced when two animals are placed in a cage and shocked. He also mentions, but does not deal with, interspecific aggression in which one of the species is a food object of the other.

Valzelli suggests two major categories of aggression. His first category is "spontaneous aggression," which includes both intra- and interspecific aggression and which he suggests is common in the animal kingdom. His second category is "induced aggression," which refers to those methods used to evoke aggression in the laboratory, including cerebral lesions, painful stimulation, and isolation.

In 1968 the present author attempted to classify the different types of aggressive behavior on the basis of the types of stimuli that elicit an aggressive response (Moyer, 1968). The following classes were tentatively suggested: predatory, inter-male, fear-induced, irritable, territorial, maternal, instrumental, and sex-related.

Further study indicates that to be most useful this classification should be revised. Territorial aggression, for example, appears to be not a single kind of aggression, but a complex of behaviors with different underlying physiological mechanisms. (See Chapter 7.) Further, a definition of the kinds of aggression simply on the basis of the eliciting stimuli seems now to be too restrictive.

The kinds of aggression vary on a number of different dimensions; in order to understand this complex phenomenon it is necessary to consider each dimension. Each dimension will be discussed and some examples will be given to show that it is useful in making a differentiation. It will then be possible to define the various aggressive behaviors on the basis of those dimensions.

DIMENSIONS ON WHICH THE KINDS OF AGGRESSION VARY
Types of Stimulus Situations

The types of stimulus situations that elicit hostile behavior are usually different for the different kinds of aggression. Thus aggression may generally be considered to be stimulus-bound. In many classes of aggression the stimulus situation to which the animal reacts with hostility is remarkably specific. As indicated on p. 131, a male mouse will attack another male but will generally not attack a female or a juvenile (Scott & Fredericson, 1951). A rat will attack a strange member of the same species but will seldom react aggressively to a member of its own group (Barnett, 1963;

Eibl-Eibesfeldt, 1961a). The mouse-killing laboratory rat not only refuses to attack the experimenter, but rarely attacks a rat pup. In fact, the kinds of small animals attacked by a given rat are quite specific. In one experiment almost 100 percent of male hooded rats attacked and killed frogs or small turtles, 45 percent killed a young chicken, but only 10 to 20 percent killed mice (Bandler & Moyer, 1970).

Aggression evoked by electrical stimulation of the brain also shows evidence of being stimulus-bound. Stimulation of the lateral hypothalamus of the cat results in effective and persistent attacks on a rat. However, the more the stimulus animal deviates from the natural prey of the cat, the less sustained the attack is likely to be. Hypothalamic stimulation of the cat will produce brief attacks on a dead rat and the cat will show only passing interest in a stuffed rat or a block of wood about the size of a rat (Wassman & Flynn, 1962; Levison & Flynn, 1965).

Although the range of stimuli that elicit certain kinds of aggression is extremely narrow, for other kinds it is quite broad. Except in situations involving intense arousal, inter-male aggression is shown only toward another male conspecific. In certain types of irritable aggression, however (see Chapter 6), the animal may attack any animate object within reach and under conditions of high arousal may also attack inanimate objects.

Topography of the Response

There are some obvious differences in the response patterns that animals show in different aggression-inducing situations. Several investigators have pointed out that the topography of the behavior in predatory attack by the cat is quite different from a type of aggression that has been called affective. Predatory aggression involves little, if any, emotional display. The cat does not hiss or growl, but slinks close to the floor and makes a silent, deadly attack on the rat. However, in the so-called affective aggression there is evidence of pronounced sympathetic arousal. The back arches, the tail fluffs out, the ears lay back against the head, the animal hisses and growls and may attack in a flurry of scratching and biting (Wassman & Flynn, 1962; Roberts & Kiess, 1964; Hutchinson & Renfrew, 1966).

As indicated on p. 5, the topography of the aggressive response in the deer is quite different when the fighting response is elicited by another male (inter-male aggression) from when it is elicited by predators. In the first instance the male deer confront one another with lowered head and the locking of antlers. Attacks by predators, however, are met by striking out with the front hooves (Tinbergen, 1953).

Sex

In most species certain types of aggression are manifest by only one of the sexes, but the tendency to other kinds of aggressive behavior is the same for both. This, then, is another dimension on which the kinds of aggression may vary. The differential tendency of the sexes to aggress in certain situations is frequently a function of the physiological differences between them.

It is well recognized that there is considerable potential for intraspecific aggression among males and that this potential is a function of the hormonal and neurological differentiation between the sexes. For example, the intraspecific fighting in mice is in general restricted to the males and does not appear until the mouse is sexually mature (Frederickson, 1950). Testosterone injections given to immature mice result in fighting in males but do not have that effect on females (Levy & King, 1953; Levy, 1954). Thus this effect of the male hormone is dependent on the particular organization of the male brain.

Aggressive behavior in defense of the young is primarily, although not exclusively, a female characteristic. In many species the mother will attack any male that approaches the nest, including in some instances her mate. This behavior may depend on the particular hormone balance related to lactation.

Reinforcing Properties

As indicated in Chapter 1, the opportunity to behave aggressively against an appropriate target is in some instances reinforcing. Activity in a given neural system for aggression may produce either positive or negative affect, which is another way in which the kinds of aggression differ.

Interactions with Other Behavior Tendencies

As indicated in the outline of the model in Chapter 1, there are neural systems in the brain that constitute the substrates for complex behaviors other than aggression. These neural substrates interact with the systems for aggressive behavior. However, the evidence indicates that the neural systems for the different kinds of aggression interact differently with the neural substrates for other behavior. The kinds of aggression can also vary on this dimension and can contribute to the definition of the different types. For example, there is evidence that an interaction exists between the neural substrate for hunger and the one for predatory aggression. However, there is little evidence that the substrate for hunger interacts with the neural systems for fear-induced, sex-related, or inter-male aggression.

Physiological Characteristics

All the preceding dimensions ultimately depend on the physiological differences that underlie the different kinds of aggressive behavior. Some of the evidence for the different physiological properties of the different kinds of aggression have already been mentioned. Subsequent chapters will deal with the details of the neurology and endocrinology of each kind. In this section detailed physiology is considered only as it is related to the sensory and motor aspects of the particular types.

DEFINITIONS AND CHARACTERISTICS OF DIFFERENT KINDS OF AGGRESSION

It should be emphasized that the following system of classification is and must remain for some time a tentative one. Much more research needs to be directed specifically at the problem of differentiating among the various kinds of aggression before the most useful classification scheme can be achieved. However, this system is a start and can be modified later as research findings dictate.

The classes of aggression here defined are predatory, inter-male, fear-induced, irritable, maternal, instrumental, and sex-related. These classes of aggression are certainly not mutually exclusive. It is entirely possible, in the real world, that a particular instance of aggression may involve more than one of the preceding classes. Thus irritable aggression may augment inter-male aggression, with the result that the intensity of the aggressive response is increased. The position is taken here, however, that different neural and endocrine bases exist for each of the preceding aggression classes and that the manipulation of the physiological variables inhibits or facilitates the classes of aggression differentially. Also, our understanding of the interactions among these various classes of aggression should be enhanced as we understand the details of the neural and endocrine bases.

Predatory Aggression

Most simply defined, *predatory aggression* is the attack behavior that an animal directs against its natural prey. It is aggressive in that it leads to the injury or destruction of the prey. Aside from that, predation has little in common with the other classes of aggression discussed here (Delgado, 1966; Carthy & Ebling, 1964). A knowledge of the predatory tendencies of a given animal does not enable one to predict the aggressiveness of that animal toward other types of targets, such as a conspecific or a human. Some animals, such as the bull and the hippopotamus, that are very aggressive in other contexts are herbivores and have no predatory tendencies.

Lorenz (personal communication) has suggested that predatory behavior should not be considered as a kind of aggression at all, but as an entirely different type of behavior. However, predatory behavior does fit our general definition of aggression (p. 2). Further, behavior that is obviously predatory is very frequently referred to in the literature as aggressive. The following references are a few of many examples: Myer and White, 1965; Karli and Vergnes, 1963; Bandler, 1969; and Roberts and Kiess, 1964. Predation is also confused with other types of aggressive behavior (Ardrey, 1962; Didiergeorges et al., 1966). (Also see the discussion by Eibl-Eibesfeldt, 1967 and 1970, p. 315.) It therefore seems essential to include it in the classification system and to provide a sufficiently precise description to eliminate further confusion.

Types of Stimulus Situations Eliciting Predatory Aggression

The stimulus situation that elicits predatory aggressive behavior is the presence of the natural prey object. Movement on the part of the prey, though not essential for eliciting attack by experienced killers, increases the probability of attack (Fox, 1969a; Tinbergen, 1950; Clark, 1962; Eibl-Eibesfeldt, 1961b, Van Hemel & Colucci, 1973). Other aspects of the environment as long as they are neutral (i.e., do not evoke any other incompatible motivational state) are irrelevant to this kind of aggression. In this respect predatory aggression differs from maternal aggression, which usually requires the presence of the young in addition to the object to be attacked.

Relatively little is known about specific stimulus characteristics of a given prey object that make it an acceptable natural prey for particular mammals. Within a species it is possible to have considerable variability in the types of animals attacked. The laboratory rat is one of the few animals that has been systematically studied in this regard. Karli (1956), in an excellent study, established that both wild Norway rats and the domesticated laboratory rats prey on mice. Seventy percent of the wild rats killed mice and ate them, whereas only about 12 percent of the laboratory rats killed.[1] Karli's findings on the domesticated rats have been generally confirmed by Myer and others (Myer, 1964; Bandler & Moyer, 1970). Kreiskott (1969) indicates that the percentages of killers may vary from 1 to 20 percent. On the basis of these and many other studies it has been tacitly assumed that the tendency to predation has generally been bred out of the laboratory rat.

Recent work, however, indicates that this animal is highly predatory,

---

[1] For a good discussion of the predatory nature of mouse killing by rats, see O'Boyle, 1974.

but is selective in the type of prey it attacks. Some rats attack hamsters and small rabbits (Kreiskott, 1969). In a study that confirmed the work of Karli regarding the percentage of rats that kill mice, it was also shown that many of the animals that showed no predatory tendency toward the mouse would attack a variety of other small animals, including young chickens, frogs, and turtles (Bandler & Moyer, 1970).

It is probably safe to assume that neither the animals in the Bandler and Moyer experiment nor their ancestors for many generations were given opportunities for predatory behavior. However, the killing behavior was quick and efficient. Most kills were made in the first 30 minutes and over half in the first 10. The killing response was surprisingly specific, usually involving a bite through the cervical regions of the spinal cord. It will be noted, however, that the cervical regions of the spinal cord in the mouse, chick, and frog are remarkably lacking in absolute stimulus similarity. Even the turtle, which has no exposed spinal cord, was attacked most frequently at the head end of the shell.

The frog and turtle, which elicit the greatest number of attacks, are also quite dissimilar. The frog is mobile, soft, and resilient and has appendages readily available for attack. The turtle is immobile, hard, unyielding, smooth and rounded, and lacks appendages. It is possible that there are olfactory cues common to both animals that elicit attack, but Myer (1964) showed that mouse killing is not immediately eliminated by olfactory bulbectomy.

The details of how the nervous system codes which type of stimulus complex will innately elicit a particular type of motor attack have not been worked out, and because of their complexity are not likely to be well understood in the near future. However, some work has been done that begins to define some of the mechanisms involved. Rats that kill mice will not kill rat pups (Myer & White, 1965). For reasons that are not clear, this inhibition is not observed in rats induced to kill by lateral hypothalamic stimulation (Woodworth, 1971). The odor of the pups has an inhibitory effect on the predatory behavior. If the odor of the pup is masked by coating the pup with oil of lavender or if the odor is eliminated by placing the pup in an airtight polyethylene envelope, a significant number of mouse-killing rats will kill the rat pups. Rats made anosmic by olfactory bulbectomy did not differentiate between mice and rat pups as they had prior to the operation. However, some of the olfactory-lesioned animals showed a general waning of all killing after the lesions (Myer, 1964).

The work of Myer shows why the rat pup is not attacked (olfactory inhibition), but it does not indicate why the mouse is attacked. A number of studies on lower animals indicate that the predatory response is activated by specific stimulus characteristics of the prey. These releasing stimuli are referred to as "key stimuli" (Eibl-Eibesfeldt, 1970). Thus the predatory water beetle reacts to the olfactory stimulus of meat extract but not to the visual pattern of its tadpole prey (Tinbergen, 1955), and the prey-catching response of the toad is released only by the movement of objects about the size of the insects on which it usually feeds. It does not respond to an appropriate nonmoving insect immediately in front of it, but it can be made to snap at moving pieces of paper or stone if they are of the correct size (Eibl-Eibesfeldt, 1970). Predatory behavior is released in garter snakes by chemical substances that characterize the articular prey that in their natural environment constitutes their major source of food (Burghardt, 1967).

The predatory responses of the higher animals are obviously much more complex and it seems unlikely that they are "released" in the same sense as the reflex bug-catching response of the toad or the attack of the snake. In the rat, for example, no particular sensory channel is essential to the predatory response. Mouse-killing rats continue to kill in the combined absence of olfactory, visual, and auditory sensations (Karli, 1961).

Because of the work in the laboratory of J. P. Flynn, more is known about the sensory mechanisms involved in predatory behavior in the cat than about those in any other animal. The general procedure of Flynn and his colleagues has been to use nonpredatory cats and induce aggressive behavior by the electrical stimulation of particular brain sites. This technique provides them with an animal preparation that gives highly reliable responses under the control of the experimenter and that thus can be studied in great detail. It is necessary to assume that the neurological and behavioral changes occurring during brain stimulation are similar to the changes occurring during natural predatory behavior. The types of behavior patterns described by Flynn are very similar to those found in nature, which makes the assumption seem quite reasonable. It does, however, remain to be validated.

Levison and Flynn (1965) showed that cats that promptly attack rats during electrical stimulation of the lateral hypothalamus show a reduction in attack intensity and persistence directly proportional to the degree to which the stimulus object differs from a rat. The cats seldom attacked a styrofoam or foam rubber block and would make only half-hearted attacks on a toy dog or a stuffed rat.

Similar results have been obtained during electrical stimulation of the posterior lateral hypothalamus of the rat. Rats were tested in the presence of a live frog, a dead frog, a small rubber mouse, and a live mouse. During stimulation the rats showed no tendency to attack the mice. They attacked the dead frog significantly more often than the rubber mouse and the live frog significantly more often than the dead one. The attacks on the toy mouse and the dead frog were generally terminated after a single bite. Attacks on the live frog were terminated only on the death of the frog (DeSisto, 1970). Woodworth (1971) obtained similar results with a different set of stimulus animals.

The particular senses involved in the location of the rat by the cat and in the biting response during hypothalamic stimulation have also been specified. Vision and tactile cues from the forepaws and snout are critical to the location of the rat, but olfaction plays little role. Both vision and tactile stimulation are involved in the biting response (MacDonnell & Flynn, 1966b).

Sensorimotor Interactions

As indicated on p. 5, there is an interaction between the sensory input and the motor output that accounts for the particular patterning of the motor responses in a given kind of aggressive behavior. What is currently known about this interaction in the cat is well summarized in a paper by Flynn et al. (1971). Activity in the neural system for predation (in this series of experiments the activity was initiated by electrical stimulation) results in the activation of specific sensory and motor systems that control the particulars of the behavior. These systems then function in a manner similar to reflexes except that resultant behavior is quite complex. Flynn et al. refer to them as "patterned reflexes."

In the experimental conditions used by these investigators a cat was restrained in a bag inside a plastic box from which its head protruded. When a mouse was presented to the cat during stimulation of the predatory attack site of the hypothalamus, the animal lunged at the mouse (i.e., at the sight of the mouse, the cat opened its mouth and rapidly moved its head in the mouse's direction). The frequency of the response in some cats was a function of the intensity of the hypothalamic stimulation and the response did not occur under control, nonstimulation, conditions. The behavior is regarded as a patterned reflex rather than a generalized "aggressive drive state" because the response shows a significant laterality. The probability of a lunge is significantly greater when the mouse is presented to the eye contralateral to the point of hypothalamic stimulation (Bandler & Flynn, 1971). If the stimulation had resulted in an "aggressive drive state," one would expect the attack tendencies to be the same, regardless of the side of the animal on which the mouse was presented.

Different portions of the neural system for predation activate different patterned reflexes. The visual system may or may not be effective in mediating the motor pattern of mouth opening, depending on which hypothalamic attack site is stimulated. In an experiment by MacDonnell and Flynn (1966b), the infraalveolar and infraorbital branches of the trigeminal nerve were cut. This left the motor system for biting intact and the cats ate solid food as usual. However, when a hypothalamic attack site was stimulated with a rat present, some of the animals bit the rat (one bite), whereas others approached the prey and rubbed their muzzles on the rat's back but did not open their mouths to bite. Whether the visual stimulation mediated the bite response depended on the specific point in the hypothalamus that was stimulated. Thus at point A, the biting response during stimulation was dependent on sensory feedback of a tactile nature from the cat's muzzle. At point B, however, it was dependent on visual feedback and could be eliminated by blindfolding the cat.

The specific pathways involved in the influence of hypothalamic activity on the visual system are not yet known, but there is physiological evidence to show that the visual system is influenced by that stimulation. If the optic tract is electrically stimulated, evoked potentials can be recorded from the visual cortex, optic radiations, lateral geniculate nucleus and superior colliculus. These evoked potentials are altered by the stimulation of attack sites in the hypothalamus. The changes in evoked potential occur whether the midbrain reticular formation is intact or not, demonstrating that the hypothalamic influence is not mediated by that system (Chi & Flynn, 1968). Another study showed that the responses of individual cells in the visual cortex to stimuli such as slits of light and moving edges could also be altered by hypothalamic stimulation. In some cells hypothalamic stimulation enhanced the response, in others the activity was decreased, and in still others the activity was unchanged (Vanegas et al., 1969–1970).

These studies demonstrate the effect of hypothalamic activity on the visual system. The effect of such activity on the tactile system in the muzzle of the cat as shown by the MacDonnell and Flynn (1966a) study has already been discussed (p. 6). Bandler and Flynn (1972), more recently, have demonstrated in the cat that there is a patterned reflex for striking that is elicited by a light touch to the forelimb. This reflex occurs in the nonpredatory cat only during stimulation of the hypothalamic portion of the predatory system. The size of the receptive field from which striking can be elicited varies with the intensity of the hypothalamic stimulation. As the intensity of that stimulation is increased, the receptive field expands over successive forelimb dermatomes. This sensitivity also shows laterality in that the receptive field of the paw contralateral to the side of the hypothalamic stimulation is larger than that of the ipsilateral paw.

It has also been shown that the motor portion of the patterned reflex for biting is influenced by stimulation of the hypothalamic attack sites. Direct stimulation of the motor nucleus of the trigeminal nerve, which innervates the jaw muscles, results in jaw closure. If at the same time a particular attack site of the hypothalamus is stimulated, the magnitude of the response is increased (Flynn, 1967).

Summary of Stimulus Factors in Predation

The preceding discussion makes it clear that it is not possible to consider in isolation the stimulus input eliciting an aggressive response. There is a constant interaction among the sensory systems, the motor systems, and the central integrating mechanisms. Each of these systems can be considered individually only for expository convenience. However, the evidence strongly suggests that a very limited number of relatively complex stimuli produce specific changes in the sensory mechanisms. These changes interact with the motor mechanisms that have been specifically tuned for complex coordinated and patterned reactivity by the central neural system for predation. The relevant stimulus complexes are those of the animal's natural prey. The less similar the stimuli are to the prey, the less the probability that the resultant sensory change will influence or be influenced by the activity in the rest of the neural system.

Response Topography in Predatory Aggression

The topography of the predatory response has been studied in a number of species and is in general readily differentiated from the response patterns of other kinds of aggressive behavior. [See Fox (1969a) for a discussion of the differences in the topography of predatory and inter-male aggression in canidae.] Some of the characteristics of predation in the cat have already been mentioned (p. 133) and are described in detail by Leyhausen (1956). Although domestic cats attack their prey by biting the back of the neck, lions, accordings to Shaller (1969), kill large prey by strangulation or suffocation.

Eisenberg and Leyhausen (1972) studied the prey-catching behavior of a wide variety of animals. They present detailed protocols for many of them and suggest that the killing response for carnivores can be broken down into the following movements: initial approach, biting, pinning, pinning and rolling, biting and shaking, or biting and tossing. In this study, as in the one already cited (p. 137), the killing bite was most often directed toward the anterior portion of the prey, although canidae generally seize the prey around the abdomen or thorax (Fox, 1969a). The authors suggest that the precise aiming of this response is developed through learning, but the response itself is the result of an innate tendency for the animal to strike slightly ahead of a moving prey. This hypothesis is based in part on some testing with a young genet. If a dead mouse were pulled backward by the tail, the genet would strike at the base of the tail, indicating that the differentiation was based on the movement rather than on the neck per se. The hypothesis has not been formally tested.

Eibl-Eibesfeldt (1963, quoted in Eibl-Eibesfeldt, 1970) suggests that the tendency to bite the back of the neck is learned on the basis of trial and error. The young polecat will attack the posterior end of a fleeing rat. However, with experience it learns that the rat cannot bite back if it is grabbed at the back of the neck. The biting and shaking portion of the response may also be derived from the efforts of the predator to avoid counterattack by the prey during a series of learning experiences (Eisenberg & Leyhausen, 1972).

There can be little doubt that some learning is involved in the development of the response topography of predation. The final form of the response must result from an interaction between the innate proclivities and experience. However, experience with killing is not essential to the manifestation of the response. Effective, if not skilled, killing is reported for many predators that have never been exposed to any prey (Bandler & Moyer, 1970; Eisenberg & Leyhausen, 1972). Cats isolated from birth will attack rats (although less vigorously and less persistently than those non-isolated) when electrically stimulated in the lateral hypothalamus (Roberts & Bergquist, 1968).

Predator's Sex and Predatory Aggression

Since predatory behavior is associated with sustenance in many animals, it is not surprising that both sexes display it. In studies in which a formal comparison has been made, it has been reported that the sexes do not differ significantly in their tendency to predatory aggression (Karli, 1956). Fox (1969a) studied predatory behavior in both sexes in several species of canidae, including the wolf, coyote, gray fox, and dog, and indicates no appreciable differences between the sexes in their predatory activity. Some studies have reported sex differences in predatory behavior. Female Long-Evans rats tended to kill mice more frequently than their male litter mates (Paul et al., 1971), and Butler (1973) have reported that only one of seven strains of mice studied showed sex differences in the tendency to kill crickets. Baboons are also predatory, but most of the predation is done by the males. During ten months of observation, 49 olive baboons were observed to catch and eat 47 small animals. The adult males caught and ate all but three of the prey. Adult females captured three hares but only one of the females was able to keep and eat most of the animal she caught (Harding, 1973).

Reinforcing Properties of Predatory Aggression

The opportunity to display predatory aggression appears to be positively reinforcing if the appropriate prey is used. In the maze-learning study cited, mouse-killing and non-mouse-killing rats were used. The potential reward available to the rats after the appropriate response in the maze were either rat pups or mice. The mouse-killing rats showed significant learning to the goal box of the maze that contained the mouse they killed, whereas the nonkilling rats showed significant learning to the goal box containing the rat pup. Other types of prey were not available in these studies, but it seems likely that non-mouse killers would learn a maze in order to arrive at a goal box containing a frog or turtle. Rats will kill frogs repeatedly, with the killing response itself as the only reinforcement (i.e., they are not permitted to eat the killed prey). In one experiment frogs were presented to rats at 3-minute intervals. Some of the animals killed up to 30 frogs before they stopped killing. The rat resumed killing on the following day (Houston, DeSisto, & Meyer, 1969).

Mouse-killing rats also perform other instrumental responses to obtain the opportunity to kill. What might be described as a mouse-o-mat was used in studies by Van Hemel (Van Hemel, 1970; Van Hemel & Meyer, 1970; Van Hemel, 1972). An experimental chamber was fitted with a Plexiglas key. Pressure on the key closed a circuit that activated a motorized wheel containing caged mice. Each key activation resulted in the automatic introduction of a mouse into the chamber. Mouse-killing rats quickly learned the key-pressing response with no reinforcer other than the presentation of the mouse and the opportunity to kill. Similar findings were obtained in a frog-o-mat during posterior lateral hypothalmic stimulation in the rat. The animals quickly learned to press a lever that activated the frog dispenser and provided them with a frog to be killed. After good performance was obtained on a continuous reinforcement schedule, the subjects were readily trained to FR-4 and FR-5 schedules during the same training session (DeSisto, 1970).

As indicated in the model (p. 10), tendencies to the various kinds of aggression wax and wane over time as a function of the activity in or sensitivity of the underlying neural substrates. A study by Roberts and Kiess (1964) seems to indicate that the reinforcement properties of the opportunity for predatory attack depend on activity in the neural substrate for predation. Cats that did not normally attack rats were implanted with stainless steel electrodes in the lateral hypothalamus. Stimulation of those sites reliably produced predatory attack behavior. The cats were then given Y-Maze training during stimulation. The stimulation was turned on in the start box and continued while the animals were in the maze; they were given an opportunity to learn to approach the goal box containing a rat that could be attacked. The possibility that the termination of the stimulation could be rewarding in itself was conrolled for by giving an equal number of forced trials to both arms of the maze. All the animals learned on the free trials to approach the arm of the maze containing the rat. During trials without stimulation the habit deteriorated and none of the cats showed attack behavior. These authors conclude that the "performance of the attack was rewarding and that the central readiness for attack elicited by the stimulation possessed motivational and cue properties salient in the evocation of the learned responses leading to prey."

Stimulation of the same area of the brain that produces an attack on the mouse by the rat has been shown to be aversive in that the rat will bar-press at a rate of 400 to 1000 responses per hour to escape continuous stimulation of that site. One animal in this study displayed self-stimulation at a rate of 3000 responses per hour, although it would also bar-press to terminate continuous stimulation. Some of the animals in this study showed stimulation-induced predatory aggression, and some showed irritable aggression toward the mouse; it is not clear in the paper which of the rats were tested for aversive or reinforcing aspects of the stimulation. The intensity of current required to produce the self-stimulation and the stimulation escape was half that necessary to elicit attack (King & Hoebel, 1968).

In a study that showed that lateral hypothalamic stimulation facilitated predatory frog killing in the rat, it was also shown that the animals would respond at a rate of 8000 to 10,000 responses per hour to receive stimulation in the same area. However, the current intensity required to elicit self-stimulation was two to five times as great as that required to facilitate killing. No evidence was found to show that this stimulation was aversive (DeSisto, 1970). Woodworth (1971) also showed that 10 out of 12 electrodes that elicited predatory-type attack behavior in rats would also support self-stimulation. In this case the current level used was above the minimum threshold for attack, but not greater than the optimal attack threshold. The durations, however, were shorter. Panksepp (1971c) induced both predatory attack and affective attack by stimulating different sites in the hypothalamus. He then showed that the rats would self-stimulate for current intensities and durations that produced predation but would escape from stimulation that produced affective attack. The difficulties in the interpretation of this kind of data have been discussed earlier (p. 16).

Interactions of Predatory Aggression with Other Behavior Tendencies
There appears to be a relationship between the physiological status that produces eating behavior and that which produces predatory aggression, but the relationship is not yet clear. Eating and predatory attack can both be induced by stimulation of the same area of the lateral hypothalamus (Hutchinson & Renfrew, 1966). However, more intense stimulation is required to induce eating. Thus the same neurons are not necessarily involved. The more intense stimulation may spread and activate additional neurons. It has also been shown that there are sites in the hypothalamus that result in predatory attack when stimulated but that do not result in eating behavior, regardless of the intensity of stimulation (Flynn et al., 1970).

The Hutchinson and Renfrew study shows that there is an anatomical proximity for the predatory and eating response patterns, but there is evidence that predatory behavior is not based on hunger. A hungry but non-rat-killing cat will eat cat food in the presence of a rat with no manifest tendency to attack. However, if the lateral hypothalamic portion of the predatory system is activated, the hungry cat will leave the food and attack the rat (Roberts & Kiess, 1964; Flynn et al., 1970).

Both stimulus-bound feeding and stimulus-bound killing can be produced by hypothalamic stimulation in the rat. These neural systems appear to be relatively independent. Stimulation-bound feeders do not manifest any attack tendencies when stimulated in the presence of a mouse and the stimulation-bound killers do not eat either the dead prey or food pellets during hypothalamic stimulation that produces killing (King & Hoebel, 1968). Natural frog killers that are also stimulus-bound feeders will respond to stimulation in the presence of both food and a frog by eating rather than killing. If the test is repeated on successive days, there is evidence that the rats may kill a frog while being stimulated in the feeding area. Most of the time during stimulation, however, is devoted to eating, and the rat eats the food pellets and shows no tendency to eat the frog it has just killed (DeSisto, 1970).

Predation and eating in cats are differentially affected by different lesions in the caudal midbrain. Lesions involving the reticular formation of the mesencephalon and the nucleus reticularis pontis oralis result in a hyperpredatory syndrome. Although there is some differentiation on the basis of the stimulus input, the predatory behaviors are not limited to the animal's normal prey. Cats with the preceding lesions stalked around their cages in a persistent manner. "Prey carrying" could be elicited by lightly touching the animal's lips with some object that could be carried. If a wooden ruler was used the animals would seize it but carry it for only a few steps. However, if the object more closely resembled normal prey—a warm, moist towel, for example—the cat would carry it to a corner of the cage, deliver several hard bites, and then attempt to eat it. Normal prey such as mice and rats were treated in a similar manner. The normal eating behavior of these animals was disrupted. They never showed the normal feline eating pattern. Although they consistently carried normal prey, they frequently did not kill it, and they never ate the prey that they did kill. They reacted to horse meat as though it were prey, carrying it to a corner, biting it hard, and then swallowing whatever remained in the mouth. The weight of these animals was relatively unaffected (Randall, 1964). In the same study it was shown that more ventral and lateral lesions in the midbrain considerably increased eating behavior. Predation was also increased, but only if the animals had been deprived of food for a 24-hour period. These animals gained considerable weight.

Further evidence for the differential neurological basis of eating and predation is supplied by experiments from Karli's laboratory. Bilateral lesions in the lateral hypothalamus that abolish feeding behavior in the rat only temporarily inhibit predatory aggression (Karli & Vergnes, 1964b). On the other hand, lesions of the ventromedial hypothalamus that produce hyperphagia do not necessarily produce an increase in mouse killing. Of 29 rats that showed behavioral changes after lesioning, only five manifested both clear hyperphagia and interspecific aggression. The other 24 showed one or the other of these changes in behavior. Hyperemotionality was also a common result of the operation, indicating that the mouse killing that did occur may not have been typically predatory (Eclancher & Karli, 1971).

It has also been shown that nonkiller rats will not kill mice even though they are starved (Karli, 1956). Similar results have been reported for the predatory mouse *Onychomys* by Clark (1962). However, one study has shown that starvation did induce muricide in some nonkilling rats (Lorenz, 1972). Both cyclic food deprivation (Whalen & Fehr, 1964) and competition over food (Heimstra & Newton, 1961; Heimstra, 1965) tend to increase the percentage of rats that kill mice. More recently it has been demonstrated that a two-week schedule of food deprivation significantly increases the percentage of rats that kill mice and a significant portion of the killers continue killing after being food satiated for two or more weeks. Nondeprived rats are much less likely to kill. It was also clearly shown in this experiment, however, that a history of water deprivation had no effect on the rat's muricidal tendencies (Paul et al., 1971).

Another indirect relationship between hunger and predation was demonstrated in an experiment by Johnson et al. (1970a). Hunger does not normally induce frog killing in a nonkilling laboratory rat. However, if that rat has had the experience of watching a rat kill frogs, it will kill when placed on 24-hour food deprivation.

Hunger is evidently not essential for the manifestation of predatory behavior, since many predators continue to kill long after their capacity to eat the prey has been exceeded (Kruuk, 1972). They kill even when satiated and some kill prey after prey even though they are never permitted to eat the animals they have killed (Huston et al., 1969). However, it is still possible that the same factors that influence eating behavior also influence predatory behavior. Food deprivation in the killer or in the hypothalamically stimulated predator may shorten the killing latency or lower the required stimulation threshold.

This hypothesis has been recently confirmed by DeSisto. Natural frog-killing rats were tested for killing while on an ad lib feeding schedule and after 48 hours of food deprivation. Each animal was given five killing trials at 2-minute intervals on a given day. The latencies for both attack and kill were significantly reduced during the deprivation condition. Under the ad lib conditions the rats showed a significant decrease of the killing response over the five trials. However, in the deprivation condition no such decrease occurred, and the rats continued to kill in less than 10 seconds (DeSisto, 1970).

Fear responses tend to interfere with predatory aggression. In most laboratory studies on predation it is necessary to adapt the animal to the testing situation in order to obtain reliable predation; otherwise the strangeness of the environment results in freezing or cautious exploratory behaviors while the prey is ignored (Huston et al., 1969). Karli (1956) reports that wild rats, which are highly reliable killers of mice, show a considerable delay in. the killing response if they are transferred from their habitual environment to a new one. In 'another study rats previously established as mouse killers were given an opportunity to kill in the home cage, a cage with a rat odor, a neutral cage, and a cage with mouse odor. The more the environment differed from the home cage, the more the percentage of rats that did not kill increased (Avis & Treadway, 1971).

Baenninger (1967) produced conditioned fear in mouse-killing rats by giving them a series of tone shock trials. When the subjects were tested in the presence of the mouse, the conditioned stimulus of the tone inhibited the predatory response. However, the presentation of the unconditioned stimulus of shock overcame the inhibition and produced killing.

The direct electrical stimulation of particular areas of the midline thalamus (in the path of the inferior thalamic peduncle and its terminal regions in the dorsomedial and reticular nuclei) result in retreating behavior characteristic of a fear response in the cat. The animal does not show behavioral arrest and does not respond with violent escape movements. It retreats from a stimulus rat or from the experimenter cautiously yet alertly watching stimulus objects in the environment. Stimulation of these "fear-inducing" areas functions to block the predatory aggression response produced by lateral hypothalamic stimulation (MacDonnell & Flynn, 1968).

Response Decrement After Successive Kills

The practice of all types of consummatory responses results in response decrement if continued. The response is inhibited for some period of time and the presentation of the same stimulus complex does not elicit the response. Response decrement after sexual responding is a well-recognized phenomenon and has been well studied (Wilson et al., 1963; Fowler & Whalen, 1961; Schein & Hale, 1965; Fisher, 1962). Less is known about the reduction of the predatory response, but it has also been studied. If mouse-killing rats are provided with a mouse once a day, they continue to kill almost indefinitely (Moyer & Bandler, unpublished). In an experiment by Myer and Baenninger (1966) it was reported that experienced mouse-killing rats killed 15 successive mice when presented with one mouse every 30 minutes. Further, once the rat begins consistent killing, that response is remarkably stable. Rats that have reached the criterion of killing on ten successive days kill consistently when tested after intervals of up to 150 days (Myer, 1971). However, if the interval between presentations is shortened, the killing response tends to drop out.

Kulkarni (1968) increased the number of opportunities to kill to seven per day and found that some consistent mouse killers discontinued killing after a few episodes and that the response decrement was inversely related to the length of time permitted between consecutive kills. Bandler (1969) has shown that the attack and kill latencies of some rats are significantly increased by a training procedure that involves the presentation of five successive prey objects per day at intervals of 1 minute between presentations. Although the latencies increased, the response did not disappear. As already indicated, frog killing by rats is highly persistent, with some rats killing as many as 30 frogs in succession.

The automatic mouse dispenser developed by Van Hemel (1970) provides the opportunity to study response decrement in predation in a situation in which the rate of prey presentation is determined by the killing animal rather than the experimenter. A mouse is delivered whenever the rat presses a Plexiglas key. Four rats were studied during 10-hour sessions in this apparatus. Response inhibition, defined as a 15-minute interval of nonresponding, occurred after 47 to 144 minutes. During that time the rats obtained and killed between 32 and 57 mice. During the rest of the session, an average of 41 more mice were obtained and killed. An analysis of the results indicated that the rats obtained and killed several mice in rapid succession and then paused for rather prolonged periods. All these animals recovered from the response decrement effect within a 24-hour period.

The rate at which the various components of the predatory response disappear during satiation has also been studied (Lorenz, 1966). In general, the loss of the responses occurs in reverse order. The killing bite is inhibited first, followed by the capture, chasing, and orientation toward the prey. Lorenz (1966) suggests that this is adaptive in that it permits the greatest amount of practice of the components that lead to the capture of a vital resource for the animal.

Predation Response Loss After Early Exposure to Prey

A number of studies have been done in which the predator and the prey have been raised together, with the general result that the propensity of the predator for killing that particular kind of prey was significantly reduced. In the classic study of Kuo (1930) cats were raised with rats and none of the cats killed companion rats. Only three of 18 killed other rats. More recently, similar experiments have been conducted using rats and mice as subjects. When these two species are raised together, almost no rats show a predatory tendency toward the mouse (Galef, 1970a; Myer, 1969). Birds do not elicit attack from cats if those two species are raised together (Kuo, 1967). However, one must be careful about drawing general conclusions from these experiments because the predatory tendencies studied were not particularly strong.

Many domestic cats have minimal predatory proclivities and, depending on the particular strain, only 10 to 20 percent of laboratory rats kill mice. Further, the mouse is not the preferred prey of those rats that do kill mice (Bandler & Moyer, 1970). Thus the importance of early experience in the inhibition of predatory behavior may well be overemphasized. A more complete understanding may be achieved by studying a stronger genetically determined response tendency.

A more appropriate prey for the laboratory rat is the frog, which under optimal conditions is attacked by nearly 100 percent of the animals (Bandler & Moyer, 1970; DeSisto & Huston, 1970a). An experiment using rats and frogs was attempted by Johnson et al. (1970a, 1970b, 1972) and Johnson (1972). Rats were reared with frogs in a variety of conditions. In one group the rats were maintained on a raft in a bathtub containing frogs that also had access to the platform. In another group the frogs were maintained in a pan of water inside the rat cage and the species had an opportunity to interact. In the third group the rats were provided with visual exposure to the frogs that were maintained in a glass jar in the rat's cage. Finally, the frogs were separated from the rats in a wire enclosure that did not permit direct contact between the animals. Control groups included rats raised in social isolation and rats raised with peers with no exposure to frogs.

The experiment proceeded well until the rats were about 50 days of age. Up until that time the two species interacted and were frequently observed to sit side by side on the platform in the bathtub. However, when the rats were 50 days of age a frog skeleton was discovered on the platform and from that time on the frogs stayed in the water. After that point, "Rats began to patrol the edge of the platform in an effort to snare passing frogs, and they became so skillful that replacement frogs were quickly captured and devoured. (One rat drowned, apparently from falling off of the platform while trying to catch a frog)" (Johnson et al., 1970a). The frogs living in the cage with the rats did not fare much better. Up until 52 days of age, the rats and frogs interacted well. After that age, however, the rats were seen to chase the frogs around the water, ultimately killing them. Replacement frogs were also quickly killed. After the rats were 75 days of age the experimenters stopped replacing the frogs and the animals in those two experimental groups had no further contact with frogs until the testing session when they were 95 days of age.

None of the conditions of this experiment in which frogs and rats were

Table 3
Results of Arena Tests with Frogs

Rearing condition	Proportion of killers %
Total social isolation	80.0
Raised with peers	49.1
Group A: raised with peers and with frogs on platform	80.0
Group B: raised with peers and with frogs in large cages	100.0
Group C: raised with peers and frogs with frogs protected	76.9
Group D: isolated rats raised with protected frogs	94.1

Adapted from R. N. Johnson, M. J. DeSisto, & A. B. Koenig, Social and developmental experience and interspecific aggression in rats. *Journal of Comparative and Physiological Psychology*, 1972, *79*, 239. Copyright by the American Psychological Association. Reprinted by permission.

reared together decreased the tendency of the rats to prey on the frogs. In fact, the following table shows that early association with frogs increased the amount of killing. The difference between the group raised with peers with frogs protected and the group raised without exposure to frogs was significant at the 0.01 level of confidence.

It can be concluded from many experiments that early prolonged exposure to the stimulus complex of the prey can be a force in the inhibition of predatory aggression. However, it appears that some genetically determined predatory tendencies are too potent to be inhibited by early experience with the prey.

Additional Experiential Factors in Predation
The role of experience with objects of prey is somewhat more complex than is indicated by the early experience studies cited. A more recent study by Paul et al. (1973) has shown that the effect of experience with prey on predatory tendencies depends on the intrinsic stimulus properties of the prey object, the aggressive history of the subject and the subject's state of arousal during the inhibitory experience. Naive rats are unlikely to kill rat pups. However, if rats are given considerable experience in mouse killing and then presented with a rat pup, they are quite likely to kill it *unless* they were exposed to rat pups before the mouse-killing experience. A generalized tendency not to kill either mice or rat pups can be induced by providing the rat with exposure to rat pups, but the development of that inhibition depends on the arousal state of the subject during the exposure period. The generalized tendency not to kill occurs only if the rat is satiated at the time of exposure. If the animal is hungry during the exposure, mouse killing is not significantly inhibited.

Summary of Predatory Aggression

Predatory aggression can be defined by the following characteristics. It is elicited by the relatively narrow range of stimuli that constitute the animal's natural prey object. No other factor in the environment is relevant to this response as long as a competing motivational state is not activated. The topography of the predatory response is species-specific but in general is quiet and efficient and involves very little affective display. There is generally no differentiation between the sexes in regard to predatory aggression. The opportunity to kill prey animals has been shown to support several different kinds of learning and can therefore be considered reinforcing. Predation is inhibited by fear. It is not dependent on hunger but natural tendencies to kill can be enhanced by food deprivation. Predatory tendencies can be reduced by repeated killing responses that occur during a short period. However, recovery takes place a short time later. Nonkilling experience with prey may reduce the predatory tendencies, but the role of experience in the inhibition of predation is a complex one.

Although some of the preceding factors may overlap with other kinds of aggression, this particular constellation of characteristics is unique to predatory aggression.

Inter-Male Aggression

From mouse to man, with few exceptions, the male of the species is more aggressive than the female[2] and the most frequent target of that hostility is a male conspecific to which the attacker has not become habituated. Inter-male aggression is unique and can be differentiated from other types of hostile behavior on the basis of the kinds of stimuli that elicit it, the stimuli that inhibit it, the species-specific topography, and its particular physiological basis.

Although there are particular situations in which the female can display intense and effective aggression (in the defense of the young, for example), in most day-to-day encounters among animals it is the male that shows the highest and most consistent level of spontaneous aggression. Calhoun (1962), in his extensive study of a rat colony under seminatural conditions, came to the conclusion that males actively "seek" competitive situations. He based this conclusion on the observation that the number of male-male conflicts was far beyond what could be ex-

---

[2] Exceptions to this general rule include hamsters and gibbons. When hamsters are tested in pairs in a neutral area, considerable agonistic behavior occurs with overt fighting in about half the cases. However, no sex differences are discernible (Payne & Swanson, 1970). After extensive field observations, Carpenter (1940) has concluded that male and female gibbons are generally equally dominant and aggressive.

pected on the basis of chance encounters. The number of conflicts between two females, however, was within the range of chance interactions, and the agonistic contacts between pairs of males and females was so low that Calhoun concluded that the sexes tend to avoid conflict with one another. A number of other investigators have arrived at similar conclusions (Barnett, 1963; Seward, 1945a).

It has been repeatedly shown that pairs of male mice placed together in a neutral environment promptly engage in fighting, and if the animals are relatively well matched, the fight may be intense and result in wounding. Fredericson (1949) found that spontaneous fighting between ten pairs of male mice occurred in 100 percent of the time in over 13 trials. However, when females were tested in the same apparatus under the same conditions, only one pair of mice manifested spontaneous aggression (Fredericson, 1952). In an attempt to develop an aggressive strain of mouse, Lagerspetz (1964) found so little spontaneous fighting among females that it was necessary to do her selective breeding entirely on the basis of the behavior of the males. The tendency for pairs of male mice to fight is so strong and so consistent that it has frequently been used as a dependent variable in the testing of drug effects on aggression (Valzelli, 1967).

In most of the species that have been studied it has been found that the male is the more aggressive sex. Among the Pacific pilot whales (*Globicephala scammoni*) the young males are described as tattered with scars, both new and healing, and there appears to be good evidence that the wounds result from attacks by older males. Bull sperm whales fight by grappling with their jaws and these fights reach such intensity that they result in broken, dislocated, or twisted jaws (Norris, 1967).

Under certain conditions, such as the crowding that results during high tide on a narrow beach, aggression among male elephant seals may reach such dramatic proportions that the whole social structure is disrupted, with resulting chaos (Bartholomew, 1967). Matthews (1964) describes the aggressive social interactions of the hippopotamus, deer, musk-ox, seals, walruses, wolves, and a variety of Australian marsupials; in each case he attributes the bulk of the aggressive behavior to the males.

Among nonhuman primates most of the aggressive behavior that does occur is manifest by males. For example, Thompson (1967) studied fascicularis macaques and observed dyadic encounters within and between sexes in a laboratory situation and reports that the principal interaction between pairs of males consisted of biting or rough handling of one male by the other. Pairs of females manifested almost no aggressive behavior, but spent their time in grooming and inspecting one another. In male-female pairs the males initiated most of the social interactions, which involved mounting, grooming, and anogenital inspection with relatively little hostile behavior.

Although there are some species differences, the naturalistic observations of a variety of nonhuman primates tends to support the laboratory findings that indicate that intraspecific aggression is displayed more by the males than by the females (Kummer, 1968; Chance & Jolly, 1970; Carpenter, 1964). A number of additional studies are cited in Gray (1971).

Humans are no exception to this general zoological principle. Although hostile behavior is by no means the exclusive province of the male, he is the primary perpetrator of violent crimes. One of the major findings of the National Commission on the Causes and Prevention of Violence (1969) is stated in unequivocal terms, "Violent crime in the city is overwhelmingly committed by males." In 1968, for example, the homicide rate in the United States was five times higher for males than it was for females and the rate for robbery was 20 times higher.

It has been suggested that the trait that has the greatest statistical significance in differentiating criminals from noncriminals is that of sex status (Cressey, 1961). Broom and Selznick (1957, p. 639) summarize the particular propensity of the male for all types of criminal behavior as follows: "Compared with females, males have a great excess of crimes in all nations, all communities within nations, all age groups, all periods of history for which we have statistics and all types of crime except those related to the female sex, such as abortion."[3]

Although actual fighting does not generally occur until endocrine maturation takes place, the males in some species seem to have an early predisposition to rough-and-tumble play that simulates adult aggressive behavior. Among chimpanzees and baboons males spend considerably more time engaging in aggressive play than do females (Hamburg, 1971a). Infant male rhesus monkeys wrestle and roll and engage in sham biting significantly more than do females, and from 2½ months of age, males show more threat responses than do females. These results were obtained during the study of infant monkeys raised with inanimate surrogate mothers who could hardly transmit cultural differences to the young (Harlow, 1965a). Sexual dimorphism in regard to frequency of threat, rough-and-tumble play, and chasing play in the infant rhesus has also been confirmed by Goy (1968); it seems unlikely that this difference between the sexes is due to blood levels of testosterone since that hormone is undetectable in the blood at that age (Resko, 1967). Furthermore, these sex differences are maintained even though the males are castrated at 3 to 4 months of age (Goy, 1966). Field studies have also confirmed the tendency for the young male monkey (old world) to engage in the rough-and-tumble play (DeVore, 1965).

Human children also show sex differences in aggressive tendencies at

[3] In man, of course, there are potent social and environmental influences on the aggressive behavior displayed by the males, but the sex differences are clear.

a very early age. Large amounts of data have been collected in various parts of the United States on the amount and kinds of aggression displayed in relatively standardized doll play situations and there is a clear distinction between the sexes on these variables as early as the age of 3. Boys spend more time in aggressive play than do girls and the type of aggression shown by boys tends to be more vigorous, destructive, and hurtful than that shown by the girls (Sears, 1965). Careful observation of nursery school children reveals that boys more frequently engage in mock hostile play than do girls. This activity involves rough contact with considerable running, chasing, jumping up and down, and laughing (Blurton, 1969). Preschool boys manifest more physical aggression than do girls (McIntyre, 1972). It has also been reported that boys up to the age of 6 or 7 in a Melanesian society show much more rough-and-tumble play than do girls (Davenport, 1965).

Response Topography in Inter-Male Aggression

A number of authors have emphasized the stereotyped ritualized nature of fights between male conspecifics (Lorenz, 1964; Eibl-Eibesfeldt, 1967, 1970; Fox, 1969b; Ardrey, 1966). The behaviors displayed by fighting males are characteristic of the species and differ considerably from aggressive behavior involved in the capture of prey or defense against predators.

The response sequences characteristic of intermale aggression have been referred to as fixed action patterns, and although there is some increase in the precision of the movements and an increase in coordination with practice, there is little evidence that these response sequences are learned. Eibl-Eibesfeldt (1961a) raised male, wild Norway rats in isolation so they would not have an opportunity to learn fighting responses through social interactions. After adulthood the isolates were matched with strange, socially reared males and fighting ensued almost immediately. Eibl-Eibesfeldt reports, "The patterns of display, tussling and biting were essentially the same in the case of the inexperienced rats as in the case of those who had been brought up with other rats and were faced by an outsider. The steps in the ritual are apparently innate and fixed behavior patterns; many of the movements seem to be available to each rat like tools in a toolkit." Other investigators have also shown that learning is not essential to the manifestation of aggressive responses (Scott, 1942; Lagerspetz & Talo, 1967; Poole, 1966).

Among canids attack is frequently directed against the hackle or scruff of the neck, and this particular response tendency occurs even though the animals have been visually deprived as pups (Fox, 1969b).

The pattern of aggressive responses in the rat has been studied by a number of investigators (Calhoun, 1962; Grant, 1963; Eibl-Eibesfeldt,

1961b; Barnett, 1963, 1969). One of the best descriptions of this response topography is given by Barnett (also see most recent edition Barnett, 1975). After describing the threat posture he says,

> The next stage is that of *leaping* and *biting*. This can be followed in detail only by means of high speed filming. The attacker springs in the air and comes down on his opponent, repeatedly striking him by rapidly adducting his extended forelimbs; he also bites usually an ear or limb or the tail, less often the skin of the face, rump or belly. Typically a bite is exceedingly brief; as soon as the jaws close they open again and the rat leaps back. Rarely very aggressive *norvegicus* males bite and hold on. A leap and bite is followed as a rule by a second or two of violent movement on the part of both rats, toward the opponent on the part of the attacker, evasive on the part of the other rat, until both become disoriented. These brief bouts are followed by longer intervals in which both rats adopt a defensive attitude, or possibly a stance as if boxing. Functionally, biting is obviously a pain-causing stimulus likely to evoke flight in the animal attacked, if non-violent sign-stimuli have failed to do so.
>
> In many fights there is complete sequence of stereotyped actions, and this might suggest that the different motor components of the total pattern are related to each other in a specific way. However, tooth chattering, threat-posturing, leaping and biting may each occur independently of the others: There is no fixed chain or "hierarchical organization" of the components of fighting behavior in wild rats.[4]

The ritualistic aspect of inter-male aggression can also be readily seen in higher animals. An excellent description of the fighting topography in the baboon is given by Kummer:

> Fighting technique consists of each opponent aiming bites at the shoulder or neck of the other. Among hundreds of such scenes we have only seen a male actually take hold of another's coat on two occasions. The analysis of films shows that the animals fence rapidly with open jaws without really touching each other and that the heads are often held back. During a fight each opponent also hits out at the face of the other with his hand, usually missing here as well. The biting and hitting ritual goes on with tremendous speed for a few seconds, silently, the opponents facing each other. Then, one of them turns to flee. At this moment the other often snaps out at him, producing an occasional scratch on the anal region. The vigorous chasing, interrupted by some more fencing, usually lasts no longer than 10 seconds. Most fights come to an end when one opponent flees.[5]

The threat response is also a portion of the topography of inter-male aggression. Unless an opponent responds to threat with a submissive posture, a fight is likely to ensue. The threat of the squirrel monkey is

[4] S. A. Barnett, *A Study in Behavior*. London, Methuen, 1963, p. 87.
[5] H. Kummer, *Social Organization of Hamadryas Baboons: A Field Study*. Basel, Karger, 1968.

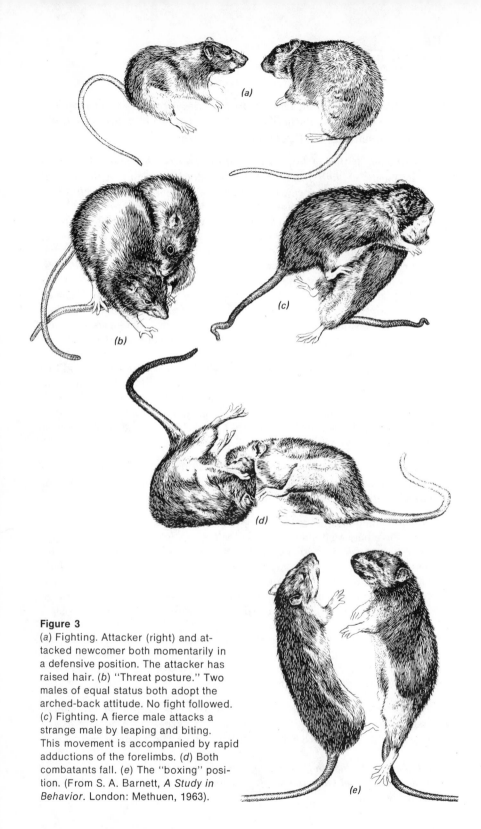

Figure 3
(a) Fighting. Attacker (right) and attacked newcomer both momentarily in
a defensive position. The attacker has
raised hair. (b) "Threat posture." Two
males of equal status both adopt the
arched-back attitude. No fight followed.
(c) Fighting. A fierce male attacks a
strange male by leaping and biting.
This movement is accompanied by rapid
adductions of the forelimbs. (d) Both
combatants fall. (e) The "boxing" position. (From S. A. Barnett, *A Study in
Behavior*. London: Methuen, 1963).

particularly easy to observe and consists of a genital display in which one monkey approaches another and bends over it, making penile thrusts toward the second animal (Candland et al., 1970; Ploog, 1967). Candland et al. have produced one of the few studies on an autonomic component of inter-male engagements. As inter-male encounters result in a status hierarchy, the results show that heart rate is related to status order in a curvilinear fashion, with the middle-ranking animals showing the lowest heart rate. A similar relationship has been found in the domestic chicken (Candland et al., 1969).

The behavior patterns displayed during inter-male aggression have now been studied in a number of species, including the mouse (Clark & Schein, 1966; Banks, 1962; Warne, 1947; Brown, 1953) the lemming (Allin & Banks, 1968) and the mink (MacLennon & Bailey, 1969). Much of this material has been summarized by Eibl-Eibesfeldt (1970, 1961a, 1967).

Minor Damage from Inter-Male Contests

One of the most remarkable characteristics of inter-male aggression is the relatively small amount of injury that occurs during fighting. In other kinds of aggression, the animal uses its available weapons as effectively as possible to dispatch the antagonist. As indicated, the terminal behavior in the predatory aggression sequence is the killing of the prey. Most typically, there is a bite directed at the cervical spine, which is both efficient and lethal. In contests between males, however, the fighting behaviors have evolved in such a way that the encounters result in a demonstrable superiority of one animal over the other with little physical damage. At a given stage in the conflict one of the animals may flee and his opponent is unlikely to pursue for any distance, or the defeated animal may assume a posture that results in the inhibition of aggression on the part of the victor. In other instances the attack is aimed at portions of the opponent's anatomy that have evolved in such a way as to minimize injury.

Fighting among male elephant seals, for example, is vigorous and intense. It is conducted with the large upper canine teeth, which have considerable potential for damage. The bulls are frequently wounded and the older, more dominant veterans of many encounters display a large number of wrinkled scars in the neck region, where the attacks are directed. However, the elephant seal is well equipped by tough skin and fat pads to take a great deal of punishment in that part of the body (Matthews, 1964).

The agonistic behavior between males of the same species is highly ritualized and stereotyped. Again the nature of the response is such that the possibility of serious wounding is minimized. Among fallow deer (*Dama dama*), rival stags engage in vigorous fighting. Their encounters consist of headlong charges against one another. However, they charge only when facing, with the result that the contact is antler to antler. An attack is never directed against the more vulnerable parts of the body. Fighting among male giraffes is common. They engage in neck-to-neck pushing matches or they swing their heads against the opponent's body or legs. They do not, however, attack with their sharp and dangerous hooves, which are reserved for defense against predators. The oryx and other antelopes may have extremely sharp horns for use in interspecific defense. In intraspecific interactions they are used only to lock the heads of the animals together during inter-male pushing contests (Cloudsley-Thompson, 1965).

Another aspect of the hostile interactions among male conspecifics that tends to minimize serious injury is the role of learning. After a limited number of agonistic contacts between a given pair of animals a dominance-submission relationship is set up between them. When this is accomplished the probability of actual fighting is diminished because the more submissive animal has learned to respond to anticipatory aggressive responses (threat behavior) with submission or escape, which terminates the encounter. Thus the threat gestures functionally replace actual fighting.

In spite of the several safeguards that have evolved to minimize serious consequences from intraspecific conflict, "fractricidal accidents" do occasionally occur and some animals are badly wounded. Pederson (1962, quoted in Matthews, 1964) reports that a bull musk-ox is sometimes killed as a result of fractures in the frontal part of the skull received during an inter-male head-butting match. Bull elephants have been killed as a result of a tusk stab by a rival. Defeated hippos have died from heart penetration by the tooth of another male (Cloudsley-Thompson, 1965). In the fights between seals an eye may be burst or knocked out, and rarely an animal is killed (Bartholomew, 1967). Fights between male gibbons sometimes result in serious wounds, including broken bones (Carpenter, 1940). All these examples, however, are the exception rather than the rule.

Stimulus Situations Eliciting Inter-Male Aggression

Although males are more aggressive in many situations, a strange male conspecific constitutes a unique aggression-eliciting stimulus complex in a large number of animal species (Aberts & Galef, 1973). One male may attack another male but interact peaceably with other animals or humans. Gibbons will feed in the same general area with macaques and langurs without conflict but will not tolerate the approach of other male gibbons (Carpenter, 1940). The Mongolian gerbil makes an excellent pet because its reactions to humans is gentle and without hostility (Ginsburg & Braud, 1971). However, if two strange males are placed together in a cage, blood will be drawn in a few minutes, and when there is no escape, one of them may be killed. According to Matthews (1964) the barred bandicoot (*Perameles*), a marsupial from South Australia, becomes very tame and gentle toward humans during captivity but is desperately pugnacious among its own kind.

It is relatively rare that females of any species elicit aggression from the male. Barnett (1963) indicates that even when strange rats intrude on an established colony, it is the mature males and not the females or juveniles that are attacked by the residents. Under conditions of high population density, the amount of fighting among mice increases significantly. Some of the more dominant mice roam about the area, attacking other colony members without provocation. Once again, however, females and immature mice are ignored (Lloyd & Christian, 1967). In a fighting situation male mice attack males more frequently and longer than do females (Lee, 1970).

The Role of Olfaction in Inter-Male Aggression

The role of odors in releasing or eliciting particular behaviors is well established. Chemically complex substances (pheromones) are produced in specialized body organs by one member of a species and function as a powerful determinant of behavior by other members, which has survival value for the species.

It has been determined recently that the sexual status of higher organisms is communicated by pheromones and that the tendencies to sexual behavior are controlled in part by these chemical substances. Further, the pheromone production can be manipulated by altering the endocrine status of the animal. Free-ranging rhesus monkeys display a distinct seasonal rhythm. During the nonbreeding season the males can be returned to a sexually activated state by exposing them to females that have been brought into estrus by the administration of estradiol benzoate (Vandenbergh, 1969). Male rhesus monkeys show no interest in females that have been given estrogen as long as the males are maintained in an anosmic state by nasal olfactory plugs of treated gauze. When olfaction is restored, however, they will work persistently (press a lever 250 times) in order to obtain access to the female (Michael & Keverne, 1968). This persistent approach behavior by the male can be reduced by administering progesterone to the female. On the basis of these and other experiments, Michael and Keverne postulated a pheromone produced by the female that communicated her endocrine status to the male. In 1971 they chemically identified the substance and demonstrated that it was contained in the vaginal secretions of the female (Michael et al., 1971).

Since certain aggressive behaviors are sexually specific and since sexual status has been shown to be communicated chemically, it appears reasonable to suspect that aggression may in part be under the control of olfactorily acting pheromones. Tollman and King (1956) suggested this possibility to explain the sex differences in aggression among mice. The role of olfaction in inter-male aggression in this species was confirmed in an experiment by Ropartz (1967, 1968). He found a statistically significant increase in latency of attack and a reduction in the mean number of attacks when the male mice were scented with French perfume and placed in a fighting situation. When he removed the olfactory bulbs from mice that had fought earlier, aggression was completely eliminated. When these same bulbectomized mice were subject to attack by a highly trained fighter mouse, they did not even show defensive aggression. They either fled or adopted a submissive posture. (Also see Richardson & Scudder, 1970.) More recently it was shown that male mice trained to be aggressive manifested significantly less tendency to attack male conspecifics treated with the spray deodorant Man Power than they did nondeodorized controls (Lee, 1970; Lee & Brake, 1971). The normally intense fighting between male hamsters is also eliminated along with other social behaviors by olfactory bulb lesions (Murphy & Schneider, 1970).

Pheromones and Sex Differences in Aggression in the Mouse
A well-conceived series of experiments has now demonstrated that inter-male aggressive behavior in mice is under the control of a pheromone, and although it has not as yet been chemically identified, a physiological source has been located. Mice that have habituated to one another and thus do not fight will do so when placed in a strange cage if that cage has been soiled by strange mice (Archer, 1968). This finding was substantiated more recently by Mugford (1973), who showed that male fighter mice manifested more aggression toward castrated opponents in home cages of either single or stable groups of male mice than they did in clean cages. He also found that odors deposited by either single or groups of female mice greatly reduced fighting. If an established mouse whose presence does not elicit fighting is rubbed with the perineal region of a strange mouse, it will once again elicit attack responses from companion mice. However, the amount of aggressive behavior between two strange mice is reduced if one of them is rubbed with the perineal region of a mouse already known to the other (Mackintosh & Grant, 1966). Ropartz (1967) showed that the behavior of male mice is affected by the odor of the urine from other mice but not by that from the excrements. The general activity of these animals as measured by photoelectric cells increased when they were exposed to the urine odor.

The preceding findings lead Mugford and Nowell (1970a) to postulate that the transport mechanism for the aggression-eliciting cues was through the urine. Their hypothesis was confirmed by an experiment in which they applied the urine of mice of different sex, endocrine, and dominance status to the coat of castrated male mice. The results of that experiment are listed in Table 4 and can be summarized as follows. Castrated male mice treated with water elicit only a modest amount of attack behavior from an intact isolated male mouse. However, if the castrated male is wet with the urine of a mouse that has previously been shown to be an aggressive and dominant animal, the amount of elicited aggression is significantly increased. Wetting the castrate victim mouse with the urine of an intact but submissive mouse results in an attack by the aggressor mouse that is of an intensity between the experimental conditions cited. It is further interesting to note that a castrate mouse wet with the urine of a female mouse is essentially protected from attack. The amount of aggression is significantly less than under all other experimental conditions. Dixon and Mackintosh (1971) also showed that the level of aggression between intact, strange male mice is significantly reduced if one of the partners is rubbed with the urine of an adult female. (Also see Connor, 1972.)

Table 4

Mean Scores of Test Isolate Mice on Four Measures of Aggression, When Their Opponents Were Given Different Urine/Water Treatments

	Source of urine applied to standard castrate opponents				
	Aggres-sive	Sub-missive	Castrate	Water	Female
Latency measure					
Mean test session score with treatment	87.2	93.0	109.0	108.6	149.5
Mean change in score following treatment	−30.7*	−11.6	+2.5	11.1	+55.9*
Accumulated attack score					
Mean test session score with treatment	18.1	19.6	14.8	13.4	6.7
Mean change in score following treatment	+3.6	+1.6	−1.04	−1.8	−10.9*
Bites score					
Mean test session score with treatment	10.0	9.9	8.4	6.4	3.3
Mean change in score following treatment	+2.4†	+1.0	−0.4	−0.7	−5.8†
Number of fights out of 25					
Number with treatment	20	16	15	13	12
Change in number following treatment	+4	+1	−4	−4	−9

After R. A. Mugford & N. W. Nowell, Pheromones and their effect on aggression in mice, *Nature,* 1970, *226,* 967.

* $p < 0.025$; † $p < 0.05$. (Probability values [one-tailed] derived from analysis by the Wilcoxon sign test for correlated samples.)

It can be concluded from these studies that the urine of an intact male mouse contains an endocrine-dependent pheromone that elicits attack from another male. Dominant males evidently produce larger amounts of this pheromone than do submissive animals and the urine of females contains a pheromone that has an inhibitory effect on male aggression. The pheromone is endocrine dependent in the sense that the organ of secretion is under the control of some endocrine mechanism.

Hormonal Control of Aggression-Related Pheromones in Mice
Further experimentation has provided additional information on the endocrine basis for these aggression-eliciting and aggression-inhibiting pheromones. The female's protection from aggression by the male is dependent on some factor produced by the ovaries because the urine from spayed females contains no antiaggression pheromone and does not inhibit attack by aggressive males. However, the production of this pheromone is evidently not dependent on the particular phase of the menstrual cycle because the urine from estrous and diestrous mice contain similar amounts of antiaggression substances. Although it is not yet known which ovarian hormone is responsible for the aggression-inhibiting pheromone, it is clear that estrogen is not responsible. Urine from spayed donor females that have been given high doses of estrogen applied to victim mice significantly increases the tendencies for aggressive males to attack them (Mugford & Nowell, 1971a). Although the ovaries evidently contribute to the production of an antiaggression pheromone, they are not the only source of aggression-inhibiting cues provided by the female. Males show no more tendency to attack an ovariectomized female than they do a normal one (Mugford & Nowell, 1971c).

Testosterone appears to be the hormonal agent responsible for the production of the aggression-eliciting pheromone. As indicated, the amount of this pheromone is reduced by the castration of male mice, and Lee and Brake (1971) have shown that intact male mice are more aggressive toward sham-operated males than toward castrated males and toward castrate males injected with testosterone (Lee & Brake, 1972). Female mice, either spayed or intact, injected with testosterone propionate, are attacked by aggressive males significantly more than are control-injected animals. However, the pheromonal substance is apparently released from androgen-dependent tissue rather than being an excreted androgen metabolite because there is a delay of ten days between the beginning of the testostrone injection and the maximal effect (Mugford & Nowell, 1970b, 1972).

Anatomical Origin of Aggression-Related Pheromones
At least one of these androgen-dependent pheromone-producing tissues has been identified. The preputial glands, located in the prepuce or penile

foreskin, are modified sebaceous glands. These glands are heavier in dominant than in subordinate male mice (Bronson & Marsden, 1973). If the glands are removed from one of a pair of male fighters, the amount of fighting is increased, with the attacks being initiated by the operated animal (McKinney & Christian, 1970). This finding is interpreted as being due to the lack of the aggression-elicited pheromone in the operated animal and its increased sensitivity to that odor. There is evidence that the preputial glands atrophy after castration and, as previously indicated, urine from castrated males applied to the coats of other castrates results in only moderate attack from aggressive opponents.

In the female mouse the preputial glands are referred to as clitoral glands and are vestigial. However, they are highly sensitive to testosterone propionate in that they will manifest a fivefold increase in size during a series of androgen injections. The aggression of males toward testosterone-injected females is decreased but not eliminated by the removal of the preputial glands (Mugford & Nowell, 1971b). [Although androgenized females elicit attack from males, they are not themselves aggressive (Tolman & King, 1956), which may account for the Mugford and Nowell (1971b) results and that of McKinney and Christian (1970).]

The tendency, although reduced, for males to attack androgenized preputilectomized female mice must indicate that there is some other source for the aggression-eliciting pheromone, and there may, of course, be more than one. Grant and Mackintosh (1963) have suggested that a gland under the chin may have that function, since prefighting behavior in mice frequently involves sniffing of that area. However, there also appears to be an androgen-sensitive tissue other than the preputial glands that release the substance into the urine because males attack other castrate males that have been coated with the urine of testosterone-injected females even though the preputial glands of these females have been excised (Mugford & Nowell, 1971b).

Further Influence of Odors on Aggression

The influence of odors on inter-male aggression in mice has been considered here in some detail because that species has been most intensively studied and that research can serve as a model for the investigation of pheromonal phenomena in other species. There can be no doubt that odor influences behavior in general and aggressive behavior in particular in many species. Although the details have not yet been worked out, it would appear likely that many of the inter-male encounters previously described are based on reactions to pheromones that are dependent on the sexual and endocrine status of the animals in conflict.

There is also evidence that aggression among males is enhanced by odors not characteristic of the males themselves. The amount of fighting in an established colony of rats is significantly greater (on the order of

twice as much) during the breeding season than during the winter months
(Calhoun, 1962) and there is a great deal of fighting with a high mortality
rate in artificial colonies of wild rats of mixed sex. In all-male colonies,
however, fighting is relatively rare and when it occurs it is mild. This appears to be accounted for, at least in part, by the increased tendency for
males to fight in the presence of the odor of estrus females. Males tend to
be attracted to a female in estrus and to localities where she leaves her
scent. That increases the contact rate among the males and that contact is
likely to be hostile (Barnett, 1967a, 1967b; Barnett et al., 1968). (Eisenberg, 1962, reports similar findings in mice.)

Careful study by Barnett (1963) has shown that although the males
fight in the presence of an estrus female, they do not fight over the female.
He described a typical example in which males that normally lived
peaceably together engaged in fighting only after a female in proestrus
had withdrawn from the scene and entered a next box. Barnett concludes
that the presence of the female in some way lowers the threshold for
fighting among males. It seems likely that this is due to an aggression-
promoting pheromone produced by the estrus female, although evidence
specific to that hypothesis is not yet available.

The Role of Vision in Inter-Male Aggression

Specific visual stimuli function to release aggressive behavior in certain
submammalian species. An English robin attacks a tuft of red feathers
whether those feathers are attached to the breast of a real robin or not
(Lack, 1943), and the male stickleback responds aggressively to the
crudest model of another stickleback as long as it has the releasing
stimulus of the red underbelly (Tinbergen, 1948). (For a detailed discussion of the role of stimuli in the release of fixed action patterns in lower
animals, see Hinde, 1966.)

Although mammals do, in certain circumstances, appear to respond to
threat responses with counterthreat, there is as yet little experimental
evidence relating to visual releasers of aggression such as are found in
species lower on the phylogenetic scale. Movement, however, may be a
contributing visual stimulus. It appears that the attention of an aggressive
mouse can be directed toward a victim by movement, and Calhoun
(1956) and Lagerspetz (1964) both suggest that motion per se appears
to be a stimulus initiating attack in that species. A similar conclusion may
be derived from studies on the rat, guinea pig, and hamster (Alberts &
Galef, 1973; Calhoun, 1962; Grant & Mackintosh, 1963). It may be that
freezing is an effective method of inhibiting attack because movement is
an important component of aggression-releasing stimuli.

Although visual signals are not prepotent in the activation of aggression
in the animal receiving the signal, there are visual signs that play a role
in the termination of inter-male aggressive interactions. Male golden

hamsters have a black marking on the chest that is a morphological sign stimulus indicating aggressive propensities. This marking tends to be displayed when the animal assumes an offensive stance and is covered by the lighter forearms during defensive postures. The dark chest markings, when exposed, precipitate flight in other male hamsters and the strength of the flight tendency is related to the size of the black marking on the opponent. If the marking is intensified and extended with black hair dye, the dyed animal is significantly more likely to win in inter-male encounters because his opponent is more likely to flee. The marked animal also shows more aggressive behavior than its opponent, which may be due to the aggression-elicited flight behavior displayed by the victim (Grant et al., 1970).

Stimulus Situation Inhibiting Inter-Male Aggression

Inter-male aggression is unique in that it can be blocked or inhibited by specific, generally species-specific stimulus input. The defeated animal successfully avoids serious injury by engaging in particular ritualized behaviors that function to prevent further attack by the superior contestant. These behaviors have been referred to as submissive (Matthews, 1964) or appeasement (Lorenz, 1966) responses. Schenkel (1967) has characterized "active submission" in the wolf and dog as "impulses and effort of the inferior toward the friendly harmonic social integration," or as a request for "love" from the superior animal. It is important to recognize that one need not project such complex cognitive-affective mental states onto animals in order to recognize that a particular behavior in one animal has a high probability of eliciting a particular behavior on the part of a responding animal. The terms *submission, appeasement, love,* and so on, are descriptive of mental states recognizable by humans. They may, of course, have nothing at all to do with the mental states (if any) that are concurrent in animals behaving in the manner described as submissive, appeasing, and so on.

Although the intent and the derivation of these ritualized aggression-inhibiting responses have been variously interpreted, there can be little doubt that active, ongoing inter-male aggression can be immediately blocked by the assumption of a particular stance or posture by the defeated animal. The ethological literature is replete with examples (Darwin, 1896; Eibl-Eibesfeldt, 1961a, 1970; Cloudsley Thompson, 1965; Lorenz, 1966). Lorenz (1966) devotes an entire chapter ("Behavioral Analogies to Morality") to descriptions of various aggression-inhibiting signals. The wolf, it is said, turns its head away from its opponent and offers the jugular vein, which immediately inhibits further aggression from its rival. Or when the fight is clearly lost, the weaker wolf throws itself on its back, exposing all the vulnerable parts of the body to the victor, who "cannot" then follow up his advantage (Matthews, 1964).

Detailed observations on the mouse indicate that the defeated animal "sits on its rump and rears without displaying the aggressive face." The posture is accompanied by vocalization. The submissive animal does not attempt to bite the attacker, but may push it away with the front feet. This posture reduces the aggressiveness of the attacker. If the defeated mouse attempts to flee, the victor follows for some distance in hot pursuit, with the result that the fleeing mouse is frequently bitten on the rump (Brain & Nowell, 1970a). Brain and Nowell also indicate that the inhibition of aggression by posturing is found only in inter-male aggression. The submissive posture in several laboratory animals is described by Grant and Mackintosh (1963). Grant (1963) constructed ethograms of the social behavior of the rat and showed that the submissive posture occurs as a response much more frequently than it is responded to. The opposing animal most frequently reacts to submission by refraining from further social behavior and by moving away from the social interaction. Aggression-inhibiting postures have also been described in detail by Barnett (1963) and Seward (1945a).

In the rat, and evidently in other rodents, the submissive posture is accompanied by a particular pattern of ultrasounds. Long pulses up to 3400 msec duration at about 25 kHz appear to occur during the long exhalations of submissive animals. Aggressive behavior is reduced in encounters where these particular ultrasounds were produced (Sales, 1972).

Although submissive postures are, in general, species-specific, it is likely that there are cross-species similarities. It has been shown, for example, that the hostile behavior of the Mongolian gerbil toward intruders of different species (rat or mouse) is inhibited if the intruding animal assumes a submissive posture (Ginsburg & Braud, 1971).

Submissive Behavior and the Principle of Antithesis

The submissive postures, in general, tend to be quite different from those displayed during threat or actual fighting, and it may be that there are few components in the submissive posture that elicit aggression. Darwin (1896), in developing his principle of antithesis in emotional expression, emphasized that gestures of greeting and gestures of affection present a stimulus pattern that is quite the opposite of the pattern presented during threat. In the anecdotal method of the times he presents some rather convincing examples. "When a dog approaches a strange dog or man in a savage or hostile frame of mind, he walks upright and very stiffly; his head is slightly raised, or not much lowered; the tail is held erect and quite rigid; the hairs bristle, especially along the neck and back; the pricked ears are directed forwards and the eyes have a fixed stare."

Darwin suggests that the demeanor of the friendly greeting dog is just the reverse of threat.

(a)

(b)

Figure 4
(a) Dog approaching another dog with hostile intentions. (b) The same in a humble
and affectionate frame of mind. (From C. Darwin, *The Expression of Emotions in
Man and Animals.* New York: D. Appleton, 1896.)

Instead of walking upright, the body sinks downward or even crouches, and
is thrown into flexous movements; his tail, instead of being held stiff and upright, is lowered and wagged from side to side; his hair instantly becomes
smooth; his ears are depressed and drawn backwards, but not closely to the
head; and his lips hang loosely. From the drawing back of the ears, the eye-

lids become elongated, and the eyes no longer appear round and staring. [See Figure 4.]

An analysis of many of the submissive postures manifest by mammals seems to indicate that, at least in a general way, Darwin's principle of antithesis appears to hold (Eisenberg, 1963). The animal that appears large in threat appears small in submission. The erect stance of threat is replaced by the supine posture of submission. The canines, which in many species are prominently displayed during threat, are hidden, covered, or turned away during gestures of appeasement.

Submissive Behavior as a Remotivating Display

However, it seems likely that more is involved in the act of submission than merely the absence of aggression-eliciting stimuli. Lorenz (1966) makes the salient point that in the aroused and "angry" animal there is considerable emotional momentum and that the shift from one motivational state to another tends to be gradual rather than abrupt. Thus it seems that the appeasement postures provoke direct response inhibition on the part of the attacking animal.

Nothing is known as yet about the neurological mechanisms underlying the aggression-inhibiting capacity of submissive postures. However, the descriptive literature available suggests the possibility that elements of the submissive pose function to activate neural systems that are incompatible with the neural system for intermale aggression. Morris (1964) has referred to the submissive gestures as "remotivating displays"; that is, the submissive posture elicits from the attacking animal a response that is incompatible with further attack behavior. He suggests that an important component in the display in many species is pseudoinfantile and pseudosexual behavior. The behavior of the submissive wolf is frequently identical to the food begging of a puppy. Or, as indicated previously, the wolf may roll on its back and remain still. Such behavior does expose the vulnerable belly, but perhaps more important, it constitutes a "ritualized presentation for cleaning of the anal region," as is common in puppies (Fox, 1969b). The submissive wolf may urinate, which elicits an actual cleaning response on the part of the dominating victorious animal (Eibl-Eibesfeldt, 1970).

A frequent component of submissive behavior in a number of subhuman primates involves sexual presentation. That is, the submissive animal turns and presents the hindquarters to the dominant animal (Kreveld, 1970; Chance & Jolly, 1970; Altman, 1962; Hall & DeVore, 1965). The presentation posture results in the elicitation of a perfunctory mounting response, which is incompatible with continued attack.

Aggression-inhibiting postures have not evolved in all species of animals. Neither the cotton rat (Bunnell & Smith, 1966) nor the dove (Lorenz, 1966), for example, seem to have developed such mechanisms; consequently, when escape is not possible, aggression may lead to the death of one of the animals. In general, however, in species in which efficient weapons of defense or of predation have evolved, there has been a parallel development of aggression-inhibiting mechanisms. The resultant value to the species is obvious in that intraspecific confrontations do not generally have serious or lethal consequences.

Stimulus Habituation as an Inhibitor of Inter-Male Aggression

It is well recognized that inter-male aggressive behavior is relatively rare in established colonies of animals in which there has been a prolonged interaction. Littermate mice raised together generally do not fight and it is only with difficulty that they can be induced to fight (Scott & Fredericson, 1951; Clark, 1962). The rate of hostile interactions is significantly lower for caged cotton rats (*Sigmodon hispidus*) if they are taken from naturally occurring organized populations than if the groups are composed of strangers (Wolfe, 1968). Male cats that have been adapted to one another almost never fight (Green et al., 1957). The same finding has been reported for the wild Norway rat (*Rattus norvegicus*) (Barnett, 1963; Galef, 1970a; Barnett, 1969). However, animals that have lived together without conflict readily attack a strange male conspecific. Further, if males are raised together and little or no fighting occurs during this time and if they are then separated for a period of time, intense fighting occurs when they are once again placed in the same cage (Clark, 1962).

Although there have been no well-controlled studies to confirm it, it has been conjectured that rats attack strangers but not colony members on the basis of the unique odor of the intruder (Barnett, 1963, 1969). The colony members appear to take on a distinctive odor that does not elicit aggressive tendencies on the part of other colony members. Novelty is one of the most important features in the elicitation of attack, as Galef (1970a) has shown. Littermates raised together become familiar with any aggression-eliciting odors of their cage mates during the prepubescent period prior to the development of aggressive tendencies, with the result that those odors do not elicit aggression when the fighting tendency has matured. This interpretation is somewhat different from that of Scott and Fredericson (1951), who hypothesize that the lack of fighting among familiar animals is due to a response inhibition. That is, the animal learns a habit of not fighting because it has not fought. Scott suggests further that such an animal could be trained to fight, but it would be anticipated that even after training, the fighting would be somewhat less severe. Such an explanation would predict that animals in a peaceful colony would not attack noncolony members. That, as indicated previously, does not appear to be the case. Galef (1970a) says, "The response to intruders by members of the established colony is also well established. These intruders, who are identical in every respect except for their familiarity to colony members, are almost invariably the recipients of savage attacks."

The techniques used by Mugford and Nowell (p. 160) would be useful in isolating the role of habituation to odors as a limiting factor in inter-male aggression.

Reinforcing Properties of Inter-Male Aggression

There are several lines of evidence to indicate that the opportunity to engage in inter-male aggression may be positively reinforcing to the participants. The opportunity for one male to attack another will suffice to support the learning of new response patterns. Male mice trained as fighters using the "dangling" procedure of Scott (1958) learned a position response in a T-maze when the only reinforcer used was the opportunity to attack a "victim" mouse. When the reinforcer was withdrawn, the response extinguished and the position response was reversed when the victim mouse was moved to the opposite side of the T (Tellegen et al., 1969).

It has also been shown that trained fighters run faster in a runway if the running behavior results in a 5-second opportunity to attack a victim mouse. The starting latency for these animals is shorter than that of controls; they acquire the running response in fewer days and take longer to extinguish than do control subjects (Legrand, 1970). Further, Fredericson (1949, 1951) showed many years ago that the latency for "spontaneous" fighting between male mice decreased over days when they were permitted to fight once a day. If a fight between mice is interrupted, the victorious mouse will push open a door and run from one compartment to another to get at its opponent, as will one of a pair of evenly matched mice. The only reward for this behavior is the opportunity to continue the fight. The latency of this response is significantly shorter than that of either defeated mice or mice not involved in an aggressive incident (Lagerspetz, 1964). If a fight immediately precedes a trial, aggressive mice will also cross an electrified grid to get at a defeated opponent. Again there is no reward available except the opportunity to fight (Lagerspetz, 1964).

Inter-male aggression has been produced in primates, *M. mulatta*, by direct hypothalamic stimulation. It appeared to be a relatively clear-cut inter-male type because the stimulated animal when confined to a primate chair made no attempt to attack the experimenter. When in a colony situation, the brain stimulation resulted in an attack on another male, but a female also present in the cage was not subjected to attack. In at least some sites in which the stimulation resulted in aggression, the animal would self-stimulate, implying that stimulation, if not positive, could hardly be defined as aversive (Robinson et al., 1969).

Interactions of Inter-Male Aggression with Other Behavior Tendencies Although there does seem to be some relationship between predatory aggression and eating tendencies (p. 146), no such relationship appears to exist between that response tendency and inter-male aggression. Mice that have been deprived of either food or water do not show an increase in intermale fighting (Ginsburg & Allee, 1942). Hungry mice fight over food, but the amount of fighting produced appears to be less than that which occurs in spontaneous inter-male encounters (Fredericson, 1950; Fredericson et al., 1955). The activity is directed at the acquisition of the food and not at the competing animal, as is found in inter-male fights, indicating that the response topography is different. Further, females show this competitive type of fighting, but rarely fight "spontaneously" (Fredericson, 1952).

There is a relationship between the tendencies to inter-male aggression and the tendencies to sexual behavior. Both of these behavior tendencies depend in part on an intact gonadal endocrine system (see Chapter 8).

Neither tendency appears in the male until gonadal maturity occurs. Aggressive reactions among members of a given species are determined in part by the sexual status of the individuals involved. In mice, at least, the sexes produce different odors that elicit or inhibit aggression from a male.

In most species inter-male aggression is increased during the breeding season (Cloudsley-Thompson, 1965). The relationship between inter-male aggressive behavior and the sexual status of females has already been discussed.

Sexual satiation has no effect on aggressive tendencies in the mouse (Lagerspetz, 1964; Gustafson & Winokur, 1960) or in the rat (Hall & Klein, 1942), although it has been reported that a temporary reduction in aggressive behavior between cats resulted from sexual experience (Gantt, 1950). Naive male mice that have initial contact with a female tend to react with mounting tendencies when placed with a male. If the initial experience is with a male, they show a tendency to attack when placed with a female. However, these differences disappear when the mouse has had adequate experience with both sexes (Lagerspetz, 1964).

Although there is little direct evidence on the problem, there is some suggestion that stimuli that produce fear reactions tend to inhibit inter-male aggressive behaviors. Animals that have been selectively bred for "timidity" or "fearfulness" manifest significantly less aggressive behavior in a male-male interaction than those selected for "nonemotionality or fearlessness" (Hall & Klein, 1942).[6] Similar findings have been reported for the mouse (Lagerspetz, 1964). Davis (1933) reports that a rat in its

[6] Timidity, fearfulness, or emotionality were operationally defined as the rat's tendency to limit activity and to defecate in a large open field.

home cage is more likely to attack a strange rat than when it is a visitor in the stranger's cage. He suggests that this may be due to the fact that the novel stimuli of the strange cage activate the neural system for fear, which is incompatible with the neural system for inter-male aggression (p. 9).

Jones and Nowell (1973) systematically studied the amount of aggressive behavior shown by mice under different levels of novelty of the fighting environment. The results show a significant increase in aggressive behavior with progressively more familiar environments. Familiar olfactory cues enhanced aggression more than did familiar visual cues. The investigators explained their results in terms of the conflict between attack and competing behaviors.

Learning plays an important role in inter-male aggression and may serve to alter the innate behavior tendencies of a given animal. The negative reinforcement involved in defeat during inter-male aggression results in a decrease in aggressive tendencies (Kahn, 1951; Lagerspetz, 1964), and the rapidity with which mice learn submissive reactions to other mice is in part a function of the length of the fighting bouts (Levine et al., 1965). Moreover, the earlier in the animal's life that defeat occurred, the greater was the decrease in inter-male aggression (Kahn, 1951).

In an established colony where animals have a frequent opportunity to interact, it is easy to see that the learning mechanisms of reward and punishment could account for the development of dominance hierarchies. A given animal could easily learn to respond to the cue complex of one animal in the colony with aggressive responses, but to another with avoidance, submission, or aggression-inhibitory responses. Further, anticipatory fighting postures or threats, since they precede the attack response, may function to elicit a submissive posture in a previously defeated animal. Thus an actual fight may be avoided.

Dominance may be specific to particular situations. For example, the most dominant animal is not necessarily one that kills the prey that is available to several animals in a group (Baenninger & Baenninger, 1970). Among gorillas one animal may be dominant in a feeding situation whereas another may be dominant in play or during grooming (Carpenter, 1964).

Additional Influence on Inter-Male Aggression

Much of what is known about inter-male aggressive behavior is derived from laboratory studies of different strains of mice, and it is important not to overgeneralize on the basis of a single species. However, these studies do provide a basis for hypotheses to be tested on other animals.

Several investigators have shown that early experiences have a significant effect on the aggressive behavior of the mouse, although the use of different strains and measuring techniques makes these studies difficult to interpret. Mice that are handled during the first few days of life have a shorter latency for fighting in adulthood than do those left undisturbed (Levine, 1959). This is interpreted by Levine as indicating that the handled animals, having had early experience with mildly stressful stimuli, have a higher threshold for emotional susceptibility than do the non-handled ones and are thus less affected by the strangeness of the fighting situation. On the other hand, more intense stimulation (painful tail pinching or the injection of a control substance such as sesame oil) tends to retard the maturation of the aggressive response (Lagerspetz & Talo, 1967).

If mice from a nonaggressive strain are cross-fostered to a female from a more aggressive strain, there is a greater amount of spontaneous aggression manifest when these pups are tested during adulthood. At this time, however, it is not possible to determine whether the maternal influence is due to behavioral differences in the handling of the pups or to hormonal influences transmitted through the milk during the nursing process (Southwick, 1968).

Many investigators have demonstrated that aggressive behavior in male mice is intensified on most dimensions if the mice are isolated for some period of time before being matched (Scott & Fredericson, 1951; Scott, 1958; Kahn, 1954; Welch, 1967). (Many more studies will be found in Garattini & Sigg, 1969.) Levine et al. (1965), for example, have shown that 45 percent of the mice isolated for one week will fight when placed together. However, after four weeks of isolation, 78 percent will fight, after nine weeks of isolation, 100 percent will fight. This increased tendency to fight can be reversed by housing the animals in groups for five to ten weeks (Cairns & Nakelski, 1971).

Isolated and grouped mice differ both in their hormonal status and in their brain chemistry. These differences may account in part for the behavioral differences and are discussed later. However, it also seems likely that familiarity with the aggression-eliciting cues of cage mates may play a role in the reduction of aggressiveness in grouped animals. Although the bulk of the evidence confirms the potent influence of isolation on aggressiveness, at least two early studies found a decrease in aggression after the mice were isolated (King & Gurney, 1954; King, 1957).

Summary of Inter-Male Aggression

Inter-male aggression can be defined by the following characteristics. As the term implies, inter-male aggression is characteristic of the male sex and is found in a wide variety of species. The topography of this response tends to be highly stereotyped and ritualized. Relatively little serious wounding takes place during bouts between male conspecifics because the attack is generally directed at a well-protected portion of the opponent's body.

Except in certain rare conditions of extreme arousal, inter-male aggression is elicited only by the total stimulus complex of another male of the same species. Odor plays a particularly important role as an eliciting stimulus in some species, and visual stimuli are of importance in others. Inter-male aggression is particularly characterized by the fact that specific postures on the part of a defeated animal function to inhibit further aggression by the victor.

The evidence available indicates that the opportunity for one male to attack another functions as a reinforcer and supports further learning. The aggressive behavior between males is generally enhanced during the breeding season; although in many instances the males have an increased tendency to fight in the presence of a female, they do not fight over her. Fear-eliciting stimuli tend to inhibit inter-male aggression, but it is relatively unaffected by food or water deprivation. Learning plays an important role in maintenance of dominance, which may be established through the tendencies for inter-male aggression. Such early experiences as stress, social contact, and isolation are also variables that influence this type of aggressive behavior.

GENERAL SUMMARY

Aggression is not a unitary phenomenon and our understanding of this general class of behavior can only come when the different kinds have adequately operational definitions. Much of the confusion and conflicting studies in the literature are due to the fact that different authors call different behaviors by the same name. In this chapter it is tentatively suggested that there are the following kinds of aggressive behavior: predatory, inter-male, fear-induced, irritable, maternal, sex-related, and instrumental.

The kinds of aggression vary on a number of dimensions. The stimulus situation that elicits the behavior is different for the different aggression types. An animal's reaction to its natural prey is quite different from its reaction to another male conspecific. Both behaviors fit under the general definition of aggression indicated in Chapter 1, but they are clearly distinguishable. The kinds of aggression can also be differentiated on the basis of the response topography; that is, the particular patterns of behavior differ from one kind of aggression to another.

Females are more prone than males to display certain types of aggressive behavior (e.g., maternal aggression), inter-male aggression is, of course, the province of males. The opportunity to behave aggressively is, in some instances, positively reinforcing and supports new learning. The activity in a given neural system for aggression may produce either positive or negative affect. The various kinds of aggression interact differently with other behavior tendencies. For example, there is an interaction between the neural substrate for predatory aggression and that for hunger. However, no such interaction appears to exist between hunger and some of the other kinds of aggressive behavior. Finally, each of the different kinds of aggression has a unique physiological substrate.

This chapter also contains a detailed discussion of predatory aggression (summarized on page 151) and of inter-male aggression (summarized on page 173). In Chapter 6 the other five types of aggression are covered.

6

Kinds of Aggression
II. Fear-Induced,
Maternal, Irritable,
Sex-Related

This chapter will cover the remaining types of aggression in an attempt to define them and indicate the various dimensions along which they differ.

FEAR-INDUCED AGGRESSION
Stimulus Factors Eliciting Fear-Induced Aggression
In its purest form fear-induced aggression is always preceded by attempts to escape. Thus one of the components of the stimulus situation that elicits this type of aggressive behavior is some degree of confinement in which the defensive animal is cornered and is unable to escape. In that situation the animal turns and attacks the attacker. A second component of the stimulus situation is, of course, the presence of some threatening agent. This type of aggression can be differentiated from all others in that it is always preceded by escape attempts. The term *fear* is merely descriptive of behavior and does not imply that it is possible to know how a given animal "feels" at the time it is behaving. Fear-induced aggression always involves an emotional component that includes specific patterns of autonomic arousal. A detailed study of the topography of fear-induced aggression will involve an analysis of those autonomic components. Although such an analysis has not yet been undertaken, some of the components such as piloerection have been frequently mentioned.

The confinement or barrier to escape that is involved in fear-induced aggression may be of two types. Escape may be prevented by actual physical barriers such as the confines of a cage, or the tendency to flee may be blocked by a strong attachment to some element of the environment, most frequently a conspecific. For example, females of many species have a strong attachment to their own young and manifest a form of fear-induced aggression if they are threatened in the nest area. (See the following discussion of maternal aggression.) The tendency to flee in response to a threat occurs as a function of the proximity of the threatening agent; that is, when some critical "flight distance" is breached. (Hediger, 1950, provides a summary table of flight distances for a number of wild animals.) If pursuit does not occur and the animal's movements are not restricted, flight successfully solves the immediate problem and no aggression occurs. However, if the animal is very suddenly aware (surprised) that its personal space (see following discussion of personal space as territory) has been invaded, it may react with a sudden burst of defensive or fear-induced aggression. Herrero (1970) provides an interesting example of this phenomenon in the grizzly bear.

Response Topography in Fear-Induced Aggression
Although there have been some analyses of the response topography in fear-induced aggression, they are limited to a relatively few animals and have not been nearly as extensively documented as have similar analyses for predatory aggression. Leyhausen (1956), who has studied the cat under both natural and seminatural conditions, indicates that the initial reaction when the animal perceives a threatening agent is the disruption of ongoing activities and flight when that is possible. If escape is not an available response, the cat faces the enemy and hisses with an open mouth while showing piloerection and pupillodilation. The topography of fear-induced aggression in the cat is quite distinct from that labeled "attack" by Leyhausen, in which piloerection, dilation of the pupil, and hissing are frequently absent. In attack, hissing is generally replaced by a low growl.

A squirrel that is about to attack pulls its ears back and produces a chattering sound with its front teeth. The reaction is quite different, however, if the animal is cornered and on the defensive. In that case it squeals and raises its ears (Eibl-Eibesfeldt, 1970).

The development of the fear-induced aggressive response has been studied in the New Zealand rabbit by stimulating one side of the body with a blunt probe. The components of the response include an oriented jump toward the side of stimulation; hind limb thrust; vocalization; stabbing out with the forelimb, striking the ground with the hind limb, directed escape, and biting attack. Biting attack and vocalization occurred when the animal was cornered or when it was in the presence of its young. The components of this complex response appeared at different stages in the rabbit's development. Similar behavior has been described for the antelope jackrabbit, black-tailed jackrabbit, and the European hare (Fox and Apelbaum, 1969).

Defensive threat is a frequent component of the behavior of the cornered animal. This threat response usually involves a display of weapons available to the animal such as teeth and claws. It also includes postures that make the animal appear larger (Eibl-Eibesfeldt, 1970). The ears of the squirrel, for example, have tufts of hair on their tips and when the ears are raised during the defensive threat posture, the apparent size of the animal is enhanced.

The topography of fear-induced aggression has been compared with that of the "rage response" or irritable aggression in a number of experiments showing that the neurological bases of these behaviors are different. This material is discussed later in the section on the physiology of the different kinds of aggression.

All Defensive Aggression Is Not Fear-Induced

In a number of animals the reaction to external threat is not flight. The animal may stand its ground, threaten, and even attack when confronted by some hostile agent. A group of wild chimpanzees exposed to a stuffed leopard reacted by yelling, barking, and leaping up and down. A few fled the area but returned shortly and joined the majority, which charged the leopard brandishing large sticks and broken-off trees, which they threw at the predator. Although the chimps were described as showing fear symptoms between charges, the aggression was elicited in the absence of cornering (Kortlandt & Kooij, 1963, quoted in Chance and Jolly, 1970). The chimpanzee rarely attacks a man, but the relatively peaceful gorilla, if it becomes highly aroused during a threatening display toward a human, may attack, even though it is not cornered (Reynolds, 1965; Schaller, 1963).

In a baboon troop large predators such as lions and cheetahs evoke different responses based on age and sex. When the troop is threatened, the females and young flee to nearby trees. The large males, however, turn and face the threat and move to a position between the predator and the rest of the troop. They engage in aggressive display, showing their large canine teeth. Few predators attack in the face of such a formidable defense (Washburn, 1966; Hamburg, 1971b; Kummer, 1968).

Although there have been no physiological studies directly concerned with this type of aggressive reaction in the face of threat, it seems likely that the substrates of this behavior differ from that of the pure fear-induced aggression. It is probably more closely related to irritable aggression, discussed later.

Aggression Is Not the Only Response of the Cornered Animal
There are classes of responses to extreme fear other than aggression. The cornered animal may continue to cower, may assume submissive postures, may freeze, may faint, or may enter a cataleptic state. Fear-induced aggression is only one of many possible responses. Detailed studies will have to be undertaken to determine the variables contributing to one or the other of these reactions.

Under certain conditions the animal's response to threat is neither aggression nor flight. Among baboons, for example, a submissive animal, either male or female, may respond to the threat of a dominant male not by escape but by an approach to the threatening male. This response, according to Kummer (quoted in Chance, 1966) results from the tendency for the members of the troop to approach the highest ranking male in any threatening situation (Bernstein, 1964). The tendency is strong enough to evoke the same response even though it is the dominant male that is doing the threatening. It is suggested that this behavior is derived from the infant's reaction of approaching the mother during times of stress. Chance indicates that this reaction functions to bind the animals into a group because it replaces escape tendencies with approach. A similar response tendency has been found in macaques, and Barnett and Evans (1965) have reported that under certain circumstances, attacked rats may repeatedly approach the aggressor in a nonbelligerent fashion.

The Role of Habituation in Fear-Induced Aggression
Novelty is one of the most important stimulus characteristics likely to elicit flight in a variety of wild animals and seems to contribute to the probability that the animal will behave aggressively when cornered. Barnett (1958) has described the wild rat as "neophobic" and has shown that a novel stimulus in the environment is avoided even when that avoidance causes a drastic reduction in food intake.

It has also been shown that the wild rat will avoid a human handler if possible and will savagely attack when its escape is blocked by some kind of barrier (Stone, 1932; Yerkes, 1913). The laboratory rat is far less fearful but its behavior will be similar to the wild species in certain circumstances. It has been shown by several investigators (Rasmussen, 1938; Stone, 1932; and Farris & Yeakel, 1945) that gradual exposure to humans permits the animals to habituate to that stimulus complex with the result that the explosive avoidance response as well as the savageness is reduced. This has been most recently and most systematically investigated by Galef (1970a), who demonstrated that the reduction in aggressiveness was due to the prepubertal handling of the rats and not to other environmental variables such as the type of mother (wild or albino) or the type of siblings with which it was raised. In this experiment the reduction in aggressiveness produced by handling was specific to fear-induced aggressiveness. It had no effect on inter-male or predatory aggression. Although systematic research has not been done on other animals, the importance of habituation or "taming" in the reduction of fear-induced aggression is well recognized by animal trainers and zoological garden directors. The process of habituation may also be relatively specific to a given individual, not immediately generalizing to all humans (Hediger, 1950).

Summary of Fear-Induced Aggression

Fear-induced aggression occurs when an animal is unsuccessful in its attempts to escape from some threatening agent. There is some evidence that the topography of this response is different from other types of aggressive behavior. It involves particular patterns of autonomic responding as well as defensive threat responses, which usually involve the display of the animal's available weapons. Defensive reactions in some animals are probably more closely related to irritable aggression than fear-induced, in that they attack well before they are cornered. There are many responses to extreme fear other than fear-induced aggression, including freezing, fainting, and submissive posturing. Both novelty and habituation are important in fear-induced aggression in that they influence the tendency for the elicitation of the fear reaction.

MATERNAL AGGRESSION

A mother animal with young will behave aggressively toward a large number of intruders. It has been suggested that this strong tendency to aggression is characteristic of all vertebrate mothers (Beach, 1948). Although maternal aggressive behavior may not be universal, there is abundant evidence that it is a characteristic of many species. In general, the stimulus situation that elicits this type of aggression involves the proximity of some threatening agent to the young of that particular female. Thus both the young and the threatening agent are a part of the necessary stimulus complex, differentiating this class of aggression from all others. It is generally true that as the mother gets further from her young, the tendency to aggression decreases. The probability of attack is also frequently a function of particular stimulus characteristics of the young, and the hormonal status of the mother. The attack waxes and wanes as the hormones associated with the birth process fluctuate.

Although relatively few detailed experimental studies of maternal aggressivity have been conducted, there is considerable qualitative documentation of the phenomenon. Grizzly bear sows with cubs account for 82 percent of all the bear attacks on hikers and campers in the national parks of Canada and the United States (Herrero, 1970).

A few days before giving birth, the female mouse may be so aggressive that it will kill any males that are unable to escape from her ferocious and unrelenting attack (Brown, 1953). After the birth of the litters in the laboratory situation, mouse mothers savagely attack a forceps placed close to the nest. The most aggressive animals cling to the rubber tips so firmly with their teeth that they can be lifted from the nest (King, 1963). Lactating female rats chase any intruder away from their nests or burrows when unweaned young are present, but that behavior is rare in other circumstances (Barnett, 1964a, 1969).

A moose cow with her calf will attack any intruder, including a large bull moose, and it will pursue the offender for a considerable distance. Altman (1963) describes a moose cow that chased a horse into the water, attacked it fiercely, and did not give up the chase until the horse was driven to another island. In another case a moose cow attacked and badly wounded a bear that was attempting to carry off her calf.

As indicated earlier, chimpanzees will attack a model leopard. However, the model will be attacked much more vigorously if it has a model baby chimpanzee as its victim. Mother chimpanzees with young are more aggressive toward the model whether it has a victim or not (Chance & Jolly, 1970).

Attacks by mothers with young are also common in squirrels (Taylor, 1966), langurs (Jay, 1963), baboons (DeVore, 1963b), snowshoe hares (Burt, 1943), rabbits (Ross et al., 1963), sheep (Hersher et al., 1963), weasels (Lockie, 1966), cats (Schneirla et al., 1963), and many other animals.

Not All Animals Show Maternal Aggression

There are some significant exceptions to the general rule that mother animals show increased attack tendencies. Of four different breeding groups of rats—the Wistar-SPF, Long-Evans, Wistar-conventional, and Sprague-Dawley—only the Wistar-SPF showed any increased aggression toward a black mouse during lactation, and only 60 percent of those animals exhibited attack behavior (Flandera & Novakova, 1971a, 1917b). Calhoun (1962) concludes that domestication has resulted in a general reduction in aggressiveness, including that associated with lactation. Some species of mice manifest no maternal aggressivity (King, 1963; Scudder et al., 1967) and some strains of rabbits show that behavior, whereas some other strains are not aggressive at all (Ross et al., 1963).

Under certain circumstances animals not only fail to show aggression toward an intruder, but actually attempt to mother it and retrieve it to the nest. Karli (1956) has reported that some lactating female rats exhibit marked maternal behavior toward a mouse, attempting to retrieve it. These animals do not become aggressive toward the mouse even though it disrupts the nest and scatters the pups. Similar findings have been reported by Revlis and Moyer (1969) and Baenninger (1969). Although many mice with pups behave as an "unrelenting tigress" toward a male (King, 1963), it has been reported that some actually attempt to grasp the male and bring it back to the nesting area (Scudder et al., 1967). Among rats that are not mouse killers, the maternal behavior may result from stimulus generalization due to the similarity of the mouse to the rat pups. This hypothesis, however, has not been systematically tested.

For reasons that are not at all clear the mother's aggression is sometimes directed toward her own young. (Of course, this is not maternal aggression as described earlier, but it occurs in the same time span.) In mice the mother not infrequently kills and cannibalizes her young, usually shortly after giving birth, but sometimes waiting as long as a week (King, 1963). In one laboratory 93 of 279 litters were killed and eaten. There is some evidence that this cannibalistic characteristic is under genetic control, and it does not seem to be correlated with the tendency for the mother to attack intruders that approach the nest area (Ross et al., 1963). Pup killing by female rats can be induced by injections of testosterone propionate and it has been suggested that the female attack on the young may be due to abnormally high endogenous androgens of adrenal origin (Davis & Gandelman, 1972).

Pup killing and cannibalism appear to have a different endocrine basis than the more common maternal aggression. Virgin mice that spontaneously kill strange pups do not do so during the lactation period following the subsequent pregnancy of these animals (Gandelman & Davis, 1973). However, the pup cannibalism that occurs during lactation in animals that are not normally pup killers may be the result of the hormonal disruption during the postpartum period. Relatively little research has been done on this problem and much more is needed.

Relationship of Maternal Aggression to
Pregnancy, Parturition, and Lactation

In most animals increased aggressiveness of the female toward intruders is directly related to pregnancy, parturition, and lactation. There is, however, a good bit of variability both within and among species. Mice become highly aggressive during the last few days of pregnancy (Brown, 1953) and remain so during the first 14 days postpartum. In one of the few experimental studies on this problem, it was shown that 86 percent of the lactating females tested between days 1 and 14 of lactation exhibited immediate and intense aggression toward either a male or a female intruder. After the fourteenth day of lactation, only 13 percent of the animals attacked, and none attacked when tested 21 days after lactation had ceased (Gandelman, 1972). These results were essentially substantiated by St. John and Corning (1973), who found that the attacks by mothers on either male or female intruders peaked by day

4 postpartum and rapidly declined after day 16. (Also see Svare and Gandelman, 1973.) Scudder et al. (1967) report that three of the four genera of mice that they studied showed aggression toward humans during the first seven or eight days postpartum.

In natural or seminatural conditions female rats drive other animals from their nests only during lactation (Calhoun, 1962; Barnett, 1964a; 1969). Endroczi et al. (1958) report that only lactating female rats will attack a frog placed in the home cage. This finding is evidently strain specific because other investigators have been unable to replicate it. (See Revlis and Moyer, 1969.) The attack behavior of non-mouse-killing female rats on mice increased from parturition and reached its maximum on the fifth day of lactation (60 percent occurrence). Thereafter the incidence of aggression decreased and it disappeared entirely by the fifteenth day of lactation. This behavior was also strain-specific and occurred in only one of the four strains studied (Flandera & Novakova, 1971b).

The female weasel, normally submissive toward the male, assumes a position of dominance from about midpregnancy until the young are about 12 weeks of age, whereupon she again becomes submissive to the male (Lockie, 1966). Similarly, the female langur may be dominant to the male during the last few weeks of pregnancy (Jay, 1963).

In sheep there is a very sensitive period immediately after birth during which the mother will show strong approach tendencies toward any lamb. However, this strong maternal drive toward all young fades within a few hours after parturition, after which the dam attempts to butt any young other than her own as well as any other sheep, male or female (Hersher et al., 1963).

The relationship between maternal aggressivity and pregnancy, parturition, and lactation in the animals discussed here implies a hormonal influence on this behavior. In some higher animals—baboons, chimpanzees, and Japanese macaques—the hormonal influences seem to be less important than the external stimulus control in the elicitation of this type of aggression. Among the baboons, for example, a baby baboon is the center of attraction for the whole troop. Females other than the mother attempt to groom the baby and respond to its distress. The older males also show great interest in the infant and are highly sensitive to any hint of distress from it. They will viciously attack any human that comes between it and the troop (DeVore, 1963b). If, because of injury, the infant baboon manifests considerable distress, the amount of threatening by the males rises considerably. They threaten each other, the females, and human observers. If the infant dies, the males may threaten the mother if she moves even a short way from her baby (Hamburg, 1971b).

The type of behavior just described might well be classified as *paternal aggression* since it appears to be elicited by a particular and relatively specific stimulus situation. However, except for a few naturalistic descriptions, relatively little is known about it.

Types of Stimulus Situations Eliciting Maternal Aggression

Few experiments have been done on mammals that attempt systematically to manipulate the stimuli most relevant to the elicitation of maternal aggression. It is therefore necessary to make inferences about the relevant stimuli from naturalistic studies and experimental work designed to study other questions.

In the turkey a very wide range of stimuli elicit attack during the time that the poults are of a given age. The turkey may be described as being in a general state of irritability, attacking almost anything that moves except turkey chicks. For the turkey the problem is not to find what stimuli elicit aggression, but to find those factors that prevent the bird from attacking its own chicks. The relevant aggression-inhibiting stimulus is the distinctive call of the turkey poult. A dumb poult will be attacked and killed, but the turkey will foster a model of a polecat (a natural predator of turkey chicks) if it has a built-in speaker that emits recorded calls of a turkey poult (Schleidt et al., 1960).

Although there are definite species differences, it is generally true that nursing mother mice are less aggressive when their young are not present; thus the presence of the young is an important variable in the elicitation of maternal aggression. Further, some stimulus complexes are more prepotent in the elicitation of aggression than others. Male mice elicit ferocious attacks from a female in the eighth day of lactation. However, if she is tested 5 hours after her pups are removed from the nest, she shows no aggression at all (Gandelman, 1972). Before the birth of their young, pregnant females can be easily chased from the nest with a 10-in. forceps. After the birth of the litters, however, some species will savagely attack the forceps (King, 1963). The mouse *Peromyscus maniculatus gracilis* will show a relatively mild attack on the forceps but is intensely aggressive toward a male mouse placed in the cage. She continues her attack even when the male shows the species-typical submissive posture. Thus the male mouse is a more potent stimulus complex for the elicitation of maternal aggression than is the inanimate forceps. The mouse *P. m. bairdii* also attacks the male but does not continue the attack with the intensity of the *gracilis* (King, 1963). Eisenberg (1962) also reports species differences in maternal aggression. The *californicus* are "defensive" of the nest even when not with the young, whereas the *maniculatus* does not react aggressively in the nest area unless she is parturient.

A series of experiments by Svare and Gandelman (1973) provides more information on the stimulus variables that elicit maternal aggression. Lactating mice in the presence of their young readily attack strange mice but rarely attack a conspecific to which they had been previously exposed. One- and 10-day-old intruders are seldom attacked, but intense aggression will be directed against 14- and 20-day-old intruders. However, if the hair of a 14-day-old intruder is removed, it is protected from attack.

A lactating female rat seems to show an increase in irritability, but her attack tendencies are limited to particular stimulus situations. As indicated earlier, she is aggressive toward all alien rats in the vicinity of her burrow. However, she also reacts aggressively, although less so, in the food pen, which may be some distance from her nest area. These aggressive tendencies in the food area are elicited only by male rats and there is remarkably little aggressive interaction among lactating females in the food pen even though their nest areas are widely separated (Calhoun, 1962).

Sheep recognize their young on the basis of visual cues, and aggression toward them is inhibited. The female sheep will butt away any other animal that approaches her regardless of age or sex. However, she exhibits the same behavior even in the absence of her young. Thus, in sheep, the young are not a critical variable in the elicitation of aggression and the state produced by the physiological changes accompanying parturition appears to be one of generalized irritability.

A similar generalized irritability apparently occurs in various cat species shortly before and after the birth of the young. Schneirla et al. (1963) suggest that the irritability increase may be due to the general "stressor" effects of parturition.

The cues that elicit both cherishing behavior and maternal (paternal) aggression in primates are, as might be expected, complex. The mother recognizes her own young and is more responsive to them than she is to young in general. Among baboons, adult females show considerable interest in young baboons. They tend to pay less attention to them when the young reach th age of about 8 months and may threaten and mildly attack these juveniles. If the young is attacked, it screeches in terror and the mother runs to its side and threatens or attacks the aggressor if it is a female of lower status (DeVore, 1963b). One of the factors that appears to elicit attention and the tendency to aggression during infant distress is the coat color of the infant. In langurs the infant's coat is brown and when it changes to gray, the adults tend to lose interest (Jay, 1963). The young of baboons, vervet monkeys, and chimpanzees also have distinctive coat colorations that serve a similar purpose.

Response Topography in Maternal Aggression
There have been few studies dealing with the response topography of this type of aggression. What little is known about it, however, seems to indicate that the response patterns are somewhat different from other

kinds of aggressive responding. In mice the maternal attack on an intruder is immediate. The female lunges at and bites the strange animal. There is no prelude of behaviors, such as genital sniffing and tail rattling, which are usually observed when two male mice are paired. The attack is continuous, consisting primarily of bites to the flanks and the neck region (Gandelman, 1972).

Generally, mother animals with mobile young move away from a possible source of conflict. For example, no person in our national parks has been molested by a sow bear with cubs if the individuals were making noise, talking loudly, or singing. The bear mother maintains an individual distance of up to several hundred yards. However, if the bear is unable to avoid an intruder (in the case of surprise, for example), she may actively attack and pursue an escaping individual. The bear need not be cornered for the attack response to occur (Herrero, 1970).

A female moose with a calf also attempts to maintain a distance from other animals. If approached too closely, however, she will carry on an attack toward the intruder and pursue it for a considerable distance. The attack is carried out with the hooves, and follows the mother's signal to the calf to heel. The signal consists of a warning posture of freezing and a "bristling" with the head lifted (Altman, 1963).

Summary of Maternal Aggression

Although relatively few experimental studies of maternal aggressive reactions have been done, there is abundant qualitative evidence for this tendency. Maternal aggression is common, but by no means universal. It appears to be reduced during the process of domestication. Maternal aggressivity, particularly in lower animals, is related to pregnancy, parturition, and lactation and appears to be hormonally based. However, in primates the response seems to be more under the control of external stimuli associated with the young and its distress calls in that aggressive reactions in response to the young occur in both nonmother females and even males. In some species the stimuli that elicit maternal aggression are quite broad and the mother may be described as generally irritable. In others, however, the presence of the young is a necessary part of the stimulus complex before aggression toward an intruder is manifest. There is some evidence that the topography of maternal aggression has distinctive features.

IRRITABLE AGGRESSION

When species differences are taken into account, it is generally possible to classify the different kinds of aggression discussed here on the basis of the kinds of stimuli that elicit them and the particular topography of the response. However, when all those kinds of aggression are accounted for, there remains a significant amount of hostile behavior that does not fit into any of the preceding categories and that is of a different physiological origin. This set of hostile behaviors is referred to as irritable aggression.

In its pure form irritable aggression involves attack without attempts to escape from the object being attacked. The most extreme form of irritable aggression is exemplified by destructive "uncontrollable rage" directed against either animate or inanimate objects. In less extreme forms it may involve only "annoyance," threat, or halfhearted attack. The stimulus situation that evokes an irritable aggression response is the presence of any attackable organism or object. The range of stimuli that may elicit this aggressive response is extremely broad and may involve inanimate as well as animate objects. The presence of the animal's young is not relevant to the evocation of irritable aggression, which differentiates it from maternal aggression. Irritable aggression is differentiated from predatory, inter-male, and sex-related aggressiveness by its inclusiveness. Animals showing irritable aggression may attack prey, conspecifics of either sex, and many other available stimuli. Predatory, inter-male, and sex-related aggression, however, are elicited only by the relevant stimuli.

Topography of Irritable Aggression

The specific behavior patterns involved in irritable aggression have not been extensively studied. One of the best descriptions of this behavior in the cat is given by Flynn et al. (1970). They refer to the behavior as affective aggression, which they differentiate from quiet biting attack (predatory aggression), and they emphasize that the cat does not manifest withdrawal or escape behaviors. The attack is produced by direct hypothalamic stimulation and involves a pattern of pronounced sympathetic arousal that is commonly regarded as indicative of "feline rage." The autonomic responses include pupillary dilation, piloerction (particularly along the middle of the back), and the tail becoming bushy and fluffed out. Their description is classic and worth quoting in full.

> If sitting, the animal leaps to its feet and begins to move with head low to the ground, back arched, claws unsheathed, hissing and/or snarling, sometimes salivating profusely, and breathing deeply. The cat either comes up to the rat directly or circles to the rear of the cage and then approaches the rat. The cat stands poised, appearing to watch the rat intensely, while the affective aspect of the reaction becomes still more pronounced. After a second or two, the cat raises a paw with claws unsheathed and then strikes with its paw in a series of swift, accurate blows. Any sudden movement of the rat serves to trigger the attack, but attack will occur even if the rat remains motionless. In some instances, the cat, instead of delivering discrete blows with a single paw, springs at the rat with a high-pitched scream and pounces,

tearing at the rat with its claws. If the stimulus is continued, the cat will savagely bite the rat, although the initial part of the attack is clearly with its claws.[1]

Detailed descriptions of the behavior patterns involved in irritable aggression in other animals are not readily available. However, if the reaction is of any appreciable magnitude, it will involve an affective component with autonomic involvement. In man this affect is recognized as anger or rage and there is some evidence that the pattern of autonomic involvement is different for anger than for other emotional responses (Ax, 1953; Schachter, 1957).

The tendency to irritable aggression is increased by several antecedent factors, including frustration, deprivation, pain, and various physiological dysfunctions.

Frustration and Irritable Aggression

Since man began to introspect on his motivational states, he has recognized that frustration (the blocking of some ongoing goal-oriented behavior) sometimes makes him angry and that the feeling of anger increases the probability that he will respond aggressively. Freud considered aggression to be a primordial reaction to frustration. In the classic treatise *Frustration and Aggression* (Dollard et al., 1939) it was suggested that aggression was always a consequence of frustration and that the occurrence of aggressive behavior always presupposed the existence of frustration. Extensive research has been devoted to this proposition and the others derived from it. Since the frustration-aggression hypothesis has been reviewed in considerable detail in a number of other places, it is not necessary to examine it in detail here. (See Buss, 1961; Berkowitz, 1962, 1969; Miller, 1941; Bateson, 1941.) It is sufficient to say that there can be no doubt that frustration does at times result in aggressive behavior.

A number of laboratory experiments using human subjects show that frustration increases aggressive tendencies. These have been summarized by Berkowitz (1962, 1969). A considerable amount of nonlaboratory evidence also relates the different types of frustrating situations to hostile behavior. These more global studies, because they cannot be well controlled, are difficult to interpret precisely, but they are a source of evidence that should not be ignored.

A number of authors have indicated that the blacks in the United States are systematically frustrated by the institutionalized racism that deprives them of self-respect and self-determination, as well as basic

---

[1] J. Flynn, H. Vanegas, W. Foote, & S. Edwards, Neural mechanisms involved in a cat's attack on a rat. In R. Whalen, R. F. Thompson, M. Verziano, & N. Weinberger (Eds.), *The Neural Control of Behavior.* New York: Academic Press, 1970, p. 138.

economic goods (Grier & Cobbs, 1968; Spiegel, 1968; Kerner, 1968). They conclude that rage and violence are a result of these frustrations.

Cross-cultural studies have shown that cultural patterns that provide for the frustration of free sexual expression, as evidenced by the tendency to punish extramarital intercourse, are significantly correlated with a number of indexes of violent and aggressive behavior including incidence of personal crime, military glory, bellicosity, and the killing and torturing of one's enemies (Textor, 1967, quoted in Ilfeld, 1969). As Ilfeld indicates, correlational studies are difficult to interpret. It may be that the hostile behavior is due to the frustration of sexual expression or to the generally restrictive and punitive customs of these cultures. In any case frustration seems to be a relevant variable.

Collective violence, which is a complex phenomenon, can, of course, be primarily instrumental, but there can be no doubt that much of it has a highly affective component and can be classed with irritable aggression. Several studies have shown that collective violence is related to deprivation. In one cross-national study of 114 political entities between 1961 and 1965, Gurr (1968) demonstrated that outbreaks of internal group violence were directly correlated with indexes of socioeconomic deprivations. Although it will be shown later that deprivation per se can increase the tendency to irritable aggression, the important factor in this group of studies on collective violence appears to be the frustration that occurs because the deprivation imposed on the individuals is unjustified and inconsistent with their expectations. Gurr (1968, 1970) refers to this as relative deprivation. Coles (1967), in discussing the effects of deprivation on black ghetto children, makes the point that the deprivation leads to violence only after the age of 12 or 14, when the child begins to compare his status with the rest of the culture and sees the jobs that he cannot get and the material things that others have but he is denied. Davies (1969) has built a theory of revolution on the general construct that collective violence results not from a simple deprivation, but from the frustration involved when masses of men in a given culture experience a wide gap between their expectations and their gratifications.

In an interesting series of studies Feierabend and Feierabend (1966, 1968) have attempted to isolate those conditions that contribute to the chances that violent behavior will occur in a given nation, and frustration has emerged as a significant variable. Political instability was found in a number of countries where various measures of frustration and deprivation were high. These measures included such variables as gross national product, literacy rate, average caloric intake, and numbers of radios, telephones, newspapers, and physicians.

Although the results are difficult to interpret, a number of studies have related child-rearing practices to the tendency for the children to manifest hostile behaviors later in life. For example, there is considerable evidence that physically aggressive and punitive parents have children who are also physically aggressive (Bandura & Walters, 1959, 1963), and there is a high probability that hyperaggressive children will have a history of physical punishment at home (Feshbach, 1971). There can be little doubt that the physical punishment and the threat of physical punishment is frustrating to the child, but it is also painful (see later discussion of the role of pain in aggression) and an aggressive parent provides a potent role model on which the child can pattern his behaviors. (For a recent evaluative survey of the role of child-rearing practices in aggressive behavior, see Johnson, 1972.)

Frustration and Irritable Aggression in Animals
A variety of techniques have been used to demonstrate in animals that one reaction to frustration is an increase in one or more measures of aggressive behavior. Lagerspetz and Nurmi (1964) used the simple procedure of teaching mice to obtain food at the end of a runway. When the response was well learned, they blocked the goal box. This frustration procedure did not result in aggressive reactions in the absence of another mouse. However, in a nonaggressive strain of mice, the frustration increased the level of aggression. In a strain bred for aggressiveness, fighting occurred whether the mice were frustrated or not and frustration did not enhance their level of aggression, which was already high.

If 6-month-old rhesus monkeys are frustrated by separating them from their mother, they show an increased tendency to manifest aggression toward a peer even though aggressive behavior is extremely rare at this age (Seay & Harlow, 1965).

Competition as Frustration Resulting in Aggression
Aggressive behavior resulting from competitive interactions may be considered as resulting from frustration. When a goal presumably attractive to two or more subjects is made available in such a way that it can be obtained by only one of them, the end result is frustration for the loser. In the natural state it has been observed that both chimpanzees and baboons will fight over premium foods. Baboons will harass adult chimpanzees in an attempt to get bananas from them. In general, however, they are unsuccessful and may then turn and attack female or juvenile chimpanzees even though those animals have no bananas (Hamburg, 1971b). Thus it appears that the frustration of unsuccessful competition results in redirected aggression.

A similar displaced aggression has been demonstrated in cats in the laboratory. The animals were required to run down a 21-ft. runway for food that could be obtained by only one of them. When there were three cats in the situation, aggression was often directed by one loser against the other. These instances of displaced aggression indicate that the frustration increases the potential for aggression even though that behavior is not instrumental in the acquisition of the goal object.

Vigorous competitive fighting over food has been reported for mice (Fredericson, 1952; Fredericson & Birnbaum, 1954; Fredericson et al., 1955) and for rats (Grossman, 1970; Grossman & Grossman, 1970) and obvious aggression results when gerbils compete for water (Boice, 1969). Boice also reports that hamsters become aggressive when competing for both water and for dominance in a tunnel.

In certain circumstances competition can result in intense aggression with severe wounding. Miller and Banks (1962) trained individual rhesus monkeys to climb on a small perch to escape a tone-signaled shock. When two monkeys were placed in the apparatus together, the competition for the perch was violent and in the early encounters some of the animals received severe lacerations.

Extinction as Frustration Resulting in Aggression
If an animal is consistently rewarded for a given response and the reward is suddenly discontinued, the result is frustration. A frequent, although not inevitable, consequence of that frustration is irritable aggression. Psychologists working with animals in learning problems have long been aware that the subjects tend to be more irritable and difficult to handle during the extinction phase of an experiment, and this has been incidentally noted. Mowrer and Jones (1943) indicate that animals during extinction "showed signs of frustration and aggression, consisting of excessively vigorous pressing of the bar, gnawing at the guards and other parts of the apparatus, jumping, and other agitated behavior."

Extinction-induced aggression was first formally studied in pigeons. The birds were trained to peck a key for food under conditions of continuous reinforcement and were then exposed to sessions of continuous reinforcement alternated with periods of extinction. During these sessions a target pigeon was restrained at the rear of the cage. All the experimental birds attacked the target animal more frequently during extinction periods than they did during earlier control periods without reinforcement. The attacks consisted of intense pecking at the head and throat of the target bird, particularly around the eyes. Feathers were pulled out, the skin was bruised, and occasionally the target bird sustained serious injury (Azrin et al., 1966). These results have been essentially confirmed by other investigators, some of whom used high fixed-ratio schedules, which, in effect, are extinction procedures (Flory, 1969, 1970; Gentry, 1968; Knutson, 1969, 1970).

Extinction-induced aggression has also been demonstrated in mammals and it has thus been shown that the attacks may be directed toward either conspecifics or inanimate objects. Rats taught to bar-press for food on a schedule of continuous reinforcement show an immediate increase in bar-pressing rate after the onset of extinction. However, during the second and third minutes of extinction the predominant response is attack on another rat in the cage. Initially, at least, the attacks were of sufficient severity to produce wounding (Thompson & Bloom, 1966). If two rats are trained on separate bars in the same cage, the fighting that results from extinction is more intense if both of the rats are extinguished at the same time than if they are extinguished one at a time (Davis & Donefeld, 1967).

A similar effect has been obtained in the runway situation. Female albino rats were trained in a straight alley for 100 percent food reward and then tested in a double straight alley in pairs on a random 50 percent schedule of reinforcement. After a 30-second interval in the goal box, they were allowed free access to one another for a period of 60 seconds. Significantly more aggression, as measured by the Hall-Klein aggression scale, occurred following nonreinforced trials than after those that were reinforced (Gallup, 1965).

It has also been reported that rats under conditions of extinction or under high fixed-ratio schedules will attack the bar that they had previously learned to press for reward (Keller & Schoenfeld, 1950, p. 328; Pear & Roy, 1971). Under conditions of extinction after responding on a low fixed-ratio schedule, monkeys will bite a rubber hose significantly more frequently than they do during control periods. Further, the frequency of biting on the rubber tube increases over the session as the fixed-ratio requirements are increased (Hutchinson t al., 1968).

Finally, humans also tend to respond aggressively to the extinction phase of a learning experiment. Male subjects between the ages of 14 and 18 were given monetary rewards on a fixed-ratio schedule for pulling a knob. At irregular intervals a noxious 68-db tone occurred which could be terminated in one of two ways, either by pressing a button that required a force of 1.5 lb of pressure or by punching a padded cushion that required a force of 20 lb. The latter was designated as an aggressive response because of the force required and the topographical similarity to human aggressive behaviors in this culture. Button pressing was the preferred response for terminating the tone during the fixed-ratio portion of the experiment and relatively few punching responses occurred. However, during the extinction phase, when the subjects were no longer rewarded for knob pulling, the punching response increased for seven of the nine subjects (Kelly & Hake, 1970). This study has been replicated by Harrell (1972), who also showed that the force of the punch as well as the frequency of the response increased during the extinction phase of the experiment.

Extinction and high levels of fixed-ratio reinforcement do not always produce aggressive behavior. Several experimenters using procedures similar to those discussed have failed to find the expected reaction

(Gentry & Schaeffer, 1969; Hymowitz, 1971; Seward, 1945a). Suffice to say that there are many possible reasons for these failures, from slight procedural differences to the use of strains with a higher threshold for either frustration or aggression. There can be little doubt that when conditions are right, a variety of sources of frustration can result in an increase in aggressive tendencies.

Deprivation and Irritable Aggression

If an individual's ongoing behavior toward a goal is blocked, he is said to be frustrated, and as shown earlier, there are many circumstances in which that frustration results in aggressive tendencies. However, if an appropriate goal object is unavailable, the individual is said to be deprived and it is generally agreed that these two situations are not the same (Berkowitz, 1962, 1969). Although frustration appears to be more likely to lead to aggression, some conditions of deprivation also increase the aggression potential.

Food and Water Deprivation

Although there is very little experimental evidence, it is common knowledge that children (and adults too) tend to become irritable when they are hungry. During periods of famine and severe food deprivation a characteristic increase occurs in a variety of hostile behaviors from thievery to violent crime. Keys et al. (1950) detail the effects of a variety of starvation and semistarvation situations from a thirteenth-century famine in Russia to the food deprivation in the Belsen concentration camp in 1945, indicating that a consistent behavior common to all these hunger experiences is irritability and aggressive behavior during the earliest stages of intense deprivation. During the later stages a lethargy ensues that reduces the impulse to any kind of activity. "Riot and rebellion are engendered by minor hunger and deprivation, but real starvation makes for relative tractability" (Keys et al., 1950, p. 785).

During the semistarvation experiments conducted on volunteers during World War II the normally friendly volunteer subjects became short-tempered and hostile.

> The even-temperedness, patience, and tolerance evidenced during the control period gave way under stress. Irritability increased to the point that it became an individual and group problem. Although the men were well aware of their hyperirritability, they were not altogether able to control their emotionally charged responses; outbursts of temper and periods of sulking and pique were not uncommon. A few had strong urges toward violence but these were controlled. The men who showed a large degree of personal and social deterioration became objects of aggression for the rest of the group [Keys et al., 1950, p. 836].

Partial food deprivation in the form of a therapeutic reduction diet was imposed on a group of mentally retarded children and their aggressive behavior was studied over a six-month period. The results showed a significant increase in the number of physically assaultive acts by the dieters against staff members or another resident as compared with a nondiet control group (Talkington & Riley, 1971). Although both of the preceding cases are instructive, it should be clear that frustration as well as deprivation may have been involved and it is not possible to determine the relative importance of the two variables.

A number of studies on animals either have failed to find a change in spontaneous aggressive behavior as a function of food deprivation or have reported a significant drop in the amount of fighting. Moderate hunger or thirst has no effect on the fighting behavior of mice (Ginsburg & Allee, 1942), but if they are deprived of food for a period of 56 hours, spontaneous fighting is eliminated (Fredericson, 1950). Two reports indicate that monkeys show a significant drop in agonistic social interactions during periods of food shortage. However, the deprivation was severe and the animals became lethargic and depressed and all types of activity were reduced (Southwick, 1969; Loy, 1970).

Food deprivation in itself may not increase the probability of hostile behavior, but there is some evidence that it serves to enhance aggressive tendencies elicited by other means. Restrained rats will bite and pull on a brass rod in front of them under conditions of tail shock, but do not do so if they are placed in the situation under various levels of food deprivation. However, deprivation plus shock results in more biting and pulling on the rod than does shock alone. Further, the number of aggressive responses tends to vary positively with the amount of deprivation (Cahoon et al., 1971). For reasons that are not at all clear, shock stimulation delivered while the rat is water deprived results in *fewer* aggressive responses than shock alone (Hamby & Cahoon, 1971). The situation is even more confused by a more recent study showing that food deprivation of rats did not affect the frequency of fighting to foot shock, but water deprivation resulted in a marked increase in that type of fighting (Creer, 1973).

Isolation can also be used to induce aggressive behavior in many animals. In rats, however, it is not a highly reliable procedure (Korn & Moyer, 1968). In one study it has been shown that isolated rats that were fed every 24 hours did not attack other rats placed in a cage with them. However, if the deprivation period was extended to 48 hours, the isolated animals reacted aggressively toward a strange animal placed in their cage (Davis, 1933). Several studies have shown that extract of marihuana will not in itself cause fighting in paired rats, nor will 20- to 22-hour food deprivation. When these treatments are combined, however, great irritability occurs with vocalization and vigorous attacks between cage mates. The aggressiveness appears within 30 to 40 minutes and persists for two to four hours. Control experiments indicate that it is the stress of hunger (and not hypoglycemia, acidosis, or lack of specific nutrients because of starvation) that facilitates the development of aggression by marihuana administration (Carlini et al., 1972; Carlini & Masur, 1969; Orsingher & Fulginitti, 1970).

Sleep Deprivation

After 37 hours of sleep deprivation people working in small groups manifested an increase in negative affect and negative behavior and, although overt aggression did not actually occur, verbal hostility clearly increased (Laties, 1961). Rats also show an increase in intraspecific aggression after prolonged sleep deprivation (Webb, 1962). Rats can be specifically deprived of the REM phase of sleep by placing them on small pedestals surrounded by water. The total relaxation that occurs when they drift into REM sleep causes them to topple into the water and awaken. Animals who have been REM deprived for seven days show dramatic increases in shock-induced fighting responses, particularly at lower shock intensities. Further, this increase in fighting frequently persists even after prolonged sleep recovery (Morden et al., 1968; Morden, Conner, Mitchell, Dement, & Levine, 1968).

Available information on the influence of REM deprivation on human behavior is much more difficult to interpret. Initial studies indicated that subjects deprived of REM sleep for as little as three to seven days showed an increase in anxiety, irritability, and difficulties in concentration (Dement, 1960; Dement & Fisher, 1963; Sampson, 1965). Later, better-controlled studies did not confirm those results and implied that the observed irritability may have been due to general sleep loss or the experimental situation (Kales et al., 1964). However, Dement (1964) reported later on two subjects who had been REM deprived for 15 and 16 consecutive nights. Both of these individuals showed an increase in irritability and anger reactions. The effect of REM deprivation on hostile tendencies is still open to various interpretations and though there is some indication that REM deprivation increases those tendencies, more research with better measures of irritability is needed before any firm conclusion can be drawn (Dement, 1965; Vogel, 1968).

Morphine Deprivation in Addicted Subjects

It is generally agreed that individuals under the influence of morphine react passively with a reduced tendency to hostile behavior. However, hyperirritability and a predisposition to violence are a part of the syndrome produced by morphine withdrawal (Tinklenberg & Stillman, 1970). It has also been shown that addicted rats (20 mg/kg/day for 20 days), caged together during withdrawal, manifest considerable aggression

(Boshka et al., 1966) and that the fighting intensity is dose related (Thor & Teel, 1968). Shocking the animals during withdrawal increases the number of aggressive responses (Davis & Khalsa, 1971a). In fact, under these circumstances the aggressive behavior can become so intense that one rat may kill its cage mate within a half-hour period (Crabtree & Moyer, 1973). The general finding of aggression increase during morphine withdrawal has been replicated many times (Borgen et al., 1970; Davis & Khalsa, 1971b; Floria & Thor, 1968; Thor & Hoats, 1970).

Social Deprivation: Isolation-Induced Aggression
Social deprivation has a profound effect on a wide variety of behavior systems. Early and prolonged isolation in monkeys severely disrupts sexual, maternal, and all other social behavior in adulthood (Harlow, 1962) and the animals tend to unrestrained, atypical aggressiveness. Almost all animals have been shown to manifest more aggression after isolation. Studies have included mice[2] (Valzelli, 1969; Welch & Welch, 1971; Charpentier, 1969), rats (Hatch et al., 1963), hamsters (Brain, 1972a), gerbils (Rieder & Reynierse, 1971; Spencer et al., 1973), opossums (Plat et al., 1967), rabbits (Wolf & Von Haxthausen, 1960), and dogs (Kuo, 1967). It has been much more rarely reported that early isolation produces a reduced tendency to fight although this has been reported for mice (King & Gurney, 1954) and for the dog (Scott & Fuller, 1965). At least one strain of laboratory rats shows no increase in irritability even after months of isolation (Rozenzweig, 1966).

Complexity of Aggressive Behavior Produced by Isolation
The fighting behavior produced by social deprivation appears to be complex and may involve several different types of aggression, as defined earlier. The response topography of isolation-induced aggression in male mice generally appears to be that involved in inter-male aggression and can be manipulated by the same kinds of variables that affect that type, such as submission on the part of the opponent. It also seems to be under the control of the pheromones that elicit this type of behavior.

It has generally been reported that isolation does not produce fighting behavior in female mice (Valzelli, 1969; Marucci et al., 1968; Giacalone et al., 1968; Anton et al., 1968; and Anton, 1969). However, in some species of mouse under particular conditions of isolation, female mice do become irritable, hyperreactive to all stimuli, and vicious (Cole & Wolf, 1970; Charpentier, 1969). They will attack other females as well as males placed in their cage. These animals are described as being highly irritable and nervous with a pronounced head-twitching response (Weltman et al., 1962, 1966, 1967, 1968). The variety of stimuli eliciting attack

---

[2] There have been literally hundreds of studies on isolation-induced aggression. Only a few have been cited here.

by isolated females seems to indicate that this is a form of irritable aggression. It is also possible, of course, that there is also an irritable component in the fighting produced in males by isolation, although it appears to be a less important factor.

In the rat there is no evidence that isolation-induced aggression is of the inter-male type. Rats paired after 4 or 14 weeks of isolation tend to ignore one another after a brief sniff (Korn & Moyer, 1968). However, evidence indicates that some strains of rats are made more reactive to many types of stimuli and are more timid and fearful (Moyer & Korn, 1965). They make frantic escape attempts and bite when cornered (Korn & Moyer, 1968; Bernstein & Moyer, 1970; see description on p. 130). This could best be described as fear-induced aggression and may be due to the animal's lack of opportunity to habituate to a wide range of strange stimuli because of the limitations of the isolation environment.

Effects of Social Deprivation in Monkeys

The aggressive behavior produced in monkeys by social deprivation can best be described as irritable since it can be elicited by a very wide range of stimuli. Animals isolated for prolonged periods will attack other monkeys of the same or opposite sex (Harlow, 1962; Harlow et al., 1966), animals of a different species (Mason & Green, 1962), and even infant monkeys, which are rarely the object of monkey aggression (Mitchell et al., 1966). In the absence of any other appropriate target, isolated animals will attack themselves with such intensity that they produce severe wounds on their own extremities (Cross & Harlow, 1965).

Social deprivation, among other things, deprives the animal of an opportunity to learn normal interanimal reactions and the meaning of various social signals. Although these limitations on social learning cannot account for the initiation of the aggressive response by the isolates, they may well explain its inappropriateness, its intensity, and its nonadaptive consequences. Normal monkeys resort to violent action relatively infrequently because, over the course of their social experience, they learn that social signals can take the place of overt action. A dominant animal can subdue a more submissive one with a gesture of threat, and a submissive one can prevent attack by assuming certain "submissive" postures. In the isolate, however, the various social signals have never been associated with a reinforcement pattern and therefore have no meaning. As a result, isolates make repeated "suicidal" attacks on large dominant males (Mitchell et al., 1966) and they fail to live up to monkey social rules by continuing violent attack on smaller monkeys even though those animals are making gestures that are usually effective in inhibiting aggression among normals (Mason, 1963). Some of this learning evidently takes place quite early in the life of the monkeys. Feral monkey mothers tend to control the behavior of their offspring with relatively little actual physical attack. They use posturing, facial signals, and vocalizations and generally precede any type of attack with a warning sign. However, mothers who themselves have been raised without mothers show frequent violent physical aggression against their offspring and do not provide warning signals beforehand (Sackett, 1968a).

Both the length and the kind of social deprivation are important in the production of hyperaggressivity in monkeys. Three months of total isolation from birth has relatively little effect of any kind (Harlow, 1965b), whereas 24 months of total isolation results in an extremely fearful, nonaggressive animal that makes no effort to defend itself from attack and reacts to all types of social stimuli with a crouching posture displayed by normal monkeys under conditions of extreme threat (Harlow & Harlow, 1962). Twelve-month isolates are also fearful and nonaggressive, although they do show pathological aggression if tested later as adults (Mitchell et al., 1966; Harlow & Harlow, 1967). Six months of isolation, however, causes full-blown sociopathic, nonadaptive aggression. These are the animals that attack all comers, brutally beating juveniles and making hopeless attacks on the large dominant males in the cage (Harlow & Harlow, 1962).

The opportunity to associate with peers during early life seems to be an important variable in preventing the development of excessive aggressiveness. Monkeys permitted the social stimulus of the mother only for an eight-month period and deprived of peer relationships show a great deal of hostility and aggression when given the opportunity as compared to those permitted association with both their peers and their mothers (Alexander, 1966).

Self-directed Attack

Perhaps the strangest effect of social deprivation on behavior is the tendency for the animals to direct painful, mutilating attacks against themselves. These animals are spontaneously aggressive and self-destructive. The behavior may be manifest when the subject is approached, but it also occurs when the animal is left alone. Harlow (1962, p. 6) indicates that they "go into violent frenzies of rage, grasping and tearing at their legs with such fury that they sometimes require medical care." Such self-destructive behavior does not develop for the first three years of life whereupon it makes a dramatic appearance. It is present in both sexes, but is more pronounced in the male (Cross & Harlow, 1965).[3]

Alleviating the Effects of Social Deprivation

The devastating effects of early social deprivation on monkeys are relatively permanent and highly resistant to a variety of therapeutic measures.

[3] A recent study has shown that under conditions of stress where no appropriate outward expression of emotion is available, some non-isolate-reared monkeys also show self-directed aggression (Erwin, Mitchell, & Maple, 1973).

It does not help, for example, to introduce the animals into the social situation on a gradual basis (Clark, 1968; Pratt, 1969), and attempts to shape adequate social responding by the negative reinforcement of inappropriate behaviors has had little effect outside the immediate experimental environment (Sackett, 1968b). If the isolated subjects are repeatedly exposed to normally raised monkeys of their own age, their symptoms are likely to be enhanced rather than relieved (Harlow et al., 1965). However, Suomi and Harlow (1972) were finally able to effect a social rehabilitation of isolates by permitting them to interact with socially normal monkeys that were three months younger than they. At 3 months of age aggressive behavior is not well developed in monkeys, but they do initiate clinging, positive-type contact. It is believed that these behavior characteristics permitted the isolated subjects to interact socially without the negative effects of aggressive contact. After six months of social interactions with the young "therapist" monkeys, the behavior of the isolates could not be distinguished from that of the normals.

Pain and Irritable Aggression

There is now a vast literature on aggressive behavior produced by the application of some pain stimulus to the individual, and several reviews of this material exist (Johnson, 1972; Azrin, 1967; Ulrich, 1967; Ulrich & Symannek, 1969; Ulrich et al., 1965).

Foot Shock and Defensive Threat in the Rat

The largest number of studies have been done using electric shock to the foot as the pain stimulus with albino laboratory rats as subjects. The technique has many advantages in that the subjects are readily available; the apparatus is simple; and it is easy to quantify both the stimulus parameters and the responses made. However, as Johnson (1972) has pointed out, it is difficult to determine what most of these experiments have to do with aggression per se. The use of shock with the laboratory rat to study aggression is much like looking under a street lamp for a dime one has lost in a dark alley. It is definitely easier, but the chances of finding it are considerably reduced.

The most common paradigm involves placing two rats in a box with a grid floor and applying shock to the feet of the animals at periodic intervals. On the application of the shock, the animals typically face one another and rear up on their hind legs in what is called a boxing posture. Each assumption of the posture is counted as one aggressive response. The number of times the boxing posture is assumed is a function of such variables as the shock intensity, chamber size, session length, animal age, and strain of the subject (Ulrich, 1966). With most strains of laboratory rat the only manifestation of social interaction is the boxing posture. None of the other components of rat fighting (Barnett, 1963; Eibl-Eibesfeldt, 1961a) such as teeth chattering, erection of the fur, flank presentation, kicking, biting, or wrestling appear as a response to the shock. Generally the boxing posture is assumed only during the shock and the animals show almost no social interaction between shocks. The rats attempt to minimize contact with the shocking grid. This may involve vigorous attempts to climb on top of the other animal. However, even this highly aroused contact activity does not involve biting or other components (Baenninger & Ulm, 1969). Finally, recent studies have shown that the boxing posture is not associated with an attack response or other factors involved in offensive aggression in the rat or mouse (Knutson & Hynan, 1972; Kimbrell, 1969). In one study in which intensive fighting was produced using morphine deprivation in combination with shock, a factor analysis of nine intercorrelated behavioral measures revealed two factors, *defensive threat* and *fighting*. All the defensive-threat measures were of a noncontact nature and included squeals and the assumption of the boxing posture (Crabtree & Moyer, 1973).

Early work on shock-induced aggression in the rat implied that the paradigm provided a good animal model for "aggressive behavior" in the general sense and that one could derive general principles about aggression through the study of that model. Would that the world were so simple. Pain, as indicated later, does sometimes produce an aggressive response but it is, of course, only one of many kinds of aggression. The response evoked by applying shock to the feet of albino rats does not appear to be aggressive at all as aggression is defined in this book. There are, of course, good reasons for studying defensive threat and the variables of which it is a function, but it is important that it be differentiated from fighting, which involves active body contact and biting.

Pain and Aggression in Other Species

Although the many studies on foot shock and defensive aggression in the laboratory rat may be of dubious value in helping us to understand aggressive behavior in general, there can be no doubt that under certain circumstances pain can lead to an intense attack. Such behavior has been demonstrated in the monkey (Delgado, 1955; Plotnik et al., 1971; Azrin et al., 1964; Azrin et al., 1963), the cat (Ulrich et al., 1964), the wild rat (Karli, 1956), and the gerbil (Dunstone et al., 1972). For obvious reasons there is little experimental literature on humans, but it is a rare individual who has not felt a flash of anger and responded with an aggressive kick after the sudden onset of pain from shins barked on a coffee table.

The aggressive response to pain is generally quick and direct and has been referred to as stereotyped or reflexive although, as Johnson

(1972) indicates, it is not highly stereotyped and can hardly be considered reflexive in the more technical sense. The most effective stimulus for eliciting this kind of aggression is a sharp, sudden pain, as characterized by electric shock. Other types of aversive stimulation, such as cold, loud noises, and heat, are much less effective in producing aggression (Ulrich & Azrin, 1962).

Types of Object Attacked in Pain-Induced Aggression

Frequently the subject's attack is directed against the source of the pain. A rat frequently bites the bars through which it is shocked. If the animal's tail is shocked, it often directs its attack against the electrodes (Scott, 1966). If another animal is available in the cage, the attack is often, although not inevitably, directed against it. Monkeys have been shown to attack other monkeys, rats, or mice when they are shocked (Azrin et al., 1964). However, non-mouse-killing wild rats do not attack a mouse, although they fight vigorously with other rats (Karli, 1956). Many species also attack inanimate objects when exposed to a sharp pain. Monkeys threaten a toy tiger (Plotnick, 1971) or attack a stuffed doll or a ball (Azrin, 1964). Shocked rats attack a lever they have learned to press during the experiment (Pear et al., 1973). Wild rats are significantly more likely to attack an unfamiliar inanimate target than they are one with which they have had experience, and the number of attacks directed toward the novel target decreases with increased exposure to it (Galef, 1970b). They also attack a familiar inanimate target more frequently if it is in an unfamiliar rather than a familiar place (Galef, 1970c).

Conditioning, Punishment, and Reinforcement
Value of Pain-Induced Aggression

Although it appears to be difficult to accomplish, there is some evidence that pain-induced aggression can be conditioned. Using the defensive posture (which, as has already been indicated, may not be aggression) as a dependent variable, Vernon and Ulrich (1966) were able to show a moderate amount of conditioning by combining the unconditioned stimulus of shock with a conditioned stimulus of a tone. It has also been shown that the boxing response could be classically conditioned to an 80-db buzzer by using both simultaneous and delayed conditioning paradigms (Creer et al., 1966). It has also been shown that the defensive posture can be conditioned by using a discrimination procedure in which the CS+ was a tone and the CS− was a click (Lyon & Ozolins, 1970). Active aggression, including biting and scratching, in monkeys has been conditioned to the apparatus. These animals were experimental subjects over a period of months and the unconditioned stimulus used was noxious brain stimulation. After a prolonged exposure to the experimental procedure the animals would make violent and aggressive attempts to escape when they were placed in the apparatus. However, this response appears to be much more closely related to fear-induced aggression in anticipation of the noxious stimulation rather than a direct conditioning of pain-induced aggression. In fact, the author refers to the phenomenon as *conditioned anxiety* (Delgado, 1955). In a later report the same author and his colleagues were unable to condition the stereotyped pain-induced aggressive response to a tone in the monkeys. They do not report whether the apparatus evoked aggressive escape responses or the fear-induced type (Plotnik et al., 1971).

Although a variety of aggressive responses can be produced by the application of pain stimulation, it is also possible to suppress an aggressive response if the application of pain is contingent on the response. Rats show fighting and stereotyped posture in response to painful mechanical tail pinch. However, response-contingent electric shock to either fore or hind paws suppressed both the fighting and the postures (Baenninger & Grossman, 1969). Squirrel monkeys subjected to tail shock show high rates of biting on an available hose, but if each bite is followed by a shock more intense that the eliciting shock, the biting behavior drops off rapidly. The biting increases once again when the punishment contingency is removed (Ulrich et al., 1969; Azrin, 1970).

The opportunity to escape from noxious stimulation is, of course, reinforcing as the many studies on avoidance show. However, the opportunity to express aggression induced by noxious stimulation can also be reinforcing and thereby support new learning. Squirrel monkeys loosely restrained in a chair and given tail shock consistently bite inanimate objects. If there is no object convenient for attack, they learn to pull a chain, which will make a ball they can bite accessible to them. If the chain pulling is not reinforced by the presentation of the ball, the response quickly extinguishes but can be reestablished by once again rewarding it with the ball presentation (Azrin et al., 1965). A rat given inescapable shocks in a T-maze will choose to run to the arm containing another rat where it engages in shock-induced fighting (Dreyer & Church, 1970).

Physiological Dysfunctions and Irritable Aggression

A number of physiological dysfunctions in man lower the threshold for and increase the probability of irritable aggressive behavior. These have been discussed in detail in Chapters 2 and 3 but should be mentioned at this point in order to give a full picture. They include rabies, the sequelae to encephalitis lethargica, hyperkinesis in children, Lesh-Nyhan syndrome, certain brain tumors, particularly in the septal temporal and hypothalamic regions, psychomotor epilepsy, premenstrual tension, hypoglycemia, certain allergies, and some types of poisoning, such as mercury.

Sex Differences in Irritable Aggression

Specific studies on the differences between the sexes in irritable aggression are lacking, probably because the different kinds of aggression have only recently been defined. However, there is considerable reason to believe that males manifest more of this trait than do females, although females are by no means free of irritable hostility. As indicated earlier (p. 151), there is evidence that the male of most species engages in more aggressive fighting and threatening behavior of all kinds. Although much male aggressive behavior is directed toward other males (inter-male aggression), it is not confined to that stimulus complex. The mature bull is just as dangerous toward the human handler as it is toward other bulls, and among humans, males account for an overwhelming percentage of the crimes of violence.

Irritable aggression in the female tends to be cyclical and associated with the reproductive phases. Some female cats become extremely aggressive toward the male during heat and immediately after coitus (Green et al., 1957). Female rats frequently attack other females in the later stages of estrus (Calhoun, 1962). Female chimpanzees tend to become irritable during periods of sexual skin swelling (Kohler, 1925). Rhesus monkeys and baboons also become generally more aggressive when sexually receptive (Michael, 1969). Wounding in caged female rhesus monkeys occurs significantly more frequently during the premenstrual period than it does during the rest of the cycle (Sassenrath et al., 1973). Finally, an increase in irritability is a common component of premenstrual tension in the human female (see Chapter 3).

Summary of Irritable Aggression

Irritable aggression can be differentiated from other types by the diversity of the types of stimuli subject to attack. In other kinds of aggression the stimulus objects eliciting aggressive behavior are relatively specific. In irritable aggression, however, the attack may be against a conspecific of either sex, against other species, or even against inanimate objects. The topography of irritable aggression is direct without escape attempts and involves a particular autonomic pattern that in many species includes pupillary dilation and piloerection. In man the affective state is recognized as anger or rage.

The tendency to irritable aggression is increased by several antecedent factors including frustration, deprivation, pain, and a variety of physiological dysfunctions. Frustration that results in irritable aggression may include the direct blocking of goal-oriented behavior as well as the frustration resulting from competition and that induced by extinction procedures (i.e., the withholding of a reinforcement that has previously repeatedly followed a particular response). Under specific conditions food deprivation, sleep deprivation, morphine deprivation in an addicted subject, and social deprivation can result in irritable aggression. Sharp, sudden pain frequently results in a brief display of irritable aggression, and the threshold for irritable aggressive behavior is lowered by a variety of bodily malfunctions from rabies to brain tumors.

Males tend to manifest more irritable aggression than females and at least some of this behavior in females is cyclical and associated with re-productive rhythms.

SEX-RELATED AGGRESSION

There can be no doubt of the relationship between sexual and aggressive behavior. Freud (1955) has suggested aggression is an essential and integral part of sexual feelings in the male. When sexually aroused, he actively subdues the female in the mating process. The woman in turn submits to the aggressive behavior and prefers to be subdued. This is presumed to be of value to the species because it enables the stronger males to make a greater proportional contribution to the gene pool.

Under optimal conditions the aggression involved in sex relations should be under sufficient control to prevent serious injury to either participant. However, because of normal biological variability sex-related aggression sometimes exceeds optimal bounds and becomes sexual violence with severe injury and frequently death as a result. The evidence for sex-related aggression abounds in the daily newspaper. Case studies are presented ad nauseum in a number of different sources (Rein-hardt, 1957; Stekel, 1929; Krafft-Ebing, 1892; Rothman, 1971), and need not be elaborated here.

Definition

It is proposed in this section that sex-related aggression should be considered as a separate class of aggressive behavior in that the stimulus situation eliciting it is relatively specific and because it most probably has a physiological basis different from other types of aggression. In spite of the prevalence of sex-related aggression and the constant and morbid interest in it (many tabloids would go out of business if a sudden universal cure were found), there is remarkably little experimental evidence on the topic.

Sex-related aggression can be defined as aggressive behavior that is elicited by the same stimuli which elicit sexual behavior. It is found primarily but not exclusively in the male, and the stimulus variables are those related to the opposite sex. Although this type of aggressive behavior assumes its most variable and bizarre forms in the human, it is also found in other species.

Sex-Related Aggression in Animals

Mating behavior in many species involves motor components that are very similar to those found in inter-male aggression or in prey catching. Fighting, including a great deal of scratching, biting, and vocalization, is an important part of the courtship process in the cat and weasel family. In some cases it is difficult to distinguish mating behavior from an intense aggressive encounter. Among ferrets and mink, mating has the characteristics of a prolonged fight which may endure for an hour or more (Etkin, 1964). The male mink grabs the female by the scruff of the neck during copulation in a manner that is very similar to the same response made during inter-male encounters (MacLennan & Bailey, 1969). Similar responses can be found in the gray fox (Fox, 1969b) and a number of carnivores and marsupials. Eisenberg and Leyhausen (1972) relate this neck grip during mating to the killing bite of predation and suggest that the potential for the lethal bite is always present but is controlled or partially inhibited during mating.

In general, aggressive courtship displays can be distinguished from true fighting by their consequences; only minor injuries are inflicted. However, sex-related aggression in animals sometimes exceeds adaptive bounds as it does in humans. Carpenter (1942) has made extensive field observations of the rhesus monkey and reports that males frequently attack estrous females. Observation of 45 estrous periods revealed that 22 females were attacked and six of them were severely wounded. One of them lost parts of both ears and received severe cuts on the arm and a number of wounds on the face and muzzle. Another had a leg wound severe enough to make her limp for several days. Others had deep thigh cuts, bruised noses, and deep gashes, and one received such a deep wound in the hip that the motor nerve was damaged and she became a permanent cripple.

Experimental work on the aggressive behavior of the male rhesus indicates the male is responding to some stimulus characteristic of phases of estrus in the female because that behavior can be manipulated by the administration of hormones to the female. Threat behavior on the part of the male is directed away from the female at one stage. When the male's sexual interest is high, the "threatening away" is more frequent and intense, and is not elicited by any particular external stimulation. The threat may be directed at a distant animal or at nothing. Females, when they are most receptive, also display threatening-away behavior. However, if their receptivity is reduced by the administration of progesterone, the threat behavior is also reduced (Zumpe & Michael, 1970). There are also hormonal states during which the aggressive behavior of the female toward the male increases (administration of estrogen and during pregnancy) but during which the male is remarkably tolerant of the female. It is speculated that aggression by the male at this time is inhibited by a female pheromone (Michael & Zumpe, 1970).

Sex-Related Aggression in Humans

The abundant clinical evidence for sex-related aggression in humans has some experimental support but even that is not unequivocal. An increase in hostile fantasy under conditions of sexual arousal has been shown by Clark (1953). A more recent study indicates that the increase in hostile fantasy (as measured by the Thematic Apperception Test) was not simply a function of a general state of arousal. Subjects who were sexually aroused by a videotape of a stimulating scene wrote stories higher in sexual and aggressive imagery than did subjects aroused by videotapes designed to stimulate anxiety or laughter (Barclay, 1971). In another study it was shown that an increase in aggressive arousal also increased sexual story themes (Barclay & Haber, 1965), indicating that the sex-aggression link works both ways.

An indirect indication of the aggression-sex relationship in the male comes from a study on bystander reactions to physical assault. Male and female undergraduates observed highly realistic spontaneous fights between two male and/or female experimenter accomplices. Significantly more males attempted to interfere and stop the fight when it was between two males. However, none of the males interfered when a male was injuring a female. These results are, of course, open to several interpretations, but the authors suggest that the males may have obtained a vicarious sexual and/or hostile gratification from seeing a male "hurt" a female (Borofsky et al., 1971).

Not all studies show an increase in hostile tendencies under sexual arousal. Measures of verbal aggressiveness taken on male college students were not significantly increased after viewing pornographic films (Mosher & Katz, 1970). At least one study has shown that sexually arousing stimuli tend significantly to decrease the number of aggressive-themes-related TAT stimulus cards. College males exposed to slides of nude females do not show as much fantasy aggression as controls (Clark & Sensiber, 1955).

The experiments cited here tell us very little about sex-related aggression in humans. They are, of course, very complex and subject to a multiplicity of interpretations. However, they exemplify the limitations of our knowledge in this area. There can be no doubt that a relationship exists between sex and aggression in humans but we know essentially nothing about the details of the relationship. This is an area of research that needs a great deal of attention.

Some indication of the relationship between sex and aggression can be gained from the physiological mechanisms involved. This material is covered in more detail in Chapter 8, but it should be mentioned here that in some instances a relationship has been established between male sex crimes and the sex hormones. Individuals with excessive sexual motivation who repeatedly get into trouble with the law either because of asocial sexual behavior or because of sadistic homosexual aggression can be brought under control by the oral administration of estrogen (Whitaker, 1959). Hawke (1950) also reports that very vicious homosexuals who brutally attacked small children and who were unstable and constantly creating disturbances could be stabilized and converted into useful citizens within the institution by castration. He also reports one case in which the beneficial antiaggression effects of castration were reversed by the administration of testosterone. (See Chapter 3 for more detail.)

Summary of Sex-Related Aggression

Sex-related aggression is elicited by the same stimuli that elicit sexual behavior. Although there is abundant clinical material on this topic, relatively few experimental studies have been conducted. Sex-related aggression has been observed in animals, and in some animals it is difficult to distinguish mating behavior from intense aggression. The studies on sex-related aggression in humans are contradictory. Some show an increase in hostile tendencies with sexual arousal, but that finding is not supported by other investigators. Sex-related aggression in humans can be reduced by a variety of techniques that reduce sexual motivation.

INTERACTIONS AMONG THE DIFFERENT KINDS OF AGGRESSION

The preceding discussions have dealt with the classes of aggression in their pure form as much as possible in order to clarify the distinctions among them. There is every reason to believe, however, that the different kinds of aggression interact with each other, and differently with other motivation states. For example, in a paper by Baenninger (1967) it was shown that a learned fear response and pain have different effects on predatory aggression in the rat. A conditioned emotional response was developed in mouse-killing rats by giving them tone-shock trials. Testing the Ss in the presence of a mouse showed that the conditioned stimulus of the tone inhibited mouse killing but the unconditioned stimulus of shock overcame the inhibition and produced killing. This appears to be the interaction of predatory and irritable aggression.

There is no theoretical reason why behavior should not be under the influence of more than one set of physiological processes. It is, in fact, probably the most common state of affairs. The possible interactions

among the different kinds of aggression and other motivational states are
extremely complex and a detailed model is needed that attempts to
specify the possible behavior outcomes of various simultaneous motivational influences. As in the preceding illustration, the tendency to
predatory behavior may be inhibited by factors that activate the physiological process associated with fear. However, the behavioral components
of predation may be facilitated by those factors that activate the mechanisms for irritable aggression. At the same time, however, the predator
is at some stage of food deprivation and the physiological processes
underlying that state are also contributing an input to the behavioral
tendency that may be either facilitating or inhibiting, depending on the
amount of deprivation. The animal is also in some state of sleep deprivation, which may also make some contribution to the behavioral outcome,
and so on, almost ad infinitum. The different intensity levels of the
various motivational states may have different influences on a particular
behavior tendency. The mechanisms involved in the interactions among
motivational states are also extremely complex. Some of the factors
involved in the physiological process of fear are particular patterns of
muscle tone. These may be directly incompatible with the muscle tension
patterns required for predation. The sensory mechanisms may also be influenced by the central processes involved in the fear reaction so that
some types of stimuli are more effective in eliciting attention from the
animal than others. There may also be direct inhibiting and facilitating
interactions among the central processes themselves. The potential complexity of the possible interactions soon exceeds the information-process-
ing capacities of the human mind. Thus it seems likely that further
progress in our understanding of these interactions will come from a
computer-modeling approach to the problem.

7

Territoriality?

In 1968 the present author suggested that it might be useful to consider territorial aggression as a separate classification in which the major stimulus variables eliciting that behavior included a territory in which an animal had established itself, and an intruder (Moyer, 1968). It was implied, further, that this type of aggression had a separate physiological basis about which little was known but which should ultimately be experimentally differentiable. As the rest of this section will show, this is not the case. It seems, in fact, that the term *territorial* may be misleading. However, the concept is widely used. It is presumed to have a great deal of explanatory power, and a number of authors have suggested that it is a fundamental concept that is useful in helping us to understand much if not all of the aggressive behavior of mankind (Ardrey, 1966; Lorenz, 1966; Storr, 1968; Tinbergen, 1968). It is therefore important that a section of this book be devoted to it.

The literature on animals is replete with examples of vigorous fighting that occurs when one individual enters the home range of another. Schenkel (1966), for example, reports several instances in which an intruder lion has been killed when it was encountered in areas that were frequently visited by a given lion pride.

In general, animals concentrate their activities in a particular spatial location. Periodically, however, they move out from the area in which they spend most of their time into less familiar grounds. If during that foray they enter the area in which a conspecific concentrates its activities, an aggressive display is likely to ensue. If the intruder does not leave there

is a high probability of a fight occurring. Further, the resolution of the
conflict will most likely involve the defeat and retreat of the animal that
is on unfamiliar ground. The animal closest to the center of its own activity range is most likely to conduct the more vigorous attack and is also
more likely to win, even though the intruder is larger, and in other situations may be more dominant and a more able and vigorous fighter.

The preceding aggression scenario has been observed and reported so
frequently and by so many investigators that there can be little doubt
that it is a behavior pattern characteristic of a wide variety of species.
However, many reports of this behavior have involved a mixture of observations and inferences about those observations. Much of the theorizing
about the meaning of these behaviors has further confused inference and
observation, with the result that a great deal more meaning has been attached to this particular aggressive interaction than the actual observations merit. One of the purposes of this section is to attempt to separate
observation from inference and put this behavior in perspective.

Definition and Motivational Inference

Territoriality is such a diverse phenomenon that a single definition seldom
includes all the behaviors considered relevant by all investigators. However, territoriality is generally considered to be different from *home range*.
The latter concept, initially formulated by Burt, includes "the area, usually
around a home site, over which the animal normally travels in search of
food" (1943, p. 351). Other authors have considered the home range to
be more inclusive, involving the "area over which an animal normally
travels in pursuit of its routine activities" (Jewell, 1966, p. 103). Even
more inclusive is the "annual home range," which includes the living areas
in different seasons of the year (Jay, 1965). Finally the "lifetime" range
has been suggested and includes the entire space over which the animal
has traveled over its lifetime (Jewell, 1966).

Although one cannot know what an animal is searching for at any given
time, as suggested by Burt's definition, the other uses of the home range
concept are generally clear, observable, and capable of being agreed on
by independent observers. The definitions of territoriality and territorial
aggression, however, are not so clear nor so easily agreed on. Unobserv-
ables are inferred by almost all definitions of these constructs. Anthropomorphic motivational states are projected to the animal and are then
treated as though they were established observations.

One of the earliest definitions suggested that "Territory is any defended area" (Noble, 1939). Many authors have adopted this definition
(Ruffer, 1968; Jewell, 1966; Brown, 1966; Bates, 1970; Ardrey, 1966; Storr,
1968; Wynne-Edwards, 1962; Washburn & Devore, 1961; Hediger, 1961,
1950; Myers and Mykytowycz, 1958; and many others). [For a historical

account of this concept, see Carpenter's excellent review (Carpenter, 1958).]

It has been repeatedly pointed out that home ranges may overlap, but territories generally do not because the various animals under study "defend" their territories and "protect" them from encroachment by conspecifics, or by male conspecifics, or by any intruder. How intensive a "defense" the animal puts up depends on the species under consideration and on how broadly the experimenter wishes to make the definition.

Motivational states are not only attributed to the territory holder but are also not uncommonly attributed to the intruder. For example, Hamilton (1947, quoted in Wynne-Edwards, 1962, p. 187) suggests that the blue wildebeest (*Gorgon taurinus*) "strongly resents" encroachment on its grazing land. He also describes an instance in which intruders are chased by a territory-holding bull and then says, "Not the least remarkable phase of the incident was the *sense of wrong-doing* exhibited by the trespassers, which displayed not the smallest tendency to offer any resistance." (Italics added.)

Defend, protect, and *resent* are all terms that are descriptive of human motivational states. When these terms are applied to animals they are inferred from the behavior, and there can be no assurance that the animal has any mental process even remotely similar to those implied by such words. Observation indicates only that many kinds of animals live within certain restricted areas and that some of them engage in fighting behavior. It can also be said that, in general, the closer they are to the center of their home range, the more likely they are to react to another animal with threatening gestures and fighting responses. It is really no more reasonable to suggest that the animal is "defending" his territory than it is to believe that the intruder is defending his God-given right to territorial expansion. Crook (1968) makes the important point that, "In animal societies, individuals do not fight because they have territories, they have territories because, among other things, they fight."

It contributes very little to our understanding of the phenomenon to suggest that certain animals have an innate tendency for territorial defense. Understanding comes only when we can specify the variables of which this behavior is a function. We need to spell out specifically the stimulus characteristics that elicit this kind of behavior in a given animal. Further, since many animals engage in aggression within the home range only at particular times in the seasonal or life cycle, it is necessary to specify the physiological state of the animal during that aggressive period.

Range of Behaviors Included in Territoriality

Although it is certainly true that a wide variety of animals in diverse circumstances do engage in aggressive behavior near the center of their

home range, there is little evidence that there is any kind of unitary instinct or innate tendency for "territorial defense." The conditions under
which home range fighting occurs are highly variable and differ on a wide
variety of dimensions. Carpenter (1958) expresses it well when he says,
"Territorial behavior apparently has great variations, these are related to
differences in species and their habits, to seasons and climates, to 'population pressures,' to social organization, to fluctuations of food supplies, to
predation, and many other factors." He indicates further, that "territoriality is of the nature of higher order, complex and dependent behavior
systems which are organized upon numerous subsystems and behavioral
determinants." It is, in fact (although this is not suggested by Carpenter),
such a catchall term for such a wide variety of behaviors that it has little
value as a unifying construct.

There have been some attempts to classify different kinds of territoriality on the basis of presumed function. Nice (1941), in reference to territories in birds, has suggested seven classes based on combinations of feeding, breeding, and nesting grounds as well as winter roosting. Others have
included communal territories (Hatch, 1966; Garrick, 1963). Burt (1943),
writing about mammals, has also suggested a classification based on function. These include territories concerned with breeding and rearing of
young and with food and shelter. He indicates further that these classes
can be subdivided. Territoriality, because it is so diverse, could, of course,
be classified in a variety of other ways.

In order to appreciate the many different response patterns that have
been referred to as territorial, some of the characteristics of this phenomenon in different species will be reviewed. This is not an attempt to survey
the entire literature on the topic, but to cite examples of animals that show
the different behaviors.[1] Since I wish to avoid the imputation of unknowable motives to animals, I will refer to what is often called territorial
defense as *central home range fighting*. Central home range refers to the
geographical area most frequented by the animal in question. In keeping
with the orientation of the rest of the book, this review deals primarily
with mammals, although there is probably much more information available on "territoriality" in birds.

Animals Subject to Attack by an Animal in His Familiar Home Range

There is considerable variability among the species in regard to what
types of stimulus animals elicit threat or attack by an individual within
its own central home range. Some species, such as the vole, are so soli-

---

[1] A number of detailed reviews with different orientations are available on this
subject, including the following: Ardrey (1966), Bates (1970), Burt (1943), Calhoun (1956), Carpenter (1958), Crook (1968), Esser (1971), Guhle (1961),
Hediger (1961), Hinde (1956), Jewell and Loizos (1966), Klopfer (1969), Nice
(1941), Tinbergen (1957), Wynne-Edwards (1962).

tary that a vigorous fight occurs when another vole is encountered, whether male or female, young or old, except during a restricted mating period (Barnett, 1964b). Among the wildebeest the fighting age occurs generally at 34 to 40 months. At this time some of the males confine their activities to a particular geographical location. Other male wildebeests that approach the area are attacked in the characteristic "tournament" behavior. Females, however, are neither threatened nor attacked (Estes, 1969). Similar behavior is found in Uganda kob (Buechner, 1961; see the superb literary description of this behavior by Ardrey, 1966), the puku *Adenota vardoni* (Vos, 1965), and, on a much smaller geographical scale, the seal (Bartholomew, 1952; Bartholomew & Hoel, 1953).

Lions do not restrict their attacks to males. Either a male or a female lion may be attacked and in some instances killed if it is encountered within the central home range of another animal·(Schenkel, 1966; Schaller, 1969). The lion, like many other animals, does not live in isolation. Thus the home ranges, including the central home ranges, may overlap with many other animals of the same species. Lions live in prides of four or five members up to 15 adults and two cubs. Rabbits (Mykytowycz, 1968), rats (Archer, 1970), mice (Eibl-Eibesfeldt, 1950), prairie dogs (King, 1955), and many primates (Carpenter, 1964) are colonial, with many animals occupying the same geographical areas. They meet and interact with one another with remarkably little agonistic behavior within the colony. However, if a conspecific that has its central home range in a different geographical location wanders into the home range of the colony, it will be attacked. Thus it is a conspecific with which the attacker has had little experience that is the object of the aggressive encounter.

Territory is sometimes defined as that area in which a given animal will not tolerate another member of the same species (Eibl-Eibesfeldt, 1970; Bates, 1970). However, in many animals the tendency to attack within the central home range is not limited to conspecifics.

There is evidence that when the home ranges of the mice *Peromyscus maniculaus bairdii* and *Mus musculus* overlap, there is a good probability that the more aggressive *Mus* will drive the *Peromyscus* from the area (King, 1957). Gerbils vigorously attack other gerbils that are not their littermates and also attack albino rats and albino mice (Ginsburg & Braud, 1971). Gibbons, particularly those that have had little contact with people, threaten any who approach their central home range (Carpenter, 1934), and Hediger (1961) describes the case of a lemur that would permit only its keeper in its cage and severely bit a volunteer assistant. Hediger suggests that in "territorial defense" even small birds and animals can be dangerous to man.

According to Barnett (1964b), a lion is not particularly dangerous to man if it has escaped from captivity and is encountered in the street. It can be driven away fairly easily. However, if the animal is in its home cage or home range, it may instantly strike down a human intruder. Thus, Barnett suggests, the wise lion tamer has the animal driven into an area already occupied by the tamer.

Sex of Animal Attacking in Central Home Range

In many species, from the mouse to the Uganda kob, fighting behavior is the particular province of the male. However, there are also many species in which the female shows the same aggressive proclivity as the male when another animal appears in the central home range. The female gibbon is just as hostile as the male (Carpenter, 1940). Wilson (1968, quoted in Eibl-Eibesfeldt, 1970) describes a confrontation between two free-ranging groups of rhesus monkeys in which several females from one group rush toward the second group and fight briefly only to retreat and then be replaced by another group of females. The female lion will participate in the attack on conspecifics within the home range (Schenkel, 1966). Female voles fight vigorously over large portions of their home range (Barnett, 1964b). In some species, such as the weasel, both sexes engage in fighting behavior within the home range, but the area in which the female will fight is much smaller and more central to her activities than that of the male (Lockie, 1966). In the marmoset a strange male will generally be attacked by the alpha male of the group. However, if the intruder is a strange female the attack is most frequently carried out by the alpha female (Epple, 1970).

Attacks Beyond the Home Range

Most observers report that fighting is restricted to the central home range and that one animal will not attack another on unfamiliar ground. Further, there is a high probability that the winner of a given fight will be the one closest to the center of its home range. There are, however, exceptions to this general rule. A group of Ceylon gray langurs may penetrate deep into the home range of another group, engage in fighting behavior, and win the encounter. However, the results of the encounter do not appreciably change the home ranges of the two groups (Ripley, 1967). Among the howler monkeys, one clan may, because of population pressure, gradually usurp the home range of another, which is then crowded into a less desirable area (Carpenter, 1934). The prairie dog is one of the few animals that appears to extend its home range by winning fighting encounters within the normal range of another colony (King, 1955).

Passive Territoriality

Calhoun (1962) suggests that lactating female rats manifest a passive "defense" of their burrows by plugging up the entrances with pebbles and dirt. The same type of behavior is described for the nursing female rabbit, which seals a nesting burrow containing young and opens it only once a day so that they can be suckled (Mykytowycz, 1968). Calhoun, however, does recognize the possibility of an underlying cause quite unrelated to a basic tendency to territorial defense when he suggests that the behavior may protect the animal from drafts. The fact that other rats are indeed kept out of the burrow may be incidental to the underlying motivation.

Temporal Territory

At least one animal, the domestic cat, is said to have a temporal territory. That is, a group of these animals, although they are essentially solitary in nature, may restrict its activities to the same geographical area. However, this area is distributed on a time-sharing basis. Thus one animal avoids using one of the well-established paths or trails through the area during the time that it is normally used by another animal. A particular cat will be more inclined to lose a fight if it challenges another on an established trail at one time of day, but may be less inclined to lose at a different time of day. However, hostile contact between animals is limited because the cats tend to avoid using the trails at the inappropriate time. The fact that another cat is in temporary possession of a given route is signaled either visually or through odors (Leyhausen, 1965; 1971). Eisenberg (1962) suggests that the same behavior probably occurs in the mouse (*Peromyscus californicus*).

Threat and Attack in Nesting Area

A number of animals make nests and manifest a strong tendency to fight with any organism that approaches the nesting area. In general, the invader loses the encounter and retreats, regardless of its relative dominance in other situations. Calhoun found, in his well-known 1962 experiment with wild rats in a large but enclosed area, that both sexes maintained harborage boxes and expelled any conspecific from the box or from the burrow leading to it. This behavior occurred most frequently in males that had succeeded in maintaining a harem and in lactating females. In the latter case two lactating females might occupy a single burrow system without fighting but they would drive away any other rats.

Female mice (*Peromyscus maniculatus*) do not engage in fighting in the nest area unless they are parturient. In the species *P. californicus*, paired males and females show a considerable tendency to fight with other mice that approach the nest, and the females of this species show this behavior whether they have young or not (Eisenberg, 1962). The tendency to fight in the nest area is highly variable among nonreproducing female mice (*P. gracilis* and *bairdii*). However, when these mice are lac-

tating they viciously attack any strange male approaching the nest area
(King, 1963).

Factors Affecting Tendency to Fight in Home Range

The tendency for an animal to threaten or fight in its home range is highly
variable, depending on both the environmental conditions and the internal physiological process of the individual. Under laboratory conditions
of high population density, mice do not restrict their activities to specific
areas. Although they do fight, the fighting is not geographically localized
(Scott, 1944). However, it has been shown that under more natural conditions, where space is available, some species of mice do live in colonies
within restricted areas and do attack noncolony members who enter the
area (Eibl-Eibesfeldt, 1950; Crowcroft, 1955). Several factors may contribute to a shift from geographically localized fighting to a dominant-
subordinate relationship within a group of animals. These include insuffi-
cient space, a lack of opportunity to emigrate, inadequate escape cover,
as well as a high population density (Archer, 1970). Vervet monkeys may
fight in their home range in one habitat but not in another (Gartlan, 1966,
quoted in Crook, 1968). A number of animals restrict their activities to a
particular geographical area only during certain times of the year, frequently during the breeding season. This is true of a number of the Pinnipedia, such as the southern fur seal, the gray seal, sea lions, and elephant
seals (Wynne-Edwards, 1962). It is also true of the Uganda kob, the
wildebeest (Estes, 1969), and in part the red deer (Darling, 1937). Male
rabbits show less tendency to confine their activities to a given area and
to fight in that area after the breeding season is over (Myers & Mykytowycz, 1958).

As indicated, fighting by females near the nest area in some animals
depends on whether or not the animal is lactating.

The area adopted for the home range is also dependent on the season
and the availability of food. The deer (Darling, 1937) and the elk (Murie,
1951) have home ranges in the mountains during the summer but migrate
to the lower ranges during the winter. The home range of howler monkeys
is dynamic and shifts over the years and within the seasons (Carpenter,
1934). Restriction of range and intensity of fighting within that range in
small carnivors depends both on the amount of food available and on the
number of competing animals (Lockie, 1966).

Personal Space as a Form of Territoriality

Many different animals, from birds (Marler, 1956) to men (Hall, 1966;
Sommer, 1969), under certain conditions, prevent the close approach of
conspecifics. The infringement of this individual distance or personal

space results in either avoidance or attack by the animals involved. Crook (1968) suggests that territoriality is a special case of spatial defense that cannot be easily separated from the maintenance of personal space. However, the tendency to maintain an individual distance may also be combined with the tendency to fight within a given home range. Carpenter (1940) indicates that gibbons have a personal space that cannot be violated but that they also fight as a group against other groups intruding into their home range.

Among some species—the moose (Altman, 1963) and bear (Herrero, 1970), for example—the mother maintains a "ring of sliding territoriality" (Altman, 1963, p. 245) or a personal space around herself and the young, and behaves aggressively toward any approaching animal.

Nonterritorial Animals

Although a number of authors are impressed by how widespread territoriality is among vertebrates (Carpenter, 1958; Ardrey, 1966), it is by no means universal. Even among closely related species, some show an attachment to a particular geographical location and a tendency to fight within it, whereas other species do not. Heller (1971), for example, studied four species of chipmunk. Two of these species, *Eutamias alpinus* and *E. amoenus*, behaved aggressively within their home range, whereas *E. minimus* and *E. Speciosus* did not. The Indian rhinoceros is highly aggressive and has an attachment to a specific geographical location throughout the year. However, the white rhino does not have a well-differentiated land area to which it confines its activities and it is much less aggressive (Cloudsley-Thompson, 1965). The black rhinoceros does not appear to be territorially inclined (Schenkel & Schenkel-Hulliger, 1969). As indicated, many seals and related animals have well-defined areas of activity during the breeding season. However, seals of the genus *Phoca* as well as some others do not manifest this behavior and do not react aggressively to conspecifics (Wynne-Edwards, 1962).

The home ranges of nutria (*Myocastor coypus*) overlap extensively, and although adults may be highly aggressive, there is no indication that this hostile behavior is restricted to a given location except that a mother with offspring is aggressive in the nesting area (Ryszkowski, 1966). Lowe (1966) has reported aggressive behavior among red deer on the island of Rhum, but he indicates that marked animals may be found in different groups at different times and that there is no evidence of group territorial behavior.

Many herding animals, primarily the ungulates, show neither the restriction of activity to a given land space nor hostile tendencies. (Wynne-Edwards, 1962, gives many examples.) Among the subhuman primates most closely related to man, many do not show aggression when encountering a strange conspecific. Among the baboons in Rhodesia, for example, the habitual daily routines tend to keep the different troops apart, but the ranges of the troops overlap to a considerable extent in some cases. There is no evidence that these animals fight with other troops when they meet (Washburn & DeVore, 1961). According to Schaller (1963), the *Gorilla gorilla* is a remarkably peaceful animal that does not engage in fighting within its home range. The monkeys of the forest fringes and the savannahs (some species of *Cercopithecus* and *Macaca*) also do not show central home range fighting (Crook, 1968). Chimpanzees are organized into troops, but interchanges in membership are not uncommon and several troops may use the same home range (Reynolds, 1965).

Scent Marking and Its Meaning

Many animals are equipped with specialized anatomical structures that produce species-specific chemical substances. These scents are distributed around the animal's home range through a variety of behaviors. Antelopes have scent glands located beside the eye (Hediger, 1949). In the gerbil the midventral sebaceous gland produces a scent (Thiessen et al., 1968). Badgers and martens have scent glands under the bases of their tails (Eibl-Eibesfeldt, 1970). Scent glands are located in the flanks of voles (Brown, 1966) and hamsters (Eibl-Eibesfeldt, 1970). Rabbits have scent glands located under the chin (Mykytowycz, 1968). Lions can release a scent along with the urine (Schaller, 1969) and many animals are said to utilize urine and fecal material for marking purposes (Brain & Nowell, 1969; Calhoun, 1962; Egan et al., 1972).

The act of depositing the scent in the environment is called marking and many investigators refer to this behavior as territorial marking. Cloudsley-Thompson suggests that some of the scent glands have evolved specifically for the purpose of marking territory and Eibl-Eibesfeldt (1970) says in a quotation from F. Goethe (1938) that scent markings are chemical property signs. The term *scent marking* is descriptive of a given animal's behavior. That is, the marmoset rubs the circumgenital area against some item in the environment, or the gerbil rubs its ventral sebaceous gland against a peg, or the dog deposits a few drops of urine on a fire plug. The result of this behavior is the deposition of a scent that can be detected and reacted to by other animals. However, to refer to this behavior as *territorial marking* imputes to the animal a motivation. [It *wants* to mark a territory to warn conspecifics that this land is occupied so that they will avoid it. Lorenz (1954), for example, compares scent marking in the dog to the song of the nightingale. The dog deposits scent in its territory in order to ward off intruders.] Such a teleological explanation is neither necessary nor particularly useful and can, in fact, be misleading. Marking may be associated with aggressive behavior and it may frequently occur within the animals' home range. However, it is also associated with other behavior patterns.

Scent Marking and Home Range

Marking is a response to certain types of stimuli in the environment and those stimuli need not necessarily be associated with the animals' central home range or "territory." Any dog owner knows that it is possible to take his pet half a world away from its home range and the dog will readily mark any post in the environment, even though that post has been previously marked by local dogs. Many members of the Canidae family mark familiar and conspicuous objects on which they have previously deposited a scent, but marking is also elicited by entirely new and unfamiliar objects (Kleiman, 1966). Marking in gerbils is actually less frequent in the central home range where the stimuli are most familiar (Higgins et al., 1967). The highest rate of ventral marking in this species occurs in a moderately novel environment (Baran & Glickman, 1970) and olfaction appears to be of prime importance because olfactory ablation essentially eliminates the marking response (Baran & Glickman, 1970; Thiessen et al., 1970). Golden hamsters (*Mesocricetus auratus*) have been shown to spend significantly more time engaged in flank marking in the cage of strange hamsters than they do in their own cage (Murphy, 1970).

Avoidance of Marked Areas

If marking is territorial in nature and designed to warn conspecifics away from the area, it would be expected that the scent marks would elicit an avoidance response from other members of the same species. In many cases, however, just the opposite reaction occurs. Gerbils show a preference for objects marked by conspecifics, that is, they will choose as nesting material paper that has been marked by another gerbil (Baran & Glickman, 1970). When gerbils mark an environment that is new to them, they show neither a preference for nor a tendency to avoid pegs that have been previously marked by a strange gerbil (Thiessen et al., 1970).

Marmosets approach and mark a perch in their cages that has been previously marked by another marmoset significantly more than they do a neutral perch or one marked with mouse urine (Epple, 1970). Both mice and rats follow regular pathways and trails in their daily excursions through their home range. These trails are well scent-marked with urine. If a given population is experimentally eliminated, the home range will be taken over by immigrants from surrounding areas. These newcomers actually utilize the marked trails and paths of the previous population to find their way around the area and show no evidence of being repelled by the earlier scent markings (Eibl-Eibesfeldt, 1950; Telle, 1966).

In some species there appears to be a tendency to avoid marked areas of other individuals. Schaller (1969) implies that lions avoid marked areas but he provides little evidence that they do. It has been suggested (Kleiman, 1966) that the avoidance of marked areas is due to the novelty of scent of the stranger. However, an interesting experiment on gerbils suggests that the avoidance of a particular scent may be a learned reaction because that scent has been associated with the negative reinforcement of defeat. If gerbils are given an opportunity to nest in boxes that contain either clean shavings or shavings that have been soiled by other gerbils, they show no preference. However, if these animals are placed in the home area of a group of gerbils and are attacked and defeated, they show a clear-cut preference for nesting in clean shavings rather than in shavings soiled by the antagonists that had defeated them earlier (Dawber & Thiessen, 1971; Thiessen & Dawber, 1972). When gerbils are given a choice in a Y-maze, they avoid the odor of an animal that has recently defeated them (Nyby et al., 1970).

Scent Marking and Other Behaviors

Although there is relatively little evidence that a strange scent produces an automatic avoidance response, it does frequently affect the animals' behavior. A strange scent frequently elicits a considerable increase in marking in a number of different species, including the sugar glider, rabbit, hamster, marmoset, duiker (Ralls, 1971). Some of these animals, including the rabbit (Mykytowycz, 1966), hamster (Eibl-Eibesfeldt, 1953), marmoset (Epple, 1970), display a threat response in connection with the increased marking.

There does appear to be a relationship between aggressive behavior and scent marking, but there is little evidence that it is related to territoriality as usually defined. In general, males mark more frequently than females, and dominant animals mark more than submissive ones. The same complexes of stimuli that elicit the marking response also tend to elicit fighting. This relationship has been considered in considerable detail by Ralls (1971), who concludes that, "Mammals mark frequently in any situation where they are both intolerant of and dominant to other members of the same species. In other words, they mark when they are likely to attack another member of the same species and are likely to win if they do attack" (p. 449).

Other Presumed Functions of Marking

It should also be pointed out that scent marking is said to have a number of functions that do not relate to territory. It may help to define a "safe" area and promote colony cohesion (Baran & Glickman, 1970). It may be important as sexual communication (Epple, 1970) and may help to reassure the animal in a strange territory (Kleiman, 1966). It may also be a mechanism for defining trails or paths (Eibl-Eibesfeldt, 1970). Ralls (1971) lists several other possible functions, including, as alarm signals, for individual or group recognition, for species or subspecies recognition, and as a primer pheromone that influences reproductive processes.

Vocalization in the Home Range

Population dispersal as well as the limitation of individuals and groups to restricted geographical locations appears to be due in part to a variety of vocal signals. There is evidence that a number of mammals, although by no means all, tend to avoid areas in which conspecifics are emitting particular calls.

The chipmunk (*Tamias striatus*) produces several kinds of vocalizations. Although home ranges of these animals overlap completely, a given chipmunk is usually dominant to others in the core area that centers around its burrow entrance. The particular sound called chipping occurs only in that immediate area, and it has been suggested that chipping may function as an agonistic signal that inhibits the approach of other chipmunks (Dunford, 1970). Roaring by lions is said to function as a signal that informs conspecifics of the location of a local pride and thus keeps them at a distance (Schenkel, 1966). This function of roaring has not, however, been experimentally demonstrated. Experimental work has shown that barking by the larger male sea lions (*Zalophus californianus*) functions to restrict both the movements and the amount of vocalization by other, smaller males (Schusterman & Dawson, 1968).

Although there are exceptions, primates very rarely show interanimal or intergroup aggressive behavior in relation to their home range or core areas. In general, however, they do restrict their activities to definable geographic areas, and family groups or troops are usually isolated from one another even though their home ranges may overlap (Bates, 1970). The groups appear to be separated by spacing mechanisms. A number of observations indicate that spacing is accomplished by a mutual repulsion or avoidance rather than as a result of actual aggression (Marler, 1968; DeVore, 1963a). Many primates, including the howler monkey (Carpenter, 1964), gibbon (Carpenter, 1940), the northern India langur (Jay, 1965), and the Callicebus (Mason, 1968), produce vocalizations that are loud enough to be audible at a considerable distance and that may contribute to the spacing process. These long-range calls occur frequently during the early morning and in the absence of any particular external triggering situations (Marler, 1968). To refer to these calls as territorial markers (Mason, 1968) or threats seems unwarranted. The calls may serve as "spatial location markers" (Bates, 1970) that provide other members of the same species with information concerning the whereabouts of conspecifics. They may then react by avoiding that location and contribute to the dispersal of those animals. [For the sake of completeness it should be pointed out that long-distance calls of some primate species do not necessarily elicit avoidance reactions. They do sometimes result in approach tendencies (Marler, 1968).]

An Alternative to Territoriality

It can be seen from the foregoing discussion that "territoriality" refers to a complex of behavior patterns that vary widely across species and within species, depending on the animal's sex, the characteristics of the intruder, the season of the year, the developmental stage of the animal, and a variety of environmental variables. There is evidence, of course, that animals do confine their activities to particular geographical locations and within a given location many animals spend a greater amount of time in so-called core areas. There is also abundant evidence that many animals engage in intraspecific fighting within home ranges and that many species tend to win encounters that are fought close to their core area; that is, the animals on unfamiliar ground are chased away, infrequently injured, and on very rare occasions killed.

It is of little explanatory value to suggest that the large variety of factors contributing to fighting within an animal's home range are related to an innate tendency or need to defend a territory. The fact that the animal closest to the center of its home range is more likely to be successful in an encounter with an intruder is certainly not evidence that territorial defense is involved. Barnett (1969), for example, has suggested that aggressive behavior in the rat is territorial because the animal must be on familiar ground before it will attack a conspecific. By the same reasoning, one should refer to territorial sexual behavior and territorial eating behavior.

Animals are more "successful" in all their behaviors when they are on familiar ground. If one wishes to study sexual behavior, predation, or simply eating and drinking, it is essential that the animal be adapted to the environment. In a strange area the predominant behavior of most animals is cautious investigation, which is incompatible with aggressive, sexual, or consummatory behavior. Exploratory behavior overrides eating or drinking even under conditions of extreme deprivation. It has been repeatedly reported that a mouse in its home cage is more likely to initiate and to win a fight against an introduced intruder. However, Urich observed in 1938 that the stranger spends most of its time investigating the unfamiliar cage whereas the home cage mouse concentrates on fighting.

As indicated in Chapter 6, there are a variety of stimulus conditions that facilitate the tendency for one male to attack another. There is also a tendency on the part of most animals to investigate and/or escape from unfamiliar situations. As suggested in Chapter 1, in the section on the interactions of various motivational states, there are a variety of ways in which motivational states can be mutually inhibitory. Thus if an animal is on unfamiliar ground, it has investigatory and escape tendencies that are incompatible with a full-blown aggressive response of whatever kind. If, under the pressure of attack, the animal flees to the familiar stimuli of its own core area, the factors producing escape and investigation tendencies are eliminated and the stimulus of its attacker elicits full and uninhibited aggressive proclivities. It is now more likely to win an encounter with the aggressor, who is now itself on unfamiliar ground and has escape and investigation tendencies to compete with its hostile behaviors. In a series of chases and counterchases it would be expected that the animals might end up at the borders of their home ranges manifesting a combination of escape and aggressive behaviors that are frequently components of the threat response.

Since, as Carpenter (1958) suggests, the so-called territorial behavior is a higher-order construct that results from the action of a variety of subsystems, it is not possible to attribute this behavior to particular physiological mechanisms. In different seasons and in different species, fighting in relation to a geographical location may be primarily between males, as in the Uganda kob (inter-male aggression); restricted to a nest area and confined to lactating females, as in certain female mice (maternal aggression); or related to the herding of a harem, as in the Pinnipedia (sex-related aggression). The amount and intensity of fighting must also undoubtedly be a function of the success or failure of these various aggressive interactions and is therefore partly instrumental aggression. The physiological substrates of each of these different kinds of aggression will be dealt with separately.

Human Aggression and the "Territorial Imperative"

The application of the concept of territorial aggression to man has resulted primarily from an attempt to extrapolate findings from animal research to the human condition. Thus if the construct is of dubious value in understanding animals, it may be even less useful in understanding man. The question, of course, is not whether man is territorial, but whether that territoriality is imperative.

There is little need to document man's tendency to become attached to geographical locations and possessions. National boundaries do exist; property lines are carefully drawn; and there are well-established legal mechanisms for establishing title to and exclusive use of property and possessions. Mental patients establish definable territories on the ward

and defend them (Esser et al., 1965), children establish and defend
territories in a playroom (Paluck & Esser, 1971), and my neighbor down
the street becomes upset if I step on his lawn. Significant portions of a
number of books have been devoted to the experimental and literary exploration of the human tendency to territoriality (Proshansky et al., 1970;
Ardrey, 1966; Esser, 1971; Montagu, 1968; Hall, 1966; Sommer, 1969).

Man not only establishes and defends territories, he does so with far
greater complexity than is apparent in lower animals. As Stea's (1965)
analysis indicates, a single individual may have a "territorial unit" in his
place of employment, another one at home, and a third at his vacation
cabin. The same individual also has a territorial domain that he shares
with other persons each of whom also has several "territorial units" only
some of which are shared by two or more individuals. This shared territory is the "territorial cluster." Each worker, for example, has an individual
territorial unit that may be the area immediately surrounding his desk but
he shares with others the territorial cluster of the department. Further, a
number of territorial clusters may be grouped into a "territorial complex,"
such as a business or a political unit, which large numbers of individuals
perceive as their own and are willing, to some extent, to protect and defend (see Figure 5).

Although it is dubious to use the concepts of *protect, defend,* and
resent in relation to animal behaviors, such motivational constructs are

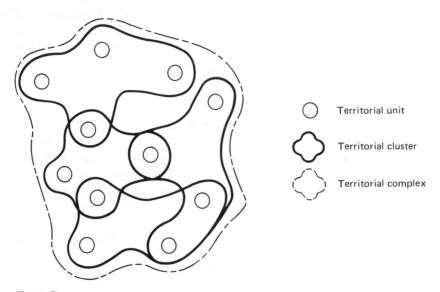

○ Territorial unit

✦ Territorial cluster

⟨✦⟩ Territorial complex

Figure 5
Complexity of territorial behavior in man. (After D. Stea, Space, territory and human
movements, *Landscape,* 1965, *15,* No. 1.)

readily applied to man and can be inferred from the individual's verbal behavior as well as directly observed in one's own introspection. The real question is not whether many men establish and defend a complexly organized set of territories but whether such a tendency is innate or built in, as it has been said to be in animals. Man does, of course, have internal impulses to aggression (Moyer, 1969), but there is little evidence that the expression of these impulses is innately related to the remarkably complex and abstract construction of territory. Certainly there is no need to invoke an "instinct" to territoriality as an explanatory principle. The analysis earlier in this chapter appears to make such an explanation untenable for animals, and it seems even less likely for man. There is abundant opportunity for man to learn an aggressive reaction to the invasion of his many territories. Such an invasion frequently involves threat, inconvenience, frustration, and deprivation. Successful aggressive action terminates these negative states, with the result that the aggressive behavior is rewarded. In the early social development of man, conflict potential was considerably enhanced as the concept of ownership of property, tools, livestock, and so on, began to develop. It seems reasonable to suggest, as Crook (1968) does, that cultural patterns of behavior would develop to regulate interactions regarding property. These behaviors would then be codified into laws of property, its use and exchange.

However, even if, for the sake of argument (and only for the sake of argument), the concept of instinctive territorial defense in man were to be granted, it would not mean that the resultant behavior would be ineradicable, as is frequently implied (Lorenz, 1966; Ardrey, 1966; Storr, 1968). As suggested in Chapter 1, powerful internal impulses of all kinds are modifiable through learning and through manipulations of the environment. Some cultures, such as the Arapesh (Benedict, 1934) and the Zunis (Mead, 1935), although manifesting other kinds of aggressive behavior, do not show territorial tendencies.

Further, the concept of instinctive territorial defense is not particularly useful in helping us understand modern war. At best, such an instinct could be offered to explain a defensive war, or why countries tend to win defensive war. (They do not, of course, as the downfall of Ethiopia in 1936 and the fall of most of western Europe in the 1940s will testify.) An "instinct" for territorial acquisition would have to be invoked to explain the expansionist policies of many national bodies. It is difficult even to find examples of animal forms exhibiting that type of behavior.

In summary, many men manifest a wide variety of highly complex territorial tendencies but there is little evidence that territorial defense is any more instinctive, innate, inevitable, or ineradicable than any other complex learned behavior. The superficial similarities between the territorial behavior of animals and that of man are analogous rather than homologous.

SUMMARY

Evidence for the concept of territorial aggression in both animals and humans is reviewed and it is concluded that the construct of territoriality is not particularly useful and has little explanatory power. The definitions of territorial aggression frequently infer unobservable, anthropomorphic motivational states. These motivational states are then projected to the animal and treated as though they were established observations. Territoriality has come to refer to a complex of diverse behavior patterns that vary widely across species and within species depending on the animal's sex, the characteristics of the intruder, the season of the year, the developmental stages of the animal, as well as a variety of environmental variables. So-called territorial aggression may, at different times and in different animals, involve *inter-male, maternal, sex-related,* and *instrumental* aggression, each of which has been shown to have a different physiological basis. It is not useful to attempt to encompass these divergent behaviors under a single innate tendency to "defend" a territory.

It is further concluded that since the construct of territoriality is of dubious value in helping us to understand animal behavior, it may be even less useful in helping us to understand the behavior of man.

8

Physiological Substrates of Different Kinds of Aggression

In earlier chapters some reference has been made to the physiological bases of the different kinds of aggression in order to help differentiate among them. In this chapter an attempt will be made to review the rather large body of knowledge on this topic in order to present a coherent picture of what is known about the physiology of each type of aggression.

Because of the nature of the material this chapter is highly technical and may be of greatest interest to research scholars who wish to extend the frontiers of knowledge. Many students may wish to skip this chapter entirely or read only the summaries at the end of the chapter. Certainly there is no need to attempt to commit this mass of detail to memory, because much of the detail will change tomorrow. This field is changing very rapidly. Laboratories all over the world are working on this problem and each month brings a mass of new data. Therefore any statement about the physiology of aggressive behaviors must be highly tentative. Further, an unbelievable amount remains to be done before we have even a moderate understanding of the details. However, it is useful to have a review of the current state of the art.

NEUROLOGICAL BASIS OF PREDATORY AGGRESSION

A considerable amount is now known about the neurology of predatory behavior in two species. Although many investigators have contributed to this store of information, the greatest amount of work has been done in two laboratories. Pierre Karli and his colleagues at the University of Strasbourg in France have been studying the neurology of predation in the rat since 1956. Karli reviewed this extensive series of experiments at the Milan conference on aggression in 1968 (Karli et al., 1969). Flynn and his students at Yale have concentrated on predatory aggression in the cat since 1962. This work was reviewed in 1967 and more completely in 1970 and 1972 (Flynn, 1967, 1972; Flynn et al., 1970). An attempt is made here to integrate the materials from these reviews and incorporate the findings of other investigators in order to summarize the material and to put it in the context of the general physiological model of aggression postulated in this book. The neurology of the sensory and motor functions in predation was discussed earlier. This section is concerned with the central integrating mechanisms. It should be recognized, of course, that the central integrating mechanisms can only be separated from the sensory and motor functions for convenience of exposition. Certainly the neurological mechanisms function as a unit.

Predatory aggression is controlled by a neural system that is a complex of neurons involving several brain levels including the amygdala, thalamus, hypothalamus, and midbrain. There are other neural systems in the brain that send fibers to the system for predation. Some of them act to facilitate the functioning of that system whereas others inhibit it.

Lateral Hypothalamus and Predation
When the neural system for predation is activated electrically, or chemically, or presumably naturally, in the presence of the animal's natural prey, predatory behavior characteristic of the species occurs with remarkable reliability. It has been shown repeatedly that cats that normally do not attack rats will do so if particular areas of the hypothalamus are stimulated. The latency of the attack depends on the intensity of the stimulation. Wasman and Flynn (1962) observed over 2500 hypothalamic stimulation trials and attack on the rat occurred in 97.6 percent of the trials. The behavior does not resemble the diffuse sham rage reaction of the decorticate animal. The response is well organized and the cat's behavior is adjusted on the basis of the behavior of the stimulus object. As Wasman and Flynn (1962, p. 62) state in their description of the cat's behavior during stimulation: "The cat's responses were clearly directed. It would pursue and invariably catch a fleeing rat. If the rat leaped in the air the cat waited and caught the rat in mid-air or when it landed. The effectiveness of the attack was attested to by the frequent deaths and injuries to the rats."

The aggressive response is dependent on the activation of the hypothalamus in that it begins when that area is electrically activated and it ceases precisely with the offset of the stimulation. The cat will terminate a bite just as the jaws are closing if the stimulation is turned off at that instant. The response to electrical stimulation at the proper hypothalamic site has the characteristic topography of predation in the cat. The attack is quiet, stalking, and primarily biting. The paws are used to hold and subdue the prey but not to strike or tear with extended claws.

As indicated earlier, the hypothalamically induced response is stimulus-bound in that the less the available stimulus resembles an appropriate prey object, the less the probability of attack. Although the stimulated animals show a preference for the typical prey (see p. 138), the response is not completely specific to that stimulus object. Cats stimulated in the lateral hypothalamus show some attack behavior toward kittens and other cats (Bandler, personal communication).

If no appropriate target for the attack is available, the same amount of hypothalamic stimulation does not result in any semblance of attack. The subject manifests arousal; it explores and sniffs and walks around in the cage, but it does not attack the wall, the food dish, or the experimenter.

In the now classic studies at Yale (Wasman & Flynn, 1962; Egger & Flynn, 1963; Adams & Flynn, 1966) it was dramatically shown that at least two kinds of aggression could be differentiated in the hypothalamus. Stimulation of the lateral hypothalamus resulted in the predatory attack, as indicated earlier. The cat would ignore the experimenter and attack a rat. However, if the medial hypothalamus was stimulated, the cat would ignore an available rat in its cage and manifest a highly directed attack on the experimenter. If a rat is available and the experimenter is not when the medial hypothalamus is stimulated, the cat will launch a directed attack on the rat. However, the fact that the rat is attacked does not make the attack predatory. The topography of the response is very different. The attack is not quiet and stalking. The cat is highly aroused manifesting all the symptoms of feline "rage" and the assault is characterized by striking out with the unsheathed claws rather than biting. As is noted below, these two kinds of aggression are sometimes confused because the object of attack is the same.

The attack behavior induced by lateral hypothalamic activation has been described in some detail because it is characteristic of brain-stimulation-induced predation and because it is a highly reliable response reported by a number of investigators in at least three species. In addition to the studies from Flynn's laboratory (Levison & Flynn, 1965; Wasman & Flynn, 1962; MacDonnell & Flynn, 1966a, 1966b; Chi & Flynn, 1971a, 1971b; Adams & Flynn, 1966), predatory or stalking attack in the cat from lateral hypothalamic stimulation has been reported by Hutchinson and Renfrew (1966), Roberts and Kiess (1964), and Roberts and Bergquist (1968).

Electrical stimulation of the lateral hypothalamus of the rat has also resulted in the typical predatory attack by the rat on the mouse. This involves the rapid and precise kill with the killing bite directed at the cervical spinal column (Vergnes & Karli, 1969; King & Hoebel, 1968; Panksepp, 1969, 1971b, 1971c). Electrical stimulation has also been shown to facilitate the frog-killing response in natural frog killers (De-Sisto, 1970; DeSisto & Huston, 1970a) and mouse killing in the natural mouse killer (Karli et al., 1969). Chemical stimulation of the same area has also been shown to elicit mouse killing in the rat (Bandler, 1969, 1970; Smith et al., 1969) and to facilitate both mouse and frog killing in natural killers (Bandler, 1969, 1970).

What appears to be predatory aggression has also been elicited in the opossum by electrical stimulation of the lateral hypothalamus. The attack on a rat involved the usual predatory components of seizing, head tossing, and killing bite and crunching, which consisted of a rhythmic biting on the head. The intensity of the attack was related to the stimulation voltage. As with the cat, stimulation in the same area also produced a similar attack on opossum pups and on adult opossums if the adults were prevented from defending themselves by having their mouths taped closed (Roberts et al., 1967).

Predatory aggression in the rat can be eliminated if extensive bilateral lesions are made in the lateral hypothalamus (Panksepp, 1971a). It is necessary, however, that the area lesioned include the anterior, medial, and posterior portions if a long-lasting suppression of the response is to be obtained (Karli & Vergnes, 1964a). The loss of the killing response may be due to the interruption of the neural system for killing, but it is undoubtedly due in part to a drastic sensory deficit (Marshall et al., 1971).

Chemical Manipulations of Predation

The evidence from experiments using chemical stimulation and peripheral drug administration have led some investigators to suggest that the neural transmitter substance involved is cholinergic. The mouse-killing response in rats can be facilitated or elicited by the direct application of carbachol, acetylcholine mixed with physostigmine, or neostigmine. (Both physostigmine and neostigmine block the action of cholinesterase, thus enhancing the action of acetylcholine.) Other types of neurotransmitters, such as norepinephrine, serotonin, and DL-5-hydroxytryptophan, did not produce this effect, nor was it produced by control substances, including sodium salts and amphetamines (Bandler, 1969, 1970; Smith et al., 1969, 1970).

Some attempts to block the natural predatory response with anticholinergic agents have been successful. Atropine methyl nitrate, an anticholinergic substance that does not readily cross the blood-brain barrier was applied directly to the lateral hypothalamic sites by Smith et al., with the result that the kill latencies of natural killers were significantly increased. The control substance sodium nitrate had no such effect. Bandler

(1970) found that the central application of atropine significantly depressed attack and kill tendencies in only two of the 13 positive hypothalamic placements. In the light of what is known about the redundancy
of the predatory aggression pathways in the brain, this result is less surprising than the more general suppression obtained by Smith et al.

Bandler also administered the cholinergic blocking agents atropine
sulfate and atropine methyl nitrate systemically and found that both of
these drugs significantly increased attack latencies in natural killers.
Atropine sulfate increased the kill latencies in the natural killing situation
and blocked the killing facilitation by the central application of carbachol
stimulation. The greater efficacy of atropine sulfate was probably due to
the fact that it passes the blood-brain barrier much more readily than
atropine methyl nitrate. Other investigators have also shown that
peripherally administered anticholinergic agents are effective in blocking
the mouse-killing response (Hoffmeister et al., 1964; Kreisskot, 1963),
and two reports indicate that cholinergic stimulation (pilocarpine) can
induce mouse killing in some nonkiller rats (McCarthy, 1966; Vogel &
Leaf, 1972; Wnek & Leaf, 1973).

Cholinergic stimulation of the amygdala has, in some cases, produced
mouse killing (Leaf et al., 1969) and the application of amitone (a
cholinesterase inhibitor) to the basal amygdala produced mouse killing
in 2 out of 12 nonkiller rats (Igic et al., 1970). Amiton applied to the
lateral septum induced mouse killing in four of 18 animals (Igic et al.,
1970). It has also been shown that predatory attack by the cat can be
elicited by intraperitoneal injections of the cholinergic agents oxotremorine or arecoline. The attack can be blocked by pretreatment with
atropine sulfate, which crosses the blood-brain barrier, but not by
atropine methyl nitrate, which does not (Bernston & Leibowitz, 1973).

More recent studies have called into question the cholinergic nature of
the predatory system. The doses of cholinergic substances required to
elicit or facilitate predation were quite high. Smith et al. (1970) used
bilateral doses of 50 μg of carbachol and 20 μg of atropine. Bandler
(1969, 1970) used 7 μg of carbachol and 15 μg of atropine. These doses
resulted in considerable parasympathetic arousal in the Smith et al. rats
and in carbachol-induced seizures in some of Bandler's animals. Lonowski
et al. (1973) applied considerably smaller doses of carbachol (2 μg) and
atropine (2.5 μg) to the anterior lateral hypothalamus of mouse-killing
rats. Although 2 μg of carbachol had previously been shown to be an
efficient dose for the elicitation of drinking in the rat (Krikstone & Levitt,
1970), it significantly *inhibited* mouse killing. The atropine, however, had
no effect even though that dose does block drinking in a thirsty rat
(Levitt & Fisher, 1966).

Wnek and Leaf (1973) were able to induce mouse killing in some rats
with pilocarpine. However, a large number of other cholinergic drugs,

including nicotine, oxotremorine, arecoline, physostigmine, neostigmine, and methacholine, were ineffective over a broad range of doses. The authors conclude "that if a central cholinergic system for selective control of killing exists in rodents, it is not easily activated."

In light of the evidence there can be little doubt that the lateral hypothalamus is intimately involved in the natural manifestations of predatory aggression. However, it is equally clear that this area is not "the center" for predation, but merely one part of a complex system. In fact, experiments show that the lateral hypothalamus is important but not essential to a well-organized pattern of attack on prey. If the hypothalamus is surgically isolated from the rest of the brain in cats, the animals will remain relatively inactive after the lesion is made. However, they can be aroused to predatory attack by the sight of a mouse or rat. In three of the cats studied, electrodes had been implanted in the mesencephalic reticular formation prior to the hypothalamic operation. On stimulation, these animals would direct their attack toward the head and neck of a stimulus mouse. They would also approach but not bite a stuffed toy dog, demonstrating that the hypothalamus was not essential for the adequate discrimination of prey objects (Ellison & Flynn, 1968).

Thalamus, Midbrain, Amygdala, and Hippocampus in Predation

A study of Chi and Flynn (1971a, 1971b) has shown the manner in which the hypothalamic portion of the neural system for predation is linked with other parts of the system. Using the usual techniques of Flynn's laboratory, they implanted electrodes in the lateral hypothalamus and located positive points that would reliably produce predatory attack in the cat. They then made electrolytic lesions at these positive sites through the implanted bipolar electrodes. The lesions were sufficiently large that stimulation of two or three times the previous intensity did not elicit the attack. Seven to 14 days after the lesions were made, the animals were sacrificed and the degenerated axons were traced out using a modified Nauta stain.

Most of the degeneration occurred in the medial forebrain bundle that connects with the midbrain tegmentum and the basal olfactory and limbic structures of the forebrain. Degeneration also occurred in the midline nuclei of the thalamus.

All of the preceding brain structures have been implicated in the neural system for predation. Stimulation of the thalamus and the ventral midbrain in the tegmental area of Tsai both result in the facilitation of predatory aggression in the rat (Bandler, 1971a, 1971b) and the elicitation of predation in the cat (MacDonnell & Flynn, 1964, 1968; Flynn et al., 1970; Bandler et al., 1972). Lesions in the ventral tegmentum eliminate the behavior (Bernston, 1972). The relationship among these structures and the hypothalamus appears to be as follows. The hypothalamic system for pre-

dation descends through the medial forebrain bundle to the ventral tegmentum and probably continues into the pontine central tegmental area
(Bernston, 1973). It also sends fibers to the midline nuclei of the thalamus. Proper functioning of the system depends on the integrity of both
of these brain areas. Bandler (1971a, 1971b) using rats has shown that
the direct application of atropine to either the midline thalamus or the
ventral midbrain tegmentum will block the facilitation of predatory aggression produced by hypothalamic stimulation with carbachol. However,
blocking the positive hypothalamic sites had no effect on the facilitation
of predation produced by the stimulation of either the thalamus or the
tegmental area. The thalamic system, however, is not dependent on the
integrity of either the hypothalamic areas or the ventral midbrain areas.
An atropine blockade of either of them does not interfere with the facilitation of predation produced by thalamic stimulation. Bandler suggests
that the thalamic system may be directed to the periventricular system and
the dorsal longitudinal fasciculus of Schultz.

Further information on the role of the midbrain in predatory aggression
in rats was obtained by Chaurand et al. (1973). They lesioned the ventromedial region of the mesencephalic tegmentum and found a transient
elimination of mouse killing. The lesions also produced transient anorexia
or aphagia and a transient depression of self-stimulation responses at
lateral hypothalamic sites. There was considerable variability in the symptoms from subject to subject. However, most of the animals recovered
mouse killing while they were still anorexic or aphagic, and while their
self-stimulation rates were below 10 percent of the preoperative level.
This study also supports the independence of the neural systems for hunger and predation.

Lesions of the midbrain sites that, on stimulation, produce predation in
the cat result in a degeneration of neurons terminating in the vicinity of
the trigeminal and facial nerves. It is conjectured that those fibers from
the midbrain terminate on Golgi I cells which then project into the trigeminal and facial nuclei via short collateral branches (Chi et al., 1973).

The thalamus does influence the hypothalamic system and functions as
one of the modulating structures for aggression (Flynn, 1967). Predatory
aggression elicited in the cat by lateral hypothalamic stimulation can be
either facilitated or inhibited by the concurrent stimulation of medial and
midline thalamic structures (MacDonnell & Flynn, 1964, 1968). Attack
facilitation is produced by stimulation of the central portion of the nucleus
medialis dorsalis and the posterior midline thalamic region. Attack can
also be elicited by stimulation on the latter site. Suppression of hypothalamic attack is most often found in the rostral midline thalamic region and
in that part of the nucleus medialis dorsalis slightly lateral to the facilita-
tory sites. Suppression of attack is also caused by stimulation of the rostral
portions of the nucleus reuniens. The specific pathways for suppression of

The Psychobiology
of Aggression

hypothalamic attack are in some doubt, although possible paths have been suggested (Siegel et al., 1972; Bandler & Flynn, 1974). Vergnes and Karli (1972) have also shown that electrical stimulation of the dorsomedial thalamus of the rat results in an inhibition of the subject's mouse-killing behavior.

The amygdala plays a critical role in the neurological basis of predation. Certain cells in the amygdala of the cat show a considerable increase in firing when a rat is introduced into the cage and cease immediately when the rat is removed. The rapid firing in these cells appears to be specific to the stimulus of a rat and is not elicited by movement or general cerebral activation (Sawa & Delgado, 1963). (Also see Jacobs & McGinty, 1972.) Early studies showed that total bilateral amygdalectomy eliminated predatory tendencies in the cat (Summers & Kaelber, 1962) and in the rat (Woods, 1956; Karli, 1956). This finding was confirmed by Galef (1969). Recently, much more refined lesioning and stimulation techniques have provided more detailed information on the influence of this complex structure. (See Figure 6.)

The letters in the following text refer to that figure. Predatory aggression in the cat produced by stimulation of the lateral hypothalamus is enhanced by stimulation of the dorsolateral section of the posterior portion of the lateral nucleus of the amygdala (a). The same response is inhibited by stimulation of the junction of the magnocellular portion of the basomedial nucleus of the lateral nucleus of the amygdala (b). This is the same area that on stimulation has produced an aggressive response in cats characterized by an intense emotional display (Egger & Flynn, 1963, 1967).[1] Lesions of the preceding suppressor areas produce response facilitation of the hypothalamically induced predation (Egger & Flynn, 1967). It has also been shown that stimulation of specific sites in the medial portion of the periamygdaloid or prepyriform cortex results in a suppression of lateral hypothalamic predatory attack in the cat (Siegel et al., 1972), as does stimulation in the medial aspect of the prefrontal cortex (Siegel et al., 1974).

In the rat predatory aggression appears to be facilitated in the central nucleus (f), since killers with ablation of that nucleus completely lose the tendency to kill mice (Horovitz et al., 1966; Karli & Vergnes, 1965; Vergnes & Karli, 1964). That tendency is blocked by the direct application of either imipramine or thiazesim to the same area (Horovitz & Leaf, 1967). Imipramine also blocks after discharge from the medial basal amygdala (G&E) (Penaloza-Rojas et al., 1961) and inhibits the mouse-killing response when administered systemically (Horovitz, 1965; Horovitz et al.,

---

[1] Egger and Flynn only elicited display from the amygdala at intensities that produced signs of afterdischarges in the EEG. Thus the localization of the stimulation effects in the amygdala may not be very precise.

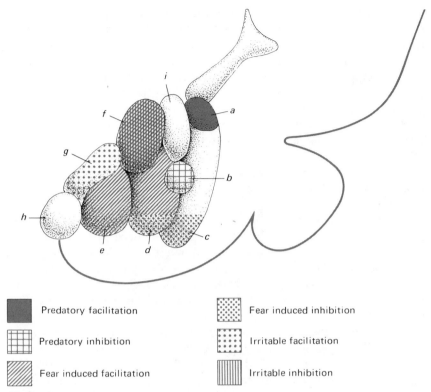

■	Predatory facilitation	▦	Fear induced inhibition
⊞	Predatory inhibition	⋮	Irritable facilitation
▨	Fear induced facilitation	‖‖	Irritable inhibition

Figure 6
Schematic of the nuclei of the amygdala associated with different kinds of aggression (explanation in text). (a) Dorsal portion of lateral nucleus; (b) medial part of lateral nucleus and lateral part of basal nucleus; (c) lateral nucleus; (d and e) basal nuclei; (f) central nucleus; (g) medial nucleus; (h) cortical nucleus; (i) putamen central amygdaloid complex

1966). This central nucleus control is conveyed to the lower brain areas through the ventral amygdalofugal system and not by way of the stria terminalis (Vergnes & Karli, 1964). Mouse killing by rats is also inhibited by electrical stimulation of the amygdala, but this appears to be a generalized motor inhibition and is not restricted to particular nuclei (Karli et al., 1969).

There is some evidence that the amygdaloid inhibitory system for predatory aggression in the rat utilizes catecholamines as neurotransmitters. Nerve terminals containing and releasing catecholamines in the amygdala have been identified (Fuxe, 1965; Fuxe & Gunne, 1964). The direct bilateral application of norepinephrine to the amygdala blocked mouse killing in natural killer rats. The direct application of *d*-amphetamine, which is not metabolized as rapidly as norepinephrine and which evidently acts by releasing endogenous catecholamines, was more effective in the inhibition of that response (Leaf et al., 1969).

Other areas of the brain that have a modulating influence on the neural systems for predation include the midbrain reticular formation, the hippocampus, the olfactory bulbs, the septum, and the cingulate gyrus. Stimulation of the hippocampus augments the predatory aggression induced by lateral hypothalamic stimulation in the cat, but stimulation of the dorsal hippocampus suppresses that response (Siegel & Flynn, 1968). Hippocampal seizures do not appear to disrupt the attack tendency in the cat (Wasman & Flynn, 1966) but will disrupt mouse killing by a rat if the mouse is presented in the initial phases of the seizure discharge (Karli et al., 1969).

The role of the septum in predatory aggression remains to be clarified. Septal stimulation inhibits hypothalamically induced attack in the cat (Siegel & Skog, 1970). However, several investigators have reported that septal lesions in the rat do not induce mouse killing in rats that preoperatively do not kill mice (Karli, 1960; Karli et al., 1969; Malick, 1970). More recently it has been shown that if septal-lesioned rats are tested for mouse killing on the first day after the operation, they do kill. Siegel and Leaf (1969) describe the behavior as a typical predatory kill in which the rat disposes of the mouse with a single cervical bite. Miczek and Grossman (1972), however, describe the kill as an "affective" one in which the rat's biting is not specifically directed to the back of the neck and includes numerous bites all over the body. Since rats with septal lesions manifest other aggressive tendencies, the Miczek and Grossman findings are not unreasonable. It is possible, however, that slightly different lesion locations might account for the different results of Siegel and Leaf. Miley and Baenninger (1972) report that nonkiller rats with septal lesions will kill mice if they are given noncontingent shocks in the presence of the mouse. The result could be due either to the activation of the system for irritable aggression or to the enhancement of the predatory system by the arousing effects of shock. An analysis of the topography of the response that might shed some light on this problem is not reported by Miley and Baenninger.

Stimulation of the anterior cingulate gyrus tends to have an inhibitory effect on predatory attack in the cat induced by hypothalamic stimulation, but stimulation of the posterior cingulate has no such effect. Since there are no known direct connections between the anterior cingulate and the hypothalamus, the modulating influence of the cingulate must be mediated indirectly, perhaps through the medial dorsal nucleus of the thalamus, which, as previously indicated, does play a role in predation in the cat (Siegel & Chabora, 1971).

Stimulation of the caudate nucleus of the cat also results in the suppression of hypothalamically induced predatory aggression. However, the mechanisms appear to be somewhat different. The stimulation affects only the direction of the attack. The animal is activated and moves around the cage, sometimes even stepping on the rat, but it does not carry out the attack. The minor autonomic arousal produced by the hypothalamic stimulation remains unaffected (Plumer & Siegel, 1973). This finding is in keeping with other studies that show that caudate stimulation disrupts several kinds of directed behavior. (See Plumer & Siegel, 1973, for details.)

Predatory attack in the cat induced by hypothalamic stimulation is augmented by the simultaneous activation of the midbrain reticular formation either through direct electrical stimulation or by the administration of amphetamine (Sheard & Flynn, 1967; Sheard, 1967). In the rat, however, there is evidence that the systemic administration of amphetamines will block mouse killing (Kulkarni, 1968b; Horovitz et al., 1965; and Horovitz et al., 1966). The physiological basis of this discrepancy between the species is not clear.

Finally, it has been shown that electrical stimulation of the rostral fastigial nucleus of the cerebellum of the cat results in predatory attack on a rat (Reis et al., 1973). Stimulation of the site at a lower intensity results in feeding, and stimulation at an even lower intensity results in grooming. Bilateral lesions of the sites result in eliminating the behaviors without evident motor deficit.

Olfactory Bulbs and Predation

The role of the olfactory bulbs in predatory behavior is not clear. Olfaction is not essential for the manifestation of predation in either the rat or the cat. However, it has been shown that total, bilateral, olfactory bulbectomy will convert 50 percent to 100 percent of non-mouse-killing rats into killers (Didiergeorges et al., 1966; Karli et al., 1969; Vergnes & Karli, 1963, 1965). The mouse killing observed in this series of experiments may not have been of the predatory type. There is now considerable evidence from experiments by Bernstein and Moyer (1970), Spector and Hull (1972), Bugbee and Eichelman (1972), Cain and Paxinos (1974), and Cain (1974), as well as from the experiments by Karli and his colleagues that olfactory ablation produced affective or irritable rather than predatory aggression. The olfactory-lesioned rats in the Bernstein-Moyer study did not show a greater incidence of either mouse killing or frog killing. They did, however, show a significant increase in the tendency to bite a gloved hand that was thrust at them. Although Karli et al. (1969) did not systematically measure any type of aggression except mouse killing, there are a number of indications that the lesioned animals in that study reacted with considerable emotionality. The topography of the killing response was not the typical quiet, quick kill of predation. The kill "usually has the aspect of a compulsory 'disinhibited' reaction, the rat biting the mouse all over the body and covering it with blood from head to tail" (Karli et al., 1969). The lesioned rats placed in group cages show violent intra-specific aggression for a few days after the operation (Didiergeorges et al., 1966). It has also been reported that the lesioned subjects that became killers were generally more vicious and emotional than those that did not (Didiergeorges et al., 1966). None of the preceding behaviors is char-acteristic of the precise, well-organized, nonemotional response of preda-tion.

There is also indirect evidence from the work of Karli that olfactory lesions affect a kind of aggression that is not predatory. He has shown that androgens appear to have no effect on natural predatory behavior. Castration does not block mouse killing in a natural killer, nor do exogenous androgens induce killing in a nonkiller (Karli, 1958). There is considerable evidence, however, that the androgens do play a role in inter-male aggression (see below). There is also some experimental and clinical evidence that supports the importance of androgenic hormones in irritable aggression. Thus the findings of Didiergeorges and Karli (1967) to the effect that castration and unilateral adrenalectomy reduce the percentage of nonkilling rats that are converted into killers by olfactory lesions and that these castrated nonkillers can be induced to kill after testosterone injections may reflect the effect of the androgens on what appears to be irritable aggression. In the experiment by Bernstein and Moyer (1970) olfactory lesions made the rats irritable but did not increase mouse killing.

The preceding hypotheses appear reasonable but the issue is further confused by an experiment by Bandler and Chi (1971). They did not find an increase in irritable aggression after olfactory lesions. The lesions did, however, suppress frog killing in natural frog killers and mouse killing in natural mouse killers, but they induced mouse killing in some nonkillers. Partial olfactory bulb lesions facilitated inter-male aggression in the rats, but complete olfactory ablations suppressed it. Thorne et al. (1973) also failed to find changes in irritable aggression. They did, however, find an increase in predatory mouse killing in Long-Evans rats but not in Wistar, Holtzman, or Sprague-Dawley rats. Only further research can clarify this welter of contradictory findings.

ENDOCRINOLOGY OF PREDATION

Relatively little is known about the endocrine influences on predation. The studies by Karli and his colleagues on the role of the adrenals and the gonads in mouse killing probably relate to irritable rather than predatory aggression. There is now in the literature one prototype study from J. P. Flynn's laboratory that will set the pattern for a great many studies in the future on all types of aggression as well as predatory. Inselman-Temkin and Flynn (1973) manipulated peripheral hormone levels in the cat and studied the effects of those manipulations on the latency for the cat to attack an anesthetized rat after electrical stimulation of the hypothalamus. All but two of the 12 sites studied in this experiment produced quiet biting or predatory attack. Five female and five male cats were used. Gonadectomy decreased the attack latencies in females and increased them in males. The luteinizing hormones estradiol and testosterone had the opposite effects; that is, they increased the attack latencies in females and decreased them in males. These results are most probably due to the sensitization or desensitization of the neural system for attack by the the hormones involved. For example, an increase in the intensity of the stimulation could result in a latency comparable to that found during the pregonadectomy period. The differential effects of the endocrine manipulations on the sexes are interpreted as being due to the fact that the hormones are acting on different types of neural substrates in the male and the female. This is reasonable in that there is abundant evidence that the nervous systems of the sexes differ as a result of exposure to different hormone balances early in life. (See the section on permanent effects of early endocrine manipulations on inter-male aggression, p. 249.) The role of the endocrines in the sensitization of the neural system for predation is particularly interesting in the light of the equivocal data on sex differences in predatory behavior (see p. 142).

A recent study has shown that predation (frog killing) in the rat is not androgen dependent. Bernard (1974) injected testosterone proprionate in non-frog-killing rats on alternate days for a month and failed to induce frog killing in any of the subjects. He also castrated killer rats and injected others with testosterone proprionate. Neither procedure had an effect on the latency of killing when compared with appropriate controls (also see Karli, 1958). Whether the latency to kill under brain stimulation would be changed by the endocrine manipulations is not known.

ENDOCRINOLOGY OF
INTER-MALE AGGRESSION

More is known about the endocrinology of inter-male aggression than about any other type. Some of this material has been covered in the section on the production of pheromones in mice (p. 160). Even though mice are the only species in which aggression-eliciting and aggression-inhibiting pheromones have been demonstrated, it is possible that differential pheromone production is a mechanism through which the endocrine status functions to produce changes in aggressive tendencies in other species. Additional studies on the relation between pheromones and aggression will help to clarify the constant interactions between the organism's internal state and the external stimulus input that results in hostile behavior.

Sexual Maturity and Inter-Male Aggression

There is now abundant evidence that the male sex hormones play a critical role in the development and maintenance of the inter-male aggressive response. As indicated in Chapter 5, there are distinct differences in the play activities of young males and females of many species, including man. The play of the males involves much more vigorous physical activity and there is more mock combat and sham biting. However, until sexual maturity occurs, the interactions among these juveniles are well tempered in intensity, with the result that there is seldom any pain inflicted by either participant. Fighting in earnest only occurs after the male gonads become functional. In the rat there is a heightened increase in hostile behavior after the descent of the testes (at 86 to 115 days of age) and overt antagonism is rarely observed before that time. Further, prepubescent males do not elicit unrestrained aggressive behavior from adults. The juveniles may be driven from the home burrow or from a food source by a mature animal, but they are seldom bitten. Instead they are attacked and may be knocked over and trounced with all four feet. It is rare, however, that the younger rat is wounded in this type of encounter (Calhoun, 1962). The physiological basis for this reaction by the adults is not yet understood. It may, of course, be due to the lack of an aggression-eliciting pheromone but this has not been experimentally confirmed. After puberty, fighting among rats becomes serious and frequently includes a considerable emotional component (Seward, 1954a). Similar findings have also been reported for mice (Lagerspetz & Talo, 1967; Fredericson, 1950) and for mink (MacLennon & Bailey, 1969). The direct measurement of plasma androgens and onset of fighting in mice reveals that the initiation of inter-male aggression occurs at a time when the secretion of androgens is increasing (McKinney & Desjardins, 1972).

If the androgen level in immature male mice is raised by testosterone injections there is a significant increase in the amount of aggression (Levy & King, 1953), or the aggression reaction appears earlier (Lagerspetz & Talo, 1967). A similar finding has been reported in primates. Two of six juvenile male macaques, after testosterone injections, showed more than double the amount of aggressive behavior observed during control periods (Kling, 1968). Exogenous androgens given to immature female mice, however, do result in a facilitation of aggressive behavior (Levy, 1954).

*Effects of Castration and Androgen Replacement on
Inter-Male Aggression*

When the level of androgens in the bloodstream is reduced by castration there is a decrease in the manifest aggression between males in many species. (Although this review is primarily concerned with mammals, there is considerable evidence for the role of the gonads in inter-male aggression in lower vertebrates. See Beach, 1948; Collias, 1944; and Guhle, 1961, for reviews of this literature.)

The classic experiment on this problem was done by Beeman in 1947. She demonstrated that male mice show considerable aggressive behavior when they are placed together after a period of isolation. She scored instances of tail rattling, parrying, mincing, attacking, and fighting as aggressive behaviors. Mice that were castrated either prior to puberty or after 60 days of age, when they were sexually mature, showed essentially no aggressive behavior when a period of 25 or more days intervened between the operation and the initial pairings. In a total of 396 encounters experienced by castrated mice of two different strains, the only indication of aggression consisted of two instances of tail rattling. This is contrasted with the behavior of normal male albino mice that showed 833 tail rattles, 104 minces, 431 attacks, and 230 fights in a series of 130 encounters, and normal male C57 black mice that engaged in tail rattling 226 times, showed 180 minces, 884 attacks, and 518 fights during 240 encounters.

The particular importance of the role of the androgenic hormone in the fighting reaction was demonstrated through the use of replacement therapy. Approximately half of the castrated animals in both strains were given subcutaneous implants of 15-mg pellets of testosterone propionate under ether anesthesia. Four days after the testosterone implantation there was a dramatic increase in the fighting behavior of these animals. Twelve out of 14 of the C57 black mice receiving the pellets of male hormone and all 11 albino mice exhibited aggressive behavior during the encounters when the hormone was present. The aggressive behavior of castrated animals receiving implanted control pellets of dextrose did not change.

After three weeks the mice with the implanted pellets were once again anesthetized and the pellets were removed, with a resulting drastic reduction in the manifestations of aggression. Of the seven C57 black mice that experienced encounters after the removal of the pellets, only two showed any evidence of aggression, and in one of those there was reason to believe that the testosterone pellet was not completely removed. Among the four albino mice there was only one instance of tail rattling and one of mincing during the encounters after the pellets were removed. (Beeman's results are summarized in Table 5.)

Many studies have now essentially confirmed these basic findings. The spontaneous aggressive behavior between males is reduced by castration

Table 5
Aggressive Behavior of Mice: Normals, Castrates, and Castrates Implanted with Testosterone Propionate or Dextrose Pellets

Strain	Set	No. mice per Set	Activity in first 6 rounds of encounters						Activity in second 6 rounds of encounters						Activity in third 6 rounds of encounters				
			Tail rattle	Parry	Mince	At-tack	Fight	Treat-ment	Tail rattle	Parry	Mince	At-tack	Fight	Treat-ment	Tail rattle	Parry	Mince	At-tack	Fight
Albino ♂	I	3	0	0	0	0	0	T.P.*	138	1	26	79	58	—	—	—	—	—	—
♂	II	4	0	0	0	0	0	T.P.	267	1	24	117	104	T.P. out	1	0	1	0	0
♂	VI	4	2	0	0	0	0	T.P.	187	0	23	79	26	—	—	—	—	—	—
♂	III	4	0	0	0	0	0	Dextrose	0	0	0	0	0	—	0	0	0	0	0
♂	VIII	4	0	0	0	0	0	Dextrose	0	0	0	0	0	—	0	0	0	0	0
♂	VII	4	0	0	0	0	0	—	—	—	—	—	—	—	—	—	—	—	—
Normal ♂	V	4	49	0	1	7	1	—	209	1	18	169	102	—	125	0	28	70	20
Normal ♂ operated	IX	4	215	0	23	100	56	—	175	1	34	85	51	—	—	—	—	—	—
C57 black ♂	II	3	2	0	0	0	0	T.P.	27	8	29	48	18	T.P. out	3	0	0	3	0
♂	IX	3	0	0	0	0	0	T.P.	1	0	15	35	0	—	—	—	—	—	—
♂	I	4	0	0	0	0	0	T.P.	59	13	86	150	87	T.P. out	22	0	26	47	0†
♂	V	4	0	0	0	0	0	T.P.	90	14	38	158	129	—	—	—	—	—	—
♂	IV	3	0	0	0	0	0	Dextrose	0	0	0	0	0	—	—	—	—	—	—
♂	VIII	4	0	0	0	0	0	Dextrose	0	0	0	0	0	—	—	—	—	—	—
♂	XI	4	0	0	0	0	0	—	—	—	—	—	—	—	—	—	—	—	—
Normal ♂	III	4	38	8	11	117	43	—	29	9	37	129	36	—	25	7	30	87	24
Normal ♂	VII	4	17	13	11	176	145	—	67	6	38	112	69	—	—	—	—	—	—
Normal ♂ operated	VI	4	27	12	49	147	129	—	—	—	—	—	—	—	—	—	—	—	—

From E. A. Beeman, The effect of male hormone on aggressive behavior in mice, *Physiological Zoology*, 1947, *20*, p. 384. By permission of the University of Chicago Press.
* Testosterone propionate.
† All aggressive behavior in third six rounds was displayed by Mouse No. 2, whose androgen pellet was removed in three pieces.

and can be restored by appropriate doses of male hormones. It has been confirmed for mice (Urich, 1938; Suchowsky et al., 1969, 1971; Sigg et al., 1966; Sigg, 1969; Edwards, 1968, 1970a; Bevan et al., 1958a; Kochakian, 1941; Anton et al., 1968; Bevan et al., 1958b; Yen et al., 1962; Erpino & Chappelle, 1971) and it has also been demonstrated in the rat (Riege, cited in Seward, 1945a; Beach, 1945; Barfield et al., 1972), in the gerbil (Sayler, 1970), and in the hamster (Vandenberg, 1971). Of course, individuals involved in the practical problems of animal husbandry have known for centuries that castration of males produces docility in a wide variety of species, from the camel to the bull.

All types of androgens are not equally effective in restoring aggressive behavior in castrated males. Fighting among castrate mice was facilitated by treatment with testosterone, dihydrotestosterone, or androstenedione. However, testosterone was the most potent of the three. All three of these androgens stimulated growth of the seminal vesicles and preputial glands, but the potency in these peripheral tissues did not parallel the potency in the behavioral tests (Luttge & Hall, 1973).

It is interesting, however, that castration does not appear to inhibit the development of aggression in the dog as measured by the frequency of social fighting or the dominance position arising from competition for females or bones (LeBoeuf, 1970). Testosterone given to castrated macaque monkeys did not result in a change in the hierarchical status of subordinate animals. However, the hierarchies had been well established before the testosterone administration (Mirsky, 1955). Castration has been shown to affect the behavior of rhesus macaques but there is considerable individual variability that evidently depends in part on the types of social experiences the animal has. Ten young males from the free-ranging colony of Cayo Santiago Island off Puerto Rico were castrated, and it was shown that the castrates tended to associate with one another, responded more to immature monkeys, and in general had a lower dominance status. However, some who formed coalitions did engage in fighting and were successful, even against larger animals (Wilson, 1968; referred to in Hamburg, 1971c).

Influences of Exogenous Androgens on Noncastrates

Although aggression can be reduced by castration and restored by androgen replacement, it does not necessarily follow that exogenous testosterone administered to the noncastrate will result in a potentiation of aggressive tendencies. This problem has been little studied, but within limits it does appear that androgens may enhance aggression. A dose of 1 mg per animal of testosterone propionate results in an increase in aggressive behavior in intact isolated mice, according to Suchowsky et al. (1971). However, these authors, using a similar dosage and procedure, did not find such an increase in an earlier study (Suchowsky et al., 1969). Isolated intact mice that are either nonaggressive or moderately aggressive show an increase in aggression when treated with 2.5 mg of testosterone (Banerjee, 1971).

The effect of exogenous androgens undoubtedly depends on the dosage, and the exogenous androgens must interact with the individual animal's endogenous androgen level. There is some evidence that large doses of androgens may have anesthetic properties (Davis, 1964). This may account for the reduction in fighting after sizable doses of androgens to isolated mice (Bevan et al., 1958a; Bevan et al., 1958b).

Relationship Between Endogenous Androgen Levels and Aggressive Behavior

Indirect evidence of the relationship between endogenous levels of androgens and aggressive behavior can be derived from studies of the seasonal fluctuations of this type of behavior in primates. Wilson and Boelkins (1970), in a study of the colony of rhesus monkeys on Cayo Santiago Island, have shown that high levels of aggression (as measured by amount of wounding and deaths) occur most frequently in males during the mating season and in females during the birth season. These authors cite evidence to show that the testis is larger during the breeding season (Sade, 1964) and that the relative spermatogenesis occurs during the spring birth season and maximum spermatogenesis during the mating season (Conaway & Sade, 1965). They conclude from these data that the most plausible interpretation of the elevated frequencies of aggression during the mating season is indirectly due to the hormonal changes at that time in the mature males. Alexander (1970) also reports seasonal changes in the behavior of adult male Japanese monkeys, indicating that increases in affiliative behavior result from the seasonal withdrawal of androgens.

The plasma testosterone levels of male rhesus monkeys have been shown to correlate with a number of agonistic behaviors. Threatening and chasing behavior and being submitted to by another member of the colony all correlate significantly with testosterone plasma levels. Submissive behavior is negatively correlated with testosterone level, but not significantly so. This is interpreted as indicating that an animal with a high frequency of aggressive contacts with his subordinates will generally show a higher testosterone level, regardless of how frequently he responds submissively to those above him in the dominance hierarchy. (See Table 6.) Dominance rank within the colony is also correlated with plasma testosterone concentration. The animals in the highest quartile had significantly higher testosterone levels than those animals lower in the hierarchy (Rose et al., 1971). (See Figure 7.)

Table 6
Testosterone and Behavior

A. Testosterone and behavioral correlations	
Total aggression	0.469
Noncontact aggression	0.515
Receives submission	0.516
Tension	0.534
Dominance rank	0.350 (rho)
Submission	−0.320 NS
B. Behavioral intercorrelations	
Aggression and receives submission	0.543
Aggression and dominance rank	0.710 (rho)
Submission and dominance rank	−0.650 (rho)
Aggression and tension	0.334 NS
Tension and dominance rank	0.490 (rho)

All correlations listed are Pearson's r except those shown as ρ, which are Spearman's rank-order correlations. All are significant to at least $p < 0.05$, except those followed by NS. For all correlations, $n = 34$.

From R. M. Rose et al., Plasma testosterone, dominance rank and aggressive behavior in male rhesus monkeys, *Nature*, 1971, *231*, 367.

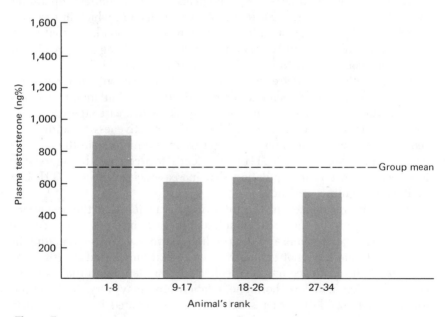

Figure 7
Mean ±s.c. for each quartile of the dominance rank order. The most dominant animals, rank order 1 to 8, had significantly higher testosterone concentrations than those in the lower quartiles. (From R. M. Rose et al., Plasma testosterone, dominance rank and aggressive behavior in male rhesus monkeys, *Nature*, 1971, *231*, 367.)

Isolation of mice that results in a dramatic increase in aggression occurs with a concomitant increase in androgen production and a reduction in ACTH release (Brain & Nowell, 1971). Thus isolation-induced aggression may be a function of the endogenous androgens.

The Role of Other Hormones in Inter-Male Aggression

Although the experimental results are not completely consistent, it is possible to sketch a tentative picture of the role that other endocrine glands play in inter-male aggression. However, the evidence available so far permits only a fairly low level of explanation. A number of studies show the effects of various endocrine manipulations, but very little is known about the mechanisms through which these hormones have their effect. For example, a variety of pituitary-adrenal manipulations influence the course of inter-male aggression. It is also known, however, that pituitary-adrenal manipulations also affect various kinds of fear-motivated behavior (Brain, 1972b; di Giusto et al., 1971). According to the model presented in Chapter 1, the hormonal effects might result from their direct action on the neural system for aggression, either increasing or decreasing its threshold. On the other hand, the effects might be indirect, operating through the neural system for fear-motivated behavior, which in turn has an effect on the neural system for aggression. There is evidence that there is an inverse relationship between fear and inter-male aggression (Brain & Nowell, 1969; Brain & Nowell, 1970b; Svare & Leshner, 1973).

Briefly, inter-male aggression is essentially dependent on circulating androgens in the bloodstream, and any endocrine manipulation that limits the quantity of circulating androgens tends to decrease aggressive responding. Also, any process that blocks the effectiveness of androgens reduces the tendency to inter-male aggression. An increase in the adrenocorticotrophic hormone (ACTH) also tends to decrease the aggressive tendencies, and any manipulation that increases circulating ACTH also inhibits the fighting tendency.

It must be recognized in the following discussion that the secondary effects of a given endocrine manipulation are inferred from earlier physiological experiments and the resultant hormonal levels circulating in the bloodstream have not generally been directly measured. Further, almost all of this evidence has been collected on rodents, and the resultant proposed micromodel of hormone relationships may very well not be totally generalizable to other species. It is also limited by the fact that most of the experimental work has been done on isolation-induced aggression, which may not be pure inter-male.

As previously shown, testicular androgens are critical to the development of aggression between males. It is therefore not surprising that hypophysectomy completely prevents the development of fighting be-

havior in isolated mice. This effect is evidently due to the lack of gonadotrophic hormone, because aggressiveness does develop in hypophy-
sectomized mice given subcutaneous implants of testosterone (17.5 mg
per mouse) (Sigg, 1969).

Although one study that used a single dose of estrogen failed to find it
(Gustafson & Winokur, 1960), it has now been reported several times that
estrogenic compounds tend to inhibit inter-male aggression in intact male
mice (Anton et al., 1968; Suchowsky et al., 1969, 1971; Banerjee, 1971).
However, it has also been reported that estradiol administered to isolated
castrated male mice restored the suppressed aggressive tendency. Thus it
appears that the estrogenic blockage of fighting behavior in intact mice
may be due to the estrogenic suppression of the gonadotrophic hormone
in the pituitary, which inhibits endogenous androgen production (Edwards & Burge, 1971). [It should be noted that Suchowsky et al. (1969)
failed to find facilitation of aggression in castrated mice by estradiol, but
they used only 0.01 the dosage that Edwards and Burge (1971) did when
they got maximal effect.]

Progesterone and progesteronelike compounds also block aggression in
intact male mice (Suchowsky et al., 1969). However, this action appears
to result from the antagonism of the effects of androgens in the central
nervous system because the simultaneous administration of testosterone
propionate and progesterone to castrated male mice does not result in the
restoration of fighting. However, the progesterone does not block the
effects of the testosterone on seminal vesicle growth (Erpino & Chappelle,
1971; Luttge, 1972). It should be emphasized here that without considerably more research, interpretations must be highly tentative. For example,
high estrogen doses may be androgenic in their action and there is considerable interconvertibility of many hormones (e.g., progesterone is a
common precursor of many steroid hormones).

There are several lines of evidence indicating that ACTH tends to
block inter-male aggression. ACTH-injected, isolated, adult male mice are
significantly less aggressive in a standard fighting situation than are injected controls (Brain et al., 1971). One of the effects of adrenalectomy
is an increase in ACTH levels in the blood because ACTH production by
the pituitary is released from inhibition by the adrenal hormones (Cox et
al., 1958). It would follow then that fighting should be reduced by
adrenalectomy. Some investigators have failed to find this relationship
(Burge & Edwards, 1971; Welch, 1968). However, the more common finding has been that although adrenalectomy does not eliminate inter-male
fighting in the mouse, it does significantly reduce it (Brain et al., 1971;
Harding & Leshner, 1972; Walker & Leshner, 1972; Svare & Leshner,
1972; Leshner & Walker, 1972).

Various kinds of stress affect the pituitary adrenal axis with a resultant
increase in ACTH output, and it has been shown that several stressors

result in an inhibition of inter-male fighting. The stress of an injection procedure in isolated male mice results in a depression of a composite aggression score, and even the handling of the mouse without the actual injection increases the latency to attack (Brain & Nowell, 1970a). Adult buck rabbits frequently fight viciously and to the death if caged together. However, if these animals are anesthetized and permitted to recover together in the same cage, the fighting behavior is suppressed for several weeks (Cherkin & Meinecke, 1971). Brain (1971a) has suggested that this finding is due to the fact that most anesthesia procedures are stressful and that the stress increases. ACTH output, which then produces the fighting suppression.

Another possible interpretation is that the fighting inhibition is due to some kind of a habituation phenomenon so that the animals no longer respond to aggression-eliciting cues after having been exposed to them during a period in which they were incapable of fighting. However, if the aggression suppression is in fact due to anesthesia stress, it is not clear whether the suppression is due directly to the increase in ACTH level or to some other mechanism. It is also known that a number of stressors reduce the level of plasma testosterone. (This could be due to an indirect effect of an increase in ACTH levels as indicated later.) Male rhesus monkeys exposed to severe social defeat by being placed in an established colony showed a drastic reduction in plasma testosterone levels (an 80 percent drop below baseline). The testosterone level remained markedly depressed for up to nine weeks (Rose et al., 1972). These authors cite other studies indicating that testosterone levels appear to fall in other stressful situations such as ether anesthesia and foot shock in the rat (Bardin & Peterson, 1967; Bliss et al., 1972), surgery in humans (Matsumoto et al., 1970), and the stressful phase of officer candidate training in the army (Kreuz et al., 1972).

The effects of stress in the reduction of inter-male fighting may also be mediated indirectly through adrenal androgens. During stress the plasma testosterone produced by the gonads decreases but the production of androstenedione by the adrenals is increased. These two androgens have a similar molecular structure and may compete for the same receptor cites in the brain. Androstenedione, however, is a less potent androgen in some senses than testosterone and may further inhibit the mechanism for inter-male aggression. (This hypothesis is developed in some detail in regard to male sex behavior by Ward, 1972.)

Dexamethasone, which is a powerful blocker of ACTH, causes an increase in fighting behavior in male mice (Brain et al., 1971), and although the drug has no effect on the aggressiveness of mice that have been both adrenalectomized and castrated, it does restore the fighting behavior of those that have only been adrenalectomized (Walker & Leshner, 1972). The later finding supports the idea that the aggression suppression pro-

duced by adrenalectomy is due to the increase in ACTH output. Hydrocortisone, another adrenal glucocorticoid that suppresses ACTH output,
has also been shown to increase fighting behavior in isolated male mice
(Banerjee, 1971; Kostowski et al., 1970).

The relationship between the pituitary-adrenal system and the pitui-
tary-gonadal system in the production of inter-male aggression is complex
and needs more study. One attempt to sort out these relationships is a
series of studies by Leshner and his colleagues. They have shown that the
fighting behavior of adrenalectomized mice is restored by corticosterone,
which evidently inhibits ACTH production. However, if the mice are both
castrated and adrenalectomized, neither corticosterone nor testosterone
alone is sufficient to restore fighting. Given in combination, however, they
are effective in this regard. Dexamethasone restores the fighting of
adrenalectomized mice but is not effective in restoring aggression in either
castrated mice or castrated-adrenalectomized mice, which seems to indicate that the excess of ACTH produced by adrenalectomy may act by
suppressing endogenous androgens. And there is evidence that this does
occur, at least in guinea pigs (Bullock & New, 1971). However, the ACTH
may also have some independent suppressing effect because exogenous
testosterone does not restore the aggressiveness of mice that have been
both castrated and adrenalectomized (Svare & Leshner, 1972; Walker &
Leshner, 1972; Leshner & Walker, 1972; Harding & Leshner, 1972) or
simply adrenalectomized (Leshner et al., 1973). The independent aggression suppression action of ACTH is further supported by the finding
that ACTH decreases the fighting of intact mice and those with controlled
levels of corticosterone and/or testosterone (Leshner et al., 1973).
Further, it has been shown that ACTH reduces aggressiveness in mice at
doses that have no effect on the weight of the testes, ventral prostate, or
the preputial glands (Brain, 1971b). Evidently the entire ACTH mole-
cule is necessary to produce fighting suppression since none of the frac-
tions thus far tested (ACTH 4-10, ACTH1-10, and ACTH 4-10-phe) had
an effect (Brain and Poole, 1974). The same authors have also shown that
the effects of ACTH on isolation-induced aggression are strain-dependent,
affecting some strains but not others. This finding is likely to lead to continuing confusion in the literature on this problem.

Permanent Effects of Early Endocrine
Manipulations on Inter-Male Aggression

The changes induced by the endocrine manipulations discussed so far are
essentially reversible. The deficits produced by adult castration can be
restored by testosterone injections, and the changes induced by hormone
injections disappear when the material is fully metabolized. However, as
indicated in Chapter 1, certain endocrine manipulations early in life have
a permanent irreversible effect on aggressive behavior in adulthood. This

has been demonstrated for shock-induced aggression (Conner & Levine, 1969; Conner et al., 1969; Powell, 1971), but most of the work has related to the type of aggressive behavior defined here as inter-male.

There are certain critical periods during which some biochemical influences can permanently alter the direction of the development of the nervous system. The result is an adult animal whose nervous system is either more or less sensitive to the influence of various blood chemistry components, and to particular types of complex sensory input. In considering the evidence for this phenomenon, it is once again important to recognize that most of the experimental work has been done on a single species, the mouse, and that the specific paradigm has generally involved some measure of isolation-induced aggression. Considerable caution must therefore be exercised in generalizing to other species. The limited amount of work done on other animals seems to indicate that the general construct of permanent nervous system alterability by endocrine manipulations in early life is valid, but it is also clear that there are significant differences in the specific details.

Most of the experimental manipulations that have an effect on aggressive behavior also influence some aspects of sexual behavior. However, this discussion will be limited to aggression.

Masculinizing the Feminine Nervous System

Nature appears to have a general rule for the nervous system of mammals. If left alone it will develop into one that is characteristically feminine (Money & Ehrhardt, 1972). In order for a male type of system to be formed, some exposure to androgens at particular developmental periods is necessary. In the normal course of development in the genetic male, the nervous system comes under the influence of the available testicular androgens. In the genetic female no androgens are available and consequently the female nervous system develops. Thus any manipulation that subjects the nervous system to adequate androgen influence at the proper time will result in what is essentially a masculine nervous system in a genetically feminine soma.

It has now been repeatedly demonstrated that perinatal androgens [usually in the form of testosterone propionate (TP)] administered to females results in permanent changes in the responsivity of the nervous system to androgens administered in adulthood. A large number of these studies are reviewed in Bronson and Desjardins (1971). As indicated earlier in this chapter, female mice seldom display spontaneous fighting. However, if they are given a single early androgen treatment (10 to 100 μg of TP) and are again treated as adults (50 to 100 μg), they display fighting that is quite comparable to that displayed by normal male mice (Edwards, 1968; Edwards & Herdon, 1970; Bronson & Desjardins, 1969, 1970). It is important to note that the mice do not display spontaneous aggression in adulthood unless they are given an androgen treatment as adults. In this respect the treated females are also like normal males. As indicated earlier, males do not begin to fight seriously until sexual maturity when the levels of circulating testosterone increase.

The developing nervous system is not indefinitely malleable. The effectiveness of androgen stimulation declines rapidly from birth through the first 12 days. A single androgen injection on the day of birth is more effective in producing fighting among females in adulthood than is a single dose at day 10. However, the day 10 androgen treatment is more effective than a control injection of oil (Edwards, 1969). In an extensive parametric study Bronson and Desjardins (1970) showed that a single injection of TP is more effective on the day of birth than it is on days 3, 6, or 12, and that single doses become ineffective sometime between day 12 and day 24. Prolonged treatment with TP can alter the sensitivity of the female nervous system to later androgen treatment. Female mice gonadectomized at 30 days of age and administered 100 μg of TP daily for 20 days did show more aggression than oil-injected controls when tested under androgen influence 45 days later (Edwards, 1970b). Thus very small amounts of androgens are effective during certain critical periods but relatively massive amounts are necessary later.

Since there are two types of androgens produced by the testis of the neonatal rat (testosterone and androstenedione), the nervous system defeminization could be due to the action of either one. However, it has been shown that the effect is probably due to testosterone or one of its metabolites. After androgen administration in adulthood, female mice that had been given either testosterone propionate or testosterone on days 1, 2, and 3 after birth fought significantly more than controls given oil. However, the subjects given androstenedione shortly after birth did not fight more than controls (Edwards, 1971). Testosterone propionate is more effective than testosterone, probably because of its more prolonged action (Edwards, 1971).

Female mice are also masculinized and show more fighting when given estradiol benzoate on the day of birth or at 3 days of age (Edwards & Herndon, 1970; Bronson & Desjardins, 1969). Thus neonatal estrogenization appears to mimic the effects of neonatal androgenization. However, there is also evidence that estradiol benzoate given to 3-day-old male mice tends to inhibit aggression in adulthood (Bronson & Desjardins, 1971).

In at least one type of fighting situation it has been shown that androgens, either early or late, are not critical to the initiation of fighting of either male or female castrate mice. In the so-called bully test, in which the stimulus animal is a significantly smaller mouse, the larger castrate will attack even though it has had no replacement androgens. However, when paired with a mouse of equal size, fighting never occurs unless the androgen level is adequate (Edwards, 1969). This may be an exception to all the preceding findings, or it may be that this is a different kind of aggressive behavior in which the attacking mouse is reacting to quite a different set of stimulus variables. More insight on this problem might be obtained by testing for pheromone changes (see later discussion).

The strain of the animals is also an important variable influencing the effects of early endocrine manipulations. The early androgenization of female mice makes them aggressive in response to androgen stimulation in adulthood only if the males of that strain are normally aggressive (Vale, Ray & Vale, 1972). There are, of course, differences in the aggressive tendencies of different strains of mice (Southwick & Clark, 1968). In the more passive animals the nervous system is evidently organized in such a way that the mechanisms for inter-male fighting have very high thresholds even under the influence of the androgen levels achieved during maturity in the male. Androgen given to females of a passive strain evidently does not make them more masculine (from the standpoint of aggression at least) than the normal males of that strain.

There is evidence from one study that at least part of the effect of early androgenization of females is due to changes in the pheromone output. Androgen-treated females are significantly more frequently attacked by trained male fighters than are oil-treated controls. Further, if castrated males, which are usually not subject to attack, are treated with the urine of early-androgenized females, they elicit attack from fighters. However, treatment with the urine of oil-treated controls has no such effect. When androgen-treated females were exposed to mature, native males for a five-day period, five of seven were killed. None of the oil-treated animals were killed (Lee & Griffo, 1972). Although no attempt was made to measure pheromone changes directly, this experiment provides good presumptive evidence of pheromone actions.

Feminization of the Genetic Male

The nervous system of the genetic male is presumably masculinized by the action of minute amounts of androgens circulating in the bloodstream during early life. Thus any manipulation that reduces the level of those androgens will block that process. There are now a number of studies indicating that neonatal castration is an effective procedure for preventing normal masculinization in male mice (Edwards, 1969; Bronson & Desjardins, 1969; Peters & Bronson, 1971; Peters et al., 1972; Miley, 1973). Once again, there is evidently a critical period after which this treatment is no longer effective. In mice it appears that the masculinization of the nervous system is completed sometime between the second and the sixth day after birth. Castration 12 hours after birth is more effective than castration at two days after birth in preventing fighting in male mice given androgens in adulthood. Castration after six days, however, is no more effective than a sham operation (Peters et al., 1972).

The mouse is different in this respect from the rhesus monkey. Genetic male rhesus monkeys castrated on the day of birth and tested at three and one-half to nine months of age are clearly different from female counterparts on such measures as threat, play initiation, and rough-and-tumble and chasing play (Goy, 1966). There is some indication that no testosterone circulates in the neonatal monkey as it does in rodents (Goy, 1968).

The normal aggressiveness in adult male isolated mice can also be permanently blocked during a relatively short critical prenatal period. The male offspring of female mice injected with a combination of norethynodrel and mestranol (as a synthetic progestational-estrogenic compound) on the tenth day of pregnancy were significantly less aggressive than control male offspring and those treated on days 7, 12, 15, and 17 of pregnancy. This treatment did not produce any genital abnormalities. Nothing is known about the mechanism for this effect and further study of prenatal influences are well indicated (Abbatiello & Scudder, 1970).

Prenatal Masculinization in Monkeys
Relatively little work has been done on the masculinizing effects of endocrine manipulation in primates and no direct measures of overt injurious aggression have been taken in the studies that have been done. However, there is some indication that the aggressiveness of primates can be altered by prenatal rather than postnatal manipulations. This work has been well summarized in a paper by Goy in 1968. If 600 to 700 mg of testosterone propionate is administered to pregnant rhesus monkeys over a 25- to 50-day period after the thirty-ninth day of pregnancy, the genetically female offspring will be pseudohermaphroditic with a well-developed scrotum and a small but complete penis. The behavior of these animals is also altered in a masculine direction. They display frequencies of performance of rough-and-tumble play and chasing play that either are intermediate or overlap extensively with the normal male standards. During the entire 150 days of observation the masculinized females always scored higher on these variables than normal control females.

Mechanisms of Early Androgenization Action
Although a number of physiological processes are affected by androgens in the neonate, essentially nothing is known about the particular mechanisms by which those androgens influence later aggressive behavior. Some hypotheses are discussed briefly in papers by Bronson and Desjardins (1971) and Hamburg (1971c). There is evidence in the rat and the ring dove that neonatally administered androgens do accumulate in

specific brain areas. Intravenously injected, tritium-labeled testosterone is quickly metabolized and selectively located in the hypothalamus and in the pituitary gland. The testosterone metabolite dihydrotestosterone is also selectively located in those tissues (Stern, 1970).

Early-administered testosterone also appears selectively to affect RNA metabolism, particularly in the anterior hypothalamus and the amygdala, both of which have been shown to play a role in aggressive behavior and gonadotropin release (Clayton et al., 1970). Early testosterone has also been shown to have long-lasting effects on RNA synthesis in the forebrain but not the midbrain of rats (Shimada & Gorbman, 1945).

Finally, newborn rats show sex-dependent chronological changes in serotonin concentration in the whole brain, and these changes can be altered by early castration and testosterone injections (Ladosky & Gaziri, 1969).

All these data are little more than suggestive of the directions that future research might take and provide us with very little insight into the basic mechanisms involved.

Neurology of Inter-Male Aggression

Relatively little is known of the details of the neurology of inter-male aggression. A great many studies have been done on the effects of various neurological manipulations on dominance relationships but these are very difficult to evaluate because of the interaction between the inter-male fighting tendencies and the individual animal's prior social experience. It has been shown, for example, that septal lesions enhance the aggressiveness of a dominant hamster. However, the same lesions increase the submissiveness of a submissive hamster (Sodetz & Bunnell, 1967a). In the socially naive hamster, however, septal lesions specifically facilitate inter-male aggression. Septal hamsters, unlike septal rats, do not show hyperemotionality and are not aggressive toward human handlers (Sodetz & Bunnell, 1967a, 1967b).

Chemical stimulation of the septal area in the naive hamster indicates that submissive behavior is increased by catecholaminergic stimulation whereas inter-male aggression is increased by catecholamine antagonists. Cholinergic stimulation decreases aggression without increasing submissive responses, and an anticholinergic again increases aggressiveness (Sodetz, 1967).

Lesions in the lateral hypothalamus and combined lesions of the lateral and medial hypothalamus of the male rat completely eliminate the tendency for a previously aggressive animal to attack another male placed in its home cage. Ventromedial lesions alone, however, have no effect on the behavior (Adams, 1971). Although it is not entirely clear, what appears to be inter-male aggression in rats is significantly reduced by small lesions in the periamygdaloid cortex, the cortical amygdaloid nucleus (*H* in Figure 7), or the bed nuclei of the stria terminalis. The same lesions had no effect on either shock-induced fighting or mouse killing (Miczek et al., 1974).

Midbrain reticular lesions at the level of the inferior colliculus [MRF (IC)] appear specifically to enhance inter-male fighting in the rat whereas midbrain lesions at the level of the superior colliculus have no effect. MRF (IC) animals showed an intense form of fighting with sufficiently hard biting to cause wounds when they were confronted with another male. Fighting also occurred when the MRF (IC) animal was confronted with a female rat, but that fighting was in response to the female's attacks after the male had attempted vigorous mounting. The midbrain lesions had no effect on either shock-induced aggression or mouse killing (Kesner & Keiser, 1973).

One study using electrical stimulation of the hypothalamus of the rhesus monkey appears to be concerned with pure inter-male aggression to the exclusion of any other type. A remote telestimulator was used and the points stimulated were in the anterior portion of the lateral hypothalamus and in the preoptic region. The experimental subjects were two male rhesus monkeys that had been shown to be submissive to the test males during control periods. During the test periods the experimental animal was caged with the dominant test animal and its female consort. Initially, the test male displayed clearly dominant responses. It paced the cage with tail erect and actively aggressed against the experimental monkey. It also monopolized all the sexual and grooming responses of the female. The experimental animal reacted with the typically submissive pattern including grimacing and crouching when approached by the dominant monkey. Direct hypothalamic stimulation of the experimental animal in both groups resulted in a vicious directed attack on the dominant male. It is important to note that the stimulated animal showed no tendency to attack the female and no tendency to attack inanimate objects. Further, it showed no fear reactions and no escape tendencies. Thus this aggression could not be considered to be generalized irritable aggression or fear-induced aggression. The test animal reacted to these attacks as though they were normal monkey behavior and counterattacked vigorously. Following the tenth stimulation in one group and the forty-third stimulation in the second, the dominance roles between the two animals were reversed. The formerly dominant test animal began to give shrill screams each time it was attacked. The now-dominant experimental male paced freely about the cage, mounted the female, and was groomed by her (Robinson et al., 1969).

Another point of considerable interest is that one of the three points that produced attack behavior also supported self-stimulation. That is, the monkey bar-pressed at a rate of at least 50 presses per minute on a lever that produced stimulation at that point. The other two points yielded reliable escape behavior.

The results of this study are so clear-cut and the stimulus object so specific that it appears to be excellent evidence for a relatively specific neural system for inter-male aggression. Experimental animals similar to the ones used in this study would be excellent preparations for the study of the actions of hormones on neural systems, an area where almost no information is currently available.

In a follow-up study by Alexander and Perachio (1973) it was shown that stimulated males attacked other males more frequently than females, and subordinate targets of either sex were attacked more frequently than dominant targets. In this experiment females were attacked, but at equal current levels the attacks of 'one experimental animal on the dominant male were considerably more intense than those directed at a dominant female. Other experimental animals who did attack females often threatened and chased the male before attacking the more accessible female. The greater tendency to attack a subordinate rather than a dominant animal seems to be a good example of an interaction between a learned inhibition and activity in the neural system for inter-male aggression.

One study has been concerned with the endocrine-neural interactions in inter-male aggression. Castrated male rats that showed a loss of aggression against an intruder in the home cage had that behavior restored when they received bilaterally implanted 25-gauge testosterone propionate filled tubes in either the hypothalamus or the caudate putamen nucleus. The largest amount of aggression was shown in the animals with caudate putamen implants. Since this study is reported only as an abstract, it is difficult to evaluate it. However, it is an excellent research technique that should be followed up (Christie & Barfield, 1973).

NEUROLOGY OF
FEAR-INDUCED AGGRESSION

Conjecture about the physiological basis of fear-induced aggression must be tentative at best. The limited number of conditions under which animals are usually studied makes it difficult to determine from published reports whether the aggression being studied is fear-induced or irritable because it is frequently not possible to determine whether the animal would have tried to escape prior to developing aggressive tendencies had the opportunity been available. Both fear-induced and irritable aggression have strong affective components, which leads to further confusion between them.

Amygdala and Fear-Induced Aggression

Since fear-induced aggression is always preceded by escape attempts, any experimental manipulation that reduces the number of stimuli from which the animal tends to escape should also reduce the tendency to that particular kind of aggressive behavior. This seems to account for part, although not all, of the reduction in aggressiveness in animals with amygdaloid lesions. A number of studies have shown that fear ractions (escape tendencies) are drastically reduced in a variety of animals after amygdalectomy. Weiskrantz (1956) summarizes nicely the reduction in fear that accompanies amygdalectomy in the monkey. This typifies the findings for a variety of animals in a number of different studies.

> Postoperatively there was an immediate and unmistakable difference in appearance and behavior between AM (amygdalectomized) operates and controls. The AM animals permitted petting and handling without visible excitement, or even approached and reached for observers. On the other hand, control operates continued to display their fear and hostility toward humans by running to the farthest corner of the cage, frequently urinating and defecating, grimacing, and screeching. The AM operates were also altered in their reactions to sticks and gloves, handling and chewing them without hesitation. Controls showed the same violent behavior toward these objects as they had preoperatively [p. 385].

The same author also showed that fear responses conditioned prior to the operation extinguished more rapidly in amygdalectomized animals than they did in controls. These findings have been essentially confirmed in other studies on nonhuman primates (Rosvold et al., 1954; Schreiner & Kling, 1953; Kling et al., 1968), as well as in the cat (Schreiner & Kling, 1953; Schreiner & Kling, 1956; Shealy & Peele, 1957) the wild Norway rat (Karli, 1956; Wood, 1958; Galef, 1970a), and the lynx and agouti (Schreiner & Kling, 1953). (See Kling, 1972, for an excellent detailed review of this material.) Normal albino rats freeze and remain immobile in the presence of a cat even though they have had no prior experience with that animal. However, if the rat is amygdalectomized, its behavior in the presence of the cat is not inhibited and it approaches the cat without reluctance. In one case an amygdalectomized rat climbed onto the cat's back and head and began to nibble on the cat's ear. The resultant attack by the cat only momentarily inhibited the rat, which again crawled back on the cat's back as soon as it was released (Blanchard & Blanchard, 1972).

For the sake of completeness it should be pointed out that amygdalectomy has not, in all instances, resulted in a reduction of fear-type behavior and fear-induced aggression. Bard (1950) gives protocols of two cats subjected to amygdalectomy which showed intense escape reactions and subsequent aggression. Two of the animals in the series by Schreiner and Kling (1953) also showed an increase in fear. In the latter case the authors were unable to determine any differences between the lesions of those animals and 18 others in the series. One of the animals in the Bard (1950) study and both in the Schreiner and Kling (1953) study did not develop the increased fear reaction for more than a month after the operation. The reasons for these individual differences resulting from amygdalectomy are not clear, but several authors have offered hypotheses to explain them (Goddard, 1964; Weiskrantz, 1956; Summers & Kaelber, 1962). The amygdala and fear-induced aggression will be discussed in more detail later.

In the preceding studies the animals were observed in the laboratory setting. Somewhat different findings are obtained when the amygdalectomized animals are released among normal animals in a natural setting, or in a natural group in a large cage. In general, the subjects do show a lack of fear or escape responses in relation to man, but they tend to avoid social interactions with other animals and become social isolates. The dominance rank of the operated animals is reduced and they manifest inappropriate social behaviors which elicit aggression from the normal animals (Kling & Cornell, 1971; Kling et al., 1968). In a completely natural setting, operated animals released into their own group withdrew from all attempts by their peers to interact with them. The operates appeared fearful and eventually left the group (Kling et al., 1970). Briefly, the amygdalectomized animals in a fairly normal social setting appear to show an *increase* in fear in all social interactions.

In an attempt to resolve the discrepancy between the apparent loss of fear of man and the increase in fear of normal social interactions with other monkeys, Kling (1972) suggests the interesting hypothesis that the removal of the amygdala results in an inability to comprehend complex visual input. The inability to sort out visual communications may result in a state of "depersonalization" such as has been reported in some human patients after amygdalotomy. Kling's argument for the importance of visual input in the amygdalectomy syndrome is supported by an experiment performed by Downer (1962) and confirmed by Barrett (1969) in which split-brain monkeys with a unilateral amygdalectomy showed the syndrome typical of that operation only when the eye on the intact side was closed. The symptoms were reversed when that eye was opened.

The Temporal Lobe, Cingulate Gyrus, Septum, and Hippocampus and Fear-Induced Aggression

Fear-induced aggression has also been reduced in monkeys (Turner, 1954) and in phalangers (Adey et al., 1956) by lesions in the temporal lobe not involving the amygdala. Rhesus monkeys subjected to bilateral ablation of either the anterior third of the temporal lobes or the prefrontal cortex lying anterior to the frontal eye fields showed a severe disruption of all social behavior including fear-induced aggression. The animals failed to retreat from a human observer and in some cases approached the observer to obtain food (Franzen & Myers, 1973; Myers, 1972).

The cingulate gyrus appears to be involved in fear-induced aggression. Anterior cingulectomy in the monkey produces a temporary reduction in fear and an increase in docility (Glees et al., 1950; Kennard, 1955a; and Ward, 1948). These animals are variously described as being tame, uncompetitive, socially indifferent, and as having lost their shyness of man. Stimulation in the same region, however, makes monkeys anxious and irritable (Anand & Dua, 1955, 1956). More recent studies by Franzen and Myers (1973) and Myers (1972) did not confirm these results. At this point there is no indication as to why. Cingulate lesions in the cat, however, have no effect on either flight reactions or defense (Ursin, 1969).

Septal lesions may temporarily facilitate both fear-induced and irritable aggression. In the rat septal lesions cause hyperemotionality, including increased escape tendencies and aggressive behavior (Brady & Nauta, 1953, 1955; King, 1958; King & Meyer, 1958). The threshold for escape and the threshold for aggression in a social situation are both lowered by septal ablations (Bunnell et al., 1966; Bunnell & Smith, 1966). However, it is not clear from these studies whether the aggressive behavior is the result of blocking the escape response. Schnurr (1972) has shown that the septal syndrome is mediated by the dorsal nuclei and structures of the anterior septal area. Rats with lesions of the more posterior septal nuclei did not differ from control animals. Although she refers to the syndrome as septal rage, her measure consists of ratings of the intensity of the animal's escape response with the highest score given to the animal that bit the gloved hand during vigorous escape attempts. One study indicates that, in the mouse at least, the septal syndrome involved primarily fear-induced aggression. Male mice with septal lesions showed exaggerated attempts to escape capture and vigorous biting when restrained. However, in intraspecific aggression encounters the septal animals were readily defeated by controls or sham operated animals and showed very little inclination to fight (Slotnick & McMullen, 1972).

MacLean and Delgado (1953) describe a case of fear-induced aggression in the monkey resulting from prolonged stimulation of the rostral hippocampus.

> [It] was accompanied by behavior that resembled generalized agitation and the attempt to escape from some threatening situation. It might be accompanied by a piercing cry, biting at the lead off cable, protective movements of the hands and head, and backward cringing movements of the body. If the animal were held, he would ferociously bite at the examiner's glove. The biting activity and generalized agitation would outlast the duration of the stimulation (p. 95).

Kaada et al. (1953) also give an incidental report of escape reactions closely associated with aggression resulting from stimulation in the hippocampus.

The Hypothalamus and Fear-Induced Aggression

The hypothalamus is involved in both fear-induced aggression and in irritable aggression but many of the details remain to be worked out. A number of studies have shown that this brain area is involved in escape or flight responses but few studies have involved the systematic study of the animal's response to having escape blocked. Hess (1964, p. 54), in his discussion of the defense zone of the hypothalamus, implies that fear-induced aggression will result from interference with the animal's flight. Although the quotation has an anthropomorphic tone, it can be readily translated into specific behaviors.

> In the concrete case, it seems that by stimulation of moderate degree, evidently particularly in the marginal region of the defense zone, the cat is led to looking around (Hunsperger, 1956; Roberts, 1958). If she sees a way out, she immediately jumps off the experimental table and tries to reach safety in a corner or underneath an object. If there is not a way out, she chooses another reaction that promises protection; she opposes the enemy and tries to avoid the danger by threatening gestures or swiftly executed attack.

Stimulation in the anterior hypothalamus results in aggression only in cornered cats, whereas ventromedial hypothalamic stimulation produces a rage reaction that appears to be uncontaminated by escape tendencies (Yasukochi, 1960). According to Kling and Hutt (1958), lesions in the ventromedial hypothalamus in cats result in aggression only if escape is blocked. Wheatley (1944), however, has shown that these lesions may result in extreme savageness without escape tendencies. It is evident that attempts to separate the functions of such a very small and functionally congested area as the hypothalamus will result in confusion. Romaniuk (1965) indicates that aggression and escape are organized in the hypothalamus on a dorsoventral basis. He has found that stimulation of the ventral part of the medial hypothalamus produces aggression in the cat whereas stimulation of the dorsal part of the medial hypothalamus produces an attempt to escape. He did not, however, corner the escaping animals to determine whether they would become aggressive.

The Relationship Among the Amygdala, Hypothalamus, and Midbrain in Fear-Induced Aggression

A careful series of studies conducted over a number of years by Brown and several different colleagues provides some insight into the neurology of fear-induced aggression and to some extent into the interactions between irritable and fear-induced aggression. These investigators, using electrical stimulation of the brains of freely moving unanesthetized cats, have studied three basic patterns of behavior that appear to be related to the natural behavior of the cat. Stimulation has produced growling, hissing, and flight. Growling in normal cat behavior is associated with attack unmixed with escape tendencies (irritable aggression). Hissing is characteristic of a defense reaction when the animal is confronted with a superior opponent. Flight involves an aroused response with autonomic components and a quick retreat from the situation (Leyhausen, 1956). These three types of response could be separately elicited at threshold levels of brain stimulation (Brown et al., 1969a) and were grossly similar when elicited in different parts of the brain, that is, the midbrain, hypothalamus, and forebrain (Hunsperger & Bucher, 1967). However, stimulation at one-and-one-half times threshold frequently yielded combined patterns indicating that the neural systems for these different reactions have considerable anatomical proximity. Above-threshold stimulation of a growling point resulted in a response in which growling and hissing alternated. Points yielding flight resulted in a combined hissing-flight reaction on suprathreshold stimulation (Brown et al., 1969a). Simultaneous stimulation of two points that had yielded the same type of reaction resulted in a facilitation (spatial summation) of the effects evoked. Latencies of the responses were reduced and the reactions were intensified (Brown et al., 1969b). In the hypothalamus the growling reactions were obtained from the region of the tuber, whereas the hissing responses were elicited from points above the tuber. Flight reactions resulted from stimulation in the intermediate zone extending from the level of the preoptic area to the mammillary bodies.

Caution must be used in interpreting these studies because most of them were conducted without external targets for attack and the interpretations are based on affective expressions that are presumed to be a part of the aggressive encounter. Some of these emotional expressions could also occur as a result of pain induced by the stimulation or by the uniqueness or strangeness of the sensations produced by the stimulation. It is risky to infer that a given behavioral pattern is being affected when the behavior itself is not observed, and as indicated earlier, the behavior will not be expressed in full unless there is a specific target in the environment to which the animal can respond.

Fortunately, these investigators also did some testing of the animals with an appropriate external stimulus, either a stuffed cat, dog, or fox. Stimulation in the presence of the dummy resulted in appropriate, well-organized, and directed aggressive behaviors.

Although it is not possible to separate out completely the irritable from the fear-induced reactions in these experiments, it can generally be concluded that these combined reactions are organized at three levels of progressively increasing importance situated in the amygdala, the hypothalamus, and the central gray of the midbrain. Behavior patterns evoked by hypothalamic stimulation are unaffected by bilateral amygdaloid lesions, but those produced by amygdaloid stimulation were abolished by ipsolateral lesions of the appropriate areas of either the midbrain or the hypothalamus. Further, the patterns evoked by hypothalamic stimulation can be blocked by midbrain lesions, but those evoked by midbrain stimulation are not blocked by hypothalamic lesions (Hunsperger, 1956; Fernandez de Molina & Hunsperger, 1962; Fernandez de Molina & Hunsperger, 1959). A more recent study by Berntson 1972) supports the preceding work showing that bilateral midbrain lesions block hypothalamically induced hissing (and to a lesser extent growling). Unilateral lesions do not affect the response induced by contralateral electrodes indicating that the hypothalamic efferents for the hissing response are primarily homolateral but partially crossed.

A final study that implicates the midbrain in what is probably fear-induced aggression was done by Adams (1968a, 1968b). Recordings were made of the activity of single nerve cells in cats defending themselves from attacks by other cats. Defense was defined as hissing or striking back at the attacking cat. Ninety-five cells located in areas previously shown to be important in affective attack or defense were studied. Control measures included recording while the cat was lifted and dropped, had its forelimb pulled, had its tail punched, and was presented with flashes and clicks and other sensory stimulation. The cells in the midbrain appeared to be most closely associated with affective defense. The four cells that changed only during affective defense were in the midbrain.

A large number of studies have shown that stimulation of various brain areas results in escape behavior on the part of the subjects. These studies have been well summarized in a variety of reviews (Akert, 1961; Brady, 1960; Brown & Hunsperger, 1963; Hess, 1964) and need not be reviewed in detail here. In general, however, it is not possible to determine whether these escape behaviors would have resulted in aggression if the subject had been cornered or prevented from escaping.

ENDOCRINOLOGY OF
FEAR-INDUCED AGGRESSION

Essentially nothing is known about the endocrine basis of fear-induced aggression. It seems likely, however, that certain endocrine balances might sensitize the brain areas that control this type of response to external stimulation. A combined approach using brain stimulation and peripheral endocrine manipulation may turn out to be a sensitive tool for the investigation of this problem. When brain areas are located that produce escape behavior followed by fear-induced aggression, endocrine manipulations can be undertaken to determine whether the involved brain areas are sensitized or desensitized by the endocrine changes.

PHYSIOLOGY OF
MATERNAL AGGRESSION

Although there is good evidence that maternal aggression is a frequently observed phenomenon in many species, essentially nothing is known about the physiology of this class of behavior. In many species, although not all, the tendency to attack intruders in the presence of the young appears to be related to the hormonal changes that occur during the postpartum period. Gandelman (1972) has suggested that the postpartum aggressive behavior of mice may be the result of the relatively high levels of prolactin present during that period. The waning of the aggressive tendencies in the mice that he studied corresponded with the declining levels of prolactin. That is a reasonable hypothesis but it has not yet been subjected to experimental test.

It is interesting that so little has been done on the problem of maternal aggression, although the phenomenon has been recognized for centuries and many of the techniques for its investigation have been available for many years. This area of research has the potential for a large number of Ph.D. dissertations.

NEUROLOGY OF
IRRITABLE AGGRESSION

As indicated in the discussion of fear-induced aggression, it is frequently difficult to determine from experiments designed to deal with other problems what particular kind of aggression is being observed. It is therefore not possible to delineate the neurological basis of irritable aggression with any confidence. There are, however, a number of experiments from which tentative conclusions may be drawn. In the interpretation of these studies it is necessary to keep in mind the studies on aggression induced by aversive stimulation (see p. 199). It is always possible that a given experimental manipulation may activate neural systems comparable to those that produce the conscious experience of pain when activated in man. Thus the aggression produced may be secondary to the activation of the "pain" systems (Plotnik et al., 1971). Delgado (1966) has considered this problem in some detail and concludes that the "cerebral mechanisms for the perception of pain and for aggressive behavior have a different anatomical and physiological organization . . ." (p. 679). This conclusion is based on a number of experiments showing that animals stimulated in certain brain areas make responses similar to those made when they are subjected to external aversive stimulation. Aggression does not necessarily follow brain stimulation in those areas. Stimulation in other areas elicits aggressive behavior that is not accompanied by behavior resembling responses evoked by aversive stimulation. However, whether the animals feel pain or anger, can, of course, never be more than a conjecture.

The Role of the Hypothalamus in Irritable Aggression

Several investigators have reported aggressive behavior with evidence of considerable sympathetic arousal on stimulation of the ventromedial hypothalamus (VMH), thus implicating this brain area in irritable aggression. The stimulated animal may attack either the experimenter or another animal (Wasman & Flynn, 1962; Yasukochi, 1960; Nakao, 1958; Glusman & Roisin, 1960; Adams & Flynn, 1966; Sheard & Flynn, 1967). If hypothalamic sites from which irritable or affective attack can be elicited are lesioned, the subsequent neural degeneration can be traced. Chi and Flynn (1971a, 1971b) have shown that the degeneration is essentially confined to the periventricular system that connects the medial hypothalamus and the central gray of the midbrain. King and Hoebel (1968) have reported some instances of affective attack not typical of predation by a rat on a mouse during electrical stimulation of the lateral hypothalamus. Consistent affective or irritable attack by the rat on the mouse has also been reported during stimulation of the anterior lateral hypothalamus. These animals attacked live mice and other rats, but not dead mice (Panksepp & Trowill, 1969; Panksepp, 1971c).

Occasional reports have indicated attacks on an "hallucination" during VMH stimulation (Brown & Hunsperger, 1963; Yasukochi, 1960). However, the larger amount of evidence indicates that the aggressive response is stimulus-bound and that some stimuli are preferred to others. A live rat is preferred to a dead one and attacks on a stuffed rat or toy dog are not sustained (Wasman & Flynn, 1962). Only pupillary dilation and slight snarling results during stimulation in the absence of an object for attack (Nakao, 1958).

Irritable aggression produced by VMH stimulation is enhanced by simultaneous stimulation in the midbrain reticular formation, just as predatory aggression resulting from lateral hypothalmic stimulation is (Sheard & Flynn, 1967). This implies that an aroused animal will respond more quickly and intensely to the stimuli eliciting irritable aggression than will an unaroused animal. There are also areas in the midbrain that when stimulated alone result in irritable aggression (Skultety, 1963; Delgado, 1966).

As indicated, irritability without escape tendencies is produced by VMH lesions (Wheatley, 1944; McAdam & Kaelber, 1966; Glusman et al., 1961; Kaelber et al., 1965; Anand & Brobeck, 1951; Ingram, 1939). VMH lesions also enhance shock-induced aggression (Grossman, 1972a). After the operation only one-tenth the intensity of shock is needed to induce fighting and the operated rats show considerable spontaneous fighting between shocks. However, what appears to be inter-male aggression is unaffected by the lesions (Adams, 1971). Irritable aggression has also been reported in humans with tumors in the hypothalamic regions (Wheatley, 1944; Vonderahe, 1944). It has been suggested that the hyperirritability resulting from VMH lesions may be due to irritative scar tissue (Glusman & Roisin, 1960). However, more recent research appears to indicate that the effect is the result of the interruption of a suppressor fiber system that runs through the VMH (Grossman, 1972b). Knife cuts that sever the connections between the ventromedial and lateral hypothalamus and the VMH and the anterior lateral hypothalamus result in a hyperirritable pattern of behavior quite similar to that produced by the VMH lesions. However, cuts made anterior and posterior to the VMH produce either no effects or equivocal effects (Sclafani, 1971; Paxinos & Bindra, 1972). It has also been shown that cats made savage by VMH lesions are again made docile by lesions in the midbrain, specifically in the medial lemniscus and the spinothalamic tracts, or in the central gray. In the latter case, however, the docility was temporary (Kaelber et al., 1965; Glusman et al., 1961).

One can only conclude from these lesion studies that the medial hypothalamus is in some way involved in the neural system for irritable aggression. The mechanisms producing the effect have not yet been worked out. The increased aggression may, as Grossman suggests, be due to the interruption of suppressor fibers. However, other interpretations are possible. The VMH-lesioned animal may have a lowered pain threshold; it may be hyperresponsive to all stimuli or the sensory input may be distorted in some way. Or irritative scar tissue may be activating distant portions of the brain. Any of the preceding factors may contribute to the observed hyperirritability.

Although the preceding evidence clearly indicates that the hypothalamus is involved in irritable aggression, it does not appear to be essential to that function. After a considerable number of attempts, Ellison and Flynn (1968) were able to isolate the hypothalamus from the rest of the brain by rotating two small knives positioned in the brain in opposite directions through 360° several times. The operation was successful on four cats. These animals were inactive after the lesion but could be aroused by a pinch on the tail and were capable of making well-directed attacks on the offending object. One cat also reacted with well-directed aggression in response to stimulation of the central gray around the aqueduct.

The Role of the Cingulum and Olfactory Bulbs in Irritable Aggression

The cingulum is involved in aggressive behavior but there are species differences. Irritable aggression is increased in cats either by stimulation or lesions in the cingulum (Anand & Dua, 1956; Kennard, 1955a, 1955b). The latter finding may be due to resulting irritative lesions. Cingulate lesions also produce irritable aggression in dogs. This irritability may result from hypersensitivity to tactile stimulation (Brutkowski et al., 1961). Cingulectomy in monkeys reduces fear and makes them more docile (Kennard, 1955a). Cingulectomy has been used to treat uncontrollable violence in man. Although these patients are more easily irritated after the operation, their outbursts are milder and less sustained (LeBeau, 1952; Tow & Whitty, 1953; Whitty et al., 1952).

Our understanding of the role of the olfactory bulbs in irritable aggression is at best confused and has already been covered in the discussion of their relationship to predation (p. 237). One additional study on mice serves only to confuse the issue further. Removal of the olfactory bulbs eliminated pain-induced aggression in male mice. This effect, however, does not appear to be related to the pheromone responsible for inter-male fighting. Intact mice adulterated with an odorant that reduced aggressive behavior in home cage fighting tests had no effect in the pain-induced fighting situation (Fortuna & Gandelman, 1972).

The Role of the Amygdala in Irritable Aggression

As indicated earlier, the amygdala is involved in the neural circuitry for several kinds of aggressive behavior and the effects of stimulation and lesions operate through the hypothalamus and midbrain. The details of the relationships among the various brain levels remain to be worked out, although beginnings have been made (Egger & Flynn, 1967; Fernandez de Molino & Hunsperger, 1962; Clemente & Chase, 1973). Although there are some conflicting reports in the literature and some indications of species differences, studies on the amygdala exemplify the different neurological bases of various kinds of aggressive behavior and support the contention that it is possible to facilitate one kind of aggression and suppress another with the same manipulation. It would seem, for example, that stimulation of an area in the lateral portion of the basal nucleus of the amygdala of the cat would facilitate fear-induced aggression, but inhibit both predatory and irritable aggression.

Early studies showed that total bilateral amygdalectomy raised the threshold for at least three different kinds of aggressive behavior. Irritable aggression is dramatically reduced. Amygdalectomized cats do not aggress even when suspended by their tails or when they are generally roughed up (Schreiner & Kling, 1953). Amygdalectomy also eliminated predatory aggression (see p. 234) and fear-induced aggression (see p. 257).

There are now several reviews of the literature dealing with the role of the amygdala in various kinds of aggressive behavior (Kaada, 1972; Kling, 1972; Karli et al., 1972; and Zbrozyna, 1972). The following section takes a slightly different approach in an attempt to sort out the role of the different amygdaloid nuclei in the different kinds of aggression as defined in this book.

Stimulation of the central nucleus (*f*) (letters in this section refer to Figure 7) results in fear and escape responses in the dog (Fonberg, 1965) and the cat (Wood, 1958; Anand & Dua, 1956). The latter will escape if possible but becomes aggressive when cornered. The direct application of carbachol to the same nucleus in the cat inhibits a "rage" reaction resulting from carbachol stimulation of the hypothalamus (Deci et al., 1969). The cat's reaction to stimulation in the basal nuclei (*d, e*) is similar. However, Fonberg (1965, 1968) has reported that stimulation of the more ventral portion of the basal and lateral nuclei results in fear inhibition in dogs.

Lesions in the central nucleus produce irritable aggression in cats (Wood, 1958) and in dogs (Fonberg, 1965). The cat does not show escape behavior; it will cross the room and engage in fights with another cat. The dog does not attack spontaneously but shows great irritability to normal restraints and once started in a rage response becomes more and more wild, exhibiting what Fonberg calls an avalanche syndrome. Both Wood and Fonberg have suggested that the central nucleus may have inhibitory functions and releases aggressive behavior when it is lesioned.

Once again, it should be pointed out that the increase in aggression resulting from lesions in the central nucleus does not necessarily mean that it has specific inhibitory functions. It may, of course, but there are a number of other possible interpretations. The avalanche syndrome, for example, could result from some type of hypersensitivity. If the dog is moved to activity as a reaction against the restraints, greater activity results in more stimulation from the restraints with increasing reaction to them. There are, of course, a variety of suppressor mechanisms in the brain. However, the relevant experiments have not been done to show that a suppressor system is involved in this instance.

Stimulation of the medial nucleus (*g*) seems to result in irritable aggression without escape tendencies in both the cat and the dog. Since the cat was tested without a particular object of attack, the results are somewhat difficult to interpret, but the responses included hissing, growling, claw extension, and pupillary dilation (MacLean & Delgado, 1953). Lesions in this same general area in the dog result in tameness (Fonberg, 1965), whereas stimulation in the same area in the dog results in the "opposite of tameness." Fonberg refers to the reaction as defensive but makes no mention of escape tendencies.

The experiments of Ursin and Kaada (1960) using stimulation in cats support, in general, the preceding findings but seem to show more overlap of irritable and fear-induced aggression particularly in the central nucleus (*f*). Their general conclusions were that the rostral part of the lateral nucleus and the central nucleus were involved in the system for fear reactions, whereas the more ventromedial and caudal parts of the amygdala contribute to the anger reaction.

The lesion experiments done by Ursin (1965) have in general supported those findings and show clearly that fear and anger reactions are anatomically separable. The same general flight and aggression mechanisms also appear to exist in the primate brain (Ursin, 1972). Contrary to those findings, however, Allikmets (1966) was unable to differentiate among the amygdaloid nuclei that produced fear and anger reactions on electrical stimulation. He suggested that the reaction to stimulation depended on the individual differences in the cats. The docile ones showed fear, whereas the more resistive ones showed signs of strong aggression.

Interpretation of the preceding findings must remain tentative until further research is done that recognizes the different types of aggression and tests for them specifically while manipulating the particular amygdaloid nuclei. It does not appear possible to reconcile the results of all the studies done on the amygdala, but several points seem to stand out. Fear-induced, irritable, and predatory aggression are probably controlled in part by separate but overlapping anatomical areas. Fear-induced is, in general, located more dorsally, laterally, and rostrally, whereas irritable is more ventral, medial, and caudal. Predatory aggression control is located in the more dorsal portion of the amygdala.

It also seems possible in the light of the results of Fonberg (1965), Wood (1958), and Egger and Flynn (1967) that a portion of the amygdaloid area controlling fear also has inhibitory functions in relation to the irritable and predatory areas. There is no indication at the moment whether the inhibition acts through the facilitating areas of the amygdala, through the lower brain areas, or through some other mechanism.

Affective reactions and behavior associated with irritable aggression have also been produced in humans by electrical stimulation in the amygdaloid region. (See Chapter 2.)

The Hippocampus and Irritable Aggression

A number of other brain areas are evidently involved in the neural circuitry of irritable aggression but much more research is needed before it will be possible to understand the interrelations among these areas. Hippocampal lesions increase the aggressiveness of cats toward conspecifics and toward the experimenter (Green et al., 1957). That this result may be due to irritative effects of the lesions is supported by the finding that the aggressiveness decreases over time. A more recent study on rats shows that animals with hippocampal lesions show less shock-induced fighting (defined as fighting, lunging, striking, or biting) than do operated controls. The lesioned animals also show a greatly reduced tendency to assume the boxing stance usually found in the shock box situation. However, hippocampal lesioned animals do show more inclination to attack a prod with which they have been shocked (Blanchard et al., 1970). The different reactions in the two shock situations may be due to the fact that there are different neural systems for these two different aggressive reactions. Or, as Blanchard et al. suggest, the reduced fighting in the shock box may result from the fact that the lesioned animals have less of a tendency to assume the immobile boxing posture from which the shock-induced attacks on another animal are usually launched. At least one study seems to show that irritable aggression results from stimulation of the rostral hippocampus by acetylcholine (MacLean & Delgado, 1953).

The Septum and Other Brain Areas Involved in Irritable Aggression

The septum is a complex structure that sends and receives fiber tracts from several different parts of the brain. Therefore studies that involve lesions in the septal area are difficult to interpret. It is unlikely that the septal region as a whole has a unitary effect on any particular type of aggression. However, a number of studies have been done that indicate that the septal region is involved in some way. Since most of these experiments involved massive septal lesions, any interpretation must be made with caution.

As indicated earlier, septal lesions in rats produce a temporary increase in that animal's tendency to make highly irritable attacks on a mouse, which is distinctly different from the typical predatory response. They also show increased fighting in the shock-induced situation. If the animals are tested 15 days after surgery rather than immediately, neither of these aggressive tendencies occur. However, rats tested during the critical 15-day period do not lose their tendency to kill mice after the 15 days (Miczek & Grossman, 1972). It has generally been found that the syndrome produced by septal lesions is temporary and seldom lasts more than a week or so. At least one study has shown, however, that rats with septal lesions are more reactive in the shock-induced aggression situation as much as 85 days after the operation (Wetzel et al., 1967). However, this may be a secondary effect due to the subject's increased sensitivity to shock (Lints, 1965; Lints & Harvey, 1969). The septal syndrome of hyperreactivity, which evidently involves more than one kind of aggressive behavior, is not altered by adrenalectomy, gonadectomy, or hypophysectomy (Montgomery et al., 1971). The so-called septal rage syndrome may be limited to a few species. Squirrel monkeys do not show it (Buddington et al.,

1967), nor do guinea pigs or cotton rats (Sodetz et al., 1967), and hamsters, although changed by the operation, are not hyperreactive (Sodetz & Bunnell, 1967a, 1967b).

Irritable aggression can be inhibited by the stimulation of several brain areas but only a limited amount of work has been done on this problem. Stimulation at some points in the head of the caudate nucleus reduces aggressive behavior in the monkey (Delgado, 1960, 1963). Caudate stimulation also eliminates the irritable or affective attack of the cat on the rat produced by medial hypothalamic stimulation. As with predatory aggression, however, the cat appears to be quite capable of making the attack, but it does not adequately direct the attack to the rat. No competing motor responses were observed and the autonomic reactivity produced by the hypothalamic stimulation was not affected (Plumer & Siegel, 1973). Stimulation of certain areas of the midbrain also suppress attack induced by hypothalamic stimulation in the cat (Sheard & Flynn, 1967).

ENDOCRINOLOGY OF IRRITABLE AGGRESSION

There is evidence that both the endocrine system and the nervous system are involved in the control of irritable aggression but little is known about the interactions between the two. In one study it was shown that castration controlled both the hypersexuality and the aggressive behavior of amygdalectomized cats (Schreiner & Kling, 1953). These same experimenters reported a drastic increase in irritable aggression in two docile, spayed, but otherwise normal female cats after the administration daily of diethylstilbestrol. However, this finding has never been replicated.

Androgenic hormones appear to play a role in irritable aggression. It is well known that intact male domestic animals such as the bull and the stallion react aggressively not only toward other males, but toward human handlers as well. Castration makes them relatively docile. However, this problem has been little studied in the laboratory. Castration has been shown to reduce but not eliminate the irritable aggression produced in rats by foot shock (Hutchinson et al., 1965). A number of studies have failed to show consistent differences between the sexes in shock-induced aggression (Ulrich & Azrin, 1962; Powell, 1967; Powell et al., 1970; Powell, 1971). However, it has been shown in other studies that in the shock box situation males tend to maintain the boxing posture longer than females. The male tendency to fight increases over sessions whereas the fighting of females decreases. Males fight frequently between shocks but females rarely do. Finally, females need a warm-up period within a session before they begin to fight, whereas males fight immediately (Conner & Levine, 1969; Conner et al., 1969). The different findings among the various studies appear to be due to procedural differences. Conner et al., for example, used several different shock and temporal parameters.

Endocrine manipulations in early life have an effect on shock-induced aggression similar to the effects on spontaneous aggression in mice. Neonatally castrated rats manifest a female pattern of behavior in the situation and do not change behavior if given androgens in adulthood. However, animals castrated shortly after weaning do show an increase in fighting after androgen replacement. Weaning castrates fight less than normals but more than neonatal castrates (Conner & Levine, 1969; Conner et al., 1969). Female rats given testosterone injections within 24 hours after birth fight more than normals (Powell, 1971).

There is some evidence that the plasma level of testosterone in rhesus monkeys is related to irritable aggression. Animals that inhibited aggressive behavior in the presence of more dominant animals in the hierarchy showed evidence of tension, which included the shaking and banging of objects as well as yawning and teeth grinding. The tension indicators correlated with testosterone, $r = 0.534$ (Rose et al., 1971).

It is possible that amygdalectomy produces a reduction in aggression through the endocrine system. A number of studies have shown that amygdalectomy produces testicular atrophy and thus the output of androgenic hormones (Goddard, 1964). It has been shown that juvenile *M. mulatta* manifest less rough-and-tumble play after amygdalectomy and that such play, particularly sham biting, is increased after the administration of exogenous testosterone (Kling, 1968).

In spite of the fact that female mammals are, in general, far less aggressive than are males, in a number of situations females are aggressive and that behavior is frequently associated with the reproductive hormones. Female mink reach the peak of their aggression after the breeding season and that behavior change related to the formation of the corpus luteum (MacLennan & Bailey, 1969). Female rhesus monkeys (*Macaca mulatta*) show a significant increase in aggressive behavior when given subcutaneous injections of estrogen. Progesterone also increases female aggressive behavior, but the effect appears to be an indirect one because the female is less receptive to male mounting attempts (Michael & Zumpe, 1970). When females were given both estrogen and progesterone, their aggressive behavior was very greatly increased (Michael, 1969).

The female golden hamster is unusual among mammals in that she is generally more aggressive than the male. Ovariectomized females are significantly less aggressive than intact ones but show an increase in aggression in response to progesterone. However, neither testosterone propionate nor estradiol benzoate is effective in restoring the fighting tendency (Payne & Swanson, 1972).

There are a number of suggestions from clinical endocrinology impli-

cating endocrine mechanisms in irritable aggression in humans. These
have been discussed in Chapter 3.

Although androgens definitely appear to play a role in irritable aggression, they do not seem to be the only endocrine mechanisms involved.
There is abundant evidence that a variety of stressful conditions increase
the tendency to aggressive behavior. However, there is also evidence that
stress results in a reduction in the testosterone levels in the bloodstream
of males, with a consequent reduction in inter-male fights. It seems likely
that interaction occurs between the nonandrogenic hormones resulting
from stress and the neural system for irritable aggression, and that those
hormones sensitize that system to lower its activation threshold. Although
no research has been done as yet on that hypothesis, it would seem to be
a profitable course to pursue.

SUMMARY OF THE PHYSIOLOGICAL SUBSTRATES OF THE DIFFERENT KINDS OF AGGRESSION
Predatory Aggression

The neurology of predation in the cat and rat, despite some differences, is
quite similar. The general picture is that there is an innately organized[2]
neural system for predation involving neurons in the lateral hypothalamus,
midbrain, amygdala, and hippocampus. When this neural system is activated, electrically, chemically, or naturally, in the presence of an appropriate prey object, species-characteristic combinations of patterned reflexes occur that constitute a well-directed attack on the prey. Some
lesions that interrupt the continuity of the system eliminate the predatory
response. The neural system is redundant in that it is bilaterally represented, and there appears to be more than one system. The lateral hypothalamus, for example, is undoubtedly important in normal predation, but
is evidently not essential to the manifestation of the response. The neural
system for predation receives both facilitating and inhibiting inputs from
various portions of the brain. Facilitating mechanisms have been identified
in the ventral hippocampus, dorsolateral amygdala, midbrain reticular
system, and thalamus. Inhibiting mechanisms are found in the dorsal hippocampus, baso-medial-lateral amygdala, thalamus, and septum.

Relatively little is known about the endocrinological basis of predation.

Inter-Male Aggression

Androgens are critical to the development and maintenance of inter-male
aggression. The behavior does not appear until the onset of sexual matur-

[2] Although there is as yet little information on the development of the predatory
response, it is clear that the animal needs no experience with either prey or conspecifics to manifest the complete, albeit somewhat clumsy, killing of a natural prey
under appropriate electrical brain stimulation (Roberts and Berquist, 1968).

ity. Aggression between males can be eliminated by castration and restored by androgen therapy, and the level of aggression is related to the amount of endogenous androgen in the bloodstream. There is an inverse relationship between the circulating levels of adrenocorticotrophic hormone (ACTH) and the tendency to aggression, and any manipulation that increases ACTH also inhibits the fighting behavior between males. Stress, which increases ACTH levels, reduces inter-male aggression. Various adrenal hormones that block ACTH also facilitate fighting. Aggression between males is blocked by the estrogens and progesteronelike compounds.

Endocrine manipulations conducted early in life have a permanent irreversible effect on aggressive behavior in adulthood. Females are masculinized by testosterone injections given in the first few days of life and react to androgens in adulthood with the typical male fighting response. Genetic males, however, are permanently feminized by early castration and do not show aggression after androgen injections in adulthood. Much of the preceding information is based on inter-male fighting in mice. There are indications that other species do not follow the pattern in all details.

Much less is known about the neurology of inter-male aggression. However, it appears that the hypothalamus, particularly the anterior portion, is involved.

Fear-Induced Aggression

Fear-induced aggression is reduced by lesions in the cingulate gyrus and total bilateral amygdalectomy but increased by stimulation of parts of the hypothalamus, hippocampus, midbrain, and specific nuclei of the amygdala. It is increased by septal lesions, at least in mice. The interrelationships of all of these brain areas have not yet been worked out, but there is evidence that among the amygdala, hypothalamus, and central gray, the level of importance in the organization of this response proceeds from rostral to caudal. Behavior patterns evoked by hypothalamic stimulation are not affected by amygdala lesions, but those produced by amygdala stimulation are abolished by hypothalamic lesions. Lesions in the midbrain block aggressive behavior induced by hypothalamic lesions, but the reverse is not true.

Essentially nothing is known about the endocrine basis of fear-induced aggression.

Irritable Aggression

Irritable aggressive behavior can be produced by stimulation in the anterior and medial hypothalamus and by lesions in the ventromedial nuclei of the same structure. The latter effect appears to be due to the interruption of a tract of suppressor fibers because the same result can be produced by selective knife cuts that sever the connections between the VMH and the lateral hypothalamus. Lesions in hypothalamic areas that produce irritable attack result in degeneration confined to the periventricular system, which connects the medial hypothalamus with the central gray of the midbrain. The hypothalamus is important in but not essential to irritable aggressive behavior since that behavior can still occur after the hypothalamus is isolated from the rest of the brain.

The cingulum and the olfactory bulbs are involved in irritable attack behavior but there are species differences in the effects produced. The irritable response can be induced by both lesions and chemical stimulation of the hippocampus and the lesion effect is probably due to irritative scar tissue. The role of the amygdala is complex. The irritable reaction can be activated or inhibited by stimulation or lesions of particular nuclei, and there is a reciprocal inhibitory relationship between those nuclei involved in fear-induced and irritable aggression. The syndrome produced by septal lesions appears to involve irritable aggression in some species.

Androgens definitely appear to play a role in irritable aggression. Other hormones appear to be involved, but little research has been done to determine their precise role.

9

Some Theoretical Considerations

One test of any model of behavior is the kind of predictions that it makes and whether it makes different predictions from other models currently available. In this final chapter an attempt will be made to point up the difference between this model and others. There will be no attempt to summarize all the various theories of aggression. This has been done with varying degrees of bias by a number of other authors (Corning & Corning, 1971; Bandura, 1973; Berkowitz, 1962; Kaufman, 1970; Megargee, 1969). Our concern will be only with the major differences between the theoretical position taken in this book and other theories.

Aggression as a Drive

There is currently a great deal of controversy about whether or not there is an aggressive drive. According to some theorists, such as the psychoanalysts (Freud, 1933, and more recently Storr, 1968), the drive results from an innate, undefined mechanism. A similar position is held by a group of ethologists led by Konrad Lorenz (1966). Other authors (Dollard et al., 1939, and more recently, Feshback, 1964) maintain that the aggressive drive is produced by frustration that results when goal-directed behavior is blocked. In either case there is a buildup of an aggressive force, or "energy," which continues to accumulate until reduced by hostile expression or some substitute behavior.

One of the principal difficulties with the aggressive drive position is that its proponents tend to treat the inside of man as a black box and develop their positions on the basis of behavior alone. Drive is an intervening variable that may have some usefulness as a descriptive term but that has relatively little value as a predictor of behavior. It is essentially an expression of ignorance of the internal or physiological mechanisms that underlie basic behaviors. As Barnett and Evans (1965) have suggested, "Sometimes we get the impression that whenever anything relevant is discovered by physiological research, 'drive' makes a further retreat into obscurity" (p. 241).

Scott (1971) addresses himself to the inadequate physiological base for the aggressive drive model when he says,

> There is no known physiological mechanism by which any large amount of energy can be accumulated in the nervous system. Therefore, hydraulic models of motivation are chiefly valid only in that they may represent subjective interpretations of motivation; in short, how it feels to be motivated. The entire organism is, of course, a mechanism by which energy can be accumulated and stored. However, such energy is not specific to any particular kind of behavior and does not represent motivation (p. 27).

Scott is, of course, correct when he suggests that energy can be accumulated and stored. He is also correct in indicating that available energy is not specific to any particular kind of behavior. However, there are mechanisms that direct the available energy into particular channels, with the result that there can be an accumulating potential for hostile expression. One of the major functions of the nervous system is to give direction to the utilization of energy resources. Abundant evidence has been presented to show that there are neural systems for various types of aggression and that those neural systems can be progressively sensitized by a variety of factors, such as changes in the blood chemistry. Thus there are indeed physiological mechanisms that permit the gradual increase in the potential for aggressive behavior, that is, the energy available to the organisms has a greater probability of being expressed in a hostile manner. The end result is essentially what one might expect if there were an accumulation of "aggressive energy." These physiological mechanisms can provide for either a relatively transient increase in the tendency to hostility or a prolonged or chronic behavior tendency. For example, a precipitous drop in blood sugar can induce fighting and aggressive behavior in a man but he can "become quite civilized" when the proper blood sugar level is restored (Gloor, 1967b). The tendency to inter-male aggression is gradually increased with increasing titers of testosterone in the bloodstream during puberty and lasts for a prolonged period.

However, it should be obvious from the discussion in earlier chapters that a continuing accumulation of "aggressive energy," relievable *only* by the expression of aggression, is not in keeping with the physiological evidence. The hypoglycemic patient described may have intense, irrational, and progressively mounting feelings of hostility. However, if, because of early inhibitory training or lack of an appropriate external target, he does not behave aggressively, a glass of orange juice will return him to the ranks of the rational and his internal tendencies to hostility will be eliminated without ever having been expressed. A woman who has intense feelings of irritability during her premenstrual period because of her particular hormone balance may very well be able to keep her behavior under control and not display hostility. As the endocrine cycle continues and her hormone balance returns to normal, the neural system for irritability is desensitized and she loses her aggressive tendencies, whether she has expressed her hostility or not.

External Versus Internal or Spontaneous Stimulation to Aggression

Much of the controversy in aggression theories revolves around whether or not the tendency to hostility ever arises spontaneously in the absence of some relevant external stimulation. Lorenz (1966), Storr (1968), and Bettelheim (1967), of course, accept as given, the spontaneity of internal impulses to aggression; others (Montague, 1966; Hinde, 1967; Scott, 1971; Bandura, 1973) reject it. Scott is most explicit when he says, "In the absence of external stimulation internal arousal (*to aggression*) will not occur" (Scott, 1971, p. 21). Since there is sometimes confusion on what is meant by *spontaneous* (Tinbergen, 1968) it is well to define it. Scott's definition is a useful one:

> I shall therefore define what I mean by spontaneous internal stimulation. In the first place, all stimulation, whether external or internal, consists of changes. An internal change that is produced by physiological or metabolic processes independently of outside stimulation is "spontaneous," and such a change which in some way activates the nervous system is "spontaneous stimulation" (Scott, 1971, p. 27).

In the model proposed in this book it has been suggested that spontaneous activation of the neural systems for aggression may indeed occur. It is also suggested that aggressive behavior is generally stimulus-bound, that is, the organism engages in aggressive behavior only in the presence of an appropriate target. The idea that aggression is stimulus-bound is not incompatible with the concept of spontaneous activation. It has long been accepted that there is spontaneous stimulation to other basic behaviors, such as hunger, thirst, and sex (Scott, 1971). However, these behaviors are also stimulus-bound; like aggression, they do not occur in a vacuum. As the present author has suggested (Moyer, 1969), "A deprived animal neither makes random chewing movements nor attempts to eat all available objects. Regardless of the intensity of the internal state produced by deprivation, the animal responds to a very limited set of stimuli with an eating response. It eats only food" (p. 105).

What kinds of evidence exists for the spontaneous activation of the neural systems for aggression? The evidence is exactly the same as that available for the spontaneous activation of the neural systems for ingestive behavior. An animal with a presumed active neural system for ingestive behavior is offered food. If it eats, the presumption is confirmed. If one is willing to accept the introspective report of humans as evidence, we can all agree that we have at times "felt" hungry. Again we presume that the neural system relating to ingestive behavior has been spontaneously active. However, who among us is unable to report having had irrational "feelings" of irritability that, as nearly as we can tell, are unrelated to external reality? If anything, hostile behavior is less stimulus-bound than eating behavior. Hungry men do not eat rocks, but angry men do at times strike walls.

There are numerous examples in Chapters 2 and 3 of physiological processes that result in the activation of the neural systems for aggressive behavior. When these physiological changes take place the individual reports feelings of anger and hostility even though he can sometimes recognize that there is no adequate environmental provocation. Solomon and Kleeman (1971) offer a number of other examples.

It is important to note that the potential for spontaneous activation of the neural systems for hostility does not mean that hostile behavior is inevitable or that it cannot be controlled. Nor does it mean that man is "inately depraved" or "evil," as suggested by Montagu (Montagu, 1966, 1968). Man is as he is, and his physiological mechanisms are beyond good and evil.

The "instinct" theorists (Lorenz, 1966; Storr, 1968; Tinbergen, 1968), who accept the idea that the urge to aggression may arise spontaneously, are pessimistic about the usefulness of controlling man's innate tendencies by educational means or by reducing or eliminating the various social instigations to hostility such as the frustrations and deprivations endured by significant portions of the world population. Berkowitz (1962), in reacting to Freud's idea of an innate aggressive drive, indicates that the implications for social policy are obvious: "Civilization and moral order ultimately must be based on force, not love and charity" (p. 4). Although that conclusion may be drawn from some theories that recognize a spontaneous internal activation of aggression potential, it is clearly not an implication from the model under discussion in this book. There are three considerations in this model that invalidate that interpretation. First, although feelings of hostility do sometimes arise spontaneously, they are also readily evoked by frustration or aversive external stimulation. Secondly, aggressive behavior is amenable to learned inhibition, just as any other behavior is. However, the amount and type of inhibitory training necessary for hostility control may be much different for different people. An individual with a chronic behavior tendency to hostility because of the low threshold of his neural systems regulating that behavior may need intensive inhibitory training. In a limited number of pathologically aggressive individuals, such as Charles Whitman, educational measures may be of no value at all and the underlying neurological pathology may need to be corrected.

Finally, there is no aggressive energy to be drained off (see below) and there is *no necessity* for aggressive feelings to be expressed. When the activity in the neural systems for hostility is decreased or eliminated, the available energy sources (not hostile energy, of course) of the organism are directed to some other endeavor by other neural systems.

Diffuse Arousal as an Argument Against Biologically Based Aggression

Some authors argue against a specific physiological substrate for feelings of anger and hostility on the basis of the relatively diffuse nature of visceral arousal during emotional states. (See, in particular, Bandura, 1973, p. 55.) It is seldom possible to determine from physiological records of autonomic nervous system activity whether an individual is experiencing fear or anger. Some experimenters have found differences in autonomic patterns during emotional arousal (Ax, 1953; Schachter, 1957), but it is clear that these differences are minimal. Further, Schachter and Singer (1962), in a classic experiment, have shown that subjects autonomically aroused by adrenalin injections tend to assign an emotional label to that arousal that depends on the environmental cues available to them. Thus even though the autonomic arousal pattern was the same for all subjects, those interacting with an angry stooge felt more angry than controls and those interacting with a stooge behaving in a euphoric manner felt happier than controls. This experiment shows that when subjects are autonomically aroused and they do not have a reasonable explanation for that arousal, they label the state in terms of the cognitions available to them.

The experiment does not prove, as Schachter and Singer are careful to point out, that there are no physiological differences among the various emotional states. However, this experiment has been badly misinterpreted many times to support the position that since there is little differentiable autonomic arousal among the various emotional states, the *only* way in which emotions are differentiated is on the basis of cognitions. In a much quoted *Science* article by Lennard et al. (1970) the Schachter-Singer experiment is cited to prove that psychotropic drugs can have no specific emotion-altering effect. Drug effects, according to Lennard et al., can only produce diffuse physiological reactions, which are then interpreted on the basis of the patient's cognitions.

The fallacy in these misinterpretations of the Schachter-Singer experiment is the assumption that the *only* determinant of emotion is the individual's interpretation of how his viscera feel. Within limits the emotions experienced are a function of which neural systems in the brain are active. King's patient (see p. 55) had her feelings of hostility turned on and off at the flick of a switch that activated amygdaloid stimulation. Her external environment did not change, but her hostile emotional reactions could be activated or deactivated, depending on whether or not a particular neural system was active. Many other examples of specific emotions activated by direct brain stimulation can be found in Chapter 2.

If the only contributing factor to feelings of emotion were the interpretation of autonomic arousal, one would expect individuals with spinal cord lesions that blocked the autonomic afferents to be without emotion. That does not, however, appear to be the case (Hohman, 1966). In a study of 25 adult males with spinal cord lesions it was shown that although there was a reduction in the intensity, the duration and peripheral sensations associated with emotions, the individual still reported having emotional experiences. This is exactly what one would expect if it is assumed that subjective affective experience results when particular neural systems are activated and that the activation of those neural systems also results in autonomic arousal that feeds back into the reticular activating system and in some measure perpetuates activity in the active neural system. (See Chapter 1.)

This argument is not to deny the importance of environmental or cognitive determination of affective states. In the normal course of events the neural systems that control the various emotional states are heavily influenced by environmental input. It is a common experience for one to be tired, frustrated, and highly irritable from a bad day at the office but to achieve a state nearing euphoria at a social function with good friends a few hours later. In summary, the model that best fits the available data is an interactive one. Feeling states and the correlated behaviors are most frequently a result of an interaction between the activity (or reactivity) of complex neural systems in the brain and the individual's cognitive reactions to external events. There is always some interaction involved but in any particular situation either the internal or the external conditions may have a predominant influence.

Since the Lennard et al. (1970) paper is directed against the specific effects of all psychotropic drugs and since the present author has considered a whole series of drugs that have been demonstrated to have at least moderately specific antihostility effects, it may be useful to comment further on the Lennard et al. paper. First, there is' much that the authors say that is true. Psychoactive drugs are frequently abused by laymen and this includes the neurotic middle-aged housewife as well as the "hippie" in his commune. They are also misused, abused, and prescribed for the wrong reasons by *some* physicians who hold a much too simplistic view of their action and depend entirely on the drug house inserts for their limited knowledge of the drug effects. It is also true that *some* pharmaceutical companies take advantage of the ignorance of physicians and make exaggerated claims for their various drugs. However, this does not mean that drugs cannot be used wisely or that they cannot have *relatively* specific effects.

The proper prescription of drugs depends, of course, on what is perceived as being wrong with the patient. If it is felt that a patient is excessively hostile because he has a faulty "cognitive map" of the world and that as a result of unfortunate training he perceived much of his environment to be threatening, a therapeutic program geared to re-education may very well be in the patient's best interest. However, if it is felt that the patient has a particularly low threshold for the activation of his neural substrates for anger, the best therapeutic regimen may very well be the prescription of one of the antihostility drugs. In many cases, of course, a dual therapy may be optimal.

Similar reasoning would apply to other psychological dysfunctions. If an individual has a reactive depression because he has just lost his wife in an automobile accident, it would be a disservice to put him on an antidepressant drug like amitriptyline. First, it would be unlikely to be effective. If he were given a high enough dosage, it would sedate him and induce him to spend a significant amount of time sleeping, which could prevent him from engaging in the kinds of social interactions that would enable him to put his loss into perspective and begin to adapt to it. This is the kind of "misuse" that Lennard et al. refer to, and their comments are valid for a variety of mood or emotional states. On the other hand, if the individual has an endogenous depression that results from an imbalance in the norepinephrine levels in the amygdala and/or the hypothalamus, it is a disservice to give him social interaction therapy or psychotherapy. It is highly unlikely to help him in the least. If he is put on amitriptyline, however, he has about an 80 percent chance of coming out of the depression within three weeks whether anything else is done to him or not and whether or not his environment has been changed.

Is It Dangerous to Control Aggression?

It has been suggested that attempts to control aggressive behavior may not be in man's best interest. Lorenz indicates that there is an inextricable link between hostility and affiliation: "Thus intraspecific aggression can certainly exist without its counterpart, love, but conversely there is no love without aggression" (Lorenz, 1966, p. 217). This argument and others leads him to the conclusion that the elimination of aggressive tendencies would be a disastrous step, eliminating or severely limiting ambition, artistic and scientific endeavors, and "countless other equally indispensable behavior patterns," including laughter. Hinde (1967) has already emphasized that there is relatively little evidence to support this point of view. Lorenz (1964) has cited the evidence that in the course of evolution, tendencies to intraspecific aggression and social bonding have developed together. However, it is an unwarranted extrapolation from that argument to take the position that social bonding or "love" is necessarily *dependent* on a viable system for hostility.

There is no physiological support for such a model. In the discussion of the arousal system in Chapter 1, evidence was cited to show that the arousal system enhances but does not initiate activity in the neural systems for aggression. It is quite possible to activate a variety of positive non-aggressive responses without initiating tendencies to aggression. In fact, the evidence seems to indicate that the activation of some of the neural bases for what Lorenz calls "indispensable behavior patterns," which would include love and laughter, tends to inhibit aggressive tendencies. Lesions in the neural substrates for aggression may, in fact, release from inhibition a variety of affiliative tendencies. The vicious monkeys of Kluver and Bucy (1937) given temporal lobectomies not only lost their excessive hostility toward the experimenter, but became overtly friendly and initiated attempts to play with the experimenter. One of the pathologically hostile patients of Heimberger et al. (1966) who received a partial amygdalectomy not only had his tendencies to aggression drastically reduced, but was seen to laugh for the first time in his life.

A number of authors have claimed, on the basis of an aggressive energy model, that aggression is valuable. Anger is presumed to serve constructive ends because it energizes behavior. Thus it is said that the scientist who becomes angry at his apparatus works hard to fix it (Feshback, 1971) or that the Dutch have successfully directed their "aggressive urge" against the sea and now have valuable land (Tinbergen, 1968). These arguments are based on the faulty assumption that the only source of energy available to man is an "aggressive energy." It is implied that unless the scientist were angry at his broken apparatus, he would sit quietly and look at it, which is obviously not the case. Many people work hard and enthusiastically with no hint of anger. The fact that an angry person may also work hard is irrelevant. Further, the internal cues of anger may very well function as a distractor that provides a less than optimal environment for problem solving. Further, there is no physiological basis for the concept that the source of man's energy is a reserve of hostility.

Catharsis is another principle derivable from the hydraulic model of aggression. The tendency to aggression is viewed as an inevitable, continuously mounting pressure to express hostility. Since the pressure is inevitable, the only solution to the problem of aggression control must involve some method of draining off the "aggressive energy." Thus it is suggested that the individual engage in aggressive competition as a participant in sports, for example, or vicariously as an observer of competitive sports.

The model presented in this book does not lead one to that conclusion. In fact, it leads to just the opposite prediction. Aside from instrumental aggression, the tendency to behave in a hostile manner is a function of the sensitivity of particular neural systems as they interact with the external environment. If those systems are not firing spontaneously, there is no "aggressive energy" to be drained off. If, however, they are sensitized, hostile feelings and behaviors are likely to be increased rather than decreased by competitive sports. In competition there is a winner and a loser, and losing is frustrating. Winning also involves frustrations on the way to the goal. As we have postulated, frustration tends to activate the sensitized neural system for irritable aggression, and the competitive activity provides the opponent as a convenient target for the expression of that generated hostility. The competition also generates a high level of arousal that tends to amplify the activity in the neural system for aggression once it is started. Unless the individuals involved have well-learned inhibitory tendencies, the result may be, and frequently is, violence.

In May, 1964, a riot, precipitated by a referee's decision, erupted at a soccer match in Lima, Peru, killing a number of spectators; the war between El Salvador and Honduras has been traced to a soccer match between those two countries (Lever, 1969); and additional outbreaks of violence have occurred at soccer matches in Great Britain and at boxing matches in New York's Madison Square Garden (Goldstein & Arms, 1971). Goldstein and Arms (1971) did an interesting study that showed that an observer's hostility increased significantly after watching a competitive sport (football) and further that the increase in hostility did not interact with the individual's preferred outcome of the game. No such increase in hostility was found for observers of a gymnastic meet (Goldstein & Arms, 1971).

Competitive sports may have many values, but the model presented here indicates that the general reduction of aggressive tendencies is not one of them.

Space does not permit a review of the vast research and the general problem of catharsis as a means of reducing tendencies to hostility. However, it is clear that it is by no means generally effective and there is much additional evidence that aggression, either vicarious or other-wise, may increase the tendency to further aggression (see Berkowitz, 1970; Hokanson, 1970; Bramel, 1970).

Some Further Implications

It can be seen from the preceding discussion that an understanding of the physiology of aggressive behavior provides some new insights into the complex problem of aggression and introduces a somewhat different view of man. This view reintroduces the importance of physiological mechanisms as a contributor to the determination of behavior. Environ-mental conditions and learning are powerful factors that influence be-havior, but they clearly operate on a soma that may enhance or reduce their effects. There are wide individual differences in physiology among men. These differences are at times powerful determinants of behavior.

Man has always recognized that behavior can be changed by altering an individual's environment or his experience. It must now be recognized that behavior can be changed, sometimes drastically, by altering his internal milieu. That conclusion is now inescapable. The implications of this view of man are profound, and it will change history. Our understanding of physiological mechanisms underlying behavior is in its infancy. However, knowledge is accumulating at an ever-increasing rate. Airplanes are now being built that are longer than the entire initial flight of the Wright brothers. If there is a comparable increase in our understanding of the physiology of behavior, and there is every reason to believe that there will be, powerful new forces for influencing man's destiny will be available. The increase in our knowledge of atomic forces moved man into a new era. The increase in our understanding of the physiology of behavior will move us into another, and the effects will be even more profound.

Appendix

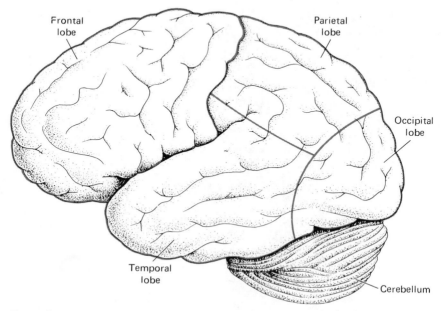

Figure A
Lobes of the brain—lateral aspect

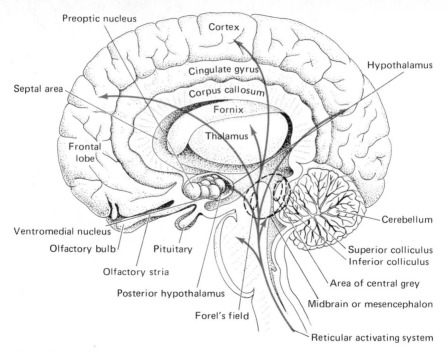

Preoptic nucleus

Cortex

Cingulate gyrus

Hypothalamus

Corpus callosum

Septal area

Fornix

Thalamus

Frontal lobe

Ventromedial nucleus

Cerebellum

Olfactory bulb

Pituitary

Superior colliculus
Inferior colliculus

Olfactory stria

Area of central grey

Posterior hypothalamus

Midbrain or mesencephalon

Forel's field

Reticular activating system

Figure B
Lobes of the brain—medial aspect

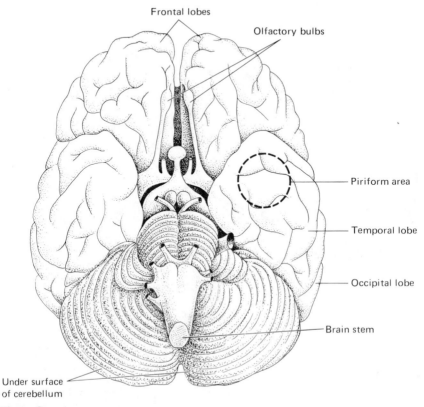

Frontal lobes

Olfactory bulbs

Piriform area

Temporal lobe

Occipital lobe

Brain stem

Under surface
of cerebellum

Figure C
Lobes of the brain—ventral aspect

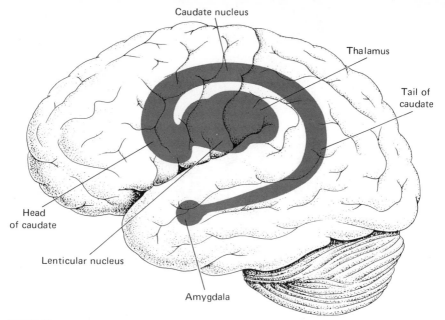

Figure D
Caudate nucleus—amygdala relationship with the rest of the brain

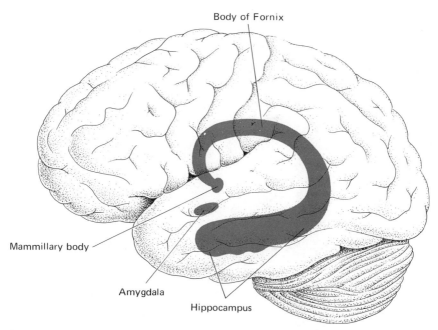

Figure E
Mammillary body, fornix, and hippocampus relationship with the rest of the brain

Glossary

Ablation   The removal of a portion of the body or brain.

Abulia   Loss of will power.

Acetylcholine   A neurotransmitter in the central nervous system also liberated by the preganglionic and postganglionic endings of the parasympathetic fibers and from the preganglionic fibers of the sympathetic nervous system.

Addison's disease   Chronic adrenocortical insufficiency.

Adrenal androgen   Androgenic substances that originate in the adrenal cortex, including dehydroepiandrosterone, androstenedione, and possibly testosterone.

Adrenalectomy   Surgical removal of the adrenal glands.

Adrenergic   Relating to the action of adrenalin or to the nerve fibers (sympathetic) that liberate sympathin.

Adrenocorticotrophic hormone (ACTH)   A hormone produced by the anterior pituitary gland that acts on the adrenal cortex, producing the release of the adrenocortical hormones.

Agnosia   Loss of sensory ability to recognize objects.

Aldosterone   A steroid hormone produced by the adrenal cortex.

Amitriptyline   Elavil. An antidepressant drug that also has a tranquilizing effect that helps to control the anxiety and agitation often found in depression.

Amphetamine   Benzedrine. A central nervous system stimulant with an action similar to the sympathomimetic amines. Used in treatment of minimal brain dysfunction, narcolepsy, and obesity.

Amphetamine phosphate   Same action and uses as amphetamine.

Amphetamine sulfate   Benzedrine sulphate. *See* amphetamine.

Amygdala   A nuggetlike mass of gray matter in the anterior portion of the temporal lobe. It is composed of eight separate, identifiable nuclei. (See Figures D and E in the Appendix)

Amygdalectomy   A surgical procedure in which the amygdalae are lesioned.

Androgens   A generic term for an agent, usually a hormone (e.g., testosterone or androsterone) that stimulates the activity of the accessory sex organs of the male, encourages the development of the male sex characteristics.

Androstenedione   An androgen isolated from the adrenal cortex.

Angioedema   A noninflammatory swelling that may occur in any portion of the body.

Anorexia   Loss of appetite.

A-norprogesterone   A recently developed antiandrogenic substance.

Anticholinergic   Antagonistic to the action of parasympathetic or other cholinergic fibers.

Anticonvulsants   Any drug that reduces the probability of seizures or seizure activity in the brain.

Antidepressant   Any drug useful in the control of depression.

Aphagia   Pathological loss of appetite.

Arecoline   A colorless alkaloid from the betel nut.

Athetosis   A pathological condition in which there is constant movement of a writhing and involuntary nature. It most commonly involves the hands and fingers but may also affect the feet and toes.

Atropine methyl nitrate   An anticholinergic drug that does not readily cross the blood-brain barrier.

Atropine sulfate   An anticholinergic drug that crosses the blood-brain barrier.

Automatism   A state in which the individual's behavior occurs independent of his own willful processes. The behaviors are involuntary and are often purposeless and may be foolish or harmful.

Autonomic nervous system   That portion of the peripheral nervous system that regulates those body functions not usually under voluntary control, such as the visceral changes that occur during emotion. It includes the sympathetic and parasympathetic divisions.

Barbiturates   A class of sedative drugs derived from barbituric acid. Used as sedatives, hypnotics, or anticonvulsants. Includes at least 60 clinically useful drugs, such as phenobarbital, secobarbital, butobarbital. Used by drug abusers as a "downer." Can be addictive.

Benadryl   A potent antihistaminic agent. Also has anticholinergic and sedative effects.

Benzodiazepines   A group of drugs used for their antihostility, anticonvulsant, and skeletal-muscle-relaxing properties. The most commonly used are chlordiazepoxide (Librium), diazepam (Valium), and oxazepam (Serax). Used for control of tension, irritability, anxiety, and related symptoms.

Bulimia   Excessive appetite.

Carbachol   A parasympathetic stimulant that has actions similar to acetylcholine but is longer-lasting.

Carcinoma   Any of the various types of cancer.

Catecholamines   A group of hormones, including epinephrine, norepinephrine, and dopa, that function as neurotransmitters.

Caudate nucleus A portion of the basal ganglia. The head of the caudate n. is located in the anterior portion of the lateral ventricle. The tail of the caudate projects caudally over the thalamus into the temporal lobe, where it ends in the amygdala. (See Figure D in the Appendix.)

Centermedianum Refers to the central medial nucleus of the thalamus.

Central gray A collection of cell bodies located in the dorsal midbrain. (See Figure B in the Appendix.)

Chlordiazepoxide Librium. *See* benzodiazepines.

Chlormadinone acetate A progesterone derivative. With estrogen it is used as an oral contraceptive.

Chlorpromazine Thorazine. The first major tranquilizer developed. Used in the control of agitation, anxiety, tension, and confusion, associated with the neuroses and such psychotic conditions as schizophrenia, manic phase of manic-depressive states and senile psychosis. Has a definite antihostility effect.

Cholinergic Relates to the action of acetylcholine or to the nerve fibers that use acetylcholine as a neurotransmitter.

Cholinesterase An enzyme widely distributed in the body. Breaks down acetylcholine into the inactive choline and acetic acid.

Chorea A disorder involving irregular spasmodic movements of the limbs and facial muscles. Not under voluntary control. Most commonly occurs during childhood.

Chromosome A rodlike body in the nucleus of the cell that contains the genes responsible for hereditary traits.

Chronic brain syndrome A group of symptoms resulting from irreversible impairment of cerebral function. Involves loss of memory, loss of orientation, affective disturbances. Irritability, anger, and rage are the most dominant moods.

Cingulum An arch-shaped convolution of cortical substance that lies above the corpus callosum. It begins below the anterior portion of the corpus callosum and curves around it, turning downward behind the corpus callosum, where it has a narrow connection with the hippocampal gyrus. (See Figure B in the Appendix.)

Clitoral glands Glands located in the area of the clitoris.

Corticosterone A steroid produced by the adrenal cortex. Controls sodium and potassium metabolism and induces glycogen deposition in the liver.

Cortisol A hormone of the adrenal cortex. The most potent glucocorticoid.

Cryosurgery Surgery that uses reduced temperature. Used in some forms of brain surgery for cell destruction.

Cyproterone acetate A synthetic steroid that blocks the action of androgens.

Dehydroisoandosterone One of the androgens that has been isolated in male urine.

Dexamethasone A synthetic analogue of cortisol. Used as an anti-inflammatory agent. Inhibits ACTH production.

Dexedrine Dextroamphetamine sulfate. A central nervous system stimulant related to amphetamine.

Diazepam Valium. *See* Benzodiazepines.

Diethylstilbestrol *See* stilbestrol.

Digit symbol test A substitution test in which digits are equated with geometric figures. The task is to write the correct digit under each of the geometric figures which are presented in irregular order.

Dihydrotestosterone A semisynthetic steroid which has considerable androgen activity.

Dilantin Sodium diphenylhydantoin. An anticonvulsant that reduces seizure tendencies. Has a distinct antihostility effect in some patients.

Diestrous That period between the periods of desire in female mammals.

Diuretic Any agent that promotes urine secretion.

Dopamine Hydroxytyramine. An intermediate in tyrosine catabolism. The precursor of norepinephrine and epinephrine.

Dyscontrol syndrome A pattern of behavior that may involve irrational brutality and other offenses of an aggressive nature. May be caused by limbic system lesions.

Dysrhythmia Defective rhythm. Used in reference to a faulty rhythm in the EEG.

Edema An accumulation of excessive amounts of clear watery fluid in the tissues.

Electroshock treatments Electroconvulsive therapy. A treatment for psychoses in which an electric current is passed through the head, resulting in convulsions. Now usually used for severe depression.

Endocrine glands Ductless glands that secrete hormones directly into the bloodstream.

Ergotropic Refers to the syndrome characterized by sympathetic discharges and associated with increased activity of the motor apparatus.

Estradiol The most potent naturally occurring estrogen in mammals.

Estradiol B.P.C. A form of estradiol benzoate.

Estradiol valerianate Has the same general uses as estradiol. It is administered by intramuscular injection and has a more prolonged duration of action.

Estrogen A general term for all substances that produce estrus. They usually produce a growth of the female secondary sexual characteristics.

Estrus A condition of heat in the lower mammals in which the female readily accepts the male and is ready for pregnancy.

Ethogram The precise catalog of all the behavior patterns of an animal.

Fasciculus of Schutz A group of fibers in the central gray that connect hypothalamic nuclei with the nuclei of the midbrain reticular system.

Fluphenazine Prolixin. A potent antipsychotic agent that has particularly prolonged effects. A phenothiazine derivative similar in action to chlorpromazine.

Fornix A prominent band of fibers running between the mammillary bodies in the hypothalamus and the hippocampus. It follows along the under surface of the corpus callosum and over the medial portion of the thalamus. (See Figures B and E in the Appendix.)

FR-4 and FR-5 Schedules of reinforcement in which the subject receives a reinforcement after four, or five responses.

Fugue A period during which an individual has a complete loss of memory and physically leaves his normal life situation. When he returns to the normal state, his behavior during the fugue state is forgotten.

Gliosis   An overgrowth of or tumor of the neuroglia.

Glucocorticoid   A class of adrenal corticoids that promote glycogen deposition in the liver and have an anti-inflammatory action.

Gonadotrophic hormone   A hormone that promotes gonadal growth and function.

Grand mal seizure   A seizure involving loss of consciousness and tonic contractions of major muscle groups. This is followed by repeated, generalized clonic jerking.

Haloperidol   Haldol. A major tranquilizer not related to the phenothiazines. Useful in a wide variety of neurotic and psychotic states. Specifically improves particular aspects of psychotic behavior, such as anxiety, withdrawal, hostility, suspiciousness, hallucinations, and uncooperativeness.

Hemiparesis   Paralysis that affects only one side of the body.

Hormone   A complex chemical substance formed in one place in the body (usually in the endocrine glands) and carried by the blood to its site of action in a different portion of the body.

Huntington's chorea   A hereditary disorder of a chronic nature that usually begins between the ages of 30 and 50 years. It is characterized by irregular spasmodic movements of the limbs and facial muscles. It is accompanied by a gradual loss of mental capacity.

Hydrocortisone   *See* cortisol.

Hyperinsulinism   A condition of excess insulin in the bloodstream. Results in hypoglycemia.

Hyperkinetic child syndrome   *See* minimal brain dysfunction.

Hyperphagia   Excessive eating.

Hypoglycemia   An inadequate concentration of glucose in the circulating blood for normal functioning.

Hypothalamus   A group of nuclei at the base of the brain around the third ventricle. (See Figure B in the Appendix.)

Hypothyroidism   Inadequate production of the thyroid hormone.

Ictal   Relating to or produced by a seizure.

Idiosyncratic reaction   A susceptibility to a drug, food, or allergen that is peculiar to an individual person.

Imipramine   Tofranil. An antidepressant drug.

Inferior colliculus   A collection of cells located on the dorsal aspect of the midbrain or mesencephalon. It is concerned with auditory reflexes. (See Figure B in the Appendix.)

Infraorbital   Below the orbital cavity or eye socket.

Insulin   A hormone produced by the Islands of Langerhans in the pancreas. It promotes glucose utilization and protein synthesis.

Interictal   The interval between seizures.

Islands of Langerhans   Cells in the pancreas that secrete insulin directly into the bloodstream.

Klinefelter syndrome   A chromosome abnormality in which there is a chromosome count of 47. The sex chromosome constitution is XXY.

Kluver and Bucy syndrome   A group of symptoms produced by extensive lesions in the temporal lobes. It involves an inability to recognize familiar objects, hypersexuality, and a dramatic increase in tameness.

Korsakoff's syndrome   A disorder characterized by hallucinations, loss of memory, and imaginary reminiscences. Frequently involves marked agitation.

Lateral geniculate body   A complex nucleus on the lateral part of the posterior end of the thalamus. About 80 percent of the fibers of the optic tract end here.

Lesch-Nyhan syndrome   A group of symptoms resulting from a disorder of purine metabolism. It involves excessive aggressiveness and self-destructive tendencies.

Lesions   Circumscribed tissue damage.

Leukotomy   An operation that involves cutting the white matter of the frontal lobe of the brain.

Levarterenol bitartrate   L-Norepinephrine bitartrate. *See* Norepinephrine.

Leydig cell   Interstitial cells in the testes that produce testosterone.

Lipiodol   A trade name for a 40 percent solution of iodine in poppy oil. Used to produce opacity in x-ray films.

Lithium carbonate   A drug with antihostility properties. Usually used in the treatment of manic-depressive states.

Lobectomy   Removal of a lobe; for example, temporal lobectomy refers to the removal of the temporal lobe of the brain.

Luteinizing hormone (LH)   A gonadotrophic hormone of the pituitary. Plays a role in follicle development and in the development of the corpus luteum.

Mamillary bodies   Large nuclei of the hypothalamus located just posterior to the optic chiasm. (See Figure E in the Appendix.)

Medial forebrain bundle   A large fiber tract containing ascending and descending fibers connecting the ventromedial rhinencephalic areas with the preoptic and lateral hypothalamus.

Medial lemniscus   A large bundle of fibers running from the nucleus gracilis and cuneatus to the ventrolateral nucleus of the thalamus. Carry proprioceptive sense.

Medroxyprogesterone   A progesterone-type substance that is effective orally as well as parenterally. It is more potent than progesterone. Used with estrogens as an oral contraceptive.

Mesencephalon   The midbrain. (See Figure B in the Appendix.)

Mestranol   An estrogen used in many oral contraceptives.

Methacholine   A parasympathomimetic derived from acetylcholine.

Methamphetamine hydrochloride   Related to amphetamine but has a greater stimulating effect on the central nervous system. Used by drug abusers to obtain and retain a "high." Excessive use may result in amphetamine psychosis.

Midbrain   A short, constricted segment of the brain that connects the pons and cerebellum to the forebrain. The ventral portion contains the cerebral peduncles. The dorsal portion is referred to as the midbrain tegmentum. (See Figure B in the Appendix.)

Midbrain reticular formation   That part of the reticular activating system that has nuclei in the midbrain. (See Figure B in the Appendix.)

Midbrain tegmentum   *See* midbrain.

Minimal brain dysfunction   *Also called* hyperkinesis. A syndrome that does not have a single cause and involves hyperactivity, inability to pay attention, and frequently aggressive behavior. Usually found in children.

Motor aphasia A loss in the ability of verbal expression by either writing or speaking.

Narcolepsy A syndrome involving a sudden uncontrollable tendency to fall asleep.

Nauta stain A histological technique that was developed to stain degenerating small unmyelinated terminals (terminal boutons).

Necrosis Cell death within any given tissue. Results from irreversible damage to the cell nucleus.

Negri bodies Dark bodies found in the cytoplasm of nerve cells that contain the rabies virus. Their precise nature is unknown.

Neophobia Fear of that which is novel. Characteristic of wild rats.

Neoplasms A term interchangeable with *tumor.*

Neostigmine A synthetic compound that can be used as a reversible cholinesterase inhibitor.

Neurotransmitters Chemical substances stored in the synaptic vesicles in the presynaptic axon terminals. They are released into the synaptic junction on stimulation of the nerve and serve to activate the postsynaptic nerve.

Nicotine An alkaloid derived from tobacco. In small doses it inhibits autonomic ganglia and myoneural junctions. At large doses it depresses them.

Nitrazepam One of the benzodiazepines.

Nocturnal jactations Extreme restlessness during sleep.

Norepinephrine Noradrenaline. A hormone secreted by the adrenal medulla. Also considered to be a neurotransmitter in the brain and the autonomic nervous system.

Norethynodrel A progestin that is orally active and has some estrogenic activity.

Nucleus reuniens The most ventrally located of the midline nuclei of the thalamus.

Occipital Refers to the occiput, the back of the head or to the occipital lobe of the brain. (See Figure A in the Appendix.)

Oestrus *See* Estrus.

Olfactory bulbectomy Surgical removal of the olfactory bulbs.

Oligophrenia Feeblemindedness.

Optic radiations A group of fibers arising from the nerve cells in the lateral geniculate body passing through the occipital part of the internal capsule.

Optic tract Fibers running backward and lateralward from the posterolateral angles of the optic chiasma.

Oxazepam Serax. *See* benzodiazepines.

Palsy Refers to a variety of types of paralysis.

Parkinsonian Relating to Parkinson's disease (paralysis agitans). A neurological disorder caused by degeneration of the basal ganglia. Characterized by rhythmical tremor, rigidity, poverty of movement, and masklike face.

Periaqueductal gray matter Gray matter around the cerebral aqueduct, which is a narrow canal connecting the third with the fourth ventricle. (See central gray in Figure B.)

Perifalciform regions   An area located in the posterior portion of the temporal bone of the skull.

Perineal region   The area between the vulva and the anus in the female and the scrotum and the anus in the male.

Periventricular system   A system of fibers arising from the posterior hypothalamic area. Some of these fibers terminate in the midline and dorsomedial thalamus. The majority project toward the brainstem, ending in the tectal or tegmental nuclei of the midbrain, pons, and medulla.

Perphenazine   Trilafon. A phenothiazine similar to chlorpromazine in action.

Petit mal   A brief loss of consciousness sometimes associated with mild twitching of the mouth and eyelids. Occurs in milder forms of epilepsy.

Phenothiazine   The basic chemical from which a large number of tranquilizers or antipsychotic agents have been developed, including chlorpromazine.

Pheromones   A complex chemical substance released by one individual which produces a species specific reaction on other members of the same species.

Physostigmine   *Also called* eserine. A reversible inhibitor of cholinesterase, thus preventing the destruction of acetylcholine.

Pilocarpine   A parasympathomimetic agent.

Pituitary   A two-lobed endocrine gland that lies at the base of the brain just below the hypothalamus. Secretes a large number of hormones that affect the other endocrine glands.

Pituitary adrenal axis   Refers to the interactions between the pituitary gland and the adrenal gland. Corticotrophic hormones from the pituitary cause the release of certain corticoids from the adrenal cortex, which in turn inhibit further pituitary action.

Placebo   An inert substance used to duplicate an active drug in a controlled drug study. Sometimes used in medicine to effect changes caused by suggestion.

Plethysmograph   An instrument for recording changes in volume in any portion of the body.

Pneumoencephalography   A diagnostic procedure in which the cerebrospinal fluid is replaced by air and an X-ray picture is taken of the brain.

Polydypsia   Pathological thirst resulting in excessive drinking.

Polyuria   Excessive production of urine.

Preoptic   Most anterior set of nuclei in the hypothalamus. Participate in temperature regulation. (See Figure B in the Appendix.)

Prepuce   The foreskin that more or less completely covers the glans of the penis.

Preputial glands   Glands associated with the prepuce.

Primidone   Mysoline. An anticonvulsant used in the control of *grand mal,* psychomotor, and focal epileptic seizures.

Proestrus   That period in the estrus cycle that just precedes estrus.

Progesterone   A hormone secreted by the corpus luteum. Used to correct abnormalities in the menstrual cycle.

Propericiazinine   A phenothiazine derivative particularly useful in the control of aggressive manifestations.

Provera   Medroxyprogesterone acetate.

Psychomotor epilepsy Epilepsy associated with temporal lobe dysfunction. Attacks are associated with consciousness impairment and amnesia. Some psychomotor epileptics may display aggressive behavior during an attack.

Psychosurgery An operation of the brain for the purpose of treating a mental disorder.

Radiculitis Inflammation of a spinal nerve root at the point of entrance to the spinal column.

Reciprocal inhibition The inhibition of a given set of muscles when the antagonistic set is activated.

Reciprocal innervation A neural mechanism by which when the motor neurons to a given muscle are reflexly excited, the motor neurons supplying antagonistic muscles are inhibited by the same sensory input.

Rhinencephalic Refers to the rhinencephalon or olfactory brain. In man this includes the rudimentary olfactory lobe, which consists of the olfactory bulb and peduncle, the paraolfactory area, the subcallosal gyrus, and the anterior perforated substance.

Rosenzweig Picture Frustration Test A test to determine the type of aggressive reaction to frustration.

Rostral Fastigial nucleus Tectal nucleus of the cerebellum buried deep in the white matter of each side of the cerebellum.

Scotoma An isolated area within the visual field where vision is absent or blurred.

Sebaceous glands Glands in the skin that produce an oily, fatty substance known as sebum.

Seminal vesicles Two pouches located between the bladder and the rectum that secrete a fluid to be added to the secretion of the testes.

Senile dementia Loss of mental capacity that comes with old age.

Sensory aphasia A loss of the ability to comprehend printed or spoken words.

Septal Syndrome Results from lesions in the septal region and involves exaggerated startle response, increased irritability, and aggressiveness.

Septum A thin-walled structure separating the lateral ventricles, placed between the fornix and the corpus callosum. (See Figure B in the Appendix.)

Serotonin 5-Hydroxytryptamine. An important neurohumor in brain function. Also produced in other parts of the body and functions as a vasoconstrictor.

Sexual dimorphism The somatic differences between males and females that occur as a consequence of sexual maturation.

Sham rage Refers to the very low threshold for a rage reaction produced by decortication.

Sodium diphenylhydantoin *See* Dilantin.

Spermatogenesis The process of the development and formation of spermatozoon.

Sphenoid bone A bat-shaped bone situated at the base of the skull anterior to the temporal and occipital bones.

Spinothalamic tracts Lateral spinothalamic tract runs from the spinal cord to the thalamus, mediates pain and temperature senses. Ventral spinothalamic tract also runs from the spinal cord to the thalamus and mediates impulses of touch.

Stereotaxic instrument   A device that can be accurately manipulated in three dimensions. Used for making precise brain lesions through a small opening in the skull.

Steroids   Any of a group of compounds including many hormones characteristically having the carbon-atom ring structure of the sterols.

Stilbestrol   *Also called* diethylstibestrol. A nonsteroid crystalline compound that possesses estrogenic activity when given either orally or by injection.

Stria terminalis   A major fiber bundle that projects from the amygdaloid nuclei to the preoptic and anterior hypothalamic areas.

Substantia nigra   A mass of gray matter shaped like a crescent in cross section. Extends from the border of the pons into the subthalamic region. A part of the extrapyramidal system.

Superior colliculus   A collection of cells located on dorsal aspect of the midbrain or mesencephalon. It is concerned with visual reflexes. (See Figure B in the Appendix.)

Taylor Manifest Anxiety Test   A paper and pencil test derived from the Minnesota Multiphasic Inventory, designed to assess anxiety levels.

Tegmental area of Tsai   In the ventral midbrain just ventral to the red nucleus.

Tegmentum   The ventral portion of the midbrain.

Temporal lobectomy   Removal of the temporal lobes of the brain.

Teratoma   A neoplasm composed of multiple tissues some of which are not normally found in the organ in which it arises.

Testosterone   The male hormone. An androgenic steroid obtained from the tissue of the testes.

Testosterone propionate   Has the same action as testosterone but is more pronounced and longer acting than testosterone.

Thalamus   A large ovoid mass of gray matter situated on either side of the third ventricle. Serves as a relay station for sensory stimuli to the cortex. Also has integrative and nonspecific functions. (See Figure B and D in the Appendix.)

Thematic Apperception Test   A projective test in which the subject is asked to make up stories about a series of pictures.

Theta Waves   EEG waves of 4- to 7-cycles-per-second. Have been interpreted as a possible sign of inhibitory activity.

Trifluoperazine   Stelazine. A phenothiazine derivative particularly useful in the control of apathy.

Thioridazine   Mellaril. A phenothiazine derivative with action similar to that of chlorpromazine.

Tractotomy   The surgical sectioning of any nerve tract.

Tranquilizers   *Also called* ataractic. A drug that produces a peaceful frame of mind by reducing anxiety and psychotic reactions. Major tranquilizers include the phenothiazine derivatives and others. The minor tranquilizers include, among others, the benzodiazepines.

Tremor   Shaking or trembling.

Trigeminal nerve   Fifth cranial nerve. Sensory functions serve face, sinuses, and teeth. Motor functions serve muscles of mastication.

Trochar   A sharp, pointed instrument enclosed in a cannula—used for implanting drug pellets under the skin.

Tropotropic   Refers to the syndrome characterized by parasympathetic effects. Associated with lessened activity and responsiveness of the somatic nervous system.

Wais   *See* Wechsler Adult Intelligence Scale.

Wechsler Adult Intelligence Scale   A test battery for intelligence. Also called Wechsler-Bellevue Scale and WAIS.

Uncus   The hooked portion of the hippocampal gyrus that lies on the basal surface of the brain medial to the temporal lobe.

Urticaria   Hives. An eruption of itching wheals. A frequent reaction to allergens.

Visual cortex   That portion of the cerebral cortex relating to vision. In the area of the calcarine fissure in the occipital lobe.

XYY syndrome   A chromosome abnormality in which the sex chromosome constitution is XYY. These individuals are tall and are said to have problems with impulse control.

Bibliography

Abbatiello, E. & C. L. Scudder. The effect of northynodrel with mestranol treatment of pregnant mice on the isolation-induced aggression of their male offspring. *International Journal of Fertility*, 1970, *15*, 182–189.

Abbott, P., A. Blake, L. Vincze. Treatment of mentally retarded with thioridazine. *Diseases of the Nervous System*, 1965, *26*, 583–585.

Abrahamson, E. M. & A. W. Pezet. *Body, mind, and sugar.* New York: Henry Holt, Rinehart and Winston, 1951.

Adams, D. B. Cells related to fighting behavior recorded from midbrain central gray neurophil of cat. *Science*, 1968a, *159*, 894–896.

Adams, D. B. The activity of single cells in the midbrain and hypothalamus of the cat during affective defense behavior. *Archives Italiennes de Biologie*, 1968b, *106*, 243–269.

Adams, D. B. Defence and territorial behaviour dissociated by hypothalamic lesions in the rat. *Nature*, 1971, *232*, 573–574.

Adams, D. B. & J, P. Flynn. Transfer of an escape response from tail shock to brain-stimulated attack behavior. *Journal of the Experimental Analysis of Behavior*, 1966, *9*, 401–508.

Adey, W. R., N. C. R. Merrilless, & S. Sunderland. The entorhinal area: Behavioral, evoked potential, and histological studies of its inter-relationships with brain stem regions. *Brain*, 1956, *79*, 414–438.

Aird, R. B. & T. Yamamoto. Behavior disorders of childhood. *Electroencephalography and Clinical Neurophysiology*, 1966, *21*, 148–156.

Akert, K. Diencephalon. In D. E. Sheer (Ed.), *Electrical stimulation of the brain.* Austin: University of Texas Press, 1961, pp. 288–310.

Alberts, J. R. & B. G. Galef. Olfactory cues and movement: Stimuli mediating intraspecific aggression in wild Norway rat. *Journal of Comparative and Physiological Psychology,* 1973, *85,* 233–242.

Aldersberg, D. & H. Dolger. Medico-legal problems of hypoglycemic reactions in diabetes. *Annals of Internal Medicine,* 1938–1939, *12,* 1804–1805.

Alderton, H. & B. A. Hoddinott. A controlled study of the use of thioridazine in the treatment of hyperactive and aggressive children in a children's psychiatric hospital. *Canadian Psychiatric Association Journal,* 1964, *9,* 239–247.

Alexander, B. K. The effects of early peer-deprivation on juvenile behavior of rhesus monkeys. Doctoral dissertation, University of Wisconsin, 1966.

Alexander, B. K. Parental behavior of adult male Japanese monkeys. *Behaviour,* 1970, *36,* 270–285.

Alexander, M. & A. A. Perachio. The influence of target sex and dominance on evoked attack in rhesus monkeys. *American Journal of Physical Anthropology,* 1973, *38,* 543–547.

Allen, M., G. Shannon, & D. Rose. Thioridazine hydrochloride in the behavior disturbances of retarded children. *American Journal of Mental Deficiency,* 1963, *68,* 63–68.

Allikmets, L. Kh. Behavioral reactions to electrical stimulation of amygdala in cats. *Zhurnal Vysshei Nervnoi Deyatel 'nosti imeni I. P. Pavlova,* 1966, *16,* 119–127.

Allin, J. T. & E. M. Banks. Behavioural biology of the collared lemming *Dicrostonyx groenlandicus* (traill): I. agonistic behaviour, *Animal Behaviour,* 1968, *16,* 245–262.

Allison, T. S. & S. L. Allison. Time-out from reinforcement: Effect on sibling aggression. *Psychological Record,* 1971, *21,* 81–86.

Alpers, B. J. Relation of the hypothalamus to disorders of personality. *Archives of Neurology and Psychiatry,* 1937, *38,* 291–303.

Altman, M. Naturalistic studies of maternal care in the moose and elk. In H. L. Rheingold, *Maternal behavior in mammals.* New York: Wiley, 1963, pp. 233–253.

Altmann, M., E. Knowles, & H. D. Bull. A psychosomatic study of the sex cycle in women. *Psychosomatic Medicine,* 1941, *3,* 199–225.

Altman, S. A field study of the sociobiology of rhesus monkeys, *Macaca mulatta. Annals of the New York Academy of Science,* 1962, *102,* 338–435.

Anand, B. K. & J. R. Brobeck. Hypothalamic control of food intake in rats and cats. *Yale Journal of Biology and Medicine,* 1951, *24,* 123–140.

Anand, B. K. & S. Dua. Stimulation of limbic system of brain in waking animals. *Science,* 1955, *122,* 1139.

Anand, B. K. & S. Dua. Electrical stimulation of the limbic system of the brain ("visceral brain") in the waking animal. *Indian Journal of Medicinal Research,* 1956, *44,* 107–119.

Anderson, E. W. Psychiatric complications of hypoglycemia in children. *Lancet,* 1940, *2,* 329–331.

Anderson, R. Psychological differences after amygdalotomy. *Acta Neurologica Scandinavica,* Supplement, 1970, *46,* 94.

Anderson, R. Differences in the course of learning as measured by various memory tasks after amygdalotomy in man. In E. Hitchcock, L. Laitinen, & K. Vaernet (Eds.), *Psychosurgery*. Springfield, Ill.: Thomas, 1972, pp. 177–194.

Andy, O. J. Neurosurgical treatment of abnormal behavior. *American Journal of Medical Sciences*, 1966, *252*, 132–138.

Andy, O. J. Thalamotomy in hyperactive and aggressive behavior. *Confinia Neurologica*, 1970, *32*, 322–325.

Andy, O. J. & M. F. Jurko. Thalamotomy for hyperresponsive syndrome: Lesions in the centermedianum and intralaminar nuclei. In E. Hitchcock, L. Laitinen, & K. Vaernet (Eds.), *Psychosurgery*, Springfield, Ill.: Thomas, 1972a, pp. 127–135.

Andy, O. J. & M. F. Jurko. Hyperresponsive syndrome. In E. Hitchcock, L. Laitinen, & K. Vaernet (Eds.), *Psychosurgery*. Springfield, Ill.: Thomas, 1972b, pp. 117–126.

Anton, A. H. Effects of group size, sex, and time on organ weights, catecholamines and behavior in mice. *Physiology and Behavior*, 1969, *4*, 483–487.

Anton, A. H., R. P. Schwartz, & S. Kramer. Catecholamines and behavior in isolated and grouped mice. *Journal of Psychiatric Research*, 1968, *6*, 211–220.

Arai, N., Y. Shibata, & A. Akahene. Electroencephalographic analysis of behavior problem children. *Acta Criminologiae et Medicina Legalis Japonica*, 1966, *32*, 143–152.

Archer, J. The effect of strange male odor on aggressive behavior in male mice. *Journal of Mammalogy*, 1968, *49*, 572–575.

Archer, J. Effects of population density on behaviour in rodents. In J. H. Crook (Ed.), *Social behaviour in birds and mammals*. London: Academic Press, 1970, pp. 169–210.

Ardrey, R. *African genesis*. London: Collins, 1962.

Ardrey, R. *The territorial imperative*. New York: Atheneum, 1966.

Arthurs, R. G. & E. B. Cahoon. A clinical and electroencephalographic survey of psychopathic personality. *American Journal of Psychiatry*, 1964, *120*, 875–877.

Avis, H. H. & J. T. Treadway. Mediation of rat-mouse interspecific aggression by cage odor. *Psychonomic Science*, 1971, *22*, 293–294.

Ax, A. The physiological differentiation of fear and anger in humans. *Psychosomatic Medicine*, 1953, *15*, 433–442.

Azrin, N. H. Aggression. Paper presented at the meeting of the American Psychological Association, Los Angeles, September, 1964.

Azrin, N. H. Pain and aggression. *Psychology Today*, 1967, *1*, 27–33.

Azrin, N. H. Punishment of elicited aggression. *Journal of the Experimental Analysis of Behavior*, 1970, *14*, 7–10.

Azrin, N. H., R. R. Hutchinson, & D. F. Hake. Pain induced fighting in the squirrel monkey. *Journal of the Experimental Analysis of Behavior*, 1963, *6*, 620.

Azrin, N. H., R. R. Hutchinson, & D. F. Hake. Extinction induced aggression. *Journal of the Experimental Analysis of Behavior*, 1966, *9*, 191–204.

Azrin, N. H., R. R. Hutchinson, & R. McLaughlin. The opportunity for aggression as an operant reinforcer during aversive stimulation. *Journal of the Experimental Analysis of Behavior*, 1965, *8*, 171–180.

Azrin, N. H., R. R. Hutchinson, & R. D. Sallery. Pain aggression toward inanimate objects. *Journal of the Experimental Analysis of Behavior*, 1964, *7*, 223–228.

Bach-Y-Rita, G. & J. R. Lion. Episodic dyscontrol: A study of 130 violent patients. *American Journal of Psychiatry*, 1971, *127*, 1473–1478.

Bach-Y-Rita, G., J. R. Lion, & F. R. Ervin. Pathological intoxication: Clinical and electroencephalographic studies. *American Journal of Psychiatry*, 1970, *127*, 698–703.

Baenninger, R. Contrasting effects of fear and pain on mouse-killing by rats. *Journal of Comparative and Physiological Psychology*, 1967, *63*, 298–303.

Baenninger, R. Independence of parturition and mouse-killing by female rats. *Psychonomic Science*, 1969, *15*, 144–145.

Baenninger, L. P. & R. Baenninger. "Spontaneous" fighting and mouse killing by rats. *Psychonomic Science*, 1970, *19*, 161.

Baenninger, R. & J. C. Grossman. Some effects of punishment of pain-elicited aggression. *Journal of the Experimental Analysis of Behavior*, 1969, *12*, 1017–1022.

Baenninger, R. & R. R. Ulm. Overcoming the effects of prior punishment on interspecies aggression in the rat. *Journal of Comparative and Physiological Psychology*, 1969, *69*, 628–635.

Bailey, P. Discussion. In M. Baldwin & P. Bailey (Eds.), *Temporal lobe epilepsy*. Springfield, Ill.: Thomas, 1958, p. 551.

Bailey, P. & F. A. Gibbs. The surgical treatment of psychomotor epilepsy. *Journal of the American Medical Association*, 1951, *145*, 365–370.

Baker, R. K. & S. J. Ball. *Mass media and violence*, Vol. IX. A report to the National Commission on the Causes and Prevention of Violence, Washington, D.C.: U.S. Government Office, 1969.

Baker, R. R. The effects of psychotropic drugs on psychological testing. *Psychological Bulletin*, 1968, *69*, 377–387.

Balasubramaniam, V., B. Ramamurthi, K. Jagannathan, & S. Kalyamaraman. Stereotaxic amygadalotomy. *Neurology India*, 1967, *15*, 119–122.

Balasubramaniam, V., P. B. Ramanujam, R. S. Kanada, & B. Ramamurthi. Stereotaxic surgery for behavior disorders. In E. Hitchcock, L. Laitinen, & K. Vaernet (Eds.), *Psychosurgery*. Springfield, Ill.: Thomas, 1972, pp. 156–163.

Ban, T. A. *Psychopharmacology*. Baltimore: Williams & Wilkins, 1969.

Banay, R. S. Pathologic reaction to alcohol, Vol. I. Review of the literature and original case reports. *Quarterly Journal of Studies on Alcohol*, 1944, *4*, 580–605.

Bandler, R. J. Facilitation of aggressive behavior in the rat by direct cholinergic stimulation of the hypothalamus. *Nature*, 1969, *224*, 1035–1036.

Bandler, R. J. Cholinergic synapses in the lateral hypothalamus for the control of predatory aggression in the rat. *Brain Research*, 1970, *20*, 409–424.

Bandler, R. J. Direct chemical stimulation of the thalamus: Effects on aggressive behavior in the rat. *Brain Research*, 1971a, *26*, 81–93.

Bandler, R. J. Chemical stimulation of the rat midbrain and aggressive behaviour. *Nature*, 1971b, *229*, 222–223.

Bandler, R. J. & C. C. Chi. Effects of olfactory bulb removal on aggression: A reevaluation. *Physiology and Behavior*, 1971, *8*, 1–5.

Bandler, R. J., C. C. Chi, & J. P. Flynn. Biting attack elicited by stimulation of the ventral midbrain tegmentum of cats. *Science*, 1972, *177*, 364–366.

Bandler, R. J. & J. P. Flynn. Visual patterned reflex present during hypothalamically elicited attack. *Science*, 1971, *171*, 817–818.

Bandler, R. J. & J. P. Flynn. Control of somatosensory fields striking during hypothalamically elicited attack. *Brain Research*, 1972, *38*, 197–201.

Bandler, R. J. & J. P. Flynn. Neural pathways from thalamus associated with regulation of aggressive behavior. *Science*, 1974, *183*, 96–99.

Bandler, R. J. & K. E. Moyer. Animals spontaneously attacked by rats. *Communications in Behavioral Biology*, 1970, *5*, 177–182.

Bandura, A. *Principles of behavior modification*. New York: Holt, Rinehart and Winston, 1969.

Bandura, A. Analysis of modeling processes. In A. Bandura (Ed.), *Theories of modeling*. New York, Atherton Press, 1970.

Bandura, A. *Aggression: A social learning analysis*. Englewood Cliffs, N.J.: Prentice-Hall, 1973.

Bandura, A. & A. C. Huston. Identification as a process of incidental learning. *Journal of Abnormal and Social Psychology*, 1961, *63*, 311–318.

Bandura, A. & R. H. Walters. *Adolescent aggression*, New York: Ronald Press, 1959.

Bandura, A. & R. H. Walters. *Social learning and personality development*. New York: Holt, Rinehart and Winston, 1963.

Banerjee, U. Influence of some hormones and drugs on isolation induced aggression in male mice. *Communications in Behavioral Biology*, 1971, *6*, 163–170.

Banks, E. M. A time and motion study of prefighting behavior in mice. *Journal of Genetic Psychology*, 1962, *101*, 165–183.

Baran, D. & S. E. Glickman. "Territorial marking" in the Mongolian gerbil: A study of sensory control and function. *Journal of Comparative and Physiological Psychology*, 1970, *71*, 237–245.

Barbeau, A. Dopamine and mental function. In S. Malitz (Ed.), *L-DOPA and behavior*. New York: Raven Press, 1972, pp. 9–33.

Barclay, A. M. Linking sexual and aggressive motives: Contributions of "irrelevant" arousals. *Journal of Personality*, 1971, *39*, 481–492.

Barclay, A. M. & R. N. Haber. The relation of aggression to sexual motivation. *Journal of Personality*, 1965, *3*, 462–475.

Bard, P. Central nervous mechanisms for the expression of anger in animals. In M. L. Reymert (Ed.), *Feelings and emotions: The Mooseheart Symposium*. New York: McGraw-Hill, 1950, pp. 211–237.

Bardin, C. W. & R. E. Peterson. Studies of androgen production by the rat: Testosterone and androstenedione content of blood. *Endocrinology*, 1967, *80*, 38–44.

Bardwick, J. M. *Psychology of women*. New York: Harper & Row, 1971.

Barfield, R. J., D. E. Busch, & K. Wallen. Gonadal influence on agonistic behavior in the male domestic rat. *Hormones and Behavior*, 1972, *3*, 247–259.

Barnett, S. A. Experiments on "neophobia" in wild and laboratory rats. *British Journal of Psychology*, 1958, *49*, 195–201.

Barnett, S. A. *A study in behavior*. London: Metheun, 1963.

Barnett, S.A. Social stress. In J. D. Carthy & C. L. Duddington (Eds.), *Viewpoints in Biology*. London: Butterworth, 1964a, pp. 170–218.

Barnett, S. A. The biology of aggression. *Lancet*, 1964b, *8*, 803–807.

Barnett, S. A. Rats. *Scientific American*, 1967a, *216*, 78–85.

Barnett, S. A. Attack and defense in animal societies. In C. D. Clemente & D. B. Lindsley (Eds.), *Aggression and defense: Neural mechanisms and social patterns*, Vol. V, *Brain Function*. Los Angeles: University of California Press, 1967b, pp. 35–36.

Barnett, S. A. Grouping and dispersive behavior among wild rats. In S. Garattini & E. B. Sigg (Eds.), *Aggressive behavior*. New York: Wiley, 1969, pp. 3–14.

Barnett, S. A. *The rat: A study in behavior*. Chicago: Chicago University Press, 1975.

Barnett, S. A. & C. S. Evans. Questions on the social dynamics of rodents. *Symposium of the Zoological Society of London*, 1965, *14*, 233–248.

Barnett, S. A., C. S. Evans, & R. C. Stoddart. Influence of females on conflict among wild rats. *Journal of Zoology*, 1968, *154*, 391.

Barrett, J. E. & A. DiMascio. Comparative effects on anxiety of the "Minor Tranquilizers" in "high" and "low" anxious student volunteers. *Diseases of the Nervous System*, 1966, *27*, 483–486.

Barrett, T. W. Studies of the function of the amygdaloid complex in *M. mulatta*. *Neuropsychologia*, 1969, *7*, 1–12.

Barsa, J. & J. C. Saunder. Comparative study of chlordiazepoxide and diazepam. *Diseases of the Nervous System*, 1964, *25*, 244–246.

Bartholomew, A. A. Perphenazine (Trilafon) in the immediate management of acutely disturbed chronic alcoholics. *Medical Journal of Australia*, 1963, *1*, 812–814.

Bartholomew, G. A., Jr. Reproductive and social behavior of the northern elephant seal. *University of California Publications in Zoology*, 1952, *47*, 369–472.

Bartholomew, G. A., Jr. Discussion of paper by K. S. Norris, Aggressive behavior in Cetacea. In C. D. Clemente & D. B. Lindsley (Eds.), *Aggression and defense: Neural mechanisms and social patterns*, Vol. V, *Brain Function*. Los Angeles: University of California Press, 1967, pp. 232–241.

Bartholomew, G. A., Jr., & P. G. Hoel. Reproductive behavior of the Alaska fur seal, Callorhinus ursinus. *Journal of Mammalogy*, 1953, *34*, 417–436.

Bassoe, P. The auriculotemporal syndrome and other vasomotor disturbances about the head: "Auriculotemporal syndrome" complicating diseases of parotid gland; angioneurotic edema of brain. *Medical Clinics of North America*, 1932, *16*, 405–412.

Bates, B. C. Territorial behavior in primates: A review of recent field studies. *Primates*, 1970, *11*, 271–284.

Bateson, G., III. The frustration-aggression hypothesis and culture. *Psychological Review*, 1941, *48*, 350–355.

Bayrakal, S. The significance of electroencephalographic abnormality in behavior-problem children. *Canadian Psychiatric Association Journal*, 1965, 10, 387–392.

Beach, F. A. Bisexual mating behavior in the male rat: Effects of castration and hormone administration. *Physiological Zoology*, 1945, *18*, 195–221.

Beach, F. A. *Hormones and behavior.* New York: Harper & Row, 1948.

Beardmore, T. D., I. H. Fox, & W. N. Kelley. Effect of allopurinol on premidine metabolism in the Lesch-Nyhan syndrome. *Lancet*, 1970, *2*, 830–831.

Beeman, E. A. The effect of male hormone on aggressive behavior in mice. *Physiological Zoology*, 1947, *20*, 373–405.

Bender, L. *Aggression, hostility, and anxiety in children.* Springfield, Ill.: Thomas, 1953.

Benedict, R. *Patterns of culture.* Boston: Houghton Mifflin, 1934.

Bennett, R. M., A. H. Buss, & J. A. Carpenter. Alcohol and human physical aggression. *Quarterly Journal of Studies on Alcohol*, 1969, *39*, 870–876.

Berkowitz, L. *Aggression: A social psychological analysis.* New York: McGraw-Hill, 1962.

Berkowitz, L. Experiments on automatism and intent in human aggression. In C. D. Clemente & D. B. Lindsley (Eds.), *Aggression and defense: Neural mechanisms and social patterns*, Vol. V, *Brain Function*, Los Angeles, University of California Press, 1967, pp. 243–266.

Berkowitz, L. *Roots of aggression.* New York: Atherton Press, 1969.

Berkowitz, L. Experimental investigations of hostility catharsis. *Journal of Clinical and Consulting Psychology*, 1970, 35, 1–7.

Bernard, B. K. Frog killing (Ranicide) in male rat: Lack of effect of hormonal manipulations. *Physiology and Behavior*, 1974, *12*, 405–408.

Bernstein, H. & K. E. Moyer. Aggressive behavior in the rat: Effect of isolation and olfactory bulb lesions. *Brain Research*, 1970, *20*, 75–84.

Bernstein, I. S. Role of the dominant male rhesus monkey in response to external challenges to the group. *Journal of Comparative and Physiological Psychology.* 1964, *27*, 404–406.

Berntson, G. G. Blockade and release of hypothalamically and naturally elicited aggressive behaviors in cats following midbrain lesions. *Journal of Comparative and Physiological Psychology*, 1972, *81*, 541–554.

Berntson, G. G. Attack, grooming, and threat elicited by stimulation of the pontine tegmentum in cats. *Physiology and Behavior*, 1973, *11*, 81–87.

Berntson, G. G. & S. F. Leibowitz. Biting attack in cats: Evidence for central muscarinic mediation. *Brain Research*, 1973, *51*, 366–370.

Bettelheim, B. Children should learn about violence. *Saturday Evening Post*, 1967, *CXL*, 10–12.

Bevan, J. M., W. Bevan, & B. F. Williams. Spontaneous aggressiveness in young castrate C_3H male mice treated with three dose levels of testosterone. *Physiological Zoology*, 1958a, *31*, 284–288.

Bevan, W., W. F. Daves, & G. W. Levy. The relation of castration, androgen therapy and pretest fighting experience to competitive aggression in male C57 BL/10 mice. *Animal Behavior*, 1960, *8*, 6–12.

Bevan, W., G. W. Levy, J. M. Whitehouse, & J. M. Bevan. Spontaneous aggressiveness in two strains of mice castrated and treated with one of three androgens. *Physiological Zoology*, 1958b, *30*, 341–349.

Bevilacqua, A. R. & S. C. Little. Fourteen and six per second dysrhythmia with proven hypothalamic disease. *Electromyography and Clinical Neurophysiology*, 1961, *13*, 314.

Billig, H. E., Jr., & C. A. Spaulding. Hyperinsulinism of menses. *Industrial Medicine*, 1947, *16*, 336–339.

Bingley, T. Mental symptoms in temporal lobe epilepsy and temporal lobe gliomas. *Acta Psychiatrica et Neurologica Scandinavica*, Supplementum 120, 1958, *33*, 1–151.

Blanchard, D. C. & R. J. Blanchard. Innate and conditioned reactions to threat in rats with amygdaloid lesions. *Journal of Comparative and Physiological Psychology*, 1972, *81*, 281–290.

Blanchard, R. J., D. C. Blanchard, & R. A. Fial. Hippocampal lesions in rats and their effect on activity, avoidence, and aggression. *Journal of Comparative and Physiological Psychology*, 1970, *71*, 92–102.

Blau, A. Mental changes following head trauma in children. *Archives of Neurology and Psychiatry*, 1937, *35*, 723–769.

Bleicher, S. J. Hypoglycemia. In M. Ellenberg & H. Rifkin (Eds.), *Diabetes mellitus, theory and practice*. New York: McGraw-Hill, 1970, pp. 958–989.

Bliss, E. L., A. Frichat, & L. Samuels. Brain and testicular function. *Life Science*, 1972, *11*, 231–238.

Blum, R. H. *Mind-altering drugs and dangerous behavior: Alcohol*. Task Force Report on narcotics and drug abuse, Washington, D.C.: U.S. Government Printing Office, 1967, pp. 29–49.

Blum, R. H. Drugs and violence. In D. J. Mulvihill, M. M. Tumin, & L. A. Curtis (Eds.), *Crimes of violence:* A staff report to the National Commission on the Causes and Prevention of Violence, Vol. 13, Washington, D.C.: U.S. Government Printing Office, 1969, pp. 1462–1523.

Blumer, D. The temporal lobes and paroxysmal behavior disorders. *Szondiana*, 1967, *7*, 273–285.

Blumer, D. Hypersexual episodes in temporal lobe epilepsy. *American Journal of Psychiatry*, 1970, *126*, 1099–1106.

Blumer, D. & C. Migeon. Treatment of impulsive behavior disorders in males with medroxy-progesterone acetate. Paper presented at the annual meeting of the American Psychiatric Association, May, 1973.

Blurton Jones, N. G. An ethological study of some aspects of social behaviour of children in nursery school. In D. Morris (Ed.), *Primate Ethology*. London: Doubleday, 1969, pp. 437–463.

Boelkins, C. R. & J. F. Heiser. Biological bases of aggression. In D. N. Daniels, M. F. Gilula, & F. M. Ochberg (Eds.), *Violence and the struggle for existence*. Boston: Little, Brown, 1970, pp. 15–52.

Boice, R. Social dominance in gerbils and hamsters. *Psychonomic Science*, 1969, *16*, 127–128.

Bolton, R. Aggression and hypoglycemia among the Qolla: A study in psychobiological anthropology. *Ethnology*, 1973, *12*, 227–257.

Bonkalo, A. Electroencephalography in criminology. *Canadian Psychiatric Association Journal*, 1967, *12*, 281–286.

Borgen, L. A., J. H. Khalson, W. T. King, & W. M. Davis. Strain differences in morphine-withdrawal-induced aggression in rats. *Psychonomic Science*, 1970, *21*, 35–36.

Borofsky, G. L., G. E. Stollak, & L. A. Messe. Sex differences in bystander reactions to physical assault. *Journal of Experimental and Social Psychology*, 1971, *7*, 313–318.

Boshka, S. C., H. M. Weisman, & D. H. Thor. A technique for inducing aggression in rats utilizing morphone withdrawal. *Psychological Record*, 1966, *16*, 541–543.

Bostow, D. E. & J. B. Bailey. Modification of severe disruptive and aggressive behavior using brief timeout and reinforcement procedures. *Journal of Applied Behavior Analysis*, 1969, *2*, 31–37.

Brady, J. V. Emotional behavior. In J. Field, H. W. Magoun, & V. E. Hall (Eds.), *Handbook of physiology*, Vol. 3. Washington, D.C.: American Physiological Society, 1960, pp. 316–318.

Brady, J. V. & W. J. H. Nauta. Subcortical mechanisms in emotional behavior: Affective changes following septal forebrain lesions in the albino rat. *Journal of Comparative and Physiological Psychology*, 1953, *46*, 339–346.

Brady, J. V. & W. J. H. Nauta. Subcortical mechanisms in emotional behavior: The duration of affective changes following septal forebrain lesions in the albino rat. *Journal of Comparative and Physiological Psychology*, 1955, *48*, 412–420.

Brain, P. F. Possible role of the pituitary/adrenal axis in aggressive behaviour. *Nature*, 1971a, *233*, 489.

Brain, P. F. Some endocrine effects on fighting behaviour on isolated male albino mice. *Journal of Endocrinology*, 1971b, *51*, 18–19.

Brain, P. F. Effects of isolation grouping on endocrine function and fighting behavior in male and female golden-hamsters (*Mesocricetus* auratus waterhouse). *Behavioral Biology*, 1972a, *7*, 349–357.

Brain, P. F. Mammalian behavior and the adrenal cortex: A review. *Behavioral Biology*, 1972b, *7*, 453–477.

Brain, P. F., C. M. Evans, & A. E. Poole. Studies on the effects of cyproterone acetate administered both in early life and to adults on subsequent fighting behaviour and organ weight changes in male albino mice. *Acta Endocrinologica, and Supplementium*, 1973, *177*, 286.

Brain, P. F. & N. W. Nowell. Some behavioral and endocrine relationships in adult male laboratory mice subjected to open field and aggression tests. *Physiology and Behavior*, 1969, *4*, 945–947.

Brain, P. F. & N. W. Nowell. Some observations on intermale aggression testing in albino mice. *Communications in Behavioral Biology*, 1970a, *5*, 7–17.

Brain, P. F. & N. W. Nowell. Activity and defaecation related to aggressiveness and adrenal stress response in adult male laboratory mice. *Physiology and Behavior*, 1970b, *5*, 259–261.

Brain, P. F. & N. W. Nowell. Isolation versus grouping effects on adrenal and gonadal function in albino mice, 1: The male. *General and Comparative Endocrinology*, 1971, *16*, 49–154.

Brain, P. F., N. W. Nowell, & A. Wouters. Some relationships between adrenal function and effectiveness of a period of isolation in inducing intermale aggression in albino mice. *Physiology and Behavior,* 1971, *6,* 27–29.

Brain, P. F. & A. E. Poole. The role of endocrines in isolation induced intermale fighting in albino laboratory mice, 1: Pituitary-adrenocortical influences. *Aggressive Behavior,* 1974, *1,* 39–69.

Bramel, D. The arousal and reduction of hostility. In J. Mills (Ed.), *Experimental Social Psychology.* London: Macmillan, 1970, 33–120.

Breamish, P. & L. Kiloh. Psychosis due to amphetamine consumption. *Journal of Mental Science,* 1960, *106,* 337–343.

Breggin, P. R. Psychosurgery for the control of violence: A critical review. Paper presented at the Houston Neurological Symposium on neural bases of violence and aggression, March 9–11, 1972.

Bremer, J. *Asexualization.* New York: Macmillan, 1959.

Brewer, C. Homicide during a psychomotor seizure: The importance of airencephalography in establishing insanity under McNaughten rules. *Medical Journal of Australia,* 1971, *1,* 857–859.

Brill, H. Postencephalitic psychiatric conditions. *American Handbook of Psychiatry,* Vol. II. New York: Basic Books, 1959, pp. 1163–1174.

Brill, H. Drugs and aggression. *Medical Counterpart,* 1969, *1,* 33–38.

Bronson, F. H. & C. Desjardins. Aggressive behavior and seminal vesicle function in mice: Differential sensitivity to an androgen given neonatally. *Endocrinology,* 1969, *85,* 971–974.

Bronson, F. H. & C. Desjardins. Neonatal androgen administration and adult aggressiveness in female mice. *General and Comparative Endocrinology,* 1970, *15,* 320–325.

Bronson, F. H. & C. Desjardins. Steroid hormones and aggressive behavior in mammals. In B. Eleftheriou & J. Scott (Eds.), *The physiology of aggression and defeat.* London: Plenum Press, 1971, pp. 43–64.

Bronson, F. H. & H. M. Marsden. Preputial gland as an indicator of social dominance in male mice. *Behavioral Biology,* 1973, *9,* 625–628.

Broom, L. & P. Selznick. *Sociology: A text with adapted readings.* New York: Harper & Row, 1957.

Brown, C. *Manchild in the promised land.* New York: Macmillan, 1965.

Brown, J. L. & R. W. Hunsperger. Neuroethology and the motivation of agonistic behaviour. *Animal Behavior,* 1963, *11,* 439–448.

Brown, J. L., R. W. Hunsperger, & H. E. Rosvold. Defence, attack, and flight elicited by electrical stimulation of the hypothalamus of the cat. *Experimental Brain Research,* 1969a, *8,* 113–129.

Brown, J. L., R. W. Hunsperger, & H. E. Rosvold. Interaction of defence and flight reactions produced by simultaneous stimulation at two points in the hypothalamus of the cat. *Experimental Brain Research,* 1969b, *8,* 130–149.

Brown, L. E. Home range and movement of small mammals. In P. A. Jewell & C. Loizos (Eds.), *Play, exploration and territory in mammals.* London: Academic Press, 1966, pp. 85–107.

Brown, R. Z. Social behavior, reproduction, and population changes in the house mouse (*Mus musculus* L.). *Ecological Monographs,* 1953, *23,* 217–240.

Brutkowski, S., E. Fonberg, & E. Mempel. Angry behavior in dogs following bilateral lesions in the genual portion of the rostral cingulate gyrus. *Acta Biologica Experimentalis*, 1961, *21*, 199–205.

Bucher, B. & O. I. Lovaas. Use of aversive stimulation in behavior modification. In M. R. Jones (Ed.), *Miami symposium on the prediction of behavior, 1967: Aversive stimulation*. Coral Gables, Fla.: University of Miami Press, 1968, pp. 77–145.

Buddington, R., F. King, & L. Roberts. Emotionality and conditioned avoidance responding in the squirrel monkey following septal injury. *Psychonomic Science*, 1967, *8*, 195–196.

Buechner, H. K. Territorial behavior in the Uganda kob. *Science*, 1961, *133*, 698–699.

Bugbee, N. J. & B. S. Eichelman. Sensory alterations and aggressive behavior in the rat. *Physiology and Behavior*, 1972, *8*, 981–985.

Buki, R. A. The use of psychotropic drugs in the rehabilitation of sex-deviated criminals. *American Journal of Psychiatry*, 1964, *120*, 1170–1175.

Bullock, L. P. & M. I. New. Testosterone and cortisol concentration in spermatic adrenal and systemic venous blood in adult male guinea pigs. *Endocrinology*, 1971, *88*, 523–626.

Bunnell, B. N., J. R. Bemporad, & C. K. Flesher. Septal forebrain lesions and social dominance behavior in the hooded rat. *Psychonomic Science*, 1966, *6*, 207–208.

Bunnell, B. N. & M. H. Smith. Septal lesions and aggressiveness in the cotton rat, *Sigmodon hispidus*. *Psychonomic Science*, 1966, *6*, 443–444.

Burge, K. G. & D. A. Edwards. The adrenal gland and the pre- and post-castrational aggressive behavior of male mice. *Physiology and Behavior*, 1971, *7*, 885–888.

Burgess, A. *A clockwork orange*. New York: Norton, 1962.

Burghardt, G. M. Chemical cue preferences of inexperienced snakes: Comparative aspects. *Science*, 1967, *157*, 718–721.

Burnand, G., H. Hunter, & K. Hoggart. Some psychological test characteristics of Klinefelter's syndrome. *British Journal of Psychiatry*, 1967, *113*, 1091–1096.

Burt, W. H. Territoriality and home range concepts as applied to mammals. *Journal of Mammalogy*, 1943, *24*, 346–354.

Buss, A. *The psychology of aggression*. New York: Wiley, 1961.

Buss, A. H. & A. Durkee. An inventory for assessing different kinds of hostility. *Journal of Consulting Psychology*, 1957, *21*, 343–349.

Butler, K. Predatory behavior in laboratory mice: Strain and sex comparisons. *Journal of Comparative and Physiological Psychology*, 1973, *85*, 243–249.

Cahoon, D. D., R. M. Crosby, S. Dunn, M. S. Herrin, C. C. Hill, & M. McGinnis. The effect of food deprivation on shock elicited aggression in rats. *Psychonomic Science*, 1971, *22*, 43–44.

Cain, D. P. Olfactory bulbectomy: Neural structures involved in irritability and aggression in the male rat. *Journal of Comparative and Physiological Psychology*, 1974, *86*, 213–220.

Cain, D. P. & G. Paxinos. Olfactory bulbectomy and mucosal damage: Effects on copulation, irritability, and interspecific aggression in male rats. *Journal of Comparative and Physiological Psychology,* 1974, *86,* 202–212.

Cairns, R. B. & J. S. Nakelski. On fighting in mice: Ontogenetic and experiential determinants. *Journal of Comparative and Physiological Psychology,* 1971, *74,* 354–361.

Calhoun, J. B. A comparative study of the social behavior of two inbred strains of house mice. *Ecological Monographs,* 1956, *26,* 81–103.

Calhoun, J. B. The ecology and sociology of the Norway rat. (U.S. Department of Health, Education and Welfare, Public Health Service Publication No. 1008.) Washington, D.C.: U.S. Government Printing Office, 1962.

Campbell, H. E. The violent sex offender: A consideration of emasculation in treatment. *Rocky Mountain Medical Journal,* 1967, *64,* 40–43.

Campbell, M. B. Allergy and behavior: Neurologic and psychic syndromes. In F. Speer (Ed.), *Allergy of the nervous system.* Springfield, Ill.: Thomas, 1970a, pp. 28–46.

Campbell, M. B. Treatment of nonallergic factors. In F. Speer (Ed.), *Allergy of the nervous system.* Springfield, Ill.: Thomas, 1970b, pp. 239–254.

Campbell, M. B. Allergy and epilepsy. In F. Speer (Ed.), *Allergy of the nervous system.* Springfield, Ill.: Thomas, 1970c, pp. 59–78.

Candland, D. K., D. C. Bryan, B. L. Nazar, K. J. Kopf, & M. Sendor. Squirrel monkey heart rate during formation of status orders. *Journal of Comparative and Physiological Psychology,* 1970, *70,* 417–423.

Candland, D. K., D. B. Taylor, L. Dresdale, J. M. Leiphart, & S. P. Solow. Heart rate, aggression and dominance in the domestic chicken. *Journal of Comparative and Physiological Phsychology,* 1969, *67,* 70–76.

Carlini, E. A., A. Hamaoui, & R. M. W. Martz. Factors influencing aggressiveness elicited by marihuana in food deprived rats. *British Journal of Pharmacology,* 1972, *44,* 794–804.

Carlini, E. A. & J. Masur. Development of aggressive behaviour in rats by chronic administration of Cannabis sativa. *Life Science,* 1969, *8,* 607–720.

Carpenter, C. R. A field study of the behavior and social relations of howling monkeys. *Comparative Psychology Monographs,* 1934, *10,* 1–168.

Carpenter, C. R. A field study in Siam of the behavior and social relations of the gibbon. *Comparative Psychology Monographs,* 1940, *16,* 1–212.

Carpenter, C. R. Sexual behavior of free ranging Rhesus monkeys (*Macaca mulatta*). *Journal of Comparative Psychology,* 1942, *33,* 113–142.

Carpenter, C. R. Territoriality: A review of concepts and problems. In A. Roe & G. G. Simpson (Eds.), *Behavior and evolution.* New Haven: Yale University Press, 1958, pp. 224–250.

Carpenter, C. R. *Naturalistic behavior of nonhuman primates.* University Park, Pa.: Pennsylvania State University Press, 1964.

Carrick, R. Ecological significance of territory in the Australian magpie (*Gymnorhina tibicen*). *Proceedings XIII International Ornithology Congress,* 1963, 740–753.

Carthy, J. D., & F. J. Ebling. *The natural history of aggression.* New York: Academic Press, 1964.

Cazzullo, C. L. Psychiatric aspects of epilepsy. *International Journal of Neurology,* 1959, *1,* 53–65.

Challas, G. & W. Brauer. Tourette's disease: Relief of symptoms with R 1625. *American Journal of Psychiatry*, 1963, *120*, 283–284.

Chance, M. R. Resolution of social conflict in animals and man. In A. de Reuck & J. Knight (Eds.), *Conflict in society*. Boston: Little, Brown, 1966, pp. 16–35.

Chance, M. & C. Jolly. *Social groups of monkeys, apes and men*. New York: Dutton, 1970.

Chao, D., J. Sexton, & S. D. Davis. Convulsive equivalent syndrome of childhood. *Journal of Pediatrics*, 1964, *64*, 499–508.

Chapel, J. L., N. Brown, & R. L. Jenkins. Tourette's disease: Symptomatic relief with haloperidol. *American Journal of Psychiatry*, 1964, *121*, 608–610.

Chapman, W. P. Studies of the periamygdaloid area in relation to human behavior. *Research Publications of the Association for Research in Nervous and Mental Disease*, 1958, *36*, 258–277.

Chapman, W. P., H. R. Schrpeder, G. Geyer, G. Brazier, M. A. B. Fager, J. L. Poppen, H. C. Solomon, & P. I. Yakovler. Physiological evidence concerning importance of the amygdaloid nuclear region in the integration of circulatory function and emotion in man. *Science*, 1954, *120*, 949.

Charpentier, J. Analysis and measurement of aggressive behavior in mice. In S. Garattini & E. B. Sigg (Eds.), *Aggressive behaviour*. New York: Wiley, 1969, pp. 86–100.

Chatz, T. L. Management of male adolescent sex offenders. *International Journal of Offender Therapy*, 1972, *2*, 109–115.

Chaurand, J. P., P. Schmitt, & P. Karli. Effects de lésions du tegmentum ventral du mésencephale sur le comportement d'aggression rat-souris. *Physiology and Behavior*, 1973, *10*, 507–515.

Cherkin, A. & R. O. Meinecke. Suppression of fighting behavior in rabbits by paired emergence from anaesthesia. *Nature*, 1971, *231*, 195–196.

Chi, C. C., R. J. Bandler, & J. P. Flynn. Neuroanatomic projections related to biting attack elicited from ventral midbrain in cats. Unpublished manuscript.

Chi, C. C. & J. P. Flynn. The effects of hypothalamic and reticular stimulation on evoked responses in the visual system of the cat. *EEG* and *Clinical Neurophysiology*, 1968, *24*, 343–356.

Chi, C. C. & J. P. Flynn. Neural pathways associated with hypothalamically elicited attack behavior in cats. *Science*, 1971a, *171*, 703–705.

Chi, C. C. & J. P. Flynn. Neuroanatomic projections related to biting attack elicited from hypothalamus in cats. *Brain Research*, 1971b, *35*, 49–66.

Christie, M. H. & R. J. Barfield. Restoration of social aggression by androgen implanted into brain of castrated male rats. *American Zoologist*, 1973, *13*, 1267.

Clapham, B. An interesting case of hypoglycemia. *Medico-Legal Journal*, 1965, *33*, 72–73.

Clark, D. L. Immediate and delayed effects of early, intermediate, and late social isolation in the Rhesus monkey. Unpublished doctoral dissertation, University of Wisconsin, 1968.

Clark, K. B. The pathos of power: A psychological perspective. *American Psychologist*, 1971, *26*, 1047–1057.

Clark, L. D. Experimental studies of the behavior of an aggressive predatory mouse, *Onychomys leucogaster*. In E. L. Bliss (Ed.), *Roots of behavior*. New York: Harper & Row, 1962, pp. 179–186.

Clark, L. H. & M. W. Schein. Activities associated with conflict behavior in mice. *Animal Behaviour*, 1966, *14*, 44–49.

Clark, R. A. The effects of sexual motivation of phantasy. *Journal of Experimental Psychology*, 1953, *44*, 391–399.

Clark, R. A. & M. R. Sensibar. The relationship between symbolic and manifest projections of sexuality with some incidental correlates. *Journal of Abnormal and Social Psychology*, 1955, *50*, 327–334.

Clayton, R. B., J. Kogura, & H. C. Kraemer. Sexual differentiation of the brain: Effects of testosterone on brain RNA metabolism in newborn female rats. *Nature*, 1970, *226*, 810–812.

Clemente, C. D. & M. H. Chase. Neurological substrates of aggressive behavior. *Annual Review of Psychology*, 1973, *53*, 329–356.

Cloudsley-Thompson, J. L. *Animal conflict and adaptation*. Chester-Springs, Pa.: Dufour, 1965.

Coca, A. F. *The Pulse Test: The secret of building your basic health*. New York: Lyle Stuart, 1959.

Cohen, S. Thioridazine (Mellaril): Recent developments. *Journal of Psychopharmacology*, 1966, *1*, 1–15.

Cohen, S. Abuse of centrally stimulating agents among juveniles in California. In F. Sjoqvist & M. Tuttle (Eds.), *Abuse of central stimulants*. New York: Raven Press, 1969, pp. 165–180.

Cohn, R. & J. E. Nardini. The correlation of bilateral occipital slow activity in the human EEG with certain disorders of behavior. *American Journal of Psychiatry*, 1958, *115*, 44–54.

Cole, H. F. & H. H. Wolf. Laboratory evaluation of aggressive behavior of the grasshopper mouse (*Onychomys*). *Journal of Pharmaceutical Sciences*, 1970, *59*, 969–971.

Cole, J. O., S. C. Goldberg, & J. M. Davis. Drugs in the treatment of psychosis: Controlled studies. In P. Solomon (Ed), *Psychiatric drugs*. New York: Grune & Stratton, 1966, pp. 153–180.

Coles, R. Violence in ghetto children. *Children*, 1967, *14*, 101–104.

Collias, N. E. Aggressive behavior among vertebrate animals. *Physiological Zoology*, 1944, *17*, 83–123.

Comstock. G. A. & E. A. Rubinstein (Eds.), *Television and social behavior*, Vol. 3: *Television and adolescent aggressiveness*. Washington, D.C.: U.S. Government Printing Office, 1972.

Conaway, C. H. & D. S. Sade. The seasonal spermatogenic cycle in free ranging rhesus monkeys. *Folia Primatologica*, 1965, *3*, 1–12.

Connell, P. H. *Amphetamine psychosis*. London: Oxford University Press, 1958.

Conner, R. L. & S. Levine. Hormonal influences on aggressive behaviour. In S. Garattini & E. B. Sigg (Eds.), *Aggressive behaviour*. New York: Wiley, 1969, pp. 150–163.

Conner, R. L., S. Levine, G. A. Wertheim, & J. F. Cummer. Hormonal determinants of aggressive behavior. *Annals of the New York Academy of Science*, 1969, *159*, 760–776.

Conners, C., R. Kramer, G. Rothschild, L. Schwartz, & A. Stone. Treatment of young delinquent boys with diphenylhydantoin sodium and methylphenidate. *Archives of General Psychiatry*, 1971, *24*, 156–159.

Connor, J. Olfactory control of aggressive and sexual behavior in the mouse (*Mus musculus* L.) *Psychonomic Science*, 1972, *27*, 1–3.

Coppen, A. & N. Kessel. Menstruation and personality. *British Journal of Psychiatry*, 1963, *109*, 711–721.

Corning, P. A. & C. H. Corning. Toward a general theory of violent aggression. *Social Science Information*, 1971, *11*, 7–35.

Cox, G. S., J. R. Hodges, & J. Vernikos. The effect of adrenalectomy on the circulating level of adrenocorticotrophic hormone in the rat. *Journal of Endocrinology*, 1958, *17*, 177–181.

Crabtree, J. M. & K. E. Moyer. Sex differences in fighting and defense induced in rats by shock during morphine withdrawal. *Physiology and Behavior*, 1973, *11*, 337–343.

Creer, T. L. Hunger and thirst in shock-induced aggression. *Behavioral Biology*, 1973, *8*, 443–437.

Creer, T. L., E. W. Hitzing, & R. W. Schaeffer. Classical conditioning of reflexive fighting. *Psychonomic Science*, 1966, *4*, 89–90.

Cressey, D. R. Crime. In R. K. Merton & R. A. Nisbet (Eds.), *Contemporary Social Problems*. New York: Harcourt Brace Jovanovich, 1961, pp. 21–76.

Crichton, M. *The terminal man*. New York: Bantam Books, 1972.

Crook, J. H. The nature and function of territorial aggression. In M. F. A. Montague (Ed.), *Man and aggression*. London: Oxford University Press, 1968, pp. 141–178.

Crook, W. G., W. W. Harrison, S. E. Crawford, & B. S. Emerson. Systemic manifestations due to allergy: Report of fifty patients and a review of the literature on the subject. *Pediatrics*, 1961, *27*, 790–799.

Cross, H. A. & H. F. Harlow. Prolonged and progressive effects of partial isolation on the behavior of Macaque monkeys. *Journal of Experimental Research in Personality*, 1965, *1*, 39–49.

Crowcroft, P. Territoriality in wild house mice, *Mus musculus*. *Journal of Mammalogy*, 1955, *36*, 299–301.

Currier, R. D., S. C. Little, J. F. Suess, & O. Andy. Sexual seizures. *Archives of Neurology*, 1971, *25*, 260–264.

Dalton, K. Menstruation and acute psychiatric illness. *British Medical Journal*, 1959, *1*, 148–149.

Dalton, K. Schoolgirls' misbehavior and menstruation. *British Medical Journal*, 1960, *2*, 1647–1649.

Dalton, K. Menstruation and crime. *British Medical Journal*, 1961, *3*, 1752–1753.

Dalton, K. *The premenstrual syndrome*. Springfield, Ill.: Thomas, 1964.

Daniels, D. N., M. F. Gilula, & F. M. Ochberg. *Violence and the struggle for existence*. Boston: Little, Brown, 1970.

Darling, F. F. *A herd of red deer: A study in animal behaviour*. London: Oxford University Press, 1937.

Darling, H. F. Haloperidol in 60 criminal psychotics. *Diseases of the Nervous System*, 1971, *32*, 31–34.

Darwin, C. *The expression of emotions in man and animals.* New York: D. Appleton, 1896 (authorized edition).

Davenport, W. Sexual patterns and their regulation in a society of the southwest Pacific. In F. A. Beach (Ed.), *Sex and behavior.* New York: Wiley, 1965, pp. 164–207.

Davies, J. C. The J-curve of rising and declining satisfactions as a cause of some great revolutions and a contained rebellion. In H. D. Graham & T. R. Gurr (Eds.), *Violence in America: Historical and comparative perspectives,* Vol. II. A report to the National Commission on the Causes and Prevention of Violence, Washington, D.C.: U.S. Government Printing Office, 1969, 547–576.

Davis, D. E. The physiological analysis of aggressive behavior. In W. Etkin (Ed.), *Social behavior and organization among vertebrates.* Chicago: University of Chicago Press, 1964, pp. 53–74.

Davis, F. C. The measurement of aggressive behavior in laboratory rats. *Journal of Genetic Psychology,* 1933, *43,* 213–217.

Davis, H. & I. Donefeld. Extinction induced social interaction in rats. *Psychonomic Science,* 1967, *7,* 85–86.

Davis, P. G. & R. D. Gandelman. Pup-killing produced by the administration of testosterone propionate to adult female mice. *Hormones and Behavior,* 1972, *3,* 169–173.

Davis, W. M. & J. H. Khalsa. Increased shock induced aggression during morphine withdrawal. *Life Science,* 1971a, *10,* 1321–1327.

Davis, W. M. & J. H. Khalsa. Some determinants of aggressive behavior induced by morphine withdrawal. *Psychonomic Science,* 1971b, *24,* 13–15.

Davison, H. M. Allergy of the nervous system. *Quarterly Review of Allergy and Applied Immunology,* 1952, *6,* 157–188.

Dawber, M. A. & D. D. Thiessen. Territoriality as a factor in forced migration and reproductive isolation. Paper presented at the American Association for the Advancement of Science, Philadelphia, December, 1971.

Deci, L., M. K. Varszegi, J. Mehes. Direct chemical stimulation of various subcortical brain areas in unrestrained cats. In K. Lissak (Ed.), *Recent developments of neurobiology in Hungary,* Vol. II: *Results in neurophysiology, neuropharmacology and behaviour.* Budapest: Akademiai Kiado, 1969, pp. 1–211.

DeHaas, A. M. *Lectures on epilepsy.* Netherlands: Elsevier, 1958.

DeHaas, A. M. Epilepsy in criminality. *British Journal of Criminology,* 1963, *3,* 248–257.

de la Vega Llamosa, A. Los equivalentes del delito y su importancia en nuestro medio. Thesis presented at Universidad Nacional Autonoma de México, Mexico City, 1966.

Delgado, J. M. R. Cerebral structures involved in transmission and elaboration of noxious stimulation. *Journal of Neurophysiology,* 1955, *18,* 261–275.

Delgado, J. M. R. Modification of social behavior induced by remote controlled electrical stimulation of the brain. XXI International Congress of Physiological Science, 1959, 75.

Delgado, J. M. R. Emotional behavior in animals and humans. *Psychiatric Research Reports,* 1960, *12,* 259–271.

Delgado, J. M. R. Cerebral heterostimulation in a monkey colony. *Science,* 1963, *141,* 161–163.

Delgado, J. M. R. *Evolution of physical control of the brain.* New York: The American Museum of Natural History, 1965a.

Delgado, J. M. R. Evoking and inhibiting aggressive behavior by radio stimulation in monkey colonies. *American Zoologist,* 1965b, *5,* 642.

Delgado, J. M. R. Chronic radiostimulation of the brain in monkey colonies. *Proceedings of the International Union of Physiological Sciences,* 1965c, *4,* 365–371.

Delgado, J. M. R. Aggressive behavior evoked by radio stimulation in monkey colonies. *American Zoologist,* 1966, *6,* 669–681.

Delgado, J. M. R. Aggression and defense under cerebral radio control. In C. D. Clemente and D. B. Lindsley (Eds.), *Aggression and defense: Neural mechanisms and social patterns,* Vol. V., *Brain function.* Los Angeles: University of California Press, 1967, pp. 171–193.

Delgado, J. M. R. *Physical control of the mind.* New York: Harper & Row, 1969a.

Delgado, J. M. R. Aggression in free monkeys modified by electrical and chemical stimulation of the brain. Paper presented at the Symposium on aggression, Interdepartmental Institute for Training in Research in the Behavioral and Neurologic Sciences, Albert Einstein College of Medicine, New York, 1969b.

Delgado, J. M. R. Modulation of emotions by cerebral radio stimulation. In P. Black (Ed.), *Physiological correlates of emotion.* New York: Academic Press, 1970, pp. 189–202.

Delgado, J. M. R., H. Hamlin, & W. P. Chapman. Technique of intracerebral electrode placement for recording and stimulation and its possible therapeutic value in psychotic patients. *Confinia Neurologia,* 1952, *12,* 315–319.

Delgado, J. M. R., V. Mark, W. Sweet, F. Ervin, G. Weiss, G. Bach-Y-Rita, & R. Hagiwara. Intracerebral radio stimulation and recording in completely free patients. *Journal of Nervous and Mental Diseases,* 1968, *147,* 329–340.

Dement, W. C. The effect of dream deprivation. *Science,* 1960, *131,* 1705–1707.

Dement, W. C. Experimental dream studies. In Academy of Psychoanalysis, *Science and Psychoanalysis,* Vol. 7. New York: Grune & Stratton, 1964, pp. 129–184.

Dement, W. C. Studies on the function of rapid eye movement (paradoxical) sleep in human subjects. In *Aspects anatomo-fonctionnels de la physiologie du sommeil* (Lyon Conference, September 1963), Éditions du Centre National de la Recherche Scientifique, 1965, pp. 571–608.

Dement, W. C. & C. Fisher. Experimental interference with sleep cycle. *Canadian Psychiatric Association Journal,* 1963, *8,* 400–405.

Denham, J. Psychotherapy of obsessional neurosis assisted by Librium. Topical problems of psychotherapy. *Supplementum ad Acta Psychotherapeutica et Psychosomatica,* 1963, *4,* 195–198.

DeSisto, J. M. Hypothalamic mechanisms of killing behavior in the laboratory rat. Dissertation, Tufts University, 1970.

DeSisto, J. M. & J. P. Huston. Facilitation of interspecific aggression by subreinforcing electrical stimulation in the posterior lateral hypothalamus. Presented at the Eastern Psychological Association Meeting, Atlantic City, 1970a.

DeSisto, J. M. & J. P. Huston. Effect of territory on frog-killing by rats. *Journal of General Psychology*, 1970b, *83*, 179–184.

Deutsch, H. *The psychology of women*. New York: Grune & Stratton, 1944.

DeVore, I. Comparative ecology and behavior of monkeys and apes. In S. L. Washburn (Ed.), *Classification and human evolution*. New York: Wenner-Gren Foundation, 1963a, pp. 301–319.

DeVore, I. Mother-infant relations in free-ranging baboons. In H. L. Rheingold (Ed.), *Maternal behavior in mammals*. New York: Wiley, 1963b, pp. 305–335.

DeVore, I. (Ed.), *Primate behavior: Field studies of monkeys and apes*. New York: Holt, Rinehart and Winston, 1965.

Dicks, D., R. D. Myers, & A. Kling. Uncus and amydala lesions: Effects on social behavior in the free-ranging rhesus monkey. *Science*, 1969, *165*, 69–71.

Didiergeorges, F. & P. Karli. Hormones stéroides et maturation d'un comportement d'adression interspecifique du rat. *Comptes Rendus des Séances de la Société de Biologie*, 1967, *161*, 179.

Didiergeorges, F., M. Vergnes, & P. Karli. Privation des afferences olfactives et agressivité interspecifique du rat. *Comptes Rendus des Séances de la Société de Biologie*, 1966, *160*, 866.

Dietze, H. J. & G. E. Boegele. The 14 and 6 per second positive spikes in the EEG and their relation to behavioral disturbances in children and adolescents. *Acta Paedopsychiatrica*, 1963, *30*, 392–401.

diGiusto, E. L., K. Cairncross, & M. G. King. Hormonal influences on fear-motivated responses. *Psychological Bulletin*, 1971, *75*, 432–444.

DiMascio, A. & J. E. Barrett. Comparative effects of oxazepam in high and low anxious student volunteers. *Psychosomatics*, 1965, *6*, 298–302.

DiMascio, A., R. I. Shader, & J. Harmatz. Psychotropic drugs and induced hostility. *Psychosomatics*, 1969, *10*, 27–28.

Dinnen, A. Homicide during a psychomotor seizure. *Medical Journal of Australia*, 1971, *1*, 1353.

Dismang, L. H. & C. F. Cheatham. The Lesch-Nyhan syndrome. *American Journal of Psychiatry*, 1970, *127*, 671–677.

Dixon, A. K. and J. H. Mackintosh. Effects of female urine upon the social behaviour of adult male mice. *Animal Behaviour*, 1971, *19*, 138–140.

Dollard, J., L. W. Doob, N. E. Miller, O. H. Mowrer, & R. R. Sears. *Frustration and aggression*. New Haven, Conn.: Yale University Press, 1939.

Downer, C. J. L. Interhemispheric integration in the visual system. In V. B. Mouncastle (Ed.), *Interhemispheric relations and cerebral dominance*. Baltimore: Johns Hopkins Press, 1962, pp. 87–100.

Dreyer, P. L. & R. M. Church. Reinforcement of shock-induced fighting. *Psychonomic Science*, 1970, *18*, 147–148.

Duffy, C. T. & A. Hirshberg. *Sex and crime*. New York: Doubleday, 1965.

Duncan, G. G. The antidotal effect of anger in a case of insulin reaction (hypoglycemia) in a diabetic. *Canadian Medical Association*, 1935, *33*, 71.

Dunford, C. Behavioral aspects of spatial organization in the chipmunk, *Tamias striatus. Behaviour,* 1970, *36,* 215–231.

Dunn, G. W. Stilbestrol induced testicular degeneration in hypersexual males. *Journal of Clinical Endocrinology,* 1941, *1,* 643–648.

Dunstone, J. J., J. T. Cannon, J. T. Chickson, & W. K. Burns. Persistence and vigor of shock-induced aggression in gerbils (*Meriones unguiculatus*). *Psychonomic Science,* 1972, *28,* 272–274.

Eclancher, F. & P. Karli. Comportement d'agression interspecifique et comportement alimentaire du rat: Effets de lésions des noyaux ventromedians de l'hypothalamus. *Brain Research,* 1971, *26,* 71–79.

Edwards, D. A. Mice: Fighting by neonatally androgenized females. *Science,* 1968, *161,* 1027–1028.

Edwards, D. A. Early androgen stimulation and aggressive behavior in male and female mice. *Physiology and Behavior,* 1969, *4,* 333–338.

Edwards, D. A. Effects of cyproterone acetate on aggressive behaviour and the seminal vesicles of male mice. *Journal of Endocrinology,* 1970a, *46,* 477–481.

Edwards, D. A. Post neonatal androgenization and adult aggressive behavior in female mice. *Physiology and Behavior,* 1970b, *5,* 465–467.

Edwards, D. A. Neonatal administration of androstenedione, testosterone or testosterone propionate: Effects on ovulation, sexual receptivity and aggressive behavior in female mice. *Physiology and Behavior,* 1971, *6,* 223–228.

Edwards, D. A. & K. G. Burge. Estrogenic arousal of aggressive behavior and masculine sexual behavior in male and female mice. *Hormones and Behavior,* 1971, *2,* 239–245.

Edwards, D. A. & J. Herndon. Neonatal estrogen stimulation and aggressive behavior in female mice. *Physiology and Behavior,* 1970, *5,* 993–995.

Egan, O., J. R. Royce, & W. Poley. Evidence for a territorial marking factor of mouse emotionality. *Psychonomic Science,* 1972, *27,* 272–274.

Egger, M. D. & J. P. Flynn. Effect of electrical stimulation of the amygdala on hypothalamically elicited attack behavior in cats. *Journal of Neurophysiology,* 1963, *26,* 705–720.

Egger, M. D. & J. P. Flynn. Further studies on the effects of amygdaloid stimulation and ablation on hypothalmically elicited attack behavior in cats. In W. R. Adey & T. Tokizane (Eds.), *Progress in brain research,* Vol. 27. Amsterdam: Elsevier, 1967, pp. 165–182.

Eibl-Eibesfeldt, I. Beitrage zur Biologie der Haus- und der Ahrenmaus nebst einigen Beobachtungen an andere Nagern. *Zeitschrift fur Tierphychologie,* 1950, *7,* 558–587.

Eibl-Eibesfeldt, I. Zur ethologie des hamsters (*Cricetus cricetus* L.). *Zeitschrift fur Tierpsychologie,* 1953, *10,* 204–254.

Eibl-Eibesfeldt, I. The fighting behavior of animals. *Scientific American,* 1961a, *205,* 112–122.

Eibl-Eibesfeldt, I. The interactions of unlearned behavior patterns and learning in mammals. In J. F. Delafresnaye, *Brain mechanisms and learning.* Oxford: London, 1961b, pp. 53–73.

Eibl-Eibesfeldt, I. Angeborenes und Erbowbenes im Verhalten einiger Sauger. *Zeitschrift fur Tierpsychologie,* 1963, *20,* 705–754.

Eibl-Eibesfeldt, I. Ontogenetic and maturational studies of aggressive behavior. In C. D. Clemente & D. B. Lindsley (Eds.), *Aggression and defense: Neural mechanisms and social patterns,* Vol. V. *Brain function.* Los Angeles: University of California Press, 1967, pp. 57–94.

Eibl-Eibesfeldt, I. *Ethology: The biology of behavior.* New York: Holt, Rinehart and Winston, 1970.

Eibl-Eibesfeldt, I. *Love and hate.* New York: Holt, Rinehart and Winston, 1972.

Eisenberg, B. C. Etiology: Inhalants. In F. Speer (Ed.), *Allergy of the nervous system.* Springfield, Ill.: Thomas, 1970, pp. 143–197.

Eisenberg, J. F. Studies on the behavior of *Peromyscus maniculatus gambelii* and *Peromyscus californicus parasiticus. Behaviour,* 1962, *19,* 177–207.

Eisenberg, J. F. The behavior of heteromyid rodents. *University of California Publication in Zoology,* 1963, *69,* 1–114.

Eisenberg, J. F. & P. Leyhausen. The phylogenesis of predatory behavior in mammals. *Zeitschrift fur Tierpsychologie,* 1972, *30,* 59–93.

Eleftheriou, B. E. & J. P. Scott (Eds.), *The physiology of aggression and defeat.* New York: Plenum Press, 1971.

Ellingson, R. J. Incidence of EEG abnormality among patients with mental disorders of apparently non-organic origin: Critical review. *American Journal of Psychiatry,* 1955, *114,* 263–275.

Ellinwood, E. H. Amphetamine psychosis: I. Description of the individuals and process. *Journal of Nervous and Mental Diseases,* 1967, *144,* 273–283.

Ellinwood, E. H. Assault and homicide associated with amphetamine abuse. *American Journal of Psychiatry,* 1971, *127,* 1170–1176.

Ellis, D. P. & P. Austin. Menstruation and aggressive behavior in a correctional center for women. *Journal of Criminal Law Criminology and Police Science,* 1971, *62,* 388–395.

Ellis, H. *Psychology of sex.* New York, Brooks, 1937.

Ellison, G. D. & J. P. Flynn. Organized aggressive behavior in cats after surgical isolation of the hypothalamus. *Archives Italiennes de Biologie,* 1968, *106,* 1–20.

Endroczi, E. K. Lissak, & G. Telegdy. Influence of sexual and adrenocortical hormones on the maternal aggressivity. *Acta Physiologica Academiae Scientiarum Hungaricae,* 1958, *14,* 353–357.

Epple, G. Quantitative studies on scent marking in the marmoset (*Callithrix jacchus*). *Folia Primatologica,* 1970, *13,* 48–62.

Epstein, A. W. Disordered human sexual behavior associated with temporal lobe dysfunction. *Medical Aspects of Human Sexuality,* 1969, February, 62–68.

Erpino, M. J. & T. C. Chappelle. Interactions between androgens and progesterone in mediation of aggression in the mouse. *Hormones and Behavior,* 1971, *2,* 265–272.

Ervin, F. The biology of individual violence: An overview. In D. J. Mulvihill, M. M. Tumin, & L. A. Curtis (Eds.), *Crimes of violence,* Vol. 13. A staff report submitted to the National Commission on the Causes and Prevention of Violence, Washington, D.C.: U.S. Government Printing Office, 1969.

Ervin, F. R. Discussion in workshop on regulation of behavior. In P. N. Williams (Ed.), *Ethical issues in biology and medicine*. Cambridge, Mass.: Schenkman, 1973, pp. 179–180.

Ervin, F. R., V. H. Mark, & J. Stevens. Behavioral and affective response to brain stimulation in man. In J. Zubin & C. Shagass (Eds.), *Neurobiological aspects of psychopathology*. New York: Grune & Stratton, 1969, pp. 54–65.

Erwin, J., G. Mitchell, & T. Maple. Abnormal behavior in non-isolate-reared rhesus monkeys. *Psychological Reports*, 1973, *33*, 515–523.

Esser, A. H. (Ed.), *Behavior and environment: The uses of space by animals and men*. New York: Plenum, 1971.

Esser, A. H., A. S. Chamberlain, E. D. Chapple, & N. S. Kline. Territoriality of patients on a research ward. In J. Wortis (Ed.), *Recent advances in biological psychiatry*, New York: Plenum, 1965, *7*, pp. 36–44.

Estes, R. D. Territorial behavior of the wildebeest (*Connochaetes taurinus* Burchell, 1823). *Zeitschrift fur Tierpsychologie*, 1969, *26*, 284–370.

Etkin, W. Reproductive behavors. In W. Etkin (Ed.), *Social behavior and organization among vertebrates*. Chicago: University of Chicago Press, 1964, pp. 75–116.

Evans, D. R. Specific aggression, arousal and reciprocal inhibition therapy. *Western Psychologist*, 1970, *1*, 125–130.

Evans, D. R. & M. T. Hearn. Anger and systematic desensitization: A follow-up. *Psychological Report*, 1973, *32*, 569–570.

Fabrykant, M. & B. L. Pacella. Association of spontaneous hypoglycemia with hypocalcemia and electrocerebral dysfunction. *Archives of Internal Medicine*, 1948, *81*, 184–202.

Falconer, M. A. Discussion. In M. Baldwin & P. Bailey, *Temporal lobe epilepsy*. Springfield, Ill.: Thomas, 1958, pp. 286–295.

Falconer, M. A. The pathological substrates of temporal lobe epilepsy and their significance in surgical treatment. In E. Hitchcock, L. Laitinen, & K. Vaernet (Eds.), *Psychosurgery*. Springfield, Ill.: Thomas, 1972, pp. 46–54.

Falconer, M. A. Reversibility by temporal-lobe resection of the behavioral abnormalities of temporal-lobe epilepsy. *New England Journal of Medicine*, 1973, *289*, 451–455.

Falconer, M. A., D. Hill, A Meyer, & J. L. Wilson. Clinical, radiological, and EEG correlations with pathological changes in temporal lobe epilepsy and their significance in surgical treatment. In M. Baldwin & P. Bailey, *Temporal lobe epilepsy*. Springfield, Ill.: Thomas, 1958, pp. 396–410.

Falconer, M. A., A. Meyer, D. Hill, & W. Mitchell. Treatment of temporal lobe epilepsy by temporal lobectomy: A survey of findings and results. *Lancet*, 1955, *268*, 827–835.

Farris, E. J. & E. H. Yeakel. Emotional behaviour of gray Norway and Wistar albino rats. *Journal of Comparative Psychology*, 1945, *38*, 108–118.

Feirabend, I. K. & R. L. Feirabend. Aggressive behaviors within politics 1948–1962: A cross-national study. *Journal of Conflict Resolution*, 1966, *10*, 249–272.

Feirabend, I. K. & R. L. Feirabend. Conflict, crisis and collision: A study of international stability. *Psychology Today*, 1968, *1*, 26–32.

Feldman, P. E. Analysis of the efficacy of diazepam. *Journal of Neuropsychiatry,* 1962, *3,* 62–67.

Fenton, G. W. & E. L. Udwin. Homicide, temporal lobe epilepsy and depression: A case report. *British Journal of Psychiatry,* 1965, *11,* 304–306.

Ferinden, W. E. Behavioristic psychodrama: A technique for modifying aggressive behavior in children. *Group Psychotherapy and Psychodrama,* 1971, *24,* 102–106.

Fernandez de Molina, A. & R. W. Hunsperger. Central representation of affective reactions in forebrain and brain stem: Electrical stimulation of amygdala, stria terminalis, and adjacent structure. *Journal of Physiology,* 1959, *145,* 251–265.

Fernandez de Molina, A. & R. W. Hunsperger. Organization of the subcortical system governing defense and flight reactions in the cat. *Journal of Physiology,* 1962, *160,* 200–213.

Feshbach, S. The function of aggression and the regulation of the aggressive drive. *Psychological Review,* 1964, *71,* 257–272.·

Feshbach, S. Aggression. In P. H. Mussen (Ed.), *Carmichael's Manual of Child Psychology,* Vol. II. New York: Wiley, 1970, pp. 159–259.

Feshbach, S. Dynamics of morality of violence and aggression: Some psychological considerations. *American Psychologist,* 1971, *26,* 281–291.

Feshbach, N. & S. Feshbach. The relationship between empathy and aggression in two age groups. *Developmental Psychology,* 1969, *1,* 102–107.

Feshbach, S. & R. D. Singer. *Television and aggression.* San Francisco: Jossey-Bass, 1971.

Field, L. H. & M. Williams. The hormonal treatment of sexual offenders. *Medicine, Science and the Law,* 1970, *10,* 27–34.

Fish, B. Drug therapy in child psychiatry: Psychological aspects. *Comparative Psychiatry,* 1960, *1,* 55–61.

Fisher, A. E. Effects of stimulus variation on sexual satiation in the male rat. *Journal of Comparative and Physiological Psychology,* 1962, *55,* 614–620.

Flandera, V. & V. Novakova. Interspecific aggressive behavior of rats with mice during the period of lactation. *Physologise Bohemoslovencia,* 1971a, *20,* 61.

Flandera, V. & V. Novakova. The development of interspecies aggression of rats towards mice during lactation. *Physiology and Behavior,* 1971b, *6,* 161–164.

Florea, J. & D. H. Thor. Drug withdrawal and fighting in rats. *Psychonomic Science,* 1968, *12,* 33–34.

Flory, R. K. Attack behavior as a function of minimum inter-food interval. *Journal of the Experimental Analysis of Behavior,* 1969, *12,* 825–828.

Flory, R. K. Attack behavior in a multiple fixed-ratio schedule of reinforcement. *Psychonomic Science,* 1970, *16,* 156–157.

Flynn, J. P. The neural basis of aggression in cats. In D. Glass (Ed.), *Neurophysiology and emotion.* New York: Rockefeller University, 1967, pp. 40–59.

Flynn, J. P. Patterning mechanisms, patterned reflexes, and attack behavior in cats. In J. K. Cole & D. D. Jensen (Eds.), *Nebraska Symposium on Motivation 1972.* Lincoln, Neb.: University of Nebraska Press, 1972.

Flynn, J. P., S. B. Edwards, & R. J. Bandler. Changes in sensory and motor systems during centrally elicited attack. *Behavioral Science*, 1971, *16*, 1–19.

Flynn, J., H. Vanegas, W. Foote, & S. B. Edwards. Neural mechanisms involved in a cat's attack on a rat. In R. Whalen, R. F. Thompson, M. Verzeano, & N. Weinberger (Eds.), *The neural control of behavior*. New York: Academic Press, 1970, pp. 135–173.

Fonberg, E. Effect of partial destruction of the amydaloid complex on the emotional-defensive behavior of dogs. *Bulletin de l'Academie Polanaise des Sciences Cl. II.*, 1965, *13*, 429–431.

Fonberg, E. The role of the amygdaloid nucleus in animal behaviour. *Progress in Brain Research*, 1968, *22*, 273–281.

Foote, R. M. Diethylstilbestrol in the management of psychopathological states in males. *Journal of Nervous and Mental Diseases*, 1944, *99*, 928–935.

Fortuna, M. & R. Gandelman. Elimination of pain-induced aggression in male mice following olfactory bulb removal. *Physiology and Behavior*, 1972, *9*, 397–400.

Fowler, H. & R. E. Whalen. Variation in incentive stimulus and sexual behavior in the male rat. *Journal of Comparative and Physiological Psychology*, 1961, *54*, 68–71.

Fox, M. W. Ontogeny of prey-killing behavior in Canidae. *Behaviour*, 1969a, *35*, 259–272.

Fox, M. W. The anatomy of aggression and its ritualization in Canidae: A developmental and comparative study. *Behaviour*, 1969b, *35*, 242–258.

Fox, M. W. & J. Apelbaum. Ontogeny of the orienting-jump response of the rabbit. *Behaviour*, 1969, *35*, 77–83.

Foxx, R. M. & N. H. Azrin. Restitution: A method of eliminating aggressive-disruptive behavior of retarded and brain damaged patients. *Behaviour Research & Therapy*, 1972, *10*, 15–27.

Frank, J. D. *Sanity and survival*. New York: Random House, 1967.

Franzen, E. A. & R. E. Myers. Neural control of social behavior: Prefrontal and anterior temporal cortex. *Neuropsychologia*, 1973, *11*, 141–157.

Frederichs, C. & H. Goodman. *Low blood sugar and you*. New York: Constellation International, 1969.

Fredericson, E. Response latency and habit strength in relationship to spontaneous fighting in C57 black mice. *Anatomical Record*, 1949, *105*, 29.

Fredericson, E. The effects of food deprivation upon competitive and spontaneous combat in C57 black mice. *Journal of Psychology*, 1950, *29*, 89–100.

Fredericson, E. Time and aggression. *Psychological Review*, 1951, *58*, 41–51.

Fredericson, E. Aggressiveness in female mice. *Journal of Comparative and Physiological Psychology*, 1952, *45*, 254–257.

Fredericson, E. & E. A. Birnbaum. Competitive fighting between mice with different hereditary backgrounds. *Journal of Genetic Psychology*, 1954, *85*, 271–280.

Fredericson, E., C. D. Fink, & J. R. Parker. Elicitation and inhibition of competitive fighting in food deprived mice. *Journal of Genetic Psychology*, 1955, *86*, 131–141.

Freed, H. *The chemistry and therapy of behavior disorders in children*. Springfield, Ill.: Thomas, 1962.

Freeman, W. Psychosurgery. *American Journal of Psychiatry*, 1965, *121*, 653–655.

Freeman, W. & J. M. Williams. Human sonar: The amygdaloid nucleus in relation to auditory hallucinations. *Journal of Nervous and Mental Disease*, 1952, *116*, 456–462.

Fregly, A. R., M. Bergstedt, & A. Graybiel. Relationships between blood alcohol, positional alcohol nystagmus and postural equilibrium. *Quarterly Journal of Studies on Alcohol*, 1967, *28*, 11–21.

Freud, S. *New introductory lectures on psychoanalysis*. New York: Norton, 1933.

Freud, S. *The complete psychological works of* . . ., Vol. 18, chap. 3. London: Hogarth Press, 1955.

Friedman, R. C., R. M. Richart, & R. L. Vande Wiele (Eds.), *Sex differences in behavior*. New York: Wiley, 1974.

Fuxe, K. Evidence for the existence of monoamine neurones in the central nervous system: IV. The distribution of monoamine terminals in the central nervous system. *Acta Physiologica Scandinavica*, 1965, Suppl. *247*, 64.

Fuxe, K. & L. Gunne. Depletion of the amine stores in brain catecholamine terminals on amygdaloid stimulation. *Acta Physiologica Scandinavica*, 1964, *62*, 493.

Galef, B. G. The effects of amygdalectomy on timidity and aggression in the wild rat. Paper presented at the Eastern Psychological Association, Philadelphia, April, 1969.

Galef, B. G. Aggression and timidity: Responses to novelty in feral Norway rats. *Journal of Comparative and Physiological Psychology*, 1970a, *70*, 370–381.

Galef, B. G. Target novelty elicits and directs shock-associated aggression in wild rats. *Journal of Comparative and Physiological Psychology*, 1970b, *71*, 87–91.

Galef, B. G. Familiarity of target location as a factor in shock-associated aggression of wild rats. *Psychonomic Science*, 1970c, *19*, 299–300.

Gallup, G., Jr. Aggression in rats as a function of frustrative nonreward in a straight alley. *Psychonomic Science*, 1965, *3*, 99–100.

Gandelman, R. Mice: Postpartum aggression elicited by the presence of an intruder. *Hormones and Behavior*, 1972, *3*, 23–28.

Gandelman, R. & P. G. Davis. Spontaneous and testosterone-induced pup killing in female Rockland-Swiss mice: The effect of lactation and the presence of young. *Developmental Psychobiology*, 1973, *6*, 251–257.

Gantt, W. H. In H. G. Wolff (Ed.), *Life Stress and Bodily Disease. Proceedings of the Association for Research in Nervous and Mental Disease*, Vol. 29. Baltimore: Williams & Wilkins, 1950, pp. 1030–1050.

Garattini, S. & E. B. Sigg (Eds.), *Aggressive Behaviour*. New York: Wiley, 1969.

Gardos, G., A. DiMascio, C. Salzman, & R. I. Shader. Differential actions of chlordiazepoxide and oxazepam on hostility. *Archives of General Psychiatry*, 1968, *18*, 757–760.

Gartlan, J. S. Ecology and behaviour of the vervet monkey. Ph.D. thesis, Lolui Island, Lake Victoria, Uganda, Bristol University Library, 1966.

Gastaut, H. Interpretation of the symptoms of "psychomotor" epilepsy in relation to physiologic data on rhinencephalic function. *Epilepsia*, 1954, *3*, 84–88.

Gastaut, H., J. Roger, & N. Lesevre. Différentiation psychologique des épileptiques en fonction des formes electro-cliniques de leur maladie. *Revue de Psychologie Appliquee*, 1953, 3, 237–249.

Gattozzi, A. A. Lithium in the treatment of mood disorders. (U.S. Department of Health, Education, and Welfare.) Washington, D.C., U.S. Government Printing Office, 1970.

Gellhorn, E. *Autonomic imbalance and the hypothalamus*. Minneapolis: University of Minnesota Press, 1957.

Gentry, W. D. Fixed-ratio schedule-induced aggression. *Journal of the Experimental Analysis of Behavior*, 1968, *11*, 813–817.

Gentry, W. D. & R. W. Schaeffer. The effect of FR response requirement on aggressive behavior in rats. *Psychonomic Science*, 1969, *14*, 236–238.

Giacalone, E., M. Tansella, L. Valzelli, & S. Garattini. Brain serotonin metabolism in isolated aggressive mice. *Biochemical Pharmacology*, 1968, *17*, 1315–1327.

Gianutsos, G., M. D. Hynes, S. K. Puri, R. B. Drawbaugh, & H. Lal. Effect of apomorphine and nigrostriatal lesions on aggression and striatal dopamine turnover during morphine withdrawal: Evidence for dopaminergic supersensitivity in protracted abstinence. *Psychopharmacologia*, 1974, *34*, 37–44.

Gibbens, T. C., D. A. Pond, & D. A. Stafford-Clark. Follow-up study of criminal psychopaths. *Journal of Mental Science*, 1959, *105*, 108–115.

Gibbs, E. L. & F. A. Gibbs. Electroencephalographic evidence of thalamic and hypothalamic epilepsy. *Neurology*, 1951, *1*, *136–144*.

Gibbs, F. A. Subjective complaints and behavior disturbances associated with 14/6 per second positive spikes. *Electroencephalography and Clinical Neurophysiology*, 1955, 7, 315–316.

Gibbs, F. A., L. Amador, & C. Rich. Electroencephalographic findings and therapeutic results in surgical treatment of psychomotor epilepsy. In M. Baldwin & P. Bailey (Eds.), *Temporal lobe epilepsy*. Springfield, Ill.: Thomas, 1958, pp. 358–367.

Gibbs, F. A. & E. L. Gibbs. Borderline epilepsy. *Journal of Neuropsychiatry*, 1963a, *4*, 287–295.

Gibbs, F. A. & E. L. Gibbs. Fourteen and six per second positive spikes. *Electroencephalography and Clinical Neurophysiology*, 1963b, *15*, 4.

Gillies, H. Murder in West Scotland. *British Journal of Psychiatry*, 1965, *111*, 1087–1094.

Ginsberg, H. J. & W. G. Braud. A laboratory investigation of aggression behavior in the Mongolian gerbil (*Meriones unguiculatus*). *Psychonomic Science*, 1971, *22*, 54–55.

Ginsburg, B. & W. C. Allee. Some effects of conditioning on social dominance and subordination in inbred strains of mice. *Physiological Zoology*, 1942, *15*, 485–596.

Glaser, E. M. *The physiological basis of habituation*. London: Oxford University Press, 1966.

Glaser, G. H., R. J. Neuman, & R. Schafer. Interictal psychosis in psychomotor-temporal lobe epilepsy: An EEG psychological study. In G. H. Glaser (Ed.), *EEG and behavior.* New York: Basic Books, 1963,,pp. 345–365.

Glass, G. S., G. R. Heninger, M. Lansky, & K. Talan. Psychiatric emergency related to the menstrual cycle. *American Journal of Psychiatry,* 1971, *128,* 705–711.

Glees, P., J. Cole, C. Whitty, & H. Cairns. The effects of lesions in the cincular gyrus and adjacent areas in monkeys. *Journal of Neurology, Neurosurgery and Psychiatry,* 1950, *13,* 178–190.

Gleser, G. C., L. A. Gottschalk, R. Fox, & W. Lippert. Immediate changes in affect with chlordiazepoxide. *Archives of General Psychiatry,* 1965, *13,* 291–295.

Gloor, P. In discussion of a paper by Eibl-Eibesfeldt, I. Ontogenetic and maturational studies on aggressive behavior. In C. D. Clemente & D. B. Lindsley (Eds.), *Aggression and defense: Neural mechanisms and social patterns,* Vol. V, *Brain function.* Los Angeles: University of California Press, 1967a, pp. 57–94.

Gloor, P. Discussion of brain mechanisms related to aggressive behavior by B. Kaada. In C. D. Clemente & D. B. Lindsley (Eds.), *Aggression and defense: Neural mechanisms and social patterns,* Vol. V, *Brain function.* Los Angeles: University of California Press, 1967b, pp. 116–127.

Glusman, M. & L. Roisin. Role of the hypothalamus in the organization of agonistic behavior in the cat. *Transactions of the American Neurological Association,* 1960, 177–179.

Glusman, M., W. Won, E. I. Burdock, & J. Ransohoff. Effects of midbrain lesions on "savage" behavior induced by hypothalamic lesions in the cat. *Transactions of the American Neurological Association,* 1961, 216–218.

Goddard, G. V. Functions of the amygdala. *Psychological Bulletin,* 1964, *62,* 89–109.

Goddard, G. V. Long term alteration following amygdaloid stimulation. In B. Eleftheriou (Ed.), *The neurobiology of the amygdala.* New York: Plenum, 1972, pp. 581–596.

Goethe, F. Beobachtungen uber das absetzen von witterungsmarken beim baummarder. *Deut Jager,* 1938, 13.

Goldensohn, E. S. EEG and ictal and postictal behavior. In G. H. Glazer (Ed.), *EEG and behavior.* New York: Basic Books, 1963, pp. 293–314.

Goldstein, J. H. & R. L. Arms. Effects of observing athletic contests on hostility. *Sociometry,* 1971, *34,* 83–90.

Golla, F. L. & R. S. Hodge. Hormone treatment of the sexual offender. *Lancet,* 1949, *256,* 1006–1007.

Goodman, L. S. & A. Gilman. *The pharmacological basis of therapeutics.* New York: Macmillan, 1965.

Gottlieb, P. M. Neuroallergic reactions to drugs. In F. Speer (Ed.), *Allergy of the nervous system.* Springfield, Ill.: Thomas, 1970a, pp. 134–142.

Gottlieb, P. M. Allergic neuropathies and demyelinative disease. In F. Speer (Ed.), *Allergy of the nervous system.* Springfield, Ill.: Thomas, 1970b, pp. 79–121.

Gottschalk, L. A. Phasic circulating biochemical reflections of transient mental content. In A. J. Mandell & M. P. Mandell (Eds.), *Psychochemical research in man*. New York: Academic Press, 1969, pp. 357–378.

Gottschalk, L. A., G. C. Gleser, & K. J. Springer. Three hostility scales applicable to verbal samples. *Archives of General Psychiatry*, 1963, *9*, 254–279.

Gottschalk, L. A., G. C. Gleser, K. J. Springer, S. Kaplan, J. Shanon, & W. D. Ross. The effects of perphenazine on verbal behavior: A contribution to the problem of measuring the psychologic effect of psychoactive drugs. *Archives of General Psychiatry*, 1960, *2*, 632–639.

Gottschalk, L. A., G. C. Gleser, H. W. Wylie, & S. M. Kaplan. Effects of imipramine on anxiety and hostility levels. *Psychopharmacologia*, 1965, *7*, 303–310.

Goy, R. W. Role of androgens in the establishment and regulation of behavioral sex differences in mammals. *Journal of Animal Science*, 1966, *25*, Supplement, 21–35.

Goy, R. W. Organizing effects of androgen on the behaviour of Rhesus monkeys. In R. P. Michael (Ed.), *Endocrinology and human behavior*. London: Oxford University Press, 1968, pp. 12–31.

Grant, E. C. An analysis of the social behaviour of the male laboratory rat. *Behaviour*, 1963, *21*, 260–281.

Grant, E. C. & J. H. Mackintosh. A comparison of the social postures of some common laboratory rodents. *Behaviour*, 1963, *21*, 246–259.

Grant, E. C., J. H. Mackintosh, & C. J. Lerwill. The effect of a visual stimulus on the agonistic behavior of the golden hamster. *Zeitschrift fur Tierpsychologie*, 1970, *27*, 73–77.

Gray, J. A. Sex differences in emotional behaviour in mammals including man: Endocrine bases. *Acta Psychologica*, 1971, *35*, 29–46.

Graziano, A. M. & J. E. Kean. Programmed relaxation and reciprocal inhibition with psychotic children. *Proceedings of the 75th Annual Convention of the American Psychological Association*, 1967, pp. 253–254.

Green, J. D., C. D. Clemente, & J. de Groot. Rhinencephalic lesions and behavior in cats. *Journal of Comparative Neurology*, 1957, *108*, 505–536.

Green, J. R., R. E. Duisberg, & W. B. McGrath. Focal epilepsy of psychomotor type: A preliminary report of observation on effects of surgical therapy. *Journal of Neurosurgery*, 1951, *8*, 157–172.

Greenbaum, J. V. & L. A. Lurie. Encephalitis as a causative factor in behavior disorders of children. *Journal of the American Medical Association*, 1948, *136*, 923–930.

Greenberg, I. M. & M. Pollack. Clinical correlates of 14 and 6/sec. positive spiking in schizophrenia patients. *Electroencephalography and Clinical Neurophysiology*, 1966, *20*, 197–200.

Greene, R. & K. Dalton. The premenstrual syndrome. *British Medical Journal*, 1953, *1*, 1007–1014.

Greenhill, J. P. & S. C. Freed. The mechanism and treatment of premenstrual distress with ammonium chloride. *Endocrinology*, 1940, *26*, 529–531.

Greenwood, J. Hypoglycemia as a cause of mental symptoms. *Pennsylvania Medical Journal*, 1935, *39*, 12–16.

Grier, W. H. & P. Coggs. *Black rage*. New York: Basic Books, 1968.

Gross, M. D. & W. C. Wilson. Behavior disorders of children with cerebral dysrhythmia. *Archives of General Psychiatry*, 1964, *11*, 610–619.

Grossman, C. Laminar cortical blocking and its relation to episodic aggressive outbursts. *A.M.A. Archives of Neurology and Psychiatry*, 1954, *71*, 576–587.

Grossman, S. P. Chemically induced epileptiform seizures in the cat. *Science*, 1963, *142*, 409–410.

Grossman, S. P. Avoidance behavior and aggression in rats with transections of the lateral connections of the medial or lateral hypothalamus. *Physiology and Behavior*, 1970, 5, 1103–1108.

Grossman, S. P. Aggression, avoidance, and reaction to novel environments in female rats with ventromedial hypothalmic lesions. *Journal of Comparative and Physiological Psychology*, 1972a, *78*, 274–283.

Grossman, S. P. The ventromedial hypothalmus and aggressive behaviors. *Physiology and Behavior*, 1972b, 9, 721–725.

Grossman, S. P. & L. Grossman. Surgical interruption of the anterior or posterior connections of the hypothalamus: Effects on aggressive and avoidance behavior. *Physiology and Behavior*, 1970, 5, 1313–1317.

Guhle, A. M. Gonadal hormones and social behavior in infrahuman vertebrates. In W. C. Young & G. W. Corner (Eds.), *Sex and internal secretions*. Baltimore: Williams & Wilkins, 1961, pp. 1240–1267.

Gunn, J. & G. Fenton. Epilepsy, automatism and crime. *Lancet*, 1971, *1*, 1173–1176.

Gurr, T. R. A causal model of civil strife: A comparative analysis using new indices. *American Political Science Review*, 1968, *42*, 1104–1124.

Gurr, T. R. *Why men rebel*. Princeton, N.J.: Princeton University Press, 1970.

Gustafson, J. E. & G. Winokur. The effect of sexual satiation and female hormone upon aggressivity in an inbred mouse strain. *Journal of Neuropsychiatry*, 1960, *1*, 182–184.

Guttmacher, M. The normal and the sociopathic murderer. In M. Wolfgang (Ed.), *Studies in homicide*. New York: Harper & Row, 1967, pp. 114–135.

Hall, C. S. & S. J. Klein. Individual differences in aggressiveness in rats. *Journal of Comparative and Physiological Psychology*, 1942, *33*, 371–383.

Hall, E. T. *The hidden dimension*. Garden City, N.Y.: Doubleday, 1966.

Hall, K. R. L. & I. DeVore. Baboon social behavior. In I. DeVore (Ed.), *Primate behavior*. New York: Holt, Rinehart and Winston, 1965, pp. 53–110.

Hamburg, D. A. Psychobiological studies of aggressive behavior. *Nature*, 1971a, *230*, 19–23.

Hamburg, D. A. Aggressive behavior of chimpanzees and baboon in natural habitats. *Journal of Psychiatric Research*, 1971b, *8*, 385–398.

Hamburg, D. A. Recent research on hormonal factors relevant to human aggressiveness. *International Social Science Journal*, 1971c, *23*, 36–47.

Hamburg, D. A. & D. T. Lunde. Sex hormones in the development of sex differences in human behavior. In E. Maccoby (Ed.), *The development of sex differences in human behavior*. Palo Alto, Calif.: Stanford University Press, 1966, pp. 1–24.

Hamburg, D. A., R. H. Moos, & I. D. Yalom. Studies of distress in the menstrual cycle and postpartum period. In R. P. Michael (Ed.), *Endocrinology and human behaviour*. London: Oxford University Press, 1968, 1–349.

Hamby, W. & D. D. Cahoon. The effect of water deprivation upon shock elicited aggression in the white rat. *Psychonomic Science,* 1971, *23,* 50–53.

Hamilton, J. S. *Wildlife in South Africa.* London: Cassell, 1947.

Hampton, W. H. Observed psychiatric reactions following use of amphetamine and amphetamine-like substance. *Bulletin of the New York Academy of Medicine,* 1961, *37,* 167–175.

Harding, C. F. & A. Leshner. The effects of adrenalectomy on the aggressiveness of differently housed mice. *Physiology and Behavior,* 1972, *8,* 437–440.

Harding, R. S. Predation by a troupe of olive baboons. *American Journal of Physical Anthropology,* 1973, 587–591.

Harlow, H. F. The heterosexual affectional system in monkeys. *American Psychologist,* 1962, *17,* 1–9.

Harlow, H. F. Sexual behavior in the rhesus monkey. In F. A. Beach (Eds.), *Sex and behavior.* New York: Wiley, 1965a, pp. 234–266.

Harlow, H. F. Total social isolation: Effects of Macaque monkey behavior, *Science,* 1965b, *148,* 666.

Harlow, H. F., R. O. Dodsworth, & M. K. Harlow. Total isolation in monkeys. *Proceedings of the National Academy of Sciences,* 1965, *54,* 90–96.

Harlow, H. F. & M. K. Harlow. Social deprivation in monkeys. *Scientific American,* 1962, *207,* 137–146.

Harlow, H. F. & M. K. Harlow. The young monkeys. *Psychology Today,* 1967, 40–47.

Harlow, H. F., W. D. Joslyn, M. G. Senko, & A. Dopp. Behavioral aspects of reproduction in primates. *Journal of Animal Sciences,* 1966, *25,* 49–65.

Harrell, W. A. Effects of extinction on magnitude of aggression in humans. *Psychonomic Science,* 1972, *29,* 213–215.

Harris, S. Hyperinsulinism and dysinsulinism. *Journal of the American Medical Association,* 1924, *83,* 729–733.

Harris, S., Jr. Hyperinsulinism. *Southern Medical Journal,* 1944, *37,* 714–717.

Hatch, A., G. S. Wiberg, T. Balzas, & H. C. Grice. Long-term isolation in rats. *Science,* 1963, *142,* 507.

Hatch, J. Collective territories in Galapagos mockingbirds with notes on other behavior. *Wilson Bulletin,* 1966, *78,* 198–207.

Haward, L. R. Differential modifications of verbal aggression by psychotropic drugs. In S. Garattini & E. B. Sigg (Eds.), *Aggressive behaviour.* New York: Wiley, 1969, pp. 317–321.

Hawke, C. C. Castration and sex crimes. *American Journal of Mental Deficiency,* 1950, *55,* 220–226.

Hearn, M. T. & D. R. Evans. Anger and reciprocal inhibition therapy. *Psychological Reports,* 1972, *30,* 943–948.

Heath, R. G., et al. *Studies in schizophrenia,* Cambridge, Mass.: Harvard University Press, 1954, pp. 83–84.

Heath, R. G. Correlations between levels of psychological awareness and physiological activity in the central nervous system. *Psychosomatic Medicine,* 1955, *17,* 383–395.

Heath, R. G. Brain centers and control of behavior—man. In J. H. Nodine &

J. H. Moyer (Eds.), *Psychosomatic medicine: First Hahnemann Symposium.* Philadelphia: Lea & Febiger, 1962, pp. 228–240.

Heath, R. G. Electrical self-stimulation of the brain in man. *American Journal of Psychiatry,* 1963, *120,* 571–577.

Heath, R. G. Developments toward new physiologic treatments in psychiatry. *Journal of Neuropsychiatry,* 1964a, *5,* 318–331.

Heath, R. G. Pleasure response of human subjects to direct stimulation of the brain: Physiologic and psychodynamic considerations. In R. G. Heath (Ed.), *The role of pleasure in behavior.* New York: Harper & Row, 1964b, pp. 219–244.

Heath, R. G. & R. Guerrero-Figueroa. Psychotic behavior with evoked septal dysrhythmia: Effects of intracerebral acetylcholine and gamma aminobutric acid. *American Journal of Psychiatry,* 1965, *121,* 1080–1086.

Heath, R. G. & W. A. Mickle. Evaluation of seven years experience with depth electrode studies in human patients. In E. R. Ramey & P. S. O'Doherty (Eds.), *Electrical studies on the unanesthetized brain.* New York: Harper & Row, 1960, pp. 214–247.

Heath, R. G., R. R. Monroe, & W. A. Mickle. Stimulation of the amygdaloid nucleus in a schizophrenic patient. *American Journal of Psychiatry,* 1955, *111,* 862–863.

Hediger, H. Saugetierterritorien und ihre Markierung. *Bijdr tot de Dierkde,* 1949, *28,* 172–184.

Hediger, H. *Wild animals in captivity: An outline of the biology of zoological gardens.* London: Butterworth's Scientific, 1950.

Hediger, H. P. The evolution of territorial behavior. In S. L. Washburn (Ed.), *Social life of early man.* Chicago: Aldine, 1961, pp. 34–57.

Heimburger, R. F., C. C. Whitlock, & J. E. Kalsbeck. Stereotaxic amygdalotomy for epilepsy with aggressive behavior. *Journal of the American Medical Association,* 1966, *198,* 165–169.

Heimstra, N. W. A further investigation of the development of mouse killing in rats. *Psychonomic Science,* 1965, *2,* 170–180.

Heimstra, N. W. & G. Newton. Effects of prior food competition on the rat's killing response to the white mouse. *Behaviour,* 1961, *17,* 95–102.

Heise, G. A. & E. Boff. Taming action of chlordiazepoxide. *Federal Proceedings,* 1961, *20,* 393.

Heller, H. C. Altitudinal zonation of chipmunks (*Eutamias*): Interspecific aggression. *Ecology,* 1971, *52,* 312–319.

Henry, C. E. Positive spike discharges in the EEG and behavior. In G. H. Glaser (Ed.), *EEG and behavior.* New York: Basic Books, 1963, pp. 315–344.

Herreca, M. A. El visteo, *Revista Del Instituto de Investigaciones y Docencia Criminologicas,* 1965–1966, *9,* 85–92.

Herrell, J. M. A use of systematic desensitization to eliminate inappropriate anger. *Proceedings of the Annual Convention of the American Psychological Association,* 1971, *6,* 431–432.

Herrero, S. Human injury inflicted by grizzly bears. *Science,* 1970, *170,* 593–598.

Hersher, L., J. B. Richmond, & A. U. Moore. Maternal behavior in sheep and goats. In H. L. Rheingold (Ed.), *Maternal behavior in mammals.* New York: Wiley, 1963, pp. 203–232.

Hess, W. R. The biology of mind. Chicago: University of Chicago Press, 1964.

Hetherington, E. M. & N. P. Wray. Aggression, need for social approval and humor preferences. *Journal of Abnormal and Social Psychology,* 1964, *68,* 685–689.

Hetherington, R. F., P. Haden, & W. J. Craig. Neurosurgery in affective disorder: Criteria for selection of patients. In E. Hitchcock, L. Laitinen, & K. Vaernet (Eds.), *Psychosurgery.* Springfield, Ill.: Thomas, 1972, pp. 332–345.

Higgins, T. J., S. E. Glickman, & R. L. Isaacson. Effects of hippocampal lesions on some selected behavior patterns in the Mongolian gerbil. Paper presented at the meeting of the Psychonomic Society, Chicago, November, 1967.

Hill, D. Cerebral dysrhythmia: Its significance in aggressive behaviour. *Proceedings of the Royal Society of Medicine,* 1944, *37,* 317–328.

Hill, D. EEG in episodic psychiatric and psychopathic behavior. *Electroencephalography and Clinical Neurophysiology,* 1952, *4,* 419–442.

Hill, D., D. A. Pond, W. Mitchell, & M. A. Falconer. Personality changes following temporal lobectomy for epilepsy. *Journal of Mental Science,* 1957, *103,* 18–27.

Hill, D. & W. A. Sargant. A case of matricide. *Lancet,* 1943, *1,* 526–527.

Hill, D. & D. Watterson. Electro-encephalographic studies of psychopathic personalities. *Journal of Neurology and Psychiatry,* London, 1942, *5,* 47–65.

Himmelhock, J., J. Pincus, G. Tucker, & T. Detre. Sub-acute encephalitis: Behavioral and neurological aspects. *British Journal of Psychiatry,* 1970, *116,* 531–538.

Hinde, R. A. The biological significance of the territories of birds. *Ibis,* 1956, *98,* 340–369.

Hinde, R. A. *Animal behaviour.* New York: McGraw-Hill, 1966.

Hinde, R. A. The nature of aggression. *New Society,* 1967, *9,* 302–304.

Hirose, S. Mentally abnormal offenders and psychosurgery. *Acta Criminologiae et Medici nae Legalis Japonica,* 1968, *34,* 186–195.

Hirose, S. The case selection of mental disorder for orbitoventromedial undercutting. In E. Hitchcock, L. Laitinen, & K. Vaernet (Eds.), *Psychosurgery.* Springfield, Ill.: Thomas, 1972, pp. 291–303.

Hitchcock, E., G. W. Ashcroft, V. M. Cairns, & L. G. Murray. Preoperative and postoperative assessment and management of psychosurgical patients. In E. Hitchcock, L. Laitinen, & K. Vaernet (Eds.), *Psychosurgery.* Springfield, Ill.: Thomas, 1972, pp. 164–176.

Hoefnagel, D. Seminars on the Lesch-Nyhan Syndrome: Summary. *Federation Proceedings,* 1968, *27,* 1042–1046.

Hoffmeister, Von F., H. Kreiskott, & W. Wirth. Untersuchungen mit zentral wirksamen anticholinerica. *Arzneimittel-Forschung,* 1964, *14,* 482–486.

Hohmann, G. W. Some effects of spinal cord lesions on experienced emotional feelings. *Psychophysiology,* 1966, *3,* 143–156.

Hokanson, J. E. Psychophysiological evaluation of the catharsis hypothesis. In E. I. Megargee & J. E. Hokanson (Eds.), *The dynamics of aggression.* New York: Harper & Row, 1970, pp. 74–86.

Holloway, R. L. Human aggression: The need for a species specific framework. In M. Fried, M. Harris, & R. Murphy (Eds.), *War*. New York: Natural History Press, 1968, pp. 29–48.

Hoobler, B. R. Some early symptoms suggesting protein sensitization in infancy. *American Journal of Diseases of Children*, 1916, *12*, 129–135.

Horovitz, Z. P. Psychoactive drugs and the limbic system of the brain. *Psychosomatics*, 1965, *6*, 281–286.

Horovitz, Z. P. & R. Leaf. The effects of direct injections of psychotropic drugs into the amygdala of rats and its relationship to antidepressant site of action. In H. Brill, J. O. Cole, P. Deniker, H. Hippius, & P. B. Bradley (Eds.), *Neuropsycholopharmacology. Proceedings of 5th International Congress of the Collegium Internationale Neuropsychopharmacologicum, ICS, 129,* Excerpta Medica, Amsterdam, 1967, 1042.

Horovitz, A. P., J. J. Piala, J. P. High, J. C. Burke, & R. C. Leaf. Effects of drugs on the mouse-killing (muricide) test and its relationship to amygdaloid function. *International Journal of Neuropharmacology*, 1966, *5*, 405–411.

Horovitz, Z. P., P. W. Ragozzino, & R. C. Leaf. Selective block of rat mouse-killing by antidepressants. *Life Sciences*, 1965, *4*, 1909–1912.

Hughes, J. R. A review of the positive spike phenomenon. In W. P. Wilson (Ed.), *Applications of electroencephalography in psychiatry*, Durham, N.C.: Duke University Press, 1965, pp. 54–101.

Hunsperger, R. W. Affektreaktionen auf elektrische Reizung in Hirnstramm der katze. *Helvetica Physiologica et Pharmacologica Acta, Basel*, 1956, *14*, 70.

Hunsperger, R. W. & V. M. Bucher. Affective behaviour produced by electrical stimulation in the forebrain and brain stem of the cat. *Progress in Brain Research*, 1967, *27*, 125–127.

Huston, J. P., M. J. DeSisto, & E. P. Meyer. Frog-killing by rats as influenced by territorial variables. Paper presented at the Eastern Psychological Association Meetings, Philadelphia, April, 1969.

Hutchinson, R. R., N. H. Azrin, & G. M. Hunt. Attack produced by intermittent reinforcement of a concurrent operant response. *Journal of the Experimental Analysis of Behavior*, 1968, *11*, 489–495.

Hutchinson, R. R. & J. W. Renfrew. Stalking attack and eating behavior elicited from the same sites in the hypothalamus. *Journal of Comparative and Physiological Psychology*, 1966, *61*, 360–367.

Hutchinson, R. R., R. E. Ulrich, & N. H. Azrin. Effects of age and related factors on the pain aggression reaction. *Journal of Comparative and Physiological Psychology*, 1965, *59*, 365–369.

Hymowitz, N. Schedule-induced polydipsia and aggression in rats. *Psychonomic Science*, 1971, *23*, 226–228.

Igic, R., P. Stern, & E. Basagic. Changes in motivational behavior after application of cholinesterase inhibitors in the septal and amygdala region. *Neuropharmacology*, 1970, *8*, 73–75.

Ilfeld, F. W. Overview of the causes and prevention of violence. *Archives of General Psychiatry*, 1969, *20*, 675–689.

Ingram, W. R. The hypothalamus: A review of the experimental data. *Psychosomatic Medicine*, 1939, *1*, 48–91.

Inselman-Temkin, B. R. & J. P. Flynn. Sex-dependent effects of gonadal and gonadotropic hormones on centrally-elicited attack in cats. *Brain Research*, 1973, *60*, 393–410.

Ivey, M. E. & J. M. Bardwick. Patterns of affective fluctuation in the menstrual cycle. *Psychosomatic Medicine*, 1968, *30*, 336–345.

Jacobs, T. J. & E. Charles. Correlation of psychiatric symptomatology and the menstrual cycle in an outpatient population. *American Journal of Psychiatry*, 1970, *126*, 148–152.

Jacobs, B. & D. J. McGinty. Participation of the amygdala in complex stimulus recognition and behavioral inhibition. Evidence from unit studies. *Brain Research*, 1972, *36*, 431–436.

Jacobsen, E. The clinical effects of drugs and their influence on animal behavior. *Revue de Psychologie Appliquée*, 1961, *11*, 421–532.

Janowsky, E. S., R. Gorney, & A. J. Mandell. The menstrual cycle: Psychiatric and ovarian-adrenocortical hórmone correlates: Case study and literature review. *Archives of General Psychiatry*, 1967, *17*, 459–469.

Jarrard, L. Personal communication, 1970.

Jasper, H. H. & T. Rasmussen. Studies of clinical and electrical responses to deep temporal stimulation in man with some consideration of functional anatomy. *Association for Research in Nervous and Mental Diseases Proceedings*, 1958, *36*, 316–334.

Jay, P. Mother-infant relations in langurs. In H. L. Rheingold (Ed.), *Maternal Behavior in Mammals*. New York: Wiley, 1963, pp. 282–304.

Jay, P. The common langur of north India. In I. DeVore (Ed.), *Primate behavior*. New York: Holt, Rinehart and Winston, 1965, pp. 197–249.

Jenkins, R. L. & B. L. Pacella. Electroencephalographic studies of delinquent boys. *American Journal of Orthopsychiatry*, 1943, *13*, 107–120.

Jewell, P. A. & C. Loizos (Eds.), *Play, exploration and territory in mammals*. London: Academic Press, 1966.

Jirgl, M., J. Drtil, & J. Cepelak. The influence of propericiazine on the behavior of difficult delinquents. *Activitas Nervosa Superior*, 1970, *12*, 134–135.

Johnson, R. N. *Aggression in man and animals*. Philadelphia: Saunders, 1972.

Johnson, R. N., M. J. DeSisto, & A. B. Koenig. Social and developmental experience and interspecific aggression in rats. Paper presented at the American Psychological Association Meeting, September, 1970a, Miami Beach, Fla.

Johnson, R. N., M. J. DeSisto, & A. Koenig. Social experience and interspecies aggression in rats. *Proceedings of the 78th Annual Convention of the American Psychological Association*, 1970b, 231–232.

Johnson, R. N., M. J. DeSisto, & A. B. Koenig. Social and developmental experience and interspecific aggression in rats. *Journal of Comparative and Physiological Psychology*, 1972, *79*, 237–242.

Jonas, A. D. *Ictal and subictal neurosis: Diagnosis and treatment*. Springfield, Ill.: Thomas, 1965.

Jones, M. S. Hypoglycemia in the neuroses. *British Medical Journal*, 1935, 945–946.

Jones, N. & G. Blurton. An ethological study of some aspects of social behaviour of children in neursery school. In D. Morris (Ed), *Primate ethology*. London: Doubleday, 1969, pp. 437–463.

Jones, R. B. & N. W. Nowell. The effect of the familiar visual and olfactory cues on the aggressive behaviour of mice. *Physiology and Behavior, 1973, 10,* 221–223.

Kaada, B. R. Brain mechanisms related to aggressive behavior. In C. D. Clemente & D. B. Lindsley (Eds.), *Aggression and defense: Neural mechanisms and social patterns,* Vol. V, *Brain Function.* Los Angeles: University of California Press, 1967, pp. 95–134.

Kaada, B. R. Stimulation and regional ablation of the amygdaloid complex with reference to functional representations. In B. E. Eleftheriou (Ed.), *The neurobiology of the amygdala.* New York: Plenum, 1972, pp. 205–282.

Kaada, B. R., J. Jansen, & P. Andersen. Stimulation of the hippocampus and medial cortical areas in unanesthetized cats. *Neurology, 1953, 3,* 843–857.

Kaelber, W. W., C. L. Mitchell, & J. S. Way. Some sensory influences on savage (affective) behavior in cats. *American Journal of Physiology, 1965, 209,* 866–870.

Kahn, I. S. Pollen toxemia in children. *Journal of the American Medical Association, 1927, 88,* 241–242.

Kahn, M. W. The effect of severe defeat at various age levels on the aggressive behavior of mice. *Journal of Genetic Psychology, 1951, 79,* 117–130.

Kahn, M. W. Infantile experience and mature aggressive behavior of mice: Some maternal influences. *Journal of Genetic Psychology, 1954, 84,* 65–75.

Kalant, O. J. *The amphetamines: Toxicity and addiction.* Springfield, Ill.: Thomas, 1966.

Kales, A., F. S. Hoedemaker, A. Jacobson, & E. L. Lochtenstein, Dream deprivation: An experimental reappraisal. *Nature, 1964, 204,* 1337–1338.

Kalin, R., D. C. McClelland, & M. Kahn. The effects of male social drinking on fantasy. *Journal of Personality and Social Psychology, 1965, 1,* 441–452.

Kalina, R. K. Use of diazepam in the violent psychotic patient: A preliminary report. *Colorado GP, 1962, 4,* 11–14.

Kalina, R. K. Diazepam: Its role in a prison setting. *Diseases of the Nervous System, 1964, 25,* 101–107.

Kamm, I., & A. Mandel. Thioridazine in the treatment of behavior disorders in epileptics. *Diseases of the Nervous System, 1967, 28,* 46–48.

Karli, P. The Norway rat's killing response to the white mouse. *Behavior, 1956, 10,* 81–103.

Karli, P. Hormones stéroides et comportement d'aggression interspecifique rat-souris. *Journal de Physiologie et de Pathologie Generale, 1958, 50,* 346–357.

Karli, P. Septum, hypothalamus posterieur et agressivite interspecifique rat-souris. *Journal de Physiologie, 1960, 52,* 135–136.

Karli, P. Rôle des afferences sensorielles dans le déclenchement du comportement d'aggression interspecifique rat-souris. *Comptes Rendus des Séances de la Société de Biologie, 1961, 155,* 644.

Karli, P. & M. Vergnes. Rôle du rhinencephale dans le controle du comcortement d'aggression interspecifique rat-souris. *Journal de Physiologie, 1963, 55,* 272–273.

Karli, P. & M. Vergnes. Nouvelles données sur les bases neurophysiologiques du comportement d'aggression interspecifique rat-souris. *Journal de Physiologie*, 1964a, *56*, 384.

Karli, P. & M. Vergnes. Dissociation experimentale du comportement d'aggression interspecifique rat-souris et du comportement alimentaire. *Comptes Rendus des Séances de la Société de Biologie*, 1964b, *158*, 650–653.

Karli, P. & M. Vergnes. Role des differentes composantes du complexe nucleaire amygdalien dans la facilitation de l'aggressivité interspecifique du rat. *Comptes Rendus des Séances de la Société de Biologie*, 1965, *159*, 754.

Karli, P., M. Vergnes, & F. Didiergeorges. Rat-mouse interspecific aggressive behavior and its manipulation by brain ablation and by brain stimulation. In S. Garattini & E. B. Sigg (Eds.), *Aggressive behaviour*. New York: Wiley, 1969, pp. 47–55.

Karli, P., M. Vergnes, F. Eclancher, P. Schmitt, & J. P. Chaurand. Role of the amygdala in the control of "Mouse-killing" behavior in the rat. In B. E. Eleftheriou (Ed.), *The neurobiology of the amygdala*, New York: Plenum, 1972, pp. 553–580.

Kasanin, J. Personality changes in children following cerebral trauma. *Journal of Nervous and Mental Diseases*, 1929, *69*, 385–406.

Kastl, A. J. Changes in ego functioning under alcohol. *Quarterly Journal of Studies on Alcohol*, 1969, *30*, 371–383.

Kaufman, H. *Aggression and altruism*. New York: Holt, Rinehart and Winston, 1970.

Keating, L. E. Epilepsy and behavior disorder in school children. *Journal of Mental Science*, 1961, *107*, 161–180.

Keller, J. F. & W. N. Schoenfeld. *Principles of behavior*. New York: Appleton-Century-Crofts, 1950.

Kelley, W. N. Hypozanthine-guanine phosphoribosyltransferase deficiency in the Lesch-Nyhan syndrome and gout. *Federation Proceedings*, 1968, *27*, 1047–1052.

Kelly, J. F. & D. F. Hake. An extinction-induced increase in an aggressive response with humans. *Journal of the Experimental Analysis of Behavior*, 1970, *14*, 153–164.

Kennard, M. A. The cingulate gyrus in relation to consciousness. *Journal of Nervous and Mental Disease*, 1955a, *121*, 34–39.

Kennard, M. A. Effect of bilateral ablation of cingulate area on behaviour of cats. *Journal of Neurophysiology*, 1955b, *18*, 159–169.

Kennedy, F. Cerebral symptoms induced by angioneurotic edema. *Archives of Neurology and Psychiatry*, 1926, *15*, 28–33.

Kennedy, F. Allergic manifestations in the nervous system. *New York Journal of Medicine*, 1936, *36*, 469–474.

Kennedy, F. Allergy and its effect on the central nervous system. *Archives of Neurology and Psychiatry*, 1938, *39*, 1361–1366.

Kepler, E. J. & F. P. Moersch. The psychiatric manifestations of hypoglycemia. *American Journal of Psychiatry*, 1937, *14*, 89–110.

Kerner, O. *Report of the National Advisory Commission on civil disorders*, New York: Bantam Books, 1968.

Kesner, R. P. & G. Keiser. Effects of midbrain reticular lesions upon aggression in the rat. *Journal of Comparative and Physiological Psychology*, 1973, *84*, 194–206.

Kessler, S. & R. H. Moos. The XYY karyotype and criminality: A review. *Journal of Psychiatric Research*, 1970, 7, 153–170.

Keys, A., J. Brozek, A. Henschel, O. Michelsen, & H. L. Taylor. *The Biology of human starvation*. Minneapolis: University of Minnesota Press, 1950.

Killeffer, F. A. & E. Stern. Chronic effects of hypothalamic injury. *Archives of Neurology*, 1970, *22*, 419–429.

Kiloh, L. G., R. S. Gye, R. G. Rosenworth, D. S. Bell, & R. T. White. Stereotactic amygdaloidotomy for aggressive behaviors. *Journal of Neurology, Neurosurgery and Psychiatry*, 1974, *37*, 437–444.

Kimbrell, G. McA. Relationship of the upright agonistic posture in the foot shock situation to dominance-submission in male C57BL/6 mice. *Psychonomic Science*, 1969, *16*, 167–168.

King, F. A. Effects of septal and amygdaloid lesions on emotional behavior and conditioned avoidance responses in the rat. *Journal of Nervous and Mental Disease*, 1958, *126*, 57–63.

King, F. A. & P. M. Meyer. Effects of amygdaloid lesions upon septal hyperemotionality in the rat. *Science*, 1958, *128*, 655–656.

King, H. E. Psychological effects of excitation in the limbic system. In D. E. Sheer (Ed.), *Electrical stimulation of the brain*. Austin: University of Texas Press, 1961, pp. 477–486.

King, J. A. Social behavior, social organization, and population dynamics in a black-tailed prairiedog town in the Black Hills of South Dakota. Contributions to Laboratory of Vertebrate Biology, University of Michigan, 1955.

King, J. A. Relationships between early social experience and adult aggressive behavior in inbred mice. *Journal of Genetic Psychology*, 1957, *90*, 151–166.

King, J. A. Maternal behavior in *Peromyscus*. In H. L. Rheingold (Ed.), *Maternal behavior in animals*. New York: Wiley, 1963, pp. 58–93.

King, J. A. & N. L. Gurney. Effect of early social experience on adult aggressive behavior in C57BL/10 mice. *Journal of Comparative and Physiological Psychology*, 1954, *47*, 326–330.

King, M. B. & B. G. Hoebel. Killing elicited by brain stimulation in rat. *Communications in Behavioral Biology*, 1968, *2*, 173–177.

Kislak, J. W. & F. A. Beach. Inhibition of aggressiveness by ovarian hormones. *Endocrinology*, 1955, *56*, 684–692.

Kittler, F. J. The effect of allergy on children with minimal brain damage. In E. Speer (Ed.), *Allergy of the nervous system*. Springfield, Ill.: Thomas, 1970, pp. 122–133.

Kleiman, D. Scent marking in the Canidae. In P. A. Jewell & C. Loizos (Eds.), *Play, exploration and territory in mammals*. London: Academic Press, 1966, pp. 167–177.

Kletschka, H. D. Violent behavior associated with brain tumor. *Minnesota Medicine*, 1966, *49*, 1853–1855.

Kline, N. Drugs are the greatest practical advance in the history of psychiatry. *New Medical Materia*, 1962, 49.

Kling, A. Effects of amygdalectomy and testosterone on sexual behavior of male juvenile macaques. *Journal of Comparative and Physiological Psychology*, 1968, *65*, 466–471.

Kling, A. Effects of amygdalectomy on social-affective behavior in nonhuman primates. In B. E. Eleftheriou (Ed.), *The neurobiology of amygdala*. New York: Plenum, 1972, pp. 511–536.

Kling, A. & R. Cornell. Amygdalectomy and social behavior in the caged stump-tailed macaque (*M. speciosa*). *Folia Primatologica*, 1971, *14*, 190–208.

Kling, A., D. Dicks, & E. M. Gurowitz. Amygdalectomy and social behavior in a caged-group of vervets (*C. aethiops*). *Proceedings of the 2nd International Congress of Primateology*, Atlanta, Ga., 1968, *1*, 232–241.

Kling, A. & P. J. Hutt. Effect of hypothalamic lesions on the amygdala syndrome in the cat. *AMA Archives of Neurology and Psychiatry*, 1958, *79*, 511–517.

Kling, A., J. Lancaster, & J. Benitone. Amygdalectomy in the free-ranging vervet. *Journal of Psychiatric Research*, 1970, *7*, 191–199.

Klopfer, P. M. *Habitats and territories: The study of the use of space by animals*. New York: Basic Books, 1969.

Kluver, H. & P. C. Bucy. "Psychic blindness" and other symptoms following bilateral temporal lobectomy in Rhesus monkeys. *American Journal of Physiology*, 1937, *119*, 352–353.

Kluver, H. & P. C. Bucy. An analysis of certain effects of bilateral temporal lobectomy in rhesus monkey with special reference to "psychic blindness." *Journal of Psychology*, 1938, *5*, 33–54.

Kluver, H. & P. C. Bucy. Preliminary analysis of functions of the temporal lobes in monkeys. *Archives of Neurology and Psychiatry*, 1939, *42*, 979–1000.

Knott, J. R. Electroencephalograms in psychopathic personality and murders. In W. Wilson (Ed.), *Applications of electroencephalography in psychiatry*, Durham, N.C.: Duke University Press, 1965, pp. 19–29.

Knott, J. R. & J. S. Gottlieb. Electroencephalogram in psychopathic personality. *Psychosomatic Medicine*, 1943, *5*, 139–142.

Knutson, J. F. Aggression during the time-out and fixed-ratio components of multiple schedules of reinforcement. Doctoral dissertation, Washington State University, Ann Arbor, Mich., University Microfilm, 1969.

Knutson, J. F. Aggression during the fixed-ratio and extinction components of a multiple schedule of reinforcement. *Journal of the Experimental Analysis of Behavior*, 1970, *13*, 221–231.

Knutson, J. F. (Ed.), *The Control of Aggression*. Chicago: Aldine, 1973.

Knutson, J. F. & M. T. Hynan. Influence of upright posture on shock elicited aggression in rats. *Journal of Comparative and Physiological Psychology*, 1972, *81*, 927–306.

Kochakian, C. D. The rate of absorption and effects of testosterone propionate pellets on mice. *Endocrinology*, 1941, *28*, 478–484.

Kohler, W. *The mentality of apes*. London: Routledge & Kegan Paul, 1925.

Kopp, M. E. Surgical treatment as sex crime preventive measure. *Journal of Criminal Law and Criminology*, 1938, *28*, 692–706.

Korn, J. H. & K. E. Moyer. Behavioral effects of isolation in the rat: The role of sex and time of isolation. *Journal of Genetic Psychology*, 1968, *113*, 263–273.

Kortlandt, A. & Kooji, M. Protohominid behavior in primates. *Symposium of the Zoological Society of London*, 1963, *10*, 61–88.

Kosman, M. E. & K. R. Unna. Effects of chronic administration of the amphetamines and other stimulants on behavior. *Clinical Pharmacology and Therapeutics*, 1968, *9*, 240–254.

Kostowski, W., W. Rewerski, & T. Piechocki. Effects of some steroids on aggressive behaviour in mice and rats. *Neuroendocrinology*, 1970, *6*, 311–318.

Krafft-Ebing, R. *Psychopathic Sexualis*. Philadelphia: Davis, 1892.

Kramer, J. C., V. S. Fischman, & D. C. Littlefield. Amphetamine abuse. *Journal of the American Medical Association*, 1967, *201*, 305–309.

Kreiskott, H. Some comments on the killing response behaviour of the rat. In S. Garattini & E. B. Sigg (Eds.), *Aggressive .behaviour*. New York: Wiley, 1969, pp. 56–58.

Kreisskott, W. Einflus vonPharmaka auf das Beutefanguerhalten der Ratte. *Archives fur experimentalishe Pathologiche and Pharmaka*, 1963, *245*, 255–256.

Kreuz, L. E. & R. M. Rose. Assessment of aggressive behavior and plasma testosterone in a young criminal population. *Psychosomatic Medicine*, 1972, *34*, 321–332.

Kreuz, L. E., R. M. Rose, & J. R. Jennings. Suppression of plasma testosterone levels and psychological stress. *Archives of General Psychiatry*, 1972, *26*, 479–482.

Kreveld, D. A. A selective review of dominance-subordination relations in animals. *Genetic Psychology Monographs*, 1970, *81*, 143–173.

Krikstone, B. J. & R. A. Levitt. Interactions between water deprivation and chemical brain stimulation. *Journal of Comparative and Physiological Psychology*, 1970, *71*, 334–340.

Kruuk, H. Surplus killing by carnivores. *Journal of Zoology*, London, 1972, *166*, 233–244.

Kuehn, J. L. & J. Burton. Management of the college student with homicidal impulses. *American Journal of Psychiatry*, 1969, *125*, 1594–1599.

Kulkarni, A. S. Satiation of instinctive mouse-killing by rats. *Psychological Record*, 1968a, *18*, 385–388.

Kulkarni, A. S. Muricidal block produced by 5-hydroxytryptophan and various drugs. *Life Sciences*, 1968b, *7*, 125–128.

Kummer, H. *Social organization of Hamadryas baboons: A field study*. Chicago: University of Chicago Press, 1968.

Kuo, Z. Y. The genesis of the cat's response toward the rat. *Journal of Comparative Psychology*, 1930, *11*, 1–35.

Kuo, Z. Y. *The dynamics of behavior development: An epigenetic view*. New York: Random House, 1967.

Lack, D. *The life of the robin*. London: Cambridge University Press, 1943.

Ladosky, W. & L. C. J. Gaziri. Brain serotonin and sexual differentiation of the nervous system. *Neuroendocrinology*, 1969, *6*, 168–174.

Lagerspetz, K. Genetic and social causes of aggressive behavior in mice. *Scandinavian Journal of Psychology*, 1961, 2, 167–173.

Lagerspetz, K. Studies on the aggressive behavior of mice. *Annales Academiae Scientiarum Fennicae*, 1964, Series B, *131*, 1–131.

Lagerspetz, K. & R. Nurmi. An experiment on the frustration-aggression hypothesis. *Reports from the Institute of Psychology, University Turku*, 1964, No. 10, 1–8.

Lagerspetz, K. & S. Talo. Maturation of aggressive behaviour in young mice. *Reports from the Institute of Psychology, University of Turku*, 1967, No. 28, 1–9.

Laschet, U. Antiandrogentherapie der pathologisch gesteigerten und abartigen sexualitat des mannes. *Sonderdruck aus Klinische Wochenschrift*, 1967, *45*, 324–325.

Laschet, U. Antiandrogen in the treatment of sex offenders: Mode of action and therapeutic outcome. In J. Zubin & J. Money (Eds.), *Contemporary sexual behavior: Critical issues in the 1970's*, Baltimore: Johns Hopkins Press, 1973, 311–319.

Laschet, U., L. Laschet, H. R. Fetzner, H. U. Glaesel, G. Mall, & M. Naab. Results in the treatment of hyper- or abnormal sexuality of men with anti-androgens. *Acta Endocrinologica*, 1967, Suppl. 119, *54*.

Laties, V. G. Modification of affect, social behavior and performance by sleep deprivation and drugs. *Journal of Psychiatric Research*, 1961, *1*, 12–25.

Leaf, R. C., L. Lerner, & Z. P. Horovitz. The role of the amygdala in the pharmacological and endocrinological manipulation of aggression. In S. Garattini & E. B. Sigg (Eds.), *Aggressive behaviour*. New York: Wiley, 1969, pp. 132–142.

LeBeau, J. The cingular and precingular areas in psychosurgery (agitated behaviour, obsessive compulsive states, epilepsy). *Acta Psychiatrica et Neurologica, Kjobenhavn*, 1952, 27, 305–316.

LeBoeuf, B. J. Copulatory and aggressive behavior in the prepuberally castrated dog. *Hormones and Behavior*, 1970, *1*, 127–136.

Ledesma, J. A. & J. L. Paniagua. Circumvolution del cingulo y agresividad. *Actas Luso-Espanolas de Neurologia y Psiquiatria*, 1969, 28, 289–298.

Lee, C. T. Reactions of mouse fighters to male and female mice, intact or deodorized. *American Zoologist*, 1970, *10*, 56.

Lee, C. T. & S. C. Brake. Reactions of male fighters to male and female mice, untreated or deodorized. *Psychonomic Science*, 1971, *24*, 209–211.

Lee, C. T. & S. C. Brake. Reaction of male mouse fighters to male castrates treated with testosterone propionate or oil. *Psychonomic Science*, 1972, 27, 287–288.

Lee, C. T. & W. Griffo. Early androgenization and aggression pheromone in inbred mice. *American Zoologist*, 1972, *12*, 659–660.

Lefkowitz, M. M. Effects of diphenylhydantoin in disruptive behavior: Study of male delinquents. *Archives of General Psychiatry*, 1969, 29, 643–651.

Legrand, R. Successful aggression as the reinforcer for runway behavior of mice. *Psychonomic Science*, 1970, 20, 303–305.

LeMaire, L. Danish experience regarding the castration of sexual offenders. *Journal of Criminal Law and Criminology*, 1956, 47, 294–310.

Lennard, H. L., L. J. Epstein, A. Bernstein, & D. C. Ransom. Hazards implicit in prescribing psychoactive drugs. *Science,* 1970, *169,* 438–441.

Lennox, W. G. & M. A. Lennox. *Epilepsy and related disorders,* Vol. 1. Boston: Little, Brown, 1960.

Lerner, L. J. Hormone antagonists: Inhibitors of specific activities of estrogen and androgen. *Recent progress in hormone research,* Vol. 20. New York: Academic Press, 1964, pp. 435–490.

Lerner, L. J., A. Bianchi, & A. Borman. A-Norprogesterone an androgen antagonist. *Proceedings of the Society for Experimental Biology and Medicine,* 1960, *103,* 172–175.

Lesch, M. & W. L. Nyhan. A familial disorder of uric acid metabolism and central nervous system function. *American Journal of Medicine,* 1964, *36,* 561–570.

Leshner, A. I. & W. A. Walker. The adrenals and intermale aggression. Paper presented at the Psychonomic Society Meeting, November, 1972.

Leshner, A. I., W. A. Walker, A. E. Johnson, J.·S. Kelling, S. J. Kreisler, & B. B. Svare. Pituitary adrenocortical activity and intermale aggressiveness in isolated mice. *Physiology and Behavior,* 1973, *11,* 705–711.

Le Vann, L. J. Haloperidol in the treatment of behavioral disorders in children and adolescents. *Canadian Psychiatric Association Journal,* 1969, *14,* 217–220.

Le Vann, L. J. Clinical comparison of haloperidol with chlorpromazine in mentally retarded children. *American Journal of Mental Deficiency,* 1971, *75,* 719–723.

Lever, J. Soccer: Opium of the Brazilian people. *Trans-action,* 1969, *7,* 36–43.

Levine, L., C. A. Diakow, & G. E. Barsel. Interstrain fighting in male mice. *Animal Behaviour,* 1965, *13,* 52–58.

Levine, S. Emotionality and aggressive behavior in the mouse as a function of infantile experience. *Journal of Genetic Psychology,* 1959, *94,* 77–83.

Levison, P. K. & J. P. Flynn. The objects attacked by cats during stimulation of the hypothalamus. *Animal Behaviour,* 1965, *13,* 217–220.

Levitt, R. A. & A. E. Fisher. Anticholinergic blockade of centrally induced thirst. *Science,* 1966, *154,* 520–522.

Levy, J. V. The effects of testosterone propionate on fighting behaviour in C57BL/10 young female mice. *Proceedings of the West Virginia Academy of Science,* 1954, *26,* 14.

Levy, J. V. & J. A. King. The effects of testosterone propionate on fighting behaviour in young male C57BL/10 mice. *Anatomical Record,* 1953, *117,* 562–563.

Leyhausen, P. *Verhaltensstudien an Katzen.* Berlin: P. Varey Verl., 1956.

Leyhausen, P. The communal organization of solitary mammals. *Symposium of the Zoological Society of London,* 1965, *14,* 249–263.

Leyhausen, P. Dominance and territoriality as complemented in mammalian social structure, In A. H. Esser (Ed.), *Behavior and environment: The use of space by animals and men.* New York: Plenum, 1971, pp. 22–33.

Lichtenstein, P. E. Studies of anxiety. II: The effects of lobotomy on a feeding inhibition in dogs. *Journal of Comparative and Physiological Psychology,* 1950, *43,* 419–427.

Lints, C. E. Changes in sensitivity to electric shock following central nervous system lesions in the rat. Unpublished doctoral dissertation, University of Chicago, Chicago, 1965.

Lints, C. E. & J. A. Harvey. Altered sensitivity to footshock and decreased brain content of serotonin following brain lesions in the rat. *Journal of Comparative and Physiological Psychology*, 1969, *67*, 23–31.

Lion, J. R. *Evaluation and management of the violent patient.* Springfield, Ill.: Thomas, 1972.

Lion, J. R. & G. Bach-Y-Rita. Group psychotherapy with violent outpatients. *International Journal of Group Psychotherapy*, 1970, *20*, 185–191.

Lion, J. R., G. Bach-Y-Rita, & F. R. Ervin. The self-referred violent patient. *Journal of the American Medical Association*, 1968, *205*, 503–505.

Lion, J. R., G. Bach-Y-Rita, & F. R. Ervin. Violent patients in the emergency room. *American Journal of Psychiatry*, 1969, *125*, 1706–1711.

Livingston, K. E. Cingulate cortex isolation for the treatment of psychoses and psychoneuroses. *Research Publication of the Association for Research in Nervous and Mental Disease*, 1951, *31*, 374–378.

Livingston, S. Epilepsy and murder. *Journal of the American Medical Association*, 1964, *188*, 172.

Lloyd, C. W. Problems associated with the menstrual cycle. In C. W. Lloyd (Ed.), *Human reproduction and sexual behavior.* Philadelphia: Lea & Febiger, 1964, 490–497.

Lloyd, C. W. Treatment and prevention of certain sexual behavioral problems. In C. W. Lloyd (Ed.), *Human reproduction and sexual behavior.* Philadelphia: Lea & Febiger, 1964b, pp. 498–510.

Lloyd, C. W. & J. Weisz. Hormones and Aggression. Paper presented at Houston Neurological Symposium on Neural Bases of Violence and Aggression, Houston, Texas, March 9–11, 1972.

Lloyd, J. A. & J. J. Christian. Relationship of activity and aggression to density in two confined populations of house mice *Mus musculus. Journal of Mammalogy*, 1967, *48*, 262–269.

Lockie, J. D. Territory in small carnivores. In P. A. Jewell & C. Loizos, *Play, exploration and territory in mammals.* London: Academic Press, 1966, pp. 143–165.

Logan, J. C. Use of psychodrama and sociodrama in reducing excessive Negro aggression. *Group Psychotherapy and Psychodrama*, 1971, *24*, 138–149.

Lombroso, C. T., I. M. Schwartz, D. M. Clark, H. Muensch, & J. Barry. Ctenoids in healthy youths: Controlled study of 14- and 6-per-second positive spiking. *Neurology*, 1966, *16*, 1152–1158.

Lond, M. T. & L. C. Johnson. Fourteen- and six-per-second positive spikes in a nonclinical male population. *Neurology*, 1968, *18*, 714–716.

Lonowski, D. J., R. R. Levitt, & S. D. Larson. Effects of cholinergic brain injection on mouse killing or carrying by rats. *Physiological Psychology*, 1973, *1*, 341–345.

Looker, A. & C. K. Conners. Diphenylhydantoin in children with severe temper tantrums. *Archives of General Psychiatry*, 1970, *23*, 80–89.

Loomis, T. A. & T. C. West. The influence of alcohol on automobile driving ability: An experimental study for the evaluation of certain medicolegal aspects. *Quarterly Journal of Studies on Alcohol,* 1958, *19,* 30–46.

Lorenz, K. *Man meets dog.* London: Methuen, 1954.

Lorenz, K. Ritualized fighting. In J. D. Carthy & F. J. Ebling (Eds.), *The natural history of aggression.* New York: Academic Press, 1964.

Lorenz, K. *On aggression.* New York: Harcourt Brace Jovanovich, 1966.

Lorenz, R. J. Effects of differential preweaning social isolation on emotional reactivity and stress tolerance in the rat. *Developmental Psychobiology,* 1972, *5,* 201–213.

Lowe, V. P. Observations on the dispersal of red deer on Rhum. In P. A. Jewell & C. Loizos (Eds.), *Play, exploration and territory in mammals.* London: Academic Press, 1966, pp. 211–218.

Loy, J. Behavioral responses of free-ranging rhesus monkeys to food shortage. *American Journal of Physical Anthropology,* 1970, *33,* 263–271.

Ludwig, A. M., A. J. Marx, P. A. Hill, & R. M. Browning. The control of violent behavior through faradic shock. *The Journal of Nervous and Mental Disease,* 1969, *148,* 624–637.

Luttge, W. G. Activation and inhibition of isolation induced intermale fighting behavior in castrate male CD-1 mice treated with steroidal hormones. *Hormones and Behavior,* 1972, *3,* 71–82.

Luttge, W. G. & N. R. Hall. Androgen-induced agonistic behavior in castrate male Swiss-Webster mice: Comparison of four naturally occurring androgens. *Behavioral Biology,* 1973, *8,* 725–732.

Lyght, C. E. (Ed.), *The Merck manual of diagnosis and therapy.* West Point, Pa.: Merck, 1966.

Lyon, D. D. & D. Ozolins. Pavlovian conditioning of shock-elicited aggression—a discrimination procedure. *Journal of Experimental Analysis of Behavior,* 1970, *13,* 325–331.

McAdam, D. W. & W. W. Kaelber. Differential impairment of avoidance learning in cats with ventromedial hypothalamic lesions. *Experimental Neurology,* 1966, *15,* 293–298.

McCarthy D. Mouse-killing in rats treated with pilocarpine. *Federation Proceedings,* 1966, *25,* 385.

McClearn, G. E. Biological bases of social behavior with particular reference to violent behavior. In D. J. Mulvihill, M. M. Tumin, & L. A. Curtis (Eds.), *Crimes of violence,* Vol. 13. A staff report submitted to the National Commission on the Causes and Prevention of Violence, Washington D.C., U.S. Government Printing Office, 1969, pp. 979–1016.

McCord, W. & J. McCord. *Psychopathy and delinquency.* New York: Grune & Stratton, 1956.

McCord, W., J. McCord, & A. Howard. Familial correlates of aggression in nondelinquent male children. *Journal of Abnormal and Social Psychology,* 1961, *63,* 493–503.

MacDonald, J. W. *The murderer and his victim.* Springfield, Ill.: Thomas, 1961.

MacDonnell, M. F. & J. P. Flynn. Attack elicited by stimulation of the thalamus of cats. *Science,* 1964, *144,* 1249–1250.

MacDonnell, M. F. & J. P. Flynn. Control of sensory fields by stimulation of hypothalamus. *Science,* 1966a, *152,* 1406–1408.

MacDonnell, M. F. & J. P. Flynn. Sensory control of hypothalamic attack. *Animal Behaviour*, 1966b, *14*, 399–405.

MacDonnell, M. F. & J. P. Flynn. Attack elicited by stimulation of the thalamus and adjacent structures of cats. *Behaviour*, 1968, *31*, 185–202.

McIntyre, A. Sex differences in children's aggression. *Proceedings of the Annual Convention of the American Psychological Association*, 1972, 7, 93–94.

McKinney, E. D. & J. J. Christian. Effect of preputialectomy on fighting behavior in mice. *Proceedings of the Society of Experimental Biology and Medicine*, 1970, *134*, 291–293.

McKinney, T. D. & C. Desjardins. Androgens, fighting and mating during postnatal maturation in male house mice. *Biology of Reproduction*, 1972, 7, 112.

Mackintosh, J. H. & E. C. Grant. The effect of olfactory stimuli on the agonistic behavior of laboratory mice. *Zeitschrift fur Tierpsychologie*, 1966, *23*, 584–587.

MacLean, P. D. New findings relevant to the evolution of psychosexual functions of the brain. In J. Money (Ed.), *Sex research: New developments*. New York: Holt, Rinehart and Winston, 1965, pp. 197–218.

MacLean, P. D. & J. M. R. Delgado. Electrical and chemical stimulation of frontotemporal portion of limbic system in the waking animal. *Electroencephalography and Clinical Neurophysiology*, 1953, 5, 91–100.

MacLennan, R. R. & E. D. Bailey. Seasonal changes in aggression, hunger and curiosity in ranch mink. *Canadian Journal of Zoology*, 1969, *47*, 1395–1404.

Malamud, N. Psychiatric disorders with intracranial tumors of the limbic system. *Archives of Neurology*, 1967, *17*, 113–123.

Maletzky, B. M. The episodic dyscontrol syndrome. *Diseases of the Nervous System*, 1973, pp. 178–185.

Malick, J. B. A behavioral comparison of three lesions—induced models of aggression in the rat. *Physiology and Behavior*, 1970, 5, 679–681.

Mandell, A. J. & M. P. Mandell. Suicide and the menstrual cycle. *Journal of the American Medical Association*, 1967, *200*, 792–793.

Mandell, M. Cerebral reactions in allergic patients. Case histories and provocative test results. Paper presented at the 25th Annual Congress, American College of Allergists Section on Neurologic Allergy, Washington, D.C., April 18, 1969.

Mans, J. & M. Senes. Isocarboxazid, RO 5-0690 or chlordiazepoxide and RO 4-0403 a thioxanthene derivative. Study on their individual effects and their possibilities of combination. *Journal de Medicine de Bordeaux*, 1964, *141*, 1909–1918.

Marinacci, A. A. A special type of temporal lobe psychomotor seizures following ingestion of alcohol. *Bulletin of the Los Angeles Neurological Society*, 1963, *28*, 241–250.

Mark, V. H. & F. R. Ervin. *Violence and the brain*. New York: Harper & Row, 1970.

Mark, V. H., F. R. Ervin, & W. H. Sweet. Deep temporal lobe stimulation in man. In B. E. Eleftheriou (Ed.), *The neurobiology of the amygdala*. New York: Plenum, 1972, pp. 485–507.

Mark, V. H., F. R. Ervin, W. H. Sweet, & J. Delgado. Remote telemeter stimulation and recording from implanted temporal lobe electrodes. *Confinia Neurologica*, 1969, *31*, 86–93.

Mark, V. H. & R. Neville. Brain surgery in aggressive behavior. *Journal of the American Medical Association*, 1973, *226*, 765–772.

Mark, V. H., W. H. Sweet, & F. R. Ervin. The effect of amygdalotomy on violent behavior in patients with temporal lobe epilepsy. In E. Hitchcock, L. Laitinen, & K. Vaernet (Eds.), *Psychosurgery.* Springfield, Ill.: Thomas, 1972, pp. 135–155.

Marler, P. R. Studies of fighting in chaffinches. (3) Proximity as a cause of aggression. *British Journal of Animal Behaviour*, 1956, *4*, 23–30.

Marler, P. Aggregation and dispersal: Two functions in primate communication. In P. Jay (Eds.), *Primates.* New York: Holt, Rinehart and Winston, 1968, pp. 420–438.

Marshall, J. F., B. H. Turner, & P. Teitelbaum. Sensory neglect produced by lateral hypothalamic damage. *Science*, 1971, *174*, 523–525.

Marucci, F., E. Mussini, L. Valzelli, & S. Garattini. Decrease in N-Acetyl-L-Asparatic acid in brain of aggressive mice. *Journal of Neurochemistry*, 1968, *15*, 53–54.

Mason, W. A. The effects of environmental restriction on the social development of rhesus monkeys. In C. H. Southwick (Ed.), *Primate social behavior.* New York: Van Nostrand, 1963, 161–173.

Mason, W. A. Use of space by *Callicebus* groups. In P. Jay (Ed.), *Primates.* New York: Holt, Rinehart and Winston, 1968, pp. 200–216.

Mason, W. A. & P. C. Green. The effects of social restriction on the behavior of rhesus monkeys: IV. Responses to a novel environment and to an alien species. *Journal of Comparative and Physiological Psychology*, 1962, *55*, 363–368.

Masserman, J. H. *Behavior and neuroses.* Chicago: University of Chicago Press, 1943.

Matsumoto, K., K. Takeyasu, S. Mitzutiani, Y. Hamanaka, & T. Vozumi. Plasma testosterone levels following surgical stress in male patients. *Acta Endocrinologica*, 1970, *65*, 11–17.

Matthews, L. H. Overt fighting in mammals. In J. D. Carthy & F. J. Ebling (Eds.), *The natural history of aggression.* London: Academic Press, 1964, pp. 23–32.

Mead, M. *Sex and temperament in three primitive societies.* New York: Morrow, 1935.

Megargee, E. I. A critical review of theories of violence. In D. J. Mulvihill, M. M. Tumin, & L. A. Curtis (Eds.), *Crimes of violence*, Vol. 13. A staff report submitted to the National Commission on the Causes and Prevention of Violence, Washington, D.C., U.S. Government Printing Office, 1969, pp. 1038–1115.

Mempel, E. The effect of partial amygdalectomy on emotional disturbances and epileptic seizures: Preliminary report. *Polish Medical Journal*, 1971, *10*, 969–974.

Menninger, K. A. *The crime of punishment.* New York: Viking Press, 1968.

Michael, R. P. Effects of gonadal hormones on displaced and direct aggression in pairs of rhesus monkeys of opposite sex. In S. Garattini & E. B. Sigg (Eds.), *Aggressive behaviour*. New York: Wiley, 1969, pp. 172–178.

Michael, R. P. & E. B. Keverne. Pheromones in the communication of sexual status in primates. *Nature*, 1968, *218*, 746–749.

Michael, R. P., E. B. Keverne, & R. W. Bonsall. Pheromones: Isolation of male sex attractants from a female primate. *Science*, 1971, *172*, 964–966.

Michael, R. P. & D. Zumpe. Aggression and gonadal hormones in captive rhesus monkeys (*Macaca mulatta*). *Animal Behavior*, 1970, *18*, 1–10.

Miczek, K. A., T. Brykczynski, & S. P. Grossman. Differential effects of lesions in the amygdala, periamygdaloid cortex, or stria terminalis on aggressive behaviors in rats. *Journal of Comparative and Physiological Psychology*, 1974, *87*, 760–771.

Miczek, K. A. & S. P. Grossman. Effects of septal lesions on inter- and intra-species aggression in rats. *Journal of Comparative and Physiological Psychology*, 1972, *79*, 37–45.

Miley, W. M. Some effects of androgens in intermale fighting by laboratory mice in a spontaneous dominance situation. Unpublished doctoral dissertation, Temple University, Philadelphia, 1973.

Miley, W. M. & R. Baenninger. Inhibition and facilitation of interspecies aggression in septal lesioned rats. *Physiology and Behavior*, 1972, *9*, 379–384.

Miller, N. E. The frustration-aggression hypothesis. *Psychological Review*, 1941, *48*, 337–342.

Miller, R. E. & J. H. Banks. The determination of social dominance in monkeys by a competitive avoidance method. *Journal of Comparative and Physiological Psychology*, 1962, *55*, 137–141.

Miller, R. E., J. V. Murphy, & I. A. Mirsky. The modification of social dominance in a group of monkeys by interanimal conditioning. *Journal of Comparative and Physiological Psychology*, 1955, *48*, 392–396.

Minigrino, S. & E. Schergna. Stereotaxic anterior cingulotomy in the treatment of severe behavior disorders. In E. Hitchcock, L. Laitinen, & K. Vaernet (Eds.), *Psychosurgery*. Springfield, Ill.: Thomas, 1972, pp. 258–263.

Mirsky, A. F. The influence of sex hormones on social behavior in monkeys. *Journal of Comparative and Physiological Psychology*, 1955, *48*, 327–335.

Mises, R. & H. Beauchesne. Essai de la perphenazine chez l'enfant, et l'adolescent. *Annales Medice Psychologiques*, 1963, *2*, 89–92.

Mitchell, G. D., E. J. Raymond, G. C. Ruppenthal, & H. F. Harlow. Long-term effects of total social isolation upon behavior of rhesus monkeys. *Psychological Reports*, 1966, *18*, 567–580.

Molof, M. J. Differences between assaultive and non-assaultive juvenile offenders in the California Youth Authority. *Research Report No. 51*, State of California, Department of Youth Authority, February, 1967.

Money, J. Use of an androgen-depleting hormone in the treatment of male sex offenders. *The Journal of Sex Research*, 1970, *6*, 165–172.

Money, J. & A. A. Ehrhardt. *Man and woman: Boy and girl*. Baltimore: Johns Hopkins Press, 1972.

Monroe, R. R. Episodic behavioral disorders—schizophrenia or epilepsy. *Archives of General Psychiatry*, 1959, *1*, 205–214.

Monroe, R. R. *Episodic behavioral disorders: A psychodynamic and neuro-physiologic analysis.* Cambridge, Mass.: Harvard University Press, 1970.

Monroe, R. R. Drugs in the management of episodic behavioral disorders. Paper presented at the Houston Neurological Symposium on the Neural Bases of Violence and Aggression, March 9–11, 1972.

Montagu, M. F. A. *On being human.* New York: Hawthorn Books, 1966.

Montagu, M. F. A. (Ed.), *Man and aggression.* London: Oxford University Press, 1968.

Montgomery, R. L., M. K. Berkut, E. F. Grubb, & D. L. Westbrook. Hormonal influence on behavior in brain lesioned male rats. *Physiology and Behavior,* 1971, 7, 107–111.

Moore, M. W. Extra-respiratory tract symptoms of pollinosis. *Annals of Allergy,* 1958, *16,* 152–155.

Moos, R. The development of a menstrual distress questionnaire. *Psychosomatic Medicine,* 1968, *30,* 853–867.

Morden, B., R. Conner, W. Dement, & S. Levine. Aggressive behavior and REM sleep deprivation in the rat. *Psychophysiology,* 1968, *4,* 379–380.

Morden, B., R. Conner, G. Mitchell, W. Dement, & S. Levine. Effects of rapid eye movement (REM) sleep deprivation on shock induced fighting. *Physiology and Behavior,* 1968, *3,* 425–432.

Morris, D. In discussion of L. H. Matthews—overt fighting in mammals. In J. D. Carthy & F. J. Ebling (Eds.), *The natural history of aggression.* London: Academic Press, 1964, pp. 33–38.

Morton, J. H. Premenstrual tension. *American Journal of Obstetrics and Gynecology,* 1950, *60,* 343–352.

Morton, J. H., H. Addition, R. G. Addison, L. Hunt, & J. J. Sullivan. A clinical study of premenstrual tension. *American Journal of Obstetrics and Gynecology,* 1953, *65,* 1182–1191.

Mosher, D. L. & H. Katz. Pornographic films, male verbal aggression against women and guilt. (Unpublished manuscript, summarized in Commission on Obscenity and Pornography.) Washington, D.C.: U.S. Government Printing Office, 1970.

Mowrer, O. H. & H. Jones. Extinction and behavior variability as functions of effortfulness of task. *Journal of Experimental Psychology,* 1943, *33,* 364–386.

Moyer, K. E. Kinds of aggression and their physiological basis. *Communications in Behavioral Biology,* 1968a, *2,* 65–87.

Moyer, K. E. Brain research *must* contribute to world peace. *Fiji School of Medicine Journal,* 1968b, *3,* 2–5.

Moyer, K. E. Internal impulses to aggression. *Transactions of the New York Academy of Sciences,* 1969, *31,* 104–114.

Moyer, K. E. *The physiology of hostility.* Chicago: Markham, 1971a.

Moyer, K. E. The physiology of aggression and the implications for aggression control. In J. L. Singer (Ed.), *The control of aggression and violence: cognitive and physiological factors.* New York: Academic Press, 1971b.

Moyer, K. E. A preliminary physiological model of aggression. In B. Eleftheriou and J. P. Scott, *The physiology of aggression and defeat.* New York: Plenum, 1971c.

Moyer, K. E. The physiological inhibition of hostile behavior. In J. F. Knutson (Ed.), *The control of aggression: Implications from basic research.* Chicago: Aldine, 1973.

Moyer, K. E. Sex differences in aggression. In R. C. Friedman, R. M. Richart, & R. L. Vande Wiele (Eds.), *Sex differences in behavior.* New York: Wiley, 1974.

Moyer, K. E. A physiological model of aggression: Does it have different implications? In W. S. Fields (Ed.), *Neural bases of violence and aggression.* St. Louis: Green, 1975.

Moyer, K. E. & J. H. Korn. Behavioral effects of isolation in the rat. *Psychonomic Science,* 1965, *3,* 503–504.

Mugford, R. A. Intermale fighting affected by home-cage odors of male and female mice. *Journal of Comparative and Physiological Psychology,* 1973, *84,* 289–295.

Mugford, R. A. & N. W. Nowell. Pheromones and their effect on aggression in mice. *Nature,* 1970a, *226,* 967–968.

Mugford, R. A. & N. W. Nowell. The aggression of male mice against androgenized females. *Psychonomic Science,* 1970b, *20,* 191–192.

Mugford, R. A. & N. W. Nowell. Endocrine control over production and activity of the anti-aggression pheromone from female mice. *Journal of Endocrinology,* 1971a, *49,* 225–232.

Mugford, R. A. & N. W. Nowell. The preputial gland as a source of aggression-promoting odors in mice. *Physiology and Behavior,* 1971b, *6,* 247–249.

Mugford, R. A. & N. W. Nowell. Relationship between endocrine status of female opponents and aggressive behavior of male mice. *Animal Behaviour,* 1971c, *19,* 153–155.

Mugford, R. A. & N. W. Nowell. The dose-response to testosterone propionate of preputial glands, pheromones and aggression in mice. *Hormones and Behavior,* 1972, *3,* 39–46.

Mulder, D. & D. Daly. Psychiatric symptoms associated with lesions of temporal lobe. *Journal of the American Medical Association,* 1952, *150,* 173–176.

Muller, M. Alcoholismo y criminalidad. *Revista del Instituto de Investigaciones y Docencia Criminologicas,* 1965–1966, *9,* 51–69.

Mulvihill, D. J., M. M. Tumin, & L. A. Curtis (Eds.), *Crimes of violence,* vol. 12. (A staff report submitted to the National Commission on the Causes and Prevention of Violence.) Washington, D.C.: U.S. Government Printing Office, 1969.

Murdoch, B. D. Electroencephalograms, aggression and emotional maturity in psychopathic and non-psychopathic prisoners. *Psychologia Africana,* 1972, *14,* 216–231.

Murie, O. J. *The elk of North America.* Washington, D.C.: Stackpole and Wildlife Management Institute, 1951.

Murphy, M. R. Territorial behavior of the caged golden hamster. *Proceedings of the 78th Annual Convention of the American Psychological Association,* 1970, pp. 237–238.

Murphy, M. R. & G. E. Schneider. Olfactory bulb removal eliminates mating behavior in the male golden hamster. *Science,* 1970, *167,* 302–304.

Myer, J. S. Stimulus control of mouse killing rats. *Journal of Comparative and Physiological Psychology*, 1964, 58, 112–117.

Myer, J. S. Associative and temporal determinants of facilitation and inhibition of attack by pain. *Journal of Comparative and Physiological Psychology*, 1968, 66, 17–21.

Myer, J. S. Early experience and the development of mouse-killing by rats. *Journal of Comparative and Physiological Psychology*, 1969, 67, 46–49.

Myer, J. S. Experience and the stability of mouse killing by rats. *Journal of Comparative and Physiological Psychology*, 1971, 75, 264–268.

Myer, J. S. & R. Baenninger. Some effects of punishment and stress on mouse killing by rats. *Journal of Comparative and Physiological Psychology*, 1966, 62, 292–297.

Myer, J. S. & R. T. White. Aggressive motivation in the rat. *Animal Behaviour*, 1965, 13, 430–433.

Myers, K. & R. Mykytowycz. Social behaviour in the wild rabbit. *Nature*, 1958, 181, 1515–1516.

Myers, R. E. Role of prefrontal and anterior temporal cortex in social behavior and affect in monkeys. *Acta Neurobiologiae Experimentalis*, 1972, 32, 567–579.

Mykytowycz, R. Observations on odoriferous and other glands in the Australian wild rabbit, *Oryctolagus cuniculus* L., and the hare, *Lepus europaeus* P. I. The anal gland, II. The inguinal gland, III. Harder's lacrimal and submandibular glands. *CSIRO Wildlife Research* (Canberra), 1966, 11, 11–29.

Mykytowycz, R. Territorial markings by rabbits. *Scientific American*, 1968, 218, 116–126.

Nakao, H. Emotional behavior produced by hypothalamic stimulation. *American Journal of Physiology*, 1958, 194, 441–418.

Narabayashi, H. Stereotactic amygdalectomy for behavior disorders with or without skull EEG abnormality. 2nd International Congress of Neurological Surgery. Abstracts and descriptions of contributions to the scientific program, October 14–20, 1961. *Excerpta Medica International Congress*, Series 36, pp. E125–E126.

Narabayashi, H. Stereotaxic amygdalotomy. In B. Eleftheriou (Ed.), *The neurobiology of the amygdala*. New York: Plenum, 1972, pp. 459–483.

Narabayashi, H., T. Nagao, Y. Saito, M. Yoshido, & M. Nagahata. Stereotaxic amygdalotomy for behavior disorders. *Archives of Neurology*, 1963, 9, 1–16.

Narabayashi, H. & M. Uno. Long range results of stereotaxic amygdalotomy for behavior disorders. 2nd International Symposium Stereoencephalotomy, *Confinia Neurologica*, 1966, 27, 168–171.

Nash, H. *Alcohol and caffeine: A study of their psychological effects*. Springfield, Ill.: Thomas, 1962.

Nathan, P. E., N. C. Zare, E. W. Ferneau, & L. M. Lowenstein. Effects of congener differences in alcoholic beverages on the behavior of alcoholics. *Quarterly Journal of Studies on Alcohol*, Supplement No. 5, 1970, 87–100.

National Commission on the Causes and Prevention of Violence. *To establish justice, to insure domestic tranquility* (Final Report). Washington, D.C., U.S. Government Printing Office, 1969.

Neidermeyer, E. & J. R. Knott. The incidence of 14 and 6 per second positive spikes in psychiatric material. *Electroencephalography and Clinical Neurophysiology*, 1962, *14*, 285–286.

Neuman, F., H. Steinbeck, & J. D. Hahn. Hormones and brain differentiation. In L. Martini, M. Motta, & F. Fraschini (Eds.), *The Hypothalamus*. New York: Academic Press, 1970, pp. 569–603.

Neuman, F., R. Von Berswordt-Wallrabe, W. Elger, & H. Steinbeck. Activities of antiandrogens: Experiments in prepuberal and puberal animals in foetuses. In J. Tamm (Ed.), *Testosterone: Proceedings of the workshop conference, April 1967, Tremsbuettel*. Stuttgart: Georg Thieme Verlag, 1968, pp. 134–143.

Neuringer, C. & J. L. Michael (Eds.). *Behavior modification in clinical psychology*. New York: Appleton-Century-Crofts, 1970.

Nice, M. M. The role of territory in bird life. *American Midland Naturalist*, 1941, *26*, 441–487.

Noble, G. K. The role of dominance in the social life of birds. *Auk*, 1939, *56*, 263–273.

Norris, K. S. Aggressive behavior in Cetacea. In C. D. Clemente & D. B. Lindsley (Eds.), *Aggression and defense: Neural mechanisms and social patterns*, Vol. V, *Brain Function*. Los Angeles: University of California Press, 1967, pp. 243–266.

Nuffield, E. J. Neuro-physiology and behavior disorder in epileptic children. *Journal of Mental Sciences*, 1961, *107*, 438–458.

Nyby, J., D. D. Thiessen, & P. Wallace. Social inhibition of territorial making in the Mongolian gerbil (*Meriones unguiculatus*). *Psychonomic Science*, 1970, *21*, 310–312.

Nyhan, W. L. Human purine metabolism and behavior. *Engineering and Science*, 1970, *33*, 45–49.

Nyhan, W. L., J. A. James, A. J. Teberg, L. Sweetman, & S. Nelson. A new disorder of purine metabolism with behavioral manifestations. *Pediatrics*, 1969, *74*, 20–27.

O'Boyle, M. Rats and mice together: Predatory nature of rats' mouse-killing response. *Psychological Bulletin*, 1974, *81*, 261–269.

Obrador, S. Observations and reflections on psychosurgery at different levels. In E. Hitchcock, L. Laitinen, & K. Vaernet (Eds.), *Psychosurgery*. Springfield, Ill.: Thomas, 1972, pp. 83–86.

Orsinger, O. A. & S. Fulginiti. Effects of *Cannabis sativa* on learning. *Pharmacology*, 1970, *3*, 337–344.

Ounsted, C. Aggression and epilepsy rage in children with temporal lobe epilepsy. *Journal of Psychosomatic Research*, 1969, *13*, 237–242.

Paige, K. E. The effects of oral contraceptives on affective fluctuations associated with the menstrual cycle. Unpublished doctoral dissertation, University of Michigan, Ann Arbor, 1969.

Paluck, R. J. & A. H. Esser. Controlled experimental modification of aggressive behavior in territories of severely retarded boys. *American Journal of Mental Deficiency*, 1971, *76*, 23–29.

Panksepp, J. The neural basis of aggression. Unpublished doctoral dissertation, University of Massachusetts, Amherst, 1969.

Panksepp, J. Effects of hypothalamic-lesions on mouse-killing and shock-induced fighting in rats. *Physiology and Behavior*, 1971a, *6*, 311–316.

Panksepp, J. Drugs and stimulus-bound attack. *Physiology and Behavior*, 1971b, *6*, 317–320.

Panksepp, J. Aggression elicited by electrical stimulation of hypothalamus in albino-rats. *Physiology and Behavior*, 1971c, *6*, 321–329.

Panksepp, J. & J. Trowill. Electrically induced affective attack from the hypothalamus of the albino rat. *Psychonomic Science*, 1969, *16*, 118–119.

Pauig, P. M., M. A. Deluca, & R. G. Osterheld. Thioridazine hydrochloride in the treatment of behavior disorders in epileptics. *American Journal of Psychiatry*, 1961, *117*, 832–833.

Paul, L., W. M. Miley & R. Baenninger. Mouse killing by rats: Roles of hunger and thirst in its initiation and maintenance. *Journal of Comparative and Physiological Psychology*, 1971, *76*, 242–249.

Paul, L., W. M. Miley, & N. Mazzagatti. Social facilitation and inhibition of hunger induced killing by rats. *Journal of Comparative and Physiological Psychology*, 1973, *84*, 162–168.

Paxinos, G. D. Bindra. Hypothalamic knife cuts: Effects on eating, drinking, irritability, aggression and copulation in the male rat. *Journal of Comparative and Physiological Psychology*, 1972, *79*, 219–229.

Payne, A. P. & H. H. Swanson. Agonistic behaviour between pairs of hamsters of the same and opposite sex in a neutral observation area. *Behaviour*, 1970, *36*, 259–269.

Payne, A. P. & H. H. Swanson. The effect of sex hormones on the aggressive behaviour of the female golden hamster (*Mesocricetus auratus Waterhouse*). *Animal Behaviour*, 1972, *20*, 782–787.

Pear, J. J., J. E. Moody, & M. A. Persinger. Lever attacking by rats during free operant avoidance. *Journal of the Experimental Analysis of Behaviour*, 1972, *18*, 517–523.

Pear, J. J. & G. W. Roy. Operandum attacking may contribute to schedule effects on response rate. *Perceptual and Motor Skills*, 1971, *33*, 849.

Pearson, O. P. Reproduction in the shrew (*Blarina brevicauda Say*). *American Journal of Anatomy*, 1944, *75*, 39–93.

Pedersen, A. *Polar animals* (translated from the French by Gwynne Vevers). London: Alwin, 1962.

Penaloza-Rojas, J. H., G. Bach-Y-Rita, H. F. Rubio-Chevannier, & R. Hernandez-Peon. Effects of imipramine upon hypothalamic and amygdaloid excitability. *Experimental Neurology*, 1961, *4*, 205–213.

Penfield, W. & H. Jasper. *Epilepsy and the functional anatomy of the human brain*. Boston: Little, Brown, 1954.

Pennington, V. M. Meprobamate (Miltown) in premenstrual tension. *Journal of the American Medical Association*, 1957, *164*, 638–640.

Pennington, V. M. The phrenotropic action of perphenazine amytriptyline. *American Journal of Psychiatry*, 1964, *120*, 1115–1116.

Persky, H., K. D. Smith, & G. K. Basu. Relation of psychologic measures of aggression and hostility to testosterone production in man. *Psychosomatic Medicine*, 1971, *33*, 265–277.

Persky, H., M. Zuckerman, & G. C. Curtis. Endocrine function in emotionally disturbed and normal men. *Journal of Nervous and Mental Disease,* 1968, *146,* 488–497.

Peters, P. J. & F. H. Bronson. Neonatal androgen and the organization of aggression in mice. *American Zoologist,* 1971, *11,* 621.

Peters, P. J. & F. H. Bronson, & J. M. Whitsett. Neonatal castration and intermale aggression in mice. *Physiology and Behavior,* 1972, *8,* 265–268.

Piness, G. & H. Miller. Allergic manifestations in infancy and childhood. *Archives of Pediatrics,* 1925, *42,* 557–562.

Platt, J. J., L. W. Sutker, & W. T. James. Social facilitation of eating behavior in young opossums. The effects of isolation. Paper presented at the Annual Meeting of the Society for Philosophy and Psychology, Roanoke, Va., 1967.

Ploog, D. W. The behavior of squirrel monkeys (*Saimiri sciureus*) as revealed by sociometry, bioacoustics, and brain stimulation. In S. A. Altman (Ed.), *Social communication among primates.* Chicago: University of Chicago Press, 1967.

Plotnik, R., D. Mir, & J. M. R. Delgado. Aggression noxiousness and brain stimulation in unrestrained rhesus monkeys. In B. E. Eleftheriou & J. P. Scott (Eds.), *The physiology of aggression and defeat.* New York: Plenum, 1971, pp. 143–222.

Plumer, S. I. & J. Siegel. Caudate-induced inhibition of hypothalamic attack behavior. *Physiological Psychology,* 1973, *1,* 254–256.

Poblete, M., M. Palestini, E. Figueroa, R. Gallardo, J. Rojas, M. I. Covarrubias, & Y. Doyharcabal. Stereotaxic thalamotomy (lamella medialis) in aggressive psychiatric patients. *Confinia Neurologica,* 1970, *32,* 326–331.

Podobnikar, I. G. Implementation of psychotherapy by Librium in a pioneering rural-industrial psychiatric practice. *Psychosomatics,* 1971, *12,* 205–209.

Podolsky, E. The chemical brew of criminal behavior. *Journal of Criminal Law, Criminology and Police Science,* 1955, *45,* 675–678.

Podolsky, E. The chemistry of murder. *Pakistan Medical Journal,* 1964, *15,* 9–14.

Pool, J. L. The visceral brain of man. *Journal of Neurosurgery,* 1954, *11,* 45–63.

Poole, T. B. Aggressive play in polecats. In P. A. Jewell & C. Loizos (Eds.), *Play, exploration and territory in mammals.* New York: Academic Press, 1966, pp. 23–37.

Pounders, C. M. The allergic child. *Southern Medical Journal,* 1948, *41,* 142–146.

Powell, D. A. The interaction of some environmental and developmental variables in shock-elicited aggression. Unpublished doctoral dissertation, Florida State University, Tallahassee, 1967.

Powell, D. A. The effects of castration, neonatal injections of testosterone, and previous experience with fighting on shock-elicited aggression. *Communications in Behavioral Biology,* 1971, *5,* 371–377.

Powell, D. A., T. Silverman, J. Francis, & N. Schneiderman. The effects of sex and previous experience with fighting on shock elicited aggression. *Communications in Behavioral Biology,* 1970, *5,* 51–56.

Pratt, C. L. The developmental consequences of variation in early social stimulation. Unpublished doctoral dissertation, University of Wisconsin, Madison, 1969.

Proshansky, H. M., W. H. Ittelson, & L. G. Rivlin (Eds.), *Environmental psychology: Man and his physical setting,* New York: Holt, Rinehart and Winston, 1970.

Ralls, K. Mammalian scent marking. *Science,* 1971, *171,* 443–449.

Ramey, E. R. & D. S. O'Doherty (Eds.), *Electrical studies on the unanesthetized brain.* New York: Harper & Row, 1960.

Randall, L. O., G. A. Heise, W. Schallek, R. E. Bagdon, R. Banziger, A. Boris, R. A. Moe, & W. B. Abrams. Pharmacological and clinical studies on Valium. *Current Therapeutic Research,* 1961, *3,* 405–425.

Randall, L. O., W. Schallek, G. A. Heise, E. F Keith, & R. E. Bagdon. The psychosedative properties of methaminodiazepoxide. *Journal of Pharmacology and Experimental Therapeutics,* 1960, *120,* 163–171.

Randall, W. L. The behavior of 'cats (*Falis catus* L.) with lesions in the caudal midbrain region. *Behaviour,* 1964, *23,* 107–139.

Randolph, T. G. Ecologic mental illness—psychiatry exteriorized. *Journal of Laboratory and Clinical Medicine,* 1959, *54,* 936.

Randolph, T. G. *Human ecology and susceptibility to the chemical environment.* Springfield, Ill.: Thomas, 1962.

Randy, R. W., P. H. Crandall, & R. Walter. Chronic stereotactic implantation of depth electrodes for psychomotor epilepsy. *Acta Neurochirurgica,* 1964, *11,* 609–630.

Rasmussen, E. W. Wildness in rats: Heredity or environment? *Acta Psychologica,* 1938, *4,* 295–304.

Razavi, L. Cytogenetic and dermatoglyphic studies in sexual offenders, violent criminals and aggressively behaved temporal-lobe epileptics. *Comprehensive Psychiatry,* 1973, *14,* 86–87.

Reeves, A. G. & F. Blum. Hyperphagia, rage and dementia accompanying a ventromedial hypothalamic neoplasm. *Archives of Neurology,* 1969, *20,* 616–624.

Refsum, S., J. Presthus, Aa. Skulstad, & S. Ostensjo. Clinical correlates of the 14 and 6 per second positive spikes. *Acta Psychiatrica et Neurologica Scandinavica),* 1960, *35,* 330–344.

Reinhardt, J. M. *Sex perversions and sex crimes.* Springfield, Ill.: Thomas, 1957.

Reis, D. J., N. Doba, & M. A. Nathan. Predatory attack, grooming, and consummatory behavior evoked by electrical stimulation of cat cerebellar nuclei. *Science,* 1973, *182,* 845–847.

Report of the National Advisory Commission on Civil Disorders. New York: Bantam Books, 1968.

Report of the President's Commission on Crime in the District of Columbia. Washington, D.C.: U.S. Government Printing Office, 1966.

Resko, J. A. Plasma androgen levels of the rhesus monkey: The effects of age and season. *Endocrinology,* 1967, *81,* 1203–1212.

Resnick, O. The psychoactive properties of diphenylhydantoin: Experiences with prisoners and juvenile delinquents. *International Journal of Neuropsychiatry,* 1967, Suppl. 2 S20–S47.

Resnick, O. The use of psychotropic drugs with criminals. In W. O. Evans & N. S. Kline (Eds.), *Psychotropic drugs in the year 2000: Use by normal humans.* Springfield, Ill.: Thomas, 1971, pp. 109–127.

Revlis, R. & K. E. Moyer. Maternal aggression: A failure to replicate. *Psychonomic Science,* 1969, *16,* 135–136.

Reynolds, V. Some behavioral comparisons between the chimpanzee and the mountain gorilla in the wild. *American Anthropologist,* 1965, *67,* 691–706.

Ribero, S. L. Menstruation and crime. *British Medical Journal,* 1962, *1,* 640–641.

Richardson, D. & C. L. Scudder. Effect of olfactory bulbectomy and enucleation on behavior of the mouse. *Psychonomic Science,* 1970, *19,* 277–279.

Rieder, C. A. & J. H. Reynierse. Effects of maintenance conditions on aggression and mating behavior of the Mongolian gerbil (*Meriones unguiculatus*). *Journal of Comparative and Physiological Psychology,* 1971, *75,* 471–475.

Rimm, D. C., J. C. DeGroot, P. Boord, J. Heiman, & P. V. Dillow. Systematic desensitization of an anger response. *Behavioral Research and Therapy,* 1971, *9,* 273–280.

Ripley, S. Intergroup encounters among Ceylon gray langurs. In S. A. Altmann (Ed.), *Social communication among primates.* Chicago: University of Chicago Press, 1967.

Roberts, W. W. Both rewarding and punishing effects from stimulation of posterior hypothalamus of cat with same electrode at the same intensity. *Journal of Comparative and Physiological Psychology,* 1958, *51,* 400–407.

Roberts, W. W. Hypothalamic mechanisms for motivational and species-typical behavior. In R. E. Whalen, R. F. Thompson, M. Verzeano, & N. M. Weinberger (Eds.), *The neural control of behavior.* New York: Academic Press, 1970, pp. 175–208.

Roberts, W. W. & E. Bergquist. Attack elicited by hypothalamic stimulation in cats raised in social isolation. *Journal of Comparative and Physiological Psychology,* 1968, *66,* 590–596.

Roberts, W. W. & H. O. Kiess. Motivational properties of hypothalamic aggression in cats. *Journal of Comparative and Physiological Psychology,* 1964, *58,* 187–193.

Roberts, W. W., M. I. Steinberg, & L. W. Means. Hypothalamic mechanisms for sexual, aggressive and other motivational behavior in the opossum, *Didelphus virginiana. Journal of Comparative and Physiological Psychology,* 1967, *64,* 1–15.

Robinson, B. W., M. Alexander, & G. Bowne. Dominance reversal resulting from aggressive responses evoked by brain telestimulation. *Physiology and Behavior,* 1969, *4,* 749–752.

Rocky, S. & R. O. Neri. Comparative biological properties of SCH 12600 (6-chloro 4, 6 pregnadien 16-methylene 17-α-01-3, 20-dione-17 acetate) and chlormadinone acetate. *Federation Proceedings,* 1968, *27,* 624.

Romaniuk, A. Representation of aggression and flight reactions in the hypothalamus of the cat. *Acta Biologiae Experimentalis* (Warsaw), 1965, *25,* 177–186.

Ropartz, P. Mise en evidence du role de l'olfaction dans l'addressivite de la souris. *Rev. Comp. Anim.,* 1967, *2,* 97–102.

Ropartz, P. The relation between olfactory stimulation and aggressive behaviour in mice. *Animal Behaviour*, 1968, *16*, 97–100.

Rose, R. M., T. P. Gordon, & I. S. Bernstein. Plasma testosterone levels in the male rhesus: Influences of sexual and social stimuli. *Science*, 1972, *178*, 643–654.

Rose, R. M., J. W. Holaday, & I. S. Bernstein. Plasma testosterone, dominance rank and aggressive behavior in male rhesus monkeys. *Nature*, 1971, *231*, 366–368.

Rosenberg, B., A. E. Edwards, & R. A. Hill. Relationship between peripheral vascular state, personality, and adaptive response under effects of alcohol. *Proceedings of the 74th Annual Convention of the American Psychological Association*, 1966, pp. 207–208.

Rosenberg, P. H. Management of disturbed adolescents. *Diseases of the Nervous System*, 1966, *27*, 60–61.

Rosenfeld, A. 10,000-to-one payoff. *Life Magazine*, 1967, *63*, 121–128.

Rosenzweig, M. R. Environmental complexity, cerebral change, and behavior. *American Psychologist*, 1966, *21*, 321–331.

Ross, A. T. & V. A. B. Jackson. Dilantin sodium: Its influence on conduct and on psychometric ratings of institutionalized epileptics. *Annals of International Medicine*, 1940, *14*, 770–773.

Ross, S., P. B. Sawin, M. X. Zarrow, & V. H. Denenberg. Maternal behavior in the rabbit. In H. L. Rheingold (Ed.), *Maternal behavior in mammals*. New York, Wiley, 1963, pp. 94–121.

Rosvold, H. S., A. F. Mirsky, & K. H. Pribam. Influences of amygdalectomy on social behavior in monkeys. *Journal of Comparative Physiological Psychology*, 1954, *47*, 173–178.

Rothballer, A. B. Aggression, defense and neurohumors. In C. D. Clemente & D. B. Lindsley (Eds.), *Aggression and defense: Neural mechanisms and social patterns*, Vol. V, *Brain Function*. Los Angeles: University of California Press, 1967, pp. 135–170.

Rothman, G. *The riddle of cruelty*. New York: Philosophical Library, 1971.

Rowe, A. H. Allergic toxemia and migraine due to food allergy. *California and Western Medicine*, 1930, *33*, 785–793.

Rowe, A. H. Clinical allergy in the nervous system. *Journal of Nervous and Mental Diseases*, 1944, *99*, 834–841.

Rud, E. Spontaneous hypoglycemia with peculiar psychic disturbance. *Acta Medica Scandinavica*, 1937, *91*, 648–655.

Ruffer, D. G. Agonistic behavior of the northern grasshopper mouse (*Onychomys leucogaster breviauritus*). *Journal of Mammalogy*, 1968, *49*, 481–487.

Rylander, G. Clinical & medico-criminological aspects of addiction to central stimulating drugs. In F. Sjoqvist & M. Tottie (Eds.), *Abuse of central stimulants*. New York: Raven Press, 1969, pp. 251–271.

Ryszkowski, L. The space organization of nutria (*Myocastor coypus*). In P. A. Jewell & C. Loizos (Eds.), *Play, exploration and territory in mammals*. London: Academic Press, 1966, pp. 259–275.

Sackett, G. P. Abnormal behavior in laboratory reared rhesus monkeys. In

M. W. Fox, *Abnormal behavior in animals.* Philadelphia: Saunders, 1968a, pp. 293–331.

Sackett, G. P. The persistence of abnormal behavior in monkeys following isolation rearing. In R. Porter (Ed.), *The role of learning in psychotherapy.* London: Churchill, 1968b, pp. 3–25.

Sade, D. S. Seasonal cycle in size of testes of free ranging *Macaca mulatta.· Folia Primatologica,* 1964, *2,* 171–180.

St. John, D. & P. A. Corning. Maternal aggression in mice. *Behavioral Biology,* 1973, *9,* 635–639.

Sales, G. D. Ultrasound and aggressive behaviour in rats and other small mammals. *Animal Behaviour,* 1972, *20,* 88–100.

Sampson, H. Deprivation of dreaming sleep by two methods: I. Compensatory REM time. *Archives of General Psychiatry,* 1965, *13,* 79–86.

Sands, D. E. Further studies on endocrine treatment in adolescence and early adult life. *Journal of Mental Science,* 1954, *100,* 211–219.

Sands, D. E. & G. H. A. Chamberlain. Treatment of inadequate personality in juveniles by dehydroisoandrosterone. *British Medical Journal,* 1952, *2,* 66–68.

Sano, K. Fornicotomy. *Folia Psychiatrica et Neurologica Japonica,* 1957, Suppl. 5, 57–58.

Sano, K. Upper mesencephalic reticulotomy in epilepsy and behavior disorders. *Neurologia,* 1960, *2,* 138–146.

Sano, K. Sedative neurosurgery: With special reference to posteromedial hypothalamotomy. *Neurologia medico-chirurgica,* 1962, *4,* 112–142.

Sano, K. Sedative stereoencephalotomy: Fornicotomy, upper mesencephalic reticulotomy and posteromedial hypothalamotomy. *Progress in brain research,* Vol. 21B, *Correlative neuroscience,* Part B: *Clinical studies.* Amsterdam: Elsevier, 1966, pp. 350–372.

Sano, K., S. Hiroaki, & Y. Mayanagi. Results of stimulation and destruction of the posterior hypothalamus in cases of violent aggressive and restless behaviors. In E. Hitchcock, L. Laitinen, & K. Vaernet (Eds.), *Psychosurgery.* Springfield, Ill.: Thomas, 1972, pp. 57–75.

Sano, K., M. Ogashiwa, & H. Sekino. Clinical and physiological data obtained in stereotaxic surgery of the hypothalamus. *Australian Association of Neurologists, Proceedings Reports, II Congress Asian and Oceanian Association of Neurology,* 1968, pp. 267–275.

Sano, K., M. Yoshioka, M. Ogashiwa, B. Ishijima, & C. Ohye. Postermedial hypothalamotomy in the treatment of aggressive behaviors. *2nd International Symposium on Stereoencephalotomy, Confinia Neurologica,* 1966, *27,* 164–167.

Sassenrath, E. N., T. E. Rowell, & A. G. Hendricks. Perimenstrual aggression in groups of female rhesus monkeys. *Journal of Reproduction and Fertility,* 1973, *34,* 509–411.

Sawa, M. & J. M. R. Delgado. Amygdala unitary activity in the unrestrained cat. *Electroencephalography and Clinical Neurophysiology,* 1963, *15,* 637–650.

Sawa, M., Y. Ueki, M. Arita, & T. Harada. Preliminary report on the amygdaloidectomy on the psychotic patients, with interpretation of oral-emotional manifestations in schizophrenics. *Folia Psychiatrican et Neurologica Japonica,* 1954, 7, 309–329.

Sayed, Z. A., S. A. Lewis, & R. P. Brittain. An electroencephalographic and psychiatric study of 32 insane murders. *British Journal of Psychiatry,* 1969, *115,* 1115–1124.

Sayler, A. Effect of antiandrogens on aggressive behavior in gerbil. *Physiology and Behavior,* 1970, *5,* 667–671.

Schachter, J. Pain, fear, and anger in hypertensives and normotensives: A psychophysiological study. *Psychosomatic Medicine,* 1957, *19,* 17–29.

Schachter, S. & J. E. Singer. Cognitive, social and physiological determinants of emotional state. *Psychological Review,* 1962, *69,* 379–399.

Schaffer, N. Personality changes induced in children by the use of certain antihistaminic drugs. *Annals of Allergy,* 1953, *11,* 317–318.

Schaller, G. B. *The mountain gorilla: Ecology and behavior.* Chicago: University of Chicago Press, 1963.

Schaller, G. B. Life with the king of beasts. *National Geographic,* 1969, *135,* 499–519.

Scheckel, C. L. & E. Boff. Effects of drugs on aggressive behavior in monkeys. *Excerpta Medica International Congress Series No. 129, Proceedings of the 5th International Congress of the Colleagium Internationale Neuropsychopharmacologicum,* 1966, pp. 789–795.

Schein, M. W. & E. B. Hale. Stimuli eliciting sexual behavior. In F. A. Beach (Ed.), *Sex and behavior.* New York: Wiley, 1965, pp. 440–474.

Schenkel, R. Play, exploration and territoriality in the wild lion. In P. A. Jewell & C. Loizos (Eds.), *Play, exploration and territory in mammals.* London: Academic Press, 1966, pp. 11–22.

Schenkel, R. Submission: Its features and functions in the wolf and dog. *American Zoologist,* 1967, *7,* 319–329.

Schenkel, R. & I. Schenkel-Hilliger. *Ecology and behavior of the black rhinoceros.* Hamburg: Parey, 1969.

Schleidt, W., M. Schleidt, & M. Magg. Storungen der Mutter-Kind-Beziehung bei Truthuhnern durch Gehoverlust. *Behaviour,* 1960, *16,* 254–260.

Schneider, W. F. Psychiatric evaluation of the hyperkinetic child. *Journal of Pediatrics,* 1945, *26,* 559–570.

Schneirla, T. C., J. S. Rosenblatt, & E. Tobach. *Maternal behavior in mammals.* New York: Wiley, 1963, pp. 122–168.

Schnurr, R. Localization of the septal rage syndrome in Long-Evans rats. *Journal of Comparative and Physiological Psychology,* 1972, *81,* 291–296.

Schou, M. The metabolism and biochemistry of lithium. In S. Garattini & M. N. Dukes (Eds.), *Antidepressant drugs.* Amsterdam: Excerpta Medica Foundation, 1967, pp. 80–83.

Schreiner, L. & A. Kling. Behavioral changes following rhinencephalic injury in cat. *Journal of Neurophysiology,* 1953, *16,* 643–658.

Schreiner, L. & A. Kling. Rhinencephalon and behavior. *American Journal of Physiology,* 1953, *16,* 643–658.

Schreiner, L. & A. Kling. Rhinencephalon and behavior. *American Journal of Physiology,* 1956, *184,* 486–490.

Schusterman, R. J. & R. G. Dawson. Barking, dominance, and territoriality in male sea lions. *Science*, 1968, *160*, 434–436.

Schwab, R. S., W. H. Sweet, V. H. Mark, R. N. Kjellberg, & F. R. Ervin. Treatment of intractable temporal lobe epilepsy by stereotactic amygdala lesions. *Transactions of the American Neurological Association*, 1965, *90*, 12–19.

Schwade, E. D. & S. C. Geiger. Abnormal EEG findings in severe behavior disorder. *Diseases of the Nervous System*, 1956, *17*, 307–317.

Schwade, E. D. & S. C. Gieger. Severe behavior disorders with abnormal electroencephalograms. *Diseases of the Nervous System*, 1960, *21*, 616–620.

Schwade, E. D. & O. Otto. Homicide as a manifestation of thalamic or hypothalamic disorder with abnormal electroencephalographic findings. *Wisconsin Medical Journal*, 1953, *52*, 171–174.

Schwadron, R. Scaramuzzo gets 15–20 years for manslaughter. *The Times Herald Record*, March 30, 1965.

Sclafani, A. Neural pathways involved in the ventromedial hypothalamic lesion syndrome in the rat. *Journal of Comparative and Physiological Psychology*, 1971, *77*, 70–96.

Scott, J. P. Genetic differences in the social behavior of inbred strains of mice. *Journal of Heredity*, 1942, *33*, 11–15.

Scott, J. P. Social behavior, range and territoriality in domestic mice. *Proceedings of the Indiana Academy of Science*, 1944, *53*, 188–195.

Scott, J. P. Dominance and the frustration-aggression hypothesis. *Physiological Zoology*, 1948, *21*, 31–39.

Scott, J. P. *Aggression*. Chicago: University of Chicago Press, 1958.

Scott, J. P. Agonistic behavior of mice and rats: A review. *American Zoologist*, 1966, *6*, 683–701.

Scott, J. P. Hostility and aggression in animals. In E. L. Bliss (Ed.), *Roots of behavior*. New York: Harper & Row, 1962, pp. 167–178.

Scott, J. P. Theoretical issues concerning the origin and causes of fighting. In B. E. Eleftheriou & J. P. Scott (Eds.), *The physiology of aggression and defeat*. New York: Plenum, 1971, pp. 11–42.

Scott, J. P. & E. Fredericson. The causes of fighting in mice and rats. *Physiological Zoology*, 1951, *24*, 273–309.

Scott, J. P. & J. L. Fuller. *Genetics and the social behavior of the dog*. Chicago: University of Chicago Press, 1965.

Scott, W. G. The theory of significant people. *Public Administration Review*, 1973, *33*, 308–313.

Scoville, W. B. & B. Milner. Loss of recent memory after bilateral hippocampal lesions. *Journal of Neurology, Neurosurgery and Psychiatry*, 1957, *20*, 11–21.

Scudder, C. L., A. G. Karczmar, & L. Lockett. Behavioral development studies on four genera and several strains of mice. *Animal Behaviour*, 1967, *15*, 353–363.

Sears, R. R. Development of gender role. In F. A. Beach (Ed.), *Sex and behavior*. New York: Wiley, 1965, pp. 133–163.

Seay, B. & H. F. Harlow. Maternal separation in the rhesus monkey. *Journal of Nervous and Mental Diseases*, 1965, *140*, 434–441.

Seignot, J. N. Un cas de maladie des tics de Gilles de la Tourette guere par le R 1625. *Annales Medico-Psychologiques*, 1961, *119*, 578–579.

Sells, S. B. Gottschalk-Gleser Content analysis scales. In O. K. Buros (Ed.), *Mental measurements yearbook*, Vol. 1. Highland Park, N.J.: Gryphon Press, 1972.

Sem-Jacobsen, C. W. Depth-electrographic observations related to Parkinson's disease. *Journal of Neurosurgery*, 1966, *24*, 388–402.

Sem-Jacobsen, C. W. *Depth-electrographic stimulation of the human brain and behavior*. Springfield, Ill.: Thomas, 1968.

Sem-Jacobsen, C. W. & A. Torkildesen. Depth recording and electrical stimulation in the human brain. In E. R. Ramey & D. S. O'Doherty (Eds.), *Electrical studies on the unanesthetized brain*. New York: Harper & Row, 1960, pp. 275–290.

Serafetinides, E. A. Aggressiveness in temporal lobe epileptics and its relation to cerebral dysfunction and environmental factors. *Epilepsia*, 1965, *6*, 33–43.

Serafetinides, E. A. Psychiatric aspects of temporal lobe epilepsy. In E. Niedmeyer (Ed.), *Epilepsy, modern problems in pharmacopsychiatry*. New York: Karger, 1970, pp. 155–169.

Servais, J. Étude clinique de quelques cas de troubles psychosexuels chez l'homme, traités par un inhibiteur de la libido: La methyloestrenolone. *Acta Neurologica et Psychiatrica Belgica*, 1968, 407–415.

Seward, J. P. Aggressive behavior in the rat: I. General characteristics; age and sex differences. *Journal of Comparative Psychology*, 1945a, *38*, 175–197.

Seward, J. P. Aggressive behavior in the rat: III. The role of frustration. *Journal of Comparative Psychology*, 1945b, *38*, 225–238.

Shader, R. I., A. H. Jackson, & L. M. Dodes, The antiaggressive effects of lithium in man. *Psychopharmacologia*, 1974, *40*, 17–24.

Shah, S. A. & L. H. Roth. Biological and psychophysiological factors in criminality. In D. Glaser (Ed.), *Handbook of criminology*. Chicago: Rand McNally, 1974.

Shainess, N. A reevaluation of some aspects of femininity through a study of menstruation: A preliminary report. *Comprehensive Psychiatry*, 1961, *2*, 20–26.

Shannon, W. R. Neuropathic manifestations in infants and children as a result of anaphylactic reactions to foods contained in their dietary. *American Journal of Diseases of Children*, 1922, *24*, 89–94.

Shealy, C. & J. Peele. Studies on amygdaloid nucleus of cat. *Journal of Neurophysiology*, 1957, *20*, 125–139.

Sheard, M. H. The effects of amphetamine on attack behavior in the cat. *Brain Research*, 1967, *5*, 330–338.

Sheard, M. H. Behavioral effects of p-chlorophenylalanine in rats: Inhibition by lithium. *Communications in Behavioral Biology*, 1970a, *5*, 71–73.

Sheard, M. H. Effect of lithium on foot shock aggression in rats. *Nature*, 1970b, *228*, 284–285.

Sheard, M. H. The effect of lithium on behavior. *Comments on Contemporary Psychiatry*, 1971a, *1*, 1–6.

Sheard, M. H. Effect of lithium on human aggression. *Nature*, 1971b, *230*, 113–114.

Sheard, M. H. & J. P. Flynn. Facilitation of attack behavior by stimulation of the midbrain of cats. *Brain Research*, 1967, *4*, 324–333.

Sheer, D. E. (Ed.). *Electrical stimulation of the brain.* Austin: University of Texas Press, 1961.

Shimada, H. & A. Gorbman. Long lasting changes in RNA synthesis in the forebrains of female rats treated with testosterone soon after birth. *Biochemical and Biophysical Research Communications,* 1945, *38,* 423–430.

Shuntich, R. J. & S. P. Taylor. The effects of alcohol on human physical aggression. *Journal of experimental research in personality,* 1972, *6,* 34–38.

Siegel, A., R. J. Bandler, & J. P. Flynn. Thalamic sites and pathways related to elicited attack. *Brain behavior and evolution,* 1972, *6,* 542–555.

Siegel, A. & J. Chabora. Effects of electrical stimulation of the cingulate gyrus upon attack behavior elicited from the hypothalamus in the cat. *Brain Research,* 1971, *32,* 169–177.

Siegel, A., J. Chabora, R. Troiano. Effects of electrical stimulation of pyriform cortex upon hpyothalamically elicited aggression in cat. *Brain Research,* 1972, *47,* 497–500.

Siegel, A. R., H. Edinger, & H. Lowenthal. Effects of electrical stimulation of medial aspect of prefrontal cortex upon attack behavior in cats. *Brain Research,* 1974, *66,* 467–479.

Siegel, A. & J. P. Flynn. Differential effects of electrical stimulation and lesions of the hippocampus and adjacent regions upon attack behavior in cats. *Brain Research,* 1968, *7,* 252–267.

Siegel, A. & D. Skog. Effect of electrical stimulation of the septum upon attack behavior elicited from the hypothalamus in the cat. *Brain Research,* 1970, *23,* 371–380.

Siegel, D. & R. C. Leaf. Effects of septal and amygdaloid brain lesions on mouse killing. Paper presented at the Eastern Psychological Association, Philadelphia, 1969.

Siegfried, J. & A. Ben-Shmuel. Neurosurgical treatment of aggressivity: Stereotaxic amygdalotomy versus leukotomy. In K. E. Hitchcock, L. Laitinen, & K. Vaernet (Eds.), *Psychosurgery.* Springfield, Ill.: Thomas, 1972, pp. 214–218.

Sigg, E. B. Relationship of aggressive behaviour to adrenal and gonadal function in male mice. In S. Garattini & E. B. Sigg (Eds.), *Aggressive behaviour.* New York: Wiley, 1969, pp. 143–149.

Sigg, E. B., C. Day, & C. Colombo. Endocrine factors in isolation induced aggressiveness in rodents. *Endocrinology,* 1966, *78,* 679–684.

Silverman, D. Implication of the EEG abnormalities in the psychopathic personality. *Archives of Neurology and Psychiatry,* 1949, *62,* 870–873.

Singer, J. L. (Ed.). The control of aggression and violence cognitive and physiological factors. New York: Wiley, 1971.

Skelton, W. D. Alcohol, violent behavior, and the electroencephalogram. *Southern Medical Journal,* 1970, *63,* 425–466.

Skinner, B. F. *Beyond freedom and dignity.* New York: Knopf, 1971.

Skultety, F. M. Stimulation of periaqueductal gray and hypothalamus. *Archives of Neurology,* 1963, *8,* 608–620.

Sletten, I. W. & S. Gershon. The premenstrual syndrome: A discussion of its pathophysiology and treatment of lithium ion. *Comprehensive Psychiatry,* 1966, *7,* 197–206.

Slotnick, B. M. & M. F. McMullen. Intraspecific fighting in albino mice with septal forebrain lesions. *Physiology and Behavior*, 1972, *8*, 333–337.

Small, J. The organic dimensions of crime. *Archives of General Psychiatry*, 1966, *15*, 82–89.

Small, J. G., V. Milstein, & J. R. Stevens. Are psychomotor epileptics different? *American Medical Association Archives of Neurology*, 1962, *7*, 187–194.

Small, J. G. & I. F. Small. 14 & 6 second positive spikes. *Archives of General Psychiatry*, 1964, *11*, 645–650.

Smith, D. E., M. B. King, & B. G. Hoebel. Killing: Cholinergic control in the lateral hypothalamus. *Proceedings of the 77th Annual Convention of the American Psychological Association*, 1969, pp. 895–896.

Smith, D. E., M. B. King, & B. G. Hoebel. Lateral hypothalamic control of killing: Evidence for a cholinoceptive mechanism. *Science*, 1970, *167*, 900–901.

Smith, S. W. Trifluoperazine in children and adolescents with marked behavior problems. *American Journal of Psychiatry*, 1965, *122*, 702–703.

Smolev, S. R. Use of operant technique for the modification of self-injurious behavior. *American Journal of Mental Deficiency*, 1972, *76*, 296–305.

Sodetz, F. J. The social behavior and aggressiveness of the hamster following the application of chemicals to the septal region of the forebrain. Unpublished doctoral dissertation, University of Florida, Gainesville, 1967.

Sodetz, F. J. & B. N. Bunnell. Interactive effects of septal lesions and social experience in the hamster. Paper presented at the meeting of the Eastern Psychological Association, Washington, D.C., 1967a.

Sodetz, F. J. & B. N. Bunnell. Septal ablation and the social behavior of the golden hamster. Paper presented at the meeting of the Midwestern Psychological Association, Chicago, 1967b.

Sodetz, F. J., E. Matalka, & B. N. Bunnell. Septal ablation and affective behavior in the golden hamster. *Psychonomic Science*, 1967, *7*, 189–190.

Solomon, P. & S. T. Kleeman. Medical aspects of violence. *California Medicine*, 1971, *114*, 19–24.

Sommer, R. Personal space: The behavioral basis of design. Englewood Cliffs, N.J.: Prentice-Hall, 1969.

Sonne, C. Observations on the symptomatology of insulin poisoning, particularly its psychic effects. *Acta Medica Scandinavica* (Supplement) 1930, *34*, 223–233.

Southwick, C. H. Effect of maternal environment on aggressive behavior of inbred mice. *Communications in Behavioral Biology*, Part A. 1968, *1*, 129–132.

Southwick, C. H. Aggressive behaviour of rhesus monkeys in natural and captive groups. In S. Garattini & E. G. Sigg (Eds.), *Aggressive behaviour*. New York: Wiley, 1969, pp. 32–43.

Southwick, C. H. & L. H. Clark. Interstrain differences in aggressive behavior and exploratory activity of inbred mice. *Communications in Behavioral Biology*, 1968, *1*, 49–59.

Spector, S. A. & E. M. Hull. Anosmia and mouse killing by rats: A nonolfactory role for the olfactory bulbs. *Journal of Comparative and Physiological Psychology*, 1972, *80*, 354–356.

Speer, F. The allergic tension-fatigue syndrome. *Pediatric Clinic of North America*, 1954, *1*, 1029–1037.

Speer, F. The allergic tension-fatigue syndrome in children. *International Archives of Allergy*, 1958, *12*, 207–214.

Speer, F. The history of allergy of the nervous system. In F. Speer (Ed.), *Allergy of the nervous system*. Springfield, Ill.: Thomas, 1970a, pp. 3–13.

Speer, F. The allergic tension-fatigue syndrome. In F. Speer (Ed.), *Allergy of the nervous system*. Springfield, Ill.: Thomas, 1970b, pp. 14–27.

Speer, F. Etiology: Foods. In F. Speer (Ed.), *Allergy of the nervous system*. Springfield, Ill.: Thomas, 1970c, pp. 198–209.

Spencer, J., J. Gray, & A. Dalhouse. Social isolation in the gerbil: Its effect on exploratory or agonistic behavior and adrenocortical activity. *Physiology and Behavior*, 1973, *10*, 231–237.

Spiegel, E. A. & H. T. Wycis. Physiological and psychological results of thalmotomy. *Proceedings of the Royal Society* (Medical Supplement) 1949, *42*, 84–93.

Spiegel, E. A., H. T. Wycis, H. Freed, & C. Orchinik. The central mechanism of the emotions. *American Journal of Psychiatry*, 1951, *108*, 426–432.

Spiegel, J. P. Psychosocial factors in riots old and new. *American Journal of Psychiatry*, 1968, *125*, 281–285.

Stachnik, T. J., R. E. Ulrich, & J. H. Mabry. Reinforcement of intra- and interspecies aggression with intracranial stimulation. *American Zoologist*, 1966a, *6*, 663–668.

Stachnik, T. J., R. E. Ulrich, & J. H. Mabry. Reinforcement of aggression through intracranial stimulation. *Psychonomic Science*, 1966b, *5*, 101–102.

Stafford-Clark, D. & F. H. Taylor. Clinical and electroencephalographic studies of prisoners charged with murder. *Journal of Neurology, Neurosurgery and Psychiatry*, 1949, *12*, 325–330.

Stea, D. Space, territory and human movements. *Landscape*, 1965, *15*, 13–16.

Stedman, J. M., T. L. Peterson, & J. Cardarelle. Application of a token system in a pre-adolescent boys' group. *Journal of Behavior Therapy and Experimental Psychiatry*, 1971, *2*, 23–29.

Stehle, H. C. Thalamic dysfunction involved in destructive-aggressive behavior direct against persons and property. *Electroencephalography and Clinical Physiology*, 1960, *12*, 264–265.

Stekel, W. *Sadism and masochism: The psychology of hatred and cruelty*, Vols. I & II. New York: Liveright, 1929.

Stephens, J. H. & J. W. Shaffer. A controlled study of the effects of diphenylhydantoin on anxiety, irritability and anger in neurotic outpatients. *Psychopharmacologia*, 1970, *17*, 169–181.

Stern, J. M. Distribution and binding of ^{3}H-androgens in neural and peripheral tissues of rats and ring doves: Effects of progesterone and other steroid hormones. Unpublished doctoral dissertation, Rutgers University, New Brunswick, N.J., 1970.

Stevens, J. R. Psychiatric implications of psychomotor epilepsy. *Archives of General Psychiatry*, 1966, *14*, 461–471.

Stevens, J. R., V. H. Mark, F. Ervin, P. Pacheco, & K. Suenatsu. Deep temporal stimulation in man: Long latency, long lasting psychological changes. *Archives of Neurology*, 1969, *21*, 157–169.

Stone, C. P. Wildness and savageness in rats of different strains. In K. S. Lashley (Ed.), *Studies in dynamics of behavior*. Chicago: University of Chicago Press, 1932, pp. 3–55.

Storr, A. *Human aggression*. New York, Atheneum, 1968.

Strauss, E. B., D. E. Sands, A. M. Robinson, W. J. Tindall, & W. A. Stevenson. Use of dehydroisoandrosterone in psychiatric treatment. *British Medical Journal*, 1952, *2*, 64–66.

Strauss, I. & M. Keschner. Mental symptoms in cases of tumor of the frontal lobe. *Archives of Neurology and Psychiatry*. 1935, *33*, 986–1005.

Strauss, I. & M. Keschner. Mental symptoms in cases of tumor of the frontal lobe. *Archives of Neurology and Psychiatry*, 1936, *35*, 572–596.

Strecker, E. A. & F. Ebaugh. Neuropsychiatric sequaelae of cerebral trauma in children. *Archives of Neurology and Psychiatry*, 1924, *12*, 443–453.

Strom-Olsen, R. & S. Carlisle. Bifrontal stereotaxic tractotomy. In E. Hitchcock, L. Laitinen, & K. Vaernet (Eds.), *Psychosurgery*. Springfield, Ill.: Thomas, 1972, pp. 278–288.

Strom-Olsen, R., S. L. Last, & M. B. Brody. Results of prefrontal leucotomy in thirty cases of mental disorder. *Journal of Mental Science*, 1943, *89*, 165–181.

Sturup, G. K. Correctional treatment and the criminal sexual offender. *Canadian Journal of Correction*, 1961, *3*, 250–265.

Suchowsky, G. K., L. Pegrassi, & A. Bonsignori. The effect of steroids on aggressive behaviour in isolated male mice. In S. Garattini & E. B. Sigg (Eds.), *Aggressive behaviour*. New York: Wiley, 1969, pp. 164–171.

Suchowsky, G. K., L. Pegrassi, & A. Bonsignori. Steroids and aggressive behavior in isolated male and female mice. *Psychopharmacologia*, 1971, *21*, 32–38.

Sugarman, A. A., B. H. Williams, & A. M. Alderstein. Haloperidol in the psychiatric disorders of old age. *American Journal of Psychiatry*, 1964, *120*, 1190–1195.

Summers, T. B. & W. W. Kaelber. Amygdalectomy: Effects in cats and a survey of its present status. *American Journal of Physiology*, 1962, *203*, 1117–1119.

Suomi, S. J. & H. F. Harlow. Social rehabilitation of isolate-reared monkeys. *Developmental Psychology*, 1972, *6*, 487–496.

Sutherland, H. & I. A. Stewart. A critical analysis of the premenstrual syndrome. *Lancet*, 1965, *1*, 1180–1183.

Svare, B. B. & R. Gandelman. Postpartum aggression in mice: Experiential and environmental factors. *Hormones and Behavior*, 1973, *4*, 323–334.

Svare, B. B. & A. I. Leshner. The adrenals and testes: Two separate systems affecting aggression. Paper presented at the 43rd Annual Meeting, Eastern Psychological Association, Boston, 1972.

Svare, B. B. & A. I. Leshner. Behavioral correlates of intermale aggression and grouping in mice. *Journal of Comparative and Physiological Psychology*, 1973, *85*, 203–210.

Sweet, W. H., F. Ervin, & V. H. Mark. The relationship of violent behaviour to focal cerebral disease. In S. Garattini & E. B. Sigg (Eds.), *Aggressive behaviour*. New York: Wiley, 1969, pp. 336–352.

Takala, M., T. A. Pihkanen, & T. Markkanen. *The effects of distilled and brewed beverages: A physiological, neurological and psychological study*. The Finnish Foundation for Alcohol Studies, Helsinki, Publication No. 4, 1957.

Talkington, L. W. & J. B. Riley. Reduction diets and aggression in institutionalized mentally retarded patients. *American Journal of Mental Deficiency*, 1971, *76*, 370–372.

Taylor, D. C. Aggression and epilepsy. *Journal of Psychosomatic Research*, 1969, *13*, 229–236.

Taylor, J. C. Home range and agonistic behavior in the grey squirrel. In P. A. Jewell & C. Loizos (Eds.), *Play, exploration and territory in mammals*. New York: Academic Press, 1966, pp. 229–236.

Taylor, S. P. & C. B. Gammon. The effects of type and dose of alcohol on human physical aggression. *Journal of Personality and Social Psychology*, 1975, *32*, 169–175.

Telle, H. J. Beitrag zur Kenntnis der verhaltensweise bei ratten, vergleichend dargestellt bei *Rattus norvegicus* und *Rattus rattus*. *Zeitschrift fuer Angewandt Zoologie*, 1966, *9*, 129–196.

Tellegen, A., J. M. Horn, & R. G. Legrand. Opportunity for aggression as a reinforcer in mice. *Psychonomic Science*, 1969, *14*, 104–105.

Terrell, M. S. Response to trifluoperazine and chlorpromazine singly and in combination, in chronic "Back-Ward" patients. *Diseases of the Nervous System*, 1962, *23*, 41–48.

Terzian, H. Observations on the clinical symptomatology of bilateral partial or total removal of the temporal lobes in man. In M. Balwin & P. Bailey (Eds.), *Temporal lobe epilepsy*. Springfield, Ill.: Thomas, 1958, pp. 510–529.

Terzian, H. & G. D. Ore. Syndrome of Kluver and Bucy reproduced in man by bilateral removal of the temporal lobes. *Neurology*, 1955, *5*, 378–380.

Textor, R. B. *A cross cultural summary*. New Haven, Conn.: Human Resources Area Files Press, 1967.

Thiessen, D. D. & M. Dawber. Territorial exclusion and reproductive isolation. *Psychonomic Science*, 1972, *28*, 159–160.

Thiessen, D. D., H. C. Friend, & G. Lindzey. Androgen control of territorial marking in the Mongolian gerbil. *Science*, 1968, *160*, 432–433.

Thiessen, D. D., G. Lindzey, & J. Nyby. The effects of olfactory deprivation and hormones on territorial marking in the male Mongolian gerbil (*Meriones unguiculatus*). *Hormones and behavior*, 1970, *1*, 315–325.

Thompson, N. S. Some variables affecting the behaviour of irus macaques in dyadic encounters. *Animal Behaviour*, 1967, *15*, 307–311.

Thompson, T. & W. Bloom. Aggressive behavior and extinction induced respone rate increase. *Psychonomic Science*, 1966, *5*, 335–336.

Thor, D. H. & D. L. Hoats. Morphine-amphetamine-induced fighting and interim socialization. *Psychonomic Science*, 1970, *21*, 156–158.

Thor, D. H. & B. G. Teel. Fighting of rats during post-morphine withdrawal: Effect of prewithdrawal dosage. *The American Journal of Psychology*, 1968, *81*, 439–442.

Thorne, B. M., M. Aaron, & E. E. Latham. Effects of olfactory ablation upon emotionality and muricidal behavior in four rat strains. *Journal of Comparative and Physiological Psychology*, 1973, *84*, 339–344.

Tinbergen, N. Social releasers and the experimental method required for their study. *Wilson Bulletin*, 1948, *60*, 6–52.

Tinbergen, N. The hierarchial organization of nervous mechanisms underlying instinctive behavior. In *Physical mechanisms in animal behavior: symposium of the society for experimental biology (No. 55)*. New York: Academic Press, 1950, pp. 305–312.

Tinbergen, N. Fighting and threat in animals. *New Biology*, 1953, *14*, 9–24.

Tinbergen, N. *Tiere untereinander*. Berlin: Parey, 1955.

Tinbergen, N. The functions of territory. *Bird Study*, 1957, *4*, 14–27.

Tinbergen, N. On war and peace in animals and man. *Science*, 1968, *160*, 1411–1418.

Tinklenberg, J. R. & R. C. Stillman. Drug use and violence. In D. N. Daniels, M. F. Gilula, & F. M. Ochberg (Eds.), *Violence and the struggle for existence*. Boston: Little, Brown, 1970, pp. 327–366.

Tintera, J. W. The hypoadrenocortical state and its management. *New York State Journal of Medicine*, 1955, *55*, 1869–1876.

Tintera, J. W. Stabilizing homeostasis in the recovered alcoholic through endocrine therapy: Evaluation of the hypoglycemia factor. *Journal of the American Geriatrics Society*, 1966, *14*, 126–150.

Tobin, J. M., I. F. Bird, & D. F. Boyle. Preliminary evaluation of Librium (Ro 5-0690) in the treatment of anxiety reactions. *Diseases of the Nervous System, Supplement*, 1960, *21*, 16–19.

Toch, H. *Violent man*. Chicago: Aldine, 1969.

Tolman, J. & J. A. King. The effects of testosterone propionate on aggression in male and female C57BL/10 mice. *British Journal of Animal Behaviour*, 1956, *4*, 147–149.

Torghele, P. R. Premenstrual tension in psychotic women. *Lancet*, 1957, *77*, 163–170.

Tow, P. M. & C. W. Whitty. Personality changes after operations on the cingulate gyrus in man. *Journal of Neurology, Neurosurgery, and Psychiatry*, 1953, *16*, 186–193.

Traldi, S. Use of fluphenazine enanthate in chronic schizophrenia. *Folia Medica*, 1966, *53*, 261–277.

Travis, L. E. & J. M. Dorsey. Effect of alcohol on the patellar tendon reflex. *Archives of Neurology and Psychiatry*, 1926, *21*, 613–624.

Treffert, D. A. The psychiatric patient with an EEG temporal lobe focus. *American Journal of Psychiatry*, 1964, *120*, 765–771.

Tupin, J. P. Lithium use in nonmanic depressive conditions. *Comparative Psychiatry*, 1972, *13*, 209–214.

Tupin, J. P. & T. L. Clanon. Lithium and aggression control, personal communication.

Tupin, J. P., D. B. Smith, T. L. Clanon, L. I. Kim, A. Nugent, & A. Groupe. The long-term use of lithium in aggressive prisoners. *Comprehensive Psychiatry*, 1973, *14*, 311–317.

Turner, E. A. Cerebral control of respiration. *Brain*, 1954, *77*, 448–486.

Turner, E. A. Bilateral temporal lobotomy for psychomotor epilepsy. *1st International Congress of Neurological Science*, 1959, 2, 240–241.

Turner, E. A. Operations for aggression: Bilateral temporal lobotomy and posterior cingulectomy. In E. Hitchcock, L. Laitinen, & K. Vaernet (Eds.), *Psychosurgery*. Springfield, Ill.: Thomas, 1972, pp. 204–209.

Turner, W. J. Therapeutic use of diphenylhydantoin in neuroses. *International Journal of Neuropsychiatry*, 1967, 3, 94–105.

Turns, D., H. C. Denber, & D. N. Teller. Preliminary clinical study of propericiazine. *Journal of New Drugs*, 1965, 5, 90–93.

Tuttle, W. W. The effect of alcohol on the patellar tendon reflex. *Journal of Pharmacology and Experimental Therapeutics*, 1924, 23, 163–172.

Ullrich, H. Immer noch alkohol in der jugendkriminaltat. *Kriminalistik*, 1967, 21, 518–522.

Ulrich, R. E. Pain as a cause of aggression. *American Zoologist*, 1966, 6, 643–662.

Ulrich, R. E. Unconditioned and conditioned aggression and its relation to pain. *Activities Nervosa Superior*, 1967, 9, 80–91.

Ulrich, R. E. & N. H. Azrin. Reflexive fighting in response to aversive stimulation. *Journal of the Experimental Analysis of Behavior*, 1962, 5, 511–520.

Ulrich, R. E., S. Dulaney, M. Arnett, & K. Mueller. An experimental analysis of nonhuman and human aggression. In J. F. Knutson (Ed.), *Control of aggression: Implications for basic research*. Chicago: Aldine, 1973.

Ulrich, R. E., R. R. Hutchinson, & N. M. Azrin. Pain-elicited aggression. *The Psychological Record*, 1965, 15, 111–126.

Ulrich, R. E. & B. Symannek. Pain as a stimulus for aggression. In S. Garattini & E. B. Sigg (Eds.), *Aggressive behaviour*. New York: Wiley, 1969, pp. 59–69.

Ulrich, R. E., M. Wolfe, & S. Dulaney. Punishment of shock-induced aggression. *Journal of the Experimental Analysis of Behavior*, 1969, 12, 109–1015.

Ulrich, R. E., P. C. Wolff, & N. H. Azrin. Shock as an elicitor of intra- and interspecies fighting behavior. *Animal Behaviour*, 1964, 12, 14–15.

Umbach, W., Y. K. Kim, & M. Adler. Follow-up on stereotaxically treated patients with abnormal behavior. In E. Hitchcock, L. Laitinen, & K. Vaernet (Eds.), *Psychosurgery*. Springfield, Ill.: Thomas, 1972, pp. 210–213.

Urich, J. The social hierarchy in albino mice. *Journal of Comparative Psychology*, 1938, 25, 373–413.

Ursin, H. The temporal lobe substrate for fear and anger. *Acta Psychichiatrica et Neurologica Scandinavia* (Kjobenhavn), 1960, 35, 278–296.

Ursin, H. The effect of amygdaloid lesions on flight and defense behavior in cats. *Experimental Neurology*, 1965, 11, 61–79.

Ursin, H. The cingulate gyrus: A fear zone. *Journal of Comparative and Physiological Psychology*, 1969, 68, 235–238.

Ursin, H. Limbic control of emotional behavior. In E. Hitchcock, L. Laitinen, & K. Vaernet (Eds.), *Psychosurgery*. Springfield, Ill.: Thomas, 1972, pp. 34–45.

Ursin, H. & B. R. Kaada. Functional localization within the amygdaloid complex in cat. *Electroencephalography and Clinical Neurophysiology*, 1960, 12, 1–20.

Vaernet, K. & A. Madsen. Stereotaxic amygdalotomy and basofrontal tractotomy in psychotics with aggressive behaviour. *Journal of Neurology, Neurosurgery and Psychiatry*, 1970, 33, 858–863.

Vaernet, K. & A. Madsen. Lesions in the amygdala and the substantia innominata in aggressive psychotic patients. In E. Hitchcock, L. Laitinen, & K. Vaernet (Eds.), *Psychosurgery.* Springfield, Ill.: Thomas, 1972, pp. 187–194.

Vale, J. R., D. Ray, & C. A. Vale. Interaction of genotype and exogenous neonatal androgen: Agonistic behavior in female mice. *Behavioral Biology*, 1972, 7, 321–333.

Valenstein, E. S. *Brain control.* New York: Wiley, 1973.

Vallardares, H. & V. Corbalan. Temporal lobe and human behavior. 1st International Congress, *Neurological Science*, 1959, 201–203.

Valzelli, L. Drugs and aggressiveness. *Advances in Pharmacology*, 1967, 5, 79–108.

Valzelli, L. Aggressive behaviour induced by isolation. In S. Garattini & E. B. Sigg (Eds.), *Aggressive behaviour.* New York: Wiley, 1969, pp. 70–76.

Vandenbergh, J. G. Endocrine coordination in monkeys: Male sexual responses to the female. *Physiology and Behavior,* 1969, 4, 261–264.

Vandenberg, J. G. Effects of gonadal hormones on aggressive behavior of adult golden-hamsters (*Mesocricetus auratus*). *Animal Behaviour*, 1971, 19, 589–594.

Vanegas, H., W. Foote, & J. P. Flynn. Hypothalamic influences upon activity of units of the visual cortex. *Yale Journal of Biology and Medicine*, 1969–1970, 42, 191–201.

Van Hemel, P. E. Aggression as an incentive: Operant behavior in the mouse-killing rat. Unpublished doctoral dissertation, Johns Hopkins University, Baltimore, 1970.

Van Hemel, P. E. Aggression as a reinforcer: Operant behavior in the mouse-killing rat. *Journal of the Experimental Analysis of Behavior*, 1972, 17, 237–245.

Van Hemel, P. E. & V. M. Colucci. Effects of target movement on mouse-killing attack by rats. *Journal of Comparative and Physiological Psychology*, 1973, 85, 105–110.

Van Hemel, P. E. & J. S. Myer. Satiation of mouse killing by rats in an operant situation. *Psychonomic Science*, 1970, 21, 129–130.

Vasconcellos, J. Clinical evaluation of trifluoperazine in maximum security brain damaged patients with severe behavioral disorders. *Journal of Clinical and Experimental Pathology*, 1960, 21, 25–30.

Vergnes, M. & P. Karli. Déclenchement du comportement d'addression interspecifique rat-souris par ablation bilaterale des bulbes olfactifs. Action de l'hydroxyzine sur cette agressivité proveoquée. *Comptes Rendus des Séances de la Société de Biologie*, 1963, 157, 1061.

Vergnes, M. & P. Karli, Étude des voies nerveuses de l'influence facilitatrice exercée par les noyaux amygdaliens sur le comportement d'adression interspecifique rat-souris. *Comptes Rendus des Séances de la Société de Biologie*, 1964, 158, 856–858.

Vergnes, M. & P. Karli, Étude des coies nervauses d'une influence inhibitrice s'exerçant sur l'agressivité interspecifique du rat. *Comptes Rendus des Séances de la Société de Biologie*, 1965, 159, 972.

Vergnes, M. & P. Karli, Effets de la stimulation de l'hypothalamus de l'amygdale et de l'hippocampe sur le comportement d'aggression interspecifique rat-souris. *Physiology and Behavior*, 1969, 4, 889–894.

Vergnes, M. & P. Karli, Electrical stimulation of the dorsomedial thalamus and the rat's mouse-killing behavior. *Physiology and Behavior*, 1972, 889–892.

Vernon, W. & R. Ulrich. Classical conditioning of pain-elicited aggression. *Science*, 1966, 152, 668–669.

Vogel, G. REM deprivation. III. Dreaming and psychosis. *Archives of General Psychiatry*, 1968, 18, 312–329.

Vogel, J. R. & R. C. Leaf. Initiation of mouse-killing in non-killer rats by repeated pilocarpine treatment. *Physiology and Behavior*, 1972, 8, 421–424.

Vonderahe, A. R. The anatomic substratum of emotion. *The New Scholasticism*, 1944, 18, 76–95.

Von Pirquet, C. Allergie. *Munchener Medizinische Wochenschrift*, 1906, 53, 1457–1458.

Vos, A. Territorial behavior among puku in Zambia. *Science*, 1965, 148, 1752–1853.

Voss, H. L. & J. R. Hepburn. Patterns in criminal homicide in Chicago. *Journal of Criminal Law, Criminology and Police Science*, 1968, 59, 499–508.

Vukelich, R. & D. F. Hake. Reduction of dangerously aggressive behavior in a severely retarded resident through a combination of positive reinforcement procedures. *Journal of Applied Behavior Analysis*, 1971, 4, 215–225.

Walker. A. E. Murder or epilepsy? *Journal of Nervous and Mental Disease*, 1961, 133, 430–437.

Walker, A. E. & D. Blumer. Long term effects of temporal lobe lesions on sexual behavior and aggressivity. Paper presented at the Houston Neurological Symposium on Neural Bases of Violence and Aggression, Houston, Texas: March 9–11, 1972.

Walker, W. A. & A. I. Leshner. Role of adrenals in aggression. *American Zoologist*, 1972, 12, 652.

Wallgren, H. & H. Barry. *Actions of alcohol*, Vol. 1. Amsterdam: Elsevier, 1970.

Walter, R. R., E. G. Colbert, R. R. Koegler, J. O. Palmer, & P. M. Bond: A controlled study of the fourteen and six per second EEG pattern. *Archives of General Psychiatry*, 1960, 2, 559–566.

Ward, A. A. The cingular gyrus: Area 24. *Journal of Neurophysiology*, 1948, 11, 13–23.

Ward, A. A., H. H. Jasper, & A. Pope. Clinical and experimental challenges of the epilepsies. In H. H. Jasper, A. A. Ward, & A. Pope. *Basic mechanisms of the epilepsies*. Boston: Little, Brown, 1969, pp. 1–12.

Ward, I. Prenatal stress feminizes and demasculinizes the behavior of males. *Science*, 1972, 175, 82–85.

Warne, M. C. A time analysis of certain aspects of the behavior of small groups of caged mice. *Journal of Comparative and Physiological Psychology*, 1947, 40, 371–387.

Washburn, S. L. Conflict in primate society. In A. de Reuck & J. Knight (Eds.), *Conflict in society*. Boston: Little, Brown, 1966, pp. 3–15.

Washburn, S. L. & I. DeVore. Social behavior of baboons and early man. In S. L. Washburn (Ed.), *Social life of early man*. Chicago: Aldine, 1961, pp. 91–105.

Wasman, M. & J. P. Flynn. Directed attack elicited from hypothalamus. *Archives of Neurology*, 1962, *6*, 220–227.

Wasman, M. & J. P. Flynn. Directed attack behavior during hippocampal seizures. *Archives of Neurology*, 1966, *14*, 408–414.

Webb, W. B. Some effects of prolonged sleep deprivation on the hooded rat. *Journal of Comparative and Physiological Psychology*, 1962, 55, 791–793.

Weil, A. A. Ictal emotions occuring in temporal lobe dysfunction. *Archives of Neurology*, 1959, *1*, 101–111.

Weischer, M. L. Uber die antiagressive wirking von lithium. *Psychopharmacologia*, 1969, *15*, 245–254.

Weiskrantz, L. Behavioral changes associated with ablation of the amygdaloid complex in monkeys. *Journal of Comparative and Physiological Psychology*, 1956, *49*, 381–394.

Welch, A. S. & B. L. Welch. Isolation, reactivity and aggression: Evidence for an involvement of brain catecholamines and serotonin. In F. F. Eleftheriou and J. P. Scott (Eds.), *The physiology of aggression and defeat*. New York, Plenum, 1971, pp. 91–142.

Welch, B. L. Discussion of aggression, defense and neurohumors by A. B. Rothballer. In C. D. Clemente & D. B. Lindsley (Eds.), *Aggression and defense: Neural mechanisms and social patterns*, Vol. V: *Brain Function*. Los Angeles: University of California Press, 1967.

Welch, B. L. Report of symposium on aggressive behavior. *BioScience*, 1968, *18*, 1061–1064.

Welch, B. L. Symposium summary. In S. Garattini & E. B. Sigg (Eds.), *Aggressive behaviour*. New York: Wiley, 1969, pp. 363–370.

Welch, B. L. & A. S. Welch. Aggression and biogenic amine neurohumors. In S. Garattini & E. B. Sigg (Eds.), *Aggressive behaviour*. New York: Wiley, 1969, pp. 188–202.

Weltman, A. S., A. M. Sackler, & S. B. Sparber. Endocrine, metabolic and behavioral aspects of isolation stress on female albino mice. *Aerospace Medicine*, 1966, *37*, 804–810.

Weltman, A. S., A. M. Sackler, S. B. Sparber, & S. Opert. Endocrine aspects of isolation stress in female mice. *Federation Proceedings*, 1962, *21*, 16.

Weltman, A. S., A. M. Sackler, & R. Schwartz. Isolation induced aggressiveness and behavioral abnormalities in female mice. *American Zoologist*, 1967, 7, 794.

Weltman, A. S., A. M. Sackler, & R. Schwartz. Maternal effects on behavior and white blood cells of isolated female mice. *Life Sciences*, 1970a, 9, 291–300.

Weltman, A. S., A. M. Sackler, & R. Schwartz. Maternal effects on behavior and white blood cells of isolated female mice. *Life Sciences*, 1970b, 9, 291–300.

Weltman, A. S., A. M. Sackler, R. Schwartz, & H. Owens. Effects of isolation stress on female albino mice. *Laboratory Animal Care,* 1968, *18,* 426–435.

Wender, P. H. *Minimal brain dysfunction in children.* New York: Wiley, 1971.

Wertham, F. *Seduction of the innocent.* New York: Holt, Rinehart and Winston, 1954.

Wertham, F. *A sign for Cain.* New York: Macmillan, 1966.

Wetzel, A. B., R. L. Conner, & S. Levine. Shock-induced fighting in septal-lesioned rats. *Psychonomic Science,* 1967, *9,* 133–134.

Whalen, R. E. & H. Fehr. The development of the mouse killing response in rats. *Psychonomic Science,* 1964, *1,* 77–78.

Wheatley, M. D. The hypothalamus and affective behavior in cats. *Archives of Neurology and Psychiatry,* 1944, *52,* 296–316.

Whitaker, L. H. Oestrogen and psychosexual disorders. *Medical Journal of Australia,* 1959, *2,* 547–549.

White, G. D., G. Nielsen, & S. M. Johnson. Timeout duration and the suppression of deviant behavior in children. *Journal of Applied Behavior Analysis,* 1972, *5,* 11–120.

Whitty, C. W., J. E. Duffield, P. M. Tow, & H. Cairns. Anterior cingulectomy in the treatment of mental disease. *Lancet,* 1952, *1,* 475–481.

Wilder, B. J. The clinical neurophysiology of epilepsy: A survey of current research. *NINDB Monograph,* No. 8, 1968, 1–46.

Wilder, J. Problems of criminal psychology related to hypoglycemic states. *Journal of Criminal Psychology,* 1940, *1,* 219–233.

Wilder, J. Psychological problems in hypoglycemia. *American Journal of Digestive Diseases,* 1943, *10,* 428–435.

Wilder, J. Malnutrition and mental deficiency. *Nervous Child,* 1944, *3,* 174–186.

Wilder, J. Sugar metabolism in its relation to criminology. In S. Linduer & B. J. Seliger (Eds.), *Handbook of correctional psychology.* New York: Philosophical Library, 1947.

Williams, D. The structure of emotions reflected in epileptic emotions. *Brain,* 1965, *79,* 28–67.

Williams, D. Temporal lobe syndrome. In P. J. Vinken and G. W. Bruyn (Eds.), *Handbook of clinical neurology,* Vol. II. New York: Wiley, 1969a, pp. 700–724.

Williams, D. Neural factors related to habitual aggression. Consideration of differences between those habitual aggressives and others who have committed crimes of violence. *Brain,* 1969b, *92,* 503–520.

Williams, D. R. & P. Teitelbaum. Control of drinking behavior by means of an operant-conditioning technique. *Science,* 1956, *124,* 1294–1296.

Williams, R. J. *Biochemical individuality.* New York: Wiley, 1956.

Wilson, A. Social behavior of free-ranging rhesus monkeys with an emphasis on aggression. Unpublished dissertation, University of California, Berkeley, 1968.

Wilson, A. P. & R. C. Boelkins. Evidence for seasonal variation in aggressive behaviour by *Macaca mulatta. Animal Behaviour,* 1970, *18,* 719–724.

Wilson, J. A., R. E. Kuehn, & F. A. Beach. Modification of the sexual behavior of male rats produced by changing the stimulus female. *Journal of Comparative and Physiological Psychology,* 1963, *56,* 636–644.

Wilson, S. A. *Kinnier, Neurology,* Vol. 1. Baltimore: Williams & Wilkins, 1940.

Winfield, D. L. & O. Ozturk. Electroencephalographic findings in matricide. *Diseases of the Nervous System,* 1959, *20,* 1251–1254.

Winshel, A. W. Chlorothiazide in premenstrual tension. *International Record of Medicine,* 1959, *172,* 539–542.

Winslow, C. N. The social behavior of cats. I. Competitive and aggressive behavior in an experimental runway situation. *Journal of Comparative Psychology,* 1944, *37,* 297–313.

Wiseman, W. Four years' experience with ovulation inhibitors in clinical trial and routine use. In *Recent advances in ovarian and synthetic steroids and the control of ovarian function.* (Proceedings of a Symposium). Sydney, Australia, Globe Commercial Party Ltd., 1965.

Wnek, D. J. & R. C. Leaf. Effects of cholinergic drugs on prey-killing by rodents. *Physiology and Behavior,* 1973, *10,* 1107–1113.

Wolf, A. & E. F. Von Haxthausen. Toward the analysis of the effects of some centrally acting sedative substances. *Arzeimittel-Forschung,* 1960, *19,* 50.

Wolfe, J. L. Agonistic behavior in organized and disorganized cotton rat populations. *Science,* 1968, *160,* 98–99.

Wolfgang, M. E. *Patterns in criminal homicide.* New York: Wiley, 1958.

Wolfgang, M. E. & F. Ferracuti, *The subculture of violence.* London: Tavistock, 1967.

Wolpwitz, E. The use of thioridazine (Melleril) in cases of epileptic psychosis. *South African Medical Journal,* 1966, *40,* 143–144.

Wood, C. D. Behavioral changes following discrete lesions of temporal lobe structures. *Neurology,* 1958, *8,* 215–220.

Woods, J. W. "Taming" of the wild Norway rat by rhinencephalic lesions. *Nature,* 1956, *178,* 869.

Woods, S. M. Adolescent violence and homicide: Ego disruption and the 6 and 14 dysrhythmia. *Archives of General Psychiatry,* 1961, *5,* 528–534.

Woodworth, C. Attack elicited in rats by electrical stimulation of the lateral hypothalamus. *Physiology and Behavior,* 1971, *6,* 345–353.

Woringer, E., G. Thomalske, & J. Klingler. Les rapports anatomiques du noyau amygdalien et la technique de son extirpation neurochirurgicale. *Revue Neurologique,* 1953, *89,* 553–560.

Wynne-Edwards, V. C. *Animal dispersion in relation to social behaviour.* New York, Harner, 1962.

Yasokochi, G. Emotional response elicited by electrical stimulation of the hypothalamus in cat. *Folia Psychiatrica et Neurologica Japonica,* 1960, *14,* 260–267.

Yen, H. C. Y., C. A. Day, & E. B. Sigg. Influence of endocrine factors on development of fighting behavior in rodents. *Pharmacologist,* 1962, *4,* 173.

Yerkes, R. M. The heredity of savageness and wildness in rats. *Journal of Animal Behavior,* 1913, *3,* 286–296.

Yoshii, N., T. Ishiwara, & K. Tani. Juvenile delinquents and their abnormal EEGs 14 and 6 per second positive spikes pattern. *Medical Journal of Osaka University,* 1963, *14,* 61–66.

Yoshii, N., T. Ishiwara, & K. Tani. Juvenile delinquents and their abnormal EEGs, II. Continuous theta waves. *Folia Psychiatrica et Neurologica Japonica,* 1964, *18,* 161–167.

Yoshii, N., M. Shimolochi, & K. Tani. The electroencephalograms in juvenile delinquents. *Folia Psychiatrica et Neurologica Japonica,* 1961, *15,* 85–91.

Zbrozyna, A. W. The organization of the defense reaction elicited from amygdala and its connections. In B. E. Eleftheriou (Ed.), *The Neurobiology of the Amygdala.* New York: Plenum, 1972, pp. 597–608.

Zeman, W. & F. A. King. Tumors of the septum pellucidum and adjacent structures with abnormal affective behavior: An anterior midline structure syndrome. *Journal of Nervous and Mental Disease,* 1958, *127,* 490–502.

Zimmerman, F. T. Explosive behavior anomalies in children of an epileptic basis. *New York State Journal of Medicine,* 1956, *56,* 2537–2543.

Ziporyn, M. & H. E. Stoner. The use of fluphenazine hydrochloride (Prolixin) in acute functional psychoses. *Journal of Neuropsychiatry,* 1964, *5,* 297–299.

Ziskind, E. & W. A. Bailey. Hyperinsulinism. *Journal of Laboratory and Clinical Medicine,* 1937, *23,* 231–240.

Zumpe, D. & R. P. Michael. Redirected aggression and gonadal hormones in captive rhesus monkeys (*Macaca mulatta*) *Animal Behavior,* 1970, *18,* 11–19.

Author Index

Aaron, M., 238
Abbatiello, E., 253
Abbott, P., 90
Abrahamson, E. M., 78
Abrams, W. B., 87
Adams, D. B., 229, 254, 262, 264–265
Addison, R. G., 67
Addition, H., 67
Adey, W. R., 258
Adler, M., 48
Aird, R. B., 39
Akahene, A., 40
Akert, K., 262
Alberts, J. R., 158, 164
Aldersberg, D., 74–75
Alderstein, A. M., 92
Alderton, H., 90
Alexander, B. K., 16–17, 198, 244, 255
Alexander, M., 110, 170, 256
Allee, W. C., 171, 194
Allen, M., 90
Allikmets, L. Kh., 268
Allin, J. T., 157
Allison, S., 101
Allison, T. S., 101
Alpers, B. J., 28
Altman, M., 168, 181, 186
Altmann, M., 66, 217
Amador, L., 46
Anand, B. K., 9, 259, 265–267

Anderson, E. W., 74
Anderson, P., 260
Anderson, R., 48, 104
Andy, O. J., 46, 49, 97
Anton, A. H., 196, 243, 247
Apelbaum, J., 178
Arai, N., 40
Archer, J., 160, 213, 216
Ardrey, R., 136, 154, 209–210, 213, 217, 224–225
Arita, M., 46, 104
Arms, R. L., 283
Arthurs, R. G., 41
Ashcroft, G. W., 48
Austin, P., 67–68
Avis, H. H., 147
Ax, A., 188, 279
Azrin, N. H., 8, 16, 101, 191–192, 199–202, 270

Bach-Y-Rita, G., 53, 85–86, 90, 98–99, 102, 111, 234
Baenninger, L., 172
Baenninger, R., 142, 146–147, 150, 172, 182, 200, 202, 207, 236
Bagdon, R. E., 87
Bailey, E. D., 157, 205, 240, 271
Bailey, J. B., 101
Bailey, P., 38, 46
Bailey, W. A., 74

Baker, R. K., 102, 118
Balasubramaniam, V., 48
Ball, S. J., 102
Balzas, R., 196
Ban, T. A., 86, 90, 94
Banay, R. S., 85–86
Bandler, R. J., Jr., 6, 13, 133, 136–137, 139–140, 142, 147–149, 229–230, 232–234, 238
Bandura, A., 17–18, 96, 100, 190, 275, 277, 279
Benerjee, U., 244, 247, 249
Banks, E. M., 157
Banks, J. H., 191
Banziger, R., 87
Baran, D., 219–220
Barbeau, A., 86
Barclay, A. M., 206
Bard, P., 257–258
Bardin, C. W., 248
Bardwick, J. M., 66, 68
Barfield, R. J., 243, 256
Barett, J. E., 87, 117
Barnett, S. A., 132, 152, 155–156, 159, 164, 166, 169, 179, 183, 200, 213–214, 222, 276
Barnett, T. W., 258
Barry, H., 81, 84
Barry, J., 43
Barsa, J., 92
Barsel, G. E., 172–173
Bartholomew, A. A., 90
Bartholomew, G. A., Jr., 152, 158, 213
Basagic, E., 231
Bassoe, 73
Basu, G. K., 60
Bates, B. C., 213
Bateson, G., III, 188
Bayrakal, S., 39
Beach, F. A., 11, 147, 241, 243
Beardmore, T. D., 33
Beauchesne, H., 90
Beeman, E. A., 10, 241–242
Bell, D. S., 104, 106
Bemporad, J. R., 259
Bender, L., 43
Benedict, R., 225
Benitone, J., 258
Bennett, R. M., 69, 82
Ben-Shmuel, A., 49
Bergquist, E. H., 142, 229, 272
Bergstedt, M., 82
Berkowitz, L., 2, 100, 102, 188, 193, 275, 278, 284
Berkut, M. K., 269
Bernard, B. K., 239
Bernstein, A., 279–280
Bernstein, H., 197, 237–238

Bernstein, I. S., 179, 244, 248, 271
Berntson, G. G., 231–233, 262
Bettelheim, B., 277
Bevan, J. M., 243–244
Bevan, W., 131, 243–244
Bevilacqua, A. R., 44
Bianchi, A., 65
Billig, H. E., Jr., 68, 74
Bindra, D., 265
Bingley, T., 35
Bird, I. F., 87
Birnbaum, E. A., 191
Blake, A., 90
Blanchard, D. C., 257, 269
Blanchard, R. J., 257, 269
Blau, A., 28
Bleicher, S. J., 74
Bliss, E. L., 248
Bloom, W., 8, 192
Blum, F., 28, 78
Blum, R. H., 80, 82–83
Blumer, D., 36–37, 46, 65, 116
Blurton, J. N., 154
Boegele, G. E., 44
Boelkins, C. R., 2, 244
Boff, E., 87
Boice, R., 191
Bolton, R., 76
Bonkalo, A., 39
Bonsall, R. W., 159
Bonsignori, A., 11, 243, 247
Boody, J. E., 201
Boord, P., 102
Borgen, L. A., 196
Boris, A., 87
Borman, A., 65
Borofsky, G. L., 206
Boshka, S. C., 8, 196
Bostow, D. E., 101
Bowne, G., 16–17, 110, 170, 255
Boyle, D. F., 87
Brady, J. V., 259, 262
Brain, P. F., 65, 166, 196, 218, 246–249
Brake, S. C., 160, 162
Bramel, D., 284
Braud, W. G., 158, 166, 213
Brauer, W., 92
Brazier, G., 52
Breamish, P., 79
Breggin, P. R., 105
Bremer, J., 62–64, 66, 115
Brewer, C., 37
Brill, H., 30–32, 86, 90
Brittain, R. P., 40
Brobeck, J. R., 265
Brody, M. B., 49
Bronson, F. H., 163, 250–253
Broom, L., 153

Brown, C., 19
Brown, J. L., 261–262, 264
Brown, L. E., 210, 218
Brown, R. Z., 157, 182
Browning, R. M., 100
Brozek, J., 193
Brutkowski, S., 266
Bryan, D. C., 157
Brykczynski, T., 255
Bucher, B., 101, 261
Bucy, P. C., 46, 282
Buddington, R., 269
Buechner, H. K., 213
Bugbee, N. J., 237
Buki, R. A., 90
Bull, H. D., 66
Bullock, L. P., 249
Bunnell, B. N., 17, 168, 254, 259, 270
Burdock, E. I., 265
Burge, K. G., 247
Burgess, A., 100
Burghardt, G. M., 138
Burke, J. C., 234, 237
Burnand, G., 14
Burns, W. K., 200
Burt, W. H., 181, 212
Burton, J., 98
Bush, D. E., 243
Buss, A. J., 2, 61, 82, 87, 100, 188
Butler, K., 142

Cahoon, D. D., 41, 194
Cain, D. P., 237
Cairncross, K., 248
Cairns, H., 48, 259
Cairns, R. B., 173
Cairns, V. M., 48
Calhoun, J. B., 151, 154, 164, 181, 183, 185, 203, 214, 218, 240
Campbell, H. E., 63
Campbell, M. B., 70, 72–73
Candland, D. K., 157
Cannon, J. T., 200
Cardarelle, J., 101
Carlini, E. A., 195
Carlisle, S., 50
Carpenter, C. R., 151–152, 158, 172, 205, 211–213, 216–217, 221, 223
Carpenter, J. A., 82
Carthy, J. D., 2, 135
Cazzullo, C. L., 35
Cepelak, J., 90
Chabora, J., 234, 236
Challas, G., 92
Chamberlain, A. S., 224
Chamberlain, G. H. A., 11, 62
Chance, M. R., 153, 168, 178–179, 181
Chapel, J. L., 92

Chapman, W. P., 52
Chappelle, T. C., 243, 247
Chapple, E. D., 224
Charles, E., 66
Charpentier, J., 196
Chase, M. H., 266
Chatz, T. L., 64, 116
Chaurand, J. P., 233
Cheatham, C. F., 33
Cherkin, A., 248
Chi, C. C., 140, 229, 232–233, 238, 264
Chickson, J. T., 200
Christian, J. J., 159, 163
Christie, M. H., 256
Church, R. M., 202
Clanon, T. L., 93
Clapham, B., 74
Clark, D. L., 199
Clark, D. M., 43
Clark, K. B., 121
Clark, L. D., 136, 146, 169
Clark, L. H., 13, 157, 252
Clark, R. A., 206
Clayton, R. B., 254
Clemente, C. D., 169, 203, 266, 268
Cloudsley-Thompson, J. L., 158, 165, 171, 217–218
Cobbs, P., 189
Coca, A. F., 70
Cohen, S., 79–80, 90
Cohn, R., 39, 80
Cole, C., 259
Cole, H. F., 196
Cole, J. O., 90
Coles, R., 189
Collias, N. E., 241
Colombo, C., 12, 243
Colucci, V. M., 136
Comstock, G. A., 102
Conaway, C. H., 244
Connell, P. H., 79–80
Conner, R. L., 12, 195, 250, 269–271
Conners, C. K., 91
Connor, J., 161
Coppen, A., 67–68
Corbalan, V., 46
Cornell, R., 258
Corning, C. H., 275
Corning, P. A., 182, 275
Covarrabias, M. I., 49
Cox, G. S., 247
Crabtree, J. M., 196, 200
Crandall, P. H., 51
Crawford, S. E., 70, 72
Creer, T. L., 194, 201
Cressey, D. R., 153
Crichton, M., 112
Crook, J. H., 211, 216–218, 225

Crook, W. G., 70, 72
Crosby, R. M., 194
Cross, H. A., 197–198
Crowcroft, P., 216
Cummer, J. F., 250, 270–271
Currier, R. D., 36
Curtis, G. C., 60

Dalhouse, A., 196
Dalton, K., 11, 66–68
Daly, D., 25
Daniels, D. N., 2–3
Darling, F. F., 92, 216
Darwin, C., 165–167
Davenport, W., 154
Daves, W. F., 131
Davies, J. C., 189
Davis, D. E., 2, 244
Davis, F. C., 8, 171, 194
Davis, H., 192
Davis, J. M., 90
Davis, P. G., 182
Davis, W. M., 196
Davison, H. M., 70
Dawber, M. A., 220
Dawson, R. G., 221
Day, C., 12, 243
Deci, L., 267
DeGroot, J. C., 102, 169, 203, 268
DeHaas, A. M., 35–36, 38
De la Vega Llamosa, A., 83
Delgado, J. M. R., 9, 16–17, 50–53, 104,
    109–113, 135–136, 200, 202, 234, 259,
    263–264, 267, 269–270
Deluca, M. A., 90
Dement, W. C., 195
Denber, C., 90
Denenberg, V. H., 181–182
Denham, J., 92
Desisto, M. J., 139, 143–147, 149–150,
    230
Desjardins, C., 240, 250–253
Detre, T., 32
Deutsch, H., 68
Devore, I., 153, 168, 181, 183, 185, 210,
    218, 221
Diakow, C. A., 172
Dicks, D., 257–258
Didiergeorges, F., 136, 230, 235–238
Dietze, H. J., 44
Di Giusto, E. L., 271
Dillow, P. V., 102
DiMascio, A., 87–88, 117
Dinnen, A., 37
Dismang, L. H., 33
Dixon, A. K., 161
Doba, N., 237
Dodes, L. M., 93

Dodsworth, R. O., 197, 199
Dolger, H., 74–75
Dollard, J., 2, 188, 275
Donefeld, H., 192
Doob, L. W., 2, 188, 275
Dorsey, J. M., 84
Downer, C. J. L., 258
Doyharcabal, Y., 49
Dresdale, L., 157
Dreyer, P. L., 202
Drtil, J., 90
Dua, S., 9, 259, 266–267
Duffield, J. E., 48
Duisberg, R. E., 46
Dulaney, S., 16
Duncan, G. G., 77
Dunford, C., 221
Dunn, G. W., 11, 64
Dunn, S., 194
Dunstone, J. J., 200
Durkee, A., 87

Ebaugh, F., 28
Ebling, F. J., 2, 135
Eclancher, F., 146
Edinger, H., 234
Edwards, A. E., 84
Edwards, D. A., 12, 65, 243, 247, 250–
    252
Edwards, R., 90
Edwards, S. B., 139, 145, 187–188, 228
Egan, O., 218
Egger, M. D., 8–9, 229, 234, 266, 268
Ehrhardt, A. A., 250
Eibl-Eibesfeldt, I., 23, 133, 136–138, 141,
    154, 157, 165, 168, 177–178, 200, 213–
    214, 216, 218–221
Eichelman, B. S., 237
Eisenberg, B. C., 72
Eisenberg, J. F., 141–142, 164, 168, 184,
    205, 215
Elger, W., 65
Ellingson, R. J., 39
Ellinwood, E. H., 80
Ellis, D. P., 67–68
Ellison, G. D., 232, 265
Emerson, B. S., 70, 72
Endroczi, E., 183
Epple, G., 214, 219–220
Epstein, A. W., 36
Epstein, L. J., 279–280
Erpino, M. J., 243, 247
Ervin, F. R., 24, 28, 35, 37–38, 47–48,
    50–51, 53–54, 56–57, 77, 86, 97–99,
    104, 106–109, 111–113, 123–125
Erwin, J. C., 198
Esser, A. H., 224
Estes, R. D., 213, 216

Etkin, W., 205
Evans, C. M., 65
Evans, C. S., 164, 179, 276
Evans, D. R., 102

Fabrykant, M., 77
Fager, M. A. B., 52
Falconer, M. A., 37, 46
Farris, E. J., 179
Fehr, H., 146
Feierabend, I. K., 189
Feierabend, R. L., 189
Feldman, P. E., 87
Fenton, G. W., 37
Ferinden, W. E., 102
Fernandez de Molina, A., 262, 266
Ferneau, E. W., 81
Ferracuti, F., 82
Feshbach, N., 102
Feshbach, S., 100, 102, 190, 275, 282
Fetzner, H. R., 65
Fial, R. A., 269
Field, L. H., 64, 116
Figueroa, E., 49
Fink, C. D., 171, 191
Fish, B., 118
Fisher, A. E., 147, 231
Fisher, C., 195
Flandera, V., 181, 183
Flesher, C. K., 259
Florea, J., 196
Flory, R. K., 191
Flynn, J. P., 6–9, 133, 138–140, 144–145,
    147, 187–188, 228–229, 231, 233–234,
    236–237, 239, 264–266, 268, 271
Fonberg, E., 9, 266–268
Foote, R. M., 64, 228, 232
Foote, W., 7, 140, 145, 187–188
Fortuna, M., 266
Fowler, H., 147
Fox, I. H., 33
Fox, M. W., 136, 142, 154, 168, 178, 205
Fox, R., 92, 141
Foxx, R. M., 101
Francis, J., 270
Frank, J. D., 2
Franzen, E. A., 259
Frederichs, C., 70, 72–73
Fredericson, E., 131–132, 134, 152, 169–
    171, 173, 191, 194, 240
Freed, H., 49
Freed, S. C., 68, 99
Freeman, W., 46, 104
Fregly, A. R., 81–82
Freud, S., 188, 204, 275
Frichat, A., 248
Fulginitti, S., 195

Fuller, J. L., 196
Fuxe, K., 235

Galef, B. G., 149, 158, 164, 169, 179, 200,
    234, 257
Gallardo, R., 49
Gallup, G., Jr., 192
Gammon, C. B., 82
Gandelman, R. D., 182–184, 186, 263,
    266
Gantt, W. H., 171
Garattini, S., 12, 173, 196
Gardos, G., 88
Garrick, 212
Gartlan, J. S., 216
Gastaut, H., 37
Gattozzi, A. A., 93
Gaziri, C. J., 254
Geiger, S. C., 10, 17, 42–43
Gentry, W. D., 191, 193
Gershon, S., 66
Geyer, G., 52
Giacalone, E., 12, 196
Gibbens, T. C., 40–41
Gibbs, E. L., 42–43
Gibbs, F. A., 38, 42–43, 46
Gillies, H., 83
Gilman, A., 78, 90
Gilula, M. F., 2–3
Ginsburg, B., 158, 166, 171, 194, 213
Glaesel, H. U., 65
Glaser, G. H., 37
Glass, G. S., 66
Glees, P., 259
Gleser, G. C., 87, 90, 92
Glickman, S. E., 219–220
Gloor, P., 276
Glusman, M., 264–265
Goddard, G. V., 107, 258, 271
Goethe, F., 218
Goldberg, S. C., 90
Goldensohn, E. S., 35
Goldstein, J. H., 283
Golla, F. L., 64
Goodman, H., 70, 72–73, 90
Goodman, L. S., 78
Gorbman, A., 254
Gordon, T. P., 248
Gorney, R., 68
Gottlieb, J. S., 41
Gottlieb, P. M., 72–73
Gottschalk, L. A., 66, 87, 90, 92
Goy, R. W., 153, 253
Grant, E. C., 154, 160, 163–166
Gray, J. A., 153, 196
Graybiel, A., 82
Graziano, A. M., 102

Green, J. D., 169, 203, 268
Green, J. R., 46
Green, P. C., 197
Greenbaum, J.V., 31
Greenberg, I. M., 42–43
Greene, R., 11, 68
Greenhill, J. P., 68
Greenwood, J., 74, 77
Grice, H. C., 196
Grier, W. H., 189
Griffo, W., 252
Gross, M. D., 39, 41
Grossman, C., 44, 202
Grossman, L., 191
Grossman, S. P., 108, 191, 236, 255, 265, 269
Groupe, A., 93
Grubb, E. F., 269
Guerrero-Figueroa, R., 56
Guhle, A. M., 241
Gunn, J., 37
Gunne, L., 235
Gurney, N. L., 173, 196
Gurowitz, E. M., 257–258
Gurr, T. R., 189
Gustafson, J. E., 171, 247
Guttmacher, M., 83
Gye, R. S., 104, 106

Haber, R. N., 206
Hagiwara, R., 53, 111
Hahn, J. D., 65
Hake, D. F., 8, 101, 191–192, 200
Hale, E. B., 147
Hall, C. S., 13, 171
Hall, E. T., 216, 224
Hall, K. R. L., 168
Hall, N. R., 243
Hamanaka, Y., 248
Hamaoui, A., 195
Hamburg, D. A., 60, 67–68, 153, 178, 183, 190, 243, 253
Hamby, W., 194
Hamlin, H., 51
Hampton, W. H., 79
Harada, T., 46, 104
Harding, C. F., 142, 247, 249
Harlow, H. F., 153, 190, 196–199
Harlow, M. K., 197–199
Harmatz, J., 117
Harrell, W. A., 192
Harris, S., 68, 76
Harrison, W. W., 70, 72
Harvey, J. A., 269
Hatch, A., 196
Hatch, J., 212
Haward, L. R., 92

Hawke, C. C., 11, 63–64, 115–116, 206
Heath, R. G., 50, 52–53, 56, 109–110
Hediger, H., 177, 180, 210, 213, 218
Heim, J., 102
Heimburger, R. F., 47, 98, 104, 106, 282
Heimstra, N. W., 146
Heise, G. A., 87
Heiser, J. F., 2
Heller, H. C., 217
Hendricks, A. G., 203
Heninger, G. R., 66
Henry, C. E., 42, 44
Henschel, A., 193
Hepburn, J. R., 83
Hern, M. T., 102
Hernandez-Peon, R., 234
Herndon, J., 250
Herreca, M. A., 83
Herrell, J. M. A., 102
Herrero, S., 177, 180, 186, 217
Herrin, M. S., 194
Hersher, L., 181, 183
Hess, W. R., 260, 262
Hetherington, E. M., 49, 81
Higgins, T. J., 219
High, J. P., 234, 237
Hill, C. C., 194
Hill, D., 37, 40, 46, 74, 77
Hill, P. A., 100
Hill, R. A., 84, 90, 100
Himmelhock, J., 32
Hinde, R. A., 96, 164, 277, 282
Hiroaki, S., 48
Hirose, S., 49–50
Hitchcock, E., 48
Hitzing, E. W., 201
Hoats, D. L., 196
Hoddinott, B. A., 90
Hodge, R. S., 64
Hodges, J. R., 247
Hoebel, B. G., 144–145, 230–231, 264
Hoedemaker, F. S., 195
Hoefnagel, D., 33
Hoel, P. G., 213
Hoffmeister, Von F., 231
Hoggart, K., 14
Hohmann, G. W., 280
Hokanson, J. E., 284
Holaday, J. W., 244, 271
Holloway, R. L., 2
Hoobler, B. R., 70
Horn, J. M., 170
Horovitz, Z. P., 231, 234, 236–237
Howard, A., 100
Hughes, J. R., 42–43
Hull, E. M., 237
Hunsperger, R. W., 260–262, 264, 266
Hunt, G. M., 192

Hunt, L., 67
Hunter, H., 14
Huston, J. P., 17, 143, 146–147, 149, 230
Hutchinson, R. R., 8, 16, 133, 144, 191–192, 199–202, 229
Hutt, P. J., 260
Hymowitz, N., 192
Hynan, M. T., 200

Igic, R., 231
Ilfeld, F. W., 189
Ingram, W. R., 265
Inselman-Temkin, B. R., 239
Isaacson, R. L., 219
Ishiwara, M., 40, 43
Ittelson, W. H., 224
Ivey, M. E., 66

Jackson, A. H., 93
Jackson, V. A. B., 91, 118
Jacobs, T. J., 66, 234
Jacobsen, E., 131
Jacobson, A., 195
Jagannathan, K., 48
James, J. A., 33
James, W. T., 196
Janowsky, E. S., 68
Jansen, J., 260
Jarrard, L., 33
Jasper, H. H., 34–35, 52
Jay, P., 181, 183, 185, 210, 221
Jenkins, R. L., 40
Jennings, J. R., 248
Jewell, P. A., 210
Jirgl, M., 90
Johnson, A. E., 249
Johnson, L. C., 43
Johnson, R. N., 26, 146, 149–150, 190, 199–200
Johnson, S. M., 101
Jolly, C., 152, 168, 178, 181
Jonas, A. D., 34–35
Jones, H., 191
Jones, M. S., 74
Jones, R. B., 172
Jurko, M. F., 49, 97

Kaada, B., 9, 260, 267
Kaelber, W. W., 234, 258, 265
Kahn, I. S., 70, 72
Kahn, M. W., 17, 172–173
Kalant, O. J., 79–80
Kales, A., 195
Kalin, R., 81, 117
Kalina, R. K., 92, 117
Kalsbeck, J. E., 47, 98, 104, 106, 282
Kalyamaraman, S., 48
Kamm, I., 90
Kaplan, S., 87, 90

Karczmar, A. G., 181–183
Karli, P., 13, 15, 131, 136, 138, 142, 146–147, 181, 200–201, 228, 230, 233–239, 257, 267
Kasanin, J., 28
Kastl, A. J., 81
Katz, H., 206
Kaufman, H., 2, 275
Kean, J. E., 102
Keating, L. E., 38
Keiser, G., 255
Keith, E. F., 87
Keller, J. F., 192
Kelley, W. N., 33, 192
Kelling, J. S., 249
Kelly, J. F., 8
Kennard, M. A., 259, 266
Kennedy, F., 73
Kepler, E. J., 74–75
Kerner, O., 102, 189
Keschner, M., 27
Kesner, R. P., 255
Kessel, N., 67–68
Kessler, S., 14
Keys, A., 193
Keverne, E. B., 159
Khalsa, J. H., 196
Khalson, W. T., 196
Kiess, H. O., 15, 133, 136, 143–145, 229
Killeffer, F. A., 28
Kiloh, L., 79
Kilon, L. G., 104, 106
Kim, L. I., 93
Kim, Y. K., 48
Kimbrell, G. McA., 200
King, F. A., 27, 213, 259, 269
King, H. E., 7, 55
King, J. A., 10, 134, 156, 163, 173, 181–182, 184, 196, 213–214, 216, 240
King, M. B., 144–145, 230–231, 264
King, M. G., 248
King, W. T., 196
Kislak, J. W., 11
Kittler, F. J., 71
Kjellberg, R. N., 37, 47, 104
Kleeman, S. T., 278
Kleiman, D., 219–220
Kletschka, H. D., 24
Kline, N. S., 90, 224
Kling, A., 240, 257–258, 260, 266–267, 270–271
Klingler, J., 46
Kluver, H., 46, 282
Knowles, E., 66
Knott, J. R., 40–41, 44
Knutson, J. F., 191, 200
Kochakian, C. D., 243
Koenig, A. B., 146, 149–150
Kohler, W., 203

Kogura, J., 254
Kooij, M., 178
Kopf, K. J., 157
Kopp, M. E., 63
Korn, J. H., 130, 194, 197
Kortland, A., 178
Kosman, M. E., 79
Kostowski, W., 249
Kraemer, H. C., 254
Kraft-Ebing, R., 85, 204
Kramer, G., 91
Kramer, J. C., 79
Kramer, R., 90
Kramer, S., 196, 243, 247
Kreisler, S. J., 249
Kreiskott, H., 136–137, 331
Kreuz, L. E., 61, 248
Kreveld, D. A., 168
Krikstone, B. J., 231
Kruuk, H., 146
Kuehn, J. L., 98, 147
Kulkarni, A. S., 148, 237
Kummer, H., 152, 155, 178–179
Kuo, Z. Y., 148–149, 196

Lack, D., 164
Ladosky, W., 254
Lagerspetz, K., 13, 17, 152, 154, 164, 170–173, 190, 240
Lancaster, J., 258
Lansky, M., 66
Laschet, L., 65
Laschet, U., 65, 116
Last, S. L., 49
Latham, E. E., 238
Laties, V. G., 8, 195
Leaf, R. C., 231, 234, 236–237
LeBeau, J., 48, 266
LeBoeuf, B. J., 243
Ledesma, J. A., 48
Lee, C. T., 159–160, 162, 252
Lefkowitz, M. M., 91
Legrand, R., 170
Leibowitz, S. F., 231
Leiphart, J. M., 157
LeMaire, L., 11, 63
Lennard, H. L., 279–280
Lennox, M. A., 34
Lennox, W. G., 34
Lerner, L. J., 65, 231, 236
Lerwill, C. J., 165
Lesch, M., 33
Lesevre, N., 37
Leshner, A. I., 246, 248–249
LeVann, L. J., 92, 118
Lever, J., 283
Levine, L., 172–173
Levine, S., 12, 173, 195, 250, 269–271

Levinson, P. K., 133, 138, 229
Levitt, R. A., 231
Levy, G. W., 10, 131, 134, 244
Levy, J. V., 240
Lewis, S. A., 40
Leyhausen, P., 141–142, 177, 205, 215, 261
Lichtenstein, P. E., 14
Lindzey, G., 219
Lints, C. E., 269
Lion, J. R., 85–86, 90, 98–99, 102
Lippert, W., 92
Lissak, K., 183
Little, S. C., 36, 44
Livingston, K. E., 48
Livingston, S., 36, 38
Lloyd, C. W., 65, 68, 159
Lochtenstein, E. L., 195
Lockett, L., 181–183
Lockie, J. D., 181, 183, 214, 216
Logan, J. C., 102
Lombroso, C. T., 43
Lond, M. T., 43
Looker, A., 91
Loomis, T. A., 82
Lorenz, K., 96, 136, 146, 148, 154, 165, 168–169, 209, 218, 225, 275, 277–278, 281–282
Lovaas, O. I., 101
Lowe, V. P., 217
Lowenstein, L. M., 81
Lowenthal, H., 234
Loy, J., 194
Ludwig, A. M., 100
Lunde, D. T., 60
Lurie, L. A., 31
Luttge, W. G., 243, 247
Lyght, C. E., 29
Lyon, D. D., 201

Mabry, J. H., 14
McAdam, D. W., 265
McCarthy, D., 231
McClearn, G. E., 13, 109
McClelland, D. C., 81
McCord, J., 100, 102
McCord, W., 100, 102
MacDonald, J. W., 37
MacDonnell, M. F., 6, 8, 139–140, 147, 229, 232–233
McGinnis, M., 194
McGinty, D. J., 234
McGrath, W. B., 46
McIntyre, A., 154
McKinney, T. D., 163, 240
Mackintosh, J. H., 160–161, 163–166
McLaughlin, R., 16, 202
MacLean, P. D., 109, 259, 267, 269
MacLennan, R. R., 157, 205, 240, 271

McMullen, M. F., 259
Madsen, A., 48
Magg, M., 184
Malamud, N., 24, 27
Maletzky, B. M., 91
Malick, J. B., 236
Mall, G., 65
Mandell, A. J., 66, 68
Mandell, M. P., 66, 71, 90
Mans, J., 92
Maple, T., 198
Marinacci, A. A., 85–86
Mark, V. H., 24, 28, 35, 37–38, 47–48, 50–51, 53–54, 56–57, 97, 104, 106–109, 111–113, 123, 127–129
Markkanen, T., 81
Marler, P. R., 216, 221–222
Marsden, H. M., 163
Marshall, J. F., 230
Martz, R. M. W., 195
Marucci, F., 196
Marx, A. J., 100
Mason, W. A., 197, 221
Masserman, J. H., 14
Masur, J., 195
Matalka, E., 270
Matsumoto, K., 248
Matthews, L. H., 152, 157–159, 165
Mayanagi, Y., 48
Mazzagatti, N., 150
Mead, M., 225
Means, L. W., 230
Megargee, E. I., 275
Mehes, J., 267
Meinecke, R. O., 248
Mempel, E., 48, 266
Menninger, K. A., 126
Merrilless, N. C. R., 258
Messe, L. A., 206
Meyer, A., 37, 46, 143
Mever, E. P., 146–147
Meyer, P. M., 259
Michael, R. P., 101, 159, 203, 206, 271
Mickelsen, O., 193
Mickle, W. A., 50, 52, 56
Miczek, K. A., 236, 255, 269
Migeon, C., 65, 116
Miley, W. M., 142, 146, 150, 236, 252
Miller, H., 73
Miller, N. E., 2, 188, 275
Miller, R. E., 17, 191
Milner, B., 46
Milstein, V., 35
Minigrino, S., 48
Mir, D., 16–17, 200, 202, 263
Mirsky, A. F., 17, 243, 257
Mises, R., 90
Mitchell, C. L., 265
Mitchell, G. D., 195–196, 198

Mitchell, W., 46
Mitzutiani, S., 248
Moe, R. A., 87
Moersch, F. P., 74–75
Molof, M. J., 81
Money, J., 65, 250
Monroe, R. R., 34–36, 39, 42–43, 92, 98
Montagu, M. F. A., 2, 224, 277–278
Montgomery, R. L., 269
Moore, A. U., 181, 183
Moore, M. W., 73
Moos, R. H., 14, 67–68
Morden, B., 195
Morris, D., 168
Morton, J. H., 67–69
Mosher, D. L., 206
Moyer, K. E., 13, 15, 119, 130, 132–133, 136–137, 142, 147, 149, 182–183, 194, 196–197, 200, 209, 225, 237–238, 277
Mowrer, O. H., 2, 188, 191, 275
Muensch, H., 43
Mugford, R. A., 160–163, 170
Mulder, D., 25
Muller, M., 83
Mulvihill, D. J., 83–84
Murdoch, B. D., 40
Murie, O. J., 216
Murphy, J. V., 17
Murphy, M. R., 160, 219
Murray, L. G., 48
Mussini, E., 196
Myer, J. S., 15, 136–137, 147–149
Myers, K., 210, 216, 259
Mykytowycz, R., 210, 213, 215–216, 218, 220

Naab, M., 65
Nagahata, M., 35–47, 104, 106
Nagao, T., 35, 46, 104
Nakao, H., 264
Nakelski, J. S., 173
Narabayashi, H., 35, 47, 104
Nardini, J. E., 39
Nash, H., 81
Nathan, P. E., 81
National Commission on the Causes and Prevention of Violence, 152
Nauta, W. J. H., 259
Nazar, B. L., 157
Neidermeyer, E., 44
Nelson, 33
Neri, R. O., 65
Neuman, F. R., 65
Neuman, R. J., 37
Neuringer, C., 101
Neville, R., 112, 127–129
New, M. I., 249
Newton, G., 146
Nice, M. M., 212

Nielson, G., 101
Noble, G. K., 210
Norris, K. S., 152
Novakova, V., 181, 183
Nowell, N. W., 160–163, 166, 170, 172, 218, 246–248
Nuffield, E. J., 38
Nugent, A., 93
Nurmi, R., 190
Nyby, J., 219–220
Nyhan, W. L., 33

O'Boyle, M., 136
Obrador, S., 53
Ochberg, F. M., 2–3
O'Doherty, D. S., 51
Opert, S., 196
Orchinik, C., 49
Ore, G. D., 46, 103
Orsinger, O. A., 195
Ostensjo, S., 44
Osterheld, R. G., 90
Otto, O., 43
Ounsted, C., 38
Owens, H., 196
Ozolins, D., 201
Ozturk, O., 43

Pacella, B. L., 40, 77
Pacheco, P., 54–56
Paige, K. E., 68
Palestini, M., 49
Paluck, R. J., 224
Paneagua, J. L., 48
Panksepp, J., 144, 230, 264
Parker, J. R., 171, 191
Pauig, P. M., 90
Paul, L., 142, 146, 150
Paxinos, G., 237, 265
Payne, A. P., 151, 271
Pear, J. J., 192, 201
Pearson, O. P., 11
Pedersen, A., 158
Peele, J., 257
Pegrassi, L., 11, 244, 247
Penaloza-Rojas, J. H., 234
Penfield, W., 35, 52
Pennington, V. M., 68, 90
Perachio, A. A., 255
Persinger, M. A., 201
Persky, H., 60
Peters, P. J., 252–253
Peterson, R. E., 57, 248
Peterson, T. L., 101
Pezet, A. W., 78
Piala, J. J., 234, 237
Piechocki, T., 249
Pihkanen, T. A., 81

Pincus, J. H., 32
Piness, G., 73
Platt, J. J., 196
Ploog, 157
Plotnik, R., 16–17, 200–202, 263
Plumer, S. I., 237, 270
Poblete, M., 49
Podobnikar, I. G., 92
Podolsky, E., 68, 74
Poley, W., 218
Pollack, M., 42–43
Pond, D. A., 40–41, 46
Pool, J. L., 46
Poole, A. E., 65, 249
Poole, T. B., 154
Pope, A., 34
Poppen, J. L., 52
Pounders, C. M., 70
Powell, D. A., 250, 270–271
Pratt, C. L., 199
Presthus, J., 44
Pribam, K. H., 17, 257
Proshansky, H. M., 224

Ragozzino, P. W., 237
Ralls, K., 220–221
Ramamurthi, B., 48
Ramey, E. R., 51
Randall, L. O., 87, 145
Randolph, T. G., 70, 72
Randy, R. W., 51
Ransohoff, J., 265
Ransom, D. C., 279–280
Rasmussen, E. W., 179
Rasmussen, T., 52
Ray, D., 252
Raymond, E. J., 197–198
Reeves, A. G., 28
Refsum, S., 44
Reider, C. A., 196
Reinhardt, J. M., 204
Reiss, D. J., 237
Renfrew, J. W., 133, 144, 229
Report of the President's Commission on Crime, 80
Resko, J. A., 153
Resnick, O., 86, 88, 91
Revlis, R., 182–183
Rewerski, W., 249
Reynierse, J. H., 196
Reynolds, V., 178, 218
Ribero, S. L., 66
Rich, C., 46
Richardson, D., 160
Richmond, J. B., 181, 183
Rimm, D. C., 102
Ripley, S., 214
Rivlin, L. G., 224

Roberts, L., 269
Roberts, W. W., 15, 133, 136, 142–145, 229–230, 260, 272
Robinson, A. M., 62
Robinson, B. W., 16–17, 110, 170, 255
Robinson, W. J., 11
Rocky, S., 65
Roger, J., 37
Roisin, L., 264–265
Rojas, J., 49
Romaniuk, A., 260
Ropartz, P., 160
Rose, D., 90
Rose, R. M., 61, 244–245, 248, 271
Rosenberg, B., 84, 90
Rosenblatt, J. S., 181, 185
Rosenfeld, A., 91
Rosenworth, R. G., 104, 106
Rosenzweig, M. R., 196
Ross, A. T., 91, 118
Ross, S., 181–182
Ross, W. D., 90
Rosvold, H. E., 17, 261
Rosvold, H. S., 257
Roth, L. H., 67
Rothballer, A. B., 2, 67
Rothman, G., 204
Rothschild, G., 91
Rowe, A. H., 70, 73
Rowell, T. E., 203
Roy, G. W., 192
Royce, J. R., 218
Rubinstein, E. A., 102
Rubio-Chevannier, H. F., 234
Rud, E., 74
Ruffer, D. G., 210
Ruppenthal, G. C., 197–198
Rylander, G., 80
Ryszkowski, L., 217

Sachler, A. M., 196
Sackett, G. P., 198–199
Sade, D. S., 244
St. John, D., 182
Saito, Y., 35, 46, 104
Sales, G. D., 166
Sallery, R. D., 201
Salzman, C., 88
Sampson, H., 195
Samuels, L., 248
Sands, D. E., 11, 62, 64
Sano, K., 28, 48, 50
Sargant, W. A., 74, 77
Sassenrath, E. N., 203
Saunder, J. C., 92
Sawa, M., 46, 104, 234
Sawin, P. B., 181–182
Sayed, Z. A., 40
Sayler, A., 65, 243

Schachter, J., 188, 279
Schachter, S., 279
Schaeffer, R. W., 37, 193, 201
Schaffer, N., 70, 72
Schallek, W., 87
Schaller, G. B., 178, 213, 218
Scheckel, C. L., 87
Schein, M. W., 147, 157
Schenkel, R., 165, 209, 213–214, 217, 221
Schenkel-Hilliger, I., 217
Schergna, E., 48
Schleidt, M., 184
Schleidt, W., 184
Schmitt, P., 233
Schneider, G. E., 160
Schneider, W. F., 71
Schneiderman, N., 270
Schneirla, T. C., 181, 185
Schnurr, R., 259
Schoenfeld, W. N., 192
Schou, M., 93
Schreiner, L., 257–258, 266, 270
Schroeder, H. R., 52
Schusterman, R. J., 221
Schwab, R. S., 37, 47, 104
Schwade, E. D., 10, 17, 42–43
Schwadron, R., 75
Schwartz, I. M., 43
Schwartz, L. S., 91
Schwartz, R. P., 196, 243, 247
Sclafani, A., 265
Scott, J. P., 8, 13, 96, 120, 131–132, 154, 169–170, 173, 196, 201, 216, 276–277
Scott, W. C., 122
Scoville, W. B., 46
Scudder, C. L., 160, 253, 181–183
Sears, R. R., 2, 154, 188, 275
Seay, B., 190
Seignot, J. N., 92
Sells, S. B., 67
Selznick, P., 153
Sem-Jacobsen, C. W., 50–52, 56–57
Sendor, M., 157
Senes, M., 92
Sensibar, M. R., 206
Serafetinides, E. A., 37
Servais, J., 65
Seward, J. P., 152, 166, 193, 240, 243
Shader, R. I., 88, 93, 117
Shaffer, J. W., 91
Shagass, C., 51
Shah, S. A., 67
Shainess, N., 66
Shaller, G. B., 141, 220
Shannon, G., 90
Shannon, W. R., 70
Shanon, J., 90
Shealy, C., 257
Sheard, M. H., 7, 92–93, 237, 264, 270

Sheer, D. E., 51
Shibata, Y., 40
Shimada, H., 254
Shimolochi, M., 40
Shuntech, R. J., 82
Siegel, A., 234, 236
Siegel, J., 237, 270
Siegfried, J., 49
Sigg, E. B., 12, 173, 243, 247
Silverman, D., 40, 270
Singer, J. E., 279
Singer, R. D., 102
Skelton, W. D., 85–86
Skinner, B. F., 100
Skog, D., 236
Skulstad, A., 44
Skultety, F. M., 264
Sletten, I. W., 66
Slotnick, B. M., 259
Small, I. F., 43
Small, J. G., 35, 41, 43
Smith, D. E., 93, 230–231
Smith, K. D., 60
Smith, M. H., 168, 259
Smith, S. W., 90
Smolev, S. R., 101
Sodetz, F. J., 17, 254, 270
Solomon, H. C., 52
Solomon, P., 278
Solow, S. P., 157
Sommer, R., 216, 224
Sonne, C., 74
Southwick, C. H., 13, 173, 194, 252
Sparber, S. B., 196
Spaulding, C. A., 68, 74
Spector, S. A., 237
Speer, F., 70–73
Spencer, J., 196
Spregel, E. A., 49, 189
Springer, K. J., 90
Stachnik, T. J., 14
Stafford-Clark, D. A., 40–41
Stea, D., 224
Stedman, J. M., 101
Stehle, H. C., 43
Steinbeck, H., 65
Steinberg, M. I., 230
Stekel, W., 204
Stephens, J. H., 91
Stern, E., 28
Stern, J. M., 254
Stern, P., 231
Stevens, J. R., 35, 38, 50–51, 54, 56, 108
Stevenson, W. A., 11, 62
Stewart, I. A., 67
Stillman, R. C., 78–79, 195
Stoddart, R. C., 164
Stollak, G. E., 206
Stone, A., 13, 91, 179

Stoner, H. E., 91
Storr, A., 96, 225, 275, 277–278, 209–210
Strauss, E. B., 11, 62
Strauss, I., 27
Strecker, E. A., 28
Strom-Olson, R., 49–50
Sturup, G. K., 63–64
Suchowsky, G. K., 11, 243–244, 247
Suenatsu, K., 54, 57
Suess, J. F., 36
Sugerman, A. A., 92
Sullivan, J. J., 67
Summers, T. B., 234, 258
Sunderland, S., 258
Suomi, S. J., 199
Sutherland, H., 67
Sutker, L. W., 196
Svare, B., 183–184, 246, 249
Swanson, H. H., 151, 271
Sweet, W. H., 24, 37, 47–48, 53, 56–57,
    104, 108–109, 111–112
Sweetman, L., 33
Symannek, B., 199

Takala, M., 81
Takeyasu, K., 248
Talan, K., 66
Talkington, J. W., 194
Talo, S., 154, 173, 240
Tani, K., 40, 43
Tansella, M., 12, 196
Taylor, D. B., 157
Taylor, H. L., 38, 40, 82, 193
Taylor, J. C., 181
Teberg, A. J., 33
Teel, B. G., 196
Teitelbaum, P., 14, 230
Telegdy, G., 183
Telle, H. J., 219
Tellegen, A., 170
Teller, D. N., 90
Terrell, M. S., 91, 98
Terzian, H., 46, 103
Textor, R. B., 189
Thiessen, D. D., 218–220
Thomalske, G., 46
Thompson, T., 8, 152, 192
Thor, D. H., 8, 196
Thorne, B. M., 238
Tinbergen, N., 5, 133, 136, 138, 164, 209,
    277–278, 282
Tindall, W. J., 11, 62
Tinklenberg, J. R., 78–79, 195
Tintera, J. W., 74
Tobach, E., 181, 185
Tobin, J. M., 87
Toch, H., 102
Tolman, J., 160, 163
Torghele, J. R., 66

Torkildesen, A., 56–57
Tow, P. M., 48, 266
Traldi, S., 91
Travis, L. E., 84
Treadway, J. T., 147
Treffert, D. A., 10, 39
Troiano, R., 234
Trowill, J., 264
Tucker, G., 32
Tumin, M. M., 83–84
Tupin, J. P., 93
Turner, B. H., 91, 238
Turner, E. A., 46, 48, 258
Turns, D., 90
Tuttle, W. W., 84

Udwin, E. L., 37
Ueki, Y., 46, 104
Ullrich, H., 83, 201–202
Ulm, R. R., 200
Ulrich, R. E., 8, 14, 16, 87, 199–201, 270
Umbach, W., 48
Unna, K. R., 79
Uno, M., 47
Urich, J., 222, 243
Ursin, H., 52, 259, 267–268

Vaernet, K., 48
Vale, C. A., 252
Vale, J. R., 252
Valenstein, E. S., 27, 45, 105, 109
Vallardares, H., 46
Valzelli, L., 12, 88, 117, 131, 152, 196
Vandenbergh, J. G., 159, 243
Vanegas, H., 7, 140, 144–145, 187–188, 228, 232
VanHemel, P. E., 136, 143, 148
Varszegi, M. K., 267
Vasconcellos, J., 90–91
Vergnes, M., 136, 146, 230, 234–238
Vernikos, J., 247
Vernon, W., 201
Vincze, L., 90
Vogel, G., 195
Vogel, J. R., 231
Von Berswordt-Wallrabe, R., 65
Vonderake, A. R., 25, 265
Von Haxthausen, E. F., 196
Vos, H., 83, 213
Vozumi, T., 248
Vukelich, R., 101

Walker, W. A., 36–37, 247–249
Wallace, P., 220
Wallen, K., 243
Wallgren, H., 81, 84
Walter, R., 51
Walters, R. H., 190
Ward, A. A., 34, 48, 259

Ward, I., 248
Warne, M. C., 157
Washburn, S. L., 178, 210, 218
Wasman, M., 8, 133, 228–229, 236, 264
Watterson, D., 40
Way, J. S., 265
Webb, W., 195
Weil, A. A., 36
Weischer, M. L., 93
Weiskrantz, L., 257–258
Weisman, H. M., 8, 196
Weiss, G., 53, 111
Weisz, J., 68
Welch, A. S., 12, 196
Welch, B. L., 2, 12, 173, 196, 247
Weltman, A. S., 196
Wender, P. H., 72
Wertham, G. A., 102, 250, 270–271
West, T. C., 82
Westbrook, D. L., 269
Wetzel, A. B., 269
Whalen, R. E., 146–147
Wheatley, M. D., 260, 265
Whitaker, L. H., 64, 207
White, G. D., 101
White, R. T., 15, 104, 106, 136–137
Whitehouse, J. M., 243–244
Whitlock, C. C., 47, 98, 104, 106, 282
Whitsett, J. M., 252–253
Whitty, C., 48, 259, 266
Wiberg, G. S., 196
Wilder, B. J., 35
Wilder, J., 11, 74, 78
Williams, B. F., 243–244
Williams, B. H., 92
Williams, D., 36, 40
Williams, D. R., 14
Williams, J. M., 104
Williams, M., 64, 116
Williams, P., 125
Wilson, A., 214, 243–244
Wilson, J. A., 37, 147
Wilson, S. A., 30
Wilson, W. C., 39, 41
Winfield, D. L., 43
Winokur, G., 171, 247
Winshel, A. W., 68
Wirth, W., 231
Wiseman, W., 68
Wnek, D. J., 231
Wolf, H. H., 196
Wolfe, J. L., 169
Wolff, P. C., 16, 200
Wolfgang, M., 82–84
Wolpowitz, E., 90
Won, W., 265
Wood, C. D., 9, 257, 267–268
Woods, J. W., 234
Woods, S. M., 10, 43–44

Wordworth, C., 137, 139, 144
Woringer, E., 46
Wouters, A., 247–248
Wray, N. P., 49, 81
Wycis, H. T., 49
Wylie, H. W., 87
Wynne-Edwards, V.C., 210–211, 216–217

Yakovler, P. I., 52
Yalom, I. D., 68
Yamamoto, T., 39
Yasokochi, G., 260, 264
Yeakel, E. H., 179
Yen, H. C., 243

Yerkes, R. M., 13, 179
Yoshido, M., 35, 46, 104
Yoshii, N., 40, 43

Zare, N. C., 81
Zarrow, M. X., 181–182
Zbrozyna, A. W., 267
Zeman, W., 27
Zimmerman, F. T., 91
Ziporyn, M., 91
Ziskind, E., 74
Zubin, J., 51
Zuckerman, M., 60
Zumpe, D., 101, 206, 271

Subject Index

Abdomen, 141
Abortion, 153
Abulia, 74
Abuse, 97, 106, 114, 119, 121
Abusiveness, 37
Acetylcholine, 56, 230, 269
Acetylcholine chloride, 108
Achievement, 3
Acid base balance, 35
Acidosis, 195
ACTH. *See* Adrenocorticotrophic hormone
Activity, 194
Adaptability, 104
Addict, 80
Addiction, 109
Addison's disease, 74
Adenota vardoni, 213
Adjustment, 118, 123
Adolescent, 43, 60–61, 64–65, 90, 92
Adrenal androgen, 64, 182, 248
Adrenal corticoids, 76
Adrenalectomy, 238, 247–249, 269
Adrenalin, 76, 279
Adrenocorticotrophic hormone (ACTH)
   1–10, 249
   4–10, 249
   4–10 phe, 249
Affect, 188
   negative. *See* negative affect
   positive. *See* positive affect

Affective aggression, 133, 187
Affective attack, 264, 270
Affective defense, 262
Affective display, 151
Affective disturbance, 25, 27, 29
Affective response, 60
Affective state, 280
Affiliation, 281
Aggression. *See also* Kinds of aggression
   control, 44
   definition, 2
   inhibiting mechanism, 169
   inhibiting postures, 166
   inhibiting signals, 165
   inhibiting stimulus, 184
   symbolic, 3
Aggressive behavior, 3
Aggressive display, 209
Aggressive energy, 20, 96, 275–276, 279, 282–283
Aggressiveness, 3
Aggressive urge, 282
Aggressivity, 3
Aggressor, 179
Agitated behavior, 48, 49, 86, 90
Agitation. *See* Agitated behavior
Agnosia, 104
Agonistic behavior, 60, 151, 157–158, 213
Agonistic signal, 221
Agouti, 257

Airplane, 284
Alarm signal, 221
Alcohol, 77, 80–86, 95. *See also* Ethanol
Alcoholism, 29
Aldosterone, 68
Allergen, 59, 70, 72–73, 94
Allergic aggression, 72
Allergic reaction, 69
Allergic tension-fatigue syndrome, 70, 72
Allergy, 70–73, 98, 203
Allergy induced aggression, 72
Alpha female, 214
Alpha male, 214
Ambition, 282
Ambivalent hostility, 88, 92
Amitone, 231
Amitriptyline, 90, 281
Amnesia, 25, 34, 36, 56, 74, 85
Amphetamine, 7, 78–80, 95, 225, 235, 237
Amphetamine phosphate, 78
Amphetamine psychosis, 79–80
Amphetamine sulfate, 78
Amygdala, 9, 25, 35, 45, 47, 52, 55–58, 85, 104, 106–108, 110, 113, 124–125, 228, 231–232, 234–235, 254, 257–258, 260, 262, 266–268, 272–274, 280–281
  basal, 231, 235, 266–267
  baso-lateral, 108
  baso-medial, 234
  central nucleus, 9, 235, 266–268
  cortical nucleus, 235, 255
  lateral, 107, 109, 234–235, 268
  medial nucleus, 267
Amygdalectomy, 48, 103–105, 234, 257–258, 266, 273, 282
Amygdalofugal system, 235
Amygdalotomy, 45, 47–48, 106, 271
Anal region, 155
Androgen, 11–12, 62–63, 66, 94, 114, 162, 182, 238, 240–241, 243–244, 246–253, 271–274
Androstenedione, 60, 243, 248, 251
Anesthesia, 248
Anger, 3, 7, 10, 18–19, 22, 24, 29, 35, 37, 48, 51–53, 60, 77, 86, 91, 100, 102, 106, 112, 119–122, 125, 188, 195, 200, 203, 264, 268, 278–279, 281–282
Angioedema, 73
Animal model, 200
Animal trainer, 180
Annoyance, 187
Annual home range, 210
Anogenital inspection, 152
Anorexia, 24, 233
A-Norprogesterone, 65

Antelope, 158, 218
Antelope jackrabbit, 178
Antiaggression pheromone, 162
Antiandrogen, 65, 115–116
Anticholinergic agent, 230–231
Anticonvulsants, 41
Antidepressant, 87, 90, 281
Antihostility agent, 64–65, 88, 119–120, 281
Antihostility button, 110
Antihostility drug. *See* Antihostility agent
Antisocial behavior, 39, 63, 70, 104, 106
Antler, 133, 158
Anxiety, 34, 49, 52–53, 66, 74, 78–79, 81, 87–88, 90–94, 109, 121–122, 195, 206
Anxiety neurosis, 50
Apathy, 62, 118
Aphagia, 233
Appeasement, 165, 168
Appetite, 66, 113
Apprehension, 62
Arapesh, 225
Arecoline, 231–232
Argentina, 83
Arousal, 7, 21, 49, 106, 116, 133, 150, 174, 206, 229, 277, 279, 282–283
Arrest, 147
Arrest reaction, 9, 107
Arson, 42–43
Arteriosclerosis, 29
Artistic endeavors, 282
Asexualization, 63
Asphyxia, 29
Assault, 23, 29, 31, 37, 49, 53, 57, 61, 65, 79–81, 83–84, 92, 112, 118, 206, 229
Assaultive behavior. *See* Assault
Assaultiveness, 27, 40
Assaultive tendency. *See* Assaultiveness
Asservtiveness, 3
Asthma, 71
Athetosis, 33
Atropine, 231, 233
Atropine methyl nitrate, 230–231
Atropine sulphate, 231
Attacker, 155–156, 166
Attacking, 241–242
Attention, 185, 208
Attention span, 91
Australian marsupials, 152, 159
Automatic behavior, 36–37
Automatism, 25
Autonomic arousal, 176, 237, 280
Autonomic nervous system, 279
Avalanche syndrome, 9, 267
Aversive stimulation, 3, 8, 16, 201, 263–264. *See also* Noxious stimulation
Aversion therapy, 100–101

Avoidance, 17, 172, 179, 202, 217, 219–220
Awareness, 34, 120

Baboon, 142, 153, 155, 178–179, 181, 183, 185, 190, 203, 218
Badgers, 218
Banana, 69, 190
Barbiturates, 86
Barking, 221
Barred bandicoot, 157
Barrier, 177
Basal ganglia, 32
Bear, 181, 186, 217
Beer, 85
Beetle, 138
Behavior disorders, 35, 39, 70, 91
Bellicosity, 189
Benadryl, 72, 118
Benzodiazepines, 86–87, 92, 95, 117
Biology, 125
Bird, 149, 212, 216
Birth, 180–181, 198, 251
Birth season, 244
Biting, 155, 161, 200, 229, 269
Blackout, 39
Blacks, 188
Black-tailed jackrabbit, 178
Blood brain barrier, 230, 231
Blood chemistry, 4, 10, 12, 23, 58–59, 78, 94, 250, 276
Blood glucose. *See* Blood sugar
Blood sugar, 11, 74, 76, 94, 276
Blurred vision, 25, 42
Bobo doll, 17
Bomb release, 120
Boss monkey, 111
Bourbon, 82
Boxing matches, 283
Boxing posture, 155–156, 199–201, 269–270
Brain, 73, 77, 108, 113, 124–125, 228, 231–233, 236–237, 255, 260, 262–265, 267–268, 273–274, 280
Brain chemistry, 173
Brain damage, 22, 41–42, 44
Brain dysfunction, 39, 85, 97
Brain lesion, 44–45, 47, 58, 103, 105, 107, 114
Brain pathology, 97
Brain stem, 32
Brain stimulation, 15–17, 23, 50–53, 55–57, 107–111, 114, 125–126, 128, 131, 133, 138–140, 143–144, 147, 170, 187, 228–230, 234–235, 239, 255, 260–262, 264, 266–270, 272–273, 280
  chemical, 51, 108, 230, 254, 274
  chemical carbachol, 233, 267

chemical cholinergic, 231, 254
  noxious, 201
Brain surgery, 105
Brain trauma, 34, 57
Brain tumor, 24, 34, 204
Breeding season, 171, 174, 216–217, 244, 271
Bulimia, 46
Bull, 13, 135, 157, 203, 211, 243, 270
Bully test, 251
Burglary, 43
Burrow, 181, 185, 214–215, 221, 240
Business, 224
Buss-Durkee Hostility Inventory, 60–61, 87

Callicebus, 221
Calm, 125
Camel, 243
Canada, 180
Candy, 69, 74, 101
Canidae, 141–142, 219
Canids, 154
Canines, 168, 178
Canine teeth, 157
Cannula, 56, 116
Capture, 148
Carbachol, 230–231, 233
Carbachol-induced seizures, 231
Carbohydrate metabolism, 69
Carcinoma, 50
Carnivore, 141, 205, 216
Castration, 10–12, 62–64, 66, 128, 162–163, 207, 238, 241, 243, 248–249, 252–254, 270, 273
  chemical, 64–65
Cat, 6–7, 9, 15, 52, 107–108, 133, 138–144, 148–149, 169, 177, 181, 185, 187, 190, 200, 203, 205, 215, 228–229, 232, 234, 236–237, 239, 257, 261–262, 265–268, 270, 272
  food, 145
  wild, 44, 108
Cataleptic state, 179
Catecholamine, 235–236, 254
Catecholamine antagonist, 254
Catharsis, 103, 283
Caudate nucleus, 9, 111, 236, 270
Caudate putamen nucleus, 256
Cayo Santiago Island, 243–244
Central gray, 113, 262, 264–265, 273–274
Central home range, 212–214, 218–219
Central integrating mechanisms, 141, 228
Central nervous system, 78
Cerebellum, 237
Cerebral edema, 29, 73
Cerebral lesions, 132
Cerebral palsy, 33

Cervical bite, 131
Cervical spine, 157, 230
Challenge technique, 72
Character assassination, 3
Charity, 278
Chasing, 155
Cheetahs, 178
Chemical brain stimulation. *See* Brain stimulation chemical
Cherishing behavior, 185
Chest, 165
Chicken, 13, 133, 137, 157
Child, 17, 39, 43, 86, 90–92, 100, 154, 224
Child rearing practices, 189
Chimpanzees, 113, 158, 178, 181, 183, 185, 190, 203, 218
Chin, 163, 218
Chipmunk, 221
Chloral hydrate, 90
Chlordiazepoxide, 87–88, 92, 95
Chlormadinone acetate, 65
Chlorpromazine, 56, 92, 118
Chocolate, 71–72
Cholinergic blocking agents, 231
Cholinesterase, 230
Chorea, 33
Chromosome abnormality, 14
Chronic behavior tendency, 18–19, 21, 276, 279
Chronic brain syndrome, 29, 92
Cingulate gyrus, 27, 58, 236, 258, 266, 273–274
Cingulate lesions. *See* Cingulectomy
Cingulectomy, 48, 259, 266
Cingulotomy, 48
Cingulum. *See* Cingulate gyrus
Circumgenital area, 218
Civilization, 96–97, 100
Civil rights, 126–127
Classification, 135
Claws, 188, 229, 267
Climate, 211
Clitoral glands, 163
Clockwork Orange, 100
Cock, 13
Code of Hammurabi, 125
Cognition, 279–280
Cognitive map, 281
Cognitive restructuring, 102
Coitus, 203
Cola, 71, 72
Cold, 201
Colony, 213–214, 220, 243–245
Coma, 76, 106
Communal territories, 212
Communities, 153
Competition, 146, 190–191, 204, 243, 283
Competitive aggression, 131, 191

Compulsion, 70
Computer, 113
Computer modeling, 208
Concentration, 195
Concentration camp, 193
Conditioned anxiety, 202
Conditioned attack, 15
Conditioned emotional response, 207
Conditioned fear, 147
Conditioned stimulus, 147, 201, 207
Conditioning, 201–202
Conflict, 151–152, 157–158, 186, 210
Consciousness, 85
Conspecific, 10, 108, 133, 135, 151, 154, 158, 160, 169, 173–174, 177, 185–186, 191, 203, 209, 211, 213–218, 221–222, 268, 272
Consummatory behavior, 4, 17, 147, 222
Contraceptive, 68
Control, 96–97, 102–103, 105–107, 109–110, 112, 114, 117, 119–129
Controversy, 121
Convulsion, 27, 34, 58, 73, 107–108
Copulation, 205
Core area, 221–222
Corn, 72
Corpus luteum, 271
Cortex, 44, 52
Corticosterone, 249
Cotton rat, 168–169, 270
Counterattack, 142
Counterthreat, 164
Courtship, 205
Coyote, 142
Crickets, 142
Crime, 11, 36, 40–41, 62, 74, 80–82, 84, 128
    interpersonal, 189
    violent, 60–61, 66–67, 69, 78, 83, 97, 153, 193, 203
Criminal, 90, 92, 117, 153
Cripple, 205
Critical period, 251
Cross-cultural study, 189
Cruelty, 121
Cryosurgery, 47
Cub, 186, 213
Cue, 102, 119, 121, 143, 172–173, 185, 248, 279, 282
Culture, 23, 69, 79, 102, 119, 189, 192
Cyclic (AMP), 87
Cyproterone acetate, 65, 116

Dam, 183
Dama dama, 157
Dangling procedure, 170
Darwin, 166, 168
Death, 169, 204, 244, 248
Decorticate animal, 228

Deer, 5, 133, 152, 157, 216–217
Defeat, 172, 210, 220, 248
Defended area, 210
Defense, 169, 178, 259, 261–262
  zone, 260
Defensive aggression, 5, 160, 178
Defensive position, 156
Defensive posture, 165, 201
Defensive threat, 178, 180, 199–200
Definition, 1–2, 20, 204, 210–211, 226
Degeneration, 232, 264
Dehydroisoandosterone, 62
Delayed conditioning, 201
Delinquent, 40–41, 43, 81, 91
Delusions, 85
Denmark, 62
Dependent variable, 89
Depersonalization, 258
Depo-Provera, 65
Depression, 24, 36–37, 67–68, 74, 78, 88
  endogenous, 281
  reactive, 281
Deprivation, 14, 17, 102, 121, 147, 188–
    189, 193, 203, 208, 222, 225, 278
  food, 8, 193–194, 204, 208
  morphine, 8, 195, 200, 204
  REM, 195
  sleep, 8, 195, 204, 208
  social, 196–198, 204
  water, 146, 174, 193–194
Depth recording, 106
Dermatomes, 140
Desensitization, 11, 102
Destructive behavior. See Destructiveness
Destructiveness, 30, 39, 47, 49, 105
Determinants of behavior, 284
Deviant behavior, 101
Dexamethasone, 248–249
Dexedrine, 72, 78
Dextroamphetamine sulfate. See Dexe-
    drine
Dextrose, 241–242
Diabetes, 75
Diabetes insipidus, 104
Diagnosis, 126
Diandrone, 62
Diazepam, 87, 92, 95, 117
Diestrous, 162
Diet, 69
Diethylstilbestrol, 270
Digit symbol test, 118
Dignity, 128–129
Dihydrotestosterone, 243, 254
Dilantin, 91, 95, 118, 126
Diphenylhydantoin. See Dilantin
Disinhibited reaction, 238
Displaced aggression, 20, 190
Diuretic, 68
Dizziness, 42, 78

Docility, 46, 48, 243, 259, 265
Dog, 9, 142, 165–167, 196, 218–219, 243,
    266–267
Domestication, 181, 186
Dominance, 17, 172, 183, 191, 244–245,
    254, 258
  hierarchy, 17, 172
  status, 160
Dominant male, 131
Dopamine, 12, 87
Double-blind crossover study, 89–91
Double-blind study, 87
Dove, 168, 253
Dream study, 34
Drive, 24, 139, 275–276, 278
Drowsiness, 118
Drug, 59, 72, 78–80, 86, 88–89, 93–94,
    98, 103, 105, 117–120, 122, 126, 132,
    152, 230, 280
Drug-induced aggression, 78
Duiker, 220
Dutch, 282
Dyscontrol, 38, 77
Dyscontrol syndrome, 27
Dysrhythmia, 44

Eating behavior, 144, 222, 278
Economic exploitation, 122
Edema, 66, 73, 107
Education, 97
EEG. See Electroencephalogram
Efficiency, 123
Egg, 72
Elation, 112
Electrical stimulation, 6–7, 54, 103, 107
Electrode, 35, 53, 55–57, 85, 106, 110–
    113, 125, 144, 201, 232
Electroencephalogram, 34–35, 39–42, 58,
    71, 85–86, 91, 106, 113, 234
Electroshock treatments, 53
Elephant, 158
Elite, 122
Elk, 216
El Salvador, 283
Emotion, 121, 280–281
Emotional display, 234
Emotional expression, 166
Emotional immaturity reaction, 70
Emotional instability, 2, 8, 29, 40, 66
Emotionality, 237
Emotional stability, 126
Empathy, 102
Encephalitis, 30, 32, 53, 57
Encephalitis lethargica, 30–32, 202
Endocrine disturbance, 98
Endocrine glands, 246
Endocrine status, 159
Endocrine system, 59, 102, 270–271
Endocrinology, 60, 135, 238–239, 270

Endocrinopathy, 114
Energy, 66, 96, 276
Environment, 69, 72, 102, 119, 136, 147, 280–281, 284
Epilepsy, 34–35, 38–39, 46, 48, 50, 73, 85, 90, 98, 108, 124
  grand mal, 34–35, 42
  ideopathic, 34
  petit mal, 34
  psychomotor, 34, 38, 56, 126, 202
  temporal lobe, 34–37, 58, 65, 104
Episodic dyscontrol, 126
Ergotropic circuits, 48
Escape, 9, 130, 147, 158–159, 169, 176–177, 179–181, 187, 201–203, 223, 255–260, 262–263, 265, 267
Estradiol, 239, 247
  benzoate, 159, 251, 271
  B.P.C., 64, 116
  valerinate, 64, 116
Estrogen, 11, 64, 68–69, 94, 115, 159, 162, 207, 247, 271, 273
Estrus, 159, 162–163, 203, 205
Ethanol, 71, 84. *See also* Alcohol
Ethicists, 127
Ethics, 97, 101, 123
Ethogram, 166
Ethologists, 275
Eunuchs, 62
Euphoria, 9, 21, 24, 49, 51, 56, 74, 79, 86, 197, 280
Europe, 225
Eutamias
  alpinus, 217
  amoenus, 217
  minimus, 217
  speciosus, 217
Evoked potentials, 140
Evolution, 282
Excitability, 70
Excitement, 257
Excrement, 160
Exhibitionism, 63, 115
Exhilaration, 74
Experience, 83, 126, 142, 150–151, 284
Experimenter, 130, 133, 138, 148, 170, 229, 264, 268, 282
Exploratory behavior, 10, 147, 222
Explosive tendencies, 50
Extinction, 16, 191–192, 204
Extinction-induced aggression, 8, 191
Extramarital intercourse, 189
Extrapunitive aggression, 81

Facial nerve, 233
Facial signals, 198
Facilitation, 234, 272
Factor analysis, 200

Faintness, 76
Famine, 193
Fantasy, 206
Fantasy aggression, 3, 10, 81, 206
Fascicularis macaques, 152
Fasciculus of Schutz, 233
Fatigue, 69, 72, 76
Fear, 9, 18, 23, 36, 45–46, 48, 52–53, 62, 111, 147, 151, 171–172, 174, 176, 179–180, 207–208, 246, 255, 257–258, 266–268
Fear-flight attack reaction, 132
Fear-induced aggression, 23–24, 176–177, 180, 197, 202, 255–259, 260–263, 266, 268, 273
Feces, 56
Fencing, 155
Ferret, 205
Fetichism, 63
Fetichistic actions, 63
Fight, 155, 161, 210, 213, 242, 259
Fighter, 210
Fighting, 12–13, 16, 61, 76, 151–152, 156–158, 160, 163, 166, 169, 171, 173, 192, 194, 196–197, 200, 202–203, 205, 209, 211–212, 216, 218, 220, 223, 240–241, 246, 255, 269, 273, 276
Finland, 62
Firearms, 98–99, 103
Fixed action pattern, 154, 164
Fixed-ratio schedule, 192
Flank marking, 219
Flank presentation, 200
Flexibility, 104
Flight, 177–179, 259–261
Flight distance, 177
Fluphenazine, 91
Foam rubber block, 138
Food, 17, 69, 72, 139, 146, 171, 179, 185, 190–191, 210, 212, 240, 259, 278
  begging for, 168
Football, 283
Foot shock, 199
Force, 278
Forebrain, 232, 254, 261
Forelimb, 155
Forepaws, 139
Fornix, 50, 58
Fratricidal accident, 158
Freedom, 123
Free will, 128
Frog, 5, 137–138, 143, 149–150, 180
  Frog-o-mat, 143
  killing, 133, 144–146, 148, 230, 237–239
Frontal lobe, 27, 49, 56
  lesions, 49

FR-4 and FR-5, 143
Frustration, 2–3, 8, 11, 19, 41, 44, 102, 121, 188–191, 193–194, 203–204, 225, 275, 278, 283
  tolerance for, 91, 93
Fugue, 74
Fury, 70

Gene pool, 204
Genet, 141
Genetics, 12–14
Genital abnormalities, 253
Genital display, 157
Genital sniffing, 186
Gerbil, 65, 158, 166, 191, 196, 200, 213, 218–220, 243
Gesture, 166, 197
Ghetto, 102, 189
Gibbon, 151, 158, 213–214, 217, 221
Gilles de la Tourette disease, 92
Gin, 85
Giraffe, 158
Glazed look, 118
Glioblastoma multiforme, 27
Gliosis, 107
Globicephala scammoni, 152
Glucocorticoid, 249
Glucose, 76–77
Glucose Tolerance Test, 76
Glycogen, 76–77
Goal, 2–3, 193
Goal box, 142–143, 190, 192
Goal-directed behavior, 275
Goal object, 131, 191, 193
Golgi I cells, 233
Gonad, 238, 240–241, 248
Gonadectomy, 239, 269
Gonadotropic hormone, 64, 247, 254
Gorilla, 172, 178, 218
Gossip, 3
Gottschalk-Gliser Content Analysis Scale, 67, 87–88, 92
Grand mal. See Epilepsy, *grand mal*
Gray fox, 142, 205
Great Britain, 283
Grizzly bear, 177, 180
Grooming, 152, 172, 255
Gross National Product, 189
Group therapy, 102
Growl, 133, 177, 261–262, 267
Guilt, 43, 50
Guinea pig, 164, 249, 270
Gun. *See* Firearms
Gymnastic meet, 283

Habit, 17, 143, 169
Habitat, 216
Habituation, 169, 179–180, 248
Hackle, 154

Hall-Klein aggression scale, 192
Hallucination, 24, 39, 85, 264
Haloperidol, 91–92, 95, 118
Hamster, 137, 151, 160, 164–165, 191, 196, 218–220, 243, 254, 270
Happiness, 56, 123
Hare, 142
Harem, 62, 215, 223
Headache, 24–26, 42, 66
Head tossing, 230
Head twitching, 196
Heart rate, 157
Heat, 201
Helplessness, 86
Hemiparesis, 104
Hemorrhage, 29
Herbivores, 136
Herding animals, 217
Heredity, 12–14, 18–19, 21
Heroin addict, 118
Heterosexuality, 63
HGPRT, 33
Hierarchy, 157, 243
Hilarity, 74
Hippocampus, 29, 44, 46, 53, 55, 58, 113, 232, 236, 258–260, 268–269, 272–274
Hippopotamus, 135, 152, 158
Hiss, 133, 177, 261–262, 267
History, 284
Hives, 73
Home range, 209, 219, 221–222
Home site, 210
Homicide, 37, 80, 82–84, 153. *See also* Murder
Homosexual, 63, 65, 207
Homosexuality, 63
Honduras, 283
Hopelessness, 68
Hormone, 11, 14, 19, 21, 59, 63–66, 103, 105, 114, 116, 126, 134, 153, 162, 180, 186, 205, 239–243, 246, 256, 270, 273–274, 277
  inhibitor, 116
  therapy, 115, 128
Horn, 158
Horse, 181
Hostility, outward, 92
Hug, 101
Hunger, 17, 134, 145–146, 151, 175, 194–195, 233, 277
Huntington's chorea, 29
Hydraulic model, 276, 283
Hydrocortisone, 249. *See also* Cortisol
Hydrophobia, 29
DL-5-Hydroxytryptophan, 230
Hyperactive child, 118
Hyperactive reflexes, 78
Hyperactivity, 39, 86, 90, 92

Hyperaggressiveness. *See* Hyperaggressivity

Hyperaggressivity, 29, 77, 198

Hyperemotionality, 146, 254, 259

Hyperinsulinism, 68, 74, 76

Hyperkinesis, 202

Hyperkinetic child syndrome, 71

Hyperphagia, 24, 28, 146

Hyperresponsive syndrome, 97

Hypersensitivity, 267

Hypersexuality, 36, 103, 270

Hypnotic, 90

Hypoadrenalcorticalism, 74

Hypocrisy, 37

Hypoglycemia, 6, 11, 59, 69, 74–77, 94, 98, 195, 203
    aggression hypothesis, 76

Hypophysectomy, 246, 269

Hyposexuality, 36

Hypothalamic lesions, 48

Hypothalamus, 5, 9, 27–28, 32, 44, 58, 108, 139–140, 144, 228, 232, 236–237, 239, 254–256, 260–262, 264, 266–267, 273–274, 281
    anterior, 28, 254, 260
    lateral, 7, 133, 137–138, 142–144, 146, 228–232, 254–255, 264–265, 272, 274
    medial, 229, 254, 264–265, 270, 274
    posterior, 49, 53
    posterior lateral, 138, 143
    preoptic nucleus, 255, 261
    ventromedial, 28, 146, 260, 264–265, 274

Hypothyroidism, 74

Hysteria, 88

Iceland, 62

Ictal, 34, 36–37

Imipramine, 87, 234

Impatience, 70

Implant, 116

Impotence, 116

Impulsive control, 28, 30, 36, 39–40, 58, 88, 99, 112, 129

Impulsiveness, 30, 36–38, 43, 70, 74, 91, 122

Inanimate object, 133, 191, 203, 255

Incarceration, 126

Individual differences, 284

Infant, 183

Inferior colliculus, 255

Informed consent, 123–125, 127

Inhalants, 72

Inhibition, 8–10, 16, 18–19, 84, 88, 100, 103, 109–111, 113, 117, 137, 147, 150–151, 157, 168, 234–236, 248, 256, 267, 272, 279, 283

Inhibitory mechanisms, 28, 44

Inhibitory neurons, 20

Inhibitory system, 57
    amygdaloid, 235

Inhibitory training, 277, 279

Injury, 157, 165, 204

Insanity, 74

Insect, 138

Insight, 284

Insomnia, 78, 86

Instinct, 225, 278

Instrumental aggression, 14–15, 24, 61–62, 99, 114, 120–121, 223, 226, 283

Insulin, 74–77

Intellectual impairment, 47, 104

Intent, 2, 3, 20, 165

Interictal, 34, 37

Inter-male aggression, 5, 10–13, 16, 23, 63, 65, 133, 135, 141, 151, 154–155, 157–160, 163–165, 168–175, 180, 196, 203, 205, 223, 226, 238–241, 246, 248–249, 254, 256, 265, 272–273

Internal impulses, 96, 99, 225

Internal milieu, 284

International aggression, 100

Interpersonal aggression, 100

Interspecific aggression, 132, 146, 150

Interspecific defense, 158

Intervening variable, 276

Intoxication, 85

Intracranial pressure, 24

Intraspecific aggression, 134, 153, 195, 222, 238, 259, 281–282

Introspection, 225

Intruder, 169, 180–181, 185–186, 210, 211, 214, 222, 226, 265

Invasion, 225

Irascibility, 66, 70

Irresponsibility, 50

Irritability, 9, 11, 24, 27–29, 38, 40, 49, 53, 57, 65–70, 72, 74, 76, 78–79, 81–82, 86, 88, 91, 114, 116, 118, 184–185, 193–196, 203, 265, 277–278

Irritable aggression, 8–12, 16, 18, 20–24, 45, 62–63, 66, 70, 73, 94, 133, 135, 144, 178, 180, 186, 188, 191, 193, 197, 199, 202–204, 207–208, 236, 238, 255, 259–261, 263–274, 283

Irritative focus, 28

Islands of Langerhans, 74

Isolation, 101, 130, 132, 149–150, 154, 173–174, 194, 196–198, 213, 241, 246

Isolation-induced aggression, 12, 196–197, 246, 249–250

Jaw, 140, 229

Joy, 52

Jugular vein, 165

Juvenile, 240
Juvenile delinquents. *See* Delinquents

Kansas, 64
Kerner report, 102
Key stimuli, 137
Kicking, 200
Kindling effect, 107–108
Kinds of aggression, 3–5, 8, 16, 20–22, 45, 48, 88–89, 106, 114, 117, 131, 133–134, 151, 174–176, 178, 200, 203, 207, 226, 229, 272
   in man, 23
Kitten, 229
Klinefelter syndrome, 14
Kluver and Bucy syndrome, 103
Knife cut, 265
Korsakoff's syndrome, 29

Lactation, 74, 134, 181–184, 186
Langur, 158, 181, 183, 185, 214, 221
Larceny, 42
Latency, 146, 148, 161, 170, 173, 231, 239, 248, 261
Lateral geniculate body, 140
Laughter, 24, 206, 282
Law, 125–126, 225
   of Effect, 14
Layman, 127
Lawyer, 127
L-Dopa, 86
Leaping, 155
Learning, 4, 14–15, 17–18, 21, 23, 38, 42, 59, 62, 69, 83, 96, 99–100, 119–120, 141–142, 151, 154, 158, 172, 174, 192, 202, 225, 284
Lemming, 157
Lemur, 213
Leopard, 178, 181
Lesch-Nyhan syndrome, 32, 58, 202
Lethargy, 193
Leukotomy, 49
Levaternol bitartrate, 53
Leydig cell, 115
Libido, 64–65
Librium. *See* Chlordiazepoxide
Life cycle, 211
Limbic lobe, 24
Limbic system, 27, 29, 35, 45, 47, 57–58, 73, 77, 107, 121
Lion, 141, 178, 209, 213–214, 218, 220–221
Lion tamer, 214
Lipiodol, 47
Lip smacking, 53
Literacy rate, 189
Lithium, 68, 93, 95, 119
Litter, 181, 184
Littermates, 213
Livestock, 225

Lobotomy, 50
Loneliness, 52
Love, 19, 52, 165, 279, 281–282
Lutenizing hormone, 60
Lynx, 251

Macaque, 158, 179, 240, 243
Mamillary bodies, 261
Mammal, 136, 168, 184, 191, 212, 220–221, 241, 250, 271
Mania, 87, 93
Mankind, 123
Marihuana, 83, 194
Marmoset, 214, 218–220
Marsupials, 205. *See also* Australian marsupial
Martens, 218
Masklike face, 32
Masturbation, 63, 116
Maternal aggression, 136, 174, 177, 180, 182, 184–185, 187, 223, 226, 263
Maternal behavior, 181–182
Maternal drive, 183
Mating behavior, 205
Mating season, 244
Matricide, 43
Maze, 142–143
Maze learning, 142
Meat extract, 138
Medial forebrain bundle, 232–233
Medial lemniscus, 265
Medicine, 125
Medroxyprogesterone, 16, 116
Melanesia, 154
Memory, 29, 46–47, 52, 103–104, 118
Menstrual cycle, 66–67, 114, 162
Menstrual period, 20, 68
Menstruation, 66–68
Mental hospital, 90
Mentally retarded, 104
Mental patient, 223
Mental processes, 211
Meprobamate, 93–94, 118
Mercury, 203
Mesencephalic reticular formation, 50, 145, 232
Mesencephalon, 32, 53
Mesocricetus auratus, 219
Mestranol, 253
Metabolic disorders, 34
Metabolic processes, 10, 22
Methacholine, 232
Methamphetamine, 78–79
Mexico, 83
Midbrain, 8, 145, 228, 232–233, 254, 260–262, 264–266, 270, 272–274
   reticular formation of, 7, 108, 140, 236–237, 255, 264, 272
   tegmentum, 232

Middle age, 74
Milan Conference, 228
Milieu therapy, 101
Military glory, 189
Milk, 71–72, 173
Mincing, 241–242
Minimal brain dysfunction, 71, 78
Mink, 157, 205, 240, 271
Mock combat, 240
Model, 96
Modeling, 17, 18
Modulating structures, 9, 233
Money, 101
Monkey, 9, 15–17, 48, 107, 110, 192,
    196–198, 200–203, 218, 256–257,
    259, 270, 282
  howler, 214, 216, 221
  Japanese, 244
  Macaca mulatta, 271
  rhesus, 153, 159, 190–191, 205, 214,
    244, 248, 253, 255, 271
  squirrel, 155, 157, 202, 269
  vervet, 185, 216
  wild, 44
Mood, 48, 52, 55, 67, 71, 78, 81, 91, 107,
    125, 281
  adjective checklist, 82
  elevator, 119
Moose, 181, 186, 217
Morphine, 195–196
Morphine deprivation. *See* Deprivation,
    morphine
Mother, 134, 179–186, 190, 198, 217
Mother surrogate, 153
Motivation, 215, 218, 276
Motive, 212
Motor aphasia, 73
Motor function, 228
Motor nerve, 205
Motor neuron, 5
Motor nucleus, 140
Motor predispositional systems, 9
Motor system, 8, 9, 141
Mounting, 152
Mouse, 6, 12–16, 65, 107, 131, 134, 136–
    139, 142–147, 149, 151–152, 157,
    159–163, 166, 169–173, 181–186,
    190–191, 194, 196, 200–201, 207,
    213–216, 219, 222–223, 229, 232,
    240–244, 246, 250–251, 253, 263,
    271, 273
  killing, 15, 133, 150, 230, 234, 236–
    238, 255
  Mouse-o-mat, 143
Murder, 25, 40, 43, 65, 75, 80, 106, 115–
    117, 123, 126
Murder Inc., 120
Muricide. *See* Mouse killing
Muscle tone, 7

Muscular exhaustion, 74
Musk ox, 152, 158
Mus musculus, 213
Muzzle, 140
Myocaster coypus, 217

Narcolepsy, 78, 110
Narcotic, 83
Nasal congestion, 72
National boundaries, 223
National parks, 186
Nations, 153
Nausea, 24, 42
Nauta stain, 232
Nazi Germany, 62
Necrosis, 32
Negative affect, 16, 68, 82, 91, 134, 174,
    195
Negativism, 27, 74
Negri bodies, 29
Neonate, 12, 253
Neoplasm, 24, 28
Neostigmine, 230, 232
Nervousness, 72, 82
Nervous system, 71–73, 84, 137, 250, 252,
    276–277
Nest, 177, 181, 183–185, 215–216
Neural facilitation, 8
Neural inhibition, 9, 77
Neural system, 4–11, 14–23, 25, 27–28,
    34–36, 38, 41, 44, 51–53, 57–58, 62,
    68, 73, 84, 89, 100, 102–103, 134,
    139, 141, 168, 172, 228, 230, 232,
    236, 239, 246, 256, 263, 265, 269,
    272, 276–280, 282–283
Neurobiochemistry, 33
Neurological set, 19–21
Neurological signs, 32
Neurology, 135, 227–228, 254, 256, 260,
    263, 272–273
Neuromuscular coordination, 120
Neurons, 5, 19, 144, 228, 172
Neurosurgery, 128
Neurotic, 89, 91, 124
Neurotransmitters, 11, 235
Newspaper, 189
New York, 283
Nicotine, 232
Nightingale, 218
Nightmare, 70
Nitrazepam, 87
Nocturnal jactations, 35
Noise, 201
Non-human primates, 152–153
Nonterritorial animals, 217
Norepinephrine, 12, 230, 235–236, 281
Norethynodrel, 253
North Vietnam, 120
Norway, 62, 64, 115

Novelty, 169, 172, 179–180, 220
Noxious stimulation, 2–3, 16, 202. *See also* Aversive stimulation
Nucleus reticularis pontis oralis, 145
Nucleus reunions, 233
Nutria, 217
Nystagmus, 85

Obesity, 78
Obscenities, 92
Odor, 137, 147, 160, 163–164, 168, 171, 174, 215, 220
Offender, 65, 80, 83, 116
Offensive stance, 165
Officer candidate training, 248
Offspring, 198
Oil of lavender, 137
Olfaction, 139, 159–160, 219
Olfactory bulbectomy, 137, 219, 237–238
Olfactory bulbs, 160, 236–237, 266, 274
Olfactory cues, 137, 172
Olfactory inhibition, 137
Oligophrenia, 36, 46
"On" button, 110
Onion, 72
Onychomys, 146
Opossum, 196, 230
Opponent, 155
Oppression, 121
Optic nerve, 73
Optic tract, 140
Orange juice, 277
Orgasm, 109
Orientation, 148
Oryx, 158
Ovaries, 162
Ovulation, 66
Oxazepam, 87–88
Oxotrimorine, 231–232

Pacific pilot whale, 152
Pain, 8, 29, 33, 50, 53, 55–56, 58, 104, 109, 113, 155, 188, 190, 199–204, 207, 240, 263–265
Pain-induced aggression, 201–202, 266
Pallor, 72
Palpitation, 42
Palsy, 104
Pancreas, 74
Paradigm, 199–201, 250
Paradoxical rage, 87, 117
Paradoxical reaction, 120, 122
Paraldehyde, 90
Paralysis, 73
Paranoia, 80, 86
Parasympathetic arousal, 231
Parent, 100
Parkinsonianism, 32, 50, 78

Parkinson's disease. *See* Parkinsonianism
Parolee, 64
Paroxysmal behavior disorders, 34
Paroxysmal symptoms, 25
Parrying, 241–242
Parturient, 184
Parturition, 182, 185–186
Passive aggressiveness, 98
Passive defense, 214
Paternal aggression, 183
Path, 215, 221
Pathological intoxication, 84–86
Patterned reflex, 139–140, 272
Paw, 140, 229
Peer, 150, 190, 198, 258
Peer ratings, 76
Peevishness, 70
Penile thrusts, 157
Penis, 253
Perameles, 159
Perception, 85
Periamygdaloid cortex, 234, 255
Periaqueductal gray matter, 32
Perifalciform regions, 34
Perineal region, 160
Periventricular system, 233, 264, 274
Peromyscus
    californicus, 184, 215
    maniculatus bairdii, 184, 213, 215
    maniculatus gracilis, 184, 215
Personality, 24–25, 27–28, 30, 35, 38, 46, 50, 57–58, 62, 80, 84, 104, 124
Personal space, 177, 216–217
Peru, 283
Pervert sexual acts, 62
Phalangers, 258
Pharmaceutical agent, 122, 128
Pharmacotherapy, 117, 119
Phenmetrazine, 80
Phenothiazine, 38, 90, 92, 95
Pheromones, 159–160, 162–164, 196, 206, 221, 239–240, 252, 266
Phoca, 217
Physician, 127, 281
Physician's Desk Reference, 119
Physiological dysfunction, 202
Physostigmine, 230, 232
Pigeon, 16, 191
Pilocarpine, 231
Piloerection, 176–177, 187, 203
Pilot, 120
Pennepedin, 216, 223
Pit dogs, 13
Pituitary, 60, 64, 74, 247, 254
    adrenal axis, 247, 249
    gonadal system, 249
Placebo, 81–82, 84, 93, 109, 118
Planning, 118

Play, 153–154, 172, 240, 253, 271
   aggressive, 153–154
   doll, 154
Playroom, 224
Pleasure, 52
Plethysmograph, 84
Poisoning, 203
Polecat, 142
Political instability, 189
Political suppression, 114
Political unit, 224
Pollen, 72
Polydypsia, 115
Polyuria, 115
Population, 97, 102, 121, 127, 216, 221, 278
   pressure, 212, 214
Pornography, 206
Positive affect, 16, 19, 82, 109, 113, 125, 134, 174
Postpartum, 182–183, 263
Posture, 166, 172, 174, 178
Poult, 184
Power, 121–122
Prairie dogs, 213–214
Predation, 135–136, 139, 141, 147–148, 169, 205, 208, 212, 222, 228–232, 237–238, 272
Predator, 5, 133, 142, 146, 148, 154, 158, 178, 184, 208
Predatory aggression, 5–8, 13, 15–16, 133–136, 141–142, 144, 146–147, 150–151, 157, 171, 175, 177, 180, 187, 207, 226, 228–232, 234, 236, 264, 266, 268, 270, 272
Predatory behavior, 136
Predatory system, 9, 140
Prefrontal cortex, 234, 258
Prefrontal lobotomy, 103, 106
Pregnancy, 182, 186, 206, 253
Preludin, 80
Premenstrual period, 67, 69, 203, 277
Premenstrual syndrome, 66, 68, 94
Premenstrual tension, 4, 11, 68, 116, 202–203
Premenstruum, 67
Prenatal period, 253
Prepuce, 162
Preputial glands, 162–163, 243, 249
Prepyriform cortex, 234
Preschool, 154
Prey, 5, 133, 135–138, 140–148, 151, 154, 157, 172, 187, 205, 228–229, 232, 272
   carrying, 145
Pride, 213, 221
Primate, 170, 186, 213, 221–222, 240, 244, 253, 268
Primidone, 92

Primogyn depot, 116
Principle of antithesis, 166, 168
Prison, 61, 64, 67, 93, 106, 115, 126
Prisoner, 40, 67, 91, 93, 116
   advocate, 127
Probation, 65
Problem solving, 282
Proestrus, 164
Profanity, 92
Progestagen, 68, 115
Progesterone, 11, 65, 68, 94, 159, 206, 247, 271
Prolactin, 263
Propendiols, 93–94
Propericiazine, 90
Property, 223, 225
Prostate, 249
Protein, 69
Provera, 65
Provocation, 19–20, 37, 42, 53, 56, 121, 159, 278
Psychiatric symptoms, 24
Psychiatrist, 55, 124
Psychoactive drug. See Psychotropic drug
Psychoanalysts, 275
Psychodrama, 102
Psychological dysfunction, 281
Psychometrist, 105
Psychomotor epilepsy. See Epilepsy, psychomotor
Psychoneurosis, 94
Psychopath, 39–41, 46, 91
Psychosis, 80
Psychosurgery, 105–106, 128
Psychotec, 91–92, 117
Psychotherapy, 53, 101, 119, 281
Psychotic behavior, 56
Psychotic episodes, 24
Psychotropic drug, 88, 90, 117–119, 279–280
Puberty, 60, 240–241
Puerto Rico, 243
Puka, 213
Punishment, 16–17, 30, 67, 97, 100, 157, 172, 190, 201–202
Pupillodilation, 177, 187, 203, 261, 264
Puppy, 168
Purine, 33, 58
Pyramidal tract, 30

Qolla Indians, 76

Rabbits, 137, 177–178, 181, 196, 213, 216, 218, 220, 248
Rabies, 29, 57, 202, 204
Racism, 188
Radar, 120
Radiculitis, 73

Radio, 189
Radio-controlled brain stimulation, 110–111
Radiofrequency lesion, 47
Radio transmitter, 111–113
Rage, 9, 18, 22, 24–25, 27–29, 35–36, 38–39, 42, 46, 51, 53, 56, 65, 74, 85, 86–88, 112, 117, 178, 187–189, 198, 203, 229, 260, 267
Rape, 80
Rat, 5–8, 10, 12–15, 107, 130–133, 136, 138, 140, 142, 145, 147–151, 154, 164, 166, 171, 179, 181–182, 184, 190–192, 194–197, 199–203, 213–215, 219, 222, 228–229, 232, 234, 236–237, 239–240, 243, 248, 253–254, 259, 268–270, 272
    pup, 137, 142–143, 150, 182
Rattus norvegicus, 169
Reaction time, 82
Reasoning, 118
Rebellion, 193
Rebellious behavior, 70
Receptor site, 65
Recidivism, 41, 64
Reciprocal inhibition, 9, 102
Reciprocal innervation, 9
Redirected aggression, 190
Reduction, 281
Reflex, 84, 139–140
Reflexive aggression, 16
Regression equation, 61
Reinforcement, 8, 14–17, 20, 61, 101, 121, 131, 143, 192, 197–198, 201, 204
    continuous, 191
    negative, 199, 220
    posture, 97, 101
Relaxation, 56, 81, 195
Releasing stimulus, 164
REM, 195
Remorse, 32, 43
Remotivating display, 168
Repression, 23
Research design, 89
Response decrement, 147–148
Response inhibition, 148, 169
Restlessness, 27, 78
Restraint, 33, 36, 101, 114, 267
Reticular activating system, 6–8, 21, 280
Reticular nuclei, 147
Retina, 73
Retreat, 210
Revenge, 79
Review, 211, 228, 267
Review board, 127
Reward, 15–16, 101, 170, 172, 192
Rhinoceros, 217
Rhodesia, 218

Rigidity, 32
Riot, 193, 283
Risk, 107–108, 114
Ritual, 155
Ritualized behaviors, 165
Roaring, 221
Robbery, 153
Robin, 164
Rodent, 166, 232, 246, 253
Role model, 100, 102, 190
Role playing, 102
Rosenzweig Picture Frustration Test, 81
Rostral fastigial nucleus, 237
Rubber mouse, 138
Rump, 166
Run, 79–80
Rush, 79
Russia, 193

Sarcasm, 3
Satiation, 148
Savageness, 179, 260
Savannah, 218
Scar, 152, 157, 265, 274
Scent, 218–220
    glands, 218
    marking, 218–219
Scientific endeavors, 282
Schizophrenia, 43, 46, 50, 62–63, 80, 89, 92, 100
Scotoma, 73
Scrotum, 253
Sea, 282
Seal, 152, 158, 213, 216–217
Sea lions, 216, 221
Season, 212, 226
Sebaceous glands, 163, 218
Sedation, 121
Sedative surgery, 48
Seizure, 36, 46–47, 53, 55, 57–58, 69, 86, 91, 107–108, 236
Self-confidence, 62
Self-control, 70
Self-directed attack, 198
Self-destructive behavior, 198
Self-determination, 128, 188
Self-injury, 92, 118
Self-medication, 116
Self-mutilation, 30, 33, 58, 105
Self-respect, 188
Self-stimulation, 110, 144, 170, 233, 255
Seminal vesicles, 243, 247
Senile dementia, 29
Sensation, 280
Sensitiveness, 37
Sensitization, 11
Sensorimotor feedback, 6
Sensory aphasia, 73

Sensory deficit, 280
Sensory feedback, 140
Sensory field, 6
Sensory function, 228
Sensory input, 5, 139, 265
Sensory mechanisms, 138
Sensory systems, 6–7, 141
Septal lesions, 236, 254, 259, 274
Septal region. *See* Septum
Septal stimulation, 56
Septal syndrome, 259, 269
Septum, 53, 236, 258, 269, 272
    lateral, 231
Serotonin, 12, 230, 254
Sesame oil, 173
Sex, 64, 81, 134, 142, 207, 214, 222, 226,
    248, 277
Sex activity, 46, 63
Sex crime, 62, 64, 116, 128, 207
Sex criminal, 64
Sex differences, 142, 160, 203, 239
Sex drive, 63, 66, 116
Sex hormone, 65, 207
Sex-related aggression, 23, 65–66, 94,
    114–115, 204–207, 223, 226
Sexual aggression, 63
Sexual arousal, 65, 115–116, 206–207
Sexual behavior, 65–66, 159, 171, 204,
    207, 222, 250
Sexual communication, 220
Sexual deviation, 65, 89, 90
Sexual dimorphism, 153
Sexual excitement, 52
Sexual fantasy, 116
Sexual maturity, 60, 240, 272
Sexual motive state, 107
Sexual offenses, 30
Sexual presentation, 168
Sexual satiation, 171
Sexual status, 171
Sham biting, 153, 240, 271
Sham rage, 228
Sheep, 181, 183, 185
Shelter, 212
Shiftlessness, 50
Shock, 16, 82, 100–101, 147, 191, 194,
    200–202, 207, 236, 248, 265, 270
Shock-induced aggression, 195, 200, 202,
    250, 255, 265, 269, 271
Shyness, 259
Sibling, 101, 179
Sibling rivalry, 24
Side effects, 103–104, 107–109, 113–
    118, 122, 128
Signal, 221
Six- and fourteen-per-second positive
    spike, 42–44
Sleep, 35, 85, 110, 195. *See also* De-
    privation, sleep

Snake, 138
Snarling, 264
Sniffing, 163
Snout, 139
Snowshoe hare, 181
Soccer, 283
Social awareness, 104
Social behavior, 47, 160, 259
Social bonding, 282
Social conflict, 76
Social development, 225
Social disruption, 126
Social experience, 254
Social hierarchy, 17
Social interaction, 154, 166, 200, 258,
    281
    therapy, 281
Socialization, 38
Social learning, 197
Social organization, 212
Social position, 132
Social pressure, 83
Social rehabilitation, 199
Social signals, 197
Social stimuli, 198
Social isolate, 258
Sodium, 68, 230
Sodium diphenylhydantoin. *See* Dilantin
Sodium nitrate, 230
Solitary confinement, 47, 61, 64, 93, 114,
    127
Soma, 284
Spatial defense, 217
Species specific, 151, 166, 218
    postures, 3
Spectator, 283
Speed freak, 79
Spermatogenesis, 244
Sperm whale, 152
Sphenoid bone, 34
Sphere of influence, 122
Spinal cord, 131, 137
Spindle wave, 113
Spinothalamic tract, 265
Split brain, 258
Spontaneous aggression, 131–132, 151–
    152
Spontaneous erections, 116
Spontaneous fighting, 170, 250
Sports, 283
Squeals, 200
Stag, 157
Staggering gait, 73
Stalking attack, 229
Stallion, 270
Startle reaction, 27
Starvation, 74, 193, 195
Stereotaxic instrument, 104, 106, 110
Steroid, 65

Stickleback, 164
Stilbestrol, 11, 64
Stimulant, 78
Stimulation, 177
    threshold, 146
Stimulus-bound feeding, 145
Stimulus-bound killing, 145
Stimulus complex, 4
Stimulus object, 229
Stimulus situation, 132, 174
Stress, 11, 16, 19, 26, 44, 86, 102, 174, 179, 193, 195, 247–248, 272–273
Stria terminalis, 235, 255
Stroop Colour Word Test, 104
Stuffed doll, 201
Stuffed rat, 133, 138
Stupid, 118
Stuporous, 118
Subculture, 84
Subhuman primate, 168, 217
Subjective experience, 113
Submission, 17, 158, 165–166, 172, 245
Submissiveness, 254
Submissive posture, 155, 160, 166, 168, 179, 197
Subordinate, 17
Substantia nigra, 32
Sugar, 75
Sugar glider, 220
Suicide, 66, 123, 129
Sulking, 193
Sultan, 62
Superior colliculus, 140, 255
Super-relaxation, 107, 109, 112
Suppression, 56–57, 107
Suppressor area, 234
Suppressor system, 107, 113, 265–267, 274
Surgeon, 103
Surgery, 105–106, 110, 248
Sweating, 42
Sweden, 62
Symbol, 18, 23
Symbolic activity, 130
Sympathetic arousal, 133, 187, 264
Synaptic resistance, 5

Tactile cue, 139
Tactile stimulation, 266
Tactile system, 140
Tadpole, 138
Tail rattling, 186, 241–242
Tame, 259
Tameness, 267
Tamias striatus, 24
Taming, 180
Taming effect, 90
Target, 134–135, 151, 191, 201, 261, 277
Taylor Manifest Anxiety Test, 87

Technology, 126–127
Teeth chattering, 200
Tegmental area of Tsai, 232
Tegmentum, 233
Telephone, 189
Television, 102
Temper, 24, 30, 70, 193
Temper tantrum, 30, 39, 53, 69–71, 88, 91, 97–98, 101
Temporal lobe, 24–25, 27, 29, 32, 36–37, 41, 46–47, 53, 55, 57–58, 77, 85–86, 113, 258
Temporal lobectomy, 46–48, 282
Temporal lobe lesion. *See* Temporal lobectomy
Tension, 24, 27, 43, 49, 67, 78, 90–91, 94, 109, 116, 121, 208, 245, 271
Teratoma, 28
Terminal man, 112
Territorial aggression, 132, 209–210, 223, 226
Territorial cluster, 224
Territorial defense, 212, 214, 222, 225
"Territorial imperative," 223
Territoriality, 111, 210, 216–217, 220, 222, 225–226
    passive, 214
    temporal, 215
Territorial marking, 218, 221
Territorial unit, 224
Territory, 4, 122, 132, 177, 209, 211, 213, 224, 226
Terror, 51
Testes, 65, 240, 244, 249
Testicular atrophy, 271
Testosterone, 10–12, 60–65, 134, 153, 162, 207, 238–240, 243–245, 247–249, 251, 253–254, 271–273, 276
    tritium-labeled, 254
Testosterone propionate, 12, 162, 182, 239, 241–243, 247, 250–251, 253, 256, 271
Thalamus, 44, 49, 58, 108, 228, 232, 272
    dorsal midline, 234, 236
    inferior thalamic peduncle, 147
    midline, 147, 232–233
Thalamic lesions, 49
Thematic Apperception Test (TAT), 81, 206
Theophylline, 33
Therapist monkeys, 199
Therapy, 64, 65, 69, 91, 105, 114, 116, 118, 123, 125–126, 241, 281
Thermocoagulation, 47
Theta waves, 40
Thiazesim, 234
Thioridazine, 90
Third ventricle, 28
Thirst, 194, 277

Thorax, 141

Threat, 3, 10, 42, 98, 100, 153, 155, 158, 164, 166, 168, 172, 176–179, 183, 185, 187, 190, 197–198, 205–206, 211–212, 215, 221, 223, 225, 253 position, 156

Threshold, 10, 19, 22, 84, 94–95, 99, 107, 144, 246, 259, 261, 272, 281

Time out, 101

Timidity, 62, 171

T-maze, 170, 202

Toad, 138

Token, 101

Tools, 23, 225

Tooth chattering, 155

Topography, 5, 15, 20, 23, 133, 141–142, 151, 154–155, 171, 173–174, 176–178, 180, 185–187, 196, 203, 229, 236–237

Tournament behavior, 213

Toy dog, 138, 232

Toy tiger, 201

Tractotomy, 50

Trail, 215, 219, 221

Training, 96, 120, 148, 169

Tranquilizers, 90, 94, 105

Transynaptic change, 107

Trauma, 104

Tremor, 32, 78

Trespassers, 211

Trifluoperazine, 90

Trigeminal nerve, 139–140, 233

Trigger man, 120

Trimethyl purine, 33

Trochar, 116

Tropotropic circuits, 48

Tulane Behavioral Test, 118

Tumor, 24–25, 27–28, 44, 57, 73–74, 98, 126, 265

Turkey, 184

Turtle, 5, 133, 137, 143

Uganda kob, 213–214, 216, 223

Ultrasonic energy, 110

Ultrasound, 166

Unconditioned stimulus, 147, 201, 207

Uncus, 46

Underbelly, 164

Ungulates, 217

Unhappiness, 70, 78

United States, 180, 188

University of Strausbourg, 228

Unruliness, 70

Urine, 160–163, 218–219, 252

Urticaria, 94

Vaginal secretion, 159

Valium. See Diazepam

Vasoconstriction, 84

Verbal aggression, 33, 61, 93, 206

Verbal behavior, 2, 225

Verbal hostility, 4, 88, 92, 195

Victim, 80, 82, 84, 120, 131, 161–162, 164–165, 170, 181

Violence, 3, 22, 25, 28, 40, 48, 57, 69, 78, 80, 83, 86–87, 93, 97, 105–106, 109, 112, 114, 116–117, 121, 123, 126, 128, 189, 193, 195, 204, 266, 283

Virus, 29

Viscera, 280

Vision, 164

Visual cortex, 7, 140

Visual cue, 139, 172, 185

Visual feedback, 140

Visual field defects, 104

Visual pattern, 138

Visual system, 140

Vocalization, 166, 177, 198, 205, 221

Vodka, 82

Vole, 213–214, 217

Vomiting, 24, 42, 104

WAIS, 118

Walrus, 152

War, 121–122, 225

Warning signals, 198

Water, 191

Weakness, 69, 115

Weapon, 157, 178, 180

Weasels, 181, 183, 205, 214

Wechsler Intelligence Scale, 104

Well-being, 52

Wheat, 71

Whiskey, 85

Whitman, Charles, 25–27, 98–99, 123, 279

Whitman syndrome, 98

Wildebeest, 211, 213, 216

Winter, 164

Wolf, 142, 152, 165, 168

Word fluency, 104

World leaders, 97, 121–122

Worry, 109

Wounds, 152, 158, 197, 244, 255

Wrestling, 200

Wright brothers, 284

XYY syndrome, 14

Yale, 228

Yeast, 71

Y-maze, 15, 143, 220

Zalophus californeanus, 221

Zoophilic actions, 63

76 77 78 79   9 8 7 6 5 4 3 2 1